creation
of the
american
empire:

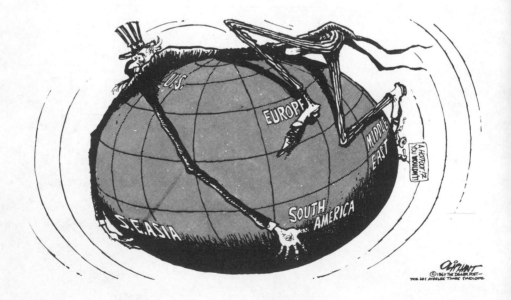

creation of the american empire:

U.S. Diplomatic History

Lloyd C. Gardner
Rutgers University

Walter F. LaFeber
Cornell University

Thomas J. McCormick
University of Wisconsin, Madison

RAND M℃NALLY & COMPANY
Chicago, New York, San Francisco, London

RAND McNALLY HISTORY SERIES

Fred Harvey Harrington, *Advisory Editor*

FOR
Fred Harvey Harrington
and
William Appleman Williams

Contents

Illustrations

Preface

WHETHER OR NOT you have ever had a formal course or read a history book, you are a historian and indeed a philosopher of history. Every day all of us give our opinions, deliver judgments, and make future plans, and every one of them is based on our understanding or ignorance of our past. The question is not whether we use history and are historians, for we have no choice in this, but whether we intelligently and accurately use the past as a guide to today and tomorrow.

Since in this respect the collective citizenry of a nation resembles the individual, since Americans as a national people comprise the most powerful political, economic, and military force the world has ever known, and since this force must be responsible and rational if it is not to destroy civilization, it follows that understanding American history is of some importance. There is no argument more potentially disastrous than that which moves from false historical analogy. Vietnam in 1965 in no way resembled Nazi Germany in 1938, and for Lyndon Johnson and his advisers to make policy in the belief that they were similar led to the tragedies in Southeast Asia after 1965. History does not repeat itself, but its process is always continuing, and it is the understanding of this process—this developing—that is crucial.

The central problem in American history is to explain the process or development, and therefore the present nature, of the American empire. On one level this requires our understanding of how the nation began physically as a string of tiny beleaguered settlements on the western rim of the Atlantic and within three hundred years encircled the globe with billions of dollars in investment capital and dozens of military bases. On another level, the problem requires us to explain how John Winthrop's and Thomas Jefferson's belief that Americans were truly the Chosen People led to the slaughter of thousands of Vietnamese civilians through indiscriminate American bombing in the 1970s.

This book attempts to trace these processes and to suggest how the problem can at least partially be unraveled by focusing upon the internal forces that have shaped American foreign policy during the past several centuries. We believe that our own study of history demonstrates that domestic pressures primarily determine foreign policy. When this policy is in turn challenged in the world arena, the response to that challenge is again determined primarily by internal factors. These factors vary from generation to generation; during the 1840s, for example, the struggle among the political parties was formative, but in the 1890s and 1930s the quest for economic salvation superseded all else.

This book differs from other texts in its emphasis on the domestic motivations of the nation's foreign policy. These motivations particularly include the economic, ideological, and at times political debates that have dominated the country's life. As authors, we are much less concerned with formal points of international contact, such as treaties, than we are with the interplay between ideology and the politico-economic elite that has framed American policies. We have tried to provide the student with an understanding of this hidden but more important 90 percent of the iceberg, without neglecting to mention the resulting international agreements or wars—the visible and more sensational 10 percent.

We have also intentionally given as much attention to the pre-1900 era as to the twentieth century. The 1780s and the 1960s, for example, receive approximately the same amount of space. And with good reason; for although most of us do not realize it, our perception of present problems, and certainly of the political and legal framework of these problems, is influenced as much by the Founding Fathers as by the historical actors of the 1960s. During the 1780s, moreover, the founders thought through their problems in a rather more exemplary and successful fashion. Marc Bloch, the great French historian whose view of and commitment to his nation's past resulted in his brutal execution for resistance to the Nazis, once observed that often distant times shape our lives considerably more than the recent past; to believe otherwise, Bloch concluded, was comparable to believing that because the moon is closer to us than the sun, the moon is therefore more important to our continuing life on this planet.

(In assessing both of these pasts, the book is "revisionist" in the root sense of that word. That is, we have questioned and revised explanations of key foreign policies given by governmental officials and many other authors of diplomatic texts. This revisionism comes in part from our assumptions about history and in part from opportunities to use primary sources that were not available or not used previously in explaining the policies.) We hope that revisionism in this sense develops new emphases and raises fresh questions, an obligation of any new history book. We are aware that this story is told through three different writing styles. We have made no effort to blend these styles because our chief concern is with the book's interpretations. We three agree on all the interpretations in the volume, and we also agree that an author's view of history is best presented in his own words.

The book is dedicated to two men who were most important in shaping this revisionist school of diplomatic history during the 1950s. In a larger context, Fred Harvey Harrington and William Appleman Williams raised unfashionable and uncomfortable questions about the direction of American policy and American historiography a decade before such questions became not only fashionable, but, unfortunately, liberal chic. Our intellectual debts to these two men are immense. Our personal obligations are even greater.

We are also indebted to Lawrence Malley and Barbara Salazar of Rand McNally, and to the several friends, particularly the late William Neuman of Goucher College, who gave detailed critiques of the manuscript.

CHAPTER 1

Men of Empire,
Children of Israel
(To 1775)

American foreign policy may be defined as the necessary relations Americans have with other nations in order to preserve and expand the prosperity of the United States. From 1776 until the 1970s Americans have attempted to increase their prosperity by using their diplomacy to obtain empire. At first, until approximately the mid-nineteenth century, they built a great continental landed empire. At the same time, however, they began developing an empire of trade around the globe. By the late twentieth century this empire had become military as well as commercial and territorial. Indeed, they had often found it impossible throughout their history to preserve the territorial and commercial empires without using military weapons. The story of how Americans expanded in less than two hundred years from a slim chain of thirteen settlements along the Atlantic coast to the superpower of the twentieth century is perhaps the most incredible secular story in human history.

That Americans have been so successful since 1776 is understandable. For in this as in most things—whether they care to admit it or not—they have been shaped by their history. Despite all their supposed peculiarities, Americans are like all other peoples in one critical matter: they cannot escape their past.

They can only hope to understand that past better in order to be happier in the present.

In attempting to understand American history this is where one begins, for from the beginnings of the nation the first settlers from Europe thought of themselves as builders of empires. Such feelings were hardly unnatural, for these people were the products, often avowed disciples, of Elizabethan England's great and developing empire. Some Americans, however, cared primarily about the empire of the soul and the community, while others coveted the empire of land and commerce. These two groups conflicted, especially in seventeenth-century New England, until by the eve of the American Revolution the merchants and land speculators had triumphed. The personification of this triumph was Benjamin Franklin. During the 1760s he participated in the successful fight to annex Canada to the British Empire, thus opening fabulous opportunities of settlement, trade, and speculation for his countrymen. That stunning success proved ironic, however. Within a decade arguments over the proper policies for the development of this hinterland created splits between American entrepreneurs and London officials. By 1774 the gap was unbridgeable. The British Empire, "that fine and noble china vase," as Franklin called it, lay in pieces. An independent American nation replaced it on the western shores of the Atlantic.

The Budding Empire

AN EMPIRE can be viewed as a group of nations, states, or colonies under the rule of a single sovereignty. By this definition the American colonies of the seventeenth century qualified as part of the British Empire. The colonies, however, varied greatly in their allegiance to the rule of the King. The first permanent settlements, made along the James River in Virginia during 1607, survived by developing a staple crop of tobacco, then selling it through British merchants to English and European markets. Most of the middle and southern colonies became large exporters of basic agricultural and raw material staples that Great Britain needed. This tie, combined with a common Anglican religion, linked many of these settlements closely to the British well before the last of the original colonies, Georgia, was founded in 1732. This set of colonies complied with the British imperial policy of mercantilism, a policy first outlined by law in 1650 and elaborated in a series of acts between 1663 and 1776.

Mercantilist policy was based on the assumption that the purpose of colonies was to enrich the mother country. The worth of a colony was measured in the amount of specie (gold and silver) it obtained for the mother country, and such specie was most systematically obtained when a colony exported more to non-British markets than it imported. Using this criterion, London officials gave the colonies southward from Maryland into the Caribbean area high marks.

Another central assumption of mercantilism, however, was that man's nature was so evil and selfish that colonials would not enrich the mother country unless they were properly controlled. This view allowed King and Parliament to make stringent laws for the regulation of colonial life. Such a policy might have led to a tight political control of London over the colonies. This did not occur, however, for during the first fifty years of the eighteenth century British governments concerned themselves with domestic and European problems, letting the colonies take their own course of development (a policy expressed by Robert Walpole, the great Prime Minister of the 1720s and 1730s, as "Let sleeping dogs lie"). By the eve of the Great War for Empire, southern colonies enjoyed well-developed representative legislatures that increasingly looked upon themselves, not Parliament, as supreme within the bounds of the colony.

Similar home rule evolved in the mid-northern colonies (Pennsylvania, New Jersey, New York) and New England. In this area, moreover, potential estrangement between colony and mother country was widened by the failure of these particular colonies to produce agricultural staples that could fit into the mercantilist scheme. These settlements instead prospered through ship-building, shipping, and other mercantile pursuits. British mercantilistic laws, however, were devised to give merchants in the home islands first preference in imperial trade, as well as to regulate tightly all trade between Great Britain and other nations. New Englanders increasingly believed they could prosper only by trading outside such rules. They consequently developed a flourishing commerce through smuggling with the French settlements in Canada and the rich French and Spanish possessions in the Caribbean.

During the several decades after the founding of the Massachusetts Bay Colony in 1630, these merchants, or "river gods," as they came to be called, had initially been restrained not so much by imperial regulations as by the socioreligious controls imposed by the Puritan leadership in the community. The first great leader of the colony, John Winthrop, warned the settlers they were embarking upon a great experiment not only for themselves, but for mankind:

Men shall say of succeeding plantacions: the lord make it like that of New England: for wee must Consider that wee shall be as a Citty Upon a Hill, the eies of all people are Uppon us; soe that if wee shall deale falsely with our god in this worke wee haue undertaken and soe cause him to withdrawe his present help from us, wee shall be made a story and a by-word through the world...tell wee be consumed out of the good land whether wee are goeing.[1]

John Winthrop

This sense of destiny, so eloquently expressed by Winthrop at the dawn of the New World's history, infused and shaped the perception that Americans have ever since had of themselves and their role in the world, a perception apparent in Thomas Jefferson's belief that Americans were the Chosen People of a new Israel, in Woodrow Wilson's phrase that the world must be made safe for democracy, and in John F. Kennedy's alarm, sounded in 1961, that "a new generation of Americans" must be prepared to fight the worldwide battle of "freedom versus tyranny." Winthrop's original call to mission differed from the later statesmen's, however, in its greater humility and larger sense of man's evil—as befitted an observant and devout Puritan.

---

[1] John Winthrop, "A Modell of Christian Charity," in Perry Miller and Thomas H. Johnson, *The Puritans* (New York, 1938), pp. 198–99. For an analysis of the theme between the 1750s and 1776, see Paul A. Varg, "The Advent of Nationalism, 1758–1776," *American Quarterly*, 16 (Summer 1964), pt. 1:169–81.

The dedication to mission explicit in the image of a "City Upon a Hill" has undergone numerous frustrations, indeed tragedies, during the nearly four centuries it has shaped American thought. Its first defeat was wrought by the "river gods" themselves. The settlers had been warned by Winthrop that the City Upon a Hill could be realized only if "wee ... be knitt together in this worke as one man, wee ... entertaine each other in brotherly Affeccion, wee ... be willing to abridge our selues of our superfluities, for the supply of others' necessities."[2] The interest of the merchants in profit through unregulated, ever expanding trade led them to disagree sharply with Winthrop's warning as well as with the observation of a later Puritan divine, Increase Mather, that "sometimes, one man by seeking to advance himself has brought great misery on the whole nation."

Hoping they could have both a free enterprise system and personal salvation, and caring more about external markets than the viability of their home community, the merchants had helped to undercut the Puritan order by the 1660s. The founders of the colony found it impossible to maintain their ideal of community in face of the temptations posed by a vast frontier area and the enticing markets of European empires along the shores of the Atlantic.

The Great War for Empire

BY THE END of the seventeenth century Americans north and south were rapidly expanding both on land and in trade. Neither religious nor political restraints, emanating from either the colonies or London, long deterred such expansion. One result was bloody warfare with the Indians, who were pushed back along the frontier. Another result was some American participation in a series of imperial wars that Britain waged against Spain and France in the early eighteenth century. After one such conflict, the Treaty of Utrecht in 1713 expanded British North America by taking Nova Scotia and Newfoundland from the French and also by opening Spanish America to British slave traders. During the War of the Austrian Succession, fought largely in Europe during the 1740s, New Englanders successfully attacked the French stronghold of Louisbourg on Cape Breton Island, gaining a key strategic area both for the exploitation of the rich fisheries in the North Atlantic and perhaps even for the conquest of Canada. To the disgust of the New Englanders, however, London officials re-

---

2 Winthrop, "Modell of Christian Charity," p. 198.

fused to support unsuccessful invasions of Canada between 1746 and 1748, and finally restored Louisbourg to the French as part of the peace settlement in 1748.

Americans bitterly believed that this loss of their foothold in Canada robbed them of tremendous opportunities for trade and land speculation in the North American interior. They refused to be deterred from moving into the disputed territory of the rich Ohio Valley. Although the area was claimed by the French, American fur traders and land speculators had increasingly penetrated the upper Ohio during the 1740s. They were met with ravaging attacks from the French and the Indian tribes that cooperated with France in attempting to keep the ever encroaching Americans from the western side of the Apalachians. In 1753 the French drove off a young surveyor named George Washington, who was charting some of those disputed lands between the Ohio River and the Alleghenies for a group of Virginia land speculators.

In response to Virginia's pleas for military aid, the British sent several Irish regiments under the command of Edward Braddock. The long-held objectives of American expansion were perfectly embodied in the planned military strategy: Braddock would clear the French out of the upper Ohio Valley, while New England militia would carry out the long-sought attack against Canada. Both campaigns failed, the northern attack when leaders from Massachusetts and New York fell to quarreling among themselves, Braddock's when the French and Indians nearly wiped out the Irish regiments and killed Braddock. After extended parliamentary debate, Great Britain decided in 1756 to wage all-out war against France. The Great War for Empire began in both Europe and America. With its initiation appeared a figure who well represented his expansive fellow Americans and who would conduct most of the important diplomatic negotiations for the rising American empire during the next thirty years.

FRANKLIN

Born in Boston in 1706, Benjamin Franklin ran away to Philadelphia, the crossroads of the colonies, when he was in his teens. Quaker merchants, with whom the ambitious young printer soon ingratiated himself, made the city prosperous and cosmopolitan. With wealth had come education, taste, and links with the urban centers of Europe. Philadelphia also controlled the opening to the vast frontier along the central Allegheny Mountains. Franklin was the personification of Philadelphia's success, and indeed of a wider colonial triumph: he became independently wealthy as a printer who shrewdly exploited

Benjamin Franklin

markets up and down the Atlantic seaboard, triumphant as a mediator between the Indians and Scotch-Irish settlers on the frontier, notable as a founder of the University of Pennsylvania and the American Philosophical Society, and politically powerful as he rose through the ranks of the Pennsylvania Assembly. He learned to know most of the colonies well, moreover, as the first successful intercolonial postmaster general, appointed by the King.

On the eve of the Great War for Empire, Franklin was a case study of a people in search of empire. Nor, as a good scientist, did Franklin neglect developing the theoretical foundation of this quest. One aspect of the theory was formulated in his *Poor Richard's Almanack*. The "penny saved is a penny earned" philosophy of Poor Richard inculcated in the colonial mind the manner in which an agrarian, newly settled community must conduct itself in the midst of scarcity, at least until enough pennies could be saved to transform it into an affluent society. Not accidentally, Poor Richard's devices were suited for a people threatened with the loss of their specie because of British mercantilist regulations. For example, Poor Richard advised money-poor Americans in 1756 to cut their purchases of expensive British imports: to mend clothes, to buy no expensive silks or chinaware, to cut down on the drinking of "Punch, Wine or Tea"; then, "at the Year's end, there will be An Hundred Thousand Pounds more Money in your country." And, he might have added, that much less in Great Britain.[3]

---

[3] "Poor Richard Improved, 1756," in *The Papers of Benjamin Franklin,* ed. Leonard W. Labaree et al., 15 vols. (New Haven, 1959–1971), 6:323–24.

Equally important, although not as widely known, was Franklin's essay of 1751, "Observations Concerning the Increase of Mankind."[4] Assuming with great accuracy that the American population would probably double every twenty years, Franklin concluded that within a century "the greatest Number of Englishmen will be on this Side of the water." Adequate land, however, must be found for this expanding people. A prince or legislator who obtains "new Territory ... or removes the Natives to give his own People Room" could be "properly called *Fathers* of their Nation," Franklin argued, "as they are the Cause of the Generation of Multitudes, by the Encouragement they afford to Marriage." Despite the population growth such territorial expansion would stimulate in America, he believed developing the frontier would also profit British merchants, for they would have an ever expanding agrarian market in which to sell the manufactured goods in Great Britain.

Three years after the publication of this essay, Franklin played the central role in an intercolonial conference at Albany called to decide upon a means of coordinating frontier policies. The Albany Congress finally failed to agree upon common policy, but the most important document advanced was Franklin's "Albany Plan of Union."[5] Anticipating the problems of 1776 to 1787 and some of the solutions found thirty-three years later at the Constitutional Convention, Franklin suggested establishing a general government, representing all the colonies, which would guide the westward drive by determining Indian and land policies. He then went considerably further by proposing that this government be given the power to levy taxes and to raise and equip a military force. Franklin had devised a government suitable for his dream of 1751, but in vesting it with such powers Franklin alienated both British officials, who were determined to have no such central government in North America, and leaders in each colony, who wanted to retain control of their own affairs.

In 1760-1761 Franklin was considerably more successful when he entered the debate over whether the British should take Canada or the rich sugar island of Guadeloupe from the nearly defeated French. At this time Franklin was a powerful agent in London for the Pennsylvania Assembly. He argued in British newspapers that Canada must be annexed, amending to this essay his 1751 analysis, which contained all of the statistics and arguments needed to buttress his preference for Canada. Franklin of course stressed the point that the interior, once settled, would provide richer pickings for British merchants and

---

4 The essay, with excellent editorial comments, can be found in ibid., 4:225-34.

5 "Albany Plan of Union," in ibid., 5:344-92. Franklin's later (1789) comments on the Albany Plan are on pp. 397-417.

manufacturers than would Guadeloupe. When London opponents to the annexation of Canada replied that the settlers in that vast hinterland could never be controlled by British authority, Franklin responded that while plentiful land would keep the settlers happy, necessary trade would tie them to the British Empire.[6]

In part because of such arguments as those advanced by Franklin, Great Britain decided to annex Canada. In addition, with the Treaty of Paris, which terminated the war in 1763, the British obtained Florida and all land westward to the Mississippi River. To compensate its Spanish allies, France gave them Louisiana west of the Mississippi River and the key port city of New Orleans. Franklin's theories were becoming real, his argument won; the British Empire emerged as the primary world power—and, ironically, was on the eve of its greatest defeat.

One Empire into Two

THE GREAT WAR FOR EMPIRE ended with the British encumbered by a large war debt. They also faced the appalling prospect of preserving peace and orderly settlement in the tremendous transmontane area of North America. The colonials meanwhile found themselves mired in an economic recession. Some determined to improve their fortunes by exploiting the new western lands. Northern and middle colony merchants meanwhile continued to gather specie through increased trade with the Spanish and French possessions in the Caribbean. Such illegal trade, indeed, had prospered even during the war against France and Spain. When the British tried to stop these outlawed cargoes in 1760–1761, merchants represented by James Otis issued a public challenge to Parliament's assumed right to regulate colonial trade.

The large war debt, the determination to exploit the western lands, Otis' challenge, and the possibility that further expansion might ignite the frontier into one flaming Indian war—all of these developments led the new British King, George III, and his shortsighted ministry to close off much of the land beyond the mountains with the Proclamation Line of 1763. The British avowedly intended to regulate settlement, thus also easing tension with the Indians. During the next ten years London officials did conclude treaties with some

---

[6] Ibid., 9:52–100; also Franklin to John Hughes, January 7, 1760, in *The Writings of Benjamin Franklin,* ed. Albert Henry Smyth, 10 vols. (New York, 1905), 4:8.

tribes, opening new lands to settlement. In 1763, however, such men as Washington believed the Proclamation Line was drawn to exclude Americans and leave the territory for pickings by British traders and speculators. One British observer had commented during the war that many men in Parliament wanted land in French America so badly that when asked for even enormous sums of money to fight France, "you would as soon hear 'No' from an old maid as from the House of Commons." Americans believed the ominous implications of that story, so much so that Washington, who in 1760 had bought up depreciated soldiers' warrants for the western lands, continued to maintain a regular agent in the upper Ohio, staking out claims even after the Proclamation Line was in effect.

In an attempt to regulate American trade within the principles of mercantilism, as well as to pay off the war debt, Parliament imposed a tax on sugar in 1764. The following year it passed legislation that forced colonials to pay for stamps necessary for the legalizing of documents and newspapers. Admiralty courts appeared in American seaports to provide the means for immediate condemnation of illegal trading. The colonies responded by directly challenging the right of Parliament to regulate their internal affairs. Delegations from nine colonies met in a "Stamp Act Congress" in New York to protest the measure, concluding with the proclamation that since they were "Englishmen," no taxes could "be imposed on them, but with their own Consent, given personally, or by their Representatives." The Americans carefully added that because of "local circumstances," they "are not, and ... cannot be, Represented in the House of Commons in Great-Britain." Violence broke out in several cities, with the unfortunate stamp agents hanged in effigy or worse.

In 1767–1768 Parliament retreated only slightly. It accepted the American distinction between Britain's right to regulate the colonies' external trade and the Americans' right to regulate internal trade (although most British officials and many Americans, including Franklin, thought the distinction specious), imposed new taxes on external trade, and in the Declaratory Act reaffirmed its power over the colonies. Americans responded to the new trade regulations by voluntarily cutting off trade with England. Some "voluntarism" was coerced by mob action. Two regiments of British troops, stationed in Boston to enforce the parliamentary measures, were confronted by a mob on March 5, 1770. In a moment of panic the British fired, killing five Americans.

The horror of the Boston Massacre frightened both sides into working to ease the tension for several years. In 1773, however, Parliament again infuriated the colonists by giving the nearly bankrupt East India Company monopoly privileges of selling tea in North America. American merchants and radical

Boston Massacre

political leaders again joined forces, the former because they realized that if Parliament could grant monopolies for one company similar favors could be given to other British traders, the latter because they realized London had made the fatal blunder of challenging both the Americans' pocketbooks and the constitutional theories enunciated at the Stamp Act Congress eight years before. Bostonians dressed as Indians dumped cargoes of tea into the harbor in December 1773 and March 1774.

The King decided to respond with full force. Parliament passed a series of acts known variously as the Coercive Acts or the Intolerable Acts, which closed Boston Harbor, weakened self-government in Massachusetts, required local citizens to quarter British troops, and changed the working of the jury system (colonial juries had freed merchants engaged in illegal trade). Of equal importance, Parliament established a separate government for the Ohio Valley, tying that area closely to a Canada that had formerly been French and was still largely Roman Catholic. Americans concluded that their political rights, economic opportunities, and religious beliefs were all under siege.[7]

---

[7] The effect of the 1774 acts on American radical leaders can be glimpsed especially in Richard Henry Lee to Arthur Lee, June 26, 1774, in *The Letters of Richard Henry Lee*, ed. James C. Ballagh, 2 vols. (New York, 1911–1914), 1:114.

On September 5, 1774, delegates from every colony but Georgia met in Philadelphia for the First Continental Congress. Radicals led by Samuel Adams of Massachusetts and Richard Henry Lee of Virginia urged immediate action but did not move for independence, knowing adequate support for a final break did not exist. Moderates led by Joseph Galloway of Pennsylvania sought a compromise. Galloway and Franklin, then on a second tour of diplomatic duty in England, hoped a solution could be found in obtaining colonial autonomy in most matters in return for vows of allegiance to the King and agreement to accept a president-general to be appointed by George III. Not unlike the British commonwealth theory that would evolve in the nineteenth century, the Galloway-Franklin plan was too early to win British acceptance and too late to obtain the support of the radicals, who were determined to take stronger action.[8] Nonimportation resolutions were again passed and committees established to maintain close contact among the colonies.

THE EVE OF ANTICOLONIAL WAR

The First Continental Congress closed by vowing "reverence and loyalty" to the King, but at least by late 1774 the American colonies had become in reality an independent empire. Between 1760 and 1775 Franklin's population theory worked out so well that the five largest American cities grew by one-third, with Philadelphia emerging as larger than any city in Great Britain except London. American merchants roamed the world in some of the best ships and along the most efficient routes of the Empire, determined to circumvent British mercantilism if it hindered their interests, as they had once undermined the Puritan community. Southerners, deeply in debt to both British and American merchants, sought to regain prosperity by moving into forbidden western lands or by selling directly to European markets, a practice outlawed by mercantilistic laws. Americans, in short, believed they possessed the economic power to force the British government to repeal the acts of 1774 as they had forced the repeal of the Stamp Act.

Not for the first or last time, Americans vastly overestimated their economic power in international affairs. But this miscalculation tended to be lost in the colonial belief that they were a Chosen People selected for a special mission, which was now being blocked by the British, whose Old World

---

[8] Franklin is especially interesting in the 1764–1775 period, for he approached his final commitment to independence only very slowly and cautiously. For his attempt to work out a dominion status for the colonies as early as 1767, see Franklin to Lord Kames, April 11, 1767, in *Writings of Franklin,* 5:16–22.

politics and society were streaked with venality and corruption during the 1760s and 1770s.[9] Overall, Americans had developed their own political institutions for more than a century, until as early as 1765 Richard Bland could argue that the original settlers brought with them "the full and absolute power of governing all the people of this place."[10]

After 1760 particularly, Americans increasingly thought of themselves as a separate people. Their allegiance to the King, that last fragile link, frayed to a thin thread on April 19, 1775, when the King's troops exchanged deadly fire with four hundred Minutemen at Concord Bridge. A Second Continental Congress hurriedly convened. In keeping with a century and a half of their history, the delegates not only prepared for independence from British colonial rule, but also prepared plans for the expansion of their already vast empire.

A larger question loomed, however. The thirteen colonies from Massachusetts through Georgia were divided by thirteen separate assemblies, each of which assumed itself sovereign within its own sphere (as Franklin had learned directly at Albany in 1754, for example), and they were divided also by the growth of black slavery, which was isolating the southern states; by the individualism of merchants, traders, and speculators, which had left both the Puritan community and the grandly designed British mercantilist empire to flounder; and by the growing number of religious sects, which had multiplied after the great revivals of the 1740s. Whether colonies such as these could become at once independent, united, and expansive remained a highly debatable question in the winter of 1775–1776.

Suggestions for Further Reading

Helpful introductory surveys on the prerevolutionary era are Max Savelle, *The Origins of American Diplomacy: The International History of Angloamerica, 1492–1763* (New York, 1967), and A. B. Darling's excellent *Our Rising Empire, 1763–1803* (New Haven, Conn., 1940); the material on the post-1763 years in Lawrence H. Gipson's magisterial and multivolumed *The British Empire Before the American*

---

9 ". . . This whole venal nation is now at market, will be sold for about two millions, and might be bought out of the hands of the present bidders (if he would offer half a million more) by the very devil himself." So wrote Franklin from London to his son, March 13, 1768 (*Writings of Franklin*, 5:117).

10 Quoted, with an excellent analysis, by Michael Kammen in "The Meaning of Colonization in American Revolutionary Thought," *Journal of the History of Ideas*, 31 (July–September 1970): 337–58.

Revolution (especially vols. 5–12) (New York, 1958–1970) is condensed in *The Coming of the Revolution* (New York, 1954).

A most profitable approach to the way these years shaped an independent American empire can be found in Richard W. Van Alstyne, *The Rising American Empire* (Chicago, 1965), and William Appleman Williams, *The Contours of American History* (Chicago, 1966). A stimulating series of essays on Americans as the supposed Chosen People is contained in Loren Baritz, *City on a Hill: A History of Ideas and Myths in America* (New York, 1964); see also Richard W. Van Alstyne, *Genesis of American Nationalism* (Waltham, Mass., 1970).

Two classic accounts on the importance of the American West are Thomas P. Abernathy, *Western Lands and the American Revolution* (New York, 1937), and Clarence W. Alvord, *The Mississippi Valley in British Politics,* 2 vols. (Cleveland, 1917).

Paul Conner has written a splendid account of Benjamin Franklin's hope for a "new American order" in *Poor Richard's Politiks* (New York, 1966); Gerald Stourzh, *Benjamin Franklin and American Foreign Policy* (Chicago, 1954), remains useful because the book overcomes its emphasis upon the overly narrow theme of security.

The best work on the political interaction between the colonies and London during the post-1750 era is Michael Kammen, *Rope of Sand* (Ithaca, N.Y., 1967), stressing the role of such lobbyists as Franklin and relating how the American interest groups lost power in shaping British policy after 1765.

See also the general bibliography at the end of this volume.

CHAPTER 2

A Virgin State
Attempts To Preserve
Its Virgin Character
(1775–1783)

The Second Continental Congress gathered at Philadelphia in May 1775. A month before, over three hundred American men had been killed or wounded at Lexington and Concord. During this agonizing spring of 1775 and until independence was declared in the summer of 1776, foreign policy was the focal point of debate. From the onset of the Revolution until peace was made in 1782, time and again the Americans confronted the fundamental, agonizing question: How much of their imperial dream would they have to bargain away in order to get the necessary aid from France to win the Revolution?

The Invasion of Canada

PERHAPS THE MOST ASTONISHING aspect of American thought was the confidence that rebellion against the world's greatest power would result not only in independence, but also in a magnificent empire controlled from Philadelphia. Franklin evinced this faith in a letter to a British friend late in 1775: "Britain, at the expense of three millions, has killed one hundred and fifty Yankees this campaign, which is twenty thousand pounds a head. . . . During the same time sixty thousand children have been born in America."[1]

The revolutionary leaders manifested this faith when they developed a plan to make Canada part of the new United States. The irony of this plan would have been hilarious had it not ended in such tragedy. The First Continental Congress, after all, had blistered the 1774 Quebec Act as "dangerous" to the "civil rights and liberties of all America" because of the encouragement given "the Roman Catholic religion and French laws." Few people disliked the Canadian French and Roman Catholics more than did the Presbyterians and Congregationalists who were in the front ranks of the revolutionary cause. Yet shortly after the Second Continental Congress convened, its leaders reasoned that in order to secure their flanks, as well as to expand their empire, they had to ask the Canadians to join them.

When the Canadians failed to step forward, Richard Henry Lee of Virginia and John and Samuel Adams of Massachusetts decided to use rougher tactics. Although they had been among the most extreme denunciators of the Quebec Act, these men now led a group in Congress determined to control the northern Roman Catholics, block the attacks of Indians sweeping down from Canada, and join together two countries that they believed formed a natural geographic unit. As Lee concluded in a letter to George Washington during the autumn of 1775, "We must have that Country with us this winter cost what it will."[2]

The cost began to be tabulated in blood in September 1775, when General Richard Montgomery led an American force toward Montreal and Colonel Benedict Arnold marched another against Quebec. Canada was to be trapped in a pincer movement. But as winter set in, supplies were exhausted, Montgomery's troops were "half-nacked," and British-Canadian resistance increased. Congress could not find the means to send immediate help. On December 31 Montgomery was killed and Arnold wounded attempting to storm Quebec. A rapid American retreat began, but the dream of annexing Canada was not to die with Montgomery. It would linger well into the twentieth century.

---

[1] Albert Henry Smyth, ed., *The Writings of Benjamin Franklin*, 10 vols. (New York, 1905), 6:430.

[2] James C. Ballagh, ed., *The Letters of Richard Henry Lee*, 2 vols. (New York, 1911–1914), 1:153.

The Need for Foreign Aid

THE DEBACLE in Canada vividly demonstrated the weakness of the Second Continental Congress. It had no navy, lacked arms and a munitions industry, and possessed neither the power to tax nor the ability to regulate a wartime economy. Long before the Congress seriously debated a declaration of independence, it began a desperate search for foreign aid. France promised to provide such assistance.

The French and Americans seemed an odd couple. For nearly two centuries the colonials had hated Frenchmen for being monarchical, Roman Catholic, and dangerous neighbors. Just a decade before, Americans had fought a full-scale war against the French. In 1775, however, the revolutionaries saw France differently. They understood that since its defeat by the Americans and British in 1763, the French court had planned revenge on England. France had built a great navy and had carefully made alliances with a number of European powers, most notably Spain. French officials wanted only a pretext to fight England, and Americans now offered the excuse.

When Americans pleaded for help in 1775, the Comte de Vergennes, the French Foreign Minister, quickly responded with a large loan. During the first year after the Declaration of Independence, France probably supplied 90 percent of American military needs, even though Vergennes had not yet formally recognized the new American government.

Early in 1776 French aid saved Congress from considerable embarrassment. By spring, however, the Americans had yet to resolve the equally difficult questions of whether to open their ports to all nations (that is, publicly proclaim that the British government no longer had authority in these ports), whether to draw up a formal declaration of independence, and how to strengthen the informal alliance with France.

Factions

THESE FOREIGN POLICY dilemmas threatened to destroy the Continental Congress, for they forced into the open deep differences among the delegates. Voting on the issues was not consistent. The membership of each faction swayed according to the issue discussed, the states affected, the political-economic interests involved. Yet a general alignment began to appear, an alignment that is crucial to the understanding of these first American foreign policies.

We can understand these and all later American policies only if we make one fundamental assumption: United States foreign policy is not shaped primarily in Europe, Asia, Latin America, or Africa. It is created at home. These policies can therefore be understood only if we comprehend the domestic politics, economics, and ideas that initially shaped the diplomacy. To believe that American foreign policy can be studied primarily by examining its effects on other areas of the globe is analogous to believing that the growth of a tree can be understood by looking closely at the top leaves and ignoring the root system. Usually foreign policies must be reshaped after they hit against the realities in other nations, but the reshaping, as well as the original formulation, is accomplished by men and women who represent certain domestic interests in the United States. Like charity, foreign policy begins at home. That, however, is the only resemblance between the two.

When the Founding Fathers confronted critical foreign policy problems, they divided along domestic political and economic lines. Sam Adams, Richard Henry Lee, John Hancock, Patrick Henry, and Thomas Jefferson generally formed one faction. This "Lee-Adams Junto," as it came to be called, was largely made up of men from Massachusetts and Virginia. They were united by a common zeal for immediate independence, distrust of a strongly centralized national government, passion for the conquest of Canada, and the desire to annex a great western empire and the Newfoundland fisheries.

The faction opposing the Junto was led initially by John Dickinson and then by Robert Morris, both from Pennsylvania. It included James Wilson, also of Pennsylvania, and Robert Livingston and John Jay of New York. This group was notable for its strong representation from the middle colonies, desire for a strong central government, fear of an immediate declaration of independence, and reluctance to become too closely tied to France (although this reluctance disappeared as the faction's appetite for empire grew). The colonies represented by this group generally lacked claims to lands beyond the Alleghenies, in contrast to Massachusetts and particularly Virginia, which held vast tracts in the West. This contrast explains in part why these men from the middle colonies cared less about western empire. At the same time, their interest in Philadelphia and New York City commerce and shipping explains their reluctance to cut their ties with the immense commercial markets of the Britsh Empire by declaring American independence.

Benjamin Franklin and John Adams usually joined the Lee-Adams Junto, although they refused to side with the ultrarevolutionaries on some issues. These two men were in especial disagreement with the Junto in their desire to create a strong central government. It was Franklin, however, who moved to the forefront of the revolutionary cause by introducing a resolution on February 26, 1776, calling for Congress to open American ports for two years to all commerce and ships. By directly repudiating British control, the resolution actually proclaimed independence. Therefore, as John Adams noted, the resolution stirred "great Spirit on both Sides."[3] After bitter debate, the Dickinson forces delayed passage of the motion for nearly six weeks. But events quickly undermined Dickinson's position. Congress soon learned that Parliament had prohibited any trade with American ports and had authorized the seizure of American ships. Of perhaps equal importance, Thomas Paine's pamphlet *Common Sense* appeared to provide backbone for many wavering colonials.

Thomas Paine

"Common Sense" Assumptions for American Foreign Policy

John Adams thought little of Paine's incendiary document. He called Paine "a Star of Disaster," and his reasons for doing so tell us much about both the

---

[3] Lyman H. Butterfield, ed., *Diary and Autobiography of John Adams,* 4 vols. (Cambridge, Mass., 1961), 3:364–65.

content of the Revolution and the central role of foreign policy. One portion of *Common Sense,* for example, attacked monarchy and proposed a democratic form of government. Like many Americans, Adams was not ready for this kind of democratic regime. He believed Paine's ideas on this subject flowed "from simple Ignorance," and urged instead a considerably more conservative structure of government.[4]

The second part of *Common Sense* proved more attractive to the acid-tongued Adams, for that section outlined the reasons the new nation could successfully become independent. Paine stressed that Americans did not need the British: "America would have flourished as much, and probably much more, had no European power had any thing to do with her." Why? "The articles of commerce, by which [America] has enriched herself, are the necessaries of life, and will always have a market while eating is the custom of Europe."

That statement had explosive political implications. "As Europe is our market for trade, we ought to form no partial connexion with any part of it," Paine warned. America's destiny was to create an empire of its own. After all, "there is something absurd, in supposing a continent to be perpetually governed by an island. In no instance hath nature made the satellite larger than its primary planet."

He then directed his fire at the open port issue. "Our plan is commerce, and that, well attended to, will secure us the peace and friendship of all Europe; because it is the interest of all Europe to have America a free port."[5]

In 1801 President Thomas Jefferson would announce that United States foreign policy rested on "peace, commerce, and honest friendship with all nations, entangling alliances with none," and thereby formulate the central principle that was to shape American diplomacy until the mid-twentieth century. Paine laid out the assumptions upon which this principle was based a quarter century before Jefferson spoke. The argument seemed irrefutable. On April 6, 1776, Congress declared American ports open to the world.

On June 7 Richard Henry Lee took the next step. He resolved in Congress that "these United Colonies are, and of right ought to be, free and independent States." The Virginian necessarily followed this resolve with another: "that it is expedient forthwith to take the most effectual measures for forming foreign Alliances." Contrary to Paine's assertion that Europe needed America, the Founding Fathers were discovering that they needed the French. Independence

---

[4] Ibid., 3:330–34.

[5] Thomas Paine, *Common Sense* (New York, 1942), pp. 23, 26–27, 31–32; Felix Gilbert, *The Beginnings of American Foreign Policy: To the Farewell Address* (New York, 1965), pp. 42–43.

and a foreign alliance were inseparable. On July 2, 1776, Congress finally accepted Lee's resolutions, but only after overcoming Dickinson's last-ditch opposition to a declaration of independence.[6]

The Model Treaty: Adams Tries
to Square the Circle

SEVERAL WEEKS EARLIER Congress had created a committee to draw up a plan for foreign alliances. The committee then asked John Adams to draft a model treaty.

In writing the document, Adams confronted a major theme (and, as has become apparent, a central problem) in American diplomatic history: How could the United States gain maximum benefits from international trade (in this case, with the French) while undertaking few if any political obligations? In other words, how could Americans make money without surrendering their political freedom of action? To United States foreign policy-makers this problem has proved to be the counterpart of the mathematician's attempt to square the circle.

Adams set out to solve the problem by using one of Thomas Paine's key points. The United States should not unite politically with either France or England. Instead, "We ought to confine ourselves strictly to a Treaty of Commerce," for "such a Treaty would be an ample compensation to France for all the aid we should want from her." He proposed the following terms:

> What Connection may We safely form with [France]?
> 1st. No Political Connection. Submit to none of her authority—receive no Governors, or officers from her.
> 2nd. No military Connection. Receive no Troops from her.
> 3d. Only a Commercial Connection, i.e., make a Treaty to receive her Ships into our Ports. Let her engage to receive our Ships into her Ports—furnish us with Arms, Cannon, Salt Petre, Powder, Duck, Steel.[7]

Adams' formulation made sense because the United States had only commerce—no meaningful diplomatic power and certainly no important military power—to offer. But it also illustrated the Americans' hope to obtain all they needed from France while giving only commerce in return and keeping their hands free politically to take all the territory they could conquer.

---

6 J. H. Powell, ed., "Speech of John Dickinson," *Pennsylvania Magazine of History and Biography*, 65:458–81.

7 *Diary of Adams*, 2:236; 3:328–29, 337–38.

After intermittent debate, Congress passed Adams' Model Treaty on September 17 with minor amendments. The resolution expressly provided that in return for American trade, France must promise that the "said United States, shall have the sole, exclusive, undivided and perpetual Possession of the Countries, Cities, and Towns, on the [North American] Continent, and of all Islands near to it" formerly under British control. That vision of empire literally knew few bounds. Besides trade, the United States would allow France to keep any West Indian islands conquered by French forces, and—wonder of wonders—would also promise that if France became involved in a war against the British as a consequence of helping the Americans, the Americans would not aid Great Britain.[8] Seldom had so much been asked of so many for so little.

REMODELING

Perfect in its natal simplicity, the Model Treaty drastically changed within three months. In late August Richard Henry Lee joined the treaty committee. During the autumn he and Sam Adams became convinced that Congress would never receive adequate French help without raising the ante. Neither man had ever been reluctant to pay a political price if in return the United States could obtain the necessary assistance to take Canada and a western empire. They did fear the prospect of large French armies within the United States, but even this reservation weakened as the British scored a major victory on Long Island, Washington hurriedly evacuated New York City, and, as the British advanced, Congress was forced to move with unmeasured tread from Philadelphia to Baltimore.

On December 30, 1776, under the lashing of Lee and Sam Adams, Congress passed a resolution that transformed the Model Treaty. Commissioners were to travel posthaste to obtain aid not only in Paris, but in Spain, Prussia, Vienna, and Tuscany. Congress now proclaimed its readiness to bargain away parts of the empire it did not yet have for immediate assistance. If, for example, France helped the United States take the fisheries, the French could even have half of Newfoundland.[9]

But Lee and Adams modified the treaty only at the cost of dividing their own faction. John Adams uttered warnings about offering France more than trade: "I don't love to be intangled in the Quarrels of Europe. I don't wish to be

---

[8] Worthington C. Ford, ed., *Journals of the Continental Congress* (Washington, D.C., 1906), 5:768–78.

[9] Ibid., 6:1054–58.

under Obligations to any of them.... Are We to be beholden to France for our Liberties?" Franklin colorfully voiced his agreement: "I have never yet chang'd the Opinion ... that a Virgin State should preserve the Virgin Character, and not go about suitoring for Alliances, but wait with decent Dignity for the Applications of others."[10]

For better or worse, the United States had begun to barter territory and political power with the hated monarchies of the Old World. Fortunately for Congress, it sent shrewd bargainers.

Ben with his beaver hat

Franklin in France

PRECEDED BY a worldwide reputation, and knowing intimately many of the leading French scientists and politicians, Franklin, who was one of the world's most urbane and cosmopolitan men, added to his popularity in Paris by appearing in plain brown clothing and wearing no powdered wig. He thus carefully played on the French fad for the "noble savage." For over six years Franklin

---

[10] Adams to James Warren, May 3, 1777, in *Letters of Members of the Continental Congress*, ed. Edmund C. Burnett, 8 vols. (Washington, D.C., 1921–1936), 2:354; Franklin to Arthur Lee, March 21, 1777, in *Writings of Franklin*, 7:35.

squeezed money out of a near-bankrupt French treasury, fitted out privateers and warships in French ports, operated an intelligence ring of American agents throughout Europe, maintained near-perfect relations with the difficult Vergennes, and still found time to publish learned essays on soil, water, and electricity.

Throughout much of 1777, however, neither Franklin's charm nor the remodeled treaty seemed to bring Vergennes closer to negotiating a formal alliance. But this stubbornness was deceiving, for Vergennes was trapped. On the one hand he feared that giving too much aid to an independent America might ultimately enable the United States to drive France and Spain from the New World in the not distant future. As early as 1775 Vergennes had warned the British ambassador in Paris that if Americans became independent they would create a great navy that could "conquer both your islands and ours," then sweep down over South America and "not leave a foot of that Hemisphere in the possession of any European power."[11] But on the other hand, the French court wanted to destroy the British Empire and had already invested too heavily in the American cause to stop short of a complete United States victory.

Three events of 1777–1778 finally led Vergennes to seal a formal alliance. First, in private conversations Franklin shrewdly emphasized the importance of a French West Indian empire, thereby providing the Foreign Minister with a rationale for sending more French aid and naval forces to those islands that served as distribution centers for the revolutionary cause. Second, the British prepared to send a peace mission to America. Vergennes could not take any chance on the outcome of negotiations if American and British officials began talking. Third, news of the American victory at Saratoga reached Paris in January 1778. This victory did not cause the Franco-American alliance, but it did influence its timing and give Vergennes an excuse to negotiate seriously with Franklin.

On February 6, 1778, Vergennes and Franklin signed two pacts. In a treaty of amity, the United States obtained most-favored-nation privileges; that is, any commercial privileges that France gave to other countries it would also give to the United States. This provision placed the United States on the same level with the leading European powers and was the first instance of a commercial principle that the United States has used throughout its history in commercial relations with other nations. In another part of the pact, the two nations agreed upon a small contraband list that closely followed Adams' Model Treaty.

---

[11] Richard W. Van Alstyne, *Empire and Independence: The International History of the American Revolution* (New York, 1965), pp. 92–93.

The second agreement, however, was a treaty of alliance which glaringly diverged from Adams' plan. Franklin had to promise not to conclude a peace or truce with the British unless the French consented. Vergennes made the same promise to Franklin. The United States not only promised to recognize any conquered West Indian islands as French, but guaranteed "from the present time and forever" the present French possessions in America and all others that Vergennes might acquire at the peace table. The price of American independence was becoming very high. These clauses destroyed any hope the Model Treaty had held out for preserving America's "Virgin Character" politically.

Franklin did extract a price. Most important, France guaranteed American independence. And the United States retained the promise of some future empire, for it was to receive all the "Northern Parts of America" taken from England, while France would also guarantee, "from the present time and forever," all other "conquests" the United States made in the war, except, of course, in the West Indies. Not only would the new nation become independent, but Britain's empire in the New World was to be destroyed and parceled out to Americans and Frenchmen, even if it took "forever."[12]

The French Trap

But Vergennes had been double-dealing. Despite the promises in the treaty, it was not in French interest to create a great American empire that might drive the French and Spanish, as well as the British, from the Western Hemisphere. Early in 1778 Vergennes sent Alexandre Gerard as the first French minister to the United States with instructions to keep constantly in mind the family alliance between the French and Spanish thrones. Translated, this meant that Gerard must do everything in his power to prevent the Americans from enlarging their territory at the expense of the Spanish Empire in Florida and the Mississippi River area. Vergennes hoped to contain the United States.

Gerard found willing allies in Congress, particularly in the faction headed by Dickinson and Robert Morris. The states represented by this faction did not have strong claims to western or southern lands, and were willing to soft-pedal territorial gains if they could obtain commercial privileges from the French. Gerard and his successor, the Chevalier de la Luzerne, soon talked Congress

---

[12] The treaties may be found in both English and French versions in *Treaties and Other International Acts of the United States of America,* ed. Hunter Miller (Washington, D.C., 1931), 2:3–27.

into dropping its ambitions for Canada and the Newfoundland fisheries in return for increased military aid. Congress even agreed to Luzerne's request that the Spanish be guaranteed "the Floridas" if in return they gave Americans free navigation rights on the Mississippi River.

The Lee-Adams Junto was infuriated. Its hope for French aid in carving out an American empire not only had proved false, but had backfired. France was fencing in the United States, and American dependence upon Luzerne's tolerance grew as the course of the war become more disastrous. During the winter of 1779–1780 the British evacuated most of the northern areas, except the vital port of New York City, and concentrated their forces in the South. In May 1780 they won a major victory at Charleston, South Carolina, then moved into a position where they could squeeze American armies between the New York and Charleston forces. The British fleet meanwhile controlled the Atlantic.

American economic power unfortunately matched that of the military. The exporting of such staples as naval supplies and rice dropped sharply because of British naval blockades and England's control of areas in the southeast where these goods were produced. The United States became increasingly dependent upon French and Spanish loans, and consequently upon Luzerne's advice. With the disappearance of revenue, paper money issued by the Congress literally became "not worth a continental."

United States leaders began to understand that the only alternative to complete dependence upon the French was a strong American central government that could tax, raise funds for an army and navy, and consequently break free of Luzerne's economic stranglehold. Such a government, however, could not be created. "But why is not this system changed?" John Jay of New York asked. "It is, in my opinion, convenient to the family compact" of the Lees and Adamses.[13] The charge was partly true. Although desiring a great empire, the Junto, with the glaring exception of John Adams, wanted no strong central government controlling that empire. Such a government would threaten the Junto's control of local politics in Virginia and Massachusetts.

In 1780–1781 the nation did take one short stride toward stronger central government. Under the threat of British occupation, Virginia tried to rally the states by finally ceding its vast claims north of the Ohio River to Congress. This cession broke the log jam that had prevented ratification of the Articles of Confederation by several states with no claims to western land. Maryland, also

---

[13] Jay to Washington, April 26, 1779, in *The Correspondence and Public Papers of John Jay,* ed. Henry P. Johnston, 4 vols. (New York, 1890), 1:209.

faced with imminent British invasion, ratified the Articles and they went into effect.

But the results soon proved disquieting. The Articles did not give Congress the powers to tax or regulate commerce. These critical weapons remained in the hands of the individual states. The historic independence and local pride of each former colony were being jealously, zealously guarded—even in the face of a threatening collapse of the revolutionary cause. Without power to tax and regulate commerce, Congress could not translate political unity into economic and military power. In 1781 the Morris faction resolved to give Congress such powers, but Virginia and Rhode Island refused to agree, thereby preventing the unanimity of states needed to amend the Articles of Confederation.

Escaping the Trap

THESE MONTHS of near-catastrophe for the rising American empire ended in the early-morning hours of October 22, 1781, when a rider brought news to Philadelphia that a main British army had surrendered at Yorktown, Virginia, three days before. Congress did not immediately recognize the full significance of the news. Peace negotiations would not commence for several months, and British troops continued to occupy several vital American ports. A full-dress debate on possible diplomatic instructions to be sent to Franklin in Paris (now joined by John Jay, who had failed in a mission to Spain, and John Adams, also unsuccessful in an attempt to pry money out of the Dutch) did not begin in Congress until almost nine months after the Yorktown triumph.

After a hectic debate the congressional factions temporarily buried their differences in order to break free of French domination. Congress decided in August 1782 to press for both the fisheries and the western lands. In Paris, Franklin and Jay knew nothing about the debate. Quite independently they used intrigue and manipulated European power balances to work out a preliminary treaty with Great Britain which created a solid base for the American empire—that empire which Franklin had coveted and planned for as early as the 1750s.

Their opportunity had arisen not as a result of the battle at Yorktown, but in the wake of two events in Europe during the spring of 1782. First, the British had held Gibraltar despite three attacks by the Spanish, inflicting heavy losses upon the navy of France's closest ally. Great Britain had therefore retained one of its most vital strategic posts and could enter peace negotiations fresh from a major naval victory. Second, in March the bitterly anti-American ministry of Lord North resigned. A new ministry, led by Lord Shelburne, assumed power and began making peace overtures to the Americans. Shelburne soon discovered indirectly from Franklin and Jay that if the negotiations were properly handled, the Franco-American alliance of 1778 might be dissolved. The United States was not interested in remaining dependent upon Vergennes and Luzerne.

On July 9, 1782, Franklin met with a British emissary, Richard Oswald, to initiate discussions. Oswald happened to be an old and compliant friend of Franklin's. Never one to underestimate either his own or his nation's ambitions, Franklin astonished even the phlegmatic Oswald by immediately presenting eight proposals. The first four, the Pennsylvanian counseled his friend, were "necessary": (1) full and complete independence of the United States and withdrawal of British troops; (2) redrawing of Canadian boundaries north of the Great Lakes instead of at the Ohio River, where they had been extended by the Quebec Act of 1774; (3) settlement of all boundaries between the United States and the loyal colonies to the north; (4) American rights to fish off the Newfoundland coast for both fish and whale.

Franklin termed the second set of four points "advisable"; that is, what he as an earnest friend of England would advise if the British hoped to win American friendship and prevent future Anglo-American wars: (1) the payment of reparations by Britain for the destruction of American towns; (2) a public apology by Parliament for "distressing those countries so much"; (3) reciprocal trading privileges between the thirteen states and the British Empire; (4) British cession to the United States of all of Canada.

When the stunned Oswald regained his composure, he sent these proposals to Shelburne, who immediately rejected all the "advisable" articles. He also balked at explicitly granting the United States independence or allowing extensive fishing rights off the Newfoundland coast.

At the beginning of September, Franklin became ill and was replaced by John Jay. With the New Yorker's appearance, the discussion topics began to shift. Jay grew less insistent on the cession of Canada and instead concentrated on acquiring the lands lying between the former colonies and the Mississippi. Above all, he demanded explicit British recognition of American independence.

The climax occurred when Jay learned that Vergennes had agreed to Spanish demands for territory south of the Ohio and control over navigation on the Mississippi. A few days later, on September 10, Oswald shrewdly passed to Jay certain captured documents proving that Luzerne was secretly working in Congress for the acceptance of the Apalachians as the western boundary.

That night Jay discovered that Vergennes's private secretary had left under cover of darkness to sail to London for a conference with Shelburne. Convinced that France and Spain were prepared to exchange America's western empire for a quick separate peace, Jay moved rapidly to beat his allies to the punch. He informed Oswald that discussions could resume immediately if Shelburne would grant de facto recognition of independence by giving the British commissioners instructions to negotiate with agents of the United States. The Prime Minister, closely watching this growing split between French and American policies, immediately complied.

By October 5 Jay and Oswald had agreed to an American boundary on the Mississippi. Within several more weeks, accord was reached on the British demand that the pro-British Loyalists who had fled America to settle in Canada or England be indemnified for property destroyed or confiscated by the revolutionaries. Then Franklin reentered the negotiations to win fishing rights along the Newfoundland coast. His clinching argument: "You know that we shall bring the greatest part of the money we get for that fish to Great Britain to pay for your manufactures." That remark was accurate as well as diplomatic.

In the preliminary treaty, signed November 3, 1782, the United States won the Mississippi as its western boundary and the St. Lawrence River and the Great Lakes as the northern demarcation. Without consulting Spain, the negotiators agreed that both Great Britain and the United States should have navigation rights on the Mississippi. The British promised to evacuate troops from the northwest posts "with all convenient speed." Finally, Spain was awarded the Floridas south of the thirty-first parallel as recompense for its frustration in failing to defeat the British at Gibraltar.

The extent of the American diplomatic triumph amazed the French and Spanish. The British concessions, Vergennes remarked, "exceed all that I should have thought possible." The Foreign Minister could not afford the luxury of anger, however, for berating the Americans could lead now to an informal alliance between the United States and Great Britain against the French. Franklin brilliantly played on this fear when he not only informed Vergennes, as he had to do, that the peace treaty had been signed without consultation with him, but then asked for another million-dollar loan. Recognizing how craftily Franklin was trapping him with the threat of an Anglo-American partnership, Vergennes accepted the preliminary treaty and even provided the loan from the impoverished French treasury. On September 3, 1783, Great Britain and the United States signed the final treaty.

The American diplomats in Paris bragged justifiably to Congress that although Spain and France had worked desperately to contain the United States, the agreed-upon boundaries "appear to leave us little to complain of and not much to desire."[14] The new nation had somehow emerged from seven years of near-defeat with both independence and empire. But observant Americans soon began to wonder whether their countrymen would be able to retain either.

Suggestions for Further Reading

Samuel Flagg Bemis, *The Diplomacy of the American Revolution* (New York, 1935), set the standard, but has now been superseded by Richard B. Morris, *The Peacemakers: The Great Powers and American Independence* (New York, 1965), and Richard W. Van Alstyne, *Empire and Independence: The International History of the American Revolution* (New York, 1965). A. B. Darling, *Our Rising Empire, 1763–1803* (New Haven, Conn., 1940), continues to be useful. All four of these volumes, however, stress international ramifications of American policy and neglect the domestic factions that produced the policy. A volume on the internal politics of foreign policy formulation during the Revolution is badly needed, and an important step toward such a study is William C. Stinchcombe's very helpful *The American Revolution and the French Alliance* (Syracuse, N.Y., 1969); Felix Gilbert, *To the Farewell Address: Ideas of Early American Foreign Policy* (Princeton, N.J., 1961), is a brilliant analysis of the intellectual formulation of that early policy. Paul A. Varg, *Foreign Policies of the Founding Fathers* (East Lansing, Mich., 1963), is good on both domestic and external factors from the Revolution to the War of 1812.

Important individuals are analyzed in John C. Miller, *Sam Adams* (Stanford, Calif., 1960), although more perceptive on Adams is William Appleman Williams' essay in *Studies on the Left,* 1 (Winter 1960):47–57. Page Smith has written a two-volume biography of John Adams (New York, 1962). The financial dilemmas are delineated in Clarence Ver Steeg's fine biography *Robert Morris* (Philadelphia, 1954) and in E. James Ferguson, *The Power of the Purse: A History of American Public Finance, 1776–1790* (Williamsburg, Va., 1961).

The crucial economic principle of American diplomacy is traced out in Vernon G. Setser's *The Commercial Reciprocity Policy of the United States, 1774–1829* (Philadelphia, 1937).

See also the general bibliography at the end of this volume.

---

[14] Adams, Franklin, Jay, and Laurens to Livingston, December 14, 1782, in *The Revolutionary Diplomatic Correspondence of the United States,* ed. Francis Wharton, 6 vols. (Washington, D.C., 1889), 6:132.

CHAPTER 3

The Imperial Constitution
(1783–1788)

Having conceived an empire, Americans were faced, as are parents of most seven-year-olds, with having to discipline it. The moment was auspicious. Americans, wrote Washington to the state governers in June 1783, are

> placed in the most enviable condition, as the sole Lords and Proprietors of a vast Tract of Continent, comprehending all the various soils and climates of the World.... They are, from this period, to be considered as the Actors on a most conspicuous Theatre, which seems to be peculiarly designated by Providence for the display of human greatness and felicity; Here, they are not only surrounded with every thing which can contribute to the completion of private and domestic enjoyment, but Heaven has crowned all its other blessings, by giving a fairer opportunity for political happiness, than any other Nation has ever been favored with.... The foundation of our Empire was not laid in the gloomy age of Ignorance and Superstition, but at an Epocha when the rights of mankind were better understood and more clearly defined, than at any former period.... At this auspicious period, the United States came into existence as a Nation, and if their Citizens should not be completely free and happy, the fault will be intirely (*sic*) their own.[1]

---

[1] "Circular to the States," June 8, 1783, in George Washington, *Writings from the Original Manuscripts Sources, 1745–1799,* ed. John C. Fitzpatrick, 39 vols. (Washington, D.C., 1931–1944), 26:484–86.

Small wonder that Americans, being human, have sometimes become irrational and bloodstained because they could not match their performance with this promise. But the first generation of independent Americans did fulfill its obligation to the promise, although only after a near-collapse of the empire in the mid-1780s.

The Breakdown of Trade—and Society

IMMEDIATELY AFTER the Revolution, American leaders viewed new commercial relationships as necessary if the United States was to survive as an independent nation. "After all," John Adams had noted privately, "the circumstances of modes, language, and religion have much less influence in determining the friendship and enmity of nations than other more essential interests. Commerce is more than all these and many more such circumstances."[2] When Franklin and Adams searched for new trade treaties with Europe, however, they found welcomes only in Morocco, Sweden, and Prussia, hardly world economic powers. The French offered little help, for although they allowed some American goods into their islands in the West Indies and France itself, fish (a vital American export) were finally substantially excluded from the Caribbean islands, and French merchants proved incapable of extending necessary long-term credit to American merchants.

The greatest commercial power, Great Britain, determined to strangle the American economy. The British were not about to reward revolution with trade preferences. They excluded American ships from the British West Indies, allowed such enumerated American goods as tobacco to enter the islands only on British ships, cut trade between the United States and Canada, and, in all, tried to ensure that Americans would provide necessary raw materials and foodstuffs to British industry while consuming the manufactures of that industry. London correctly assumed the new nation needed its trade, and that under the Articles of Confederation the American government was incapable of retaliating against British trade discriminations because the central government lacked powers to levy tariffs, pay subsidies, or in other ways encourage and regulate trade. "Our trade was never more compleatly monopolized by Great Britain when it was under the direction of the British Parliament than

---

[2] Adams to Edmond Genêt, May 17, 1780, in *The Revolutionary Diplomatic Correspondence of the United States,* ed. Francis Wharton, 6 vols. (Washington, D.C., 1889), 3:687.

it is at this moment," James Madison of Virginia wrote in sorrow in 1785.[3]

A thorough search continued for other markets. In 1784 Robert Morris fitted out the first American ship to engage in the China trade, *The Empress of China*. The Great Asian Market appeared as a vision for the first time in American history. "I fear that our Countrymen will overdue this business," Richard Henry Lee told Madison in 1785. "For now there appears every where a Rage for East India Voyages."[4] Lee's fears were justified; the Asian trade exacerbated the economic problem, for imports from the Orient, especially of luxuries, increased while the East Indies could not absorb surplus tobacco, naval stores, and other staple American exports.

The balance of trade worsened for the United States as American specie (gold and silver), already in severely short supply, left the country in large amounts to pay for imports from Great Britain and the East Indies. With money scarce and the individual states incapable of regulating their international trade, prices started to fall in mid-1784. During the four-year depression that followed, prices dropped 25 percent in the capital city of Philadelphia. Some states attempted to solve the money shortage by printing vast amounts of paper money, but without any specie to support it, the paper soon became worthless.

Other areas turned to rebellion. The most dramatic upheaval occurred in western Massachusetts, where the economic tightening led to the Shays Rebel-

Shays' Rebellion

---

[3] Madison to James Monroe, June 21, 1785, in *The Writings of James Madison*, ed. Gaillard Hunt, 9 vols. (New York, 1901), 2:147–48.

[4] Lee to Madison, May 30, 1785, in *The Letters of Richard Henry Lee*, ed. James C. Ballagh, 2 vols. (New York, 1911–1914), 2:366.

lion. The Shaysites warned the General Court sitting in Boston that the West must have more "circulating medium" and increased political power. These demands were heard; indeed, the uprising so frightened Madison and Washington in faraway Virginia that they intensified their drive for a constitutional convention to deal with this splintering of what Washington had once hopefully called "our Rising Empire."

The West Talks of Secession

REBELLIONS LIKE SHAYS' could have spread throughout the trans-Apalachian West during the mid-1780s. The area was rapidly filling with settlers. In 1779 Kentucky had approximately 200 people; by 1785 it possessed 30,000. As population grew, money seemed to become more scarce. Under the Articles, Congress demonstrated an inability to help westerners economically or to protect them against Indian attacks. The area was in turmoil. After visiting the headwaters of the Ohio River in 1784, Washington reported that the westerners "stand as it were upon a pivot; the touch of a feather would turn them any way." They could move in three directions: toward the British Empire to the north, toward the Spanish to the west and south, or toward an independent empire of their own.

In Congress, Thomas Jefferson attempted to cement the Northwest to the East in 1784 by proposing an ordinance that would establish a system through which new states, such as Kentucky, would enter the Union. But his plan proved unacceptable to both East and West. Easterners wanted more control over the Northwest than Jefferson had provided, while the West disliked his division of the area into fourteen future states; it wanted fewer, larger, and therefore more viable states. Jefferson believed westerners would not be able to govern themselves in large states, particularly since settlers were so intractable ("savages" was the term easterners often used to describe their countrymen beyond the mountains). The powers of government in such a vast realm, moreover, would be slow and difficult to wield. The Founding Fathers would face this problem again at the Constitutional Convention three years after Jefferson's proposal was defeated.

The western crisis worsened when conflict developed with Spain in 1784–1785. The northern boundaries of Florida had not been precisely defined by the 1783 peace treaty. Both Spanish soldiers and American speculators and pioneers surged into the disputed territory. To the west, Spanish officials tried to wean American settlers away from the Philadelphia government by regulating trade on the Mississippi River. Finally in 1784 Spain closed the river, "pending further settlement" of outstanding problems with the United States. With its control of the Mississippi as an unbeatable trump card, the Spanish government sent Diego de Gardoqui to negotiate settlement of a broad range of problems with the American Secretary for Foreign Affairs, John Jay.

Gardoqui announced that Spain would protect its empire against American encroachment by closing the Mississippi for twenty or thirty years. In return, he was prepared to surrender some of the disputed Florida territory, give a territorial guarantee to the United States (which would prove helpful if Great Britain attempted to stretch its Canadian boundary southward), and allow American trade with Spain and the Canary Islands, although not with the Spanish colonies in America. In making this proposal on trade, Gardoqui clearly attempted to separate eastern trading interests from the western concern over the Mississippi.

Jay decided to accept the plan. He believed that increased trade with Spain would produce badly needed specie and help lift the United States out of the depression. Having won the West at the Paris negotiations in 1782–1783, Jay was reluctant to stifle those settlements two years later, but he believed the Philadelphia government incapable of protecting the West and assumed that within twenty years the fecund and expansive Americans would gain control of the waterway regardless of Spanish objections.

Congress, however, rejected the Jay-Gardoqui pact. With a two-thirds vote needed, seven northern states supported Jay and five southern states opposed him. The division was ominous. The cohesion of the Lee-Adams Junto had dissipated and the new nation divided sectionally, North and East versus South and West. Angry Kentuckians warned that if the treaty went into effect they would join the British and open the Mississippi by force. "When once-reunited to [the British]," a Louisville writer informed Jay and Congress, "'farewell, *a long farewell* to all *your* boasted greatness,' [for then] the province of Canada and the inhabitants of these waters, of themselves, in time, will be able to conquer *you*."[5]

A Gathering Nationalism

JAY RESPONDED to his defeat by telling Congress in April 1787 that since there was "no respectable middle way between peace and war, it will be expedient

---

[5] Wharton, ed., *Revolutionary Diplomatic Correspondence,* 6:223–24.

to prepare without delay for the one or the other." Congress, however, could neither pull the nation together for war against Spain nor develop sufficient diplomatic leverage to force Spain to surrender the Mississippi without war. The Articles of Confederation placed the vital powers of regulating commerce and raising revenue in the hands of the states, but the rising problems of empire—in the West Indies, in Asia, in the trans-Apalachian area—transcended the boundaries and powers of individual states. A single state was incapable of dealing on equal terms with the empire of either Britain or Spain. Indeed, as the 1780s progressed, some Americans observed the Shays Rebellion and the disappearance of vital civil liberties in Virginia and wondered whether "these vile governments" could govern even their own states.

Provincial, if powerful, state governments were rapidly becoming irrelevant to the opportunities and problems of the 1780s. Stagecoach routes multiplied, and many of them crossed state boundaries. Steamboats made their first appearance, appropriately during the summer of 1787, when the Constitutional Convention delegates relaxed by watching a supposed madman, John Fitch, run his invention on the river at Philadelphia. Regular mail routes developed from New Hampshire to Georgia. As this external transportation revolution began, state governments proved incapable of reconciling diverse interests within their own boundaries, especially when the issue of foreign trade became involved. Regardless of state, most merchants wanted free trade and help for their shipping, while most artisans pleaded for higher tariffs to protect their products. As settlers moved inland, they needed specie, land titles, and defense against the Indians, items that individual states found difficulty in providing.

Some men, merely with their time and not ahead of it, tried to bring political institutions more in line with socioeconomic developments. James Madison and his fellow Virginian James Monroe attempted to persuade Congress to give itself powers to regulate trade. The proposal won support from merchants and chambers of commerce in New York City, Boston, and Philadelphia, but the move failed in 1785 because such legislation needed the unanimous consent of the states. Rhode Island, profiting from trade both legal and illegal, refused to place its commerce under the central government's control. On another level, Noah Webster led a group of intellectuals, including poets Joel Barlow and Timothy Dwight and historian David Ramsey, in emphasizing the importance of an American language and publicizing the nationalistic aspects of American life. Through his spellers, readers, and popular public lectures, Webster condemned the Articles of Confederation and worked for the success of the Constitutional Convention.

Meanwhile the political leaders sought ways to construct a strong union

James Madison

"by other means than State politics," as Washington wrote privately in 1783, "or ...we shall be instruments in the hands of our Enemies and those European powers who may be jealous of our greatness in Union to dissolve the Confederation."[6] Madison laid down the principle that guided this search for the proper tactics: "In fact, most of our political evils may be traced up to our commercial ones, as most of our moral may to our political."[7]

Madison, 1787: The Need
for an Extensive Empire

DELEGATES FROM twelve states finally gathered at Philadelphia between May and September 1787. (Rhode Island, difficult as always, never sent representatives.) These men were not merely politicians. Many of the leading figures were the outstanding intellectuals of their century, particularly in the area of political

[6] Washington to Hamilton, March 31, 1783, in *The Papers of Alexander Hamilton*, ed. Harold C. Syrett and Jacob Cooke, 15 vols. (New York, 1961–1969), 3:310.

[7] Madison to Jefferson, March 18, 1786, in *Writings of Madison*, 2:228–29.

theory. In this sense, the United States was blessed at its constitutional founding, for its originators were as profound as they were clever, as learned as they were articulate. A half century earlier the leading intellectuals had been the clergy. By the 1780s intellectual leadership moved with Franklin, Jefferson, Adams, and Madison into the political arena. Fortunately for Americans, it was at this juncture of their history that the Constitution was written.

Madison, "the Father of the Constitution," as he would later be called, exemplified this combination of intellect and political skill. In 1786 he left the Virginia House of Delegates, where he had served for two years, and retired to his home at Montpelier to immerse himself in the study of history, particularly the rise and fall of classical empires. He distilled this study and published much of it late in 1787 as numbers 18, 19, and 20 of the *Federalist Papers*.[8] The focus was upon the ancient Achaean League, which, he pointedly argued, fell because it had no strong central body to reconcile its factions and maintain its national coherence. From this study and his contemporary observations, Madison concluded that internal events shaped external relations. "If we be free and happy at home," he commented in 1788, "we shall be respectable abroad."

The Convention's central problem was the same one that had confronted the great political thinkers for more than two thousand years: how to create a government strong enough to protect itself against internal and external enemies, but not strong enough to destroy the legitimate and necessary freedoms of individual citizens. Such great minds as Aristotle and Montesquieu had agreed upon one starting point in this quest: a balanced republican government could more easily be constructed in a small area than over a large territory. As Montesquieu had observed nearly a century before:

> It is natural for a republic to have only a small territory. In an extensive republic, the public good is sacrificed to a thousand private views.... In a small one, the interest of the public is more obvious, better understood, and more within the reach of every citizen; abuses have less extent.

Madison disagreed with this observation. In part, he had no alternative to rejecting it, for he and his fellow delegates were faced with the problem of constructing a government for a vast empire stretching from the Atlantic to the Mississippi. Moving from the assumption that "the most common and durable source of factions has been the various and unequal distribution of property" (a phrase he used in *Federalist 10*), Madison concluded that perhaps the best way of controlling such factions was to stand Aristotle's and Montesquieu's theory on its head. If you "extend the sphere" of government, Madison wrote,

---

8 This is the first of several references to *The Federalist Papers*. They may be read in a convenient paperback edition edited by Clinton Rossiter (New York, 1961).

you take in a greater variety of parties and interests; you make it less probable that a majority of the whole will have a common motive to invade the rights of other citizens; or, if such a common motive exists, it will be more difficult for all who feel it to discover their own strength and to act in unison with each other.

This argument allowed the Virginian to advocate a strong central government. Such a government could protect its citizens against external enemies (such as Spaniards who wanted to close the Mississippi River to Americans). At the same time, if the empire was large enough, property and interests would be so diverse that no single faction could gain control of the government and destroy the freedoms of other factions. A strong central government, therefore, was not to be feared. It was to be created.

Madison and the other founders, however, added two devices to protect the empire against its seizure by one faction, or by a majority that might seek to repress a minority. The central governing unit would not possess all powers. Some were to be shared with state governments and others were to be left completely with the states. Nor was the central government to be monolithic. To ensure that even if a faction captured one branch it would have difficulty controlling the entire government, the Constitutional Convention divided the central government into an executive branch, a two-body legislature, and a judiciary, which could check one another. These devices were the essence of the "republican government" created at Philadelphia, and contrasted strongly with the dominant, single-body legislature provided by the Articles of Confederation.

In summary, a strong central government could safely be constructed because it would be checked in two ways: first, it would preside over such a large empire that far-flung factions would have great difficulty in uniting and taking over the government at the expense of minority or majority rights; second, the central government itself would be carefully divided according to function, with each part able to check the other two.

The Constitution as a "Machine" for Foreign Policy

WITH THESE fundamentals worked out, the founders proceeded to give the government the necessary powers to protect the empire. Madison posed the key commercial question when he proposed that the new government be allowed to pass commercial laws, which would govern all the states, by a mere majority. Southerners and westerners strongly protested. They feared their interests

Constitutional Convention at Philadelphia

would be sacrificed in the new Congress for the benefit of northern merchants. The impasse was finally broken by one of the major compromises at the Convention. Southern delegates dropped their demand for a two-thirds approval of commercial laws and accepted a provision allowing such acts to be passed by a mere majority. In return, northern delegates (and Madison) dropped their demand that the slave trade be immediately halted. That iniquitous business was allowed to continue for another twenty years.

The Convention devoted considerable time to a thorough discussion of the war-making power. The delegates knew that in Europe the executive (usually the King) enjoyed nearly complete authority in declaring and carrying out war. The founders, however, trusted no man completely. A belief that human nature could not be trusted because it was driven by passion, sometimes to the detriment of reason, guided the Convention when it discussed war-making powers.

It quickly distinguished between the power to "make" war and the power to "declare" war. Agreement was easily reached that the executive could better "make" war than Congress. But debate raged over which body should "declare" war. One delegate proposed the power be entrusted to the President, another wanted the Senate only to have it. George Mason of Virginia summarized the prevailing view: he "was against giving the power of war to the Executive, because [it] was not to be trusted with it; or to the Senate, because [it was] not so constructed as to be entitled to it. He was for clogging rather than facilitating war; but for facilitating peace."[9] The result was a provision requiring both houses of Congress to pass declarations of war proposed by the President, but allowing the Senate alone to approve peace treaties negotiated by the President.

The President was named "Commander in Chief of the Army and Navy of the United States." The delegates expressed little concern over giving the executive this power, for they believed Congress would control this authority through its power over the purse. But congressional prerogative in this area was also carefully circumscribed, for the legislature could "raise and support Armies, but no Appropriation of Money to that Use shall be for a longer Term than two Years" (Article 1, Section 8). In few other areas were the founders so careful about checking power. Elbridge Gerry of Massachusetts even proposed a clause in the Constitution that would prohibit a standing peacetime army of more than two or three thousand men. After discussion, Gerry dropped this scheme, but the delegates clearly had no intention of giving the central government, and particularly the President, the unrestricted power to create and maneuver such a peacetime military establishment as has been developed in the mid-twentieth century.

In a long discussion of who could best negotiate treaties with foreign powers, the Convention originally proposed to give this power only to the Senate. Fears that the Senate might represent narrow interests, however, led to a compromise: the President would make such treaties "by and with the advice and consent of the Senate ... provided two-thirds of the Senators present concur." The two-thirds rule thus provided reassurance to the South and West, a poultice needed especially after their frightening experience with the Jay-Gardoqui Treaty. Upon a motion by the eighty-two-year-old Franklin, the Convention agreed that treaties, as well as measures passed by Congress, were supreme over state law. Franklin had learned from long experience how single-state interests, unless checked in this manner, could render useless treaties made in good faith between American diplomats and foreign governments.

The Work of the Founding Fathers

THE AUTHORS of the Constitution did not primarily concern themselves with the problems of defining justice and righteousness. Madison observed simply in *Federalist 51* that "Justice is the end of government." He and the founders were

---

[9] Max Farrand, ed., *The Records of the Federal Convention of 1787,* 4 vols. (New Haven, Conn., 1937), 2:318–19.

preëminently concerned with constructing a path that would allow enlightened men to find justice, and then tried to ensure that the path would be kept open. Franklin caught the essence of the Convention's work when he referred to the new government as "our grand machine." Like all machines, it was to be a means of accomplishing great objectives, not to be the objective in and of itself.

The machine was to operate in a great empire. *Indeed, as Madison's theory explained, it could not operate properly unless it existed in a great empire.* And if, as Madison argued, the government could function only as long as the empire was large enough to separate and diversify factions, it followed that as the empire of 1787 filled with people and factions, and as imperial dimensions shrank because of new communications and more efficient governmental controls, the government could be maintained only by the further enlargement of the empire.

Gouverneur Morris, who wrote the initial draft of the Constitution, later explained that he carefully worded Article 4, Section 3, to allow vast territorial expansion of the new nation. In 1803, amidst the controversy over whether to annex the vast Louisiana Territory, Morris argued that this provision of the Constitution permitted the Union to absorb not only Louisiana but Canada as well, and, if necessary, "to govern them as provinces and allow them no voice in our councils."[10] If Morris accurately interpreted the spirit of that section, it complemented Madison's belief that republican government would expand, and would prosper as it expanded. "The larger the society, provided it lie within a practicable sphere, the more duly capable it will be of self-government," Madison wrote in *Federalist 51.* "And happily for the *republican cause,* the practicable sphere may be carried to a very great extent by a judicious modification and mixture of the *federal principle."*

The implications for foreign policy of Morris' and Madison's words are immense. Further territorial expansion meant conflict with Great Britain or Spain. Commercial expansion required confrontation with the great mercantile powers of the British and French empires. But the United States was not conceived as a static empire. Indeed, when it stagnated between 1784 and 1787, it

---

[10] Morris to Robert Livingston, December 4, 1803, quoted in *Congressional Record,* 55th Cong., 3d sess., p. 294. Article 4, Section 3, reads: "New States may be admitted by the Congress into this Union; but no new State shall be formed or erected within the Jurisdiction of any other State; nor any State be formed by the Junction of two or more States, or Parts of States, without the Consent of the Legislatures of the States concerned as well as of the Congress.

"The Congress shall have Power to dispose of and make all needful Rules and Regulations respecting the Territory or other Property belonging to the United States; and nothing in this Constitution shall be so construed as to prejudice any Claims of the United States, or of any particular State."

had, in the view of such leaders as Madison, Washington, and Hamilton, nearly dissolved.[11]

The Ordinance of 1787

THE CONVENTION provided the "machine" to pull the empire together, govern it properly, and enable it to expand. During the same summer, the Congress, still operating under the Articles of Confederation, passed legislation that implemented the imperial view of the Constitutional Convention. In July the dying Congress enacted the Ordinance of 1787. This measure outlined the steps through which territories (now the states of Ohio, Indiana, Illinois, Michigan, and Wisconsin) would move to become equal states in the Union.

The Ordinance provided that not less than three or more than five states would be established in the Northwest (or, as it would soon be called, the Old Northwest). Then it listed the stages through which the territories would pass to become states: (1) in the first stage, the settlers would be controlled by a governor, secretary, and three judges named by Congress; (2) when the population reached 5,000, the inhabitants would elect a legislature that would govern with a council of five selected by the governor (who would enjoy veto powers over the legislature) and by Congress; (3) when the population reached 60,000, the inhabitants could write a constitution and apply for admission to the Union on terms of equality with the original thirteen states. Freedom of worship and right to jury trial were guaranteed. Slavery was forbidden.

Westerners attacked the legislation, especially its first two stages, during which Congress would control the territory. The 1787 Ordinance established "colonial" governments over the Northwest Territory in a written, systematic, and detailed fashion, a feat that the British colonial government never succeeded in accomplishing at the peak of its imperial strength in the eighteenth and nineteenth centuries. Because the Ordinance required congressional control, it needed a strong central government to make it effective. That type of government was being created at the same time in Philadelphia. Article 4, Section 3 of the Constitution provided "The Congress shall have Power to dispose of and

---

[11] See Madison to Jefferson, October 24, 1787, in *The Papers of Thomas Jefferson,* ed. Julian Boyd et al., 60 vols. (Princeton, N.J., 1950–   ), 12:279–81. This Madison letter is the best short analysis of the Convention and the theory of the Constitution ever made, partly because Madison was willing to say privately what he could not say publicly.

make all needful Rules and Regulations respecting the territory or other Property belonging to the United States."

The government continued to employ the Ordinance during the next 125 years as Americans conquered a continent from Spaniards, Englishmen, Russians, Mexicans, and, let us not forget, Indian nations. The Ordinance of 1787 and the federal government created the same year were the "machines" that carried on and exploited the triumphs of American continental expansion.

Conclusion: 1776–1787

THE UNITED STATES had moved far from John Adams' Model Treaty of 1776 and the belief that its principles could be realized by a weak central government. Adams and his colleagues had hoped that by freeing world commerce, the United States would remove causes for war and enhance its own profits in peaceful trade. In elevating commercial power above military power, the Model Treaty also allowed maximum play to commerce as a diplomatic tool, while attempting to minimize naked military power, an area in which the United States was woefully weak. By 1780, however, Adams, Jay, Franklin, and their countrymen had learned that in Europe, military and political alliances determined commerce. The founders sought a means to avoid military and political alignments with Europe while at the same time playing an international political game so that American trade could flow in all directions. If that trade did not expand, domestic depression and rebellion would result, as indeed it did between 1784 and 1788.

The climax of this effort was the Constitutional Convention's decision to strengthen the American Union. This would be accomplished not by entering into alignments with Europeans, but by placing in the hands of the central government sufficient powers so that Americans would have the wherewithal to deal on equal terms with the leading commercial powers of the world. The United States was to have the power to become independent economically, for without that, political independence was of small value.

This was the awesome accomplishment of 1787: thirteen states were united, yet the individual rights of their citizens were preserved so they could expand effectively across a continent and compete economically against the world's other empires. And Americans could build their empire without having to participate in the alliances and military commitments of corrupt, monarchical Europe.

If this was American isolationism, it was isolationism that sought and achieved a worldwide empire.

Suggestions for Further Reading

Merrill Jensen, *The New Nation* (New York, 1950), is a stimulating interpretive account, now challenged in part and from various perspectives in Gordon S. Wood, *The Creation of the American Republic, 1776–1787* (Williamsburg, Va., 1969); Wood is superb for an understanding of the Founding Fathers' fears of 1785–1787. The economic problems are explained in E. James Ferguson, *The Power of the Purse: A History of American Public Finance, 1776–1790* (Chapel Hill, N.C., 1961). And the most provocative interpretation of the Constitution's formulation and ratification is Forest McDonald's *We the People: The Economic Origins of the Constitution* (Chicago, 1958). The indispensable source is Max Farrand, ed., *The Records of the Federal Convention of 1787,* 4 vols. (New Haven, Conn., 1937).

Morton Borden has edited an interesting and useful compendium of *The Antifederalist Papers* (East Lansing, Mich., 1965), giving the case against the Founding Fathers in words of the Antifederalists themselves. The Antifederalists are dissected in Jackson Turner Main, *The Antifederalists* (Williamsburg, Va., 1961).

Two of the most important delegates to the Convention have new biographies: Gerald Stourzh, *Alexander Hamilton and the Idea of Republican Government* (Stanford, Calif., 1970), especially good on the interaction between domestic institutions and foreign policy, and Ralph Ketcham, *James Madison* (New York, 1971); Irving Brant, *James Madison, the Nationalist, 1780–1787* (Indianapolis, 1948), is considerably more detailed.

The Ordinance of 1787 and its aftereffects are treated in Jack E. Eblen, *The First and Second U.S. Empires: Governors and Territorial Government, 1784–1912* (Pittsburgh, 1968).

Important relations with Great Britain and Spain are examined in several standard works: Samuel Flagg Bemis, *Jay's Treaty* and *Pinckney's Treaty* (New Haven, Conn., 1962); Arthur P. Whitaker, *The Spanish-American Frontier, 1783–1795* (Boston, 1927); and A. L. Burt, *The United States, Great Britain, and British North America, 1783–1815* (New Haven, Conn., 1940).

See also the general bibliography at the end of this volume.

CHAPTER 4

Empire Endangered (1789–1800)

The United States is now two centuries old (the world's most aged republic), but the new nation under the Constitution almost had a life span of less than a dozen years. The Union balanced on the brink of collapse in 1795–1796 and again in 1798–1799. The cause was foreign policy. The divisive question concerned which course of empire Americans should follow: could they best preserve and expand their prosperity by paying a high price to reenter their traditional markets in the British Empire, or should they attempt to create an independent commercial empire, perhaps with the aid of the French? This was not a problem easily confined to the accounting houses and stock exchanges. It quickly created hatred between Madison and Hamilton (those two key leaders who once had been so friendly that they cooperated in writing the *Federalist Papers*), hopelessly splintered the Federalist party, created explosive political factions, drove the Federalists out of power for all time in 1800, and nearly created a separation of the western states from the Union. Because of its need to expand, the new nation nearly failed to survive its first decade.

Madison's Plan of 1789

IMMEDIATELY MOVING into the leadership of the first House of Representatives, which convened in April 1789, Madison forced the central issue to the forefront of debate. He was determined to use the new constitutional powers to expand American commerce by squeezing concessions from other empires. "We possess natural advantages which no other nation does," he explained simply; "we can, therefore, with justice, stipulate for a reciprocity in commerce. The way to obtain this is by discrimination."

He proposed three steps: taxes on imports, taxes on foreign ships using American ports, and discriminating against Great Britain to force that great power to grant the United States extensive trade preferences. Madison acidly observed that British shippers enjoyed many trading privileges in the United States which American merchants were denied in British ports, especially those of the rich West Indies.[1] Congress passed the first two proposals. The third plan, however, ran into the determined opposition of Alexander Hamilton.

The thirty-two-year-old Secretary of the Treasury had rapidly become the most powerful member of George Washington's Cabinet. Born out of wedlock in the British West Indies, Hamilton had arrived in New York in 1773 to become a valued aide to General Washington and as nationalist as the most ardent native-born American. After the war he practiced law and became intimately involved with the New York City mercantile community. Like the merchants whose interests he shared, Hamilton became infuriated with the impotence of the Articles of Confederation. His preference for a strong, efficient, orderly government, as well as his extreme personal ambition, catapulted him to the front ranks of the Founding Fathers. Like Madison, Hamilton was determined that the new government should provide "safety for the people, and energy in the administration."

Federalists Fragment

BUT THE TWO MEN differed over the direction to be taken by the "energy in the administration." Both knew that the American economy, and to a large extent the stability of the political society, depended, as it had for two hun-

---

[1] Madison's 1789 speeches are in *The Writings of James Madison,* ed. Gaillard Hunt, 9 vols. (New York, 1901), 5:339–55, 357–61; 6:1–5.

dred years, upon increased trade with Great Britain. They differed over the price that should be paid for this trade. Madison wanted to pass discriminatory legislation that would coerce the British into treating Americans equitably. If the English refused to act properly, Madison would rechannel trade toward France, which had already granted reciprocal trading rights to the United States.

Hamilton refused to agree. He could not consent, given the logic of his own economic program. As Secretary of the Treasury he planned to restore public credit, establish a national bank, create manufactures, and establish a sound currency. But this program was contradictory. If, for example, he hoped to pay off the large public debt and restore national credit, he needed revenues. Some three-fourths of American revenues in the early 1790s came from duties on imports. If imports and revenues were increased, however, manufactures could hardly be supported, for their products would then have to compete in the domestic market with cheap British industrial goods. Hamilton, like Madison, faced a choice: either collect large revenues from British imports (and restore the national credit) or, as Madison urged, whip England into line by discriminating against it, encouraging manufacturing at home, and even trading with Britain's enemy, France.

Hamilton's foreign policy, like the foreign policies of all American statesmen, was determined by domestic objectives. His central domestic concern was paying off twenty years of state and national debts and restoring national credit. His plan was indirectly aided by southerners who depended upon British markets for their exports of tobacco and naval stores. With their help, Hamilton mustered congressional support in 1789 and 1790 to kill Madison's bills proposing anti-British discrimination. England's cheap imports continued to flood the United States, and Hamilton continued to collect the vital revenue.

But Madison accused the administration of nothing less than killing the nationalism of the Constitutional Convention.[2] Thomas Jefferson, the newly appointed Secretary of State, agreed with his fellow Virginian, observing sarcastically that Hamilton is "panic-struck if we refuse our breaches to every kick which Great Britain may choose to give us." Hamilton meanwhile commented bitterly that the two Virginians held "a womanish attachment to France and a womanish resentment against Great Britain."[3] Such charges confused the issue

---

[2] Madison to Jefferson, June 30, 1789, in *The Papers of Thomas Jefferson,* ed. Julian Boyd et al., 60 vols. (Princeton, N.J., 1950–   ), 15:224–27.

[3] Hamilton to Paul Carrington, May 26, 1792, in *The Papers of Alexander Hamilton,* ed. Harold C. Syrett and Jacob Cooke, 15 vols. (New York, 1961–1969), 11:39.

—and also later historians who thought the sides were being drawn along simple pro-British or pro-French lines. Neither side was pro-British or pro-French at the expense of American interests. The two groups split over the best means to expand and preserve those domestic interests, and then consequently divided over foreign policy.

The French Revolution; Or, the Dilemma of American Revolutionaries

DURING THE 1790s this debate became more explosive and embittered in the overwhelming presence of the French Revolution. While Europe focused on that upheaval, the United States was able to score important diplomatic triumphs, feats that have resulted in a popular generalization by some historians that "Europe's distresses meant American successes." The phrase oversimplifies and misleads. Over the entire period from 1790 to 1815, Americans succeeded because they strengthened and utilized the national powers that they had given their central government in 1787. Thus it was American successes, not only European distresses, that led to further American successes. Indeed, from 1790 to 1800 Europe's distresses actually created bitter divisions within the United States.

Through the first three years of the French Revolution (1789–1792), Americans were sympathetic, largely because they wanted to believe that their own "Spirit of '76" had beneficently spread across the Atlantic (and also, perhaps, out of a sense of guilt, for some remembered that the American drain on the French treasury between 1775 and 1783 had helped bankrupt it and contributed to the outbreak of the Revolution in 1789). By 1793, however, the heads that daily rolled from the guillotine and the increasing disorder and radicalism among the French led many Americans suddenly to consider themselves anti-revolutionaries. Jefferson and Madison looked on with more initial sympathy than Hamilton, but all agreed with President George Washington's sentiment that the United States should "observe a strict neutrality" while selling as much as possible to both sides.

As a prototype for other oppressed peoples, the American Revolution was apparently becoming irrelevant within a generation. Madison later observed that the French revolutionary excesses demonstrated that America remained as "the only Theatre in which true liberty can have a fair trial." In 1798 the

British Foreign Secretary, Lord Grenville, phrased this more succinctly: "None but Englishmen and their Descendants know how to make a Revolution." Madison and Jefferson, as well as Hamilton, heartily agreed.

Neutrality Is Tested by Genêt

IN APRIL 1793 full-scale war erupted between France and Great Britain. For two years (1793–1795) Spain fought alongside the British. The Washington administration feared the French would invoke the 1778 treaty and ask the United States for help. France, however, preferred to utilize the Americans as neutral carriers of French goods. Washington nevertheless ensured this neutrality on April 22, 1793, with a proclamation pledging impartial treatment of both sides.

Washington's announcement was immediately put to the test by the arrival of Citizen Edmond Genêt, the new minister from the French Republic. Jefferson and Madison initially hoped to use Genêt's popularity in a renewed effort to repeal Hamilton's policies. This was a grave miscalculation.

Genêt had hardly landed when he encouraged Americans beyond the mountains to attack Spanish territories. Some of the frontiersmen needed little encouragement. They had long been prepared to trim their allegiance to the United States if fame and fortune promised to culminate in military adventure, even perhaps in the establishment of a new western union. Appalled at Genêt's appeal to the frontiersmen, Jefferson became infuriated when the Minister proceeded to fit out fourteen privateers in American harbors to capture British ships. Genêt also openly recruited Americans to fight in Europe. He finally overreached himself by threatening to nullify Washington's Neutrality Proclamation by appealing over the President's head to the American people. At that point, Washington and a unanimous Cabinet demanded Genêt's recall.

The Frenchman's escapades dearly cost the Madison-Jefferson faction. Throughout the spring of 1793 the Virginians had argued that Congress, not the President, was the "competent body" to issue neutrality statements. They worried that through such proclamations the executive usurped congressional powers, including the right to declare war.[4] In June 1793 Hamilton, writing under the name "Pacificus," exploited Genêt's foolishness in a stinging public answer to the Jeffersonians. He cogently argued that the executive controlled foreign policy unless the Constitution specifically reserved powers to Congress.

---

4 "Letters of Helvidius," in *Writings of Madison*, 6:138–88.

The document, Hamilton observed, said nothing about Congress' power to issue neutrality proclamations.[5] Madison made an able reply, but Genêt's performance and the bloodletting in France undercut its effectiveness. To Madison's despair, the President's foreign policy powers emerged from the debate not only unimpaired but enlarged.

The Virginians Counterattack

HAMILTON WAS SCORING decisive victories when in June 1793 the British government ordered the seizure of all neutral ships carrying provisions to France or any port in Europe controlled by French armies. In November a new set of British orders-in council ruled that neutral ships could no longer carry French products to French colonies. Great Britain thereby struck hard at American shipping by challenging the revered American maritime principle that "free ships make free goods," regardless of the goods' origin or destination. Worst of all for American sensitivity, the British charged that their seamen were deserting His Majesty's ships for the tranquillity and better conditions of American vessels; they began impressing both deserters and legitimate American seamen to serve on British warships.

The moment was opportune for a renewal of Madison's demands. On January 3, 1794, Madison proposed discriminations against any nation that refused to treat the United States reciprocally. He observed that although the British sold to the United States two times more than they bought, France bought seven times more than it sold to the Americans. It was time, Madison pleaded, to aid friends like France. He admitted that his bill would help northern traders while hurting southern exporters, who had long depended upon the British market. But Madison argued that the measure would develop American manufactures, enlarge the domestic market, and create a great merchant marine.

Hamilton's forces succeeded in delaying votes on the proposals until March, when the crisis intensified. Congress learned that since November 1793 the British had seized more than two hundred American vessels in the West Indies. Angry congressmen suddenly began to consider not only Madison's plan, but an embargo bill, a measure providing for cessation of economic intercourse with England, and a proposal to stop paying debts to Britain. Hamiltonian policies overseas and at home faced a crisis.

---

[5] Hamilton's "Pacificus" letters are in *Papers of Hamilton*, vol. 15 (especially pp. 36–43).

Rebellion in the West

AT THE SAME TIME it was being challenged on the Atlantic, Washington's government also confronted an uprising in western Pennsylvania. Farmers in that area refused to pay a whiskey tax levied by Hamilton in 1791. Washington was initially reluctant to make an open display of force, but with Hamilton's urging the President called out 15,000 state militia late in 1794, quashed the rebellion, and pardoned the two ringleaders. Unlike the central government at the time of the Shays Rebellion, eight years before, the Washington government was not found wanting.

The Whiskey Rebellion was a symptom of deeper western discontents. In 1794 Edmund Randolph, who had succeeded Jefferson as Secretary of State, was convinced the British were "tampering" with American settlements in Kentucky and around Pittsburgh "to seduce them from the United States." In August 1794 General "Mad Anthony" Wayne decisively defeated several Indian tribes in the Battle of Fallen Timbers, in what is now Ohio. The discovery of several dead British citizens among the Indian bodies on the battlefield hardly improved Anglo-American relations. But most important, Wayne's victory made impossible any British hope of controlling the Northwest and demonstrated the power of the new central government to protect and control the periphery of its empire.

General "Mad Anthony" Wayne

SPAIN CANNOT LOCK UP AN OPEN FIELD

To the southwest, Spain was using a different tack to dismantle the American empire. The Spanish attempted to seduce the westerners by reopening the Mississippi, granting commercial privileges to frontiersmen who would cooperate with Spanish authorities, and opening parts of Louisiana (the area beyond the Mississippi) and Florida to settlers. Jefferson was delighted: "It will be a means of delivering to us peaceably what may otherwise cost us a war," he wrote Washington in 1791. "In the meantime we may complain of this seduction of our inhabitants just enough to make [the Spanish] believe we think it a very wise policy for them, and confirm them in it."[6]

Discontent spread through the West during the early 1790s. Specie was so scarce that trading was inhibited. Such leaders as George Rogers Clark and James Wilkinson openly talked of remedying the problems by joining the British or Spanish or establishing a separate nation. But American officials understood that Europeans did not hold the initiative. Madison knew that the "future disposition" of the settlers would "depend on the measures of the new Government."[7] Wayne's victory was one such measure.

After Spain became embroiled in the European wars, the decline of its empire accelerated. The Spanish could no longer obtain European goods to maintain ties with the Indians. American settlers roamed at will in the Floridas and Louisiana. The Spanish minister grimly informed his despairing superiors in Madrid, "You cannot lock up an open field." When the American government demanded the complete opening of New Orleans for an indefinite period, Spain was not in a position to dicker. In May 1794 the Spanish regime asked Washington to send an emissary who had treaty-making powers. The President seized this opportunity to quiet western discontent and ordered Thomas Pinckney to Spain.

The Jay and Pinckney Treaties

THREATENED BY the Madison faction in Congress and growling frontiersmen to the west, Washington sent John Jay to England to silence Congress while dis-

---

[6] Jefferson to Washington, April 2, 1791, in *Writings of Thomas Jefferson*, ed. Paul L. Ford, 10 vols. (New York, 1892–1899), 5:316.

[7] Madison to Washington, March 8, 1789, and Madison to Jefferson, March 29, 1789, in *Writings of Madison*, 5:329, 337.

patching Pinckney to placate the West. Jay hoped to remove the British from the northwest forts (which they had promised to evacuate in 1783), obtain indemnity for ship seizures in the West Indies, and increase Anglo-American trade. Jay did not enjoy a strong position. He might have threatened the British with American cooperation with Sweden and Denmark, which were then organizing a new armed neutrality to counter the British orders-in-council. But Hamilton, frightened that the negotiations might collapse, and with them his financial policy, undercut Jay by assuring the British that the United States would not join the armed neutrality.

Having few bargaining levers, Jay signed a treaty in November 1794 which transferred the northwest posts from Britain to the United States and referred several boundary and debt problems to mixed arbitration commissions. Reciprocal trade rights were to govern trade between the British Isles and the British East Indies on the one hand and the United States on the other. This concession resulted in a quick upsurge of American trade with India and Asia. But in a provision that infuriated Americans, Jay agreed to limit American commerce with the prized British West Indies to vessels of seventy tons or less, and also promised that the United States would not ship key exports, including cotton and molasses, to the West Indies in American bottoms. No mention was made of impressment, neutral rights, or British slave seizures.

Madison was deeply embittered, believing that the Jay Treaty surrendered the American right to retaliate against British trade injustice. Federalist support splintered. In the southern bastions of Federalism, long-time supporters of Hamilton deserted the party in order to fight against the provisions of the treaty which might require payment of long-standing debts to the British and its silence on the slaves that British soldiers had seized and often freed during the Revolution.

But the beleaguered President placed his authority behind the treaty, forcing it through the Senate by a vote of 20–10, the bare two-thirds needed. That body nevertheless insisted on throwing out the humiliating limitations upon the West Indian trade. In the House of Representatives, Madison again challenged the President's powers in foreign policy, arguing that the House, because of its power over appropriations, was co-equal with the Senate in regard to treaties. He demanded that the President send additional documents to the House, and his colleagues supported him by a 62–37 vote. But Washington refused to concede that the House possessed such power. Blessed by the opportune arrival of Pinckney's Treaty from Madrid, the President finally got the Jay Treaty appropriations through the House, 51–48.

Without the Pinckney Treaty, Washington might have lost his struggle with Congress. On October 27, 1795, in order to assure United States neutrality, the Spanish had agreed to open the Mississippi, to allow Americans the invaluable right to deposit goods tax-free in New Orleans for at least three years, and to surrender the disputed territory by placing the northern Florida boundary at 31°. Spain refused, however, to allow Americans to trade with Spanish colonies, nor would it grant reciprocal commercial rights. But no matter. The United States had won a sweeping victory in the West. The Senate accepted the treaty unanimously.

Key members of Congress reluctantly voted for Jay's pact because they feared that if it did not pass, northeasterners would retaliate against the Pinckney Treaty. The result could have been the secession of some southern and western areas. The passage of both treaties, however, did not quiet the aroused factions. During the mass meetings held during 1795 against the Jay Treaty, factions coalesced into various "societies" that formed the basis for the later Jeffersonian Democrat-Republican party. Washington was unable to reconcile himself to these new groups. During 1796, as he prepared to leave the presidency, he warned his countrymen about the evils that parties could create, particularly in foreign affairs.

John Jay burned in effigy

Portrait of George Washington

The Farewell Address

WASHINGTON CORRECTLY believed that France was deeply disturbed by the settlement of outstanding Anglo-American problems through the Jay Treaty. He was also right in thinking that French agents, led by Minister Pierre Adet, were attempting to elect a Francophile, preferably Jefferson, in the 1796 presidential election. But Washington was mistaken in blaming pro-French plots for the appearance of political parties. The parties had appeared spontaneously in the South and West as a reaction to his administration's policies between 1793 and 1795. Despite this spontaneity (or perhaps because of it), the President published a "Farewell Address" on the eve of the elections to warn Americans against allowing political factions to determine policy.

The Farewell consisted of two major sections. In the first, Washington urged that the checks and balances within the constitutional system would serve better than factions to maintain an orderly and just society. This led to the second theme:

> Excessive partiality for one foreign nation and excessive dislike of another, cause those whom they actuate to see danger only on one side, and serve to veil and even second the arts of influence on the other.... The great rule of conduct for us, in regard to foreign Nations, is in extending our commercial relations to have with them as little *political* connection as possible. So far as we have already formed engagements let them be fulfilled with perfect good faith. Here let us stop....

Europe has a set of primary interests, which to us have none, or a very remote relation. . . .

Our detached and distant situation invites and enables us to pursue a different course. If we remain one People, under an efficient government, the period is not far off, when we may defy material injury from external annoyance . . . when we may choose peace or war, as our interest guided by justice shall counsel.[8]

Hamilton had been heavily involved in the writing of the address, but readers did not have to know that to understand which "foreign nation" Washington had in mind. His message, in this sense, was contradictory, for while he warned against parties, he was actually aiding the Hamiltonian Federalists by condemning the Jeffersonians. Neither Washington nor anyone else could henceforth easily separate foreign policy from domestic party politics, and for a simple reason: foreign policy was formulated by property interests that worked through the parties. During the 1790s those interests lined up behind either Hamilton or Madison and Jefferson.

The Farewell Address is important less for its quixotic attack upon parties than its emphasis upon manipulating America's isolated geographic position to gain time for the development of a great empire. Survival required economic intercourse with Europe, but "as little political connection as possible" until "we [not Europe] may choose peace or war, as our interest . . . shall counsel." The Farewell was not a document of American isolationism, in large part because the United States has never been isolated, either in the 1790s or after. The address was a recipe for empire. It assumed far-reaching commercial ties. In this sense, Washington, as well as later American leaders and historians, was fundamentally wrong in believing that economics and politics could be separated. During the following seventeen years, for example, American economic ambitions would create political obligations that finally had to be paid in blood, first in cold war against the British and French, then in hot war against Great Britain.

Washington foresaw the time when Americans would become politically involved in world affairs, but he hoped that time was distant. When it did arrive, he wanted the nation to enter world politics on its own terms and with decisive power. Given this historical tradition, small wonder that Americans have moved so easily from a supposed policy of no political alignment in the nineteenth and early twentieth centuries to a policy of unilateral commitments of force around the globe after 1950. Moving from one extreme to another was

---

[8] Various drafts of the Farewell Address can be analyzed in Victor Hugo Paltsits, *Washington's Farewell Address* (New York, 1953).

rationalized by Washington a century and a half before. "Going it alone," however, had its dangers even then, as Washington's Vice-President and successor, John Adams, soon discovered.

Adams

HARSH, PROUD, VAIN, and an extremely learned man, John Adams had not increased his small personal following between 1789 and 1796. Adams and Hamilton had moved apart personally. Although they agreed generally on the need for strong government, Adams worked along Madisonian lines to create a more independent American mercantile community by discriminating against the British. He condemned New England shippers, who, like the nabobs in the British Empire, willingly accepted a subservient position in order to work within the system. Adams' determination not to be a tail to the British kite had made him less enthusiastic about the Jay Treaty than Hamilton desired.

In the acrimonious 1796 campaign, Hamilton divided the Federalists by supporting Thomas Pinckney of South Carolina for the presidency. Foreign

John Adams

affairs again were the catalyst. The South Carolina Federalists had badly split over the Jay Treaty, and Hamilton attempted to reunite the party in the South, as well as defeat Adams, by supporting the now-famous Pinckney name. Northern states, however, voted solidly for Adams, while the South over-whelmingly supported Jefferson. Adams garnered 71 electoral votes to Jefferson's 68. Under the constitutional rule then in effect, the Virginian became Vice-President.

This arrangement did not augur well for Adams. Worse, despite the obvi-ous bitterness within his own party, he surrounded himself with Cabinet mem-bers who had greater allegiance to Hamilton (then retired to law practice in New York City) than to the President. Included in the Hamiltonian, or High Federalist, faction was Secretary of State Timothy Pickering.

COLD WAR WITH FRANCE

The new President hated the "fanaticism" of the French Revolution, and Paris officials fully reciprocated Adams' feelings. Moreover, because the Jay Treaty had accepted British policy on the issues of small contraband lists and rights of neutral shipping, the French viewed the pact as a repudiation of the Franco-American alliance of 1778. Bitter that Anglo-American trade was in-creasing, France seized more than three hundred United States ships in 1796 and 1797. Anti-French sentiment flared, encouraged by Federalists who believed all-out war against France would result in long-sought favors from the British.

In the autumn of 1797 Adams attempted to still the growing storm by dis-patching three American emissaries to negotiate with the newly installed, highly corrupt French Directory, which governed the country. The diplomats were approached by three French intermediaries (later designated X, Y, and Z), accompanied by the inevitable French *femme fatale,* and demanded a large bribe for Directory officials before negotiations could begin. The three Ameri-cans flatly refused and returned home. When Adams sent documents of the "XYZ affair" to Congress, Federalists led a rising chorus against the French, and the slogan "Millions for defense but not one cent for tribute" was born. The few remaining Jeffersonians who sympathized with the Revolution became notable for their silence.

Upon Adams' request, Congress added a Department of the Navy to the executive branch. The nation began to prepare for war. Over Adams' weak objections, Congress passed the Alien and Sedition Acts, giving the President the right to expel foreigners whom he considered dangerous in wartime and forbidding any published statement that tended to "defame" the President or the federal government. Similar laws would not be passed in the United States for another 140 years; and when such laws were again legislated between 1940 and 1950, they were once more the products of domestic political figures who pointed with alarm to foreign dangers in order to stifle dissent at home.

A second front meanwhile threatened in the West. Long envious of Spain's control over Louisiana, France became increasingly interested in that vast area as a source of foodstuffs for its valuable West Indian sugar islands. The French pressured Spain to surrender the territory and also became active in stirring up discontent in the American settlements along the Mississippi. Adams began raising a ten-thousand-man army, and urged Washington to come out of retirement to command the troops. Hamilton and the High Federalists appreciated the opportunity suddenly before them. By joining Great Britain against the French, they could seize a great western empire and undercut the Jeffersonians.

ADAMS PLACES NATION ABOVE PARTY

Adams did not want British trade preferences if the price was war with France. Such a conflict would be too costly and divisive for the new nation. Nor did he want the United States to become a weak adjunct of the British Empire; after all, that was where he had started his political career in the 1760s.

Adams soon learned that the French too wanted no war with their former allies. One channel for this information was George Logan, a staunch Jeffersonian Quaker from Pennsylvania who appointed himself an emissary to Paris to settle Franco-American problems. Enraged Federalists passed the "Logan Act" in 1799, which prohibited a private American citizen from entering into unauthorized diplomatic negotiations with a foreign government. Slightly changed, the Logan Act remains law in the twentieth century.

If Adams needed a further push to end the undeclared war, it came when pressure began to build for Hamilton's appointment as field commander for the new American army. After three years of incessant trouble with the High Federalists in his Cabinet, Adams had no love for the New Yorker ("the bastard brat of a Scots peddler," he once called him). And Adams justifiably verged upon panic when he imagined Hamilton at the head of a large army roaming through the West, perhaps even "taking a squint at Mexico," as Hamilton happily planned to do, with Napoleon in France as an example of how an ambitious military commander could overthrow governments.

Against the demands for war from his own party and Cabinet, Adams decided in February 1799 to dispatch William Vans Murray, the American minister to the Netherlands, to Paris for negotiations. In a stroke Adams drastically widened the split in the Federalist party, surrendered the opportunity to forge a commercial alliance with the British, renounced the dream of empire in Florida and Louisiana, and ensured his own political death. Washington was one of the few Federalists who supported Adams, assuring the President that peace was "the ardent desire of all the friends of this uprising empire."[9]

Murray found Napoleon supremely confident after a series of smashing military victories, but the First Consul realized that peace must be maintained between France and the United States if he hoped to develop a French empire in the West Indies and perhaps even in Louisiana. After arduous negotiations, the United States agreed in the Convention of 1800 to drop its claim for some $20 million against the French for their seizure of American merchant ships. In return, the First Consul agreed to terminate the 1778 treaty. The United States thereby extricated itself from its last formal political alliance for nearly 150 years.

THE "REVOLUTION OF 1800"

Adams refused to unify the Federalists at the cost of an imperial war. A man who read history for a purpose, he understood that such conquests often have tragic denouements for governments that undertake them. By early 1800, Adams had purged Pickering and other Hamiltonians from his Cabinet. The High Federalists retaliated by supporting a separate ticket for the presidential election.

In New York, however, Aaron Burr, another of Hamilton's tormentors, successfully fought the High Federalists. With that state's vital support, Jefferson and Burr each received 73 electoral votes. Adams received 65. On the thirty-sixth ballot in the House of Representatives, Jefferson defeated Burr for the presidency. The Virginian's victory became known as the Revolution of 1800, for it marked an initial peaceful transference of political power from one party to another under the Constitution.

Jefferson's triumph was significant, but hardly a revolution. The High Federalists were on the opposite side of the political spectrum from Jefferson's Democrat-Republicans, but the Hamiltonians' plans for a western empire in 1798–1799 revealed how closely they could agree with some of Jefferson's objectives. A large majority of Americans agreed with Washington that the proper policy was to remain uncommitted to either the British or the French empire.

[9] Washington to Adams, February 1, 1799, in George Washington, *Writings from the Original Manuscripts Sources, 1745–1799*, ed. John C. Fitzpatrick, 39 vols. (Washington, D.C., 1931–1944), 37:120.

But in struggling through its first decade, the new Constitution and its first governments had endured several near-misses. The Madison-Hamilton conflict had split the Federalist party, led to a crisis with England in 1794–1795, and climaxed in undeclared war against France four years later. Through Washington's determination, Adams' statesmanship, and Jefferson's victory, these disputes had been quieted, the empire once again consolidated. The stage was set for an incredible addition to that empire.

Suggestions for Further Reading

Four volumes provide the context for the Washington administrations. Bradford Perkins, *The First Rapprochement* (Philadelphia, 1955), considers Anglo-American relations from the 1790s to 1805; Alexander De Conde, *Entangling Alliance* (Durham, N.C., 1958), analyzes Franco-American affairs down to the period of undeclared war; Joseph Charles, *The Origins of the American Party System* (Williamsburg, Va., 1956), brilliantly relates the evolving political system to foreign policies; and Felix Gilbert, *To the Farewell Address: Ideas of Early American Foreign Policy* (Princeton, N.J., 1961), is indispensable for an understanding of the ideas that shaped the foreign policies.

The critical fight over the Jay Treaty is noted in Jerald A. Combs, *The Jay Treaty* (Berkeley, 1970), again relating the struggle to domestic politics; while Samuel Flagg Bemis, *Jay's Treaty* (New Haven, Conn., 1962), is still useful. Julian P. Boyd, *Number 7: Alexander Hamilton's Secret Attempts to Control American Foreign Policy* (Princeton, N.J., 1964), demonstrates how dangerously far Hamilton went to placate the British after 1789. Pinckney's work and its background are provided in three standard volumes: Samuel Flagg Bemis, *Pinckney's Treaty* (New Haven, Conn., 1962); Arthur P. Whitaker, *The Spanish-American Frontier, 1783–1795* (Boston, 1927); and Whitaker's *The Mississippi Question, 1795–1803* (New York, 1934).

Key figures are analyzed in Douglas Southall Freeman's fine multivolume biography of Washington (New York, 1948–1957); Ralph Ketcham, *James Madison* (New York, 1971); and Dumas Malone's multivolume *Jefferson and His Time* (Boston, 1948–1971), currently covering the years to 1805.

Adams' troubled presidency and particularly the near-war with France are examined in S. G. Kurtz, *The Presidency of John Adams* (Philadelphia, 1957); Alexander De Conde, *The Quasi-War: The Politics and Diplomacy of the Undeclared War with France, 1797–1801* (New York, 1966); Peter P. Hill, *William Vans Murray, Federalist Diplomat: The Shaping of Peace with France, 1797–1801* (Syracuse, N.Y., 1971); and Marshall Smelser, *The Congress Founds the Navy, 1787–1798* (Notre Dame, Ind., 1959).

See also the general bibliography at the end of this volume.

CHAPTER 5

An "Empire for Liberty" on Land and Sea (1800–1809)

Having profited from the Federalist split, in 1801 Jefferson glanced back at the political struggles that pockmarked the 1790s and the 1800 election, then drew the appropriate conclusion: "It furnishes a new proof of the falsehood of Montesquieu's doctrine, that a republic can be preserved only in a small territory. The reverse is the truth. Had our territory been even a third only of what it is, we were gone."[1] During the next fifteen years, Jefferson and Madison would more than double the extent of that territory. This "extensive sphere," as Madison liked to term it, survived French and Spanish threats in the West, war with Great Britain, and several secessionist plots within the Union. But perhaps the empire was becoming *too* large.

Jefferson

ONE OF THE most revered and studied figures in American history, Jefferson remains complex and contradictory. The author of the Declaration of Indepen-

---

[1] Jefferson to Nathaniel Niles, March 22, 1801, in *Writings of Thomas Jefferson,* ed. Paul L. Ford, 10 vols. (New York, 1892–1899), 8:24.

dence, he privately justified slavery. A retiring, shy person, he became a political manipulator of first rank. An intellectual who loved scientific systems, he practiced a political pragmatism that culminated in the first opposition party. That party included many Americans who distrusted intellectuals but adored Jefferson. An admirer of European, especially French, culture, he was the quintessence of America and during his presidency seriously considered helping England fight France.

Such contradictions or paradoxes can partly be resolved by analyzing them in the context of their specific time and place, but they are also over-arched and reconciled by three Jeffersonian principles. Like Washington, he possessed complete faith in the future of the empire. In designing a national seal during the 1780s, Jefferson suggested that it show the Children of Israel led by a pillar of light. He believed firmly that Americans were the new Chosen People, that they had been selected to found a more perfect nation that would be the political embodiment of John Winthrop's City Upon a Hill. They were, as Jefferson said in his first inaugural address, "the world's best hope." Historians have liked to observe that the Virginian spoke of America in the future tense.

A second Jeffersonian principle can be understood if one imagines that the Children of Israel on his seal are marching southwest. He wrote Monroe in 1801:

> However our present situation may restrain us within our own limits, it is impossible not to look forward to distant times, when our rapid multiplication will expand itself beyond those limits, and cover the whole northern, if not the southern continent, with a people speaking the same language, governed in similar forms, and by similar laws; nor can we contemplate with satisfaction either blot or mixture on that surface.[2]

But he wanted more than territorial empire. To see Jefferson as an agrarian is to take too narrow a view. As a commercial farmer himself, he understood the dependence of agrarians upon commerce and manufactures. He was one of the first Americans who visualized the North American continent as an avenue to the markets of Asia and Latin America. A developed continent would also generate the power necessary to protect American commerce on the seas. "We feel ourselves strong and daily growing stronger," the new President wrote in 1801.

> If we can delay but for a few years the necessity of vindicating the laws of nature [that is, American rights] upon the ocean, we shall be the more sure

---

[2] Jefferson to Monroe, November 24, 1801, in *The Writings of Thomas Jefferson,* ed. Andrew A. Lipscomb, 20 vols. (Washington, D.C., 1903), 10:296.

of doing it with effect. The day is within my time as well as yours, when we may say by what laws other nations shall treat us on the sea. And we shall say it.[3]

This letter helps us understand Jefferson's famous words in his first inaugural address: "Peace, commerce, and honest friendship with all nations, entangling alliances with none."

Finally, Jefferson was concerned that the powers of the central government, and especially of the President, be extensive enough to preserve and enlarge the empire. Neither his well-known argument with Hamilton over presidential power during the 1790s nor his attempt to override the Alien and Sedition Acts by espousing the right of state governments to judge for themselves the justice of federal legislation reflects his later political views. Jefferson's most unfortunate political experience had been serving as governor of Virginia during the Revolution. He was highly ineffectual, in large part, he believed, because the governor could not command the state legislature to grant what was required to repulse the British and unify the state. He never forgot the lesson. Few Presidents have been as vigorous and successful in controlling, indeed subordinating, Congress to the executive branch as was Jefferson during his first term. He imposed iron discipline upon his political followers.

Thomas Jefferson with Cabinet

[3] Jefferson to William Short, October 3, 1801, in *Writings of Jefferson,* ed. Ford, 8:98.

One side of the American seal has the slogan *Novus Ordo Seclorum* (A New Order for the Ages), perfectly fitting Jefferson's conception of American destiny. The words on the other side, which the Virginian apparently suggested for the seal, are closely related: *E Pluribus Unum* (Out of Many, One). The President believed that order could not be brought out of the diverse American society without a commanding central government. In this fashion, Jeffersonianism became the political ideology for a vast pluralistic empire.

Another Western Crisis

THE EMPIRE was seriously endangered within seven months after Jefferson took the presidential oath. Napoleon had ardently pursued his plans for a New World empire, and on October 1, 1800, at San Ildefonso in Spain, he obtained Louisiana from the Spanish in return for a promise that he would give the Kingdom of Tuscany to the nephew of Charles IV of Spain. Because Napoleon was unable to deliver Tuscany for another year, the Spanish retained possession of Louisiana until October 1802.

Jefferson and Secretary of State Madison had acquiesced in Spanish control because they correctly believed Spain could not long hold off American pressures on the adjacent territory. Napoleon, however, was quite another matter, particularly when the Peace of Amiens temporarily ended the war in Europe and freed him from British interference in March 1802.

French holdings beyond the Mississippi would be highly disruptive in the American West, an area that had traditionally been sympathetic to France. George Rogers Clark and James Wilkinson, among others, incessantly schemed to align the settlements with the Spanish and French empires. The frontier states were no longer mere colonies. Kentucky's population, for example, had risen from 73,000 in 1790 to 220,000 in 1800. In 1792 it became the first trans-Apalachian territory to join the Union as a state. But specie remained scarce, and the westerners remained utterly dependent upon the Mississippi as the outlet for their surpluses. With the Peace of Amiens, the vast European wartime market closed, and reverberations of depressed prices spread throughout the American West.

Jefferson took the initiative in April 1802 with a letter to the French warning that Americans and Frenchmen could not long coexist in the West. The President hinted that if Napoleon attempted to send troops, the United States might declare war, join the British, and occupy New Orleans.[4] But he wanted only New Orleans and a return of the remaining area to Spain. Jefferson did not offer to buy all of Louisiana because the United States had neither the money to obtain it nor, he believed, the power to hold it.

PREPARING TO RACE FOR NEW ORLEANS

France did not respond satisfactorily to American entreaties in 1802, so the administration prepared to protect itself. The French Achilles' heel was obvious. A black slave revolt under the leadership of the dynamic Toussaint L'Ouverture had produced a grim situation for the French on their rich sugar island of Santo Domingo. Secretary of State Madison quickly understood that without Santo Domingo, Louisiana was useless to Napoleon. Jefferson feared, however, that United States aid to Toussaint might encourage slaves in the American South to revolt as well. The President was anxious about this possibility, but Madison refused to allow the threat to paralyze policy.

With Jefferson's reluctant consent, the Secretary of State encouraged a flow of supplies to Toussaint, all the while assuring the French of American neutrality. For more than a year Madison played the double game of aiding Toussaint while assuring France that the "United States will be guided by a strict conformity to all legitimate regulations emanating from [French] authority."[5] By the end of 1802, Toussaint's forces and a terrible yellow fever epidemic had combined to destroy French control of the island and Napoleon's hope for a New World empire. Madison now assumed that France would become more flexible in discussing Louisiana.[6]

Jefferson meanwhile accelerated military preparations in the West. Forts along the Mississippi and the Canadian boundary were rapidly stocked. Fort Adams, on the Mississippi just north of New Orleans, was fitted out with four infantry and three artillery companies, which were prepared to march on the city. If Napoleon wanted a race to New Orleans, Jefferson was prepared to run, and with a four-thousand-mile headstart. But the French ruler was encountering difficulties in moving his troops from Europe to Louisiana. An early winter in 1802 prevented one sailing, and before a second voyage could

---

[4] Jefferson to Pierre Du Pont de Nemours, April 25, 1802, in *Writings of Jefferson*, ed. Lipscomb, 10:316–18.

[5] Madison to Tobias Lear, February 28, 1802, in National Archives (Washington, D.C.), Consular, Cap Haitien, Record Group 59.

[6] Madison to Robert R. Livingston, January 18, 1803, in *The Writings of James Madison*, ed. Gaillard Hunt, 9 vols. (New York, 1901), 7:7.

embark from French shores, news arrived that Santo Domingo needed help.

And amidst hurried preparations on both sides of the ocean, the slow, unrelenting Americanization of Louisiana and New Orleans continued. By 1800 more than six thousand Americans had swarmed into upper Louisiana. Their products, including 88,000 bushels of wheat and 170,000 pounds of lead, swept down upon the New Orleans outlet. When French officials moved into New Orleans early in 1803, they immediately informed Paris that the port was monopolized not by the Spanish or French, but by Americans, "the most dreaded [commercial] rivals in the world." The officials emphasized the power held by 300,000 farmers and planters who in just twenty years had developed fabulous harvests along the eastern banks of the Mississippi and now demanded the river's outlet to the Gulf of Mexico.

AMERICAN SUCCESSES MEAN AMERICAN SUCCESSES

Late in the autumn of 1802, the Spanish finally transferred New Orleans to the French. Before they left, however, Spain announced that because of "smuggling," Americans could no longer enjoy the right of deposit at New Orleans. Early in 1803 the French reversed this decision, but the intervening months were tense for the Jefferson administration.

According to Madison's own theory, the western factions would become uncontrollable unless New Orleans were pried open. "You are aware of the sensibility of our Western citizens to such an occurrence," he told the American minister to Spain, Charles Pinckney, in November 1802. "This sensibility is justified by the interest they have at stake. The Mississippi is to them everything. It is the Hudson, the Delaware, the Potomac and all the navigable rivers of the Atlantic States formed into one stream."[7]

The administration intensified its pressure. The President attempted to quiet the aroused West by sending James Monroe (widely known to be pro-West and pro-French) to join American Minister Robert R. Livingston in Paris. The two diplomats were instructed to offer $10 million for New Orleans and Florida. The President then openly talked of a possible alliance with Great Britain if the French did not respond properly. Jefferson never went so far as to talk with London officials about the possibility of "marrying the British fleet and nation," as he once phrased the policy, but such an approach was discussed with the Cabinet, and in April 1803 Madison instructed Livingston and Monroe to initiate talks with the British if Napoleon insisted on restricting American rights to the Mississippi. For a few months in 1803 the Jeffersonians considered

[7] Madison to Pinckney, November 27, 1802, in ibid., 6:462.

forging a closer alliance with the British than had John Adams, or even Alexander Hamilton, in the 1790s.

One final blow was needed, and this was delivered by Congress. Jefferson had carefully warned in his annual message of December 1802 that if France attempted to occupy Louisiana, he would put the matter before Congress, the body possessing the power to declare war. Two months later Senator James Ross of Pennsylvania introduced resolutions asserting the American right to use the Mississippi and the port of New Orleans freely. Ross called upon Jefferson to mobilize state militia units for a march on the port if France refused to be reasonable. Although weakened by amendment, the Ross Resolutions reached Paris on April 8. Livingston immediately sent them to Napoleon's Foreign Minister, Talleyrand, with a note that considerably spiced the threats to use the militia. On or about the same day, Talleyrand received warning from the French minister in Washington that Monroe had instructions to negotiate with the British if he did not receive satisfaction in France.

NAPOLEON SELLS THE "DAMN COLONIES"

The double-barreled attack of April 8 apparently destroyed Napoleon's last doubts about selling his western empire. As early as January 12, Napoleon was discussing the comparative merits of Rousseau and Voltaire when he suddenly burst out, "Damn sugar, damn coffee, damn colonies!" He was in the proper mood to receive the American offer, and this inclination was later fixed by his decision to pursue empire through war in Europe rather than in the New World. On Easter Sunday, April 10, the First Consul announced that since the Louisiana territory was worthless without New Orleans and Santo Domingo, he wished to sell all of Louisiana. The next day Talleyrand offered the entire area to Livingston for $15 million.

The Spanish were livid with rage when they discovered the deal. In 1800, Napoleon had promised not to transfer the territory to another power; moreover, he had dallied in delivering Tuscany. But worse, without even consulting his allies in Madrid, Napoleon had now surrounded the Spanish-held Floridas with the insatiable Americans.

The French ruler cared little about Spain's displeasure. Frustration over Santo Domingo, his desire to renew war in Europe, fear of a possible Anglo-American alliance, the threat of American seizure of New Orleans, all of these things influenced Napoleon's decision. Jefferson and Madison had not waited to be rescued by Europe's distresses. When political opponents attempted to discount the administration's influence upon Napoleon's decision, Jefferson wrote that these grumblers "would be cruelly mortified could they see our files ... especially from April, 1802. They would see that tho' we could not say when war would arise, yet we said with energy what would take place when it should arise."[8]

The President obtained the $15 million, ironically, from Baring Brothers, bankers in Great Britain, the nation then preparing to war against the recipient of the $15 million. That sum, the British speculated, was a cheap price for cleansing the area west of the Mississippi of Frenchmen; besides, the Barings pocketed $3 million profit. Most important, Jefferson might henceforth be more cooperative with England. But the President now had his mind on other problems.

How to Govern an Overextensive Empire

JEFFERSON WAS SATISFIED that he had acquired a country "so extensive, so fertile," that his administration had "secured the blessings of civil and religious freedom to millions yet unborn." To obtain this vast opportunity, he did not scruple to extend his constitutional powers beyond the point justified by Hamilton and condemned by Madison and Jefferson himself during the 1790s. The President faced the immediate problem of governing the tremendous expanse between

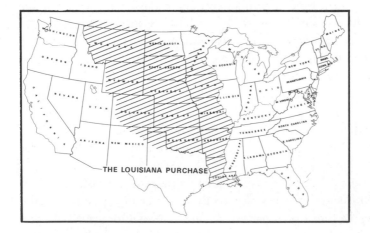

THE LOUISIANA PURCHASE

---

8 Jefferson to Horatio Gates, July 11, 1803, in *Writings of Jefferson,* ed. Ford, 8:250.

the Mississippi and the Rocky Mountains, which contained more Indians and Spaniards than Americans.

Federalists loudly announced that settlers who scrambled into the newly acquired territory would be ungovernable. "We rush like a comet into infinite space," Fisher Ames lamented. Hamilton differed only slightly. He had long sought New Orleans and criticized Jefferson for not obtaining the Floridas, but the New Yorker gave the classic criticism of Louisiana's annexation. If Americans, "more enterprising than wise," should widely disperse themselves in the vastness of Louisiana, they would not only prove themselves ungovernable, but

> by adding to the great weight of the western part of our territory, must hasten the dismemberment of a large portion of our country, or a dissolution of the Government. On the whole we think it may with candor be said, that whether the possession at this time of any territory west of the river Mississippi will be advantageous, is at best extremely problematical.[9]

Jefferson and Madison pondered this problem in 1803. Neither had expected to obtain all of Louisiana. Madison had once remarked that "a colony beyond the river could not exist under the same government" as the states on the eastern bank. Washington officials were suffering enough with the restless, specie-poor westerners. Madison had envisioned this problem in his letter to Jefferson after the Constitutional Convention, when he argued for an extensive sphere for republican government, but then carefully added that the sphere must be "practicable," that is, not overly extensive, or republican government could not remain cohesive.

Jefferson decided that Louisiana's sparse population was not ready for self-government; it would have to be ruled indefinitely from Washington through a military governor. As Madison understated the policy, the government "will leave the people of that District for a while without the organization of power dictated by the Republican theory," for their "ideas and habits" were unsuited for such a government. They would receive "every blessing of liberty" as soon "as they shall be prepared and disposed to receive it." In the meantime, the United States would retain its "parental interest."[10] With those condescending but revealing words on the way to govern the ungovernable in a great empire, Madison added yet another dimension to his political theory as well as an often forgotten chapter to Jeffersonian ideology.

---

[9] Text is in "Hamilton on the Louisiana Purchase: A Newly Identified Editorial from the *New-York Evening Post*," *William and Mary Quarterly*, 12:271, 276–77.

[10] Madison to Livingston, January 31, 1804, in *Writings of Madison*, 7:115–16.

Pickering, Burr, and Secession

THE ADMINISTRATION'S FEARS that the empire would be disrupted by over-expansion proved to be accurate, although not in the precise manner Hamilton had envisioned. Early in 1804, High Federalists decided the purchase meant an inevitable flow of political power out of their area into a vast Jeffersonian West. Thomas Pickering and other Massachusetts High Federalists approached Vice-President Aaron Burr with a plan for the secession of New England and Burr's home state of New York. Hamilton steadfastly fought the plan, and in doing so insulted Burr during the New York campaign of late spring, 1804. Burr issued a challenge that resulted in the duel that killed Hamilton.

Aaron Burr

Alexander Hamilton

After nervous excursions up and down the east coast, including visits with both French agents and Americans who were plotting secessionist schemes in the West, Burr undertook two trips beyond the mountains. During his second journey, Jefferson issued orders for his capture on the grounds that Burr was plotting a secessionist conspiracy along the Ohio and Mississippi rivers. He was brought back to Virginia, where Chief Justice John Marshall, a fervent enemy of Jefferson's, acquitted Burr by making an extremely narrow interpretation of the Constitution's definition of treason. Both Pickering's and Burr's plots had failed, but the aftereffects of the Louisiana Purchase, that supposedly glorious doubling of the empire, were unveiling themselves as in a Greek tragedy.

And this was a mere beginning. Within eleven years the New England Federalists would use the War of 1812 as an excuse to reconsider secession. Nearly a half century later, the South would leave the Union and engage in bloody civil war, in part because of fear that its slave system would be unable to exist in the former Louisiana territory. That area in mid-century was aligning with the Northeast; together, the two sections threatened to strangle the South's system.

The Floridas

ALTHOUGH THEY envisioned such possible consequences, Jefferson and Madison did not quit their search for empire. Louisiana had hardly been annexed when they attempted to interpret the 1803 treaty as including the Floridas. The Spanish and French refused to discuss the subject, but Madison was insistent. In his classic fashion, he proceeded to speak of the Floridas as he had once described the Mississippi. The United States did not need the Floridas for the land, the Secretary of State argued, but for export.

> The United States have a just claim to the use of the rivers which pass from their territories thro' the Floridas. They found their claim on like principles with those which supported their claim to the use of the Mississippi.... [Settlements on the Mobile River] are beginning; and the people have already called on the government to procure the proper outlets to foreign markets.[11]

The administration believed the Floridas of even greater value after Latin American revolutions began to erupt against Spain. The route through the Floridas into the Gulf of Mexico was a natural one for many American merchants, who finally had the opportunity to get into the markets of the crumbling Spanish Empire.

The outbreak of war in Europe prevented the President from continuing negotiations for Florida (an instance where Europe's distresses prevented possible American successes), but Jefferson never stopped envisioning the Floridas as fitting into Madison's extensive empire. When that territory, Cuba, and Canada were acquired, Jefferson wrote Madison in April 1809, the nation would be "such an empire for liberty as she has never surveyed since the creation; and I

---

[11] Madison to Livingston and Monroe, March 2, 1803, in National Archives (Washington, D.C.), Diplomatic Instructions of Department of State, 1801–1906, All Countries, vol. 6, Foreign Affairs, Record Group 59.

am persuaded no constitution was ever before so well calculated as ours for extensive empire and self-government."[12]

Warfare on the Atlantic

THE LOUISIANA PURCHASE removed or quieted foreign threats in the West. By 1805–1806 Jefferson could turn his attention to the danger posed to American commerce by the renewed Anglo-French war. With huge armies needing to be fed in Europe, United States trade spiraled upward until in 1807 it was worth $108 million in exports and $138 million in imports. In 1805, however, that commerce began to be gravely endangered. In the *Essex* case, British courts ruled that neutrals (such as Americans) could no longer legally take aboard French goods in the West Indies, unload and then reload them at an American port, and then take them through the British blockade to French ports with the justification that the goods had come from an American port. The United States was suddenly faced with the seizure of a large part of the cargoes its ships carried to France as well as with the hated impressment of seamen.

Jefferson decided the United States could not challenge the British on the high seas, especially since the President himself had decided to construct inexpensive gunboats for coastal defense rather than large oceangoing frigates. This had been a wise decision. The nation could not afford a large navy, certainly not a fleet great enough to frighten, let alone defeat, Great Britain's. Jefferson had no moral scruples against war; he willingly ordered U.S. frigates to fight the Barbary pirates to keep the Mediterranean open to American ships. But the Barbary Coast was hardly Britain. Nor was there need to spend heavily for a navy when the United States possessed another kind of power, and to Jefferson's and Madison's minds a greater one: its commerce.

In 1805–1806 the administration worked out the assumption that would guide American policy to the War of 1812: European belligerents would treat American shipping fairly because their economies, and especially their armies, were dependent upon American supplies. This assumption fitted perfectly within an old pattern of American thought, from Adams' Model Treaty through Madison's navigation acts of the 1790s. The mushrooming trade between 1804 and 1807 seemed to reaffirm the belief that American commerce sufficed to influence European diplomacy.

---

12 Jefferson to Madison, April 27, 1809, in *Writings of Jefferson*, ed. Lipscomb, 12:277.

THE NONIMPORTATION ACT OF 1806

When the Jeffersonians worked out this policy, however, they encountered unexpected problems. Southerners, for example, observed that the *Essex* decision primarily hurt New England merchants with the reexport trade. Growers of tobacco and cotton, long dependent upon European markets for their livelihood, were not anxious to surrender those markets for the sake of northern merchants. This political obstacle led the administration to propose merely a nonimportation act.

As an effort to coerce the British and French, the Nonimportation Act of March 1806 was a farce. Jefferson discovered that Americans had grown dependent upon imports from Great Britain. As a result, the act allowed the continued importation of cotton piece goods, cheap woolens, iron, gunpowder, lead, drugs, coal, and most goods imported from British colonies. Jefferson's opponent in the House, John Randolph of Virginia, called it "a milk-and-water bill, a dose of chicken broth.... You cannot do without the next Spring and Fall importations; and you tell your adversary so." It was all true.

Jefferson postponed enforcement of even this flimsy measure until he could learn the results of a diplomatic mission to London undertaken by James Monroe and William Pinckney. The British, however, understood that they, not the Americans, dealt from strength, and consequently refused to discuss such critical issues as impressment or the *Essex* decision. The two diplomats returned with such an unacceptable pact that the President refused to send it to the Senate. The administration had badly miscalculated both the diplomatic power and the self-sufficiency of the American economy.

THE EMBARGO

Some ten thousand seamen were impressed from American ships, and perhaps only a thousand were actually English deserters. The most dramatic

The Embargo

impressment episode occurred on June 22, 1807, when the British *Leopard* fired on the American *Chesapeake* just ten miles off the United States coast. Three Americans were killed and four of the *Chesapeake*'s crew impressed. The British Foreign Office soon apologized, but Americans were enraged. Jefferson refused to accept the British apology until London promised not to impress more seamen. The British could not afford to make such a promise; their fleet needed every able-bodied man it could get.

Jefferson might have gotten national support for war against the British during the last half of 1807. It was not only the *Chesapeake* affair that aroused American wrath. The British passed orders-in-council in 1806 and early 1807 announcing a blockade of Europe and prohibiting all neutral trade between French ports. Jefferson merely responded by allowing the Nonimportation Act of 1806 to go into effect and ordering British ships from American ports. But in November the situation worsened when the British proclaimed a blockade of all world ports from which British ships were excluded by England's enemies; any ships found trading with these ports could be seized. In December Napoleon retaliated with his Milan Decree, declaring that any ship that honored Britain's blockade was fair prize for the French. Unlike the British, Napoleon had no power to enforce his rule beyond the European ports controlled by his armies. Great Britain could reach as far as the West and East Indies and Latin America, areas of major American trading interest.

Late in 1807 Jefferson again rejected the idea of using military force, attempting instead to strengthen his economic weapons by obtaining an Embargo Act from Congress. This measure stopped exportation of goods, closed American ports, and allowed only coastwise trade. But once more the administration miscalculated. The British needed American goods less than they needed American markets. A good crop in 1808 further reduced British dependence upon foreign foodstuffs. Meanwhile, docks and ships either rotted in American ports or were used in smuggling operations. The embargo ironically helped accomplish Britain's objective of cutting trade between the New World and France.

For once New Englanders and southerners had a common dissatisfaction. After six years of relative quiet, political factions revived. Jefferson came under strong political attack. In the 1808 election, the Federalists, seizing the embargo as their main political issue, succeeded in tripling their electoral vote of 1804. Madison nevertheless won the presidency by a safe margin, gathering 122 electoral votes to 47 for the Federalist candidate. Significantly, the Federalists doubled their House membership, a warning that the new President could encounter strong opposition from that body.

The Final Jeffersonian Legacies

EAGERLY ANTICIPATING retirement to the tranquillity of Monticello, Jefferson cleared the docket for his successor by repealing the embargo on March 1, 1809. Three days before Madison moved into the President's mansion, Jefferson signed a measure that gave the chief executive the authority to resume trade with any belligerent that would recognize American neutral rights. This bill initially meant that although American ships could now leave port, they could not trade with Great Britain and France. But American merchants, long experienced in smuggling, viewed this nonintercourse act as an invitation to open a vast illegal trade simply by transferring their goods to British or French ships at such handy intermediate points as the Azores. Appropriately, two of the ships that regularly traveled the illegitimate routes were the *Madison* and the *Thomas Jefferson.*

The President returned to Virginia satisfied that by doubling the American empire with the Louisiana Purchase, he had secured the "blessings of liberty" for generations of his countrymen. But he worried that warfare in the Atlantic might stunt the proper development of that empire. "It is to be desired that war may be avoided, if circumstances will admit," Jefferson advised Madison in March 1809. But the Virginian's frustrations of the previous four years emerged: "War, however, may become a less losing business than unresisted depredation."[13] With this explanation of how economic ambitions created political responsibilities, Jefferson framed the alternatives for Madison's policies between 1809 and 1812.

Suggestions for Further Reading

President Jefferson and his chief advisers are examined in Dumas Malone, *Jefferson, the President (1801–1805)* (Boston, 1971), the latest volume in perhaps the definitive biography of Jefferson. Merrill Peterson's one-volume *Thomas Jefferson and the New Nation* (New York, 1970) is excellent; Lawrence Kaplan, *Jefferson and France: An Essay on Politics and Political Ideas* (New Haven, Conn., 1967), ranges before and beyond the presidential terms. See also Irving Brant's *James Madison: Secretary of State, 1800–1809* (Indianapolis, 1953) and Raymond Walters, Jr., *Albert Gallatin: Jeffersonian Financier and Diplomat* (New York, 1957), a consideration of perhaps the most talented administrator and negotiator of all Jeffersonians.

---

13 Jefferson to Madison, March 17, 1809, in ibid., 12:267.

The French side of the Louisiana story is given in the now standard account by E. W. Lyon, *Louisiana in French Diplomacy, 1759–1804* (Norman, Okla., 1934), and documented in J. A. Robertson, ed., *Louisiana Under the Rule of Spain, France, and the U.S., 1785–1807,* 2 vols. (Cleveland, 1911), while Arthur P. Whitaker splendidly depicts the background in *The Mississippi Question, 1795–1803* (New York, 1934).

Nathan Schachner, *Aaron Burr* (New York, 1937), is a rather favorable treatment of Burr, and T. P. Abernathy gives an opposing view in *The Burr Conspiracy* (New York, 1954).

Commercial problems are examined in Bradford Perkins, *Prologue to War: England and the United States, 1805–1812* (Berkeley, 1961), now a standard account, which takes particular care to delineate the British policies; Arthur P. Whitaker, *The United States and the Independence of Latin America* (Baltimore, 1941), a classic rendering of how Americans opened up markets in Latin America; R. W. Bixler, *The Open Door on the Old Barbary Coast* (New York, 1959); and Samuel Flagg Bemis, *John Quincy Adams and the Foundations of American Foreign Policy* (New York, 1949), showing how one important if atypical Federalist supported most of Jefferson's measures.

See also the general bibliography at the end of this volume.

CHAPTER 6

The Second War
for Independence
(1809–1815)

The War of 1812 might be subtitled "The Culmination of Amer-
ican History, 1763–1812." To delineate the war's causes is also to outline the
previous half century of American foreign policy: a determination to export
surpluses, the consequent struggle for enlarged markets and neutral rights, a
fixation upon expansion north and south, battles with the Indians and Great
Britain, and the traditional fear of British economic and naval power. The War
of 1812 quieted many of these disputes, but it also ironically allowed Americans
to turn inward—and toward civil war.

The Failure of Economic Diplomacy

JEFFERSON'S ADMINISTRATION had attempted to preserve American rights by
manipulating the nation's supposed economic power, first with the Nonimportation Act of 1806 and then with the embargo of 1807–1809. When these
two attempts to coerce the British and French failed, the Nonintercourse Act

[79]

of March 1809 attempted to close American ports to the ships and goods of both belligerents, but provided that trade would be restored with the belligerent that withdrew its discriminatory policy. Madison doubted the effectiveness of this act, privately asserting upon entering the presidency that he would shortly have to lead the nation to war against either Great Britain or France. He was quite correct, for the 1809 act was a failure and he soon confronted the only alternative, armed conflict.

The British had more important problems on their minds than American affairs, including the insanity of King George III, perennial Irish difficulties, and Napoleon. In 1809 London consequently attempted to ameliorate Anglo-American relations by reducing the restrictions imposed upon American exports to the continent. But this was not sufficient for Madison. He wanted all of the British orders-in-council aimed at controlling neutral trade to be immediately dropped. The embattled Foreign Office refused to go this far, so the President angrily reinstituted the Nonintercourse Act against England in March 1811. Anglo-American relations approached their nadir.

Madison's failures in dealing with the British allowed enemies in Congress to condemn him. Factions in large part dormant through the first seven years of Jefferson's presidency had suddenly arisen phoenix-like during the embargo. By midsummer 1810 Madison lost control of this proliferating opposition, even within the Democratic-Republican party, which he had helped form during the 1790s. Given his staunch belief that the presidency must be sensitive and responsible to Congress, Madison faced intense frustrations in his diplomatic efforts. He hoped for better things from the Congress to be elected in the autumn of 1810. British and French restrictions had depressed cotton and tobacco prices. "It will not be wonderful, therefore," the President remarked, "if the passive spirit which marked the late session of Congress should at the next meeting be roused to the opposite point."[1] Madison wanted to tighten the screws.

Seizing West Florida

BUT CONGRESS' first order of business in late 1811 was not commerce; it was the Floridas. American interest in the area had risen after 1805 as rebellion spread over the weakened Spanish empire in Latin America. The importance

---

[1] Madison to William Pinckney, May 23, 1810, in *The Writings of James Madison,* ed. Gaillard Hunt, 9 vols. (New York, 1901), 8:99–100.

WEST FLORIDA

EAST FLORIDA

TERRITORIES OF
EAST AND WEST FLORIDA

of the Floridas rose, moreover, as increasing numbers of Americans attempted to use the river outlets through the area in order to reach the rich markets of the Gulf of Mexico and South America. These outlets became ever more important as the West endured a severe depression between 1806 and 1810.

But again the hated British turned up. With Spanish rule overthrown in many South American areas, England had rushed in to obtain trade preferences. Madison countered by unsuccessfully attempting to undercut British influence in Brazil, then sending the first three American commercial agents to the newly independent areas in 1810. Aid to the Latin American revolutionaries was nevertheless spooned out carefully. American diplomats and businessmen neither ideologically identified with the spreading revolution nor wished to incite Napoleon and the Spanish against them.

When Napoleon placed his brother Joseph on the Spanish throne, the British threatened to defend the deposed Spanish King by protecting Spain's colonies in South America, Cuba, and Florida. American expansion southward would also, of course, be checked. Madison privately observed that such British controls could not be tolerated: "With respect to Spanish America generally, you will find that G. Britain is engaged in the most eager, and...the most reproachful grasp of political influence and commercial preference."[2] Such British ambitions were not forgotten when Madison and Congress debated the question of war in early 1812.

---

[2] Madison to Pinckney, October 30, 1810, in ibid., 8:122.

Despite British, Spanish, and French claims, West Florida was ripe for picking by the United States. Americans had swarmed into the area during the 1790s, when Spain had foolishly encouraged such immigration. By 1810 Spanish power had largely dissolved. Believing that "the Country to the Perdido, being our own, may be fairly taken possession of, if it can be done without violence," Madison ordered secret agents to tell West Floridians that if they wished to join the American union, Washington officials would act quickly and favorably. The settlers duly responded in September 1810 by capturing Baton Rouge from a phantom Spanish army, declaring the area independent, and asking for annexation. Madison carefully silenced news of the event pending the convening of Congress in November. He wanted to present the British and Napoleon with a *fait accompli.*

THE NONTRANSFER PRINCIPLE

In January 1811 Congress authorized Madison to occupy West Florida. (American authority stretched to the Pearl River only, for the settlers had not attempted to fight the Spanish garrison at Mobile.) Under the control of Henry Clay and newly arrived militant southerners and westerners, Congress warmed Madison's heart by authorizing $100,000 for presidential use if the British attempted to reclaim the territory for Spain.

Congress next passed a resolution, embodying the famous nontransfer principle, which stated that since the entire Florida territory was important for American "security, tranquillity and commerce," that area could not be allowed to "pass into the hands of any other foreign power." The resolution even provided for "temporary occupation" under "certain contingencies," and warned that otherwise East Florida must remain "subject to future arrangement" between the United States and Spain.[3] A decade later, this principle would also be applied to Cuba.

Madison attempted to make good this congressional claim by repeating the act so successfully staged in West Florida. He secretly sent elderly General George Mathews, former governor of Georgia, into East Florida to seize the area from the inside. In March 1812 Mathews carried out his mission by establishing a government that ceded the area to the United States. Madison suddenly decided he might not want it. At that moment, he was condemning the British for apparently following Mathews' strategy in New England; pro-British northeasterners were allegedly ready to cede their territory to Canada. The Gen-

---

[3] "Declaration Concerning East Florida," January 7, 1811, in *The Papers of Henry Clay,* ed. James F. Hopkins (Lexington, Ky., 1959), 1:520.

eral meanwhile met increased resistance, and much to Madison's chagrin he was not fomenting revolution covertly, but with an unfortunate flair for obtaining maximum personal publicity. The President disavowed the General ("Mathews has been playing a strange comedy, in the face of common sense, as well as of his instructions," Madison told Jefferson), but significantly the chief executive refused to drop American claims to the area that Mathews had given the United States. The territory would ultimately be returned to Spain in the treaty ending the War of 1812, but Madison and Mathews had undercut Spanish authority throughout Florida.

Madison Exhausts the Alternatives

THE AMERICAN SPHERE had been extended through West Florida, but the commercial sphere remained dangerously restricted through 1811 and early 1812. By late 1811, smuggling had so drastically reduced the effectiveness of the Nonimportation Act that influential editor Hezekiah Niles believed the measure should be retitled "An Act for the Better Encouragement of Roguery and Other Purposes." The President, moreover, carefully refrained from touching that most sensitive and exposed nerve in the Anglo-American trading system, the American grain shipments feeding the Duke of Wellington's huge armies in Spain. These shipments rose from 80,000 bushels in 1807 to more than 900,000 within five years. But as the British Empire grew more dependent upon American grain producers, Madison became more reluctant to dam these massive exports. His own analysis trapped him, for since the 1780s he had warned of the terrible political and social consequences when exports stagnated.

The President's diplomatic alternatives were narrowing as Congress prepared to meet in November 1811. The decision for or against war was at hand. In May, American war spirit soared when a forty-four-gun United States frigate, *President,* nearly destroyed a twenty-gun British sloop, *Little Belt,* off the Virginia coast. The *Chesapeake* incident had been avenged, and some Americans demanded more blood. Meanwhile American Minister William Pinckney left London in disgust after failing to settle differences with the Foreign Office.

His departure and the *Little Belt* affair occurred as the British wallowed in a depression that ruined banks and increased industrial unemployment. In an attempt to prevent further deterioration of relations, London officials restored to the *Chesapeake* the surviving seamen impressed from it in 1807 and offered to compensate them and their families. That incident was closed, but Madison attempted to settle the more important differences over neutral rights and impressment during negotiations with British Minister Augustus J. Foster in July. After these discussions failed, Madison prepared for war. He received encouragement from the newly appointed Secretary of State, James Monroe, who was pro-French and much concerned over alleged British incitement of Indians in the Old Northwest. Monroe's appearance clearly signaled new administration policies.

The Appearance of the War Hawks

MADISON AND MONROE found a new Congress convening in November 1811. Elected during the campaigns of 1810 and early 1811, it was, as Madison had prophesied the previous autumn, belligerent and ambitious. The leaders of the most militant faction, or "War Hawks," as the Federalists soon labeled them, arrived from the Southeast and West. They included Henry Clay and Felix Grundy of Kentucky and John Calhoun, William Lowndes, and Langdon Cheves of South Carolina.

Two conditions had shaped the elections in these sections. Since 1808 the Mississippi Valley had been caught in the vise of depression. Traditional western complaints, such as lack of specie and inadequate transportation and banking facilities, explained part of the problem. But westerners, observing that the depression's origins coincided with the embargo, also blamed the British and French for sealing off export markets in Europe and thereby creating great surpluses of crops in the West. When cotton dropped from twenty-five cents a pound in 1808 to eight cents in 1811, the Southeast was similarly quick to blame British and French restrictions. South Carolina proved especially vulnerable, for its cotton, rice, indigo, and tobacco accounted for more than 10 percent of the nation's exports. On December 12, 1811, in a speech to the House, John Calhoun related the depression to the need for war:

> Sir, I acknowledge the cotton of our farms is worth but little; but not for the cause assigned by the gentleman from Virginia [John Randolph, who had argued that Jefferson's embargo and Madison's nonintercourse measures were responsible for depressed prices]. The people of that section do not reason as he does; they do not attribute it to the efforts of their government to maintain the peace and independence of their country. They see, in the low price of their produce, the hand of foreign injustice; they know well, without the market to the continent, the deep and steady current of supply will glut

that of Great Britain; they are not prepared for the colonial state to which again that power is endeavoring to reduce us.[4]

This need for overseas markets explained southern and western determination to defend American rights on the high seas. New England merchants, on the other hand, cared less about the rights of the exporters, for the merchants profited from carrying the trade of other nations (including Great Britain) as well as that of the United States. For generations their dependence upon and willingness to work within the British imperial trading system (as Hamilton's program had worked) made many New Englanders reluctant to wage war against the British. Felix Grundy accentuated this sectional difference when he observed on the eve of war that the "true question" was "not the carrying trade" of the Northeast, but "the interest of the whole nation. It is the right of exporting the productions of our own soil and industry to foreign markets."

A second disquieting condition was renewed Indian attacks on both the southern and northwestern frontiers in 1809–1810. To the south, Indians attacked settlements, then frequently retreated to sanctuaries in Spanish Florida— one reason Madison gladly instigated rebellion in West Florida during 1810. The situation was considerably worse in the Northwest. Since Jefferson had accelerated a vicious Indian policy at the turn of the century, more than a hundred million acres of excellent land had been extorted from the tribes through the use of threats and cheap bribes. William Henry Harrison, governor of the Indiana territory at Vincennes, was primarily responsible for carrying out the wretched policy.

Council at Vincennes: Gen. Harrison and Tecumseh

---

[4] "Reply to Randolph," December 12, 1811, in *The Papers of John C. Calhoun,* ed. Robert L. Meriwether (Columbia, S.C., 1959), 1:83.

In 1809 he finally went too far. By playing off tribe against tribe, Harrison wrested from the Indians the Treaty of Fort Wayne, which transferred three million acres of choice Indiana land to white settlers for a mere $7,000. Frustrated by Harrison in Indiana and by warlike Sioux and Chippewa who prevented resettlement beyond the Mississippi, Indians in the Old Northwest fell under the leadership of the charismatic Tecumseh and his brother, The Prophet. They received encouragement from Canadian fur traders who had been operating south of the boundary line since the Jay Treaty, much to the anger of American settlers and traders. When attacks on white settlements commenced in 1809–1810, westerners quickly blamed both the Indians and their British friends.

The depression and Indian depredations coalesced easily with old hatred of the British to produce the election results of 1810–1811. Of the 142 members of the House, 63, mostly Democrat-Republicans, lost their seats. New men appeared, conditioned by the hatreds and insecurities boiling in the South and West. They gained control of Congress. Freshly arrived Henry Clay became Speaker. He and other newcomers organized standing committees whose chairmen were named by Clay. These committees controlled House affairs while simultaneously regaining power from the executive. Madison doubtless encouraged this reassertion of congressional power. His political theories depended upon an effective legislative arena within which factions could work out their differences. The President heartily agreed, moreover, with war measures prepared by the new leadership. Party affiliation was important; most New England Democrat-Republicans remained loyal to the administration and voted with the War Hawks. But clearly, power had swung south and west.

Clay

THE NEW thirty-four-year-old Speaker personified the southern-western alliance, for he had been born in Virginia in 1777. Receiving a license to practice law at the age of twenty, Clay rode to Lexington, Kentucky, and through land speculation and politics became involved with a section whose prosperity depended upon the exporting of hemp and tobacco. Problems of transportation and capital force-fed a booming industrial economy that turned out textiles, iron products, beer, whiskey, and powder. This environment spawned Clay's famous "American System": internal improvements, high tariffs, a national bank. These measures would expand and consolidate Kentucky's economy by tying it se-

Henry Clay

curely within the Union. Seeing no contradiction between being both a fervent Kentuckian and an ardent nationalist, Clay demanded full American rights upon the seas. He knew his state's export economy was interdependent with the mercantile and shipping communities of New England and the middle states.

During 1811 and 1812 he repeatedly emphasized the need for continued territorial and commercial expansion. Clay emphasized that the American economy depended upon exports, not imports. The British orders-in-council, he argued, thwarted these exports not primarily to starve Napoleon, but to reduce American competition to the global British trading system. "The real cause of British aggression was not to distress an enemy, but to destroy a rival," Clay believed in late 1811. Acquiescence meant accepting British rules and imports, but "the nation that imports its clothing is but little less dependent than if it imported its bread."[5]

He strongly defended Madison's seizure of West Florida. "It cannot be too often repeated," Clay observed in a speech of December 1810,

> that if Cuba on the one hand, and Florida on the other, are in the possession of a foreign maritime power, the immense country belonging to the United States, watered by the streams discharging themselves into the gulph [*sic*] of Mexico—that is one third, nay more than two thirds of the United States, comprehending Louisiana, is placed at the mercy of that power. The possession

[5] "Amendment to, and Speech on, the Bill to Raise an Additional Military Force," December 31, 1811, in *Papers of Clay,* 1:606–609.

of Florida is a guarantee absolutely necessary to the enjoyment of the navigation of those streams.[6]

His expansionism and Anglophobia easily blended. The resulting policies were advocated by a personality whose political brilliance and flair have seldom been matched in American history. A New England Brahmin, Josiah Quincy, explained Clay's force condescendingly, but not unadmiringly or inaccurately:

> Bold, aspiring, presumptuous, with a rough, overbearing eloquence, neither exact nor comprehensive, which he had cultivated and formed in the contests with the half-civilized wranglers in the country courts of Kentucky, he had not yet that polish of language and refinement of manners which he afterwards acquired by familiarity and attrition with highly cultivated men.... Such was the man whose influence and power more than that of any other produced the war of 1812.[7]

Josiah Quincy

Quincy

THE AUTHOR of that description spoke after close observation, for he unsuccessfully led the Federalist and antiwar faction against Clay and Madison. Quite in contrast to Clay, Quincy was born of a wealthy merchant family in 1772 and graduated first in his Harvard class of 1790. He became a Federalist as naturally as he breathed, and with the support of family wealth turned to politics as a profession, not, as many of his friends had done, as a hobby. Hoping to revive the Federalists after the Jefferson triumphs, he became a congressman in 1805. Six years later Quincy emerged as leader of the Federalist minority.

---

[6] "Speech on the Occupation of West Florida," December 28, 1810, in ibid., 1:514.

[7] Edmund Quincy, *Life of Josiah Quincy* (Boston, 1872), p. 255.

If Clay eulogized expansion as the cure-all for the nation's ills, Quincy warned that further expansion would destroy the Union. In a widely publicized speech against the admission of Louisiana as a state in January 1811, Quincy opposed Clay's views, Madison's theory of an extensive sphere, and the incorporation of certain races within the Union. He also prophesied the coming of the Civil War.

> I am compelled to declare it as my deliberate opinion that, if this bill passes, the bonds of this Union are virtually dissolved; that the States which compose it are free from their moral obligations; and that as it will be the right of all, so it will be the duty of some to prepare definitely for a separation—amicably, if they can; violently, if they must.... [The Constitution] was never constructed to form a covering for the inhabitants of the Missouri and the Red River country; and whenever it is attempted to be stretched over them it will rend asunder.... It was not for these men that our fathers fought.... You have no authority to throw the rights and liberties and property of this people into 'hotch pot' with the wild men on the Missouri, nor with the mixed, though more respectable, race of the Anglo-Hispano-Gallo-Americans who bask on the sands in the mouth of the Mississippi.[8]

Quincy ultimately refused to follow his own logic, for three years later, when the Hartford Convention met to discuss New England secession, Quincy refused to attend. Indeed, throughout 1811 and 1812 he tried to follow the dangerous course of opposing war against England while at the same time giving the Federalists an image of a nationalist, patriotic party. He accused the War Hawks of caring less about neutral trade than using war as an excuse to invade Canada and obtain more land for expansion. At one point, Quincy even naively believed the War Hawks were bluffing about war.[9]

His determination to be both patriotic for the sake of his party and antiwar for the benefit of his section finally ensnared him. Hating Madison and the War Hawks, Quincy nevertheless voted consistently for measures to build the army and navy in 1811 and 1812. Like the President, he personally preferred to prepare for war rather than suffer British policies. He scathingly dismissed those New England merchants who narrow-mindedly looked for aid from Great Britain:

> As to the British, there is a foolish leaning upon them among some of our friends, which, at the same time that it does little credit to their patriotism,

---

[8] "Speech on the Admission of Louisiana as a State," in *Speeches Delivered in the Congress of the United States by Josiah Quincy*, ed. Edmund Quincy (Boston, 1874), pp. 193–224, especially pp. 196, 216.

[9] Quincy to Otis, November 26, 1811, in Samuel Eliot Morison, *The Life and Letters of Harrison Gray Otis, Federalist, 1765–1848*, 2 vols. (Boston, 1913), 2:33–35.

does infinitely less to their judgment. The truth is, the British look upon us as a *foreign nation,* and we must look upon them in the same light.[10]

Such parochial views, moreover, could destroy the Federalist party, a result that Quincy hoped to avert at all costs.

He made a valiant attempt to save his party, defend New England interests, and avert war with England. More important, he placed his finger on the policy that would ultimately help tear apart the Union: expansionism. His own policies were doomed. He voted for war preparations, but refused to vote for the war declaration itself. Quincy failed to reconcile his party and sectional interests with the national drive for expansion. A tired Federalism plodded toward the dead end of the Hartford Convention, while Clay and a booming nationalism raced headlong toward war.

Madison Prepares for War

As CLAY AND QUINCY mobilized their forces, Madison capitalized upon the appearance of the War Hawks by sending a message to Congress in November 1811. In a private letter, the President summarized his paper: "The question to be decided . . . simply is, whether all the trade to which the orders are and shall be applied, is to be abandoned, or the hostile operation of them, be hostilely resisted. The apparent disposition is certainly not in favor of the first alternative."[11] He asked that the nation be prepared for war.

Congress was debating the message when news arrived that on November 7, 1811, William Henry Harrison had defeated Tecumseh at the Battle of Tippecanoe. The conflict was not decisive and the casualties on Harrison's side were heavy, but the encounter produced evidence that the British were in league with the Indians. Kentuckians wore black armbands in Congress and proposed resolutions that charged Great Britain with "inciting the savages to murder." Anti-British sentiment boiled, and Clay understood that with Tecumseh defeated, the nation could war against the British without worrying about massive Indian attacks in the Old Northwest.

The House seized the initiative on November 29, when its Foreign Affairs Committee submitted a report listing the many unsuccessful efforts to make the British behave. The paper concluded, "We ought to go to war in opposition to

---

[10] Quincy's personal record, and letter to Mrs. Quincy, March 26, 1812, in E. Quincy, *Life of Josiah Quincy,* p. 249.

[11] Madison to J. Q. Adams, November 15, 1811, in *Writings of Madison,* 8:166–67.

the Orders in Council."[12] With this as a rallying point, the War Hawks over-
came stubborn opposition to pass a small naval bill and legislation increasing
taxes to finance the war and authorizing a 25,000-man army. The War Hawks
were not always united. Clay was the only westerner to vote for a larger naval
bill, which was finally defeated by a vote of 62 to 59; other trans-Apalachian
representatives disliked the creation of a war fleet that would be manned and
controlled by New Englanders.

On March 9, 1812, Madison sent Congress papers recently purchased for
some $50,000 from a supposed British agent, John Henry. The documents
purported to show that New England leaders were secretly plotting to join
their section with British policies. When the papers were later proved to be for-
geries, Madison and Monroe barely escaped with their reputations, while the
Federalists felt doubly justified in accusing the administration of using deceit
to force a war. The immediate result, however, was a ninety-day embargo,
passed early in April. As Clay explained, the measure would "give tone to
public sentiment," and "above all powerfully accelerate preparations for the
War."

As late as May not even Clay was certain whether war would be conducted
against England, France, or perhaps both. France's seizures of American ships
ran as high as England's. Great Britain's attacks, however, were more visible:
Britannia ruled the seas, had tried to strangle American commerce for more
than thirty-five years, had impressed United States seamen, and unfortunately

Impressment of American seamen

---

[12] *Annals of Congress,* 12th Cong., 1st sess., cols. 374–77; the resulting debate is in cols.
414–20.

had loud as well as politically insensitive allies in New England. Madison closed the case in June. During the congressional debate on a war declaration, he sent documents that Clay interpreted as having "fully verified that the Indians are instigated by the British."

On June 1, Madison delivered his war message to Congress. He began by condemning British impressment, then swung into his central theme: "mock blockades" had been laid by the British so that "our commerce has been plundered in every sea, the great staples of our country have been cut off from their legitimate markets, and a destructive blow aimed at our agricultural and maritime interests." Such attacks occurred not because American commerce threatened English efforts against Napoleon, but because the trade interfered "with the monopoly which [Great Britain] covets for her own commerce and navigation." Madison had been waiting for this moment since the 1780s. He concluded by linking Indian attacks with "British traders and garrisons."[13]

The House declared for war 79–49, and after vigorous debate the Senate concurred, 19–13. The small contingent of ten western congressmen, together with Calhoun, provided the leadership; five south Atlantic states delivered necessary votes; and, in the end, representatives (primarily Democrat-Republicans) from port towns in Massachusetts, Pennsylvania, and Maryland voted for war. Federalists, personal political opponents of Madison's, and various delegates from the middle Atlantic and New England states formed the core of opposition.

Unknown to Madison and Congress, the British Ministry had repealed the orders-in-council on June 16, two days before the Senate completed action on the war resolution, in response to demands by English manufacturers, already mired in a depression, for access to American markets. Madison's nonimportation and embargo policies had finally worked, but too late. When news of the British action reached Washington several weeks later, the President refused to reconsider the war declaration. He argued that London remained obstinate on impressment. Madison also feared that a truce would only provide time for the Canadians and Indians to bolster their defenses.

War

THE CONFLICT turned into a nearly unbroken string of American disasters. The War Hawks, along with such usually astute observers as Jefferson, believed the

[13] James D. Richardson, ed., *A Compilation of the Messages and Papers of the Presidents, 1789–1897,* 10 vols. (Washington, D.C., 1900), 1:499–505.

British could quickly be brought to their senses (and some territory might be brought to the Union) by a quick conquest of Canada. Striking through the Niagara frontier area, however, American forces encountered former Loyalists of the revolutionary era who had been well treated by the British. These Canadians smashed the American army. British forces proceeded to move into American territory along the Great Lakes and in Maine. To the south, English troops drove the government from Washington and burned the capital. United States naval officers won memorable, if not diplomatically significant, victories on the Great Lakes, but no sane American ever dreamed of a decisive naval victory over England. When the British freed themselves of Napoleon in 1814, they could mobilize more than twice as many ships as the American navy had cannon.

As early as July 1812, Monroe urged London to accept an armistice based upon discontinuance of impressment and a pledge that the orders-in-council would not be reinstated. These diplomatic approaches became more urgent as New England delegates prepared to call their meeting at Hartford and the effectiveness of the government disintegrated in charred Washington buildings. Even War Hawks had had enough: "Our executive officers are most incompetent men ..." Calhoun lamented late in 1812. "We are literally boren [sic] down under the effects of errors and mismanagement."[14]

In March 1813 hope appeared. The Russian Tsar, eager to free Britain's hand so it could throw its full weight against Napoleon, proposed mediation. Madison eagerly grasped the offer. Without waiting for the British response, he ordered Albert Gallatin, James Bayard, and John Quincy Adams, the American minister to Russia, to pursue a diplomatic settlement in Europe. The President later sent Henry Clay and Jonathan Russell to join the delegation. After initially resenting the Tsar's interference, the British agreed to send emissaries to meet with the Americans at Ghent in Belgium in November 1813.

Peace

THE UNITED STATES compensated for its military disadvantages by employing a brilliant negotiating team that had the good fortune to meet second-level British diplomats. Great Britain's first team was tending to the more important problems of Napoleon and European politics at the great Vienna Conference. The American group, however, was split. Clay's frontier vibrancy clashed repeatedly with Adams' New England reserve. A division was averted only by Gallatin's

---

[14] Calhoun to Dr. James MacBride, December 25, 1812, in *Papers of Calhoun,* 1:146.

patient conciliation. More important, Clay determined to maintain American control of the Mississippi, while Adams focused on the Newfoundland fisheries as the primary diplomatic objective. Given the strength of the British position, the Americans would not be able to obtain both.

Monroe instructed the delegation to ask for the end of impressment and illegal blockades as well as for unrestricted control of the Mississippi and rights in the fisheries. He also asked for Canada, but this was only a card to be traded in the negotiations. The British stunned the Americans by demanding control of the Great Lakes, joint navigation of the Mississippi, the creation of a large Indian buffer state in the Lake Superior region, and territory in Maine and New York.

The Americans immediately rejected the British terms. Negotiations were deadlocked until November 1814, when Great Britain decided it could obtain its demands only by a costly military conquest of the Great Lakes area. An American victory at Plattsburgh Bay in September ended British hopes. English manufacturers and the powerful banking house of Baring Brothers strengthened the peace movement with demands that postwar economic troubles at home must be partially remedied by immediate access to the American market.

The defeat of Napoleon meanwhile made academic American concern over neutral rights and impressment. On Christmas Eve, 1814, the two delegations finally agreed to a peace that returned all territory captured during the war, referred questions of boundaries and fisheries to arbitration commissions, and pointedly neglected to mention neutral rights, impressment, or any British rights to the Mississippi. The Americans were relieved, but hardly overjoyed. "We lost no territory, I think no honor," Clay wrote with less than absolute certainty on Christmas Day.[15] The Kentuckian and his countrymen felt much better about their honor when they discovered several months later that General Andrew Jackson had scored a smashing victory over British troops attempting to take New Orleans on January 8, 1815. That Jackson had decimated the English force two weeks after war had been concluded neither lessened American joy nor retarded the General's future political career.

A Last Act

THE WAR OF 1812 had proven to be nearly disastrous for the United States. With relief the Senate unanimously ratified the treaty in February 1815. The last act

---

[15] Clay to Monroe, December 25, 1814, in *Papers of Clay,* 1:1007. The treaty itself is on p. 1006.

General Jackson at New Orleans

of the war was played out between 1815 and 1818. In February 1815, Madison threatened to impose trade discriminations unless Great Britain agreed to reciprocal shipping rights. Such an agreement was reached in regard to the British Isles and India in a pact of 1815, but the coveted West Indies trade remained restricted.

Two years later, in the Rush-Bagot Treaty, England and the United States agreed to begin disarmament on the Great Lakes, thereby quieting that volitile area and initiating a long period of relative peace between the United States and Canada. In the Convention of 1818, the commissions authorized at Ghent decided that the United States should have the "liberty" to fish the coasts of Newfoundland and Labrador; established the forty-ninth parallel as the U.S.-Canadian boundary from Lake of the Woods to the Rockies (thereby preventing British access to the Mississippi); renewed certain provisions of the 1815 commercial treaty; and provided that the disputed Oregon territory west of the Rockies would be "free and open" to both Englishmen and Americans.

The Treaty of Ghent and the 1817–1818 agreements vindicated the War Hawks' nationalism and killed the possible secessionist movement initiated by the Hartford Convention. With these agreements, the United States turned inward, seeking further expansion in the Floridas, in the Southwest, and along the Pacific coast. But not coincidentally, Americans simultaneously experienced the first danger signal sounded by the expansion of slavery into Missouri, that "firebell in the night," as Jefferson called it, which presaged civil war.

Suggestions for Further Reading

The most comprehensive account of events leading up to war is Bradford Perkins, *Prologue to War: England and the United States, 1805–1812* (Berkeley, 1961), while Reginald Horsman, *The Causes of the War of 1812* (Philadelphia, 1962), is a fine short analysis. A. L. Burt, *The United States, Great Britain, and British North America, 1783–1815* (New Haven, Conn., 1940), remains useful, especially on problems in the West; and two articles are indispensable: George Rogers Taylor, "Agrarian Discontent in the Mississippi Valley Preceding the War of 1812," *Journal of Political Economy*, 39 (1931):471–505, and W. H. Goodman, "The Origins of the War of 1812: A Survey of Changing Interpretations," *Mississippi Valley Historical Review*, 28 (1941):171–86.

The leading actors are examined in Irving Brant, *James Madison: The President, 1809–1812* (Indianapolis, 1956); Charles M. Wiltse, *John C. Calhoun, Nationalist, 1782–1828* (Indianapolis, 1944), the first in a splendid multivolume study; and Bernard Mayo, *Henry Clay: Spokesman of the New West* (Boston, 1937).

The problems at Ghent are well analyzed in Irving Brant, *James Madison: Commander in Chief, 1812–1836* (Indianapolis, 1961), interesting particularly for Madison's response to postwar problems; and especially Samuel Flagg Bemis, *John Quincy Adams and the Foundation of American Foreign Policy* (New York, 1949).

The problems of the New England Federalists and the appearance of some of them at the Hartford Convention are well described in David H. Fischer, *The Revolution of American Conservatism: The Federalist Party in the Era of Jeffersonian Democracy* (New York, 1965), and James M. Banner, Jr., *To the Hartford Convention* (New York, 1970).

See also the general bibliography at the end of this volume.

CHAPTER 7

The Era
of Adams
(1815–1828)

The War of 1812 enhanced American nationalism by producing a national anthem, the figure of Uncle Sam, and a peace treaty that is conveniently overlooked by those who subscribe to the popular belief that the United States never lost a war or won a peace. But the conflict also ironically intensified sectionalism. Investment in northeastern manufacturing enterprises rose to nearly $50 million by 1820. With industry came demands for higher tariffs to seal off American ports from cheap European goods. A first protective tariff was passed in 1818, and in 1828 Congress passed the highest tariff between 1789 and the Civil War.

This last measure, however, met firm opposition from the South and led to South Carolina's threatened nullification of federal acts in 1832 and 1833. The South was the backbone of the American export economy, producing vast amounts of cotton grown on large plantations with slave labor. Moreover, when southerners attempted to develop their own textile industry between 1815 and 1820, their hopes were first blunted and then destroyed by a lack of capital, an influx of cheap British goods, and finally the Panic of 1819–1821. Between 1815 and 1828 the industrializing Northeast and the raw-material-producing South split further apart over questions of internal improvements, slavery in the Louisiana Territory, and, most symbolically, the Adams-Jackson presidential campaign of 1828. This struggle increasingly centered on the problem of which section, North or South, would settle and exploit the incredibly rich western territories; for the section that controlled the West would rule the nation.

Contrary to Madison's theory in *Federalist 10,* an extensive empire did not reconcile factions, but was forcing a confrontation between those who wanted that empire to be organized according to a Jacksonian, decentralized slave system and those who demanded an Adamsonian program that restricted slavery and linked all Americans with federally sponsored internal improvements.

Adams

HISTORIANS CONSIDER John Quincy Adams the nation's greatest Secretary of State, although they give short shrift to his grand designs for consolidation of

John Quincy Adams

the Union. Adams would have thought such a divided view nonsense, for he knew his foreign policies were inseparable from his domestic plans. Both external and internal policies emanated from a mind whose learning, brilliance, and experience have had no equal among Secretaries of State. He knew six languages, European literature and theater, the classic texts in their originals, diplomatic intrigue at St. Petersburg and Paris, and how to carry on political debates with the best minds in Europe—all before the age of twenty.

Adams fervently believed that such knowledge was power. As the son of John and Abigail Adams, he was determined to use that power to realize what he believed to be the national ideals of the Revolution and the Constitution. Owing partly to this idealism and partly to his irascible temperament, Adams was hardly an ideal party member. After serving as a diplomat in the Netherlands and Prussia during the 1790s, he entered the Senate as a Federalist in 1802. He was the only Federalist senator who supported Jefferson's purchase of Louisiana, and one of the few who backed the embargo throughout 1808. For this and other sins, John Quincy was drummed out of the Federalist party in 1808 by embittered New Englanders who complained that unlike themselves, he was an "amphibious animal," one who moved on both sea and land. The dismissal occurred in time for Madison to appoint him minister to Russia. For eight years Adams distinguished himself as a diplomat at St. Petersburg and Ghent. His family background, experience, and innocence of the Hartford Convention made him the leading candidate for Secretary of State under Monroe.

Adams returned home in 1817 with a strong suspicion of Europeans: "We have ... enemies in almost every part of the world, and few or no friends anywhere. ... We are considered not merely as an active and enterprising, but as a grasping and ambitious people."[1] Neither seeking friends nor excusing ambition, he believed American empire would be realized not by European distresses or sympathy, but through the curious combination of divine will and personal self-interest. Although admittedly confused in his religious beliefs, he was driven to build an empire that he believed God meant to ordain as an example for the world. John Quincy's education fitted this conception perfectly, for he also believed the Creator worked according to fixed scientific laws; if Americans could discover and obey these laws, they could possess a nation both expansive and—a hope that was fading as it became more central in Adams' belief—free of slavery. Thus Adams' practice of reading five chapters of the Bible immediately after arising each morning was not merely ritual, but part of statecraft as he perceived it.

---

[1] John Quincy Adams to William Plumer, January 17, 1817, in *The Writings of John Quincy Adams,* ed. Worthington C. Ford, 7 vols. (New York, 1913–1917), 6:143–44.

Good Calvinist that he was, John Quincy realized that although God had willed, temporal creations were usually built by utilizing man's selfishness. To reconcile this self-interest to empire, he drew heavily from Madison, the "one living man to whom I am under greater, and more impressive personal obligations than to any other," as Adams remarked in 1832. Like Madison, he believed extensive empire both inevitable and necessary. In 1819 a member of Monroe's Cabinet reported that because Europeans believed Americans to be "ambitious," the United States should deal more moderately with Spanish and British territories in North America. "I said I doubted whether we ought to give ourselves any concern about it," Adams noted in his diary that night.

> Nothing that we could say or do would remove this impression until the world shall be familiarized with the idea of considering our proper dominion to be the continent of North America. From the time when we became an independent people it was as much a law of nature that this should become our pretension as that the Mississippi should flow to the sea.... And until Europe shall find it a settled geographical element that the United States and North America are identical, any effort on our part to reason the world out of a belief that we are ambitious will have no other effect than to convince them that we add to our ambition hypocrisy.[2]

He consequently did not believe, as Madison and Jefferson had believed, that American settlements beyond the Rockies might evolve into separate nations. In 1824 President Monroe prepared a message intimating that settlements along the Columbia River in Oregon would probably devolve from the Union. Adams and Secretary of War John Calhoun disagreed. "I thought a Government by federation would be found practicable upon a territory as extensive as this continent," the Secretary of State argued.[3] Monroe did not send that part of the message. As a New Englander, Adams valued the maritime possibilities of the Pacific, and as a believer in an American mission, he assumed the United States possessed the instruments to create an empire to the western coast.

But his faith also provided realistic limitations to the vision. In 1816 Adams learned that naval hero Stephen Decatur had proposed a toast: "Our Country: In her intercourse with foreign nations, may she always be in the right; but our country, right or wrong." Adams sharply dissented:

> I cannot ask of heaven success, even for my country, in a cause where she should be in the wrong.... My toast would be, may our country be always

---

[2] *Memoirs of John Quincy Adams, Comprising Portions of His Diary from 1795 to 1848*, ed. Charles Francis Adams, 12 vols. (Philadelphia, 1874–1877), 4:438–39.

[3] Ibid., 6:250–51.

successful, but whether successful or otherwise, always right. I disclaim as unsound all patriotism incompatible with the principles of eternal justice.[4]

God and man were to create a magnificent and ultimately free empire. With his gifts, Adams hoped to be the instrument. But his religion, diplomatic experience, and fear of slavery ringed this vision with fear and skepticism. And so John Quincy Adams arrived in Washington in 1817, "short, thick, and fat," an observer wrote. "He is regular in his habits and moral and temperate in his life. To great talent, he unites unceasing industry and perseverance, and an uncommon facility in the execution of business.... Mr. Adams is extremely plain and simple, both in his manners and habiliments."[5]

Great Britain: How to Coopt Without Cooperating

THE KEY to Adams' diplomatic tactics was his keen assessment of the world's greatest power, the British Empire. In 1817 Adams believed England to be "far more inveterate against us than it ever was before." But the new Secretary of State realized that Great Britain and the United States shared some common objectives. Both detested Spain's colonial empire with its blatant discrimination against foreign goods and its sensitivity to French pressures. Led by Russia and France, a "Holy Alliance" consisting of all European rulers except England's, Turkey's, and the Pope attempted to restore monarchical government both in Europe and in such revolutionary colonial areas as Latin America. Adams perceived that although Great Britain "admits all the pretensions of [monarchical] legitimacy," it quickly abandoned such pretensions if "a new world" opened to its commerce.[6]

Adams undertook a broad review of Anglo-American relations, and within three years quieted the common problems of armaments on the Great Lakes, the Canadian boundary in the West, Oregon, the fisheries, and certain trading rights. Adams also maintained ties with his friend Alexander, Tsar of all the Russias, with whom he had taken long walks while he was minister to St. Petersburg. A potential Russian-American alliance provided a healthy check on British ambitions in the New World.

The United States reached some accommodation with the British despite an almost holy war that Adams fought against England's attempts to exclude American trade from its empire. John Quincy hated such colonialism for many

[4] J. Q. Adams to John Adams, August 1, 1816, in *Writings of J. Q. Adams,* 6:61.

[5] Written by George Waterston, quoted in ibid., 6:519n.

[6] Adams to George Washington Campbell, June 28, 1818, in ibid., 6:377.

reasons, but particularly because he believed that trading was an inalienable right. If a nation was excluded from trade (or fishing), its national survival was threatened. (His determination to be free of British restraints, however, forced him into an embarrassing position on the international slave trade issue. Although he hated the "odious traffic" and pledged the United States to fight it, he refused in 1818 to sign a pact with England allowing reciprocal rights of search on the high seas. He trusted neither British naval officers nor British courts, and consequently undermined international cooperation on this vital question.)

John Quincy Adams demonstrated his concern with both colonialism and the expansion of American carrying trade when he set out on a crusade in 1817 to penetrate the British West Indies. A series of discriminatory measures begun at the close of Madison's administration forced England to open some of its West Indian ports to American ships in 1822. Within four years, Yankee carriers grabbed nine-tenths of the islands' commerce. But Adams was not satisfied. He demanded not only access, but actual equality with British shippers within the British Empire. When London rejected this surprising demand, the Monroe administration began again to pass discriminatory legislation in retaliation. Its patience exhausted after fifty years of dealing with Adamses, the British Ministry repealed the 1822 agreement four years later, excluding all American ships from the British West Indies. In 1830, much to John Quincy's chagrin, Andrew Jackson took a moderate approach and regained the privileges in the islands.

Adams placed the dismantling of the British Empire, and indeed all other colonial empires, at the top of his list of diplomatic priorities. He was confident that the American Revolution had signaled the beginning of the end for colonialists. He consequently battled continually against any discrimination placed on American goods or maritime rights. And the anticolonial crusade, of course, more positively promised to extend American empire in the New World, both on land and at sea.

Florida Is Parlayed into a Continent

ADAMS BRILLIANTLY EXTENDED that empire to continental proportions during protracted discussions with the Spanish minister, Luis de Onís, in 1818 and 1819. Spanish-American difficulties were numerous and Onís proved difficult. "I have seen slippery diplomatists," Adams later wrote, "...but Onís is the first man I have ever met who made it a point of honor to pass for more of a swindler than he was."[7]

The talks began with the Florida problem. During the War of 1812 the United States had completed the conquest of Florida between the Pearl and Perdido rivers to Mobile. East Florida remained in Spanish hands as the result of the Treaty of Ghent, but Adams realized that in a short time the beleaguered Spanish Empire would have to surrender the rest of Florida. Initial discussions moved slowly until the unlikely team of Adams and Andrew Jackson broke the log jam.

Monroe ordered General Jackson into East Florida to stop at the source Indian attacks upon American settlements. The General went further. Between March and May 1818 he seized nearly all the Spanish forts, expelled the Spanish governor, and executed two British citizens whom Jackson accused of instigating Indian attacks. Monroe denied that the General's orders instructed him to attack Spaniards and Englishmen. Jackson angrily replied that the orders provided a blank check, and he acted as he thought he must to protect the settlements. Spain demanded that Jackson be repudiated. The entire Monroe Cabinet agreed, with the single exception of Adams. But the Secretary of State won the day with a state paper that defended Jackson's action and scathingly characterized Spain's inability to maintain order in Florida.[8] Jefferson described it as the finest state paper in American history.

The Spanish next urgently sought aid from their British ally. England, however, refused to intervene. Jackson had gathered incriminating documents in regard to the two executed Englishmen. Adams' state paper, moreover, was adequate evidence that Spain's days in Florida were numbered. The Secretary of State correctly calculated that the British would not get involved on the losing side, especially if the disintegration of the Spanish Empire might open new commercial opportunities for London merchants.

With Spain isolated, Adams struck to remove the Spanish Empire from North America. He demanded the territory claimed by Spain to the Pacific north of the forty-first parallel. He wanted to include Texas in the bargain, but Monroe's Cabinet stopped this on the grounds that taking Texas would immediately raise a divisive debate over the expansion of slavery. In February 1819 Onís finally agreed to a treaty in which Spain ceded East Florida, recognized American possession of West Florida, surrendered its claims to Oregon and the navigation of the Mississippi to the United States, and agreed

---

[7] Ibid., 7:167.

[8] Adams to Onís, July 23, 1818, in *American State Papers, Class I: Foreign Relations* (Washington, D.C., 1834), 4:497–99.

to a southwestern boundary running along the Sabine, Red, and Arkansas rivers to the forty-second parallel and then to the Pacific. In return, the United States surrendered any rights to Texas and agreed to pay $5 million claimed by American citizens against Spain; the money, of course, never left American hands. A particular sticking point was Spain's request that Adams grant no recognition to the Latin American rebels. Although he had no intention of recognizing them immediately, Adams carefully kept the threat hanging above the Spaniards' heads throughout the negotiations, then refused to commit himself on the question in the final treaty. Largely because of that refusal, Spain delayed ratification of the pact until October 1820.

The Transcontinental Treaty was Adams' greatest triumph. It loosened many of the bonds that had inhibited American foreign policy since 1776. By removing the Spanish from Florida, gaining a vista on the Pacific, obtaining Spanish claims to Oregon, proving Adams correct in his assessment of British policy, and abolishing the obstacle posed by Spain between the United States and Latin America, the treaty permitted the United States to take the offensive in a number of areas. Ideologically the pact documented John Quincy Adams' contention that European colonies in the New World were anachronisms. Commercially the treaty provided potential outlets to Pacific and Latin American markets as well as fresh incentive for the battle against British colonial restrictions.

Henry Clay proposing the Missouri Compromise

Panic and Texas

BETWEEN THE INITIAL signing and final ratification of the Transcontinental Treaty, Americans endured several domestic crises. Late in 1818 cotton prices broke on the London market, dropping from 32.5 cents per pound to 14 cents within a period of months. Land values similarly spiraled downward after a wave of postwar speculation had created artificial prices. Banks failed, mortgages were foreclosed. The Panic of 1819–1821 gripped the nation.

One casualty was Moses Austin, a lead miner in Illinois. Austin headed southwest, and in 1821 received permission from the viceroy of New Spain, who was about to surrender to an independent Mexican government, for the immigration of Austin's family and three hundred other American families into the Mexican state of Texas. The new government proceeded to shower generous terms on the settlers: 4,428 acres of land to each farmer or cattle raiser for a total price of about $200, while Austin and his son Stephen received 26,000 acres for each hundred families they brought across the border. Mexico evidently had not closely studied the results of similar Spanish policies in Florida and Louisiana. The Mexicans required only that the immigrants be Catholic and not hold slaves, but officials winked at the first requirement and the settlers simply called their slaves "indentured servants." More than ten thousand Americans flooded into Texas during the 1820s, most arriving from adjoining American territory. Texas became a natural extension of the American frontier.

Although Adams had not wanted to concede Texas in 1819, he came under increased criticism for accepting that part of the treaty. After becoming President in 1825, Adams instructed Joel Poinsett, America's first minister to Mexico, to obtain Texas to the Brazos River or, preferably, to the Rio Grande. Mexico countered by asking for the Mississippi as a new Mexican boundary. There the negotiations deadlocked until the Texas Revolution a decade later.

"A Title Page to a Great Tragic Volume"

THE MONROE ADMINISTRATION was perhaps fortunate that the Texas issue did not arise in the early 1820s. As it was, the nation trembled during 1819 and 1820 when Missouri requested admission as a slave state. Northerners adamantly fought admission. Henry Clay finally proposed an acceptable compromise: Missouri entered with slavery while Maine came in as a free state.

The balance was thus maintained between the number of free and slave states. Slavery was forbidden in the Louisiana Territory north of latitude 36°30′. The antislave forces were hopeful they had salvaged most of the empire for the northern system.

For the first time, Adams and his countrymen had squarely faced the issue that would rip apart the City Upon a Hill. John Quincy Adams hated slavery, wondering whether "it would have been a wiser" course to have held out until the Union dissolved and either the Constitution was amended to prohibit slavery or "a new organization ... of all the white states"[9] was established. The hatred deepened as he found slavery incompatible with the imperial dream. Writing in his diary in April 1820, he

> thought the greatest danger of this Union was in the overgrown extent of its territory, combining with the slavery question.... Since the Missouri debate, I considered the continuance of the Union for any length of time as very precarious, and entertained serious doubts whether Louisiana and slavery would not ultimately break us up.

Viewing the Missouri Compromise as no compromise at all, but "a mere preamble—a title-page to a great tragic volume," Adams was determined that further expansion must be accompanied by an article prohibiting slavery in the territory acquired.[10] Such an insistence on purity could result, of course, in the secession of the South and the obliteration of Adams' North American empire.

Latin American Revolutions and July 4, 1821

DURING THE MONTHS of the panic and the Missouri Compromise, the problem of the Latin American revolutions became especially dangerous. Many merchants urged recognition in order to obtain new markets. Southerners and slave apologists like Calhoun and Clay believed an American involvement would not only spread the "spirit of '76," but move American minds off the slave controversy. Clay had told the House of "his firm belief, that there was no question in the foreign policy of this country, which had ever arisen, or which he could conceive as ever occurring, in the decision of which we had so much at stake. This interest [of Latin America] concerned our politics, our

---

9 *Memoirs of J. Q. Adams,* 5:12.
10 Ibid., 5:68; 6:502–503, 524–25, 530, 531.

commerce, our navigation."[11] President Monroe similarly urged recognition of the revolutionaries.

A spur also came from the sharp rise in trade with Latin America between 1816 and 1821. While overall American foreign commerce declined, primarily because of the panic, United States trade with the southern nations jumped approximately 25 percent to $8 million, with exports happily rising at a faster pace than imports. Perhaps of greatest economic importance, the United States merchant fleet, carrying European as well as American goods to South American ports and often on to Asia, neared the apogee of its greatness. As a New Englander who appreciated the employment and specie provided by the carrying trade, Adams valued the opening of Latin American ports to both American goods and American ships.

But through 1821 he refused to acquiesce in recognizing the revolutionary nations. He noted that trade increased despite a lack of formal recognition. More important, he deeply distrusted the revolutions, believing they bore little resemblance to the American Revolution of 1776. He observed that Americans had contended for two objectives, civil rights and political independence, but "in South America civil rights, if not entirely out of the question, appear to have been equally disregarded and trampled upon by all parties." Moreover, he doubted whether Roman Catholic countries could protect such civil rights even if they were obtained. American involvement in such unworthy causes could only lead to policy divisions within the United States. Harboring personal ambitions for the presidency, Adams wanted no more disquieting domestic issues. "As to an American system, we have it; we constitute the whole of it," he wrote in the autumn of 1820. "There is no community of interests or of principles between North and South America."[12]

On July 4, 1821, in responding to demands by Clay and others that the United States use all measures short of war to aid the revolutionaries, Adams also settled some long-standing scores with the British by publicly condemning the entire colonial system. He asserted that Latin Americans and other colonials would inevitably throw off outside domination, but the United States must not intervene in such struggles.

> America, with the same voice which spoke herself into existence as a nation, proclaimed to mankind the inextinguishable rights of human nature, and the only lawful foundations of government.... She has abstained from interference

---

11 "Remarks ..." on March 24, 1818, in *The Papers of Henry Clay,* ed. James F. Hopkins (Lexington, Ky., 1959), 2:519.

12 Adams to Alexander Hill Everett, December 29, 1817, in *Writings of J. Q. Adams,* 6:282; *Memoirs of J. Q. Adams,* 5:176–77.

in the concerns of others, even when conflict has been for principles to which she clings, as to the last vital drop that visits the heart. . . . Wherever the standard of freedom and Independence has been or shall be unfurled, there will her heart, her benedictions and her prayers be. But she goes not abroad, in search of monsters to destroy. She is the well-wisher to the freedom and independence of all. . . . She well knows that by once enlisting under other banners than her own, were they even the banners of foreign independence, she would involve herself beyond the power of extrication, in all the wars of interest and intrigue, of individual avarice, envy, and ambition, which assume the colors and usurp the standard of freedom. The fundamental maxims of her policy would insensibly change from *liberty* to *force*. . . . She might become the dictatress of the world. She would be no longer the ruler of her spirit. . . .

[America's] glory is not *dominion,* but *liberty.* Her march is the march of the mind.[13]

Within a year Adams found the Latin American situation altered. By 1822 Argentina, Chile, Colombia, Mexico, Central America, and Brazil were independent. For several years the British navy had formed an impressive obstacle to any European attempt to restore the former colonies to Spain. Such British protection was easily transformed into British trading privileges in the new nations. Unwilling to see Latin America become part of the English trading system, Adams extended recognition to the young nations in 1822. His instructions to the new American ministers, however, were studies in restraint. Fearful that Latin Americans were still "hankering after monarchy," he reiterated his doubts about the future of civil liberties on the southern continent. The instructions emphasized the necessity of obtaining equal rights with the British in the carrying trade.[14]

The Monroe Doctrine: Strategy

ADAMS' HARDHEADED ASSESSMENT of British interests and his view of commercial ties between North and South America help explain the development of the Monroe Doctrine. He realized that behind an implicit Anglo-American understanding, the United States could stake out a territorial and commercial empire in the New World.

---

13 "Address of July 4, 1821," in *John Quincy Adams and American Continental Empire,* ed. Walter LaFeber (Chicago, 1965), pp. 42–46.

14 Adams to Richard C. Anderson, May 27, 1823, *American State Papers, Class I: Foreign Relations,* 2nd ser. (Washington, D.C., 1858), 5:888–97; Adams to Rodney, May 17, 1823, in *Writings of J. Q. Adams,* 7:433–34.

James Monroe

The opportunity to claim additional rights publicly arose in 1821 when the Russian Tsar proclaimed that henceforth all the area north of the fifty-first parallel and extending one hundred miles off the coast into the Pacific would be off limits to non-Russians. The Tsar had been urged to make the announcement by the Russian-American Company, which controlled Russian territory in North America stretching from Alaska down the Pacific coast nearly to present-day San Francisco. The proclamation struck at American trading and fishing interests, which had exploited Russian America since the 1790s. As early as 1796, Americans, not Russians, monopolized the fur trading in the area, using the ports as part of a trade triangle that developed between New England, the northwest coast, and Asia. This trade sometimes resulted in a profit of as much as 500 percent for a single voyage.

In response to the Tsar's announcement, Adams called in the Russian minister on July 17, 1823. The Secretary of State "told him specially that we should contest the right of Russia to *any* territorial establishment on this continent, and that we should assume distinctly the principle that the American continents are no longer subjects of *any* new European colonial establishments."[15] The British, however, also had claims in the Northwest, particularly in Oregon.

---

[15] *Memoirs of J. Q. Adams*, 6:157, 163.

Five days later Adams consequently repeated his challenge in instructions to the American minister in London, Richard Rush: "The American continents, henceforth, will no longer be subject to *colonization*.... And the Pacific Ocean, in every part of it, will remain open to the navigation of all nations in like manner with the Atlantic." Adams warned that the United States would not suffer "the application of colonial principles of exclusion ... upon any part of the Northwest Coast of America."[16]

THE MONROE DOCTRINE: THE TACTICS

In late summer of 1823, British Foreign Secretary George Canning attempted to turn Adams' note to his own advantage. He suggested that the United States and England jointly warn the French and Spanish not to intervene in Latin America. Canning's proposal arrived while Adams was vacationing in Massachusetts, so Monroe asked Madison and Jefferson for advice. The two elder statesmen urged cooperation with Canning, but when Adams returned in November he convinced the President that a joint Anglo-American venture was neither politic nor necessary.

The Secretary of State argued that the United States did not have to tie itself to England to accomplish Canning's objectives. Without losing its freedom of action, the United States could unilaterally warn Europeans to stay away while keeping its own hands free to develop a continental empire and hemispheric trade. Adams believed it would be wise to include Englishmen among the Europeans so warned.

John Quincy had another, more grave, reservation. Canning asked that in the joint announcement both parties set a splendid example by telling the world they had no intention of annexing such areas as Cuba and Texas. Adams refused to handcuff himself in this fashion. As early as 1808 Jefferson's Cabinet had decided that since Cuba must inevitably fall into the American orbit, the island could not be transferred by Spain to either France or Great Britain. By 1815 Cuba had become a link in the developing trade with Latin America. Americans treasured it for both its strategic location and its market. Like Jefferson and Madison, Adams believed that if

> an apple severed by the tempest from its native tree cannot choose but fall to the ground, Cuba, forcibly disjoined from its own unnatural connection with Spain, and incapable of self-support, can gravitate only towards the North American Union, which by the same law of nature cannot cast her off from its bosom.[17]

16 Adams to Rush, July 22, 1823, *American State Papers, Class I: Foreign Relations*, 5:446–48.
17 Adams to Hugh Nelson, April 28, 1823, in *Writings of J. Q. Adams*, 7:372–73.

Such were the Creator's laws of nature and empire.

Adams was consequently not willing to give Great Britain a "substantial and perhaps inconvenient pledge against ourselves, and really obtain nothing in return." He did not propose to leave the future of American expansion in the hands of Great Britain.

Canning perhaps guessed at such an American response. He secretly began negotiations with the French ambassador in London, the Prince de Polignac, to reach an understanding on the Latin American situation. On October 9, 1823, France disavowed any intentions of reestablishing a colonial empire in Latin America. After discovering the Polignac Memorandum late in November, American Minister Richard Rush sent it to Washington, but it arrived too late to influence American policy. In any event, the memorandum only further documented the soundness of Adams' assumptions regarding British policy.

THE MONROE DOCTRINE: THE MESSAGE

During November the Monroe Cabinet debated whether its views on the Northwest and Latin America should be privately communicated, as Adams preferred, or announced publicly. The President favored a public announcement, and on December 2, 1823, sent a message to Congress containing three foreign policy principles: "The American Continents ... are henceforth not to be considered as subjects for future colonization by any European powers"; the United States would not tolerate any attempt by those powers "to extend their system to any portion of this hemisphere"; and, finally, the United States would not interfere "in internal concerns" of European powers.

The final point occasioned some disagreement in the Cabinet. In an original draft, Monroe had expressed sympathy with the Greek Revolution. Monroe was tapping a rich political vein, for many Americans, including such powerful congressional figures as Clay and Daniel Webster, demonstrated strong public support for the Greeks. Adams objected to Monroe's approach by urging that the message be limited strictly to an "American cause." The President rewrote the passage, carefully declaring that "in the wars of European powers in matters relating to themselves we have never taken any part, nor does it comport with our policy so to do." The message therefore left open the possibility of involvement in European wars if American interests required it. Having served as Secretary of State in 1811 and 1812, Monroe fully appreciated the importance of such a reservation.

The Monroe Doctrine was negative in warning against further European colonization or intervention in the New World. But Monroe was also saying positively that the United States expected Americans, both north and south, to exploit the opportunities of the New World. The message climaxed the triumphs of the Transcontinental Treaty, the Austins' trek to Texas, the agreement to keep Oregon open for American settlement, and the economic possibilities opened to the United States by the success of Latin American revolutionaries. In setting up "No trespassing" signs, the doctrine cleared the way for future American expansion. Monroe emphasized this theme in his concluding passage when he restated the principles of *Federalist 10:*

> This expansion of our population and accession of new States to our Union have had the happiest effect on all its highest interest. . . . It is manifest that by enlarging the basis of our system and increasing the number of States the system itself has been greatly strengthened in both its branches. Consolidation and disunion have thereby been rendered equally impracticable. Each Government, confiding in its own strength, has less to apprehend from the other, and in consequence each, enjoying a greater freedom of action, is rendered more efficient for all the purposes for which it was instituted.[18]

As Adams began to understand during the Missouri crisis, further expansion might not produce such happy endings. In the short run, however, the Monroe Doctrine proved a diplomatic triumph. Canning had been upstaged by the President, although Latin Americans recovered their pro-British sentiments after five South American nations asked the United States for aid and the Monroe administration rejected all five. Washington planned to maintain its freedom of action in Latin America as well as elsewhere. Spain and France did not try to reclaim former colonial empires, but during the next two decades European powers, including the British, seized Latin American territory on more than a half-dozen occasions without raising objections from the United States.

Adams utilized the newly announced principles to reach an accord with Russia in the Convention of 1824. The Tsar surrendered his claim to the seas off the northwestern coast and accepted 54°40′ as the southern boundary for Russian America. He thereby gave up all claims to Oregon and the San Francisco area. In return, the United States promised to regulate more closely the New Englanders who were making fortunes selling guns and liquor to the Indian tribes in Russian America. Each power granted the other reciprocal trading rights for ten years along unsettled parts of the coast. The pact signaled another major victory for the United States. Since no human force could control the New England traders, Adams had given little and in return had assured

---

18 James D. Richardson, ed., *A Compilation of the Messages and Papers of the Presidents, 1789–1897,* 10 vols. (Washington, D.C., 1969), 2:219–20.

American trading rights in the Northwest while clearing the Russians out of Oregon. That territory was now a bone only between Americans and Englishmen.

The President as Anachronism

BY THE TIME he completed negotiating the Convention of 1824, Adams was in the forefront of the presidential campaign. That election, however, proved unlike previous presidential canvasses. Since 1810 Congress had obtained increased political power while Madison and Monroe attempted to remain above party factions. By the early 1820s, this lack of leadership, the panic, and the emerging slavery issue at once sharpened and made more chaotic the chase for the presidency. Adams, Clay, William Crawford of Georgia, and Andrew Jackson of Tennessee were the leading contenders. Jackson received the largest number of popular votes, but when no one received a majority of electoral ballots, the decision was forced into the House of Representatives. Some of Clay's supporters switched to Adams, who was duly elected President. But Adams then blunderingly appointed Clay as Secretary of State. The Jacksonians viciously attacked Adams for obtaining the presidency by making a deal. The new President proceeded to demonstrate almost a total lack of political ingenuity in meeting these assaults. He rewarded enemies and forgot friends in an unsuccessful effort to reunite the factions. By 1826 he admitted that "my only course is to prepare for retirement, as I hope I am now doing."

Adams and Clay did score several diplomatic triumphs. In 1827 the 1818 Convention on Oregon was renewed, thereby keeping the area open for American settlers, who were already moving in large numbers across South Pass. At one point in these negotiations, Adams refused to accept a British offer of the Columbia River as the final boundary. In choosing to delay and take the chance that the United States ultimately would obtain both banks of that great river, the President preserved rich timber and farming lands for Americans as well as the future northern passage for American transcontinental railroads.

Adams was less successful in gaining congressional authorization to send two emissaries to a Latin American meeting at Panama. He saw the Panama Congress as an opportunity to gain liberal commercial treaties, an agreement upon freedom of the seas, and a common statement on the noncolonization principle. Secretary of State Clay hoped to work out arbitration procedures among New World nations through what he termed "Good Neighborhood" treaties. Such procedures would be most helpful if, as Adams and Clay hoped, political conflicts could be averted so that commercial relations might be fully developed. But Congress stalled Adams' request for funds until the Panama meeting was ready to adjourn. Strong opposition came from southern congressmen who fought possible trade agreements because South Americans produced many of the products grown in the southern United States. These congressmen also feared that the delegations at Panama might discuss the slave trade and the black nation of Haiti, two topics the South preferred to ignore.

Despite these several diplomatic initiatives, President Adams failed in his attempt to consolidate the empire he had helped acquire as senator, diplomat, and Secretary of State. His first annual message was an impassioned appeal for the federal government to sew the vast continent together by regulating commerce, funding an ambitious program of internal improvements, creating a great navy, establishing a national university, and encouraging scientific advancement by the establishment of astronomical observatories. But by innocently lauding European achievements in science and then pleading for the astronomical observatories by calling them "light-houses in the skies," Adams gave his political opponents a splendid opportunity to call him a monarchist and a fool, which they promptly did. He also equivocated on the sale of public lands to pay for internal improvements. Bowing to pressure for easier land prices, Adams threw this political hot potato back to Congress, where southerners and westerners prepared to give the land away for considerably lower prices.

Adams failed tragically in this attempt to refine the Hamiltonian-Madisonian nationalism so that it would irrevocably consolidate the newly acquired empire. And he lost to forces that he, of all Americans, perhaps best understood. Adams despised the centrifugal forces unloosed especially by the southern and western Jacksonians, who demanded a more decentralized government, low tariffs, cheap land, and the exclusion of the federal government from the internal improvement program. They preferred to have the states benefit from the land sales and build the canals and highways. Adams realized that such decentralization could fatally strain the continental links.

Between 1800 and 1828 Adams was a central figure in his nation's development as it acquired a continent, began to tame it with industrial and transportation innovations, formally announced the separation of the Old World from the New, and initiated an agonizing debate on slavery. Within this framework, Adams proved too radical. He urged systematic planning and enlarged governmental powers at a time when his countrymen demanded less discipline and more land, fewer governmental restraints and an easy exploitation of opportunities wherever they might be. Americans have infrequently honored radicals, even those as ordered, brilliant, and antirevolutionary as Adams. In this sense, he was the transitional figure between the Revolution and the Civil War, for he brought with him the Founding Fathers' ideals of empire and control. Indeed, he was the embodiment of those ideals. When he left the presidency to Jackson in 1828, his countrymen seized upon the empire but tragically repudiated the control.

Suggestions for Further Reading

The diplomacy of 1815–1828 makes sense only within the rapidly changing politico-economic context of the time. This framework is well analyzed in George Rogers Taylor, *The Transportation Revolution, 1815–1860* (New York, 1951); Douglass C. North, *The Economic Growth of the United States, 1790–1860* (New York, 1966); and George Dangerfield, *The Era of Good Feelings* (New York, 1952), especially good on the effects of the 1819 panic. The diplomacy is examined in Bradford Perkins' *Castlereagh and Adams: England and the United States, 1812–1823* (Berkeley, 1964), and Samuel Flagg Bemis, *John Quincy Adams and the Foundations of American Foreign Policy* (New York, 1949)

The Monroe Doctrine's background is splendidly examined in Arthur P. Whitaker, *The United States and the Independence of Latin America, 1800–1830* (Baltimore, 1941); Dexter Perkins' standard *The Monroe Doctrine, 1823–1826* (Cambridge, Mass., 1927); and J. A. Logan, Jr., *No Transfer* (New Haven, Conn., 1961). M. A. Cline, *American Attitude Toward the Greek War of Independence, 1821–1828* (Atlanta, 1930), discusses a secondary but nevertheless important part of the American reaction to European affairs.

Three older but still useful volumes dissect specific commercial problems: Vernon G. Setser, *The Commercial Reciprocity Policy of the United States, 1774–1829* (Philadelphia, 1937); Frank L. Benns, *The American Struggle for the British West India Carrying-Trade, 1815–1830* (Bloomington, Ind., 1923); and Hugh G. Soulsby, *The Right of Search and the Slave Trade in Anglo-American Relations, 1814–1862* (Baltimore, 1933).

Besides Bemis' work on Adams, useful biographies include Harry Ammon, *James Monroe* (New York, 1970), and Charles M. Wiltse, *John C. Calhoun, Nationalist, 1782–1828* (Indianapolis, 1944).

See also the general bibliography at the end of this volume.

CHAPTER 8

Liberal Capitalism
and Expansion
(1829–1844)

Andrew Jackson's elevation to the presidency in 1829 inaugurated what historians invariably characterize as an "age"—be it that of Jackson, or of laissez faire, or of liberal capitalism. Depending on one's conceptualization, the fifteen years that followed were either among the most trivial in the history of United States foreign relations or among the most epochal.

Conventional Diplomacy

IF ONE CONCEIVES of the study of foreign relations as simply the study of diplomacy—of governmental elites choosing policies that lead to specific consequences foreseen or unforeseen—then the years between 1829 and 1844 were not the stuff of which heroic epics are made. Despite occasional public furor and even loose war talk, with which American history abounds, the issues that divided the United States and other nations in that period were less than monumental. Nothing of the magnitude of Jay's Treaty or the Louisiana

Purchase or the embargo or a war for economic independence or the Transcontinental Treaty or the Monroe Doctrine was to be found.

The dynamic role of the national government in pushing commercial and territorial expansion appears somewhat tepid compared to what had gone before and what was to come. But that statement is a relative one and demands qualification. Certainly there is no evidence that the American commitment to empire—either an informal commercial empire overseas or a formal territorial empire on the North American continent—was in any way diminished during these years; nor was the period devoid of governmental action in pursuit of such imperial happiness.

Jacksonian Commercialism

CLEARLY JACKSONIANS sustained the historic American commitment to trade expansion. In an underdeveloped country where the chief obstacle to modernization had habitually been the scarcity of capital, Americans had traditionally defined the carrying trade as the chief means of filling that need. If, better yet, American ships carried American products—such as the surplus of its commercial agrarians—then the economic spread effect would be greater still. Hamilton's plans for economic growth had been based on such an analysis, though with special emphasis on expanding commercial opportunities within the British Empire. The subsequent wars spawned by the French Revolution and the revolt of the Spanish colonies in Latin America fortuitously expanded such opportunities to the West Indies, South America, and continental Europe, and made the export and reexport trade, as Douglass C. North points out, the crucial dynamic for economic growth between 1793 and 1808. And following the War of 1812—a war fought primarily to prevent restrictions on American trade expansion and hence general economic progress—it was the cotton trade that served for a quarter of a century as the prime lubricant for interregional trade within the American economy and the main engine for general growth.

CLAIMS AGAINST FRANCE

The Jackson administrations manifested their continuing concern for trade in several ways. For example, Jackson launched a campaign of bellicose diplomacy to force French payments for damages to American shipping occasioned by the Napoleonic wars between 1803 and 1815. In part the campaign reflected pressure from interested American claimants, and undoubtedly the style in which it was waged reflected not only the General's ardent nationalism and sense of presidential power, but also a desire to enhance his political image with the nation's voting constituency. But it also bore witness to the general belief that the United States' right to expand its trade as a neutral during wartime had been and would again be so important that it *had* to be upheld; hence all violators must be held (in Woodrow Wilson's later words) "strictly accountable." Great Britain had been held accountable by the sword during the war itself; now France, after the fact, was to be held accountable by the purse strings. The result, after much bickering and even a temporary break in Franco-American diplomatic relations, was a French agreement to send some 25 million francs on a transatlantic trek to this country.

OPENING THE BRITISH WEST INDIES

Jackson continued also the historic American effort to penetrate the imperial preference systems of the European empires. The wars for Latin American independence had partially opened the doors to Brazil and the former Spanish colonies, but one of the greatest commercial prizes, the British West Indies, still remained closed to American merchants and producers. John Quincy Adams, both as Secretary of State and as President, had unsuccessfully tried to pry open that prize in the 1820s. Consequently, when Jackson came to power, the British West Indies remained closed to American ships, while in retaliation American ports remained closed to British ships coming from any of the British colonies in the Western Hemisphere. Several factors coincided to end that impasse. As important as any, perhaps, was the growing British sentiment in favor of free trade, which by the next decade was to lead to dismantlement of the imperial preference system, the repeal of the Corn Laws, and increasingly specialized attention to the manufacture of high-value products. Though not yet dominant, such laissez-faire inclinations did give positive reinforcement to the move to modify the British position on the West Indies trade. Consequently, by informal agreement, Jackson repealed the retaliatory measures against British shipping in the fall of 1830, and the British government immediately followed by opening the West Indies to direct trade with the United States. Great Britain's retention of the right to impose duties on that trade, however, meant that the ultimate goal of trading with the British West Indies on the same terms as British citizens was not yet fully realized.

Jackson's opening of the West Indies represented not just a national triumph in the aggregate, but a specific triumph for certain groups inside the emerging Jacksonian coalition, especially commercial farmers selling on the world market and eastern urban merchants engaged in foreign trade. (Just as many of the merchant princes, especially those engaged in Latin American trade, had been supporters of Jefferson, so now many of the same merchants and their heirs were to be found in Jackson's political mansions.) But those same groups, supported by some manufacturers—particularly in leather goods, furniture, and crude textiles—were disappointed when the reality of commercial and marketplace expansion in the newly independent countries of South America failed to live up to their earlier roseate dreams. The vigorous commercial diplomacy of Adams and Henry Clay had produced few meaningful victories. American manufacturers found themselves cut out by superior British competition, and American agrarians found out not only that the South American market for their commodities was rather inelastic, but that many countries to the south had become leading international competitors in wheat, flour, meats, tobacco, and cotton. In their disillusionment, special interest groups did not apply much pressure to the national administration.

THE LURE OF ASIAN TRADE

But the prior boom in Latin American trade in the 1820s did have the interesting side effect of stimulating further interest in Far Eastern markets. Merchants who plied the west coast of South America were making profits that could be used to purchase tea, silks, and spices in Asian markets. And later the development of the hide and fur trades on the west coast of North America provided additional means of commercial exchange. As a consequence, increasing disillusionment with South American trade led many interest groups to assign a higher importance to the Asian trade. This was true not only of merchants; even a few agrarian producers talked of cereal markets in a food-deficient Far East, and South Carolina textile producers, then engaged in their second bout with "mill fever" (the first had come from 1808 to 1815), talked of Asian markets for coarse cloth products.

Jackson, as an honest-broker reflector of his diverse constituency, moved to give governmental support to the drive for Asian trade. His chief effort was the dispatch of Edmund Roberts in 1832 to Southeast Asia and the Far East. Roberts, a New England merchant with consular experience abroad, was to negotiate trade treaties with Siam, Muscat, Cochin China (including contemporary Vietnam), and Japan. Each treaty, consistent with American trading principles, was to be on a most-favored-nation basis, thus ensuring that America's competitors would not enjoy any discriminatory advantages. Successful in 1833 in making treaties with Siam and Muscat, Roberts failed completely at Hue. The effort to open Japan, postponed in 1833 but renewed by a second voyage in 1835, ended prematurely with Roberts' death in Macao. The unspectacular results belied the intensity of interest, an impression reinforced by the efforts of Martin Van Buren, Jackson's hand-picked heir to the presidency. In 1839, in the midst of severe economic depression (or perhaps because of it), the new President secured the necessary funds and authorization to commission Lieutenant Charles Wilkes to survey the harbors of the west coast and gather data on the Great Circle Route to the Far East, before turning south for Singapore and then home. The subsequent scientific expedition, supplemented by others, was to make the United States the most knowledgeable power in the world with regard to the great Pacific basin.

Jacksonian Continentalism

THE ACHIEVEMENTS of Jacksonion commercialism were admittedly slight. The Caribbean trade, though important, never regained its previous prominence as an economic multiplier; the Muscat and Siam trade remained negligible; the French claims settlement receives, and perhaps rightly, bare mention in history textbooks. Ironically, the national government's role in promoting the physical expansion of United States sovereignty on the North American continent was similarly unproductive; ironically in the sense that Jackson and most of his supporters were firmly persuaded that expanding the area of freedom (to use a then popular phrase), along with a favorable land-to-man ratio, was indispensable to the preservation of both democracy and prosperity.

JACKSON AND THE TEXAS REVOLUTION

Jackson's Texas policy is illustrative. That giant northern province of Mexico had long been staked out by leading Americans as a future piece of imperial real estate. Jefferson had tried to claim it as part of the Louisiana Territory purchased from France. A decade and a half later, Secretary of State Adams gave up American claims to Texas in the Transcontinental Treaty of 1819, but only with the greatest reluctance and amidst harsh criticism from expansionists like Thomas Hart Benton for making such an unwarranted sacrifice. After 1825, when he assumed the presidency, Adams himself instructed Joel R. Poinsett, his minister to Mexico and one of the leading Latin American specialists, to work for the acquisition of as much of Texas as possible. Adhering to his instructions, Poinsett offered $1 million in 1827. Going beyond the letter of his instructions, he concurrently engaged in elaborate intrigues in Mexican politics to counteract British influence, create a pro-American party among Mexican political leaders, and win acceptance for his purchase proposal. For example, as Professor A. P. Whitaker points out, he organized "York rite Masons, which were designed to neutralize the pro-British Scottish rite Masons and to serve as political clubs." It all came to nothing.[1]

Jackson, no less than his predecessors, sought to add Texas to the American imperium. The tactics pursued were the same, and initially so was the man used—Poinsett (later Secretary of War in a Democratic cabinet). Under authorization from the President, Poinsett upped the proposed price to $5 million. But already angered by his political machinations as well as by his chauvinistic conception of a United States–dominated Western Hemisphere, Mexico turned a deaf ear. Indeed, it demanded and received Poinsett's recall. His successor, Anthony Butler, continued for six years to pursue Jackson's goal of acquiring Texas, often in a manner more heavy-handed than that of his predecessor. Chiefly he manipulated Mexican financial needs both personal and public, either through bribery of Mexican leaders or by trying to foist an unrequested and probably unrepayable loan on the Mexican government. Predictably, Texas was to be the collateral. Failing in those tactics, he strongly urged Jackson to acquire eastern Texas by force or subversion. This was the part of Texas where the preconditions for a West Florida–style *putsch* were most favorable.

Unwittingly, Jacksonian diplomacy proved counterproductive by reinforcing Mexican fears about U.S. imperialism. Mexican Creoles had inherited the understandable Spanish attitude that there was no end to the United States' avarice. British diplomats in Mexico, seeking to blunt Pan Americanism, repeatedly warned Mexicans that the American colony in Texas was a Trojan horse of American empire-building; and the so-called Fredonian revolt in 1826 lent credence to that warning. Now, in the first half of the 1830s, Jackson's aggressive diplomacy, coupled with a wave of in-migration that swelled American numbers to nearly 30,000 (ten times greater than the number of Mexican inhabitants), persuaded many Mexicans of an official American plot to steal Texas away. So between 1830 and 1833 the Mexican government banned American immigration to Texas, established military garrisons to enforce its edicts, and sought to reverse the demographic situation by inducing or coercing

---

[1] Arthur P. Whitaker, *The United States and the Independence of Latin America, 1800–1830* (Baltimore, 1941), p. 593.

Mexicans to move north into Texas. (Unfortunately, the colonizers were often convicts and rarely women—hardly a viable counterpoise to the fertile Americans.) Nonetheless, many Americans, particularly members of the privileged *empresario* elite, sought to minimize freebooter cries of independence, and in 1833 worked out a détente that reopened legitimate immigration. The facts remained, however, that Texas was culturally and economically an American colony and that political accommodation with the federal government in Mexico City was tenuous and beset by mutual distrust. Rupture was perhaps probable in any case, but internal political changes in Mexico made it inevitable. Acquiring political power, which he was often to lose and hold again, Antonio López de Santa Ana set aside the constitution of 1824. It limited the size of local militias and the right to bear arms, abolished existing states (including Texas), and generally sought to create a more centralized, Napoleonic-style governmental structure. The result, among many, was the Texas revolution of 1835–1836. Its military leader was Sam Houston, long-time friend of Andrew Jackson.

American aid in making the revolution a success was probably crucial. Jackson's affirmation of neutrality was more rhetorical than real and his effort to enforce it rather feeble. In this lax context, financial speculators in Texas loans and volunteer thirsters after Texas land managed nicely to combine economic interest, democratic fervor, and anti-Mexican racism to produce men, money, and munitions for the cause of Texas independence.

In a very real way, however, the Texas revolution impeded Jacksonian diplomacy. Clearly Jackson would have preferred the simple, neat, and direct device of purchasing Texas; and, given the frequent changeovers in Mexican governments and their chronic shortage of cash, such an approach had real possibilities. But the successful revolution and the proclamation of Texas' independence muddied the waters considerably. From that point onward, any effort to annex the Republic of Texas meant possible war with Mexico; ensured conflict with Britain, which was maneuvering to maintain an independent, Anglophile Texas; and guaranteed a revival of the whole "slavery in the empire" controversy dealt with in the Missouri Compromise. Antislavery spokesmen like former President John Quincy Adams had originally favored recognition of an independent Texas on the grounds that it would contain southern expansionism and lead to the decay of the peculiar institution in the South. But when it became apparent that American recognition of Texas' independence would merely be a prelude to admission of Texas as a slave state (or states) to the Union, such opinion moved full circle. Coupled with the Whig objection to territorial expansion (save when the territory contained commercial ports of value), such opposition forced Jackson to move cautiously in the presidential election year of 1836. Only after the triumph of the Democratic party and Van Buren's election in 1836; only after ascertaining that recognition of Texas' independence would not mean war with Mexico; only after congressional resolutions favoring such a course: then and only then did Jackson finally extend recognition to the Republic of Texas. But the complications created by the revolution were to postpone the ultimate step of annexation for another decade.

THE DRANG NACH NORD: CANADA

If the urge for Texas had more vitality and attracted more Americans, the desire for Canada had more longevity and persistence. During the American Revolution itself, Americans had unsuccessfully tried persuasion, force of arms, and even the heretical affirmation of tolerance for Catholicism to secure that goal. In the negotiations that ended that confrontation, American diplomats (especially Franklin) had made acquisition of Canada an important part of the twin objectives of empire and independence. And in 1812 Americans sought that elusive goal for both strategic and imperial reasons, and assumed, wrongly as it turned out, that it was theirs for the taking.

Given the widely shared concern for acquisition of Canada, it might have seemed that the Canadian rebellion against British rule in 1837 provided the ideal opportunity to fulfill that continentalist dream. In the first place, many of the revolutionaries appeared to favor annexation to the United States. Hard hit by depression, many economic leaders saw access to the large American market (via annexation) as the panacea for their economic ills. Disturbed also by the political threat of French-Canadians, many Anglos saw annexation as a means of submerging the French in a sea of WASPs. In the second place, the rebellion seemed to stimulate much support on the American side of the border. The initial attacks on upper Canada by William Lyon Mackenzie relied heavily on American men and material in the so-called patriot force. And subsequent forays into lower Canada benefited from the substantial support of several secret societies (Hunters' Lodges being the largest) that spread from New England across upstate New York and numbered between fifty and a hundred thousand members.

Giving reinforcement were two critical incidents that grew out of the rebellion, each of the sort to stimulate chauvinism and war talk both in Great Britain and in the United States. The first involved the *Caroline,* a small American steamboat employed by the "patriots" to carry supplies and men across the Niagara frontier. In its zeal to interdict the *Caroline*'s activities, a Canadian force boarded and burned it while it was moored to American soil, thus violating American sovereignty and, as it turned out, ending the life span of one American citizen. The second incident grew out of the first. Nearly three years after the *Caroline* affair, a minor Canadian police official, Alexander McLeod, was arrested for his alleged role in the episode and brought to trial for arson and murder in a lynch-mob atmosphere before a court in Utica, New York. The first episode pricked national sensitivity on this side of the Atlantic; the second performed the same function on the other.

Finally, to cap matters, two issues either partly or wholly extraneous to the Canadian rebellion so exacerbated Anglo-American relations as to make (or so one might think) American exploitation of that uprising all the more likely. One concerned the *Creole,* an American ship engaged in the coastal slave trade (as opposed to the illegal foreign slave trade). While en route from Virginia to New Orleans, the slave "cargo" had revolted, seized the ship, and put into the British port of Nassau. Several slaves were executed for their alleged role in the death of one of the mates, but the remainder received their freedom, despite outcries and protests from the United States. More serious was the boundary dispute between Maine and the British maritime province of New Brunswick. Vaguely defined in the Peace of 1783 and still unresolved in the Peace of 1815, the boundary had long been a source of contention. British officials sought the disputed acreage to build a military and commercial short cut between the seaboard and lower Canada. Maine and Massachusetts, which shared equally in the revenue from public land sales in the area, were loath to part with the anticipated income. Bringing things to a full boil in 1838–1839 was the rivalry of Canadian and American lumbering interests over timber stands in the disputed area. The result was a conflict as colorful as it was bloodless, sometimes called the Aroostook War (after the river of the same name).

Any ordinary logician could have easily concluded that this peculiar mix of variables would inevitably produce a concerted American effort to fulfill its vision of empire to the north. He would have been wrong, for both the Democratic administration of Martin Van Buren and the Whig administration of John Tyler acted to minimize Anglo-American conflict over the issues at hand. Van Buren issued several stern proclamations promising to enforce American law rigidly against those who would compromise American neutrality; and more importantly, he dispatched General Winfield Scott to take command of the border area and try to minimize conflict. Scott then employed his own prestige with the American inhabitants, cooperated carefully with Canadian counterparts, and even employed federal money to lease or purchase equipment that otherwise might have been secured by the "patriot" supporters and the secret societies. In the succeeding Whig administration, Secretary of State Daniel Webster secured a semi-apology from the British on the *Caroline* affair, won assurances from Governor William H. Seward of New York that he would pardon McLeod if the Canadian were convicted (the Utica jury, in fact, freed him), and negotiated the Webster-Ashburton Treaty of 1842. The latter resulted from astute personal diplomacy that steered ably amidst the dangerous shoals of internal politics, competing economic interests, and sensitivity about national honor, both in Great Britain and in the United States. Though it touched on a variety of issues, its chief importance lay in the compromise settlement of the Maine boundary and the border to the west of Lake Superior. The former gave Great Britain the desired military commercial route while leaving the timber-rich Aroostook valley in American hands. The latter represented a minor readjustment that unwittingly left the rich iron ore deposits of the Mesabi Range in American control.

The task remains to account for conciliatory American actions in a situation that seemed to offer an opportunity for American expansion northward. The answers to that riddle are to be found in the localization of American interest in Canada, in the economic situation triggered by the Panic of 1837, and in the racial and cultural attitudes of white Americans. First, only a limited number of American citizens, chiefly in the border area itself, had either the vitality of interest or the ease of opportunity to give very much aid to the Canadian uprising; and the motives that prompted them to act were a curious mix seldom shared by most Americans. Second, the Panic of 1837 took away the option of risking war with Great Britain. The cotton trade with that country was the lifeblood of the American economy, and to sever that artery would have been to commit economic suicide. And finally, American cultural and racial attitudes demanded different approaches to expansion into a fellow Anglo-Saxon society. Most Americans vaguely adhered to a system sometimes called the "Great Chain of Being," which categorized and stratified human societies into various levels from savagery through barbarism to civilization. North American Indians and Mexicans were placed in the lower ranks of the vertical continuum, and could be dealt with in a peremptory fashion in the name of civilization. Canadians, especially British Canadians, were of a different and higher order by virtue of their race, language, heritage, and material achievements. This meant to many Americans that acquisition of Canada should ideally come by voluntary association, when and if the majority of Canadians perceived it to be right and proper. And given the paucity of Canadian support for the Mackenzie rebellion, it seemed that the ideal situation was not yet at hand. In the parlance of the day, the fruit was not yet ripe and ready to fall.

Domestic Changes and Foreign Policy

CONVENTIONAL DIPLOMACY between 1829 and 1844, while by no means wholly insignificant, was not of the magnitude of the diplomacy of the early 1820s or the mid-1840s. But if one conceives of the study of foreign relations as more than simply conventional diplomacy, "what one clerk said to another," then that period is enormously important. To appreciate that fact thoroughly, however, requires reaffirming an already central thesis of this book: that key events in American foreign relations often grow rather directly out of crucial changes in domestic affairs—population movements, changes in political party formation, rivalry of competing elites, changes in economic growth patterns and in economic multipliers, new ideological currents, and the like. When foreign relations are conceptualized in this way, it is possible to argue that the rapid and often unsettling domestic changes of the Jacksonian period were the catalysts for the revivified American expansionism of the mid-1840s. Specifically, American imperialism in the 1840s and after was a response to population movements on the continent, to increased interest in commercial penetration of the Pacific basin, and to endemic contradictions in the new social order of laissez-faire liberalism.

POPULATION MOVEMENTS

One of the forces promoting an imperialist policy on the part of the national government was simply that of organic growth. Generally it proceeded through four phases. First, population density, poor transportation facilities, inadequate markets, depressed farm prices, and other manifestations of general hard times combined to create centrifugal forces that sent elements of American society spinning off in various directions. Second, these elements were then pulled in centripetal fashion into other gravitational fields by factors such as proximity, the potential of new markets, liberal land policy, access to water transportation, fertile land, and the general publicity given all these things. Third, once established in alien lands, Americans remained true to their culture, their institutions, and their political processes; they rejected foreign dominance and established de facto American colonies. Fourth, relatives and friends of those colonizers, professional lobbyists, interested economic groups, and susceptible politicians began to pressure the national administration to use its foreign policy to acquire these alien lands and pull the American settlers back into the gravitational field of the mother country. The appeals were usually couched in terms of national prestige, obligations to protect American lives and property, the potential source of additional wealth to the nation, and the need to take such areas before some other nation did so. Generally the target of the last argument was Great Britain, reflecting both the intensity of Anglophobia, especially in the Democratic party, and the real fact that the British often had interests in places like Texas, California, and Oregon.

Crucial to this organic process was the course of the American economic cycle. The population movements did not follow a steady, linear pace. Instead, they came in definable waves that followed the end of hard times, which had dramatized farmers' economic plight. For example, as noted earlier, the first great migration into Texas resulted from the interaction of the Panic of 1819 and subsequent depression, on one hand, and the attraction of Mexico's liberal land policy and ready access to the Gulf of Mexico on the other. In like fashion, the depression of 1837–1842 spawned even greater migration from 1843 to 1845. The major push went into Texas once more, for reasons of proximity as much as anything else. The types attracted were many: small farmers from Missouri, Tennessee, and Kentucky; Yankee land speculators; planters and sons of planters in the deep South, seeking to rebound from the Panic of 1837; and even European groups—Germans, French, Dutch. The result was an almost quan-

Migration to the West

tum jump in Texas' population to some 100,000 by 1845. The second and much smaller push went to Oregon, where greater distance, hardships, and costs kept the numbers down. Still, by 1845 there were some six thousand Americans living in Oregon. One thousand had come in the wagon train expedition of 1843, which had demonstrated the feasibility of the trek, excited the imagination of countless Americans, and led to the "Oregon Conventions" of 1843. The tripling of migration to Oregon in 1844 bore witness to the increased interest in the region. Accounting for such attraction in the face of such obvious difficulties was the cumulative propaganda impact of missionaries, New England merchants, visionaries, and governmental agents, who for a decade had publicized the economic lure of the rich Willamette meadowlands and the promise of new markets in the Pacific.

Obviously this organic process had its impact on American foreign policy. Both Presidents Tyler and Polk readily perceived the process at work, sensed the political advantages to be gained from identifying with it, and made expansionism the cardinal tenet of their political programs. Yet just as obviously, the organic process per se did not constitute the first cause. Every president from Jefferson to John Quincy Adams had wanted Texas long before the Austins set foot in the territory. In Oregon, almost the entire American colony had settled in the Willamette Valley, an area undisputed by the British and America's for the taking. The prize for which the American government risked much was the great bay of Juan de Fuca, in a part of Oregon wholly uninhabited by American agrarians. In California, the migrations of 1843 and 1844 were minuscule and centered in the Sacramento Valley, not in the American government's prime target area, San Francisco. What this suggests is that American foreign policy makers used the population movements as much as the movements used them; that they waited for the settler migrations to provide the government with the excuse as well as the power base to fulfill objectives that had long been accepted parts of American conceptualizations of empire. Certainly the Oregon Conventions of 1818 and 1827 were based on the assumption that time and demography were on the side of the American empire. And in 1844, Tyler's Secretary of State, John C. Calhoun, even graced the policy with a name: "masterly inactivity."

EMPIRE ON THE PACIFIC

The second factor that provoked an expansionist response in the mid-1840s is a rather neglected one: the heightened American interest in commercial penetration of the Pacific. Historian Richard W. Van Alstyne has rightly concluded that "there is an epic story still to be told of this American penetration of the Pacific basin"; of "merchants, missionaries, adventurers, sea captains, naval officers and consular officials crowd[ing] into the Pacific during the nineteenth century and [spinning] a web whose strands extended to every part of the ocean."[2]

A number of coincident reinforcing developments account for this heightening of interest in the early 1840s. Significant above all others was the legal broadening of the China trade which resulted from the Opium War between China and Great Britain. Prior to that event, foreign trade in China had been limited to the Chinese port of Canton and the Portuguese leasehold of Macao. The nature of the trade in Canton was quite restricted, reflecting Chinese desire to minimize and control contact with foreign "barbarians." Foreign merchants were not permitted inside the city walls and they had to operate through a system of semiofficial bribery in order to do business. So unbending was Chinese trade policy that, significantly, the Roberts mission in the 1830s did not even include China on its agenda. The Opium War markedly changed the trading picture in China. The British, through the Nanking Treaty of 1842 and a subsequent agreement in 1843, forced China to open five new coastal ports to trade and to grant broad rights of extraterritoriality to foreign residents in those cities. The effect of the treaties was to rekindle the historic interest of westerners, from Marco Polo to the Boston firm of Bryant and Sturgis, in tapping the fabled riches of the markets of Cathay. The immediate result in the United States was the mission to China of Caleb Cushing, a Yankee lawyer with rela-

Caleb Cushing

[2] Richard W. Van Alstyne, *The Rising American Empire* (Chicago, 1965), p. 125.

tives and friends engaged in the China trade. Cushing's visit ended in the Wanghia Treaty of 1844, which formally secured for the United States all the privileges won by the British in war. Like the British treaties, it rested on the unconditional most-favored-nation clause, which ensured that Americans would receive as much preference in trade as the merchants of any other country.

The China trade was, of course, the main magnet for American attention to the Pacific coast, but a number of other factors gave it further stimulus. One was the report of Lieutenant Wilkes on his epic exploration in the Pacific. It was published in five volumes in 1845, but most of the commercially relevant findings had become known earlier. Important for American designs upon California was his description of San Francisco Bay as perhaps the world's finest port and one destined to be pivotal in the trading patterns of the Pacific. Equally important for the Oregon question was his dismissal of the mouth of the Columbia River as a viable port, in contrast to his unstinted praise of the bay at the Strait of Juan de Fuca, farther north on the forty-ninth parallel. The report simply confirmed in greater and more technical detail what interested Americans had long known, and what many more were coming to believe: that American control of those two ports (Wilkes referred to them as "two of the finest ports in the world") was indispensable if America was to have appropriate "windows to the Orient" and its trade.[3]

A more important stimulus was the Panic of 1837 and the general depression in all sectors of the American economy. Eastern merchants engaged in foreign trade were hard hit by the worldwide depression and subsequent declines in the international trade flows; given the broadening of trade rights in China, they would understandably look there for help in taking up the slack. The result was the famed era of the clipper ships, beginning, says economic historian George Rogers Taylor, in 1843 and lasting until 1860. In like vein, depressed New England textile manufacturers began to entertain the idea that there might be a market for their coarser products in China; similarly, the third round of "mill fever" in the South, from 1845 to 1850, grew partially from the belief that southern textiles would be export-oriented and that China would be one of the markets.

Increasingly interested also were commercial farmers, the champion surplus producers of them all. One of the chief attractions of the Pacific coast for migrating farmers was easy access to the sea and the consequent opportunities for an expanded market for their products in the Orient. But the potential of Asian markets attracted more than the few thousands of farmers who moved to the

---

[3] Ibid., p. 127.

Far West in 1843 and 1844. It also held heightened appeal for midwest farmers who stayed behind, the revolution in railroad transportation having raised the possibility of connecting the Mississippi Valley with the Pacific coast. Indeed, in January 1845 Asa Whitney made his first formal proposal for generous government land grants, sixty miles wide, for any group that would attempt to build a railroad from Lake Superior to Oregon. His proposal was of keen interest to Stephen A. Douglas, one of the chief spokesmen for midwest agrarians.

Stephen A. Douglas

In 1846 Douglas commented that his state of Illinois alone could meet all of America's grain needs, and he strongly urged exploration of new markets abroad. This was the same Douglas who suggested not one but three transcontinental railroads in order to blunt sectional rivalry and yet get the job done.

The actions of Whitney, a New York merchant and old China hand, and Douglas, an agrarian political representative, substantiate the analysis of historian Charles Vevier in his article "American Continentalism: An Idea of Expansion, 1845–1910."[4] Vevier stresses the crucial point that continentalism and commercialism were not separate strands of American expansion but complementary ones; that the historic drive for western land was inextricably caught up with the drive for commercial markets overseas (just as earlier agrarian longings for New Orleans reflected concern for predictable access to world markets). Henry Nash Smith, in his classic *Virgin Land,* states the same

---

[4] *American Historical Review* (1960).

theme more poetically when he notes the connection between the continentalist "myth of the garden" and the commercialist "passage to India."

Clearly the American government shared the interest in commercial expansion in the Pacific; the Wilkes expedition and the Wanghia Treaty with China offer evidence on that point. If more seems required, the Hawaiian situation perhaps supplies it. American traders and whalers had introduced American influence to the islands early in the century, and since 1820 American missionaries had greatly expanded it. While retaining their religious functions, missionaries and their sons broadened and secularized their activities: first to political roles as advisers to the native monarchy and then to economic roles as merchants and planters. (The Dole family is a good case in point.) Like the *empresario* elite in Texas, these oligarchs were not necessarily annexationists; most seemed content to build their own City Upon a Hill, independent of American control. And like New Englanders of the seventeenth century seeking to build utopia untainted by the sins of Old England, so these new Americans sought to do likewise untainted by the old American sins of slavery, frontier barbarism, and Catholic immigrants. (For example, missionary influence produced laws banning Catholic priests, restricted control of education to Protestants, and generally persecuted the "papists.") But, in a clear case of history repeating itself, these new Puritans were no more radical in their innovations than the old had been, so that by 1840 Hawaii was simply a partial replica of New England anomalously cast in the middle of the vast Pacific.

Whatever its formal political status, Hawaii was economically an American colony, ruled by a New England elite who had brought their culture with them. Awareness of this fact gave the islands a special place in the hearts of American policy-makers; Hawaii had a warm place, and further awareness of its strategic and commercial value as a halfway house to the Orient made it an even warmer one. Thus in 1842, when Hawaii feared it was in danger of becoming either a French or British protectorate and went in search of international guarantees for its independence, the Whig administration of John Tyler responded by extending the protective umbrella of the Monroe Doctrine to those islands. Declaring that the United States' interest in Hawaii's future was greater than that of any other country of the world (meaning Great Britain and France), Secretary of State Webster applied, in effect, the noncolonization clause to Hawaii by stating his opposition to European control, formal or informal, over the islands. Subsequent Democratic administrations, more inclined to active colonies than to passive protectorates, were to favor the more direct approach of annexation.

FUNCTIONAL CONFLICT IN THE SOCIAL ORDER
OF LIBERAL CAPITALISM

The most intangible of the domestic changes prompting expansion was also perhaps the most important: that is, increasing functional tension within the social structure of emerging liberal capitalism.

The passing social order of mercantilism had sought to use governmental power to chart the path to a diversified, balanced, and modernized economy at home, supplemented by a vigorous trade expansion abroad. In so doing, it sought to satisfy the functional needs of all sectors of the economy—agricultural, industrial, and commercial—by integrating their activities in mutually profitable ways. Central also to the old order had been the proposition that the economy was not to be sectionalized into an industrial Northeast, a plantation South, and a yeoman West. That would ultimately have made the last two sections simply internal colonies of an industrialized metropole. On the contrary, the development of manufacturing and the accompanying economic benefits were intended for each section, Calhoun's South Carolina and Clay's Kentucky as well as Adams' Massachusetts. Indeed, this reflected the reality of the day: that all America (the Northeast included) was mainly agricultural, and that pockets of manufacturing were to be found in all sections. It was perhaps because of this unsectionalized and integrated character that the system received seemingly consensus support at the end of the War of 1812.

The central problem of mercantilism, however, was that the economic system it envisioned was radically different from the system that existed: an export economy based on extractive and agricultural enterprises. Development from one stage to the other demanded implicitly that American society accept deferred rewards until modernization began to pay off. But many elements in that society would defer rewards only so long as they were convinced that the ongoing system worked equitably for all sectors and sections, and so long as they were not required to lower their existing standard of living.

Two key events undermined the preconditions for deferred rewards and destroyed both the mercantilist consensus and its political agent, the Republican party. One was the 1816 postwar dumping of British manufactured goods on the American marketplace. The other was the Panic of 1819 and its ensuing depression. Each played havoc with the general standard of living; each seemed to have differential impact that suggested to some that the Northeast fared better under mercantilism than other areas did. Finding neither equity nor progress under the old system, many—especially agrarians in the West and South—began to blame that system for their miseries. The National Bank became a "monster" manipulating credit policies to exploit debtor classes; federal internal improvements benefited primarily eastern interests; and the tariff artificially raised the price of goods that agrarians had to buy while impeding their reaffirmed prime function as exporters abroad.

LAISSEZ-FAIRE LIBERALISM
AND THE EXPORT ECONOMY

Disillusionment, crystallized by the events of 1816 and 1819, was the engine that created the loose Jacksonian coalition that sabotaged the federal internal improvements system (for example, the Maysville veto), destroyed the "monster" (the bank veto), and progressively began to lower the tariff in 1833. In functional terms, the coalition consisted broadly of two types: those who defined their functional roles primarily in terms of an export economy (for example, merchants engaged principally in foreign trade, commercial farmers who defined foreign markets as crucial, cotton planters integrated into the British market, and those financial, insurance, and mercantile agents whose main business was servicing exporters), and those who stood to gain from transferring the locus of power from the national to the state level (for example, state bank monopolies opposed to a national bank monopoly, or canal and railroad promoters hamstrung by the prudence and rationality of the federal internal improvements system).

Rationalizing their functional self-interests, they embraced the liberal capitalist philosophy of laissez faire and affirmed that actions based on self-interest and free competition in the marketplace and the political arena would lead automatically, if somewhat mystically, to the natural harmony of all: to the general welfare. The role of the national government was largely the negative one of removing barriers (like national banks and high tariffs) to competition. Its chief positive role was to expand the marketplace for the export sector via both continentalism and commercialism. Interestingly, such laissez-faire prescriptions did not extend to the state and local level. On the contrary, the negation of the national government's role in the economy led to a great creative release of energy at lower governmental levels. The result was a tremendous expenditure of effort and money, chiefly in investment in social overhead capital. Most important were local and state government investments in human capital (the move to mass elementary education in the North), in banking, and in the incredible "transportation revolution" that George Rogers Taylor has so superbly described. For example, between 1830 and 1839, state indebtedness rose from $26 million to $170 million. Of this, $52 million went for banking purposes and $118 million for internal improvements (33 percent for railroads and nearly 60 percent for canals). The result was more than a revolution in transportation; it was, as historian Lee Benson notes, a revolution of rising expectations, an ebullient sense of great things to come which added both verve and ferocity to the competition of the marketplace.

The essential irony of liberal capitalism is that in unleashing energy it also magnified the functional conflict that the American system had sought to sublimate and control. Just as the Hamiltonian system had created its own political opposition, so now did the Jacksonian approach. Beginning with a nucleus of Clay supporters and anti-Masons and joined by disaffected Jackson supporters in the political shakedown of the 1830s, Jackson's Whig opponents had become a truly national party by 1840 and vigorously challenged the Democrats in all elections and at all levels until 1854. What differentiated these Whigs from Democrats has been a source of historical controversy as yet unresolved. Ethnocultural differences were clearly involved, although less so than in the nativist upsurge after 1848. Class difference, crudely measured by income, may also have been a factor, although a far less compelling one than older studies asserted. More plausible is historian Joel Silbey's argument that national rather than local issues constituted the key battleground for the parties, and that in the 1830s these issues were chiefly economic (banking, tariff, transportation, and land) rather than the ethnocultural issues that came to rival them in the transformation period between 1840 and 1860 (for example, temperance, Sunday observance, and school control).

By extension, one can argue that the real distinction was functional; that Whigs tended to be those who stood to gain from a positive federal role in the economy and who put their first stress upon development of the home market (manufacturers, merchants engaged in the domestic trade, bankers servicing such activities, farmers selling primarily to local markets, and the like). Of course, such a functional analysis demands refinement, for many individuals played several functional roles simultaneously and thus felt cross-pressures. A farmer might raise wool as well as wheat; a merchant engaged in foreign commerce might also have heavy investments in manufacturing: both might be schizophrenic on the tariff issue. A worker's pocketbook interest might identify with the boss's manufacturing business, but his class and ethnocultural interest might create a counteridentity. Nevertheless, in its general thrust the Whig party clearly embraced an economic philosophy that envisioned a large and positive role for the national government.

Both in specifics and in general rationale, it resembled the old American system, with its call for high tariffs, a national banking system, and federal internal improvements. In practice, it tended to be more particularistic. It was less concerned with balance and equity than with functional self-interest. Despite popular mythology, it was also implicitly committed to a sectionalized economy that would leave the bulk of high-value manufacturing, financing, and marketing functions in northeastern hands. (Typical here was the effort of New England textile manufacturers to discourage the development of a textile industry in the South.) The one thing that Whigs did share with Democrats was a concern for commercial expansion overseas. Despite their home market orientation, many Whig manufacturers retained some investment in foreign commerce, and they were also hopeful that their cruder products might prove competitive in world markets, especially in Latin America and Asia.

THE CHALLENGE OF WHIGGERY

Until 1837, such opposition did not seriously threaten Jacksonian Democrats and the state-oriented, export-oriented sectors. But three key events joined thereafter to mount a serious challenge to the new order. First, the financial repercussions of the Panic of 1837 forced many state governments to repudiate or default on the debts they had incurred for internal improvements. Aware of how much state and local governments had overextended themselves, groups and individuals interested in improved transportation began to turn once more to the federal government for monetary support. Likewise, mismanagement of state banks and their role in creating the panic made a federal role in banking seem less an anathema. Second, a crucial shift in the economy became evident; that is, allocation of capital and labor resources began to shift perceptibly into the industrial sector. That does not imply any rapid increases in the gross national product. It does mean, however, as Douglass North points out, that the cotton trade ceased to be the prime engine for economic growth; the cotton textile industry, with its backward linkages into machine tools and its forward linkages into wholesale and retail trade, acquired that preeminent position. What this suggested, rather unhappily to Jacksonians, was that the industrial sector of the economy was becoming dominant at the expense of the export sector. Whatever balance may have existed earlier was now clearly threatened. Third, the political backlash of the Panic of 1837 drove the Democrats from power for the first time in twelve years and put a Whig administration in Washington. The Whig party was thus in a position to enhance the functional self-interests of its constituency and to return the locus of power in the political economy to the national government.

Whigs used that power to pursue two connected goals. One was to erode the export sector's support for the Democratic party; the other was to expand the domestic marketplace for domestic manufacturers. To both ends, the Whigs pushed for a renewed program of federal internal improvements and for a pre-emption law in the public domains of the West. Both measures were desired by westerners but opposed by southern Democrats; both would facilitate industrial penetration of an expanded imperial market in the West. In addition, Whigs sought further specific legislation that would aid functional groups in their coalition; particularly, they pushed for a new national bank and for a high protective tariff.

The Whigs did not get all they sought, in part because of the accident that put Vice-President John Tyler into the chief executive's office after the early death of President Harrison. Tyler was one of a small group of southern states'-righters who had found a temporary home in the Whig party after the nullification controversy of the early 1830s. True to his export economy orientation, he did much to block major parts of his party's program. As a consequence, the party got only the preemption law and repeal of the independent Treasury, that Van Buren system which had totally separated the federal government from any banking functions. Whig efforts to expand the role of the federal government in internal improvements were only marginally successful, the new tariff of 1842 was not nearly so high as the Whigs had desired, and the campaign to create a third national bank was wholly abortive. Much of what they did do was undone when the Democrats, headed by James Polk and aided by the return of prosperity, won the election of 1884. The results were to include the reinstitution of the independent Treasury system, the veto of the 1846 River and Harbor Improvements Bill, and the low-revenue tariff of 1846.

EXPANSIONISM AND THE
RESPONSE TO CHALLENGE

While the challenge of Whiggery was premature, it was felt and perceived seriously by Democrats wishing to retain political power, by functional groups threatened by its programs, and by all those who embraced a laissez-faire philosophy. These anxieties came to be focused in the Polk administration of 1845–1848, and they provoked a purposeful response aimed at warding off this and future challenges. The response was varied, but perhaps its most important facet was a conscious, militant commitment to American expansion. Such a response held the promise of several benefits to the Democratic party. In a psychological sense, the jingoism and nationalistic fervor associated with expansionism would be a diversion and an antidote to the functional unease raised by the preceding Whig administration. In a philosophic sense, Polk, like Madison earlier, believed that extending the sphere of empire would make the whole so diffuse that no factional coalition could control and dominate its course. As he put it: "Our system may be safely extended to the utmost bounds of our territorial limits, and...as it shall be extended the bonds of our Union, so far from being weakened, will become stronger."[5] And in a pragmatic sense, enlarging the imperial pie would ensure a satisfactory slice for all the functional groups within the Democratic party and preserve the party's instrumentality in the eye of its diverse constituency. Thus, in response to population movements, to heightened interest in Pacific trade, and to functional conflict in the political economy, the Polk administration was to opt for a purposeful policy of expansion. The irony and tragedy of that choice was that it would indeed weaken rather than strengthen "the bonds of our Union"; Polk's new frontier turned out to be Pandora's box.

Suggestions for Further Reading

The best general frames of reference for this period are provided by William A. Williams, *Contours of American History* (Cleveland, 1961), and Richard W. Van Alstyne, *The Rising American Empire* (Chicago, 1965).

For a general study of both domestic and diplomatic affairs in the Jacksonian period, see Glyndon G. Van Duesen, *The Jacksonian Era, 1828–1848* (New York, 1959). The most provocative monographic study of the period is Lee Benson, *The Concept of Jacksonian Democracy* (Princeton, N.J., 1961).

For the economic framework, see Douglass C. North, *The Economic Growth of the United States, 1790–1860* (New York, 1960), and George Rogers Taylor, *The Transportation Revolution, 1815–1860* (New York, 1951).

For the political context, see Joel H. Silbey, *The Shrine of Party* (Pittsburgh, 1967).

For special diplomatic studies, consult Henry Blumental, *A Reappraisal of Franco-American Relations, 1830–1871* (Chapel Hill, N.C., 1959); William C. Binkley, *The Texas Revolution* (Baton Rouge, La., 1952); Frank L. Benns, *American Struggle for the British West Indies Carrying-Trade, 1815–1830* (Bloomington, Ind., 1923); Kenneth S. Latourette, *The History of Early Relations Between the United States and China, 1784–1844* (New Haven, Conn., 1917); and Frederick Merk, *The Oregon Question: Essays in Anglo-American Diplomacy and Politics* (Cambridge, Mass., 1967).

See also the general bibliography at the end of this volume.

---

[5] William A. Williams, *Contours of American History* (Cleveland, 1961), p. 276.

CHAPTER 9

The Third Empire
(1845–1848)

In four short and ultimately tragic years in the mid-1840s the United States annexed Texas (1845), acquired the most valuable part of Oregon in strained negotiations with Great Britain (1846), and concluded a two-year war against Mexico (1846–1848) with the seizure of California and most of the present southwestern United States. The size of this area rivaled that of America's first two empires, gained in 1783 from Great Britain and in 1803 from France. The frontage of much of it on the Pacific Ocean gave it a potential value perhaps even greater than that of the others. What is singularly striking about this wave of imperialism is its conscious and purposeful character. It was not simply the product of some quixotic, irrational faith in Manifest Destiny, or merely the mechanical process of population on the move. On the contrary, to a very considerable extent it was the consequence of a deliberate foreign policy that used calculated means to achieve specific, concrete ends. As noted earlier, the main dynamics for that policy emanated from domestic pressures within American society. But as we shall have occasion to note, it also reflected (or certainly used) the alleged external threat of British imperialism.

Texas

JOHN QUINCY ADAMS' fear that recognition of Texas was simply a prelude to annexation was well founded but premature. Texans petitioning for annexation between 1836 and 1838 ran into the stone wall of American political partisanship, Van Buren's moral qualms about slavery, fear of consequent war with Mexico, and preoccupation with the Panic of 1837.

PRESIDENT TYLER AND TEXAS

By 1843, however, changing conditions led Whig President John Tyler to opt for an annexationist policy. His own southern particularism and pro-slavery ideology dictated the desirability of annexation, but more importantly, his political ambitions made it a necessity. Alienated from his party by his states'-rights proclivities and deserted by his original cabinet, Tyler was a man without a political base. But he had an acquired taste for political power and thus an urgent need for a program to broaden and strengthen his political appeal—even if it meant changing party labels. Keenly aware of the mounting pressures generated by the third great cycle of American migration into Texas, he perceived that the annexation of Texas and a general expansionist policy might be just the key he sought. Aware too that the issue had to be desectionalized if it were to bear profitable fruit, he strongly emphasized the marketplace opportunities that Texas would offer to both farmers and manufacturers, and the strategic and commercial importance of its location on the Gulf of Mexico.

John Tyler

The threat of a British protectorate in Texas seemingly played into Tyler's hands. Diplomatically recognizing Texas in 1840, Great Britain had subsequently discouraged annexation to the United States and promoted Texas' continued independence under British protection. Dominant in Mexico City since the mid-1820s, British diplomats played some role in arranging a truce between Mexico and Texas in 1842. By proffering the additional bait that British influence might gain Mexico's acceptance of Texas' independence (thus removing Texas' chief external threat), Great Britain hoped to block further American expansion to the west and south, enhance the British power position on the Gulf of Mexico, create a free trade market for its manufactures, and establish a source of raw cotton independent of the American South. Additional hopes for the abolition of slavery in Texas, a chimera that Texans cultivated, were entertained as much for practical reasons (making Texas unattractive to southern imperialists) as humanitarian ones. While an Anglo-Texas entente was genuinely appealing to some Texans, most of them, particularly in the Sam Houston faction, exploited its possibility to manipulate American fears and stimulate annexation on the best possible terms.

In a sense, Tyler was delighted to be manipulated in this way, for since the Democratic party was a hotbed of Anglophobia, any perceived British threat would increase Democratic support for his policy. Thus the issue could be structured as national and bipartisan. Why the Democratic party (in contrast to the Whig) was so virulently Anglophobic and so susceptible then to calls for preemptive expansion remains a murky matter. Economic determinants offer little insight. Whig manufacturers threatened by competition of British products were frequently Anglophiles; Democratic planters, who sold cotton primarily to Great Britain, and Western farmers, who eagerly awaited Britain's final repeal of the Corn Laws, were often anti-British. Similarly, the old canard that Democrats were the direct descendants of Anglophobic Jeffersonians and that Whigs were the lineal heirs of pro-British Federalists is contradicted by growing evidence that the new party system of the 1840s was not a direct extension of the old one, but a significantly new realignment. The only positive correlations seem to lie in ethnicity and in differing conceptions of empire. On the one hand, the Democratic party gave a readier home to new immigrants than the quasi-nativist Whigs, and this immigrant constituency, especially the Irish, was often bitterly anti-British. On the other hand, as we shall see, agrarian Democrats strongly favored continentalist expansion while Whigs did not, and Britain constituted the chief stumbling block to expansion in Texas, Oregon, and California (and later in Central America and the Caribbean). Consequently, Democrats often imagined agents of British imperialism under every rock and pebble strewn in the path of American empire-building.

Tyler, through personal spokesmen in Congress, expertly manipulated fear of British intentions, and his Secretary of State, Abel Upshur, successfully negotiated an annexation treaty with Texas by assuring Houston that it was certain to be ratified and that the United States would defend Texas if the treaty led to renewed hostilities with Mexico. Tyler's scenerio proved fatally flawed, however, as the treaty went down to overwhelming defeat in the Senate. Most accounts ascribe the debacle to Upshur's untimely death and his replacement by John C. Calhoun, already renowned as the political lawyer of slavery. Calhoun's ill-advised defense of the treaty as a bulwark against British abolitionism seemed to make Texas primarily the object of southern self-interest rather than of the national interest. Actually, partisanship rather than sectionalism scuttled the project. *All* the Whigs, including those in the South, voted against the treaty. More than two-thirds of the Democrats voted for it, and the seven who broke ranks were Van Buren men angered at their candidate's failure to secure the party nomination for the upcoming presidential election.

THE ELECTION OF 1844 AND
ANNEXATION OF TEXAS

The election of 1844 changed the whole political climate on the Texas question. The cause lay in the Democratic party's plank on expansionism and in its astute exploitation by the party candidate, James K. Polk of Tennessee. There were several beautiful things about the party call for the "reannexation" of Texas and the "reoccupation" of Oregon. First, it subsumed the specific question of Texas in the larger question of general expansion. Most especially, placing Oregon in tandem with Texas dissipated much opposition to the annexation of Texas. Second, the clever use of the prefix "re" made it appear that these territories had always rightfully and legally been America's, but had been squandered away by the proto-Whig diplomacy of John Quincy Adams: Oregon in the Convention of 1818 and Texas in the Transcontinental Treaty of 1819. And finally, party shrewdness in refusing to set a timetable for the "reacquisition" of these imperial objects and to stipulate the modes to be used enabled both jingoes and moderates to support the platform plank.

Polk's triumph in the 1844 election may not have been a mandate for expansion, but it did restore party discipline in the Senate and it did change the votes of a few southern Whigs. Aware of this change and anxious for

Demonstration for Texas annexation

history to record some achievement beside his name, lame-duck President Tyler managed to circumvent the Senate's two-thirds rule by securing annexation through majority-vote resolutions in both houses of Congress. In general, the voting pattern still followed party rather than sectional lines. Final consummation, however, awaited favorable action by Texas. Members of a small faction there still saw a better future for themselves in an independent Texas, especially if it managed to build its own empire to the Pacific coast. The larger Houston faction favored annexation but wanted better terms, such as American assumption of Texas' debts and clear support for the Rio Grande as the Texas-Mexico boundary. Unsuccessful on the debt question and encountering equivocation on the boundary issue, the Houston faction finally decided to settle for lesser terms. Joined by less reticent annexationists, Texas ratified the agreement on July 5, 1845, and joined the Union a decade after its revolution.

Oregon

SAVE FOR EASING the historian's task of organizing his material, the practice of separating the Oregon question from the issues that led to war with Mexico has little value. America's chief goals in each were the same: acquisition of the major ports on the Pacific coast and eventual settlement of their agricultural hinterlands—all as prelude to making the United States a power in Asia. The prime tactic of diplomacy used in each was the same: brinkmanship, leading to accommodation in one instance and war in the other. The issues developed simultaneously, affected each other's course, and climaxed together, with the Oregon Treaty following the launching of war on Mexico by a matter of weeks. In both cases, American diplomacy was firmly determined by one man, President James K. Polk. Often going beyond the counsel of some of his advisers (including Secretary of State James Buchanan), Polk played a bold and dangerous game, not only to advance America's commercial and continental ambitions, but to preserve and enlarge the instrumentality of the Democratic party in all sections of the country.

America's formal involvement in the Oregon Territory dated back to the Convention of 1818. Few Americans since then, whatever their functional positions or their sectional allegiances, doubted its great value, especially in relation to the Pacific trade. Jefferson Davis appreciated the importance of the bay at Juan de Fuca quite as much as William H. Seward and Thomas Hart Benton. The only real division up to 1843 had been over the means of acquiring Oregon (at least as far north as the forty-ninth parallel), and the tactic chosen was a classically simple and proven one: bide one's time until American settlement in Oregon altered power relationships there in ways that favored American pretensions over British ones. As usual, the assumption was that time, geographic mobility, and demography were on the side of American empire. Contrary to such expectations, however, the British made better use of time between 1818 and 1843, and the Hudson's Bay Company became both the dominant economic organization and the de facto governing unit for much of the territory.

POLK AND THE TENSIONS OF
POLITICS AND DIPLOMACY

The American migrations of 1843 and 1844, the consequent "Oregon fever" in the Midwest, and the specific commitment of the victorious Democratic party in 1844 to the "reoccupation" of Oregon dramatically restructured the situation. Polk thus came to office partly owing his nomination to militant expansionists like Senator Hannegan of Indiana and implicitly committed to an all-Oregon policy: that is, acquisition not only of the contemporary states of Oregon and Washington, but of the present Canadian province of British

Columbia as well. It seems probable that Polk's private attitudes on Oregon were more complex. While "all Oregon" may have been his optimum objective, securing the forty-ninth parallel and the Strait of Juan de Fuca was the distilled essence of his policy. Yet political considerations held him back from candid admission of that fact. Not only did he have conventioneering debts to repay; in addition, the prior annexation of all Texas seemed to make acquisition of all Oregon (or at least a convincing attempt at acquisition) the *sine qua non* of Democratic party viability. In all likelihood it was the unresolved tension between diplomatic goals and political expediency, between the concreteness of Juan de Fuca and the abstraction of all Oregon, that accounts for the erratic character of his dealings with Great Britain over Oregon.

RIDICULOUS EXHIBITION; OR, YANKEE-NOODLE PUTTING
HIS HEAD INTO THE BRITISH LION'S MOUTH.

Polk began his diplomatic maneuvering by proposing to the British a division of Oregon on the basis of the forty-ninth parallel. Indications are that Secretary of the Navy Bancroft had already persuaded him that the British would accept that offer. If they did accept it, he would have secured his prime commercial goal in Oregon and yet could keep his political fences intact by stressing that former American Presidents had made just such compromise offers and that he was honor-bound by precedent to offer the same compromise. The British minister to the United States, however, with neither diplomatic instructions nor much personal wisdom, rejected the overture. The immediate consequence was the heightening of Polk's unresolved tension. He had clear information from his own minister in London that the British Foreign Office was unhappy with the behavior of its man in Washington and would give serious consideration to a renewed compromise offer. Yet for Polk to pursue the matter further on his own might well seem a betrayal to specific functional and sectional groups inside the National Democratic coalition—groups that were "his" constituency in a very special way. Thus political necessity, as he perceived it, demanded that from that point onward any initiative for compromise had to come from British leaders, not from him; and it had to result in a real or apparent diplomatic victory for the United States.

THE POLKIAN PARADIGM

Reflecting these unresolved tensions as well as his own temperament, Polk's response to the Oregon question was a policy of bluster and bluff. In his State of the Union message late in 1845, he asked Congress to give Great Britain a notice of termination of joint occupancy, effective in December 1846; and he further affirmed that "Oregon must be either abandoned or maintained" and made clear that the only honorable course was to maintain it, whatever "the hazards" (i.e., war with the British).[1] At the same time, he revived the often ignored Monroe Doctrine and used it as a sacrosanct mantle to clothe, legitimate, and define America's "empire for liberty," and to make clear that he would brook no interference with its predestined fulfillment.

These stern moves, coupled with aggressive rhetoric, reflected what one might call the Polkian paradigm in foreign affairs. In terms that bring to mind the "eyeball-to-eyeball" Cuban missile crisis of 1962, Polk declared, "The only way to treat John Bull is to look him straight in the eye." And "If we hesitate, John Bull will become more grasping and arrogant."[2] In short, a hundred years before John Foster Dulles or Dean Rusk, Polk embraced the belief that accommodation is appeasement and that diplomatic victory goes only to the tough and single-minded. Unfortunately, such a strategem in foreign affairs fails as often as it works. If the adversary's national interests are marginal enough to sacrifice; if its power is so overwhelmingly strong that it can ignore the challenge if it chooses or so pathetically weak that it must capitulate without choice; if its policy-makers do not take the threats seriously or react in fright—then such tactics may be effective. But if none of these things is the case, or if they exist in an unfavorable mix, then the consequences may be

---

[1] James D. Richardson, ed., *Compilation of the Messages and Papers of the Presidents, 1789–1897*, 10 vols. (Washington, D.C., 1969), 4:397.

[2] James K. Polk, *The Diary of James K. Polk During His Presidency, 1845 to 1849*, ed. Milo M. Quaife (Chicago, 1910), 1:155.

the painful opposite of those intended. (In a contemporary example, the Cuban missile crisis of 1962, Russia, as a great nuclear superpower, would not play the "Red Rover, Red Rover, we dare you come over" game to the end because, in part, Cuba lay outside its primary sphere of national interests. Yet in the early 1950s China, then a nonnuclear power, did indeed fight the United States when American advances in North Korea threatened the vital Chinese position in Manchuria.)

In the specific case of Oregon, the dangers unleashed by Polk's brinkmanship were two. First, it raised British hackles and thus imposed limits on the diplomatic flexibility of the Foreign Office. Second, it reinforced the efforts of the more militant jingoes in Congress to formulate the Oregon termination resolution in the most aggressive and uncompromising way. In the vernacular, this threatened to open a real can of worms, for if the "ultras" had been successful, rational diplomatic discourse and agreement might have proved impossible, and any number of unanticipated consequences might have resulted. (And who is to say unequivocally that war might not have been one of them, especially if Mexican-American relations had been resolved peacefully, thus eliminating the possibility of a two-front war for the Polk administration?)

THE FACTORS WORKING
FOR COMPROMISE

Happily, events on both sides of the Atlantic intervened to ensure both Polk's salvation and his foreign policy goals. First (as he may have hoped), the political makeup of Congress resulted in a conciliatory, watered-down version of the termination resolution. Led by antiterritorial Whigs like Webster and Calhoun, by southern Democrats partly satisfied with the annexation of Texas, and by northeastern mercantile Democrats concerned primarily with port facilities, the Congress affixed a preamble that made it clear that termination was a first step not to confrontation politics but to a speedy and negotiated settlement. At the same time, the onset of war with Mexico made the United States more circumspect in its dealings with Great Britain, especially in the face of British naval mobilization. (Obviously two could play at brinkmanship.)

Meanwhile, in Great Britain, several factors coincided to make diplomatic initiative from there seem more palatable. To commence the sequence, the Hudson's Bay Company moved its headquarters from the Columbia River northward to Vancouver Island, partly because of the decline of fur trapping in the southern area and partly out of fear for the safety of its posts in the face of a growing population that loudly proclaimed its Americanism. Whatever the reasons, the move gave the impression that the area between the Columbia and the forty-ninth parallel was hardly worth contesting. In turn, British internal politics, then in the process of party formation, worked its wonders. At a crucial juncture, the Whigs were unable to form a government, in part because of the hawkish Lord Palmerston's projected role as Foreign Minister; and Peel's Tories, with the less aggressive Lord Aberdeen at the foreign policy helm, continued in power. Finally, but quite relatedly, the changing British attitudes on colonialism had their part to play. Although its colonial policy was still in transition, Great Britain by the 1840s was moving away from its past mercantilistic commitment to a formal political colonial empire overseas. Taking its place was what some have called the "imperialism of free trade"— the attitude that formal colonies were an administrative and financial burden; that British diplomacy and force would best be used to reduce the international barriers to the free flow of goods, capital, and services (the policy of what is called the free world today); and that in such a context, Britain's industrial supremacy would win it all the traditional material fruits of imperialism. In such an intellectual environment, to risk war over a colony of such dubious value as Oregon must have seemed a regressive policy indeed, especially if the forty-ninth parallel compromise gave British commercialists (like American commercialists) equal access to Juan de Fuca and entrée to the Great Circle Route to Asia.

Reacting to the dovish American preamble as a peace initiative, Lord Aberdeen proposed a draft treaty boundary that essentially followed the forty-ninth parallel, but dipped southward near the Pacific to give Vancouver Island and half of the Strait of Juan de Fuca to the British. The proposal, with slight modifications, gave Polk and most Americans most of what they wanted and more than they may have deserved. Yet even at that juncture, the exigencies of Democratic party politics compelled Polk to play a reluctant role. To his own Cabinet he declared himself certain that the British proposal ought to be rejected; and when the Cabinet systematically destroyed his position (with reasons he himself probably accepted), he simply washed his hands of the matter and passed it on to the Senate for its advice. The tactic was the complete reverse of Harry S. Truman's favorite slogan, "The buck stops here." In this case, it stopped with the Senate, and as expected, the Senate gave the treaty its overwhelming approval. Polk, however, while evading some measure of his responsibilities, contented himself with the hope that his maneuver would confer all the political liabilities of the compromise upon his Whig opponents in the Senate, while he garnered the political assets—including the loyalty of the "ultras"—for himself. In the meantime, the national interests, as he perceived them, had been served.

War on Mexico

IN THE THREE-RING imperial circus of Texas, Oregon, and the Mexican War, it was the last that rightfully and tragically occupied the center stage. It was, and is, the easiest to understand and the most difficult to confront. It is possible, to be sure, that regardless of American actions, internal Mexican politics would have produced war; that Mexico, weaker than it realized but prouder than the United States perceived, would not have caved in to American designs on California or accepted peacefully the loss of Texas. But our proper concern resides not in hypothetical Mexican behavior but in objectifiable American acts that reflected an administration commitment to expansion at Mexican expense, by diplomacy if possible, by war if necessary.

THE CARROT AND THE STICK

The initial means employed were as simple as they were contemptuous of Mexican nationalism: the classic carrot and the stick. The stick took varied forms. General Zachary Taylor, with four thousand troops (half the American regular army), was encamped in Corpus Christi at the mouth of the Nueces River, poised to move, if need be, into the debated region between there and the Rio Grande. Consul Larkin in Monterey, under between-the-lines instructions of Secretary of State Buchanan, investigated the prospects of a West Florida-style revolt in California. The western expedition of Captain Frémont, under orders not wholly clear since many were verbal and informal, similarly plunged into the waters of California politics. And American naval units operated under standing orders to seize Californian ports if war with Mexico should break out. (One unit actually took and held Monterey for two days in 1842 after receiving incorrect news of war—an embarrassment to Tyler's diplomacy but early, graphic evidence to Mexicans of the American stick.)

The carrot took the form of John Slidell's diplomatic mission to Mexico City in December 1845. Slidell trod in the still visible footsteps of Jackson's efforts to acquire California and the even more energetic efforts of the Tyler administration to purchase the same area. Like his predecessors, Slidell, acting for Polk, sought to secure as much of Mexico's northern real estate as possible:

the Rio Grande as Texas' boundary was defined as indispensable, New Mexico as desirable, and California (if one calculates on the basis of money offered as well as Polk's own private utterances) as the most important of all. The lure offered was Yankee gold, ranging from an assumption of American financial claims against Mexico on up to an additional $30 million. Such lures had failed repeatedly in the past, but Polk, with his penchant for brinkmanship, felt his varied display of force might make Mexico more prone to reason (as he defined it); that Mexico would see the handwriting on the wall, accept the inevitable, and simultaneously add some dollars to its hard-pressed treasury. To coin an old phrase, why give it away if you can sell it? Mexico, however, was too proud to turn prostitute. At a later date, the approach might well have worked. But coming less than six months after American annexation of Texas, it was an intolerable assault on Mexican sensibilities.

The failure of Slidell's mission reinforces such an analysis. Although Polk had seeming assurance from the Mexican government that it would negotiate with his representative, news of Slidell's mission and its probable intent raised such a political furor that the Mexican administration had to reject that mission or fall from power. And reject it it did, though on technical grounds rather than substantive ones, apparently in the hope of assuaging President Polk. But it fell from power anyway. Its successor, learning its political lessons well, likewise refused to treat with the American representative. By January 1846 Slidell's reports to Polk made clear his diminishing chances for success, and in March he left Mexico, certain that only war could achieve U.S. objectives.

THE DECISION FOR WAR

Polk drew the same conclusion. On January 13, after learning of the change in Mexican governments, he ordered Taylor's four thousand undertrained men out of their good defensive position at Corpus Christi and southward to the Rio Grande. After nearly two months of preparation, Taylor began the move in early March and completed it by the end of the month. In his new position he threatened the Mexican town of Matamoros, which lay under his cannon, and virtually invited Mexican retaliation. Polk banked on just that response as an excuse to open war on Mexico. But when Mexican forces were slow to take the bait, the President decided, at a lengthy Cabinet meeting in early May, to ask Congress for a war declaration anyway. The reasons he offered were many; nowhere among them was the real one. Fortunately for Polk, news arrived that very night that the awaited border conflict had finally come, so that thirty-six hours later he was able, in great self-righteousness, to ask Congress for war, in part because "American blood had been shed on American soil."[3]

The reasons for war given by Polk and sometimes accepted by subsequent historians are debatable at best. There were, to be sure, long-standing financial claims against Mexico, either for unpaid purchases or for uncompensated damages growing out of the Mexican war for independence. Yet American claims on Mexico were smaller than Britain's; indeed, they were not so large as British claims against the United States for repudiated or defaulted payments on bonds issued during the Panic of 1837, yet surely Americans would have been stunned had Britain used the claims as a reason for war on Brother Jonathan. Similarly unconvincing is Polk's emphasis on the rejection of the Slidell mission as an affront to American national honor. Polk himself well understood that the rejection was not a deliberate affront, but the unavoidable consequences of Mexican internal politics. Under such circumstances, in relations between weak and strong nations, the stronger is insulted only if it chooses to be; it can, if it wishes, ignore the affront as easily as a duck shedding water. In other words, the issue of national honor offered a useful and popular pretext for war, but hardly constituted a substantive cause. Likewise, the American insistence on the Rio Grande as the Texas-Mexico boundary is hard to justify. The disputed area was largely unsettled and its value as dubious as American claims to it. Just as few Americans had deemed the Maine-Canada boundary controversy worth a war in 1842, it seems unlikely that many more, save Texan imperialists, thought much differently about the Rio Grande issue in 1846. In short, these stated reasons, both individually and collectively, seem strained and self-serving.

The real and overriding objective can be stated in a word: California. While Polk had publicly proclaimed his expansionist designs on Oregon and Texas, his privately affirmed and most valued imperial goal was California. Only California was worth the price of a war; all other reasons were ultimately demeaning. California, with its ports of San Francisco, Monterey, and San Diego, offered America better "windows" to Pacific trade than Oregon. California, with its vast inviting valleys, offered far greater potential value than Oregon. California, not Oregon, constituted both the perfect microcosm and the perfect capstone to efforts to make commercialism and continentalism reciprocal, reinforcing, and integrated.

WAS WAR NECESSARY?

But even if California was worth a war of aggression against Mexico (a large assumption indeed), a further question remains, as historian David

---

[3] Richardson, ed., *Messages and Papers*, 4:442.

Pletcher has posed it: Was overt, planned, offensive war the only and best means of securing the imperial end? Pletcher thinks not, and in his analysis stresses the internal conditions in California in 1846; that the area was Mexican in name only and virtually autonomous in fact; that its seven thousand Spanish-speaking inhabitants were anticentralist in their attitudes toward the Mexican government, had revolted twice since 1842, and as late as 1845 had beaten back a federal effort to regain effective political control; that the seven hundred Americans, chiefly around San Francisco, were increasingly powerful in all facets of California life; and that the two thousand American settlers expected to arrive there in 1846 were but the vanguard of the mass to follow.

Under these circumstances, a number of other options were perhaps open to Polk, even after Slidell's failure. First, with the passage of time and the hoped-for cooling of Mexican anger over the annexation of Texas, the Mexican political climate might have made the sale of California feasible, since Mexico, having clearly lost control of it anyway, might well have determined to make some money out of a lost cause. (With the advantage of hindsight, one can point out, for example, that Mexico did sell Mexican soil to the United States in the so-called Gadsden Purchase of the early 1850s—despite the bitter anti-Americanism stirred by the war.) A second possibility lay in the increasing immigration and inevitable Americanization of California—a process akin to that in West Florida or "the Texas game"—which might well in time have led to annexation or an American protectorate. The process, to be sure, might have provoked Mexico to war, but at least America's actions would have been consistent with its own ideology—with the federal principle that the proper way for the empire to grow was for organized representatives of the inhabitants of a given area to propose admission to the empire voluntarily and for the inhabitants to ratify the proposal democratically. Or, finally, Mexico itself might have initiated war over the Texas question, in which case the American navy could quickly have secured the prized California ports. The means would still have been war, but at least the onus would have been on Mexico.

All of these possibilities had one thing in common: they required time, and Polk appeared to feel he had none to spare. The underlying reasons for that feeling must remain partly conjectural. The reason most often cited is his fear of British designs on California and hence the felt need to move quickly and preemptively. It is true, of course, that individual British consular and naval officials were quite interested in California and its anticipated importance to Asian trade, and that Larkin brought this fact to Polk's attention. It is true as well that rumors abounded that Britain was prepared to fund Mexico's debt, with California as collateral and ultimate repayment.

Yet it is equally true that Lord Aberdeen was not much interested in California and that a number of objectifiable facts ought to have made that clear to Polk. The British were already proving themselves conciliatory in Oregon, where British legal rights and honor were involved in ways that did not obtain in California. They had earlier repudiated an unauthorized British naval protectorate in Hawaii and further assured the United States that they had no territorial ambitions in the Pacific trading area (of which California was a part). And finally, in their efforts to end preferred treatment for the agricultural products of British colonies and to specialize further in high-value manufacturing, the British were seeking closer economic ties with the United States in the hope of making use of this country, at least temporarily, as a breadbasket. As a consequence, the British and the Americans were seeking to coordinate repeal of the British Corn Laws and passage of the exceedingly low American tariff of 1846, proposed and pushed through by Secretary of the Treasury Robert Walker. Given the priority assigned this effort by the British, it would seem unlikely that they would have jeopardized it by adventurism in California. Yet for all these objective facts, the subjective possibility remains that Anglophobia was so endemic in the Democratic party, so thoroughly pervaded all levels from party hacks to party chiefs, that Polk and his advisers wrongly perceived some ominous Redcoat menace and acted on the basis of that misperception. But still there remains also the lingering thought that, in this instance, the menacing British lion might simply have been a handy symbol to mobilize support for actions taken for other reasons; the magic button, once pushed, that would both legitimate and popularize a war of expansion.

If there were other reasons, they are probably to be found in the realm of domestic American politics. Threatened politically, functionally, and philosophically by the Whig coalition, National Democrats like Polk saw in expansion the means to minimize the threats of Whiggery and to sustain the instrumentality and viability of the Democratic party. More specifically, the acquisition of California would compensate foreign merchants and commercial farmers in Polk's constituency for the compromise he felt forced to make over Oregon. Moreover, the means of acquiring it—war—would help unify the country in an exciting national endeavor and thus subsume the nation's factional squabbles. (To borrow Richard Hofstadter's term and project it backward a century, external war would vent an internal "psychic crisis"; war and the new frontier it created would operate as the national safety valve.) This does not imply that Polk, for all his brinkmanship, was a war lover; he was not. It does mean, however, that he anticipated that this would be a miniwar, a "splendid little war" that would generate some therapeutic excitement, gain his imperial goals,

James K. Polk

and have no truly disastrous consequences for anyone—not even for Mexico, which would gain treasure for what it would not be able to hold in any case. In other words, he expected that a few quick, victorious thrusts to the Rio Grande, to Santa Fe, and into California would suffice; that the Mexicans, having felt the stick rather than simply beheld it, would reason together and capitulate. It would all be short, inexpensive, relatively painless, and to the everlasting benefit of country and party.

CONSEQUENCES, ANTICIPATED AND OTHERWISE

In an obvious sense, the American war on Mexico obtained all of Polk's objectives: more than his Whig critics wanted and less than the all-Mexico clique desired, but all he and most National Democrats sought. Texas to the Rio Grande, the Southwest Territory, and cherished California lay now within the American empire. Largely because of this staggering achievement, Polk has been lauded by many recent historians as a strong President, one of the near-greats, the only man of consequence to occupy the office between Jackson and Lincoln. The underlying reasoning for that assessment has been simple and as American as apple pie: Polk knew what he wanted, he vigorously sought it, and he got it.

Or did he? History (and this is much of its fascination) deals not with anticipated consequences alone, but with unanticipated ones as well. Polk secured his goal of commercial and territorial empire, but the frightening and unexpected results of his acts made it a Pyrrhic victory—for himself, for his party, and for his country. The quick military thrusts secured the sought-for empire, but still Mexico would not ratify reality; the penetration of the northern Mexican hinterland gave way to the landing at Veracruz and General Scott's military drive inland to Mexico City itself, and still Mexico would not negotiate. As Daniel Webster put it, "Mexico is an ugly enemy. She will not fight—and will not treat."[4] The only result was an unauthorized armistice in August 1847, which was based on terms unacceptable to Polk and which in any case quickly broke down. The only tangible consequence of that episode was Polk's alienation from his diplomatic representative, Nicholas P. Trist, and Trist's recall. Ironically, it was Trist who, ignoring the recall, successfully negotiated the Treaty of Guadalupe Hidalgo, early in 1848, which garnered Mexican acceptance of America's imperial successes. If he had not, Polk clearly would have exercised his option to escalate the war further, with yet more unpredictable consequences.

As it was, the unforeseen had already been painful enough for Polk. A short war had become a long one. A cheap war had become an enormous strain on the Treasury and the tax structure. A politically popular war for the Democratic party had become a political albatross as Whigs made the best of their position as the loyal opposition to criticize "Mr. Polk's war" while voting the money, though often belatedly, to support American troops in the field. A war that should have enhanced Polk's public stature instead made political heroes out of Whig generals and helped catapult Zachary Taylor into the White House in 1849. A war that sought to subsume internal strife raised again, for the first time since 1820, the potential polarity of wage labor versus slave labor as the famous Wilmot Proviso sought to exclude slavery from any territory acquired from the war.

By themselves these factors need not have had any more serious consequence than depriving the Democratic party of national power for four years. But the politicizing of the war, unparalleled in American history save perhaps for the Indochina war of the mid-twentieth century, made it difficult for Polk and his successors to give a satisfactory answer to one crucial question: How was this vast new empire to be organized? Or stated in terms of power relationships, who in American society was to control and benefit from it? As we have posited, Polk expected all elements to benefit from the general enlargement of the imperial pie, but the supercharged political climate created by the war and the lack of equilibrium in a dynamic, changing, growing, moderniz-

---

4 Richard W. Van Alstyne, *The Rising American Empire* (Chicago, 1965), p. 145.

ing America made agreement on the culinary slicing damnably hard to come by. An effort would be made in the Compromise of 1850, but in the end Polk and other National Democrats fell back on the only device in which they had true faith—the mechanism of the marketplace. Embracing, as we shall see, the doctrine of so-called popular sovereignty, they determined that the empire would go to the strongest and the swiftest. Already dominant in structuring the political economy of the mother country, laissez faire now became dominant in structuring the empire as well. Competition, not compromise, was to become the key determinant; and that choice, or the inability to make any better one, was to disrupt the instrumentality of the Democratic party as well as the unity of the nation-state itself. In sum, functional sectional groups competing for the spoils of empire were to compete themselves right into the Armageddon of civil war.

Suggestions for Further Reading

The best overview again is to be found in Richard W. Van Alstyne, *The Rising American Empire* (Chicago, 1965). By far the most provocative monograph is Norman A. Graebner, *Empire on the Pacific* (New York, 1955). Complementing it is Charles Vevier, "American Continentalism: An Idea of Expansion, 1845–1910," *American Historical Review* (1960).

A classic study of the myth and reality of the frontier experience in American life is Henry Nash Smith, *Virgin Land* (New York, 1959). More concerned with romantic rhetoric is William H. Goetzmann, *When the Eagle Screamed: The Romantic Horizon in American Diplomacy, 1800–1860* (New York, 1966). Concerned with the same issues are Albert K. Weinberg, *Manifest Destiny* (Baltimore, 1935), and Frederick Merk, *Manifest Destiny and Mission in American History: A Reinterpretation* (New York, 1963).

Anglo-American competition is dealt with in Ephraim D. Adams, *British Interests and Activities in Texas, 1838–1846* (Baltimore, 1910), and Willard D. Jones, *Lord Aberdeen and the Americas* (Athens, Ga., 1958).

A Mexican view of the Mexican-American conflict can be found in José Fernando Ramírez, *Mexico During the War with the United States,* ed. Walter C. Scholes, trans. Elliott B. Scherr (Columbia, Mo., 1950).

Sound biographies of two key individuals are Charles G. Sellers, *James K. Polk: Continentalist, 1843–1846* (Princeton, N.J., 1966), and Carl M. Wiltse, *John C. Calhoun: Sectionalist, 1840–1850* (Indianapolis, 1951).

The best presentation of the political framework is found in Joel H. Silbey, *The Transformation of American Politics, 1840–1860* (Englewood Cliffs, N.J., 1967).

See also the general bibliography at the end of this volume.

CHAPTER 10

The Dysfunctional Empire
(1849–1861)

Dividing Polk's empire proved fatally more difficult than appor-
tioning Jefferson's, simply because the "slavery in the empire" issue was no
longer so easily compromised. Although most Americans, both "north of slavery" and in the South, had racist attitudes, the issue of slavery itself—apart
from the question of race—had become so ideologized by the 1850s that it had
become largely a moral abstraction rather than a political question; and moral
abstractions do not easily lend themselves to political solutions. As the decade
wore on, cultural attack and counterattack led Americans to develop their
own versions of the "black legend" or the "white legend"—the inherent evil
or positive good of the institution of slavery. And what began as a debate over
slavery inevitably expanded to a debate over what constituted the good life and
the good society, for to Americans north and south, the issue of slave labor
versus wage labor ultimately involved questions of values, attitudes, life styles,
and world views. And although cavalier and Yankee had more of these in
common than many have believed, the differences were increasingly stressed,
particularly as the traditional political party structure failed to produce acceptable answers. The consequence was a cultural chasm, partly real and
partly the result of perceptual distortions.

Still, if the American political economy had been in equilibrium, traditional solutions to the problems of organizing the new empire might have

been found. Much of the ideologizing of the slavery issue, after all, was simply rationalization of functional and sectional self-interests, and if those interests had been reasonably balanced and their prospects for growth good, then another compromise like that of 1820 might have been made and might have stood up. But the America of 1850 was not the America of 1820; the balance, accidental or purposeful, which was found in the dying days of mercantilism no longer existed in the heyday of laissez faire. This latter society ("Young America," as some liked to call it) was the most dynamic and rapidly changing on the face of the earth. And the social forces at work, rather than creating countervailing forces and renewed equilibrium (as liberal economists posit that they should), created cumulative, circular reinforcement that produced yet further instability and disequilibrium. What was involved, in essence, was not a quantitative change in economic growth and reinvestment, not a takeoff stage, but a qualitative change in what was produced, where capital was invested, and how labor was employed. In these areas the changes were sharp as the winds of modernization and industrialization began to sweep the economic face of America.

Economic Disequilibrium: Metropole and Colonies

THE NORTHEAST

In no section of American society were the elements of change more dramatic and evident than in the Northeast (New England and the middle Atlantic states). When Jackson entered office in 1829, that section was still reasonably diversified. Agriculture was still important, although its decline was evident in New England. Manufacturing had survived the British deluge of 1812–1819 and renewed its growth, but its markets remained largely localized, its technology crude, and its predominant form of organization still prefactory. Overall, as earlier, mercantile and auxiliary activities remained most prominent. Especially significant was the coastal and transatlantic cotton trade.

The next two decades, however, witnessed remarkable changes. Agriculture, although still important in the middle Atlantic region, continued its downward spiral in New England, which now was forced to import much of its foodstuffs, not only from neighboring areas to the west but from Virginia and North Carolina via the coastal trade. Merchants, while still significant, found it more profitable to diversify and invest in industry, and their own commercial operations turned from the resources of farm and forest and became increasingly the handmaids of manufacturing. And most importantly,

Factories in Pawtucket, R. I.

the new industrial capitalism grew to such proportions that it came to dominate most facets of northeastern life. To an ever increasing degree, workers, farmers, bankers, and merchants found their activities integrated into the networks of an industrial marketplace economy, and often, by choice or necessity, took their political and economic cues from the captains of industry.

What made the spinning of this industrial web possible was a concentration on types of industries that went beyond the simpler modes, such as meatpacking or flour milling, where proximity to the farm product was critical; more complicated industries, like the manufacture of cotton and woolen goods, boots and shoes, and men's clothing, required greater inputs of capital—capital that only the Northeast, with long-term profits acquired through trade, could generate. The results were enterprises like cotton textile mills, which had not only forward linkages into consumer goods but backward linkages into an infant machine tool industry. Moreover, such specialized products commanded sales in distant as well as local places, so that the expanded marketplace, coupled with the double linkages, made for a beneficial spread effect that gave the whole section a much more advanced economy than that of the West or South. By 1859 the value of northern manufacturing was ten times that of southern cotton; indeed, the value of boots, leather, and iron alone surpassed the value of *all* southern staples. The capital invested in manufacturing surpassed the combined total of capital invested in southern plantations and western farms.

THE WEST

Dominance of high-value manufacturing, as well as commerce and finance, made the Northeast a metropole (mother country) that tended to colonize the economies of the West and South. In the case of the West (meaning largely the Old Northwest Territory), that dominant-subordinate relationship took the form of neo-colonial trade flows that saw high-value manufactures go west and foodstuffs and raw materials come east. Prior to 1830 much of the West remained outside a market economy and approximated pioneer self-sufficiency. What partial commercialization and specialization in cash crops existed grew out of southern demands for foodstuffs supplemented by overseas markets, especially in the West Indies and parts of Latin America. But subsequent decades saw a remarkable increase in that commercialization and specialization, partly because the southern market continued to grow as southern plantations spread into the Southwest; partly because of enlarged European markets resulting from the repeal of the Corn Laws, the Irish famines, and the exigencies of the Crimean War; but most especially because of heightened demand from the urban markets of the industrializing Northeast. As transportation was revolutionized and eastern credit extended (Charles A. Beard called them "bands of steel and gold"), western trade patterns were reoriented from a north-south to an east-west flow and the agricultural West became integrated with the metropolitan marketplace.

Still, the end result in the West was not so rigidly "colonial" as it was to be in the South. Proximity to both agricultural and mineral raw materials, local markets rapidly enlarged by mammoth population movements, the multiplying effects of the railroads, and a willingness to invest in human capital via public education—these and other conditions in the West made possible degrees of modernization not achieved in the South. The clearest manifestations were the beginnings of urbanization, from villages to bustling cities like Pittsburgh, Cincinnati, and St. Louis, and the beginnings of manufacturing, particularly in food-processing industries and related enterprises like farm-implements production. These changes, while modifying the West's subordinate position to the metropole, in turn made western attitudes and even voting behavior (on the tariff, for example) more similar to those of the East than ever before, and westerners and easterners agreed on the need to organize the western empire on the basis of free labor, free soil, and a free market.

THE SOUTH

The Staple Trap. The South's fate in the period between Jackson and Lincoln would be characterized by modern economists as a "staple equilibrium trap." The term is not used here to suggest that the South was a changeless, quasi-feudal society. On the contrary, it was marked in this period by rapid westward mobility and even by social mobility as new elites emerged in the newly developing deep South and Texas. What the term does mean is that the South was wedded, partly by choice and more largely by necessity, to a plantation economy, using slave labor and selling staples on the world market at fluctuating world market prices. Moreover, it tended toward a one-crop staple economy, since technology (the cotton gin) and an expanding world market created by industrialization, especially in Great Britain, gave cotton such great economic advantages over every other staple. By every economic index, cotton became king indeed; and by every nonmaterial assessment, the manner in which it was produced (on large-scale plantations with slave labor) and the class that presided over its production (the planter elite) came to define the life styles, values, culture, and general conceptions of the good life and the good society. Even those so socially prominent and economically important as urban merchants, bankers, and professional people ultimately took their guidance from the planter class. While they might differ over issues like banking, or might belong to the opposing political party, when it came to substantive issues that affected the viability and profitability of slavery and cotton (most especially the issue of expansion), they generally subordinated their differences to the perceived needs of the ruling class.

The difficulty with King Cotton was not the much-debated problem as to whether slavery was profitable and maintained planters in the style to which they wished to be accustomed. The real problem, as economist Douglass C. North has said, was that "the expanding income from the marketing of [cotton] outside the region induced little growth within the South. Income received there had little multiplier effect, but flowed directly to the North and West for imports of services, manufactures and foodstuffs."[1] Even for most poor southern whites, not to mention the southern blacks, the situation offered no stimulus to escape their semisubsistence existence. And even for the planter himself life became something of a treadmill existence as he continually tried to find adequate income to balance the payments of interregional and world trade flows. To break free of the treadmill, to escape the equilibrium trap, became increasingly the most pressing problem for a region that self-consciously perceived itself as an internal colony.

Solutions Considered. Three apparent recourses presented themselves. One was to get off the treadmill altogether and emulate the North's diversification

---

[1] Douglass C. North, *The Economic Growth of the United States, 1790–1860* (New York, 1960).

and industrialization; recent research indicates that a great many southerners, including planters, periodically favored such a course. But a number of factors operated against it: qualms about the kind of labor force to use (would using blacks in urban factories not erode the valued institution of slavery? would using rural poor whites not create a proletarian class to be feared?); the lack of available capital due to fixed investments in slaves and land, conspicuous upper-class consumption, and the unfavorable interregional and world terms of trade; and the lack of a sufficiently large local market induced by the plantation's inhibition of urbanization, the region's unattractiveness to European immigration, and the forced underconsumption of slaves.

The other two solutions involved refinements of the existing agricultural system. They were not necessarily exclusive, but the failure of the one made the other all the more imperative. This failure came in the South's continuing quest for a more scientific, predictable, diversified agriculture that would enable it to escape the vicious circle of intensive farming methods that exhausted the soil. As Eugene Genovese has noted in *The Political Economy of Slavery,* such efforts did not bear fruit commensurate to the energies expended. Crop rotation was rarely feasible, since economic reality usually forced the planter to pledge too much of his cotton crop as credit collateral to permit the luxury of such a device. Commercial fertilizers were too expensive in the context of available cash and credit. Manure was scarce, implements for applying it effectively were expensive, and the vast size of many plantations mitigated against its widespread use.

Failing to break the syndrome of intensive farming, the South had but one recourse: the periodic acquisition of new land—land that would be capable of sustaining a traditonal plantation staple economy, or, as in the Southwest, capable of sustaining mining industries, for which many thought slaves suitable. In either case, the expanding new South would provide a built-in market for an older South increasingly turning to the breeding and selling of slaves. Thus slavery would survive both as a social system and as a moneymaker. In short, pressing economic and social considerations required the South to expand and get its fair share of present and future pieces of American empire. And other factors gave positive reinforcement. In the obvious political terms, there was the continuing southern need to retain sufficient strength in the United States Senate to protect its regional, functional, and class interests, and acquiring new slave states was a traditional means to that end. Moreover, in a psychological sense, as a defensive South came to define slavery as a "positive good," even as the very backbone of a civilized society, the acceptance of limitations on the expansion of slavery became a contradiction in terms; one does not restrain that which is good.

Slave auction in Virginia

As a consequence of these interlocking conditions, southern planters came to perceive a need for the extension of slave labor in an expanding empire. Whether the need was inherent in the southern system, as Genovese and Beard before him have argued, is still open to debate. But there is less doubt that southern leaders, both by their rhetoric and more importantly by their behavior, indicated that they *thought* they had to expand; and it was this perceived reality, not the hindsight of contemporary scholars, that provided the basis for their actions. For example, Frank J. Kofsky, in an unpublished manuscript on "Southern Democrats and Expansionism," made a quantitative study of congressional voting behavior from 1852 to 1860, and while his findings are incomplete and thus tentative, they strongly suggest two things: (1) that by the mid-1850s, southern Democrats (including many former Whigs) were the most militantly expansionist group in the country, as reflected in their desire to acquire new territory and to employ forceful and risky methods in doing so; and (2) there was a positive statistical correlation between the extent of slaveholding in a given southern area and the tendency of its elected representatives to be militantly expansionistic. If the picture is correct, then the chief southern solution to its treadmill existence was simply to run a little faster—and farther.

Political Party Structure and Diplomacy: 1849–1855

IF THE AMERICAN ECONOMY tended to become differentiated along sectional lines, the fact remains that at least until 1855 there still remained national political parties that seemed to transcend such bifurcations: they had national constituencies in *all* sections of the country, had programs oriented to national issues, and commanded an amazing amount of cohesiveness and party-line voting. For example, the antebellum South was anything but "solid"; the Whig party, before its deterioration after 1854, never failed to gain less than 46 percent of the southern vote.

WHIGS AND EXPANSION

This partisanship was reflected not only in the pressing domestic economic issues of the day, but also in attitudes and behavior toward American expansion. Gauged statistically and in the aggregate, the Whigs, north and south, seemed opposed to further expansion of the empire, at least in a territorial sense. For example, Joel Silbey, in his *Shrine of Party,* finds that between 1848 and 1852, all the Whigs in the Senate invariably voted against measures associated with territorial expansion and acquisition, and that the same was true of 73 percent of the Whigs in the House. Most Whigs viewed continentalism as a completed process (at least until the day when·their Anglo brothers in Canada voluntarily joined the Union). If they conceived of expansion, they did so largely in terms of "conquering by commerce" overseas; that is, opening and expanding trade outlets for American enterprise. Many business Whigs, however great their investment in manufacturing, still retained diversified holdings in foreign trade firms; moreover, even those exclusively engaged in manufacturing sometimes found it difficult to hold the home market against British competition in the quasi–free trade environment of Democratic tariffs, and they defined overseas markets as a slack absorber. Consequently, they generally limited their goals to an improved consular service, an isthmian canal and/or transcontinental railroad, and an open door for trade in Latin America and the Far East. While they saw the British as their chief commercial competitors in the world arena, their own cultural Anglophilism and their belief that trade flourished best in the context of peaceful coexistence made them shy away from high-risk policies, the use of force, and the formal annexation of overseas territory. There were specific and personal exceptions to the rule, but they do not belie the general tendencies.

NATIONAL DEMOCRATS AND EXPANSION

The Democratic party, north and south, seemed to be the party of expansion: more inclined to risk-taking, the use of force, and territorial acquisition. Silbey, for example, discovered that 78 percent of Democratic senators were either militantly or moderately pro-expansionist (about half in each category), and so were 96 percent of House Democrats (with 78 percent falling in the militant grouping). Such sentiments were especially strong among the so-called Young America faction, an interesting amalgam of ideologues, propagandists, New Orleans merchants, some southern planters, and even banking, railroad, and mercantile representatives of business Democrats in New York City. Blending seemingly intense fervor for democratic institutions and processes, a paradoxical tolerance or endorsement of slavery, and a nose for profits, they created a heady brew of expansionist rhetoric and activity. But even more staid Democrats and those who, like Douglas, were only partly associated with the Young Americans continued to define expansionism in the same manner as Polk: as a way to maintain the viability of the Democratic party and to serve the interests of its functional coalition.

The one notable exception to the generalization of Democrats as expansionists is a rather intriguing one: a minority clique of southern Democrats clustered around John C. Calhoun and its leadership heirs. Given the prior assessment of the relationship between slavery and expansion, one might logically have supposed that this group—the most militant defenders of the "peculiar institution"—ought to have been appropriately expansionist as well. That they were not is best explained in terms of tactics and calculations.

SECTIONAL DEMOCRATS AND EXPANSION

Most Democrats, as Silbey classifies them, were National Democrats who took an instrumentalist view of the Democratic party. Self-conscious of the South's minority status, they saw the best means of protecting southern interests as coalition politics with northern allies in the party. Consequently they opposed the creation of sectional political movements in the South, decried southern "nationalism," and voted along party lines rather than sectional ones until the mid- to late 1850s. The much smaller Calhoun faction, which Silbey calls "Sectional Democrats," made a very different set of calculations and opted for a very different set of tactics. They did so not out of opposition to expansion, but out of a conviction that expansion could benefit southern interests only if it were accomplished in a certain way.

Simply summarized, their reasoning went like this: (1) Trusting northern Democrats, and especially western ones, to protect southern interests was political self-deceit. Western constituencies had a vested interest in preserving the western empire on a free-soil, free-labor basis, so that when the crunch came (as it inevitably would), Democratic leaders, out of political necessity, would stay with their voters and sacrifice the South. (2) The question of organizing the empire, be it slave or free, could not safely be left to the inhabitants (the popular sovereignty concept), for in such laissez-faire competition, western farmers had all the advantages of numbers and mobility. (3) Relatedly, southern slave interests would never expand effectively into areas without permanent, predictable safeguards. Slavery, like any other form of capital or property, was inherently timid; it would not venture where the environment was inhospitable and legal protection insecure. Consequently, such sectional Democrats favored expansion only if the national government, either by legislation or preferably by constitutional amendment, guaranteed the safety of slavery; or failing that, only if pro-southern filibusters had already established de facto political control (as William Walker attempted in Nicaragua and John Quitman hoped to do in Cuba).

The exception notwithstanding, most Democrats, like most Whigs, divided over expansionist issues between 1848 and 1855 largely along party lines rather than sectional ones. The point can best be made by a summary examination of overseas and continentalist issues in that period. The latter were to reveal more stark contrasts between the parties; the former often resulted in minor differences over tactics rather than ends.

Commercialism: The Pacific

WHIGS AND DEMOCRATS differed least over their interest and approaches to expanding American trade in the Pacific; indeed, such relative homogeneity carried over in the post-1855 period as the Whigs declined and the new Republican party began its meteoric ascent. All three party coalitions contained functional groups with long-standing interest in Asian commercial development, and that interest was further whetted by two developments: the California gold rush, accompanied by the rapid development of the American west coast with its Pacific ports, and the fifteen-year Taiping Rebellion in China, which so weakened Manchu rule that it fell easy prey to further enforced commercial penetration by European powers.

HITCHHIKING AGAIN IN CHINA

Bipartisan approaches to Pacific commercialism manifested themselves in many ways. For example, just as an earlier Whig administration had been quick to exploit Great Britain's forced opening of China in the Opium Wars, so a Democratic administration in the 1850s proved equally willing to play the same game of "hitchhiking imperialism." The occasion was the Taiping Rebellion. Originally the United States Department of State welcomed the rebellion, partly because of the pseudo-Christian cast of its leaders, partly out of hope that the rebels would be more receptive to Western trade than the Manchu dynasty in Peking. But it soon became evident that the longevity of the upheaval (fifteen years overall) and its violence (an estimated twenty million dead) had made China so unstable that Western trade was greatly injured and hampered.

In other senses, however, the Taiping Rebellion proved a golden opportunity to trade expansion. First, it provided the ideal excuse for yet another foreign military intervention on the grounds that the Peking regime was not protecting foreign lives and property and not living up to its commercial agreements. Second, it made that intervention relatively easy, since China was now divided, weakened, almost prostrate. Out of these preconditions came the interventions known as the Arrow Wars by Great Britain and France in 1857 and 1858. The most immediate concrete results were the Treaties of Tientsin in 1858, in which the United States and Russia joined the two European belligerents in negotiations. The treaties opened an additional eleven Chinese ports to Western trade, liberalized the rights of residence and extraterritoriality, reaffirmed the most-favored-nation arrangement, and established an inordinately low Chinese tariff on Western imports.

OPENING JAPAN

Interparty support for Pacific commercialism also manifested itself in America's opening of Japan, a nation long closed to foreign trade save for limited dealings with the Dutch and Chinese at Nagasaki. It was a Whig administration that first conceptualized and authorized the military-diplomatic mission of Matthew C. Perry to Japan in the hope that a moderate show of force would persuade the Japanese that continued isolation courted military disaster. And it was under a Democratic administration (indeed, one that added five ships to Perry's puny squadron) that Perry executed his mission, although with only partial success, since the treaty he negotiated still kept American trading rights highly restricted and controlled. And it was yet another Democratic administration that followed up Perry's opening with the even more extraordinary mission of Townshend Harris, America's first consular representative in Japan. Acting with great tact and operating within the context of a bitter internal Japanese debate over how best to deal with the threat of foreign penetration, Harris negotiated a much broadened treaty in 1858. Specifically, it opened five new Japanese ports to trade, and on a less controlled basis; affirmed the right to acquire land for residence and warehousing; extended the rights of extraterritoriality to both civil and criminal law, thus stimulating American residency by making it safer; and granted freedom of religion, which meant that American missionaries got a headstart on their European brethren. The missionary activities were of material as well as religious significance; the missionary created commercial wants that only foreign commerce could supply, for along with him went his broadcloth coat, his matches, his cigars, his callico shirts, his demonstration steam engine—all in American lines and styles.

HAWAII AND TACTICAL DIFFERENCES

Perhaps only the Hawaiian issue revealed any party differences on Pacific policy. In general, Whig administrations evidenced little interest in annexation of the islands. Generally they sustained a position first taken in 1842, that "no power ought to take possession or to seek for any undue control over the existing Government."[2] In 1849, for example, the Hawaiian government, disturbed by French threats and with the memory of British intervention only five years old, sent a diplomatic mission to gain a tripartite guarantee of its independence by Great Britain, France, and the United States; if it failed, there was strong sentiment in Hawaiian ruling circles to opt for annexation to the United States as the next best thing to independence. But the Whig administration would neither endorse the tripartite plan (that would have minimized American freedom of action) nor follow up hints of annexation. It simply confirmed its unilateral recognition of Hawaiian independence and restated, though somewhat more vigorously, its 1842 position that American interests in the islands were second to none and that it would react negatively to any efforts to eliminate or diminish Hawaiian sovereignty.

Democrats, on the other hand, were much more open to risk-taking and to outright annexation. For example, it was pro-Democratic newspapers and Democratic party officials in California that looked with most favor on schemes of filibustering expeditions to save the islands from European avarice. And it

---

[2] Richard W. Van Alstyne, *The Rising American Empire* (Chicago, 1965), p. 130.

was the Democratic administration of Franklin Pierce that dispatched David Gregg to Hawaii in 1853 on a mission that persuaded both native elites and their white American advisers that annexation was the only way to avoid internal anarchy and/or external intrusion of the sort suffered earlier by Tahiti. Unhappily for Gregg's efforts, the resulting treaty of annexation foundered on two rocks: a financial settlement for the native monarchy and chiefs which the American Senate seemed loath to subsidize, and Hawaiian insistence on entering the Union immediately as a state—a position that ran counter to the realities of American internal politics and the administration's stated policy of determining Hawaii's political status vis-à-vis the Union at a later date. In the meantime, a change in the native royal leadership in Hawaii and the cumulative impact of French and British pressure produced a switch in Hawaiian policy and closed the door on annexation for the moment. Given that fact, the Democrats simply went Whiggish and reiterated the 1842 nonalienation policy. But by that time, of course, splits in the Democratic party over the Kansas-Nebraska Bill and the party's declining political fortunes had already taken some of the steam out of Democratic aggressiveness overseas—a fact made clear by the Pierce administration's disavowal of Perry's seizure of the Bonin Islands and Okinawa following his success in Japan. By 1855 there were no apparent differences among any political groupings on either the means or the ends of American policies in the Pacific.

Commercialism and Continentalism: The Thrust to the South

NOTHING OF THE SORT could be said about America's "thrust to the south," where sectional and functional interplay produced sharp differences between Whigs and Democrats on both tactics and goals. Between 1848 and 1955 both Central America and Cuba became focal points of intense competition between the United States and Great Britain, and both American political parties had an intense interest in its outcome. The most direct conflict came in Central America, where five small republics, sandwiched between Mexico on the north and New Granada (Colombia) on the south, had earlier attempted and failed to create a viable confederation among themselves. The consequent rivalry among the republics and the internal instability of each of them made the area easy prey for stronger powers. The result was an Anglo-American power struggle, with control of future isthmian canals the chief prize for the victor. Developments in California, China, and Japan were the major stimuli for this upsurge of interest in both Britain and the United States. The related conflict over Cuba was more indirect. The American interests in the island were varied and enormous, as we shall see. The British interest was primarily strategic and negatively formulated: to keep Cuba in Spanish hands and out of the Americans', so that neither the British West Indies nor Britain's developing power base in Central America would be threatened by an American Cuba sitting astride two of the three major routes into the Caribbean.

British comment on U.S. expansionism

WHIG APPROACHES TO CUBA
AND CENTRAL AMERICA

Whig interest in the area was strictly commercial. In Whig eyes, Central America's sole worth lay in its isthmian transit routes, which offered short cuts (transportation savings) that would facilitate and make more profitable America's trade with its own west coast and the fabled markets of the Far East. Cuba's worth was twofold: its intrinsic commercial worth had always been great, and it was of strategic value as a picket guarding the entrance to the Caribbean and projected isthmian routes. Whig tactics neatly fitted the nature of Whig interests. In Cuba, the goal was continued Spanish possession on the grounds that Spain constituted no strategic threat and that its commercial policies in Cuba were tolerable. Consequently, Whig policy rarely was more than a variation on the "no transfer" theme. Many Whigs, to be sure, did state versions of the "ripe fruit" analysis, which suggested that someday control of Cuba would pass from Spain to the United States, but for the moment their chief concern was keeping the island out of British or French hands (the Caribbean version of the Whigs' Hawaiian policy). Since this approach generally coincided with Britain's, Cuba seldom became an issue between the two powers when Whigs were in office. Indeed, British schemes to encourage the abolition of slavery in Cuba in order to make the island less attractive to southern expansionists were apparently looked upon with benign favor by many northern Whigs.

British Strongholds. Anglo-American conflict, however, was unavoidable in Central America, and Whig diplomacy was necessarily more active there. When commercial-minded Americans turned attention to the isthmian areas in the late 1840s, they found that the British had already developed three focal points of power that gave them a preemptive headstart. The most unassailable was Belize, an area just south of Mexico's Yucatan peninsula long controlled by British pirates, and gradually converted into British Honduras after Spain lost even nominal control in the early nineteenth century. The second was the Bay Islands in the Bay of Honduras, which the British had secured from Honduras in 1838 by threatening bombardment; they were strategically important for defending or attacking any projected canal in the vicinity. The third was the so-called Mosquito protectorate, where the Mosquito Indians (a mixed group of Indians, Spanish pirates, and blacks) had long evaded Spanish control by cultivating ties with British Jamaica. With the Spanish collapse, the British occupied the chief port of Bluefields and gradually developed a protectorate relationship akin to that being established with the Maori tribesmen in New Zealand. Through that protectorate, the British indirectly claimed some eight hundred miles of coast that blocked Nicaraguan and Honduran access to the Caribbean, and control of Bluefields in particular gave the British dominance over the eastern terminus of any projected Nicaraguan canal.

Whig Diplomacy: The Clayton-Bulwer Treaty. The Whig reaction, which evolved partly by design and partly by pragmatic response to events in the field, was simply to counterpoise British power thrusts to create a countervailing situation, and yet to do so in ways that left room for negotiations. The aim of such talks was constant: the neutralization of the area and the structuring of Anglo-American competition on a peaceful commercial basis. The agent for countervailing actions was one Ephraim Squier, who succeeded Democrat Elijah Hise as American executive agent in Nicaragua. Squier, reacting to local conditions, launched a bitter conflict with British Consul Fred Chatfield. Each acted beyond the instructions of his own government, and Squier's moves were more akin to those of his Democratic predecessor than the State Department found comfortable.

Specifically, both Squier and Chatfield meddled overtly in the internal politics of neighboring Guatemala on the north and Costa Rica on the south; Costa Rica was of special importance since it claimed the north bank of the river that would form part of the most talked-about canal project. Both competed over isthmian rights in Nicaragua. Squier emulated Hise in making a treaty with Nicaragua which gave the United States exclusive construction and control rights over any future canal or other transit mode; Chatfield responded that the Mosquito protectorate, by British claims, controlled the eastern terminus of any Nicaraguan canal, and hence no such canal could be built without British permission and involvement. They also dueled over the western terminus, where control of Tigre Island was the key. Squier negotiated for it in his treaty; Chatfield, in response, had a British naval unit simply seize it.

Actually, the Squier-Chatfield confrontation did serve two desirable though unexpected purposes: it brought matters to a head and forced the two home offices to confront them; yet at the same time, both Squier and Chatfield had acted so much on individual initiative that each government could easily back off from overextended positions without losing face. The resulting *quid pro quo* compromise—British evacuation of Tigre Island and American scuttling of the Hise and Squier treaties—set the stage for the famous Clayton-Bulwer negotiations. In those talks, the two governments shared a willingness to see any future canal neutralized and open to all on equal terms; but disagreement over specifics marred agreement in principle. The Whig administration in the United States felt such neutralization could be predictably secure only if the British released their hold on the Bay Islands and the Mosquito protectorate; the British government, mindful of past adventurism in Central America by the Democratic party and fearful of renewal of such activities if and when the Democrats returned to power, felt a neutral isthmian route could be ensured only by British retention of some sort of power base.

The Clayton-Bulwer Treaty of 1850, which capped those long and delicate talks, reflected that conflict within consensus. Both sides promised to abstain from seeking exclusive control of any future canal or from fortifying it; both agreed to guarantee its neutrality; and both eschewed efforts to dominate any part of Central America. But it was not clear whether the last proviso meant a British promise to liquidate existing areas of British control or simply not to acquire any additional ones in the future. Unable to secure more specific commitments from the British and in no position to force them, the administration Whigs held a dual hope in the deliberately ambiguous wording: a short-range hope that it would enable the party to sell the treaty to the American public as a British backdown and an American diplomatic victory, and a long-range one that by stressing commonality and masking differences, both sides could, with time and good intentions, produce some practical, working implementation of the treaty.

DEMOCRATS AND CENTRAL AMERICA

The Democratic party approach to Cuba and Central America was markedly more militant Such militancy grew naturally out of the party's Anglophobia as well as its penchant for territorial acquisitions and the use of force. But it also reflected the fact that the party's conceptualization of American interests in those areas was broader than the Whigs'. Many Democrats, to be sure, defined those interests primarily in the same commercial terms, but a significant number, especially southerners, went beyond that and conceived of Cuba and Central America in terms of formal empire—of the legal extension of American political sovereignty and rule and the physical migration and settlement of American people (and presumably their slaves). And up to 1855 most northern Democrats, out of either conviction or the necessity of satisfying southern needs and maintaining the party's instrumentality, supported such a conceptualization. Given the nature of such large policy goals and the obstacles to their fulfillment, the tactics employed were necessarily more aggressive than the Whigs'.

The Democrats' approach to Central America had been heralded earlier by the Polk administration. Acting to outflank the developing British power base, Polk did two things. On the southern flank, he secured ratification of the Bidlack Treaty of 1846 with New Granada, which granted isthmian rights in what is present-day Panama and committed the United States to guarantee New Granada's sovereignty there. The move not only preempted British control but gave the United States an alternative to the Nicaraguan route. On the northern flank, Polk tried to exploit secessionist sentiments in the Yucatan section of Mexico by asking congressional authority to intervene there with American troops to prevent the rumored transfer of that area to Great Britain and, by implication, to gain control of the peninsula for the United States. Neither the transfer nor the intervention took place, but Polk's tactics did foreshadow the outlines of his party's more elaborated Central American policy in the early 1850s.

The occasion for formulating that policy was the Clayton-Bulwer Treaty. Leading Democrats opposed it not only at the time of its ratification but thereafter as well, and periodically called for its abrogation. The general essence of their Central American policy was insistence that Great Britain wholly abandon its base in the area and accept American hegemony there. This would mean specifically the right to build, fortify, and control any future canals unilaterally; but it would also leave the United States the option to expand physically and politically into the area if it chose to do so. It was a grandiose policy indeed, but not a very realistic one, for the United States did not command the power to dislodge the British by force, and the British in turn seemed little inclined to leave. On the contrary, in the two years following the Clayton-Bulwer Treaty, the British retained Belize, reaffirmed their protectorate over the Mosquito coast, and even formally converted some of the Bay Islands into a colony.

Whigs responded to such moves with stern protests. Their Democratic successors in the aggressively expansionist Pierce administration went a bit further. Taking advantage of British preoccupation with events that were to produce the Crimean War with Russia, the Democrats proved far more ready to employ and condone the use of force. One striking illustration came in 1854, when an American naval unit exploited a minor incident as an excuse to bombard and level the port of Greytown in the Mosquito protectorate. Turning a cold shoulder to stern British protests, the Pierce administration even produced a chauvinistic statement defending and rationalizing the act. And its disclaimers notwithstanding, the administration lent tacit support to the filibustering military expedition of William Walker in Nicaragua, while many southern Democrats as well as the Vanderbilt commercial interests gave even more direct aid. Walker, a failure in the more conventional professions of journalism, law, and medicine, turned to the more unorthodox one of filibustering in Baja California in 1853. Two years later he applied the experience thus gained by organizing a small expedition and intervening in an insurrection in Nicaragua at the behest of one side and against the British-backed opposition of the other.

Crucial to his success was Vanderbilt's decision to deny his rail and ship facilities to the pro-British faction while extending them to Walker's. As a consequence, Walker captured the capital city, hand-picked a Nicaraguan president, and made himself commander in chief; and one year later, in 1856, he combined both jobs to make himself virtual dictator. A combination of factors

—the opposition of other Central American countries, which feared Walker's expansionist designs on them; the subversive efforts of the British, who suspected Walker was simply an American agent playing the "Texas game" at their expense; and the opposition of Vanderbilt, whom Walker foolishly alienated by backing his business rivals—all led to Walker's overthrow. But it did not come before Walker reinstituted slavery in Nicaragua and laid plans to revive the slave trade; or before his efforts had generated great enthusiasm among southern leaders; or before President Pierce (a New Englander), despite strong opposition, extended diplomatic recognition to Walker's regime. The administration took that step ostensibly to counteract British influence, but in reality to sustain the instrumentality of the Democratic party in the face of increasing divisiveness.

DEMOCRATS AND CUBA

Democratic party aggressiveness and acquisitiveness were even more apparent in the case of Cuba. Not content to wait for the fruit to fall, a coalition of interests within the party pressured a series of Democratic administrations to pluck it immediately. The mercantile constituency of *De Bow's Review* in New Orleans; the Illinois Central Railroad in Chicago; New York firms like Drake Brothers and Company and the United States Mail Steamship Company: all these interconnected interests and their political spokesmen (many of them Young Americans) saw strategic, commercial, and territorial value in acquiring Cuba. Most also seemed to assume that the island would be quickly Americanized and brought into the Union as a state, presumably slave. Previously the Polk administration had tried to buy Cuba for something between $50 million and $100 million. Failing there, both the President and Secretary of State Buchanan anxiously awaited the propitious moment when conditions in Europe and Cuba would make an American coup d'état possible.

When the Democrats were ousted from power in 1849, Democratic enthusiasts for Cuba, particularly in New York and New Orleans, had to content themselves with supporting the three abortive filibustering incursions of one Narciso López. But Pierce's triumph in the 1852 election preordained bolder efforts. Hedging its bets, the new administration tried two parallel approaches. One employed August Belmont—Young American, prominent banker, and financial angel for the party. Using his manifold contacts with European bankers, including the Rothschilds, Belmont sought to use private financial leverage to persuade the debt-ridden Spanish government to dispense with Cuba—for a price. The other avenue involved the active support of prominent members of the administration for the proposed and reputedly well-financed filibustering expedition of Governor John A. Quitman of Mississippi. Both approaches were based on the premise of internal instability in Cuba, which would make it ripe for either sale or managed revolution. Both came to nothing —Belmont's for reasons unclear, Quitman's because of procrastination and organizational problems.

These two dead ends caused much administration confusion. Spurred on by the provocative counsel of the Young Americans, who occupied many key diplomatic posts, but retarded by their own skepticism as well as that of other party members, President Pierce and Secretary of State Marcy initiated bold courses but followed through on none of them. The "ultras" entertained illusions that Spain, with a bit of a shove, was itself ripe for republican revolution, and that the severing of the umbilical cord to Cuba would be its first major consequence. On another occasion, some of them felt that Spanish seizure of an American ship, the *Black Warrior,* in Havana might become the pretext for war and the forcible absorption of Cuba, or at the very least (as Pierre Soulé, Young American minister to Madrid, attempted), the opportunity for an ultimatum-bluff that might persuade Spain to part with the island. And later yet, in an act that smacked more of desperate pleading than policy initiation, Soulé and the ministers to Great Britain and France (Buchanan and John Y. Mason) composed the so-called Ostend Manifesto, which warned against the "Africanization" of Cuba (i.e., freeing the slaves) and urged "wresting [Cuba] from Spain if we possess the power."[3] To none of these endeavors did the administration lend its unequivocal support—partly because it doubted their feasibility, partly because divisiveness over the Kansas-Nebraska Act as well as the congressional defeats in the 1854 elections eroded the base for a truly militant policy. In effect, the administration had to repudiate the Ostend Manifesto and suggest that Quitman scuttle his planned expedition. Only in renewed efforts to buy the island (this time for $130 million) was the administration's Cuban policy unambiguous; but Spain, as ever, would have none of it.

Continentalism: North America

WHIG APPROACHES TO MEXICO AND CANADA

Up to 1855, divisions over continentalism in North America were also basically partisan rather than sectional. Once the western physical limits of

---

[3] House Executive Documents, 33rd Cong., 2nd sess., nos. 93, 129, 131.

the continent had been reached with the acquisition of California and Oregon, only Canada and Mexico remained as potential areas of continentalist expansion. Whigs, north and south, evidenced neither interest nor initiative in acquiring further Mexican territory, and even though most of them probably favored the annexation of Canada and assumed that one day it would occur, few seemed inclined to hurry what they defined as a natural and voluntaristic process. For example, the Whig administration of 1849–1852 coincided with an upsurge of sentiment for annexation to the United States among some prominent Anglo business leaders in Canada. The incentives were the same as they had been a decade earlier. Electoral reverses at the hands of French-Canadians made some Anglos more inclined to join the American Union and thus bury their cultural and political opponents in an overwhelming sea of Anglo-Saxons. At the same time, the economic depression created by British repeal of the Corn Laws and the loss of Canada's favored position in the imperial system led many business leaders to define annexation as the obvious means of gaining entrée to the enormous American home market, thus restoring and expanding Canadian prosperity. Yet despite the furor created by annexationist efforts in Canada itself, the Whig administration appeared to pay them little heed.

DEMOCRATIC APPROACHES TO CANADA AND MEXICO

As always, Democrats were more adventuresome and acquisitive. To be sure, this was far less true where Canadian policy was concerned. Here Democrats seemed to share with Whigs an inclination to let annexation ripen slowly and culminate by voluntary Canadian choice, rather than to attempt the more typical American gambits of war, subversion, and coercive diplomacy. But Democrats did go one step further than Whigs by signing the Canadian-American reciprocity agreement of 1854 (the Marcy-Elgin Treaty), and congressional debates indicate that some supporters of the treaty saw it as a means of furthering the cause of annexation on the grounds that closer economic ties would invariably produce closer political ones as well. More likely, the Pierce administration accepted the treaty because British harassment of American fishing boats in Canadian waters gave them no choice. And Britain's intention in pressuring for broadened Canadian access to the American market in exchange for liberalized fishing privileges was clearly to revive the Canadian economy and lessen the pressure for annexation. Indeed, the consequent collapse of the annexationist movement in Canada made it clear that British policy-makers had a far more accurate view of reality than those few Americans who saw the treaty as an opportunity to conquer by commerce.

It was over Mexican policy, however, that Democrats differed most sharply with Whigs. The Whigs' interest in Mexico was entirely commercial and limited chiefly to securing transit rights across the isthmus of Tehuantepec. To this end, they negotiated three consecutive treaties between 1850 and 1852; all were blocked by Mexican nationalism and anti-Americanism. Democrats shared the interest in Tehuantepec; indeed, Polk had tried unsuccessfully to gain transit rights there in the peace treaty of 1848. But unlike the Whigs, many Democrats, north and south, sought to carve additional territory out of the remnants of northern Mexico. Democrats had already been prominent in filibustering raids into northern Mexico, but now the expansionist Pierce administration incorporated those goals into formal diplomacy. Employing James Gadsden, a southern railroad promoter, as negotiator, the administration sought to persuade Mexico, by money or veiled threats, to part with Lower California as well as much of its northern territory, including substantial parts of present-day northern Mexican states. Politically unable to accept such unpopular terms but anxious for Yankee dollars, Santa Ana settled for somewhat less: Tehuantepec transit rights and cession of territory (intended for a southern transcontinental railroad) which today constitutes the southernmost parts of Arizona and New Mexico. Santa Ana's compensation was $10 million U.S.; his unanticipated punishment was ouster from political power.

HOW TO CONTROL THE NEW EMPIRE?

The more pressing aspect of continentalism was not where and whether to expand farther, but how to organize and control the massive empire already acquired by the Polk administration. On that crucial issue—one far more substantive than any other on the American national scene—party cohesiveness began to stretch a bit even before 1855. In particular, the Whig party began to be sectionalized over that issue; that fact, along with its ambivalence about whether or how to exploit nativist sentiments, probably explains its rapid demise in the late 1850s. In general, northern Whigs stoutly opposed organizing any part of the western empire on a slave-labor basis. Some so-called Conscience Whigs did so perhaps out of a moral repugnance to slavery. But equally compelling was the belief that an empire organized on a free-labor basis was economically more profitable to northern business interests than one organized around slavery. In particular, the yeoman commercial farmer, raising specialized cash crops and intimately integrated into a money economy, was an infinitely better customer for eastern products than the forcibly under-consuming slave. The yeoman's demands were more diversified and his effective buying power was immeasurably higher. On the other hand, many southern Whigs began to break with the party and to support moderate measures that held out some hope for the extension of slavery. As noted earlier, however much Whigs differed with Democrats in the south over issues like banking and tariffs, when the viability and survival of slavery, cotton capitalism, and the southern way of life were concerned, they acted as southerners first and Whigs second.

Democrats split far less. A few northerners took a strong antislavery stand on organizing the empire, but not so many as earlier historians believed. And, of course, sectional Democrats in the south continued to oppose any compromise on the issue short of permanent, legal, constitutional safeguards for their treasured institution, and on that ground opposed both the Compromise of 1850 and the Kansas-Nebraska Act. Most Democrats, again both north and south, sought to work out a compromise solution to the complex issues in ways that they hoped would maintain the instrumentality and unity of the party. Thus, up to 1855, Democrats as a whole continued to vote on continentalist issues in a partisan rather than a sectional way.

Unhappily for the party, its quest for a solution was marred by the inner contradiction of diverse constituencies with antithetical ambitions for the western empire. Southern Democrats, rightly or wrongly, perceived an almost continuous need for expansion of slavery into the new lands, and indeed, as we shall see, even into lands formerly closed to slavery. But the commercial agrarian wing of the party would not endure such a prospect. Slavery in the South was one thing: on moral grounds, most were indifferent to it; on economic grounds, it was actually profitable to western farmers, for the slavery/cotton syndrome ensured a large southern market for western foodstuffs. But slavery in the empire was something else. Those ever mobile and ever land-hungry farmers had their own ambitions there. They did not wish to see large blocks of it coopted by southern planters, nor did they think that slavery held much utility for them. In their racism, they doubted the capacity of blacks to engage in more diversified and scientific farming; but even if they had thought otherwise, they rightly regarded the labor costs of seasonal farm hands as much lower than the costs of maintaining slaves on a year-round basis.

DEMOCRATS OPT FOR POPULAR SOVEREIGNTY

Faced with this contradiction, Democratic leaders like Stephen A. Douglas and Lewis Cass tried to bridge it by passing the buck to the inhabitants of the empire itself. Embracing the doctrine of popular sovereignty, they said in effect that the colonists in the empire would determine their own fate—slavery or free soil—at some political stage in the process of gradual incorporation into territories and then into states. This concept underlay part of the Compromise of 1850, which, while admitting California as a free state, said that the future organization of the immense Southwest Territory would be determined by its settlers. The same concept was the whole essence of the Kansas-Nebraska Act of 1854. Effectively setting aside the old Compromise of 1820, the act reopened the remaining unorganized part of the Louisiana Territory to political competition between slavery and free-soil proponents. Passed largely by Democratic votes, north and south, the compromise measure tried to straddle two contradictory realities: (1) many southerners doubted that slavery would be very profitable in the Southwest Territory and felt that access to previously proscribed areas (like Kansas and Nebraska) was necessary for long-term survival; (2) northern Democrats, for the reasons just noted, could not directly accept that prospect and expect to survive politically with their voters. So again, in best Democratic laissez-faire fashion, it fell to the hidden hand to solve the insolvable. Thus a half century after its acquisition, even Jefferson's empire was proving as difficult to divide as Polk's.

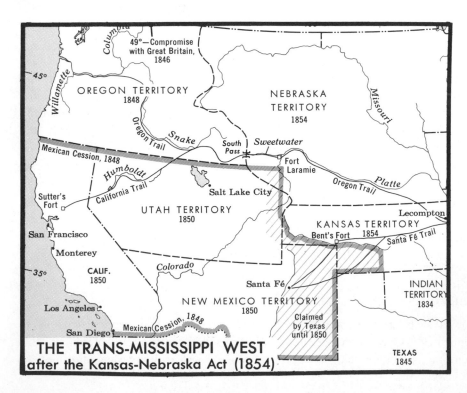

THE TRANS-MISSISSIPPI WEST
after the Kansas-Nebraska Act (1854)

EXPANSION AND THE BREAKDOWN OF
PARTY POLICY, 1855–1861

After 1855, politics increasingly became as sectionalized as the economy and conceptualizations of the good life. The Whig party disappeared from the national scene. The newly formed and rapidly developing Republican party drew its support entirely from north of the Mason-Dixon Line. But most ominous of all, the Democratic party not only lost ground to the Republican, but began to splinter on sectional lines. After nearly twenty years of amazing cohesiveness, the party found its instrumentality rapidly eroding, and with it the last major institutional link between North and South.

Democrats Divide over Continentalism. Differences over foreign policy were absolutely crucial in this fragmentation. This is especially true if one accepts Charles Vevier's contention that continentalism was simply America's internalized foreign policy,[4] for it was over the continentalist question that party bifurcations first developed. Simply put, popular sovereignty did not work as an effective way to divide the empire among interest groups. That fact of life was illustrated in the ill-fated effort to organize Kansas and bring it into the Union. Just as Calhoun had predicted, in a freely competitive, laissez-faire marketplace and political arena, the advantages of numbers and mobility resided with western yeomen and speculators; so it soon became clear that the large majority of Kansas settlers favored a free-soil, free-labor organization of their state-to-be. But southern expansionists could not accept that verdict peacefully, and the result was that abrasive exercise known as Bleeding Kansas, in which both free-soilers and slaveryites resorted to violence, and the latter in particular employed illegal political chicanery to effect a pro-slavery state constitution. Democrats paid dearly for all this by barely managing to win the presidential election of 1856 against the new Republican party.

That near disaster had antithetical impact on two groups of northern Democrats. One group (call them administration Democrats) supported President Buchanan's reasoning that the South could not be kept in the party (or even the nation) unless he could find some way of fulfilling its expansionist needs. The tactics he employed to fulfill them were, to be sure, not very ethical, especially his acceptance of the patently fraudulent pro-slave Lecompton Constitution and his ruthless use of patronage and questionable legislative tactics to seek congressional support for his policy. But ethical or not, his actions reflected a real awareness that the imperial marketplace had to be interfered with

---

[4] Charles Vevier, "American Continentalism: An Idea of Expansion, 1845–1910," *American Historical Review* (1960).

and manipulated if the South was to get its share. Western Democrats such as Douglas were forced to adopt a wholly different course. Their support of the Kansas-Nebraska Act had already hurt them politically. Since a great many of them, including Douglas, were up for reelection in 1858, they had to demonstrate to their constituencies that popular sovereignty could work honestly and effectively. In practical terms, this meant opposition to the Lecompton Constitution and an open split with southern Democrats and the administration as well.

Caribbean Policy Completes the Split.   If continentalist foreign policy first split the party, it was foreign policy overseas that helped deliver the *coup de grace*. On the one hand, the South's failure to secure Kansas as a slave state made it increasingly apparent to southern expansionist leaders that the door had been closed to any significant access to the continental empire. In their frustration, they increasingly turned their attention to Cuba, Nicaragua, and Mexico as possible areas for slave expansion. Old Kansas fire-eaters now talked more about a thrust to the south; backed their rhetoric with support for filibustering expeditions, including the last and fatal one of William Walker in 1860; and urged a vigorously expansionist policy upon the administration.

But southern expansionists did not get the foreign policy they wanted and thought they needed. To be sure, Buchanan gave them the right words, in all the inherited rhetoric of Polk and Pierce. His messages frequently talked of Cuba's place in the United States' sphere, and on several occasions he asked for congressional authorization to employ force in Central America. But rhetoric remained only that, and in the end the administration adopted a policy for the general Caribbean area which was as Whiggish as any ever employed by the late Daniel Webster.

The reasons for southern disappointment lay partly in the area of domestic politics and partly in the sphere of international diplomacy. On the home front, any revitalized expansionist thrust into the Caribbean faced two large obstacles. First of all, Republicans won control of the House of Representatives in 1858 and voted en bloc against any congressional support for Caribbean adventures. Second, while western Democrats still sometimes gave their votes to such meaningless and doomed resolutions, they did so without fervor and conviction, and no longer assigned a high priority to an aggressive foreign policy. Alienation with the South over Kansas carried over into foreign policy issues as well; the South, in western eyes, had not played by the rules, and the West no longer felt bound to them itself. Powerfully reinforcing that attitude was the hostility of western voters toward any schemes that smacked of southernism; any discerning western Democrat, then, had to soft-pedal the issue a bit. And finally, with the instrumental ties of the party already so frayed, the West was more inclined to consult its own self-interests in the Caribbean, and the essence of those interests was trade, not land. Cuba was not necessarily a piece of real estate to be owned; it was primarily a market for western foodstuffs. Nicaragua was not a place to settle in, but a place to build an isthmian canal that would expand the farmers' marketplace. In short, any aggressive foreign policy by Buchanan could count only on the support of hard-core southerners—and that was woefully shy of being enough.

Lacking the necessary power base at home, Buchanan was forced to approach Anglo-American competition in the Caribbean, especially Central America, from a much more Whiggish perspective. The problem confronted by Buchanan was that most functional groups in American society, including most of the agrarian and mercantile elements in his own party, defined American interest as primarily commercial, and commercial interest was chiefly focused on the proposed canal. But it seemed doubtful that this interest could be safeguarded and fulfilled so long as the British remained entrenched in the Mosquito protectorate and the Bay Islands. With inadequate political support to challenge the British directly and mindful of Pierce's failure to dislodge them, Buchanan had to conclude that Great Britain would not effectively vacate its power position without some kind of assurance that there was no danger of American territorial expansion in the area. He understood, that is, that the chief British interest was also commercial, but that the British believed their security could be realized only if the area was neutral—not a string of American colonies.

It was the interaction of these political and diplomatic factors that led Buchanan to abandon past Democratic party policy, with its call for abrogation of the Clayton-Bulwer Treaty and unilateral American dominance in Central America. Instead, he fell back on the original Whig position of retaining the treaty and getting British acceptance of its American interpretation. He signaled his change in three related steps: his abandonment of William Walker, his vigorous denouncement of filibustering as a means of extending American influence in Central America, and his opposition to a southern-supported resolution condemning an American naval commander involved in undermining Walker's efforts in Nicaragua. Apparently the British read these signals properly; perhaps, as well, they read the American political terrain accurately and understood the lack of support for any formal United States expansion into Central America. Whatever the reasons, they shortly thereafter concluded a series of treaties with Central American countries which seemingly abandoned the Mosquito protectorate and most of the Bay Islands. As a consequence, Buchanan was able to tell the nation in his State of the Union message in 1860 that Great Britain had accepted our interpretation of the Clayton-Bulwer Treaty, that all outstanding issues between the two countries had been resolved, and that relations had never been more amicable.

EXPANSION AND DISUNION

The die of disunion was then cast. With an expansionist South denied a share of the continental empire and cut off from any prospects of an empire overseas, the ruling classes of the South confronted two choices. First, they could accept the Republican triumph and Lincoln's election in 1860; await the inevitable Wilmot Proviso, which would permanently deny them any hope of imperial spoils; face the impending crisis of their own system; and prepare to convert to some form of free labor and make the effort to modernize their political economy. Second, they could secede from the Union, launch a southern expansion of their own, as people like Quitman had long urged, and thus retain the viability of slavery and the social structure and the good life (for elites) that it made possible. In retrospect, the first choice was obviously preferable; indeed, it essentially was the one that a defeated South would make after the Civil War. But as Genovese notes in his *Political Economy of Slavery,* if the planter elites had opted for that first choice, it "would have spelled their death as a ruling class and would have constituted moral and political suicide. Many contemporaries and many historians ever since have thought that they should have agreed to do themselves in. With this view I do not wish to argue. Neither did they."[5]

Suggestions for Further Reading

Most interesting and provocative overviews are provided by William Appleman Williams, *Contours of American History* (Cleveland, 1961), and Eugene D. Genovese, *The Political Economy of Slavery* (New York, 1961).

Again, the best economic framework is provided by Douglass C. North, *The Economic Growth of the United States, 1790–1860* (New York, 1960), and George Rogers Taylor, *The Transportation Revolution, 1815–1860* (New York, 1951).

Useful among special diplomatic studies are William L. Neumann, *America*

---

[5] Eugene D. Genovese, *The Political Economy of Slavery* (New York, 1961), p. 247.

Encounters Japan: From Perry to MacArthur (Baltimore, 1963); Basil Rauch, *American Interests in Cuba, 1848–1855* (New York, 1948); William A. Scroggs, *Filibusters and Financiers: The Story of William Walker and His Associates* (New York, 1916); Sylvester K. Stevens, *American Expansion in Hawaii, 1842–1898* (Harrisburg, Pa., 1945); Earl Swisher, *China's Management of the American Barbarians: A Study of Sino-American Relations, 1841–1861* (New Haven, Conn., 1953); Donald D. Warner, *The Idea of Continental Union: Agitation for the Annexation of Canada to the United States, 1849–1893* (Lexington, Ky., 1960); and Mary W. Williams, *Anglo-American Isthmian Diplomacy, 1815–1915* (Washington, D.C., 1916).

See also the general bibliography at the end of this volume.

CHAPTER 11

Sustaining the Vision of Commercial Empire (1861–1893)

*Diplomatic historians habitually overstudy crisis events in an end-*less syndrome of interpreting and reinterpreting America's wars, hot and cold. One of the many problems of that penchant is that each crisis event has features unique to the situation at the time it occurs, and focusing on the event alone may lead one to miss the more important dynamics of change that both precede and follow the crisis. For example, British diplomatic historians long were preoccupied with British imperialism in the seventeenth- and eighteenth-century age of mercantilism and then later with the so-called new imperialism after 1870. Like war, formal colonialism was spectacular, overt, and generally good copy. But in their preoccupation with it, British historians neglected to observe that between the stages of formal empire, Britain never stopped expanding; that expansion simply took different forms—the imperialism of free trade instead of the imperialism of colonies. But the consequences were much the same, as important countries like Brazil and Argentina became, in slightly different ways, as much controlled by Great Britain as any latter-day African colony.

Civil War Diplomacy:
Irrelevant Interlude?

Much the same kind of observation can be made about historical obsession with the American Civil War. The unique diplomatic issues raised by it were obvious: for southerners, the objective was to win the diplomatic, military, and financial support of European powers in order to tilt the balance toward southern independence; for northerners, it was quite simply to prevent that from happening. In each case, the prime object of diplomatic concern was Great Britain.

To Civil War buffs and/or those fascinated by diplomatic intrigues, the resultant narrative of Civil War diplomacy is no doubt fascinating. In reality, the story is rather simple and merits only brief telling. In essence, northern diplomacy won that contest. Great Britain respected the northern blockade of southern coasts (even in the early days of the war when it was a blockade in name only), remained generally neutral (save perhaps for de facto neglect in permitting a few Confederate commerce raiders like the *Alabama* to be built in British shipyards in violation of Britain's own laws), and failed to give the South anything approaching the crucial aid it needed. Britain did these things despite occasional war scares by the North—the most serious being the occasion when a Union warship halted the British ship *Trent* in the Caribbean and forcibly removed two prominent Confederate diplomats—and despite considerable anti-American sentiment among British leaders who rather relished the idea of seeing Britain's chief potential rival torn apart by disunion.

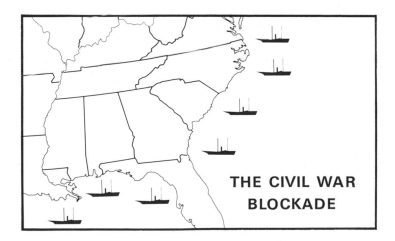

**THE CIVIL WAR
BLOCKADE**

In explaining British neutrality, historians have generally emphasized multiple factors: the division in British opinion; the general profitability in remaining neutral and selling to both sides; the adroit personal influence of Charles Francis Adams, the northern representative in London; and Britain's two-and-a-half-year stockpile of raw cotton in 1861, which made the South's embargo of its cotton (King Cotton diplomacy) an ineffectual lever for securing British aid. In the end, however, it was the military situation that was crucial. Had the war continued to go as badly for the North as it did in 1861 and 1862, it seems clear that the British would have tried to mediate the struggle in a manner that would have secured southern independence. But when the steam went out of the southern military thrust late in 1862 and the tide clearly turned in 1863, British neutrality was virtually assured.

All very interesting, one supposes. But lingering on such narrative obscures the really vital fact that the Civil War was something of a nonevent in the history of United States foreign relations. It neither changed nor stimulated nor retarded the general thrust of forces that had already been set in motion before the war and would continue apace after it.

The End of Continentalism

IT IS CLEAR that even before the war, continentalism as a force in American affairs was rapidly waning. Save for southern planters, no other functional group in American society saw much of a national or selfish need for formally colonizing new lands and opening them up to American settlement. Commercial farmers still had the last frontier on the Great Plains to exploit, and even when that frontier closed, no new wave of agrarian land hunger arose. For in an increasingly commercialized and urbanized America, the farmer was not concerned with more lands, but with the economic problems of transportation, business expertise, organization, and (most importantly) markets, as well as the social problem of how to "keep 'em down on the farm" in the face of the cities' centrifugal pull.

The fact is that even before the Civil War, the continental empire of which the Founding Fathers had dreamed stretched from sea to sea. To be sure, there still remained Canada and Mexico, but each of them served to illustrate the same pattern: an atavistic, halfhearted last gasp of continentalism followed by adoption of a new and more subtle mode of American penetration—what James G. Blaine called the "annexation of trade."[1]

---

1 Walter LaFeber, *The New Empire* (Ithaca, N.Y., 1963), p. 106.

CANADA TO THE NORTH

Take Canada, for example. Between 1866 and 1871 the United States did several things that smacked of residual continentalism. In 1866 Congress abrogated the Marcy-Elgin Treaty, at least partially on the grounds that depriving Canada of ready access to the American market might stimulate annexationist sentiments among affected Canadian interests. In 1867 Seward's purchase of Alaska carried with it the hope that British Columbia, seeing itself outflanked both to the north and to the south and widely separated by most of a continent from the rest of settled Canada, would perceive the wisdom of joining the Union. (Fifty-four-forty—and without a fight!) Between 1866 and 1870 the American government did little to stop the filibustering raids of the Anglophobic Fenian Brotherhood into Canada—raids that some Canadians thought to be American-supported efforts to terrorize them into asking for annexation, and hence peace. Finally, between 1866 and 1871, Americans periodically and sometimes officially demanded wildly extravagant financial compensation from Great Britain for its actions during the Civil War. The most extreme demand was for British payment of fully half the cost of the war on the grounds that Britain's allegedly premature recognition of Confederate belligerency and its construction of Confederate commerce raiders had prolonged the war for twice its normal course. To those pushing such demands—Charles Sumner, chairman of the Senate Foreign Relations Committee, was the most prominent and forceful—it was clear that Great Britain could pay such an exorbitant bill only by ceding Canada to the United States.

Yet all these efforts had a certain desultory and unreal quality. That they were doomed to extinction was signaled by two coinciding events. First, the British sought to organize their disunited Canadian colonies into a single confederation with a good deal of national autonomy; the act was in large part a conscious effort to lay to rest forever the ghost of American annexation. Second, in the arbitration that followed the Anglo-American Treaty of Washington in 1871, the United States in effect gave up any meaningful effort to collect indirect financial claims and settled for compensation for direct depredations to American shipping committed by Confederate raiders built in Great Britain. Almost symbolically, the act signaled the end of significant continentalist ambitions for Canada. On the contrary, it ironically ushered in several decades of friction between the United States and the new Canadian confederation over tariffs, boundaries, and fishing and sealing rights. And when those issues were finally settled, most American leaders had come around to the position that using Canada as an economic back door to the British imperial trading system was far more profitable than annexing it.

MEXICO TO THE SOUTH

Mexican-American relations followed a similar pattern. In the 1860s the chief American concern was keeping Mexico out of European hands and thus maintaining whatever future options the United States chose to exercise there. During the American Civil War, France (in the temporary company of Great Britain and Spain) had militarily intervened in Mexico on the ostensible grounds of forcing payment of debts past due. After the other two nations departed, France, under Napoleon III, sought to establish a proto-Gaullist special relationship with Mexico by intervening in that country's own civil strife on the side of clerical (and thus conservative) landholders against the secular (and thus liberal) landholders. The consequence was the establishment of a French protectorate, with a Habsburg puppet, Maximilian III, on a newly contrived Mexican throne, enforcing his good intentions with French bayonets. Hamstrung during the American Civil War by the pragmatic need to avoid pushing France into a pro-Confederate policy, Union leaders could dissent only mildly to the French gambit, though the United States, unlike most countries, did not recognize Maximilian's regime. But as the war moved clearly toward northern victory, both congressional and executive leaders spoke in increasingly harsh and militant terms against the continuing French presence; implicitly, the veiled threats were backed by the power of a large, battle-tested, and triumphant Union army. Faced with that reality, with the escalating costs of French involvement, with continuing social upheaval in Mexico itself, and with the looming danger of an aggressive Prussia, Napoleon finally decided to liquidate his Mexican adventure. Without French support, Maximilian and his regime quickly came to a fatal end.

The demise of the French protectorate left the United States with relative freedom to play its Mexican options as it saw fit. As in the Canadian situation, some American groups still labored in the dying vineyard of continentalism. This was especially true in the 1870s, when an interlocking directorate of United States Army regular officers and Texas Rangers, congressmen, and cattlemen conspired to foment a Mexican-American conflict that might lead to annexation of more of Mexico's northern territory. Regular army officers—many of them former Civil War generals since demoted several ranks—joined the plot because it seemed evident to them that there was only a limited number of American Indians to kill or corral, and once that chore was accomplished, only a war at the Mexican border (along which half the tiny American army was stationed) could save them from the oblivion of a peacetime army, with no wars to fight and no glories and promotions to win. As for the Texas interests, the cattle boom put a premium upon Mexican stock and lands, although the given reasons for their involvement were Indian raids and rustling from south of the border. Key figures in this coalition were Texas Democrats in Congress who had been prominent in arranging the deals that led to the disputed election of Republican Rutherford B. Hayes to the presidency in 1876. One of their rewards was the initial refusal of Hayes to recognize the new Mexican government of Porfirio Díaz.

But Texan elites and the minuscule officer corps were no match for the more numerous and powerful business elites throughout the country, which took a dim view of this anachronistic approach to Mexico. Mindful of the value of foreign trade and investment, which the depression of the 1870s had dramatized, and increasingly aware that the new Díaz regime held some promise of political stability and hospitality for American business ventures, numerous chambers of commerce and mining and railroad interests argued the greater efficacy of informal economic penetration. In the ensuing contest, commercialism triumphed easily over lame-duck continentalism. Hayes recognized the Díaz regime, several militant expansionists fared badly in congressional investigations, and finally Secretary of State Blaine capped it all by publicly declaring in 1881 that the United States no longer had any territorial interest in Mexico, that it viewed Mexico only as an area where it might invest its "large accumulation of capital."[2] From that point onward, the mode was once more the annexation of trade. Exploiting Díaz' liberal development policy, the United States doubled its trade in Mexico during each of the last two decades of the nineteenth century, and investments in railroads, mining, agriculture, and oil surpassed Britain's large stake to become almost equal to all other foreign investments combined. Unfortunately for Mexico, almost none of the money went into manufacturing; the railroads ran only north and south from American mines to the American market (with no beneficial spread effect for the Mexican economy); and profits from extractive industries were largely drained back to American parent companies. The relationship was far more profitable and much less burdensome to the United States than adding a few more stars to Old Glory.

Social Structure and Commercialism: The Role of Cosmopolitans

If continental expansionism expired in the postwar period, commercialism did not. On the contrary, it was sustained and revivified, and ultimately became

---

[2] Ibid., p. 51.

Burgeoning U.S. industrialism

the chief force behind America's emergence as a world power in the 1890s. This needs to be explained, for few economic preconditions existed to account for its staying power. In an America that was becoming increasingly industrialized and dominated by those who guided the industrialization, there was little objectifiable need for foreign markets in the years between 1861 and 1893. On the contrary, the domestic scene abounded with opportunities. A high birth rate, large-scale European immigration, and an even more massive migration of rural populations to cities created a vast new national urban market. The boom in railroad building also provided multiplying opportunities for the economy. And finally, if that economy occasionally became unbalanced, as it did in the Panic of 1873 and again in the downturn of the mid-1880s, it still had its own internal colonies to develop—the reconstructed South and the West's last frontier.

Any persuasive explanation of the persistence of commercialism must take into account the radical changes in the social structure brought about by urbanization, industrialization, and bureaucratization. While the social structure allowed internal social mobility, it nevertheless became increasingly stratified. That stratified structure can be seen as a vertical continuum from the local to the cosmopolitan. Those grouped at the local end of the continuum (and that would include most Americans in the late nineteenth century) had a range of activities and interests spatially confined to the geographic unit of the local community; their human consciousness and identity were rooted in and limited to that community; in the realm of foreign affairs they had little interest, information, or influence. They played almost no role in the preservation and fostering of commercial expansion.

Two other groups, however, played vital parts. One group, which we shall call the functionals, occupied the middle ranges of this vertical continuum. Unlike locals, they had a range of interests and activities, as well as a level of consciousness and identity, which transcended the limits of the inclusive local community. Instead of being organized spatially, they tended to develop a more exclusive organization on the basis of occupational function rather than geography. Typically they included interest groups in business, agriculture, and labor that collectively tried to influence markets and prices for their own benefit. The other group that was to have relevance to the continuation of commercialism was a small elite clustered at the cosmopolitan end (or top) of the social structure. These cosmopolitans had impersonal and widespread contacts and relationships; their educational experience (including such informal education as travel) had expanded their awareness; their interests, activities, and consciousness transcended the spatial limits of locals and the interest-group limits of functionals. In short, cosmopolitans were system-makers. They integrated many functional groups from widely differing geographic areas; they systematized human relationships on a large scale; they concentrated decision-making at the top. In other words, these were the men who managed America's new industrial order in both the business and the political worlds; those who did not actually engage in these activities themselves were intellectuals who observed, understood, and wrote about these social processes.

The role of the cosmopolitan in preserving commercialism lay precisely in his capacity to conceive of his society as a whole, as a system, and to anticipate and project its needs over time. In late-nineteenth-century America, most cosmopolitans could be placed in one of three categories: intellectuals; top-drawer captains of industry and finance who guided the economy down the road of vertical integration toward the elusive goal of oligopoly capitalism; and the upper echelon of the executive branch of the federal government. It was the last group that was most crucial in the years between the Civil War and the explosive 1890s, the years when America moved haltingly but continuously from commercialism frustrated to commercialism fulfilled. For it was these men in the executive branch who gave specific strategic formulation to the long-term needs of overseas commercial expansion and who had the power and occasionally the boldness to conceive and execute foreign policy designed to transform goals into achievements.

William H. Seward

WILLIAM H. SEWARD

Of those policy-makers that might be legitimately described as cosmo-politans, one was without peer: William H. Seward, Secretary of State under Presidents Lincoln and Johnson in the 1860s. It was Seward who developed an integrated and comprehensive conceptualization of American overseas expansion, a conceptualization that virtually every one of his successors in the next three decades largely accepted and acted upon. Seward's system rested upon two related premises. One was his neo-mercantilist assumption that "the nation that draws the most materials and provisions from the earth, and fabricates the most, and sells the most of productions and fabrics to foreign nations, must be, and will be, the great power of the earth." The other was his geopolitical notion that the great commercial battles would be decided in the Far East—"that empire has, for the last three thousand years...made its way constantly westward."[3] As a consequence, the one overriding goal of his foreign policy was American economic penetration of Japan, Korea, and especially China. He did not, however, seek formal colonies there; colonies would bring heavy burdens both material and spiritual. He sought instead simply what his successor and admirer, John Hay, was to call for in 1899: an open door to those markets, in which the United States would enjoy trading privileges on a nondiscriminatory, most-favored-nation basis. Confident of

[3] Ibid., pp. 25–27.

America's ever increasing industrial might, he was certain that such an open door would eventually give America the major share of that trade and the power that would flow from it.

The Far East.   Efficient connection of the American industrial base with Asia's markets led Seward to push for three related linkages. First, he strongly pushed the creation of a system of transcontinental railroads that would be tied into a system of transpacific steamship lines. Indeed, he put his own diplomacy to work in behalf of the railroad goal by pushing through the Burlingame Treaty of 1868, which facilitated the importation of cheap Chinese labor to help build the western railroads. (Later, when those railroads were built and Chinese labor competed for scarce jobs, the United States was to reverse course and move to the virtual exclusion of Chinese immigration, to the frequent embarrassment of the State Department.) Second, he endorsed the speedy building of a canal across Central America which would give much of America a money-saving short cut to Asian markets. Third, while remaining opposed to colonialism in heavily populated market areas like China, he advocated an integrated though limited system of insular imperialism. He felt the United States ought to acquire colonies, protectorates, or (at the very least) naval bases in the island perimeter of the Caribbean (Cuba, Puerto Rico, Santo Domingo, the Virgin Islands), which would give the United States strategic control over the approaches to the future canal. In the Pacific, his strategic concept was essentially one of a pincer: the United States ought to control both the northern flank of the North Pacific (the Aleutians) and the southern flank (Hawaii).

Conceptualization is one thing; implementation is quite another. Indeed, between 1861 and 1893 all of Seward's integrated schemes fell short of fulfillment. Illustrative was the developing state of American affairs in the Far East. Japan, for one, managed to escape the dependency trap of a Western Open Door policy. This was no mean feat, for in the early 1860s Japan seemed fated to relive the kind of syndrome China had experienced in the Opium and Arrow wars. Basing their actions on Japanese outrages against foreigners and failure to live up to treaty commitments, Great Britain and France resorted to military force to compel Japan to open the door still further. On a few occasions American naval units joined European powers in a show of strength, and in one instance the American sloop *Wyoming* actually sank two Japanese ships. But such an American military role was largely nominal; the United States was content to play the game of hitchhiking imperialism in Japan as well as in China. At any rate, Japan was not about to allow itself to be victimized. Beginning in 1867 with the famous Meiji restoration, political power in Japan passed to a determined elite that managed to blend traditional Japanese values with a commitment to modernization which was to produce rapid social and economic change. The chief force behind these changes was Western technology, with which Japan made itself militarily secure against any further Western efforts at coerced penetration. The chief consequence was an industrial revolution that enabled Japan to escape any potential economic colonialism, and indeed to make it a rival rather than a victim in the great game of expansion. Interestingly, the United States was the first to recognize the facts of life, and in 1878 negotiated a treaty that granted tariff autonomy to Japan. From that point onward, America's main efforts were geared not to forcing open the door to Japan, but to seeking informal Japanese cooperation in keeping open the door to China.

In Korea, American policy was more positive and successful, and yet its consequences were just as ephemeral. Beginning in the 1860s, the United States had made sporadic efforts to open the Hermit Kingdom to commercial intercourse. Finally, in 1882, Commodore Shufeldt of the United States Navy repeated Perry's gambit (with Chinese help) and made the United States the first Western power to establish trade and diplomatic relations with Korea. Subsequently America pursued a policy of maintaining Korean autonomy and the Open Door policy. Led by the remarkable Horace Allen—diplomat, missionary, and ally of American enterprise—American businessmen and especially missionaries enjoyed some instances of success in the 1880s and early 1890s. But almost from the beginning, efforts to secure American goals of autonomy and openness were ordained to fail. To China, Korea was a traditional tributary servant; to Russia it was a potential safeguard to the Trans-Siberian Railroad; to Japan it was a potential dagger pointed at the Japanese homeland. Given that political mix, an autonomous Korea (and the Open Door there) stood little chance of survival, a fact made abundantly clear by the Sino-Japanese War of 1894–1895 and more decisively so a decade later by the Russo-Japanese War.

Of all the Asian commercial prizes, then, only China held any long-term potential; happily it was the largest of the prizes and historically the most attractive. That China did remain ostensibly open and independent, however, had little to do with American actions. American diplomacy was relatively inactive, save for its efforts to assuage China's anger over ill treatment of its subjects in California and other western states and to negotiate de facto but face-saving acceptance of congressional restrictions on the immigration of Chinese. American business, save for kerosene (Standard Oil's *Oil for the Lamps of China* promotion) and some southern cotton textiles, evidenced only slight interest in any immediate development of Chinese markets. And American missionaries, while extremely active in China, had little of the success there that they were to enjoy in Korea; indeed, their presence sometimes created counterproductive xenophobic feelings among Chinese. If China remained open, it was almost entirely Great Britain's doing. Given its commercial supremacy, Great Britain defined the Open Door as in its own best interests and acted accordingly. British merchants captured the bulk of China's foreign trade; British civil servants staffed and ran the Chinese customs service; British diplomacy worked for a cooperative acceptance of the Open Door by European powers; and Britain's navy and its Indian army supplied the military muscle to boost that policy. Under those circumstances, the United States could afford the luxury of relative passivity; Americans could let the British implement American policy while waiting till conditions brought more Americans to share the interest of cosmopolitans like Seward in China's future.

The Canal. Seward's auxiliary projects—an isthmian canal in Central America and insular imperialism in the Caribbean and the Pacific—also bore mixed fruits. No substantive projects for actual construction of a canal developed. A route still had to be chosen; engineering problems had to be solved; and the government's role, either in subsidizing private promoters or in building the canal on its own, had to be determined. Save for a general inclination to favor a Nicaraguan route (a choice recommended by President Grant's Interoceanic Canal Commission in 1876), little was done to cope with these problems. Since the government (at least until 1889) showed a laissez-faire preference for a canal built by private enterprise alone, and since this proved financially impossible, none of the efforts of American outfits like the Maritime Canal Company led to much real construction progress.

The government's hands-off approach to canal financing did not reflect indifference to the canal project itself. On the contrary, the opening and successful operation of the Suez Canal in 1869 only whetted the appetites of United States policy-makers. A number of developments bore witness to this fact. One was the extremely hostile reaction to the efforts of a private French company to build a canal in Panama in the 1880s—a reaction that included a show of American naval strength off Central America and unsuccessful diplomatic arm-twisting to persuade Colombia (of which Panama was then a part) to cancel the French concession. A second example of quickening American interest was the 1885 military intervention in Panama, where American naval and Marine units helped put down an insurrection that threatened American interests in the area.

Finally there was the mounting effort to rid America of the albatross of the Clayton-Bulwer Treaty of 1850 and to have a canal that was unilaterally constructed and controlled by the United States. President Grant first took this position, more personally than officially, when he spoke at length in one of his presidential messages of the commercial cornucopia that awaited completion of an isthmian canal. His successor, President Hayes, elevated that position to official national policy. The succeeding administration made several diplomatic efforts to persuade Great Britain to abrogate or significantly amend the Clayton-Bulwer Treaty (an effort sanctioned by a congressional resolution). And when those efforts failed, that same administration simply ignored the Anglo-American agreement altogether and negotiated the Frelinghuysen-Zavala Treaty with Nicaragua, which gave the United States exclusive unilateral canal rights in that country. The treaty fell barely short of the two-thirds majority in the Senate necessary for ratification, and had it not been for the habitual party-line voting that defeated almost every treaty in the late nineteenth century, it certainly would have passed. The boldness of the government in making such a treaty and the wide extent of congressional support made it clear that the concept of a neutralized Anglo-American canal had very numbered days and that at some not too distant time the British would have to contest or concede the new American policy.

Insular Imperialism. Insular imperialism—the last link in Seward's ambitious plan—also had a rather checkered career in this transitional period. In the Caribbean, it was unfailingly frustrated. During the ten-year Cuban revolution that began in 1868, President Grant came perilously close to taking diplomatic steps that very probably would have embroiled the United States in war with Spain over Cuba's future; only lack of support and the caution of his Secretary of State pulled him up short. Both the Johnson and the Grant administrations negotiated various agreements with the Dominican Republic and Haiti for either outright annexation, protectorates, or naval bases. Every time one of these agreements managed to reach the United States Senate, the Senate declined to approve. And finally, Seward managed to negotiate a treaty for purchase of the Virgin Islands from Denmark—a treaty approved by a plebiscite of the islands' inhabitants but once more rejected by the U.S. Senate. The explanations offered for this unbroken string of fiascos are many: white supremacists' racism; the pragmatic calculation that the burdens of rule outweighed its advantages; genuine anticolonialism; the corrupt and shady character of speculative business interests involved in some of the negotiations (particularly Grant's efforts in the Dominican Republic); and the lack of sufficiently broad-based interest-group support—that is, the inability of most functionals to perceive the national interests in the Caribbean in the same way that cosmopolitans did. But analysis of congressional roll calls suggests once more that partisanship was perhaps the crucial variable. During the Johnson administration, at the height of Republican power, party splits between Radicals and Conservatives ensured factional bloc voting against anything that Johnson might propose; and from the Grant administration onward, when Republican power and Democratic power were often balanced, Democrats habitually voted against most Republican treaties. The three administrations following Grant's kept clear of the political minefield of insular imperialism. Not until 1890–1891, when the Harrison administration tried to force Haiti to part with Môle St.-Nicholas and the Dominican Republic to give up Samana Bay, did the second round of insular imperialism begin—a round that was to end more successfully, with Puerto Rico as an American colony and Cuba as an American satellite.

In the Pacific, Seward's projects came far closer to fulfillment. Securing the northern flank of the Kiska-Honolulu axis proved an easy windfall, for the purchase of Alaska in 1867 brought with it the Aleutian Islands. Extending as far westward into the northern flank of the Pacific basin as the Marshall Islands into the southern, the Aleutians gave America strategic control of the Great Circle sea approaches to Siberia, Manchuria, north China, and Japan. As the chairman of the House Foreign Affairs Committee put it in arguing for the Alaska purchase, the Aleutians would be the "drawbridge between America and Asia."[4] That the Senate approved this acquisition while disapproving those negotiated in the Caribbean owes something to many things: Seward's marvelous propaganda campaign; the idiosyncratic support of Charles Sumner, chief Radical Republican spokesman on foreign policy; the underpopulated character of Alaska, indicating that colonial burdens would be light and opportunities for WASP settlement plentiful (another Texas); the obvious fact, for all the ludicrous criticism, that the commodity bought was cheap at twice (or many times) the price; the desire not to offend the seller, Russia, mythical friend of the Union during the Civil War; and the general feeling that acquisition of Alaska made annexation of all or part of Canada somehow more likely—an objective approved, however abstractly, by virtually everyone with well-informed opinions on foreign policy.

Seward's objective on the southern flank fell short of maximum realization when his efforts to annex Hawaii failed. The countervailing balance of various business, labor, and religious groups simply made the effort impossible. Failing

---

4 Ibid., p. 29.

there, Seward did manage in 1867 to acquire Midway Island as a potentially valuable American way station between Hawaii and north China via a northwest tangent toward Japan. But Seward's successors did much to move Hawaii closer to total Americanization. The first-stage vehicle was a trick taken from Canadian-American relations: reciprocal trade treaties, specifically that of 1875 and its expanded and renewed version ratified in 1886. Fearful of a growing Hawaiian commercial orientation toward Australia and the British trading bloc, American negotiators designed the reciprocity treaties to redirect those patterns and make Hawaii "industrially and commercially a part of the United States"; not so much because of Hawaii's intrinsic economic worth, for in fact the trading arrangements largely favored the islands and not the United States, but because integrating Hawaii into the American market enhanced American strategic-political authority in that halfway house to oriental markets.[5] Indicative of such primary aims were auxiliary features of both treaties. The 1875 treaty contained a nonalienation pledge by which Hawaii promised not to alienate any of its sovereignty, however small or large, however direct or indirect, to any other nation (save the United States, of course). And the 1886 treaty added to that pledge the right to establish an American naval base at Pearl Harbor.

The effect of those treaties was to make Hawaii a virtual American protectorate. But the Harrison administration, in its revivification of insular imperialism, sought to make the relationship more literal. Taking advantage of the impending McKinley tariff, whose provisions would deprive Hawaii of its favored position in the American sugar market, Secretary of State Blaine sought to persuade Hawaii that it could have bountiful market privileges if it would reaffirm its nonalienation pledge, make the Pearl Harbor concession both permanent and exclusive, and grant the United States the right of unilateral military intervention when and if the United States saw fit. Neither in essence nor in particulars did the proposals differ much from the Platt Amendment, later forced upon a reluctant Cuba in 1902. The Hawaiian government, however, would not buy the treaty on American terms, a fact attributed to the anti-American influence of Canadian Pacific Railroad officials and to the native monarchy.

Failure of the protectorate scheme led the Harrison administration to escalate to stage three, formal annexation, especially when a change in the Hawaiian monarchy put an absolutist, antiplanter queen on the Hawaiian throne. The immediate result was a planter-led revolution, actively supported by the American minister to Hawaii, aided effectively by American naval

---

[5] Ibid., p. 142.

personnel, and tacitly encouraged by the highest officials in the American government. The ultimate result was a treaty of annexation, early in 1893, which the Harrison administration pushed on the grounds that an independent Hawaii (even one pro-planter and pro-American) might prove unstable; that other nations, like Great Britain and Japan, had designs on Hawaii, and that these had to be preempted (Texas, California, *ad infinitum* again); that Hawaii was a rich land, valuable in itself; and most importantly, that Pearl Harbor was vital to the overall American strategic scheme for the Pacific, and that its tenure could be assured only if Hawaii were firmly in American hands. Unfortunately for insular imperialists, time ran out on the outgoing administration, and the new Democratic regime of Grover Cleveland chose (as we shall see) to scuttle the treaty. But it proved only a short five-year stay of annexation.

JAMES G. BLAINE AND LATIN AMERICA

Seward's conceptualization of American commercial empire was ill developed in one sense. In his fascination and preoccupation with the Far East, he tended to give insufficient attention to another underdeveloped area that was both closer and, in the minds of many Americans, more important: Latin America. It fell to another cosmopolitan Secretary of State, James G. Blaine,

James G. Blaine

to fill that gap in the 1880s and early 1890s. Like Seward, Blaine was a Republican; like Seward, he spoke largely, though not exclusively, for industrial corporate interests in the East; like Seward, he believed that America had "developed a volume of manufactures which, in many departments, overruns the demand of the home market"; like Seward, he believed that the problem could be solved and American greatness assured by a systematic, government-supported expansion into the markets of the world.[6] Unlike Seward, he believed that the most natural and lucrative opportunities for commercial expansion lay in Latin America, not in Asia (although he was by no means indifferent to the Far East, any more than Seward was indifferent to South America).

Blaine was Secretary of State for a brief period in the early 1880s, during the short-lived Garfield administration, and then again for most of the four years of the Harrison administration, 1889–1893. During that decade he codified his thoughts about Latin America and shaped his policies accordingly. When Blaine surveyed the Latin American terrain, he was deeply troubled by two things. First and foremost, he was disturbed by the structure of that area's international trade. Specifically, he noted that while the area sold much to the United States, particularly sugar, coffee, fruits, and minerals, it did not buy a commensurate amount back. Instead, most of Latin America tended to buy its manufactured goods from Europe, principally from Great Britain. It thus became the first goal of Blaine's system of Pan Americanism to reorient those trade patterns in ways that would expand markets for American finished products in Latin America and produce a trade balance that favored the United States.

The second thing that troubled Blaine about Latin America was its political instability and internecine military strife. It disturbed him less for abstract reasons than for the very practical consideration that peace and stability were absolute prerequisites for a flourishing, expanding trade. Throughout this period there were abundant episodes to justify his concern: boundary disputes between Mexico and Guatemala; similar controversies between Argentina and Chile; and the War of the Pacific, in which Chile successfully used military force against Peru and Bolivia to acquire valuable nitrate lands. Finally, and most dramatically, there was the Chilean revolution of 1891, which brought Chile and the United States to the brink of war. The United States had been extremely unpopular in Chile for fully a decade because of the Peruvian bias of its efforts to mediate the War of the Pacific—a policy undertaken because of suspicion that British investors were behind Chile's warmaking. That residual anti-American sentiment took a giant leap forward

---

[6] Ibid., p. 106.

when the United States appeared to back an unpopular regime against which prominent Chilean congressmen and their followers had revolted. The appearance was not wholly deceiving. Finding the established regime not too unfriendly to American interests, but fearful that the revolutionary opponents were being supported by British and German elements, the United States took a number of not very neutral steps. When the anti-American insurgency ultimately triumphed, relations between the two governments remained dangerously tense. That uneasy truce was broken late in 1891 when a barroom brawl between Chileans and American sailors on leave in Valparaiso resulted in several American deaths and numerous injuries. Unseemly and irresponsible displays of incendiary rhetoric were launched from both sides, climaxed by President Harrison's virtual invitation to Congress to declare war. Only a last-minute Chilean apology and promise of compensation avoided armed conflict. In the face of such episodes, Blaine became increasingly convinced that alternatives to war had to be found. This then became the second and related goal of his Pan Americanism.

Blaine sought to realize his goals of economic expansion and political pacification through the device of an inter-American conference. Originally conceived during the brief Garfield administration, the conference did not become reality until 1889. Held in Washington and with Blaine presiding, the gathering of the hemisphere's representatives had to cope with the two main objectives of Blaine's Pan Americanism: (1) a hemispheric customs union that would facilitate industrial America's economic penetration of its underdeveloped neighbors; (2) a system of arbitration to avoid future inter-American conflicts. Latin American distrust, particularly on the part of Argentina and Chile, made it impossible for Blaine to get the kind of consensus his proposals required. Nonetheless, he did realize some minimum objectives. He did get the creation of the International Bureau of American Republics (later the Pan American Union), whose general purpose was to foster peaceful understanding among American nations. In the commercial sphere, he fell back upon the policy pushed by the Arthur administration in the early 1880s; that is, in lieu of a general customs union, he resorted to negotiation of bilateral reciprocity treaties with each individual Latin American country. Unfortunately, the protectionist McKinley tariff of 1890 forced him to use coercion in those negotiations rather than the gentle persuasion he preferred. However unwillingly, he used the coercive power Congress had put at his disposal and threatened each Latin American country with a ban on its sugar, molasses, coffee, or hides if it did not give American exports tariff advantages that he deemed sufficiently liberal. Only three of the countries approached failed to bend the knee properly.

Social Structure and Commercialism:
The Role of Functionals

UNDOUBTEDLY, it was a cosmopolitan elite, particularly in the executive branch of the national government, that played the key role between 1861 and 1893 in sustaining a vision of commercial empire. But to focus on that group alone obscures the secondary but important contribution of middle-echelon functionals in the revivification of marketplace expansionism. Functionals were especially important in the crucial transitional decade of the 1880s, when a number of special interest groups came to perceive that they had a vested interest in overseas commercial expansion. But having perceived that fact, they had to persuade a broader coalition of individuals and groups—including those with no vested interest in marketplace expansion—that such a policy was desirable. And to do that, they had to generate a conception of the national interest that transcended and yet still served their self-interest. As it turned out, the conception generated was identical to that already preserved by cosmopolitan elites; but the positive reinforcement was undeniably crucial in establishing the preconditions for the fulfilled commercialism of the 1890s.

MISSIONARIES

A half-dozen functional groups came to fit such a pattern in the 1880s; four were essentially economic groupings and two were functionally noneconomic, although the facts of life required them to think and act in economic terms. One of the latter consisted of American missionaries, especially those involved in the China missions, some of them dating back to the 1840s. Most of those missions had begun with high expectations of success; early in the mission game, a few had even approximated those expectations. But as an aggregate, American missionaries of the late nineteenth century, whether evangelical or traditional, increasingly sensed that their achievements had fallen considerably short of the mark. The result was an agonizing reappraisal that led many missionaries (though by no means all) to one conclusion: that Christianity and Western civilization (both equally difficult to define) were inseparable. To state it another way, they concluded that the chief obstacle to the spread of Christianity was the whole set of values, ethics, mores, tastes, and life styles that was the very fabric of Chinese society. Thus, before China could be Christianized, it had first to be Westernized; or, since most American missions were Protestant, it might be said more simply that the Protestant ethic had to precede the Protestant religion, or at least they had to go hand

Missionary zeal

in hand. Once this was decided, it became evident to these missionaries and their supporters that the Western penetration of China had to be markedly accelerated if they were to succeed in their self-appointed tasks. Being Americans as well as churchmen, they preferred a vanguard role for America in that penetration. Being generally anticolonial (like most Americans) and having a paternalistic attachment to Chinese integrity, they tended to prefer commercial rather than political penetration. As experienced frontiersmen, they well understood the revolutionary impact that Western technology, trade, and bureaucratic techniques had on the structures of other societies. So marketplace expansion was an eminently acceptable mode of penetration; indeed, the best of all.

This line of reasoning led mission people to several courses of action. First, it led many missionaries to do what they could personally to expand American influence. In Korea, Horace Allen and company performed ably; in Hawaii, missionaries and their entrepreneurial sons speeded the task of Americanization; in Samoa, American missionaries counteracted the influence of their English and German counterparts; in the Middle East, the missionary-founded Roberts College in Constantinople became the first, albeit small, entering wedge of American interest. Second, most of the traditional missions spread the social gospel in their day-to-day activities overseas. Rather than stressing immediate conversion, they emphasized the secular work that they had defined as a necessary preliminary to real conversion. They set up vocational schools, hospitals, retail shops, and university projects such as Yale-in-China, and undertook the education of Chinese students in America (from which they would return thinking, acting, and buying American).

Finally, like every other functional group, they made themselves into a propaganda lobby to persuade other Americans that commercial penetration of China was generally desirable. In order to accomplish this they had to go beyond saying that such penetration benefited missionaries and the process of Christianization. Such a narrow, self-interested pitch would have had minimal appeal. Instead, they had to argue that commercial expansion was in the national interest—in the interest of *all* Americans, whether or not they had any personal stake in a place like China. The arguments exploited were manifold: the sense of American mission; the white man's burden; the survival of the fittest; Manifest Destiny; Christ's command to spread the gospel—all dressed up in the latest pseudoscientific garb of social Darwinism. But all these factors were constants in American history; every expansionist thrust had historically employed them. What was new and crucial was the missionaries' seizure of an idea that had enjoyed some currency in the depression of the 1870s: that the United States industrial machine produced more than the existing home market could consume. In the 1870s this analysis had led more often than not to the conclusion that the internal colonies, the West and the South, ought to be more systematically exploited. But missionaries took that analysis and projected it on the international scene, arguing that only expansion into the world's marketplace (and what better market than mythical China?) could ensure for America the greatness history had reserved for it and bring the benefits of Western civilization to the unenlightened. So what had begun as self-interest ended in a redefinition of the nation's and the world's interest (one no doubt sincerely believed, since human beings, alone or in groups, have a marvelous capacity to transform their particular good into universal good). Thus missionaries could say with conviction that marketplace expansion served more than the needs of mission boards; and missionaries blazing trails for mammon—creating commercial wants where none had existed before—served the national interest well.

THE NAVY LOBBY

A similar pattern developed with the big-navy lobby. That lobby was an extraordinarily motley group, but the most important and most neglected element in it was the junior officer corps of the navy itself. In the 1880s that group was a classic example of status anxiety. In sociological terms, the archetypal Annapolis graduate came from the upper class, usually from a business or professional family; he was Episcopalian; he married into the eastern aristocracy; and becoming a naval officer was generally regarded as about as acceptable as going into father's firm. But in the early 1880s the naval officer's status security was threatened by austerity budget cuts that effectively froze him in his present rank; if he was ever to be promoted, someone above him had to retire or die. As a consequence, some Annapolis graduates found no room in the navy at all and had to go into civilian business; others found themselves with the prospect of remaining lifetime ensigns—hardly an acceptable position in the eyes of one's class, family, or Main Line wife.

Status-anxiety groups—if one puts any stock in current American historiography—are supposed to react irrationally to their situation. If so, the officer corps does not fit the mold. Operating informally as individuals or as committees of correspondence, or more formally inside the newly established Naval War College, which they came to dominate, the junior officers investigated thoroughly and rationally all the possible solutions to their problem. In the end, they chose the simplest and most obvious: they would have to persuade American policy-makers that a big navy was in the national interest. The reasoning was obvious: the more ships, the more commands; the more commands, the more social mobility.

Having determined upon that solution, this group did three things. First, it cultivated those businessmen and congressmen whose businesses and constituencies would most benefit from a large naval construction program. Second, realizing, like the missionaries, that a broader coalition could be assembled only by redefining the national interest, they put together all the component parts of sea-power theory that Alfred Thayer Mahan was to codify a decade later: (*a*) America suffered or was about to suffer the terrible pangs of industrial overproduction; (*b*) only a systematic expansion into the world's marketplaces could relieve that problem; and (c) only a large, wide-ranging navy could keep open the trade routes to desired markets. The result of both types of propaganda was the passage of the Navy Appropriations Bill of 1890 and the initiation of an American battleship navy—a navy geared not to coastal defense but to the more difficult chore of protecting American foreign trade. Third, like the missionaries, naval officers acted personally to expand American influence abroad, and thus give the nation a vested stake in what otherwise it might have ignored. Korea, Hawaii, Haiti: all exemplify this process. But nowhere was this phenomenon more evident than in Samoa. It was the navy that first defined Samoa as important (a harbor like the one at Pago Pago was irresistible to a seafaring man), first negotiated special relationships with Samoan tribesmen, and first interested missionaries and merchants in the islands. Only when the navy had drawn the area to the attention of cosmopolitan policy-makers did it occur to many that Samoa might be strategically placed on the trade routes to Australia and New Zealand. And thus an American government, in an age of supposed isolation, was drawn into the vortex of international politics in a manner that nearly produced conflict with its chief competitor in Samoa, Germany, and which did indeed produce a tripartite protectorate of the United States, Germany, and Great Britain over the islands —an uneasy arrangement that was to last ten years, until 1899.

MERCHANT CAPITALISTS

The four economic groups are simpler to understand and demand less attention. The most obvious were merchant capitalists, broadly defined to include merchants in the export-import business, owners of steamship lines, and shipbuilders. Disrupted by the Civil War and outdueled by the technologically more advanced British merchant marine, the American maritime service had been mired in the doldrums for many years. Obviously, then, merchant capitalists had a vested interest in any movement that might improve their economic prospects. Stirred by parallel activities of missionaries and navy men, as well as other economic groups, they trotted out the same argument of overproduction and said that the national interest, not just their own, demanded commercial empire overseas. They employed the argument to lobby for the Mail Steamship Subsidy Bill of 1891 (a far cry from the much larger and more direct subsidy they sought), and they invoked it to sanctify their own personal efforts to expand American influence overseas, most notably in Panama and Samoa.

FINANCIAL ADVENTURERS

Much the same story can be told of the American finance capitalists. Generally, large established investment firms (like the house of Morgan) had little interest in overseas investment in this period; indeed, one can argue that they did not acquire such an interest until after the Panic of 1907. In the 1880s they were largely involved in financing the last railroad boom, and in the 1890s they were preoccupied with promoting the corporate consolidation movement in heavy industry. But a significant number of smaller, more adventuresome investors did begin to wander abroad in the 1880s; the risks they took were greater—they were moving into unfamiliar and often unstable areas—but the potential jackpots were larger than anything they could earn at home. Illustrative of this wildcatting, speculative breed was Minor C. Keith, who began with a railroad in Costa Rica, developed bananas to give the railroads something to carry, plunged into steamship lines to provide transportation to American markets, and then plowed money into making American consumers banana-conscious and in setting up the market mechanisms to meet the demand he had created. The end, as John Dos Passos was to put it in *42nd Parallel,* was to make Keith "The Emperor of the Caribbean" and his United Fruit Company one of the most powerful forces in the area.

The activities of such overseas investors were significant in two ways. First, they established a pattern of investment in underdeveloped countries which was to last until the 1950s. Little money went into manufacturing or indeed into almost anything that might have a beneficial spread effect for the host economy. Instead, it went almost exclusively into extractive industries (like Mexican mining), tropical foodstuffs (like Central American bananas or Hawaiian and Cuban sugar), and rail systems to get the minerals and food specialties out easily and cheaply (like the American-controlled railroads in the Andes, the Central American republics, and Mexico). Second, when such investors encountered difficulties from either European rivals or indigenous regimes, they invariably turned to the American government for assistance. But to get that assistance they once more had to claim that their enterprises served the national interest; and like other groups, they were saved by the convenient argument of overproduction (or oversaving).

CONSUMER GOODS MANUFACTURERS

A number of industrial capitalists also perceived an advantage in marketplace expansion and argued for a redefinition of the national interest which would fit their needs. Some of them would be more aptly characterized as cosmopolitans; their role will be discussed later, in connection with the 1890s. Others saw a pressing need for foreign markets if they were to survive. Generally, this sector was made up of traditional consumer goods manufacturers who had historically engaged in rather simple fabrication processes and sold their products, such as crude cotton jeans and sheeting, largely to a rural market of commercial farmers. Quite simply, this sector was mesmerized by the emergence of the gigantic national urban market in this period; but at the same time, neither their production facilities nor their marketing techniques were geared to the more sophisticated and diversified tastes of urban consumers. The peculiar combination of greed and ignorance led many such industries, from textile firms to stove manufacturers, to overproduce on a grand scale. Stockpiling inventories made overproduction not a hypothesis but a fact for these entrepreneurs; and overseas markets were an obvious solution to their problems. If the city slickers of New York would not buy overalls, perhaps Chinese or Venezuelan peasants would. But the traditional consumer goods manufacturers, like other functional groups, had to seek a broader base of support for marketplace expansion; and like the others, they thought their solution lay in transforming their own problem of overproduction into a general economic theory that could explain the entire cyclical nature of the American economy.

AGRARIANS

Finally, a brief word about the most neglected and perhaps most important functional group of all—the American commercial farmers and the agro-industries (like meatpacking and flour milling) to which they were tied. The development of the national urban market had enormously multiplied the economic opportunities of the commercial farm sector within the United States. But other developments—the opening of the Great Plains and the diversification of the new South, the increasing use of machinery and scientific methods, the economies of scale—all kept American agriculture a giant step ahead of domestic demand. Such had been the case since the 1840s, but the 1880s contained ingredients that made it more dramatically clear: farm prices were erratic and frequently depressed; European countries, especially Germany, discriminated against American pork products and inferentially presented the possibility of discrimination against a wider range of competitive American agricultural products; and agrarians, for a host of reasons, had begun to organize themselves into Farmers' Alliances and similar organizations in efforts to make the marketplace more predictable. As William A. Williams documents in *The Roots of American Empire,* by the 1880s these organized agrarians had developed a sophisticated and reasonably comprehensive analysis of the economic problems facing the agricultural sector and of the importance of foreign markets in partially solving those problems. Moreover, they went beyond their own self-interests and pointed out, quite rightly, that a flourishing export market for agricultural commodities had important spread effects for the American economy as a whole. (One obvious connection was that a prosperous farmer was a better consumer, a fact of no small importance in a nation where more people lived on farms than in cities.) Conversely, a depressed export market had backwash effects on the general economy, and indeed, depressions in the export grain trade seemed closely correlated with the general cyclical downturns of the whole economy. Such views were widely purveyed by farm organizations and food processing industries, and there is much evidence that an increasing number of people in the industrial sector not only accepted those arguments, but borrowed them to help explain their own economic problems.

One short postscript: The importance of functional groups in generalizing from their own interests to a redefined national interest was undeniably significant, especially in reinforcing the parallel views of cosmopolitan elites. Yet that importance should not be overstated, for the simple fact remains that among both finance capitalists and more importantly industrial capitalists, only a minority perceived any pressing need for marketplace expansion overseas in the 1880s. And until some greater approximation of consensus was achieved on that score, policy-makers lacked the power base and thus the operative preconditions to support such a policy systematically and vigorously. As it turned out, one key event, and a most cataclysmic one, was to transform a minority view into a near consensus. That event was the Panic of 1893.

Suggestions for Further Reading

The best overview of the period is Walter LaFeber, *The New Empire* (Ithaca, N.Y., 1963). Also useful is Milton Plesur, *America's Outward Thrust: Approaches to Foreign Affairs, 1865–1890* (De Kalb, Ill., 1971). More narrow but richly researched is David M. Pletcher, *The Awkward Years* (Columbia, Mo., 1963).

A particularly insightful study of American social structure is found in Samuel P. Hays, "Political Parties and the Community-Society Continuum," in *The American Party Systems,* ed. William N. Chambers and Walter D. Burnham (New York, 1967). Cast in Hays's framework, two already important studies take on added significance: Fred Harvey Harrington, *God, Mammon, and the Japanese: Horace N. Allen and Korean-American Relations, 1884–1905* (Madison, Wis., 1944), and Peter Karstens, *The Naval Aristocracy* (New York, 1972).

Helpful biographical approaches to key diplomatic figures are Alice F. Tyler, *The Foreign Policy of James G. Blaine* (New York, 1935); Charles C. Tansill, *The Foreign Policy of Thomas F. Bayard, 1885–1897* (New York, 1940); and Glyndon G. Van Deusen, *William Henry Seward* (New York, 1967).

See also the general bibliography at the end of this volume.

CHAPTER 12

Economics, Ideology, and Tactics of Expansion (1893–1901)

The 1890s marked a sharp acceleration of the expansionist impulse. In a host of overseas regions, American diplomacy, arms, and trade pushed outward the nation's frontiers. American historians have generally ignored or denied any connection between this accelerated expansion of the 1890s and the historic commercialism that had preceded it. For most of them, it was a "great aberration": a kind of half-quaint, half-unhappy accident that led America temporarily away from its traditional anti-imperialism into the European mode of empire-building; but once the giddy experience had passed and rationality was restored, the argument goes, the nation set about disposing of the very empire so recently acquired. A little sin, a great redemption: the City Upon a Hill sparkled once more and America entered the twentieth century with clean hands, morally fit to fight the epic crusades against imperialism, fascism, and communism, and to create a new world order of interdependence, peace, and prosperity.

In this historiographical scenario, there were a number of alleged villains that sidetracked America into the "great aberration": the conspiracy of a few "large policy" imperialists like Theodore Roosevelt and Henry Cabot Lodge; status anxiety and social tension produced by modernization, which led in turn to a general psychic crisis that could be resolved only by turning attention outward; the boredom of a society too long at peace, fast running out of vicarious adventures on the western frontier, and not yet fully immersed in the substitutes of mass spectator sports and hyperactivity; the external actions of foreign powers like Spain, forcing unwanted choices upon a reluctant dragon; the cowardice of a mediocre President caving in to a hyped-up public opinion for the sake of political expediency. All these variant views had several things in common. They interpreted expansionism as an ephemeral phenomenon, unconnected to anything in the American experience either before or after the fact. They defined imperialism almost exclusively in formal colonial terms; hence the preoccupation with 1898 and the war with Spain, and the indifference to or ignorance of marketplace expansion and informal empire. They emphatically denied or deemphasized any possible internal economic role in expansion, and rejoiced that studies like Julius W. Pratt's *Expansionists of 1898* had rescued American historiography from the Hobsonian-Leninist trap of economic determinism.

In general, economists and economic historians let such interpretations of diplomatic historians go unchallenged. Even the econometric approach that dominated economic history in the 1960s has thus far proved of limited utility to an understanding of the economic dynamics and underpinnings of the explosive expansionism of the 1890s. Viewed through the lens of the new economic history, the two and half decades between the Panic of 1873 and the Spanish-American War was an uninterrupted period of skyrocketing production and economic growth that enabled America to surpass Great Britain in most key economic indices and become an industrial power second to none. But when one adjusts the lens to make visible the variables of income inequity, social instability, and unpredictability of the business cycle, one perceives the paradoxical outlines of a crisis inside a boom. Hence the Janus-faced image of the American economic terrain in the late nineteenth century: increasing productivity counterbalanced by falling rates of profit and periodic depressions—the crisis of uneven development.

The Economic Dynamic

THE TENDENCY toward industrial overproduction was one source of the economic crisis. Partly it grew out of the closing of traditional areas of investment, such as railroads and western lands, which flooded capital into more narrowly productive channels. But to a perhaps greater degree, surplus production was simply a projection of overcompetition—a wasteful, duplicative, almost endemic quality of laissez-faire capitalism which made the industrial order into an arena where dog ate dog as both the thirst for profit and the instinct for survival made "production, production, production, faster, greater" (as Samuel Gompers put it) "the impulse, the thought and the motive of the capitalist class."[1] The result was an economy that was chaotic, unstable, unplanned, and unpredictable. This was especially true of the consumer goods sector.

Compounding the lack of order in the economy was its lack of equity for such nonelite groups as urban laborers and farmers. Viewed from the vantage of the contemporary statistics gatherer, the plight of such groups may (or may not) appear hard; but workers and farmers defined their reality on the basis of their own perceived experiences, not through the findings of census takers. For many of them, any income gains seemed intolerably uneven and unpredictable as the result of a fluctuating market of which they often had little knowledge and less control. Moreover, even when real income demonstrably rose, it often fell short of personal expectations, particularly in comparison with the increasing shares of the nation's wealth held by industrial, financial, and mercantile entrepreneurs.

For the farmer, the complex economic problems of commercial farming grew to overwhelming proportions when he had to work them out within the context of an urban-industrial imperialism that reduced the agricultural sector to the status of an internal colony (i.e., a supplier of food and raw materials and a consumer of finished products) and subordinated him to the unpredictable, market-dictated demands of merchants, bankers, processors, and railroads. In like fashion, the worker's historic effort to avoid permanent "wage slavery" and to increase his own social mobility was complicated by a class-consciousness among capitalists which often produced overt hostility to unionism and an increasing tendency to move away from the piecework wage theories of the artisan stage to the real "wage theories" (i.e., subsistence wages) of the heavy industrial stage. The chief economic result of this inequity was the persistence of the same general patterns of income distribution and effective consumer demand, all of which exacerbated the problem of overproduction of consumer goods. The most painful manifestations of that economic crisis were the frequent and prolonged depressions that grew out of the Panic of 1873, the economic downturn in the mid-1880s, and the cataclysmic Panic of 1893. Modest

---

[1] Thomas McCormick, *China Market* (Chicago, 1967), p. 22.

by the standards of the Great Depression of the 1930s, they were unprecedented and shocking to Americans getting their first and not very pleasant taste of life in an industrialized society.

Less tangible but more fearfully felt was the social crisis. Certainly it grew out of more than just the economic crisis. It grew out of the host of social and cultural changes, disruptions, and tensions spawned by rapid industrialization and urbanization—the chaotic transition between a community-centered America and a corporate America. But the periodic downward swings of the economic cycle exacerbated the societal identity crisis and sparked more violent expressions of it. The consequent social upheaval was a frightful specter to the political elite of the day, and in the eyes of such anxious beholders, worker and farmer unrest sometimes seemed a harbinger of "revolution—and internecine war" in which "fire and sword will devastate the country."[2] The railroad strikes and urban riots of 1877 first posed the possibility of revolutionary confrontation, and the "great upheaval" of 1886 revived it in the southwestern rail tie-up and in the post–May Day hysteria labeled the Haymarket Affair. But it was not until the Panic of 1893 that elite fears became intense, widespread, and nearly unreasoning. Confronted by farmer populism, labor socialism, the traumatic Pullman boycott, textile and coal mine strikes, and the marching bonus armies, the conservative power structure could easily imagine the worst. For many of them the period became, as Harry Thurston Peck described it, one in which "those elements of dynamic discontent which had long been gathering strength, half unperceived, now loomed upon the political horizon with the black and sullen menace of a swelling thunder-cloud, within whose womb are pent the forces of destruction."[3] The social question, then—that was the rub. How to stabilize the economy and tranquilize the society? It was a question that demanded answers, particularly from those that had the most to lose by social upheaval yet also the most power to manipulate society and alter events: the business community and its political-intellectual allies.

THE SEARCH FOR ANSWERS

Effective answers, of course, required an accurate consensus as to the causes of America's recurrent economic ills. Up to the mid-1890s no such concensus existed. On the contrary, between the Panic of 1873 and that of 1893, two general explanations were offered for the behavior of the economic cycle. The favored one centered on the monetary system. Rural and urban debtors

---

[2] Ibid., p. 24.
[3] Ibid., p. 25.

blamed economic downturns on the scarcity of money and inelasticity of credit, and proclaimed greenbacks and later the free coinage of silver as the only salvation. Dominant creditor elements defended the capabilities of the gold standard and blamed hard times on easy-money inflation, which led domestic investors to hoard their gold and foreign ones to withdraw it.

Vying with that interpretation was the newer explanation that generalized overproduction led to falling prices and propelled profits into periodic stagnation (a heretical theory characterized by classical economists as an absolute impossibility). This heresy tended to follow the economic cycle itself, popping up as the downturn neared bottom and diminishing with the revival of demand and restoration of prosperity. Yet even in good times, when it was out of vogue, it continued to have its advocates in business and governmental circles, including such distinguished people as the steel magnate Andrew Carnegie. It was Carnegie who promulgated the famous Law of Surplus, which posited that the fixed costs of modern industrialization demanded constant, full productivity; that the home market could not absorb the resulting surplus; and that foreign markets offered the only solution to that contradictory situation.

Despite such celebrated advocacy and cyclical popularity, the overproduction thesis neither replaced nor subsumed the more conventional monetary explanations prior to the Panic of 1893. Indeed, even the initial reaction to it was to explain it in monetary terms and seek solutions in monetary measures. But as monetary palliatives failed, as financial panic turned to commercial depression, as economic indices seemed to indicate a state even more serious than that of the 1870s, there evolved a growing conviction that the downturn was rooted not only in the monetary system, but in the complex industrial order itself. It was this conviction that led to a concerted search for more meaningful explanations—a search made psychologically compelling by the social upheaval of 1894, the *année terrible,* which led A. D. Noyes (who experienced every panic from 1873 to 1933) to conclude that "talk of 'the country being done for'...of a future which would bring only economic decadence...came sooner after the panic of 1893" than "on any similar occasion of our times."[4]

The search for explanations led almost inevitably down the corridor marked "Overproduction." It did so because that theory had already enjoyed periods of popularity; because it benefited from influential proponents; because it jibed with the perceived reality of stockpiling inventories and stagnant demand; and because monetary and overproduction theories had never been wholly incompatible anyway. Indeed, monetary antagonists could, and increasingly did, add

---

4 Ibid., p. 30.

to their debate the question of whether a bimetallic system or a single gold standard was the best international means of fostering the sale of American surpluses abroad.

What really transformed the overproduction analysis from a minority heresy to the status of new conventional wisdom, however, was the variable of credibility. During the 1870s, when the theory first attracted significant support, there was a widespread belief that America could compete in world markets *only* during depression periods of low wages and prices; that with full recovery (and higher costs), American goods would be forced back within the confines of the home market. So the export trade might prove a temporary solution by bailing out an economy already deeply in trouble, but it could not provide a permanent, systematic solution that would help smooth out long swings in the economic cycle. But by the 1890s there was a growing self-confidence that American goods, high costs notwithstanding, could compete overseas even in good times; hence stagnation theories could be more than alleged, they and their implication could be acted upon. What largely accounted for this change in attitude was an awareness of the technological and organizational advantages brought about by retooling and corporate integration at the end of the century; advantages that more than conpensated for higher wage costs. But also, if one may speculate, there was an increasing tendency for Americans to believe their own overseas press clippings about American economic power, as Europeans began to talk about the "American invasion" of European markets and the "American Peril" (more serious than the "Yellow Peril") and to propose common European efforts to block American economic penetration. Thus, in a curious fashion, Europe's image of America became America's image of itself. As Henry Adams put it: "It is we who are now strong and Europe whose markets will be destroyed."[5]

THE CONSENSUS ON OVERPRODUCTION

The years between panic and war, between 1893 and 1898, thus produced a consensus, almost without dissent, among conservative businessmen and political leaders on the reality of an industrial glut and the pressing need for market expansion overseas to relieve it. Illustrative was the business community. Domestic merchants joined those traditionally engaged in foreign commerce in affirming the thesis. Bankers who had formerly doted on monetary questions discovered that overproduction had resulted in "the Anglo-Saxon thirst for wide

---

[5] Ibid., p. 34.

markets growing upon us."[6] And one is struck by the lack of disagreement among manufacturers along the usual lines of function, geographic location, and corporate size. Stagnationist rhetoric might have been more frenetic in the heavily depressed southern cotton textile industry, but it did not differ in substance from the outcries of either other consumer industries or heavy industries in all sections of the country. The only difference in approach concerned not the overproduction theory itself, but the tactical responses to it. Generally, large-scale units such as Carnegie Steel and Standard Oil utilized their own organizations to push surplus sales abroad. But small- to medium-sized corporations, with their higher costs and more limited resources, often pooled their efforts in broad-based trade associations. Of these, the most significant was the National Association of Manufacturers, an organization that premised its very existence and most of its actions on the conviction that "our manufacturers have outgrown or are outgrowing the home market" and that "expansion of our foreign trade is [the] only promise of relief."[7]

Broad-based business support for an overproduction theory was an indispensable prerequisite for any stepped-up market expansion abroad. But economic expansion, as America was shortly to discover, inevitably met serious obstacles abroad which could be surmounted only with government aid. Thus it is crucial to realize that principal foreign policy makers fully shared the business version of cyclical theory and (as the next chapter will illustrate) ultimately accepted the responsibility of promoting and protecting the export trade. Both Presidents Cleveland and McKinley, for example, talked often of the narrowness of "the home market" and the problem of "surplus production" beyond "consumption"; both called for a vigorous campaign to "find markets in every part of the habitable globe" and to make it "our settled purpose to open trade wherever we can."[8] Every Secretary of State between 1893 and 1898 affirmed and acted upon similar sentiments. The last of that succession, William R. Day, summed up their collective sentiments well when he counseled Congress "that the output of the United States manufacturers . . . has reached the point of large excess above the demands of home consumption." His only solution was a vigorous "commercial expansion" into "the southern half of the Western Hemisphere" and the "vast undeveloped fields in Africa and the Far East."[9]

---

6 Ibid., p. 35.
7 Ibid., p. 36.
8 Ibid., p. 37.
9 Ibid., p. 38.

THE TARIFF: CONFLICT WITHIN CONSENSUS

Illustrative of business and government promotion of expanding markets was the tariff-making of 1894 and 1897. Textbooks usually treat those tariffs as economic disasters; the Wilson-Gorman Bill of 1894 is described as emasculated by the Senate, and the Dingley tariff of 1897 is recorded as the highest in American history up to that point. All this is true as far as it goes, reflecting the fact that the tariff, more than any other issue, was traditionally a product of log-rolling by sectional and functional interests and peculiarly impervious to change. But such treatment deals only with the end product and not with the process that led up to it. Had it done that, it would have noted more emphatically that the executive branch proposals conceptualized tariff revision largely as a means of pushing the export trade; that significant numbers of legislators expounded the overproduction thesis in support of that conceptualization; and that such supporters came reasonably close to getting what they wanted despite the enormous obstacles in their way.

For example, the original 1894 proposals rested upon Cleveland's fully developed theory that freer trade would facilitate the profitable disposal of American surpluses abroad; that our stage of economic development had outstripped protectionism and put us in a position to "throw down to-day our tariff walls and defy the world's competition." As a first step in that direction, the Wilson bill aimed at a lengthy list of duty-free raw materials (such as coal, iron ore, copper, and wool). The assumption was twofold: that lower costs of raw materials used by American manufacturers would make their finished products more competitive in world markets, and that the underdeveloped nations that supplied the bulk of those raw materials would prove warm customers for American wares. The Senate did indeed emasculate the bill by virtually eliminating the free list. But the fact that a relatively free-trade bill did pass the House and that it was consciously based on the premises of what some have called free-trade imperialism makes the tariff of 1894 not all that far removed in conceptualization from the Underwood tariff of 1913.

Similarly the tariff proposals of 1897 revived and greatly expanded the concept of reciprocal trade legislated by the McKinley tariff of 1890. McKinley's theories, like Cleveland's, rested on the assumption that overproduction demanded a vigorous export trade, and that tariff revision could help bring it about. But the McKinley tariff tended to be a more pragmatic compromise between pressures for domestic protection and the need for foreign markets—a kind of adjusted protectionism. On one hand, it generally sought to maintain traditional protective barriers against the competitive exports of industrialized Europe. On the other, it aimed for reciprocal trade agreements with underdeveloped countries which would facilitate the relatively free sale of our export manufactures in exchange for one or two of the raw materials or agricultural specialties of these preindustrial extractive economies.

Pressured vigorously by important business interests, the Congress very nearly gave McKinley all he wanted. Not only did it renew the 1890 reciprocity section, but it added a much broader one: the presidency would now have discretionary powers over a two-year period to make reciprocity treaties that would either put articles on the free list, retain them there for a specified period, or reduce the duty on any article up to 20 percent. Unfortunately, the final conference bill undercut that provision by requiring that all trade agreements made by the President be submitted back to both the House and the Senate for approval, meaning that each treaty had to run the gauntlet of special interests in each house—a process that made it nearly impossible for McKinley to produce agreements acceptable to Congress. Nevertheless, the near-victory reflected in the Senate version, the administration's subsequent efforts at implementation, and McKinley's renewed and eloquent plea for expanded reciprocity in 1901— all made the tariff of 1897, both in time and conceptualization, not so far removed from the reciprocal trade agreements program of the New Deal.

In sum, the tariff bills of the 1890s illustrate that even so immovable an object as protectionism had to give a bit in the face of the growing consensus on overproduction. The fact bolsters the earlier assertion that by early 1898 a new cyclical orthodoxy had subsumed the old, and that the primary consequence was concerted agreement on the necessity of militant broad-gauged expansion into the surplus-absorbing markets of the world. In other words, the real great debate on expansion ended *before* (not after) the Spanish-American War and "America's colonial experiment" in the Caribbean and the Pacific; and it ended with little significant dissent.

The Ideology of Expansion

SOCIAL DARWINISM: IDEOLOGY AS CAUSATION?

The role of ideology in promoting expansion is more difficult to ascertain than that of economic need. Some historians have essentially argued that the end of the nineteenth century saw the emergence, popularization, and general acceptance of a new ideology that constituted a major independent causal factor in the charting of an expansionist course. The ideology in question, with all its attendant beliefs, values, and word symbols, has been labeled social Darwinism. Scholars stressing its primal importance in creating an expansionist impulse have generally gone through a certain reasoning process in reaching their conclusion. First, they have noted that certain facets of social Darwinism had imperialist implications. On the aggressive side of the coin, the concept of the survival of the fittest was easily extended to the international sphere: it was inevitable that the fittest peoples (i.e., Anglo-Saxons) would extend their dominion over the lesser peoples of the earth. On the more humanitarian side, social Darwinism added a dash of paternalism (the White Man's Burden theory): even though the fittest must conquer, they still had a duty to uplift the less fit—to teach them as much of civilization, Christianity, and democracy as they could absorb. Having noted the apparent compatibility of social Darwinism and imperialism, many historians have observed further that the evolutionary ideology was sanctified by the psuedoscientific genetics of the day; that its rhetoric became the common currency of the economic, political, and academic spokesmen of that age; and that its triumphant ascendancy coincided perfectly in time with the adoption of an imperialist policy.

But coincidence demonstrates only correlation, not necessarily cause. Such a statement is not meant to suggest that ideas and ideology can never be independent causal factors in history, only that it is not very logical to argue in that vein in the specific historical instance of American expansion in the 1890s. In the first place, it is most difficult to demonstrate that the ideology of McKinley's empire was very much different from the ideology of Polk's, save in its special jargon. Almost all of its ingredients—Anglo-Saxon racism, the sense of mission, the belief in the inevitability of organic growth—had long been part of America's value system. Even the earlier idea that the empire ought to grow by voluntary consent and association rather than by military force did not make for any real distinction between earlier expansionist concepts and those of the 1890s. Historically, the idea of voluntary consent had frequently been violated in fact and those violations simply rationalized away—as Frenchmen, Spaniards, Mexicans, and Indians could attest. The same process, no more and no less, took place in the last decade of the nineteenth century. Even the rationalization itself was not very original: that the annexation of the Philippines was based upon the implied consent of their inhabitants, a fiction stoutly maintained even in the face of bloody and explicit rebellion by those who had implicitly consented. So it seems more plausible to argue that the expansionist ideology was really a constant in American history rather than a radical new variable that suddenly popped up in the 1890s.

British comment on U.S. imperialism

Beyond that initial point, there is a second reservation: that social Darwinism could be and was used as easily by anti-imperialists as by imperialists; that racism, for example, could just as easily lead to arguments against Anglo-Saxon expansion, on the grounds that absorption of inferior peoples would mongrelize the race and dilute the purity upon which its supposed superiority depended. Hence the phenomenon, multiplied many times over, of ardent social Darwinists like Theodore Roosevelt and William Graham Sumner taking antithetical positions on the question of empire-building, yet each invoking the same philosophy to justify his stance.

Finally, one must observe the striking disparity between the grandiose rhetoric of the expansionist ideology and the simpler reality (as we shall see later) of a consciously self-limited, formal imperialism. In fact, far from accepting the heady brew of the White Man's Burden, American expansionists generally sought to impose territorial and formal limits that would lighten the burdens and responsibilities of that expansion. Put another way, American expansionists were pragmatists first and foremost, and their social Darwinism was simply (as one historian put it) "the fastest metaphor in the West."

LIBERAL CAPITALISM AS POSITIVE REINFORCEMENT

Questioning either the independence or the primacy of ideology as a causal factor in expansionism is not without its inner logic: ignoring it altogether would be absurd. People, both as individuals and as members of a group, have a need to feel that the choices they make and the courses they follow are not dictated solely by selfish desires; that what they do is not only necessary, but moral, proper, and good. In periods of gradual change, the integration of ideals and interests is as easy as it is symbiotic; departures from behavioral norms are generally slight, and the general value structure in which those modest changes occur is broad and amorphous enough to accommodate them. So the process of reconciling action and belief is relatively automatic.

But the 1890s was not a period of gradual change. To be sure, in some ways the foreign policies of that decade were simply the logical culmination of traditional commercialism. But in other ways they represented rapid and wrenching changes: in the vast acceleration of commercialism; in the systematic linkage of commercialism to industrial prosperity and social stability; and in the innovative acquisition of overseas colonies that were far removed from the North American continent and had little chance of admission to the Union as coequal states. Such changes could not have occurred had it not been for the role played by ideology—an ideology formed largely in a preindustrial period but from which selected parts were adopted and adapted to the new needs and circumstances of an industrial order. Thus, in a very real sense, the past was used to legitimate the present—to reconcile Americans to what otherwise would have seemed sharp departures from accepted norms, and to permit them to see their actions as consistent with the nation's cherished past and therefore good and proper.

Some elements of that ideological reservoir were borrowed pretty much intact and used rather literally, since they were as applicable in an industrial order as in a preindustrial one. Perhaps the classic example is the tradition often labeled "liberal capitalism" and asserted by some to have been accepted by most Americans throughout the nation's history. In a very broad sense, that assertion is probably true. From the Founding Fathers onward, most Americans had posited a direct and beneficial relationship between a system of property, profit, and trade and the loftier forms of religion, political process, and social organization. Indeed, trade was viewed as the chief avenue for transmitting religious, political, and social virtues; the act of expanding the marketplace brought into it new groups that were thereby lifted a notch higher up the Great Chain of Being from barbarism to civilization. To Americans of the 1890s, steeped for generations in such a value system, it was an easy, almost unquestioned step simply to *assume* that the expansion of American trade abroad would have a beneficent effect on the foreign participants in that trade (just as it had had at home, presumably), not only materially but spiritually as well. Thus it was easy for a politician like William McKinley to assert that the expansion of trade would act as both a "civilizer" and a "pacifier" in world affairs. And a churchman like Josiah Strong could optimistically affirm that "The world is to be Christianized and civilized," and define the process involved as nothing more than "the creating of more and higher wants." As he put it: "Commerce follows the missionary. . . . The millions of Africa and Asia are some day to have the wants of a Christian civilization."[10] Even a philosopher like young John Dewey could insist that "Wherever business in the modern sense has gone . . . the change in the political center of gravity has resulted in emancipating the individual from bonds of class and custom and in producing a political organization which depends less upon superior authority and more upon voluntary choice"—Dewey's turgid way of equating the expansion of trade with the expansion of democracy.[11] So in committing themselves to militant commercialism, Americans not only served their own material needs, but promoted peace, civilization, democracy, and Christianity as well. Self-interest was reconciled with and legitimized by the general interest.

THE FRONTIER: IDEOLOGY AS POSITIVE REINFORCEMENT

Other facets of a preindustrial ideology were employed more symbolically to sanctify industrial expansionism. Perhaps the best example of that genre was the cherished belief (whether it is myth or reality is immaterial) that the expanding western frontier had been one of the most creative causes of the good life and good society in American history. A great many Americans had engaged directly in the pioneering process; a great many others, including some confined for their lives to eastern cities, had experienced that process vicariously through the printed media. Probably most of them agreed with historian Frederick Jackson Turner's summation in the 1890s: "This perennial rebirth, this fluidity of American life, this westward expansion with its new opportunities, its continuous touch with the simplicity of primitive society, furnishes the forces dominating American character"—specifically, democracy, individualism, and nationalism. But as Turner, Strong, Roosevelt, and others pointed out with increasing frequency, the physical limits of westward expansion had long since been reached; the cattle, mining, and farming migrations had filled in the last frontier, and Indian wars raged only in the tents of Wild West shows. As Turner put it: "The frontier has gone, and with its going has closed

---

[10] Walter LaFeber, *The New Empire* (Ithaca, N.Y., 1963), p. 78.
[11] William Appleman Williams, *Contours of American History* (Cleveland, 1961), p. 404.

the first period of American history."[12] The mere assertion of that fact suggested the obvious question: If the frontier had been the fount of democracy, individualism, and nationalism, and if that frontier was now gone, what was to happen to those character traits that presumably had made America great and unique? What dynamic could possibly take the frontier's place?

For a society immersed for generations in the folklore of the frontier and its alleged life-giving qualities, the easiest answer was that only a "new frontier" would do (a phrase that still had strongly evocative qualities for millions of Americans well past the halfway mark of the twentieth century). And given the already felt need for marketplace expansion abroad, it was only natural to conclude that the new frontier would lie overseas: an international frontier would have to replace a continental frontier as the sustaining energizer for the good society. Turner himself, in 1910, saw the tie-up when he commented:

> Having colonized the Far West, having mastered its internal resources, the nation turned at the conclusion of the nineteenth and the beginning of the twentieth century to deal with the Far East, to engage in the world politics of the Pacific Ocean.... It was indeed in some respects the logical outcome of the nation's march to the Pacific, the sequence to the era in which it was engaged in occupying the free lands and exploiting the resources of the West.[13]

In praise of the Open Door Policy

---

[12] LaFeber, *New Empire,* p. 67.

[13] Frederick Jackson Turner, *The Frontier in American History* (New York, 1920), p. 315.

In certain objectifiable senses, such variations of the frontier thesis were sheer nonsense. The closing of the continental frontier, noted first in the 1880 census, had little direct bearing on the economic and social crisis of industrial America. Moreover, the new frontier overseas bore little resemblance to the old frontier at home. It envisioned no mass migrations of pioneering Americans overseas; it ultimately involved only a minimal extension of American political sovereignty. The new empire was to be far more informal and unstructured than the old.

Yet, as has been often noted, objectifiable reality is not the whole of reality, for people act on their perceptions (with all their elements of error, myth, and irrationality), not on post mortem quantifications. Whether the old frontier had really been the creative force for the best (or was it even the best?) in American character is most debatable. Whether the new frontier was an adequate substitute for the old is even more improbable. Yet the fact remains that the mind set of late-nineteenth-century Americans led them to regard the first proposition as a truism and to entertain optimistic hopes about the second. To the degree that that was so, their symbolic invocation of the frontier tradition made it possible for them to rationalize their expansionism as something far more than just materially necessary: it appeared the only likely means of preserving the traditional America of democracy, individualism, and nationalism. Thus material need and an idealistic commitment to preserve the good society went inseparably hand in hand.

The Debate over Tactics

IF CONSENSUS EXISTED on the pressing need for marketplace expansion, there nonetheless remained important and unresolved differences over the tactics and modes of that expansion. Those differences evolved around one crucial question: Did commercial expansion necessitate a formal colonial empire as an accoutrement? Would trade have to be preceded by the formal extension of American political sovereignty into overseas areas? Having to face that question led elite leaders to split into at least three discernible blocs (quantitative studies now in progress may refine those groupings even further).

ANTI-IMPERIAL EXPANSIONISTS

At one end of the spectrum were the anti-imperialists; actually "anti-imperial expansionists" would be a more accurate term, since they took second place to none in affirming the need for overseas markets. Their often incompatible leaders were upper-class easterners, Great Plains agrarians, literary rebels, mugwump journalists, and Democratic politicos. Much of their opposition to overseas expansion may simply have been idiosyncratic and individualized. But if it did have any group cohesion to it, it was probably twofold. The broader and more intangible tie was the common identification of many of these individuals and their followers with an earlier America that had not yet been fully industrialized and corporatized; all, in varying ways and degrees, were alienated from the new industrial urban order, and instinctively distrusted the invocation of old values to sanctify radically new departures. The more concrete tie was that of partisanship; many anti-imperialists were Democrats who acted not simply from principle, but from a pragmatic desire to stamp the Republican party as the imperialist party, and to profit from opposition to it.

Their answer to the elemental question was an emphatic no. America should not acquire a formal colonial empire overseas. Their reasons (or rationalizations) for that position fell into categories. The one most stressed was the general *undesirability* of formal imperialism. Under this rubric, they argued that imperialism and the democratic dogma were incompatible; that America, like Rome, could not be both an empire and a republic. And why? Because there was an essential hypocrisy involved in permitting free men to rule unfree men; and because the creation of a permanent military force, which an empire would surely demand, would threaten civilian authority—traditionally the only sure guarantor of liberty at home. Thus Americans might become as unfree as the colonials that they ruled. Second, and ironically, they argued that imperialism would mean the absorption of inferior (nonwhite) races into the American political system—a racist position that hardly jibed with their democratic idealization but which nonetheless reflected the feelings of most white Americans about "colored" peoples both at home and abroad. It was partly on this ground that many anti-imperialists fought annexation of Hawaii in the 1890s, and some of them even favored Spanish (white) control over Cuba rather than a "black republic" that might gravitate to the United States. Finally, and most perceptively, many of them argued that imperialism was undesirable simply because it would not work. Anticipating the anticolonialism of the twentieth century, they insisted that imperialism created antithetical social forces in the subject countries which would eventually undermine colonial control and make it both untenable and unprofitable. To support their position they pointed to British difficulties in India, highlighted earlier by the famous Sepoy Mutiny, and they noted that the post–Civil War experiment in internal colonialism, sometimes known as Southern Reconstruction, had proved similarly counterproductive and unsuccessful.

But anti-imperialists found colonialism more than simply undesirable; they also found it unnecessary. With only few exceptions, most of them were also free-traders or tariff revisionists, and while many of them embraced such positions out of functional self-interest or party loyalty, many did so because of an ebullient, optimistic sense of American economic supremacy. They firmly believed that America could make more, make it as well, and sell it for less than any other nation in the world. Thus, what was required was not closed empires, but a "free world" in which trade was able to flow with relatively few restrictions. In this context, it became the government's job simply to lower the tariff and encourage others to do the same; colonies would not be required. America could thus reap the material benefits of imperialism without incurring its material and spiritual burdens.

IMPERIAL EXPANSIONISTS

At the opposite end of the continuum in the debate over tactics were the so-called large-policy imperialists. Generally lumped in this group are people like Theodore Roosevelt, Alfred Thayer Mahan, Henry Cabot Lodge, and Albert Beveridge. Their response to the question of America's tactical need for a formal empire was largely affirmative, although it was not so emphatic as some historians have alleged. (Roosevelt, for example, had some early reservations about taking the Philippines.) By formal empire, however, they did not mean a large-scale physical migration into faraway lands, such as the British settlement of Australia. What they meant was administrative colonialism in the style of the British raj in India. They envisioned an administrative elite, backed by the mobility and firepower of the American military, ruling over the alien peoples of already populated lands.

Their reasons for affirming an imperialist course ran the gamut from the most quixotic to the most realpolitik. Among the most perceptive was an awareness that the days of free-trade imperialism were over; that an American move to freer trade would not work simply because the rest of the world was moving—and had been for several decades—in the opposite direction. As they surveyed the international scene, they saw clearly that the trend was toward autarkic economic policies at home (such as protectionism and trade quotas) and to formal empires and de facto spheres of influence abroad. In that context, free trade and governmental laissez faire could only court disaster in a hostile, discriminatory trade world that would not play the game according to America's rules. Accordingly, one obvious solution to that problem was to create a system of colonies and spheres of influence where American sovereignty and/or suzerainty, backed by military power, would permit Americans to monopolize markets and resources as they saw fit.

Their other reasons for embracing imperialism are a bit more murky and necessitate a more speculative approach. In the first place, it is possible to hypothesize that the leaders of this group were among the few who took the ideology of social Darwinism literally and seriously. For them, the paternalist dictum of the White Man's Burden was no idle cliché, but something real and demanding action. Viewed from that special perspective, the strictly commercial approach bordered on the immoral. Commerce might, over time, change inferior societies for the better, but it was no substitute for more direct action: building schools, roads, and hospitals, writing constitutions, holding elections. And direct efforts of this sort could be carried out effectively only in formal colonies, where America would have a free hand to do what it thought or knew to be best. For these imperialists, then, economic penetration without colonization was simply irresponsible. Only imperialism could make market expansion morally acceptable.

In a like manner, one can hypothesize that these leaders leaned toward imperialism because of their ambivalence about the value structure of industrial America. While all of them came to accept the inevitability and even desirability of an industrial, corporate society, they did have their misgivings about its tendency to elevate materialism and profit-making above all other considerations. Coming out of a Dutch patroon landed aristocracy, or out of the professional military, or out of Boston Brahminism, such men lamented what they perceived to be a drift to a shopkeeper society, primarily acquisitive and dedicated to the cultivation of the Almighty Dollar; to a nation that no longer valued martial valor and national honor or any other higher purposes; to a nation gone soft. To them, imperialism (and if need be war) was the kind of national purpose to which the whole society could commit itself, at once uniting the nation in a common cause and stiffening its backbone.

Unquestionably, the large-policy imperialists were the most colorful and fascinating opinion leaders of their day. In fact, however, their numbers were few and their influence was slight. Yet historians have lavished attention on them almost in inverse proportion to their importance, perhaps because they make such good copy; perhaps because focusing on them lends credence to the aberrational thesis of American expansion. The most famous illustration is the conspiracy theory set forth in biographies of Roosevelt and Lodge and accepted overly much and overly long by subsequent authors of textbooks. Briefly outlined, it recounts how Roosevelt, then Assistant Secretary of the Navy, accompanied by his friend Senator Lodge, sent off a series of unauthorized naval orders one Saturday morning in the absence of Roosevelt's departmental superior. Included among those orders was the famous one to George Dewey of the Asiatic squadron to put his ships in position to attack Manila when and if war broke out with Spain over Cuba. Had it not been for that order, some historians have argued, America would never have acquired the Philippines, and thus would never have become entangled in the very un-American web of imperialism. The argument, however, suffers from both inadequate research and faulty logic. It ignores the fact that the Secretary of the Navy and the President quickly learned of Roosevelt's actions and could easily have countermanded them if they went against administration policy. It ignores the fact that the Secretary did indeed countermand the majority of Roosevelt's orders (largely because they were technically incompetent), but significantly let the order to Dewey stand. And by failing to mine naval archives, those who advanced the conspiracy theory failed to discover that naval contigency plans for taking Manila had been developed months earlier, and that they had been seen and approved by administration leaders. Thus, while Roosevelt's actions may have been precipitous and unauthorized, they were hardly at odds with the large policy of the McKinley administration.

PRAGMATIC EXPANSIONISTS

The third group involved in the debate over expansionist tactics was ultimately the triumphant one. In the absence of any accepted terminology, they might simply be called pragmatic or utilitarian expansionists. Not especially moved by seemingly abstract questions of democratic dogma or martial valor, they approached the problems of expansion chiefly from a common-sense businessman's point of view. For them, expansionist tactics depended on circumstances, and might well vary from place to place and from time to time. One simply did what one had to do, but at the least possible cost. It was the kind of cost-accounting approach to expansion that the British had earlier dubbed "imperialism on the cheap"; the kind of approach that fitted well the temperament and style of President McKinley, the Republican establishment in the Senate, and the emergent industrial elites.

In practice, pragmatic expansionists generally opted for a middle-of-the-road approach to overseas expansion. On one hand, they shared with anti-imperialists a desire to minimize the burdens of expansion. On the other, they appreciated the validity of the imperialists' position that in a hostile world of economic nationalism and imperialism, the government would have to play a more active role than that envisioned by laissez-faire free-traders. Those variables considered, such pragmatists chose a course strikingly akin to that followed earlier by William H. Seward. The resulting compromise eschewed formal colonialism in heavily populated areas like China, largely on the grounds that costs and risks would outweigh any gains. But at the same time, they modified this anticolonial approach in two ways. First, they evidenced a willingness to indulge in limited amounts of insular imperialism; they would not balk at securing selected island outposts as steppingstones to major market areas. Second, they indicated a willingness to invoke governmental power in defense of American overseas interests. As least-cost expansionists, they predictably preferred the use of economic power and diplomatic maneuvering. But under certain circumstances, even military power might be employed, as it was in the Philippines and in China during the Boxer Rebellion.

By 1900, it was pretty clear that this last group had won the debate over tactics. It did so partly because it had the largest and most powerful following in American society, partly because its spokesmen had the good fortune to be in power when crucial events broke in Cuba and China. But it was triumphant also because the other, more doctrinaire groups had occasion to modify their positions. Anti-imperialists, as we shall see, were to confront a cruel dilemma in Cuba, Venezuela, Brazil, and China: a laissez-faire, hands-off policy by the government risked sacrificing American economic ambitions in important areas. At the same time, imperialists had found from their experiences with the Philippine rebellion, and with a powder-keg situation in Cuba as well, that the game of imperialism was a bit more costly, abrasive, and dangerous than they had anticipated. As a consequence, both imperialists and anti-imperialists tended to modify their positions and move to the center ground already marked out by the pragmatists. Symbolizing this near-consensus on tactics were two events late in 1900. One was the nearly unanimous approval by all three groups of the administration's Open Door policy in China. The other was the obvious failure of the Democrats to make imperialism a key issue in the election campaign of 1900. Indeed, by the last weeks of the campaign the Democratic nominee, William Jennings Bryan, backed off almost completely. Clearly the pragmatist formula was to be America's major modus operandi for expansion: the Open Door plus selective doses of insular imperialism plus real but still minimized government support of market expansion. Only future events were to demonstrate the inherent tendency of that governmental force to escalate its extent and forms.

Suggestions for Further Reading

The best introduction to the history of late-nineteenth-century economic cycles is Readings Fels, *American Business Cycles, 1865–1897* (Chapel Hill, N.C., 1959). The most useful general economic history is Edward C. Kirkland, *Industry Comes of Age: Business, Labor, and Public Policy, 1860–1897* (New York, 1960).

William Appleman Williams, *The Tragedy of American Diplomacy* (Cleveland, 1959), most successfully integrates economic change with diplomatic developments. Thomas McCormick, *China Market* (Chicago, 1967), can be used as a supplement.

Antimaterialist interpretations are best represented by Howard K. Beale, *Theodore Roosevelt and the Rise of America to World Power* (Baltimore, 1956); Richard Hofstadter, *The Paranoid Style in American Politics* (New York, 1967); Ernest R. May, *Imperial Democracy* (New York, 1961); and Julius W. Pratt, *Expansionists of 1898* (Baltimore, 1936).

The role of ideology and the debate over tactics is covered by both the Beale and Pratt monographs, as well as by Robert L. Beisner, *Twelve Against Empire: The Anti-Imperialists, 1898–1900* (New York, 1968); David Healy, *U.S. Expansionism: The Imperialist Urge in the 1890's* (Madison, Wis., 1970); Walter LaFeber, *The New Empire* (Ithaca, N.Y., 1963); Ernest R. May, *American Imperialism* (New York, 1968); and A. K. Weinberg, *Manifest Destiny* (Baltimore, 1935).

CHAPTER 13

Expansionism
in Actio
(18⁰

The most clear examples of expansionism in action in the 1890s were three: (1) the clash of the United States' Pan Americanism with alleged British obstructionism and Britain's ultimate acceptance of American hegemony in Latin America; (2) the war with Spain in 1898 in order to end the revolution in Cuba and establish an American protectorate there; and (3) the development of a vigorous diplomacy, the acquisition of Pacific islands, and ultimately the use of force in order to assure a market-hungry America of its share of that illusive thing called the China market.

Pan Americanism

PAN AMERICANISM—that search for stability and markets in Latin America— did not diminish in vitality when the Democratic administration of Grover Cleveland took office in 1893. On the contrary, it accelerated markedly; indeed, it perhaps could not have done otherwise in the midst of an American depression that increasingly caused foreign markets in underdeveloped areas to be defined as the key to American prosperity. But in that stepped-up march to American hegemony, American policy encountered obstacles in the form of European powers reluctant to abandon the strategic and economic stakes they had acquired over time. Among those powers, Great Britain was allegedly the chief villain. In the objective sense, the British had the greatest stakes to protect and the greatest power with which to protect them. In the subjective sense, American policy-makers (sometimes wrongly) perceived that the British had the will to do so: they detected a coordinated pattern of anti-Americanism in British policy which seemed calculated to deny the United States the long-deferred fruits of the Monroe Doctrine. Nowhere was this fact more clear, thought these American leaders, than in Brazil, Nicaragua, and Venezuela between 1893 and 1897.

BRAZIL

President Richard M. Nixon said in 1971 that Brazil pointed to the direction the rest of South America would take. It was a sentiment that President Cleveland and his advisers might well have accepted in the 1890s. Certainly in size, resources, numbers of European immigrants, and relative development, Brazil was the most inviting potential market in South America. It was widely believed that the reciprocity treaty with Brazil in 1891 was the most important treaty made by the United States under the reciprocity section of the McKinley tariff. And while the Cleveland administration was to prefer freer, multilateral trade to bilateral reciprocity, and therefore abrogated that treaty, it nevertheless made clear that it attached great importance to Brazilian-American commercial relations.

It was understandable, then, that the administration reacted with great anxiety to the news of revolution in Brazil in the winter of 1893. Its initial response was one of ostensible neutrality, although it steadfastly refused to grant the rebels belligerent status and would not recognize their attempted blockade of Rio de Janeiro, designed to deprive the government of its chief source of revenue.

Three factors coincided to change that policy of neutrality. One was an increasing awareness that many of the rebel leaders had openly opposed the reciprocity treaty of 1891 and evidenced no greater enthusiasm for Cleveland's brand of market penetration. The second factor was the pressure of special American business interests, headed by William Rockefeller of the Standard Oil Company, which feared the revolution would cut into present and future trade with Brazil. Finally, and perhaps most importantly, there was a growing fear among administration leaders that the British were covertly aiding the rebels and even preparing to recognize their insurgency and give overt help. Accepting skimpy evidence a bit uncritically, the administration genuinely feared a British conspiracy to unseat the pro-American government and replace it with one that would reassert the traditionally close Anglo-Brazilian economic ties.

Those developments pushed American policy from neutrality to antirevolutionary intervention. The administration named a new and more belligerent commander to head the South Atlantic squadron of the United States Navy. It instructed him to do whatever he had to do to get American ships through the rebel blockade, whether his actions interfered with rebel military activity or not. And it dispatched with him five of the squadron's six ships, giving the United States the most powerful naval detachment in Rio's harbor. When the rebel navy challenged the American presence by attempting to interdict an American merchant ship, the American commander responded with superior force to thwart the effort. Thereafter, for all intents and purposes, the rebel blockade was dead.

Whether or not American intervention was crucial in the rebels' defeat is debatable; many indigenous factors were also at work. But it is perhaps more than coincidence that the revolutionary struggle was all downhill from that point onward. Moreover, American policy-makers did what they could to encourage that plunge. Twice more Secretary of State Walter Q. Gresham sternly refused the rebels' requests for recognition of their insurgency; significantly, the British did likewise, perhaps anxious not to back a losing horse. Similarly, in February 1894, the American naval unit remained at Rio despite a yellow fever epidemic that caused nearly all other ships, including the British, to beat a safe retreat. Clearly the administration wished to maintain its influence over the course of events. Whatever, the end result was the perpetuation in power of a government that seemed not ill disposed toward increased trade with the United States—a development fully expected by American and political leaders.

NICARAGUA

Even before the Brazilian revolution faded into final oblivion, a new threat to Pan Americanism developed in Nicaragua. The Nicaraguan situation was, if anything, more complicated than the Brazilian. American interests in Nicaragua were both strategic and economic, and both centered on the

Mosquito protectorate, which had been the focal point of problems in the 1850s. The overriding interest was the projected isthmian canal route.

In 1887 the American-owned Maritime Canal Company obtained canal-building rights in Nicaragua, a project backed by all interested Americans seeking a cost-cutting transportation short cut to the Orient. The eastern terminus for the most likely route lay in the Mosquito protectorate. Yet that all-important interest was threatened on two fronts. One was the British re-assertion of their traditional role as "protectors" of the Mosquito Indians—a reassertion that led to the landing of British troops to block a Nicaraguan incursion against the region's autonomy, to the breaking of diplomatic relations in 1895 over the Nicaraguan arrest of the British proconsul, and to the occupation of strategic Corinto in the same year when Nicaragua failed to comply with a British ultimatum for indemnification. The last act particularly worried the State Department, for "suppose Great Britain demands a money indemnity which Nicaragua is unable to pay, and, as a consequence, territory is then demanded"—prime canal route territory, undoubtedly.[1]

The other threat to American interests came from Nicaragua itself. For one thing, in its continuing effort to end Mosquito autonomy and gain control of the reservation, the Nicaraguan government was not averse to threatening the United States with termination of the Maritime Canal Company concession, presumably as a means of coercing American support for its claims on the reservation. At the same time, much of Nicaragua's desire for the Mosquito area stemmed from the empty state of the government's treasury and the consequent attractiveness of revenue from that banana-rich region. But this only made matters more complicated, for 90 to 95 percent of the region's economy was controlled by American residents, most of whom rightly feared that the Nicaraguan government would discriminate against them in favor of Nicaragua's own entrepreneurs. Under the circumstances, many Americans preferred British protection to Nicaraguan incursion.

This mix of interests and threats required a delicate balancing act by the United States. On the one hand, it had to support the contention that Nicaragua had paramount rights in the Mosquito area, since to do otherwise would mean de facto acceptance of British control over a strategically sensitive region. On the other hand, it had to prevent Nicaragua from using American support for its claims on the disputed area as a legal basis for discriminatory encroachments against American business enterprises. The tactics used were varied, but

---

[1] Walter LaFeber, *The New Empire* (Ithaca, N.Y., 1963), p. 226.

they all reflected one central reality—the willingness of the administration to intervene in Nicaraguan affairs whenever American interests of any sort were threatened.

Against the British, the tactics employed were mainly a diplomatic war of words: insistence that Nicaraguan rights were supreme in the reservation, demands for absolute guarantees against any British protectorate, and inferences of a British conspiracy to terminate American canal rights. Against Nicaragua, words were also used, and more harshly than against the British. But the threat of force was not neglected: on several occasions, ominous movements of American naval forces off the Nicaraguan port of Bluefields were used to intimidate the Nicaraguan government. And the United States applied direct military force to crush insurrections against Nicaraguan authority in the Mosquito area. The last such incident, in 1896, was quite symbolic, as American Marines repeated the earlier British act of occupying Corinto while the British sat by and watched. Indeed, they not only sat by; they acquiesced in the formal incorporation of the Mosquito area into Nicaragua. Clearly the British were coming to accept American sovereignty in much of Latin America, although it remained for the resolution of the Venezuelan crisis to consummate that process.

VENEZUELA

The Venezuelan crisis of 1895–1896 climaxed a boundary dispute between Venezuela and the British colony of Guiana that had waxed and waned—mainly waned—since the 1840s. By the 1880s the quarrel had been livened considerably by the discovery of gold in the disputed territory, by the subsequent migration of settlers into the area from both Venezuela and British Guiana and the inevitable friction between settler groups, by Venezuela's increasing difficulty in commanding the allegiance of its subjects in the eastern borderlands, and by the complicating factor of Venezuela's growing and seemingly unrepayable debts to British creditors. The dispute brought periodic Venezuelan calls for arbitration, which the Americans generally supported and the British steadfastly refused—perhaps because the Venezuelan claims were so inflated that the split-the-difference tendency of arbitrators could only work to British disadvantage. By 1887 the dispute had grown to such proportions that Venezuela broke diplomatic relations with Great Britain—a state of affairs that made the boundary settlement most difficult but did relieve the Venezuelan economy of some of the pressures of British creditors.

The explosive resurgence of that crisis in 1895 and America's dramatic role in it owe their timing to several developments. First, the growing acceptance of the overproduction theory breathed new urgency into Pan Americanism and the desire for an expanded marketplace in Latin America. That some Americans viewed Venezuela as part of that marketplace was made dramatically evident by the decision of the National Association of Manufacturers to establish its first permanent warehouse of American display goods in Caracas. (Significantly, the second was to be in Shanghai.) Second, the cumulative impact of British actions in Brazil and Nicaragua had convinced American policy-makers of British opposition to Pan Americanism and led them to suspect the worst of intentions in any moves the British might make. And finally, reinforcing those suspicions and potentially threatening American trade, the British did something particularly ominous: they reversed policy on Punta Barima, the pivotal point of control over the mouth of the Orinoco River. On several occasions, even as late as 1890, the British had indicated willingness to disallow any claims to Punta Barima in any boundary settlement. Though perhaps only a diplomatic ploy, the British reversal was interpreted by many Americans as an effort to gain control over the Orinoco, which, along with its tributaries, acted as the communications artery not only for much of the Venezuelan interior, but for much of the northern third of South America as a whole. As one congressman put it, British control of the Orinoco would "revolutionize the commerce and political institutions of at least three of the South American republics.... Our trade and other relations with those people are involved in this settlement."[2]

That the Orinoco question was central to the subsequent Anglo-American confrontation can be seen from the sequence of events. In April and early May of 1895, reports arrived from both Great Britain and Venezuela that the British had reversed policy on Punta Barima. Shortly thereafter, President Cleveland held a midnight talk with Don Dickinson, a close friend, former Cabinet member, and dominant force in Michigan Democratic politics. The President displayed a detailed map of the disputed area, expressed fears about British designs on the Orinoco, and stressed the importance of that river to control of the interior. Within days, Dickinson gave a widely publicized speech that easily could have been a trial balloon sent up by the administration. In it he emphasized the importance of "open markets throughout the world to maintain and increase our prosperity," and in spread-eagle Anglophobic oratory warned against British opposition to American needs, especially as reflected in "the most extraordinary claims and movements ... in Nicaragua and Vene-

[2] Ibid., p. 249.

zuela."[3] And on May 28, Secretary of State Gresham began preparation of a protest against British actions in Venezuela.

Gresham's death interrupted that project, and it was not until July that his successor, Richard Olney, was sufficiently settled in his new role to complete Gresham's task. Given his temperament, the wording of his July 20 note to Great Britain may have been more blunt and argumentative than Gresham's would have been, but it essentially reflected the analysis and concerns of both his predecessor and President Cleveland.

Diplomatic Pyrotechnics. Olney's famous note did several things. (1) It revivified the Monroe Doctrine by paraphrasing Monroe's "two spheres" concept—the position that the New World was politically, commercially, and ideologically distinct (and superior) to the old, and that the United States could therefore not tolerate "the subjugation of any [American power] by any European power." (2) In grandiloquent language, the note then further extended the Monroe Doctrine by explicating what had always been implicit—its positive, assertive paternalism. Asserting that "today the United States is practically sovereign on this continent, and its fiat is law," Olney claimed (in what some have dubbed the Olney Corollary to the Monroe Doctrine) that the United States had the unilateral right to interpose itself in any conflict between European and American powers which in any way (by America's

Uncle Sam's position

---

[3] Ibid., p. 251.

unilateral definition) threatened American "integrity, tranquillity, or welfare." Moreover, the United States had every right to expect the parties involved to accept American "fiat" as "law." (3) It asked rhetorically whether the dispute in point potentially threatened American interests, and concluded that it clearly did: first, because of the large "domain" involved in the dispute, and second, because of the Orinoco issue, which was "of immense consequence in connection with the whole river navigation of the interior of South America." (4) It unequivocally stated that *only* "peaceful arbitration" could resolve both the boundary question and the potential threat it involved, and demanded to know if Great Britain would accept this "one feasible mode"—a mode it had continually rejected in the past.[4]

Prime Minister Salisbury, temperamentally almost a mirror image of Olney, penned the British double rejoinder. From the American viewpoint, his two replies were as infuriating as they were brilliant. In almost tutorial tones he dismissed the universalist pretensions of the hallowed Monroe Doctrine and characterized it as a unilateral and outdated proposition binding upon no one. Changing frames of reference, he chided the administration for its misuse of the Monroe Doctrine: for using it as a rationalization for an American protectorate over Latin America; for using it as a sacrosanct shield to avoid spelling out the precise nature and extent of American interests (in plain language, failing to call a spade a spade); and for misapplying it to a boundary dispute where neither the noncolonization nor "two spheres" propositions of the doctrine were historically applicable. He concluded that no other national interests save those of Venezuela and Great Britain seemed involved, and on those grounds categorically rejected the American demand for arbitration.[5]

Both the negativism and the tardiness of Salisbury's replies (they came nearly five months after Olney's note had been sent) infuriated Cleveland and Olney, and prompted Cleveland's public message of December 17, in which he defended the integrity and contemporary relevance of the Monroe Doctrine, insisted that American "rights and interests" were self-evidently involved in the boundary dispute, bemoaned Britain's lack of wisdom in rejecting the sound American suggestion of arbitration, warned against any "willful aggression" by the British upon territory the United States deemed to be Venezuelan, and called for Congress to create a commission to investigate and determine the proper boundary. Cleveland strongly intimated the possibility of war if Great Britain did not accept the commission's findings by sprinkling his message

---

[4] Ibid., pp. 260–62.
[5] Ibid., pp. 265–66.

with such phrases as "the duty of the United States ... to resist by every means in its power," "fully alive to the responsibilities incurred," "keenly realize all the consequences that may follow."[6]

For all the bellicosity of his message, Cleveland neither expected nor was prepared for war. Indeed, the message did have certain salutary effects that made a final peaceful settlement possible. First, it so neatly manipulated American national pride and sensibilities that it unified influential support behind his approach and thus enabled him to operate his diplomacy from a strong domestic base. To be sure, some clergymen, student and peace groups, and mugwumps found it too jingoistic for their tastes, but these groups were really on the periphery of power. The infinitely more important business community largely endorsed Cleveland's message. Exceptions were to be found among some eastern bankers, and a short-lived drop in the stock market did follow Cleveland's message; but it resulted less from any war scare (which few took seriously) than from financial concern over the growing threat to the gold standard and the actions of British investors, whose bearish behavior bothered eastern bankers more than the diplomacy of the British government. As for the members of the industrial and mercantile sectors of the economy, the vocal among them were nearly unanimous in their support of administration policy.

Second, Cleveland's message did persuade Great Britain that the United States viewed the situation with great gravity and was serious about making good its pretensions in the matter. Until the President's pronouncements, it is doubtful that the British fully appreciated that fact. Given their new perception of American earnestness, their awareness of American power, real and potential, in the Western Hemisphere, and their difficulties in areas of greater priority (such as South Africa), the circumstances seemed to call for a more prudent British response.

Resolution. This altered British attitude resulted in a series of diplomatic exchanges that finally produced an Anglo-American treaty in November 1896. In the process of those preliminary exchanges, the British abandoned an effort at international clarification of the Monroe Doctrine. The Americans, for their part, accepted the British proposition that titles held for fifty years or more in the disputed area would not be subject to arbitration. Those mutual concessions made, each side agreed to a five-man arbitration commission to determine the proper boundary. Two Americans, two British, and one Russian legal

---

[6] Ibid., p. 268.

authority constituted the commission; later, after outraged cries from Venezuela, one of its citizens was added to the roll.

Three things stand out about that 1896 treaty. (1) It was negotiated without the knowledge or approval of Venezuela. The object lesson was clear: American national interests, not Venezuela's, were the sole basis for American policy—a fact that explains much about Venezuela's pro-Spanish attitude during the Spanish-American War. (2) The final agreement produced by the arbitration commission fully protected those American interests. While it awarded more domain to the British, the boundary line was drawn in such a way as to exclude the British not only from the mouth of the Orinoco River, but even from its tributaries. (3) Britain's acceptance, coupled with its acquiescence in Brazil and Nicaragua, signaled the end of serious British opposition to Pan Americanism. And the payoff on British acceptance of American hegemony in the area was not long in coming. It manifested itself in Britain's pro-American attitude during the Spanish-American War. It did so as well in 1901, when the British signed the second Hay-Pauncefote Treaty, despite continued British resentment over affronts from the United States Senate which had led them to reject the first version of the treaty. In so doing, the British abrogated the half-century-old Clayton-Bulwar Treaty and gave the United States the unilateral right to build, control, and fortify any canal in the isthmian area.

The trouble in Cuba

CUBA: REVOLUTION TO WAR TO PROTECTORATE

Early in 1895 revolution broke out in Cuba against Spanish control. It grew partly out of the inequities, corruption, and broken promises of Spanish rule; it was also reinforced by economic hard times, partially caused by the American tariff of 1894, which deprived Cuban sugar of its favored status in the American market. Like most real revolutions, it was no tea party. Spain sought pacification through a series of escalating military steps that ended in a proto–concentration camp policy that brought disease, death, and despair to an astounding proportion of Cuba's people. The rebels, for their part, resorted to terrorism, guerrilla warfare, and the ultimate desperation of a burned-ground policy to devastate their own island, in the hope of making it worthless both to Spain and to American investors and their government.

The revolution affected American interests in ways that made indifference impossible. Most tangibly, it affected American strategic interests. As naval theorists and businessmen alike pointed out, Cuba was the key island in the chain that guarded the main routes into the area of the proposed isthmian canal—routes of vital importance in America's search for Asian markets. As tangible but more narrow was the American economic interest in the island itself. Cleveland, for example, publicly estimated that Americans had $50 million invested in Cuban enterprises, especially plantations, and that pre-revolutionary trade with that country had exceeded $100 million annually. Both these strategic and economic interests were really or potentially threatened by the revolution. Physical destruction and economic dislocation had virtually halted legitimate trade, while American investors saw their property destroyed and their profits liquidated—all this in the midst of an American depression that made these losses even more keenly felt. At the same time, the longer the revolution dragged on, the greater the possibility, however remote, that Spain might secure the aid of other European powers whose presence might constitute a serious threat to American designs to make the Caribbean an "American lake."

Social Structure and Differential Reactions.   The response of Americans to the revolution was differentiated, befitting the nature of the American social structure. Locals, who were normally uninformed, uninterested, and uninfluential in foreign policy issues, took an exceptional interest in the Cuban matter. Partly taking their cue from the headlines and political cartoons of newspapers that catered to the barely literate, they developed a romantic, vicarious identification with the Cuban rebels, with class overtones (the downtrodden overthrowing the yoke of the mighty) and nationalist ones as well (patriots, akin to those of 1776, doing deadly battle with yet another European empire). Over time, their sentiment for intervention increased.

Some functionals shared the locals' humanitarianism and/or paternalism, but their occupational orientation added another dimension to their attitudes. For example, Samuel Gompers, as an AFL trade unionist, adopted a pro-rebel position partly because the powerful and well-financed Cuban junto in the United States was willing to push, in exchange, for the unionization of Cuban cigar workers who had migrated to Florida. Similarly, businessmen based their attitudes on the Cuban issue partly on the size or existence of their stake in the Cuban economy, or more generally on their widely shared assumption that excessive concern over Cuba could only detract from and impair the first priority of recovery from domestic depression.

The impact of locals and functionals was not fully felt until early 1898, and even then it reinforced American policy more than it shaped it. Its only real imprint can be seen in Congress' inclination to grant belligerency status to the rebels—an opinion steadfastly ignored by both Cleveland and his Republican successor, William McKinley. Overall, it was a small cosmopolitan elite, centered in the executive branch of the government, that defined both the general thrust and the specifics of American policy, adhered to that policy with remarkable consistency through both Democratic and Republican administrations, and ultimately intervened in Cuba, less under pressure from other segments of society than from the inner and almost inexorable logic of the policy itself.

From the beginning of the revolution, elite decision-makers confronted two horrendous possibilities. One was the possibility of war with Spain, as Spanish-American relations deteriorated drastically amidst Spanish accusations that the United States deliberately belied its neutral stance by giving the Cuban junto a free hand, by failing to halt the smuggling of arms, men, and supplies into Cuba, and by using its mediation offers as a screen to mask interference in a Spanish internal matter and to usurp Spanish control in Cuba. In view of the unpredictable impact of war on economic recovery and the disturbing possibility that war with Spain might bring military confrontation with other powers as well, it seemed self-evident that war ought to be avoided if possible.

On the other hand, there was the possibility that the Cuban rebels just might oust Spain. And in view of the low esteem in which Cuban rebels were held by most American policy-makers, this possibility conjured up the further prospect of an independent Cuba that would be intolerably unstable, would not be able to protect lives and property and honor its debts, and would eventually be driven into an internecine racial and class war. Since the American government could not permit such strife to end in the establishment of a potentially radical and nationalist "black republic," the decision-makers saw no choice but to intervene and shoulder the burden of governing Cuba themselves. To an anti-imperialist like Cleveland, exercising such a colonial option was an anathema. It was only slightly less so to a utilitarian like McKinley, who evidenced little enthusiasm for embracing the same sort of revolutionary time bomb that had so recently blown up in Spain's face.

The Policy of Reasonable Delay. By late 1896, faced with such unhappy possibilities, the Cleveland administration evolved a response that might be called the "reasonable delay" policy. Its essentials were these: (1) The United States had no desire to usurp Spanish authority in Cuba; its sole foreign policy objective was "pacification" (ending the revolution), both to end unnecessary suffering and to provide the stability necessary for the protection of American economic and strategic interests. (2) The United States was willing to honor its first obligation to respect Spanish sovereignty, and therefore it would give Spain a reasonable time in which to accomplish pacification itself. ("Reasonable" was left undefined, although Cleveland had initially favored a cutoff point of December 31, 1897.) Presumably the mode of pacification was Spain's to determine, but given American doubts about a military solution, Cleveland clearly encouraged negotiated autonomy as the only viable route for Spain to follow. (3) But if "the inability of Spain to deal successfully with the insurrection [became] manifest" after a reasonable time had elapsed, the United States' obligation to Spanish sovereignty would be superseded by higher obligations to humanity and by concrete obligations to endangered American interests, and would require appropriate steps. Translated from the abstract, the policy indicated that the United States would be forced to interfere directly: politically if possible (as in Venezuela), militarily if necessary (as in Brazil).[7]

The McKinley administration, after a general review, accepted Cleveland's "reasonable delay" policy wholly unchanged. But by early summer of 1897, the administration had grown alarmed over the lack of progress in Cuba and over reports that Spain intended to resume full-scale military activities once the Cuban rainy season ended in September. This concern prompted a lengthy and emphatic note to Spain on July 16 which did three things. First, it precisely defined for Spain the nature and importance of American interests in the Cuban situation. Significantly, it added two points not emphasized before. It

---

[7] Ibid., pp. 295–97.

put forth the syllogism that American economic recovery depended upon the confidence that could be born only of predictability; the Cuban crisis caused unpredictability by perpetuating anxiety over the future—war or peace; and therefore the Cuban crisis was the chief cause of American sluggishness in recovering from the Panic of 1893. It also noted another point: that the Cuban issue had roused such popular agitation that it threatened to transform a foreign policy issue into a domestic political one. Second, it defined the "reasonable delay" policy more explicitly than ever before. Third, it closed on this ominous note: "The question arises, then, whether Spain has not already had a reasonable time to restore peace and been unable to do so."[8] Privately and informally, the administration intimated that the end of the rainy season ought to be time enough for Spain to take some concrete steps toward a negotiated settlement. At the same time, the American military refined its contingency plans in case of war, including a presidentially approved plan to attack Manila if war did occur. An elated Theodore Roosevelt concluded, and perhaps rightly, that the administration would intervene in the fall if Spain resumed futile military measures in Cuba.

Spain, however, received a reprieve as a change in governments brought to power a party committed to the creation of a home assembly in Cuba and some degree of autonomy for the island. Consequently the administration gave Spain a time extension, although McKinley warned that the United States could not contemplate an indefinite delay for the achievement of pacification. Informally, the administration intimated that the revolution should be ended by the start of the rainy season in 1898. If not, the rebellion would certainly carry on through another rainy season, since the guerrilla tactics of the rebels fared best in that period, while conversely Spain would hardly negotiate a settlement during a period of relative weakness. Thus the fall of 1898 would roll around with Cuba still operating as the psychological stumbling block to complete economic recovery and an issue in the important congressional elections in November. It was an eventuality the administration could not tolerate.

Unfortunately, Spain was unable to keep its reform promises. The ruling party's hold was so tenuous that any real innovations in Cuban policy were likely to topple it from power. In any case, reports from Havana made it clear that the rebels, after such expenditure of blood and effort, and clearly dubious about Spanish promises, would settle for nothing less than independence. Key evidence to McKinley of Spain's failure centered on the promised Cuban home assembly. Originally scheduled for January, its opening date was pushed back

---

[8] Ibid., pp. 335–36.

to May—too close to the rainy season to be of value as an institutional means of reconciliation. Moreover, revolutionary representatives were excluded from its membership, and its powers were only vaguely defined. Seeing, then, no reasonable hope that Spain could bring about pacification by the rainy season or any other time, the administration decided in early March 1898 that the United States would have to intervene to end the revolution, although it was still hoped that the intervention could be diplomatic rather than military.

Reinforcement from the Public and Business. The Cleveland-McKinley policy of reasonable delay had thus run its course by early 1898. Even if no other factors had existed, the policy probably would have led to much the same direction that McKinley was to follow. But other factors did exist, and they powerfully reinforced the drift of administration policy and certainly facilitated its implementation. One was the increase in popular sentiment for the United States to end its neutrality and take positive steps to end the revolution. Growing in strength for some time, this sentiment peaked early in 1898 with a series of inflammatory episodes that stirred anti-Spanish feeling. Chief of these was the sinking of the American battleship *Maine* in Havana Harbor during its provocative visit there—an act that many Americans irrationally assumed to be the responsibility of the Spanish. As a political leader anxious to take a strong and united party into the 1898 elections, McKinley could hardly be insensitive to such public furor. But to see him, as some have, as a spineless figure caving in to public opinion and opting for a war he did not want is a gross misreading of the historical record. That much seems evident in his effort to try diplomatic intervention first, despite public preference to shoot first and talk later, and in the fact that when he did find war necessary, he went into it on his own terms—not those of the rebel sympathizers—and for reasons wholly antithetical to theirs.

The other factor reinforcing an interventionist policy was the changing mind of the business community. Until early 1898, most businessmen preferred to maintain a low profile on the Cuban issue lest it detract from the first priority of economic recovery. But faced with some indices that recovery had been less than complete by 1898, and anxious about the future, many of the more influential in the business world changed their minds; not for abstract, humanitarian reasons, but because they had come to accept the proposition that anxiety over possible war was worse for economic conditions than the consequences of actual war. As one of McKinley's political confidants in New York City put it in a telegram that reached the President: "Big corporations here now believe we will have war. Believe all would welcome it as a relief to suspense."[9]

Interaction: War. The intersection of these factors—mass opinion, business sentiment, and the inner logic of the administration's own policy—led to the first stage of American intervention in March 1898. It was a diplomatic intervention and came in two steps. The first came on March 1 and can be interpreted either as only a gesture or as a last desperate effort to see if Spain could effect pacification. In effect, the administration, while avoiding the appearance of an ultimatum, gave Spain until April 1 to initiate steps that would end the revolution by May 1. As the American ambassador in Madrid told an influential Spanish businessman, "Finish this rebellion, no matter what your government is required to do, before the RAINY SEASON begins. . . . End it at once—end it at once—END IT AT ONCE!"[10]

Short of a capitulation that Spanish pride prohibited, there was no way for Spain to satisfy the American injunction. So, on March 27, when the predictable Spanish failure was evident, McKinley interjected his country's diplomacy more directly. In a quasi ultimatum, he insisted upon an immediate armistice, a guarantee that that armistice would last until October 1, and agreement that in the interim, "the friendly offices of the President of the United States" would mediate the conflict and presumably dictate the settlement. After some procrastination and fruitless diplomatic maneuvering, Spain finally responded on April 9 by announcing a suspension of hostilities. Often interpreted as a capitulation that McKinley chose to ignore in a cowardly acquiescence to the public thirst for war, the Spanish reply was in fact wholly unsatisfactory. It did not accept the October 1 deadline, thus leaving Spain free to resume hostilities at any time. Indeed, Spain refused to consider such a deadline unless it was solicited by the rebels—a wholly improbable occurrence. And most important, it did not accept McKinley's mediation, but continued to insist that the Cuban home assembly—an institution in name only—was the only vehicle for a negotiated settlement. In short, all Spain did was suspend hostilities at a time—the rainy season—when it always quit fighting anyway. In no way did it hold out any realistic hope that that suspension would lead to a political settlement. Consequently, McKinley was convinced that only a solution dictated and superimposed by the United States could end the revolution. So on April 11 he called upon Spain to evacuate the island peacefully,

---

9 Ibid., p. 392.
10 *Foreign Relations, 1898* (Washington, D.C., 1901), p. 284.

and asked Congress for war powers to force that evacuation if Spain declined. Spain did decline, and war was on.

Intervention: The Ground and Objectives.   Intervening militarily still left open the fundamental question: on what grounds and for what objectives? The McKinley administration had considered that question at length as early as August 1897 and decided that it had two choices. It could recognize the independence of the proclaimed Republic of Cuba and enter the war as its ally to overthrow Spain. Or "we may intervene for the protection of our own endangered interests against the malice or impotence of both contending parties."[11] The administration chose the latter course, partly because it would be easier to justify to world opinion, more largely because it was the only course consistent with the American aim of pacification. Given its assumption about the incompetence and irresponsibility of the rebels, especially the faction led by Máximo Gómez, the administration was not about to bind itself to the rebel government, oust Spain, and then quietly retire, leaving Cuba in the hands of a regime that might not be willing or able to protect American economic and strategic interests. Consequently, McKinley's war message candidly stated that the military "resort involved 'hostile constraints' upon *both* contending parties."[12] And in keeping with this sentiment during the war, the American military (under McKinley's orders) avoided formal military cooperation with the rebels; refused them any combat role, relegating them to latrine duty and supply and support; denied their leaders any participation in Spanish surrender ceremonies; retained Spanish authorities in temporary civilian posts rather than replacing them with rebels; and generally did everything possible to avoid any appearance of recognizing the legitimacy of the rebel regime.

When first made public in his war message, this policy of neutral, enforced pacification roused a storm of congressional and public protests from those few with a vested stake in Cuban independence (holders of Cuban revolutionary war bonds) and the much larger number who emotionally had come to identify with the rebels. As a result of this protest, the Senate passed the much-ignored Turpie Amendment, which declared that any military intervention had to be preceded by complete recognition of the independence of the Republic of Cuba; and that as a corollary, the United States would intervene only at that government's request, and presumably would withdraw from Cuba on the same terms. In the 51–37 vote favoring the amendment, a fair number of

[11] Alvey Adee to Secretary of State Sherman, August 19, 1897, William McKinley papers.
[12] *Foreign Relations, 1898*, p. 757.

Republican senators—especially those up for reelection—broke with the administration. But McKinley, indicating a grim determination to go to war only on his terms and for his objectives, forced the Senate to about-face. Using all the vast presidential power at his disposal, he persuaded enough Republican senators of the political safety of abstention so that a second vote of 41–35 threw out the Turpie stipulations.

To be sure, the Senate rapidly followed with the more famous Teller Amendment, promising Cuban independence. But the promise was not immediate independence to some already proclaimed government; it was a promise of eventual independence to some undefined and future Cuban government. To be more specific, its promise of independence hinged on the achievement of "pacification" in Cuba. But it was solely up to the United States to determine what constituted pacification and when it had been achieved. The Cubans themselves had no say in the matter. In short, the Teller Amendment, while promising independence, left the door wide open for an American protectorate.

A protectorate was a prospect McKinley could easily live with as the best mode of safeguarding American national interests. So the Teller Amendment was a rather sugar-coated pill to swallow. In view of public sentiment at the war's beginning, annexation seemed politically impossible anyway. But even when that sentiment grew ambivalent, as public idealization of the rebels changed to racial slurs and as military bureaucrats and vested interests began

"I can never digest that mess without straining my constitution"

to push for annexation, the President still regarded annexation as inadvisable, simply because he feared that Cuba would consider American rule, however benevolent, no more acceptable than Spain's. It was a fear reinforced by two factors: one was the increasingly overt anti-Americanism in Cuba, which grew in proportion to the length of the postwar occupation; the other was the bloody insurrection against American colonialism that began in the Philippines in 1899. The interaction of the two raised the real possibility that the United States might have to contend with two anticolonial revolutions halfway around the world from each other—an eventuality that would severely tax the nation's treasury, its military capabilities, and its ideological integrity.

Pacification Equals Protectorate. The easy victory over Spain in 1898 left McKinley with the problem of defining pacification and determining its completion. He did so in most general terms in his presidential message of December 1898, when he made it clear that pacification meant the creation of a stable, pro-American regime: one that would pay its debts, protect foreigners and their property, follow enlightened trade policies, practice thrift and industry, be just and benevolent, and generally maintain tranquillity. As he summarized it: "Until there is complete tranquillity in the island and a stable government inaugurated, American military government will continue."[13] Cutting through the rhetoric, one shrewd British observer characterized the plan as a prospectus for converting Cuba into an American Egypt.

During the next three years of American military rule, the administration, acting through Secretary of War Elihu Root, gave more specific meaning to pacification. In the short run, during the period of occupation, this encompassed several things: (1) physical reconstruction, sanitation programs, and the resumption of normal services—both to end human suffering and to make the economy viable; (2) the disarming and demobilization of the potentially dangerous rebel army, chiefly through the inducement of mustering-out pay; (3) the attempted cooptation of revolutionary leaders through the proffering of well-paid sinecures (Gómez, for example, was offered—and refused—a $5,000-a-year pro forma job as head of a committee for disabled veterans); and (4) an effort to favor the political fortunes of the more respectable (and presumably pro-American) classes by imposing literacy and property restrictions on voting rights.

The more basic goal of pacification was an institutionalization of Cuban-American relations which would continue even when occupation ended.

---

[13] David Healy, *The United States in Cuba, 1898–1902* (Madison, Wis., 1963), pp. 50–51.

Specifically, this meant the structuring of Cuba as a political satellite and the integration of the Cuban economy with the American marketplace. The first goal was accomplished with Cuban acceptance of the so-called Platt Amendment and later its incorporation into the Cuban constitution. It was gained, however, only in the face of mass public demonstration against it in Cuba, initial rejection of most of its provisions by the Cuban Constitutional Convention, and a Cuban effort to mobilize American congressional opinion against it. (The last effort failed to gain much support even from anti-imperialists or moderates, apparently because Congress realized that a protectorate was the least the administration would accept, and it somehow seemed better than outright annexation.) In the end, Cuba capitulated to the carrot (a promise not to interfere indiscriminately in Cuban internal affairs) and the stick (a threat to maintain military occupation indefinitely unless Cuba acquiesced). The results: (1) a nonalienation pledge by Cuba, similar to Hawaii's in 1875; (2) a curb on Cuba's foreign borrowing to prevent European powers from using Cuba's unpaid debts as an excuse for intervention; (3) the American right to maintain naval bases in Cuba (the origin of the installation at Guantánamo); and (4) the right of the United States to intervene in Cuba when American interests seemed endangered. As the American military commander in Cuba put it quite rightly: "There is, of course, little or no independence left for Cuba under the Platt Amendment."

The integration of the Cuban economy with the United States' involved several related developments. One was what some Cubans called the "commercial occupation." Translated, it meant an influx of Americans and their dollars into the plantation and export sectors, effectively reviving a one-crop sugar economy that had earlier shown signs of dying. A related development was the creation of a rail network. New American-owned railways were constructed, and foreign-owned lines were coerced into coordinating their activities and rates with those of the American companies. The purpose was to facilitate the movement of sugar to port facilities for export. Overall, the system had little spread effect for the Cuban economy.

The final development came with mutual ratification of a reciprocal trade treaty in 1903. Blocked in 1901 and 1902 by the American beet sugar industry, the trade agreement was finally passed when the beet sugar interests were bought out by the American Sugar Refining Company (the so-called Sugar Trust). The resulting treaty gave Cuba a 20 percent tariff break on its sugar exports to the United States; Cuba, in turn, gave a 20 percent tariff reduction on all American manufactures, and higher reductions (up to 40 percent) on selected items the United States wished to push. Implicit in the treaty was the hope that Cuba might develop into a significant marketplace—a hope never fully realized because of the maldistribution of wealth in Cuban society. Still, the treaty did have its benefits for the United States. It obviously produced dividends for the American investors who came to dominate the Cuban sugar industry by enabling Cuban sugar to be exported and sold advantageously in the United States. But the political implications of the trade arrangements were perhaps even more significant, for by controlling Cuba's major export crop and regulating the conditions of its sale, the United States gained a predominance of influence in Cuban affairs which was to endure long after the Platt Amendment (or at least most of it) passed from the scene in the 1930s.

The China Market

HOPE

The Cuban crisis coincided with another in China, which eventually proved of greater importance to American interests. It began with China's crushing defeat in the Sino-Japanese War of 1894–1895. To an America that historically had thirsted after the fabled markets of Cathay, to an America almost frenetically searching for foreign markets to cure domestic ills, China's defeat seemed God-sent. Not only did the peace treaty further liberalize China's foreign trade policies; it was also widely assumed that the ignominious defeat had finally taught China the futility of its anti-Western exclusiveness. Now China's only hope for national survival lay in emulating its conqueror through modernization and Westernization. In other words, the long-awaited "awakening of China" from its slumbering semi-isolation seemed imminent, and with it the coveted chance to convert the myth of the China market into reality. It was this belief, however unrealistic, that led American bureaucrats and businessmen, cosmopolitans and functionals, missionaries and seculars, to combine their voices in a Wagnerian crescendo of hope that peaked in 1900, and which has never ceased to shape American policy in Asia.

THREAT

For the moment, however, the horn of plenty turned out to be Pandora's box. China was no Latin America, where the United States could hope to achieve hegemony, and often did. Here the full cast of international powers played their roles, often with far greater military, political, and financial advantages than the United States'. Moreover, many of them followed overtly imperialist courses and saw in China's defeat only its vulnerability to colonial partitioning. This was especially true of Russia, France, and Germany, which preferred closed spheres of influence to open, nondiscriminatory, multilateral trade—chiefly because they lacked the competitive advantages of Britain's superior industrialization and Japan's proximity.

It was the actions of these three powers, especially Russia's, that threatened to turn American commercial dreams into a commercial nightmare between 1895 and 1901. The snowballing sequence began in 1895 when those three powers, known as the *Dreibund,* successfully intervened in Sino-Japanese peace talks and forced Japan to give up territorial demands on China and satisfy itself with a monetary indemnity. China's known inability to pay that indemnity in turn kicked off a wild scramble among the powers to secure the indemnity loans that would put China in vulnerable hock to them. The first and most important of those loans went to the Russo-French combine, probably as a political payoff for their recent diplomatic intervention. To many ob-servers, the move signaled the ascendancy of Russia over Britain in Peking's decisions. It was a conclusion greatly buttressed a year later, in 1896, when the Li-Lobanov Pact gave Russia the right to extend its Trans-Siberian Railroad across northern Manchuria. Along with it came such extraordinary commercial and monetary privileges that the pact seemed to give the Russians (and their French financial backers) de facto control of the area.

None of these plums went to Germany, the third member of the *Dreibund*. In November 1897 Germany responded to that calculated rebuff by exploiting a minor incident to seize the port of Kiaochou and force China to agree to a fifty-year German occupation of the port, plus exclusive mining and railroad rights in the entire province of Shantung. Several months later, early in 1898, the next shoe fell when Russia pushed its influence into southern Manchuria by acquiring twenty-five-year control of an extensive zone (including Port Arthur) which had important military and commercial potential. Great Britain, as the leading commercial power in China and the one most threatened by these developments, reacted vigorously. Failing to gain any international backing to support the Open Door against Russian moves, Britain turned to unilateral measures to expand and consolidate its position at Hong Kong and in the Yangtze Valley, and more importantly to counterbalance Russia's stra-tegic position at Port Arthur by acquiring a military position at Wei-hei-wei. France, in turn, expanded its formal and informal influence in the areas north of Indochina. Japan acquired an option from China on the area opposite Taiwan, and in addition secured Russian recognition of the predominant role of Japan in Korea in exchange for Japanese acceptance of the Russian zone around Port Arthur. This six-month orgy has been dubbed the "partitioning" of China, but it was by no means a complete partitioning. Many of the British, French, and Japanese moves simply created optional spheres rather than immediate, operative ones. Nonetheless, it was clear that if Germany and/or Russia moved to close the commercial door in their spheres, the result would be either war (which no one wanted) or the conversion of the optional spheres into real ones. If that happened, the "Sick Man of Asia" would almost certainly die, and along with it the United States' grandiose hopes for a new commercial frontier in the Celestial Empire.

AMERICA'S INITIAL RESPONSE

The American reaction to this evolving crisis was singularly ineffective between 1895 and 1898. The Cleveland administration hamstrung itself much of the time by its own laissez-faire orientation, which prohibited the American minister to China from directly and formally promoting American business proposals. Not until the Li-Lobanov Pact of 1896 did the government perceive the total inadequacy of this approach, and issue new instructions ordering the American minister to do anything and everything to promote American commercial interests. It was a classic too-little, too-late response.

During its first six months, the McKinley administration benefited from relative calm in China, during which it steadily, though unspectacularly, pushed American trade expansion there. But the explosion triggered by the German and Russian moves late in 1897 and early in 1898 left the administration as alarmed as it was helpless. Certainly the administration had defined China as a major target area for the trade expansion it viewed as indispensable for the American economy; certainly it had defined the Open Door as the best means for American enterprise to gain the largest possible share of the China market; certainly it perceived the dangers to that outlet in the partitioning moves. But neither the pressures of special business interests at home nor British pleas for cooperation abroad could persuade the administration to do any more than it probably would have done on its own in any case: that is, vigorously proclaim American commitment to the Open Door throughout China; inquire whether the Germans and Russians intended to honor that principle in their new spheres; and watch, wait, and hope. To do more was simply impractical. Increasingly preoccupied with Cuba, the United States lacked the Pacific commercial-military bases that the Mahanite views of the day saw as necessary for the implementation of a strong economic and diplomatic defense of the Open Door. Fortunately, the impending and almost certain conflict with Spain over Cuba gave the administration a chance to secure bases in the Pacific from which to launch an effective response to the China crisis.

INSULAR IMPERIALISM: SOME
HELP FOR THE OPEN DOOR

From the very beginning of the Spanish-American War, the McKinley administration intended to retain a foothold in the Philippines as an "American Hong Kong," a commercial entrepôt to the China market and a center of American military power in the western Pacific. The administration-approved plan to take and hold Manila was not part of a military plan to attack the Spanish navy wherever it might be found. It was a political plan to strengthen America's hand in a crisis-ridden area of the utmost importance. Any other explanation fails to account for the sequence and content of McKinley's subsequent rapid-fire decisions: (1) On May 2, before definitive confirmation of Commodore George Dewey's victory at Manila, the administration decided to send a 20,000-man army of occupation to the Philippines. (2) On May 4, three days before confirmation of the safety of Dewey's squadron, it issued a formal call for volunteers. (3) On May 11, the Cabinet, acting on McKinley's advice, approved a State Department memorandum, prepared earlier, calling for Spanish cession of Manila; the rest of the Philippines were to remain in Spanish hands. (4) On May 19, McKinley enpowered the American expedition commander to replace Spanish political rule with American, and instructed the Secretary of the Treasury to substitute American tax rates and collection for Spain's.

The decision to retain Manila was no isolated step. In an age in which coaling stations, naval bases, and cable relay points were the keys to keeping open the arteries of trade, the McKinley administration was consciously constructing an eclectic, integrated system of insular possessions that would protect America trade with Asia and maintain a military presence that would bolster its Far Eastern diplomacy. The Greater Antilles were one terminus in the chain; Manila was the other; the projected isthmian canal was to be the drawbridge. In between lay a series of way stations. Of these, Hawaii, nearly annexed by the administration in 1897, was strategically, economically, and historically the most important. The milieu created by the war made McKinley's task there, as expected, much easier. So the administration vigorously reopened the issue of annexation early in June and secured the approval of both houses of Congress (by a greater than two-thirds vote in each) within a month. In the intervening debate, administration spokesmen talked rarely of Hawaii's own worth, almost exclusively of its value as a halfway house to the Orient. Filling in the neatly spaced system were the islands of Guam (taken from Spain early in June) and Wake (occupied as the Senate completed approval on Hawaii). No other islands were taken because none were considered needed—a fact attested to by the United States' lack of interest in acquiring *all* the Mariana, Caroline, and Marshall islands from Spain, even for a modest *quid pro quo*.

The American empire of 1898, then, was a self-limiting one, taken for very calculated reasons. But what then of the United States' Philippine policy, which between May and October shifted from a desire to retain Manila alone to ambivalence to a decision to retain the entire island of Luzon to the ultimate determination to hang onto the whole archipelago? Does that development not contradict any assertion that the United States' insular imperialism was utilitarian in nature? In a word, no. First, each step was taken reluctantly, painfully, and against strong opposition within the ranks of McKinley's advisers. Territorial imperatives and social Darwinism played no visible role. Second, each shift in policy was made in response to the growing realization that Manila could not be retained without control of the surrounding area; to retain Manila was to retain all the rest. If Spain reasserted sovereignty in the rest of the archipelago, revolution—another Cuba—was a certainty. If the rebels tried to rule themselves, anarchy and chaos would be the order of the day—or so WASP policy-makers believed. And then there was Germany, with its ill-disguised hostility to American retention of the islands. If Spain retained them, it might well cede them later to Germany. (Germany had an option on Spain's Pacific possessions should Spain choose to part with them.) If the rebels ruled, the ensuing instability might provide Germany with the excuse and the opportunity to intervene. In any of these contingencies, Manila would be isolated and vulnerable, a fact driven dramatically home by detailed American military reports that pictured Manila, Luzon, and the Philippines in general as a kind of economically interdependent system in which no one part could stand alone.

THE CHOSEN ALTERNATIVE:
CONSENSUS NEUTRALIZATION

Its power base enhanced by war, the United States entered 1899 with three alternative means of preserving the possibility of expanded trade with China. One was to shut the Open Door and join in the partitioning, an option seriously considered on occasion but never affirmed, chiefly because the administration would not settle for only a slice of the China market (save as a last resort) while it still entertained hopes for the lion's share. The second was to make common cause with Great Britain and Japan—the two powers most popularly identified with the Open Door policy—and use any necessary force to make Russia and others accept the concept of nondiscriminatory trade in all of China, spheres included. But that option would have been politically unpopular at home, would have reduced America's traditional freedom of action, might have led to the international war everyone wished to avoid, and was predicated upon a commonality of interests with the British and Japanese about which McKinley rightly had strong doubts. The third alternative—and the one ultimately followed—was that of consensus neutralization of China: that is, gaining agreement among all the powers that individually and collectively their best interests would be served by exempting China from the imperializing process. That this plan—at that time, at least—was bound to fail is easy to see in retrospect. But it was based on seemingly realistic perceptions: (1) that a delicate de facto balance of power existed in the Far East between the Franco-Russian entente and the emerging Anglo-Japanese bloc; (2) that all the foreign offices of Europe were beset with fear that the China crisis might precipitate a world conflagration; and (3) that in this framework of balance and fear, if a third force dramatically insisted that the Open Door and Chinese integrity be universally accepted, and if that third force had the capacity to upset that delicate balance (as the United States certainly had in Europe's eyes after 1898), then there was some chance that consensus neutralization just might succeed.

Implementation of the third approach came in late summer and fall of 1899 with the dispatch of Secretary of State John Hay's famous Open Door notes to the interested powers. He chose the time largely because Russian policy seemed in a particularly vulnerable bind; it could not afford an outright rejection of the Open Door principle without advertising its ulterior motives—something it was not yet in a position to do. He based the content of the notes largely on a memorandum prepared by his chief adviser, W. W. Rockhill, but its general theme was one to which Hay personally had been long committed. Theoretically, the notes denied the legality of the spheres by repeatedly deprecating them as "so-called," and the preamble to the note to the British specifically referred to the need to maintain Chinese integrity. Practically, however, the notes accepted the spheres, at least temporarily, while trying to neutralize their economic impact. Specifically, the notes asked that the partitioning powers levy the same tariffs and other duties on other foreign merchants as it did on its own—no more, no less. And similarly, while accepting the right of the powers to exclusive railroad rights in specified areas, the United States insisted on the same across-the-board equality of railroad rates. In short, neither tariffs, harbor fees, railroad rates, nor any other duties were to be manipulated, in or outside the spheres and leases, in ways that would discriminate in favor of any one national group against any others.

In negotiating acceptance of the Open Door notes, Hay employed the clever technique of falling dominoes: of negotiating first with the power most likely to accept the principles involved (Great Britain), and then moving consecutively down the line to the power least likely to do so (Russia), using the cumulative force of prior acceptances to overcome each successive opposition. At the time, the results were widely hailed by Americans as a grand diplomatic triumph. Since then critics have dismissed the replies as vague, evasive, conditional, and thus meaningless. But such criticisms miss the point that Hay's accomplishment was not an end in itself and should not be evaluated as such. It was simply a first effort, however dramatic, to structure a framework within which the more traditional dynamics of diplomacy could operate. Russia's promises might be false (as Hay believed), but such public commitments offered the United States useful means to force opponents of the Open Door to use more indirect and perhaps less effective tactics; to exploit Europe's fear of war by offering a peaceful substitute to the imperial rat race; to convince un-

New member of the orchestra

believers of the earnestness of the United States' intentions and of its capabilities of manipulating, if need be, the balance of power. All these techniques and others could be and were tried, for the China market, with its vast potential, seemed well worth the effort.

THE FUSE IS LIT: CHINA AND
UNANTICIPATED CONSEQUENCES

And yet one crucial variable was left out of American calculations: China itself. Regarded merely as a passive entity, it was to have only nominal sovereignty and was to be protected paternalistically while its economy was exploited. But China would not be left out of the picture. Indeed, the ink was hardly dry on the responses to the Open Door notes when Manchuria and much of northern China erupted in a massive uprising against the foreign presence which came to be tagged the Boxer Rebellion. Foreigners, Chinese Christian converts, and foreign rails and property were attacked, and ultimately the foreign legations were besieged in their compound in Peking. The consequences for American policy were staggering. The rebellion forced the United States to precisely the military response its policies had sought to avoid. Five thousand American troops joined Japan and the European powers in an effort to free the legations and restore order. Fear that the rebellion invited further partition forced the United States to affirm more directly its support of Chinese integrity and thus indirectly to attack any policy of further sphere development—a rhetorical position it had no means of enforcing upon anyone, even past supporters of the Open Door like Britain and Japan. At the moment of deepest despair, in August 1900, the United States very nearly gave up on the Open Door altogether and prepared to accept partitioning as inevitable. And even when that dark moment passed and the rebellion was quelled, events sucked the United States into a vortex of postrebellion negotiations that were so tedious, complicated, devious, and ultimately impervious to American influence that Rockhill, the chief American negotiator, expressed fervent hopes that his country would never participate in the like again.

In the end, the Chinese "criminals" were punished, indemnities were assessed, new trade agreements were reached, and the Manchus were restored to power. All's well that ends well—except it had not ended. Settlement or not, Russian troops remained in Manchuria, and Russia only bided its time until it felt ready to take the fateful and fatal steps that were shortly to lead to war with Japan—a war that would upset the whole equilibrium upon which consensus neutralization was based. As for China itself, the existential experience of the rebellion—the intensified xenophobia generated by "barbarian" intervention, pillage, and conquest, and the heightened hostility to Manchu leadership—took China several steps closer to the revolution that lay in wait only a decade ahead, an ongoing revolution that may prove to be the most significant historical phenomenon of the twentieth century.

Suggestions for Further Reading

All the suggested readings for Chapter 12 are relevant to this chapter as well.

Interesting general studies are John A. S. Grenville and George B. Young, *Politics, Strategy, and American Diplomacy* (New Haven, Conn., 1966); Walter LaFeber, *The New Empire* (Ithaca, N.Y., 1963); and Ernest R. May, *Imperial Democracy* (New York, 1961). All three give good general coverage of Pan Americanism, Cuba, and the Spanish-American War. H. Wayne Morgan, *America's Road to Empire* (New York, 1965), focuses more sharply on the Spanish-American War. A minor classic picks up the Cuban story where most leave off: David Healy, *The United States in Cuba, 1898–1902* (Madison, Wis., 1963).

On the crucial Far East, see Charles S. Campbell, Jr., *Special Business Interests and the Open Door Policy* (New Haven, Conn., 1951); Thomas McCormick, *China Market: America's Quest for Informal Empire, 1893–1901* (Chicago, 1967); Paul A. Varg, *The Making of a Myth* (East Lansing, Mich., 1969); and Marilyn B. Young, *The Rhetoric of Empire* (Cambridge, Mass., 1968).

CHAPTER 14

The Purpose
of Power
(1900–1908)

Early in 1900 publisher William Randolph Hearst, whose New York Journal had beat the drums for war with Spain, sent word to William Jennings Bryan that the Democratic party had to abandon its current anti-imperialist posture. If we wanted to win, said Hearst's agent, Bryan would have to stop harping on the Philippines. The American people were not the "give-up kind," he continued; besides, there was a more important reason: "There are seventy millions of dissatisfied people in America. They are all anxious for some one who shall suggest measures as useful to them as McKinley is useful to the trusts and millionaires." Democrats had to prove they were more patriotic, that they were just "as ardent supporters of American expansion, as they were in the days of Jefferson."[1]

Hearst had fought a circulation war with other New York newspapers on these premises, and contributed to a real war in the process by playing on the emotions of dissatisfied Americans. Whether McKinley and the Republicans had seen the war as a means of distracting the people from their preoccupation with hard times or not, there can be no doubt of Bryan's conviction that an

---

[1] Arthur Brisbane to William Jennings Bryan, February 6, 1900, in William Jennings Bryan papers, Library of Congress.

overseas empire would lead to repression at home. "A republic can have no subjects," he said. An imperial policy meant changing "our form of government."

Bryan ignored Hearst's advice, and lost the election. He had insisted that a war of conquest in the Philippines would inevitably lead to other wars of conquest, requiring an immense military establishment, which would become, just as inevitably, "a menace to the Republic."

It might happen that way, admitted another Democratic leader, Henry Watterson, the well-known editor of the *Louisville Courier-Journal.* "We risk Caesarism, certainly; but even Caesarism is preferable to anarchism." But so far, he asserted, the nation had escaped "the menace and peril of socialism and agrarianism..." while "in every direction we multiply the opportunities of the people."[2]

McKinley's Last Messages

McKINLEY RAN on a platform of multiplying opportunities, linking domestic and foreign policies in a Republican campaign for prosperity and progress. This combination had brought the country back from the depths of depression, and would carry it forward into the new century. "We have the open door in the far East through which to market our products," he declared in an exuberant speech on March 3, 1900, and "in the last two years our sales abroad have exceeded our purchases by over one billion dollars."

The Republicans received the mandate they wanted to complete the "large policy" undertaken at the time of the Spanish-American War; i.e., the pacification of the islands newly acquired, settlement of the isthmus canal question, and the inauguration of a new trade and tariff policy better suited to the needs of a maturing industrial power.

In the previous five years, 1895–1900, the United States had increased manufactured exports by 172 percent, from $129.62 million to $353.03 million. Total exports were up 73 percent, from $793.39 million to $1.37 billion. "It is too late to argue about advantages of industrial combinations," John D. Rockefeller declared. "They are a necessity. And if Americans are to have the privilege of extending their business in all States of the Union, and into foreign countries as well, they are a necessity on a large scale...."[3]

Regardless of the reasons for going to war with Spain in 1898, Cuba and the Philippines now had to be integrated into an effort to meet European com-

---

[2] *Literary Digest,* 17 (July 2, 1898):214.

[3] *Report of the Industrial Commission,* 14 vols. (Washington, D.C., 1901), 1:796.

petition for supremacy in world markets. Between 1875 and 1900 the European powers had divided up sub-Sahara Africa and most of Southeast Asia. As these areas were consolidated into "new empires," special economic relations grew up between the metropolitian rulers and their colonies. If America was to compete, it had to be more efficient at home and abroad.

The consensus on this question was complete. McKinley was every bit as "scientific" as his successors of the Progressive Era in discussing these needs: "In this age of keen rivalry among nations for mastery in commerce, the doctrine of evolution and the rule of the survival of the fittest must be as inexorable in their operation as they are positive in the results they bring about."

Bishop J. W. Bashford of the Methodist Church in America warned the members of the Ohio legislature that their state's role in the nation's economy and in turn the nation's role in the world economy depended upon money for education:

> It is apparent to all that the leading nations of the world are entering upon a gigantic struggle for the trade of the world. It is idle to hold that the United States has already won the battle. We have only witnessed the preliminary skirmish thus far. If the United States is to become the commercial and industrial leader of the world, we must by no means neglect the preparation which England and Germany are making for the struggle.

North Carolina planter Daniel Tompkins wanted better export facilities:

> The question of overproduction would seem to be dependent on the development of foreign trade to take the goods. The cotton crop is now about ten million bales. About one quarter of this crop is manufactured in the United States. The remaining seven and a half million bales are sent abroad to be manufactured. If our export trade facilities should be made equal to those of England and Germany, then the subject would be reduced to one of our ability to compete.

America's ability to compete was McKinley's chief concern after the election of 1900. His "greatest ambition," he told Senator Robert La Follette, "was to round out his career by gaining American supremacy in world markets." That problem was on his mind as he wrote his speech for the Buffalo Pan American Exposition in September 1901. In it the President called upon Congress to forsake its traditional haggling about the tariff and settle down to write a sound reciprocity policy. He had already initiated efforts in that direction by the appointment of a special reciprocity commissioner, whose instructions were to negotiate advantageous commerical treaties with European nations. "Reciprocity," McKinley said at Buffalo, was the natural outgrowth of America's industrialization.

> What we produce, beyond our domestic consumption, must have a vent abroad. The excess must be relieved through a foreign outlet and we should sell every-

where we can, and buy wherever the buying will enlarge our sales and productions, and thereby make a greater demand for home labor.

The period of exclusiveness is past. The expansion of our trade and
commerce is the pressing problem....

At a public reception on the following day, McKinley was shot to death by
by an avowed anarchist, Leon F. Czolgosz. The speech was a fitting farewell
message to the nation, and it put the issue of imperialism in proper perspective,
as part of a larger policy, not its determinant. The assassination, on the other
hand, was a grim reminder that there were still strong undercurrents among
the "millions of dissatisfied." The Progressives had large tasks before them.

That Damned Cowboy

"I WISH that capitalists would see that what I am advocating ... is really in the
interest of property," Theodore Roosevelt wrote a newspaper editor on October
19, 1902, "for it will save it from the danger of revolution." TR backed away
from McKinley's reciprocity policy, however, because he was convinced that
the Republican party was too divided still on the tariff. He could not manage a
new tariff plan and all the other reforms he felt were more necessary. Did critics
really want him to risk turning the country over to the Democrats, whose low-
tariff notions were just as simplistic as the diehard protectionism in his own
party?

Unwilling to take that chance, TR set about finding an alternative. It had
already been spelled out by his friend Brooks Adams, who emphasized that the
only alternative policy to reciprocity was military preparedness. TR probably
would have taken this route even if he had never known Adams or read what
he had to say on the subject. As it was, Adams' advocacy of military preparedness provided him with powerful support:

> If Americans are determined to reject reciprocity in all its forms, to insist on
> their advantages, to concede nothing to the adversary; if, having driven in the
> knife, they mean to turn it in the wound, they should recognize that they
> are provoking reprisals in every form, and accept the situation with its limi-
> tations....
>
> America enjoys no immunity from natural laws. She can pay for what
> she takes, or she can fight for it, but she cannot have the earth for nothing.[4]

Of all the McKinley-Roosevelt foreign policies, however, the one Adams
found most intriguing was John Hay's Open Door policy in regard to China.

---

[4] Brooks Adams, "Reciprocity or the Alternative," *Atlantic Monthly*, 88 (August 1901):145–
55.

The stakes were immense, the outcome by no means certain. If a conflict did take place, it would probably originate there.

THE CHINESE PUZZLE

John Hay had sent the powers a second Open Door note on July 3, 1900, calling upon them not to use the Boxer Rebellion as an excuse to slice up China. They should pledge themselves to uphold the principles of "Chinese territorial and administrative integrity" and to guarantee to all nations "equal and impartial trade with all parts of the Chinese Empire." A Berlin newspaper summed up the European reaction: "The Americans regard, in a certain sense, all China as their sphere of interest."

As diplomat-historian George F. Kennan wrote fifty years later, Hay had asked everyone in the room who was not a thief to stand up. But the Secretary of State was far more sophisticated than his critics have assumed. He never expected imperial Russia, the most difficult of the powers, to commit itself to the Open Door policy. "The talk of the papers about our 'pre-eminent moral position giving us the authority to dictate to the world' is mere flap-doodle," he confided to an aide.[5] What he and McKinley sought was just enough of a response from St. Petersburg to justify the gamble that Great Britain and Japan would be encouraged enough by the American pronouncement to stand up against the Tsar's ambitions.

It *was* a complicated policy, not one blurted out by men in the grip of some psychic aberration or overpowering Anglophilia. There were plenty of reasons to doubt the ultimate success of the China policy, and McKinley and Hay did doubt it; but as Hay put it, there was no alternative but to "do everything we can for the integrity and reform of China, and to hold on like grim death to the open door...."[6]

The Russians claimed they harbored no scheme to occupy Manchuria permanently after the Boxer Rebellion was put down, but they refused to say when they would withdraw their forces. The rebellion, an antiforeign uprising by Chinese secret societies aided clandestinely by the Dowager Empress, had given the Russians an excuse to send troops into Manchuria, an area the Tsar's advisers regarded as a private preserve for the recently completed Trans-Siberian Railroad. American exporters and other poachers were not welcome.

What could the United States do? Every time the American minister in Peking urged the Chinese government to assert its rights, he was answered

---

[5] John Hay to Alvey A. Adee, September 14, 1900, in William McKinley papers, Library of Congress.

[6] John Hay, *The Letters of John Hay*, ed. Henry Adams, 3 vols. (Washington, D.C., 1908), 3:192–93.

with a question: What will America do to support China besides sending notes to the other powers? Washington was still trying to formulate a reply to that question when London and Tokyo acted, announcing their new alliance on January 30, 1902. The Anglo-Japanese alliance would eventually become an intolerable obstacle to American policy-makers, but for the moment it provided a solid base for new initiatives. Two days later, on February 1, Secretary Hay dispatched a third Open Door note to the Chinese government, protesting Sino-Russian negotiations on a Manchurian "convention." "An agreement by which China cedes to any corporation or company the exclusive right and privilege of opening mines, establishing railroads, or in any other way industrially developing Manchuria, can but be viewed with the gravest concern by the Government of the United States," wrote the Secretary. "It constitutes a monopoly, which is a distinct breach of the stipulations of treaties concluded between China and foreign powers...."

Russia naturally resented such connivance with the Anglo-Japanese entente, maintaining it desired nothing more than what other nations already claimed elsewhere— for example, Germany in the Shantung peninsula. American diplomats countered that spheres of influence anywhere in China were indeed deplorable and all nations should cooperate to eliminate them, but Manchuria was under consideration now.

Meanwhile, the Department of State launched a separate initiative on its own, the first of many efforts to strengthen China's finances and thereby increase its ability to resist future foreign inducements and threats. These efforts would not cease, in fact, until 1949, when the Chinese Communists finally established themselves in power. In January 1903, to go back to the beginning, both China and Mexico, silver-standard nations, requested United States aid in stabilizing their currencies in relation to gold-standard nations. It was to America's interest, wrote banker Charles A. Conant in the *North American Review,* to do all it could in this area for the sake of promoting "our export trade." Indeed, "the United States is perhaps more keenly interested than any other country, with the possible exception of Great Britain, in giving stability to exchange with China."

Washington sent an expert, Professor Jeremiah Jenks, to deliver its proposal: China should turn over its financial affairs to a board of foreign experts, headed by an American comptroller of currency. The British and the Japanese would also have prominent roles to play in this reorganization. Needless to say, the Russians were not happy with this idea, nor, indeed, were the other powers. And neither were Chinese leaders. One, Chang Chih-tung, read Jenks's plans with deep fear: "They are so pregnant with calamities that my heart was struck cold with fear when I read them."

Jenks never confronted Chang. He spoke no Chinese. Mistaking his hosts' cordiality and deference for consent, he sent back optimistic reports about his progress. It took him three weeks to discover that he had been talking to low-level functionaries who ran the Chinese mint. Another pattern was established for future encounters with the Chinese.

Moving on to Tokyo, Jenks found the Japanese concerned only with stopping Russia in Manchuria and Korea. Secretary Hay already knew this, and wrote Roosevelt on one occasion that if the United States would only give Japan a wink, that country would "fly at the throat of Russia in a moment." TR also heard from his closest friend, Senator Henry Cabot Lodge: "Our people everywhere are waking up to the importance of Eastern Commerce, and in certain localities the feeling is very strong." Some textile mill owners, Lodge added, were even demanding that the fleet be sent to back up American demands.[7]

Roosevelt took a strong public stand with Russia later in the summer of 1903, but it was the Japanese attack on the Tsar's fleet at Port Arthur in February of 1904 that broke the impasse. "I was thoroughly well pleased with the Japanese victory," TR wrote his son, "for Japan is playing our game." A less optimistic appraisal came from an anonymous writer in the *North American Review*: "No pen has flowed faster than Mr. Hay's since he first launched his Circular to the Powers in September, 1899; but the Chinese question, I must again insist, is not one of those cases in which the pen is mightier than the sword."

THE ASIAN TEETER-TOTTER

While some American leaders sensed that Japan was unlikely to play the American game for very long, Roosevelt felt reasonably confident that Tokyo would pursue a cautious policy. He began sounding out the Japanese on their war aims almost as soon as the guns stopped firing at Port Arthur. He did not want Russia eliminated as an Asian power, if only to put his faith in Japan beyond subjective evaluation. It irritated him that the states on the Pacific slope, especially California, seemed bent on insulting the Japanese by enacting racial laws and discriminating against Japanese immigrants. As he complained to Lodge, these were the very people who expected to gain the most from the oriental market, "and with besotted folly are indifferent to building up the navy while provoking this formidable new power—a power jealous, sensitive and

---

[7] Henry Cabot Lodge to Theodore Roosevelt, May 21, 1903, in Theodore Roosevelt papers, Library of Congress.

warlike, and which if irritated could at once take both the Philippines and Hawaii from us if she obtained the upper hand on the seas."[8]

"If, as Brooks Adams says," the President wrote, "we show ourselves 'opulent, aggressive and unarmed,' the Japanese may some time work us an injury." To confirm his understanding of Japanese willingness to strike a Far Eastern bargain, Secretary of War William Howard Taft went to Tokyo to talk with Prime Minister Taro Katsura. They quickly recognized their mutual desire to hold Japanese-American competition in check, lest it someday threaten the peace. In the Taft-Katsura Memorandum of July 27, 1905, the Japanese Prime Minister indicated that his country harbored no "aggressive designs whatever on the Philippines"; Taft responded that "his personal opinion," which he thought the President shared, was that Japanese troops should establish a "suzerainty" over Korea.

Meanwhile, Roosevelt essayed the role of peacemaker to bring the Russo-Japanese War to an end. But before agreeing to bring the antagonists together at Portsmouth, New Hampshire, TR had asked each to reconfirm its commit-

Roosevelt and peace envoys at Portsmouth

---

[8] Quoted in Howard K. Beale, *Theodore Roosevelt and the Rise of America to World Power* (Baltimore, 1956), p. 327.

ment to the Open Door policy. Of course, neither uncrossed his fingers, nor did Roosevelt really expect they would. American policy was to secure such commitments at every opportunity, over and over again if possible, and in this way perhaps transform the idea into reality. At the Portsmouth conference, TR initiated a second role that also became part of America's traditional China policy. Sometimes invited, sometimes unasked, American Presidents simply assumed everyone understood they were entitled to speak for China at international parleys. This role reached a climax nearly forty years later at Yalta, when another Roosevelt, Franklin Delano, promised that what TR had taken from Russia for Japan at Portsmouth in 1905—Port Arthur, Dairen, and certain Manchurian railroads—should now be returned to their previous owners. In neither instance was China consulted.

"The policy of economic monopoly and military aggression has had its day in Asia," rejoiced the *Journal of the American Asiatic Association,* the voice of American business interests in China, "and a new era of moral and material progress has dawned, whose brightening into the perfect day will be the central historical fact of the twentieth century." Rumors of secret Sino-Japanese understandings over Manchuria soon dampened this optimism considerably, and put off "the perfect day." It would be put off several more times during the next four decades, until the Chinese themselves changed the cycle completely in 1949.

As Japan moved to secure its postwar position in Manchuria, the United States suddenly found itself in danger of losing whatever leverage it still had with the other rivals. Back in 1895, at the time when the Russians first opened the Sino-Russian Bank to develop Manchuria, the Department of State had secured a concession on behalf of the America China Development Company for a proposed Hankow-Canton railway. Now, only a decade later, the Japanese had acquired from Russia the South Manchurian Railway, which they promptly converted into a development corporation. Meanwhile, J. P. Morgan, who had acquired control of the American concession, wanted only to convert that bankrupt holding into a quick profit through resale to the Chinese. Chagrined at this state of affairs, TR unsuccessfully tried to prevent the resale. The *New York Times* read his mind: "The matter has ceased to be a question of finance pure and simple, and has become a political problem of magnitude with several of the European powers now contending for spheres of influence in the Far East vitally concerned in its solution."

Put another way, the Progressives believed that private corporations were vested with public obligations, whether they happened to be in Minnesota, California, or China; especially if they were in China, because there they represented the interests of those who were to come after as opposed to the interests of other nations. Without either a powerful development company and/or a sphere of influence, the United States would soon find itself at a disadvantage in China. Some American policy-makers argued that the failure of the America China Development Company ruled out future efforts to secure railroad concessions; others wanted to go after a new concession at once. Roosevelt's inability to persuade the banker to reconsider no doubt had a great deal to do with his dim view of his successor's vigorous "dollar diplomacy" in China, even though Taft would bring J. P. Morgan and Company back into harness.

But TR had little time to worry about the outcome in 1905; he was too busy finishing the construction of the "Great White Fleet." It was ready in 1907, none too soon, for the anti-Japanese legislation enacted by West Coast states had stirred up some very ugly war talk on both sides of the Pacific. The exclusion of Japanese laborers from the United States was precisely the kind of thing Brooks Adams had had in mind when he warned that if the United States remained unwilling to concede anything to others by such policies, then it must prepare for war. Roosevelt sent the Great White Fleet on a world tour, and hoped it would impress not only the Japanese but other potential rivals with America's determination to play a large role in economic and political affairs.

FOR THE PRINCIPLE OF THE THING

America's direct interest in Morocco was practically nonexistent in 1906 when the German Kaiser appealed to Roosevelt to intervene in the crisis that had suddenly developed over the future of that small North African country. As part of their general settlement of Mediterranean spheres of influence, England and France had tacitly agreed that France should enjoy a free hand in Morocco. Germany leaped to the Sultan's defense, only to find itself looking into the teeth of a real war scare. Since the ostensible reason for German intervention had been protection of the Open Door policy, Wilhelm II apparently thought the best way out of a tight spot would be to call upon his old friend Theodore Roosevelt. After some hesitation, TR decided he could not refuse this appeal, and he arranged for a four-power conference to be held in Algeciras, Spain.

Three factors weighed heavily in his decision: First, he could not refuse without seeming to reject the logic of his mediation in the Russo-Japanese War. Second, he was genuinely alarmed at the threatened breakdown of the European balance of power over such an issue, and at Germany's increasing propensity to challenge British prerogatives by attempting to rearrange the status quo. And third, by posing the question as the Open Door policy versus spheres of influence, the Kaiser had made the issue something other than Morocco, or even the European balance of power. It was now a matter of principle, but principle with a special meaning to the United States.

Secretary of State Elihu Root instructed Ambassador Henry White and the American delegation on each of these concerns. They were told that the French had legitimate interests in Morocco which should be safeguarded; while the United States did not want to anger Germany, it was in American interests and the interests of world peace that the United States avoid contributing to any estrangement between Britain and France. On the Open Door principle, Root insisted that "while it is to the advantage of the powers to secure the 'open door,' it is equally vital to their interests and no less so to the advantage of Morocco that the door, being open, shall lead to something...."[9]

Elihu Root

In other words, having been invited to participate in the settlement of such affairs, the United States should serve notice that sooner or later it expected to participate fully in the economic development of the Mediterranean. After the big power crisis passed, Roosevelt put the matter of principle into its proper context in his 1906 annual message. If the Senate refused to ratify the Algeciras

---

[9] Elihu Root to Henry White, in *Foreign Relations, 1905*, pp. 678–80.

Convention, "we would be left for the first time in a hundred and twenty years without any commercial treaty with Morocco; and this at a time when we are everywhere seeking new markets and outlets for trade." Morocco never became very important for itself, but within the next four years the United States was pushing its way into the Ottoman Empire with a railroad project and into Persia's finances—much to the concern of European imperialists. During World War II, the Act of Algeciras was cited by State Department economic missions as the basis for American claims to equal opportunity all across the North African coastline.

MARE NOSTRUM

But when it came to the Caribbean, TR was no more willing than McKinley had been to grant Europe equal access to Cuba and Puerto Rico. In fact, the United States moved rapidly to impose a *Mare Nostrum* rule throughout the whole Caribbean and Central American area. The later argument over whether strategic or economic motives predominated in this campaign has troubled diplomatic historians, but it was not one of the problems that policy-makers wrestled with at the time. They were too busy.

Except for Puerto Rico, which was held simply as a non-self-governing territory, American expansion here took the form of what Europeans called administrative imperialism. American leaders sought to create a situation that gave no opportunity to European powers to intervene on any pretense. To do that it was necessary to prevent local leaders from getting into political or financial trouble vis-à-vis the Europeans. A stable government was defined by General Leonard Wood as follows: "The people ask me what we mean by a stable government in Cuba. I tell them that when money can be borrowed at a reasonable rate of interest and when capital is willing to invest in the Island, a condition of stability will have been reached."[10]

Nothing very complicated about that, so it seemed to Wood, but American policy-makers had a difficult time finding the right mix of political, economic, and military policies to keep Cuba stable. In a confused series of debates, Congress had placed a restriction, the so-called Teller Amendment, on outright annexation of Cuba when it responded to McKinley's request for a declaration of war with Spain. Hence the administration had to work out in some detail the Platt Amendment, limiting Cuban independence before the government of the island was turned over to "natives." The Platt Amendment was really

---

[10] Wood to Root, January 13, 1900, quoted in David F. Healy, *The United States in Cuba, 1898–1902* (Madison, Wis., 1963), p. 133.

fathered by Elihu Root and the War Department, but more important, it was imposed on the Cubans, as part of their constitution, without recourse or time limit. Under the Platt Amendment the Cuban government pledged itself not to enter into any treaties that might impair its sovereignty and not to incur any debts beyond its ability to repay all obligations from ordinary revenues. In addition, the United States was guaranteed the right to intervene—by force if necessary—to maintain a government "adequate for protection of life, property, and individual liberty."

The United States also insisted on reserving the right to establish naval bases in Cuba. Then, having secured its political desires, Washington negotiated a trade treaty with Havana, the Reciprocity Treaty of 1903, which for all practical purposes closed the Cuban economy to outside interests. General Wood, an advocate of annexation, commented frankly, "There is, of course, little or no independence left Cuba under the Platt Amendment."

Cuban politics under these conditions became little more than a contest between "ins" and disgruntled "outs." The outs were usually led by responsible—i.e., conservative—leaders, but their attacks upon the Havana establishment became involved in the question of Cuban-American relations. There was, in truth, no way that this situation could have been avoided, since any issue that might be discussed led back to that point. Quite naturally, too, the government in power looked for guidance to the American minister, who became a viceroy in fact, if not in name, and whose opinions and advice swung the balance. On some issues, his advice was forthcoming without solicitation. In 1905, for example, he vetoed a Cuban-British trade treaty on the grounds that it offered London significant advantages regarded as "most unsatisfactory to the United States."

The next year a revolution broke out against President Tomás Estrada Palma. Despite numerous appeals from American officials, Estrada Palma wanted nothing to do with reestablishing Cuban "independence," preferring annexation as not only more honest, but far more beneficial to his people. "The truth is," William Howard Taft lamented from Havana, "that the Cuban government has proved to be nothing but a house of cards." American troops were landed and spent the next three years propping up the house of cards again. Withdrawn in 1909, they came back in 1911 and 1917, and by proxy in later decades. Unwilling or unable to face political facts as frankly as Estrada Palma, the United States pursued a Cuban policy that prevented revolutions by preventing the kind of political development that would have given the Cubans confidence in their institutions, or a large stake in their "independence." By its own self-proclaimed standards, United States policy was a failure.

By other standards Cuban policy was more successful. The protectorate allowed the United States to maintain a naval base to secure the eastern approach to the isthmus of Panama (then part of Colombia), a vital interest thought worth any necessary cost. Following Colombia's refusal to ratify the Hay-Herran Convention of 1903 (which would have provided $10 million for Colombia in return for exclusive rights to a six-mile-wide zone across the isthmus), Washington actively encouraged a Panamanian "revolution," supported it with American ships, and blocked all efforts by Bogotá to regain control of the area. This sequence of events began when the Colombian senate held out for more money. Then the New Panama Canal Company joined forces with ambitious local figures to spawn the Republic of Panama. From its birth the new republic was promised to the United States by Philippe Bunau-Varilla, its first minister, who also just happened to be a leading official of the canal company. Bunau-Varilla had played a leading role earlier in persuading the U.S. Congress to reject a proposed Nicaraguan route, and he made good use of his $100,000 retainer to finance the Panamanian revolution. Two weeks after the revolt, on November 18, 1903, Bunau-Varilla and Secretary of State John Hay signed a treaty granting Panama the money originally intended for Colombia and the United States its canal route. But in addition Washington got the right to intervene in Panama on the same basis as in Cuba. Even had the canal never been built, the Canal Zone would have been worth a great deal simply as a well-fortified place of arms, and it proved to be so sooner than expected.

Between Cuba and Puerto Rico lies the island of Hispaniola, divided between Haiti and Santo Domingo (later the Dominican Republic). President Ulysses S. Grant had attempted to annex Santo Domingo shortly after the Civil War, but the Radical Republicans still had their hands full with the former Confederate states. Then in 1893 the San Domingo Improvement Company, a New York concern, bought Santo Domingo's foreign debt, and with it the right to collect customs revenues to satisfy their claims. In 1899 Washington sent William F. Powell to represent American interests in both Santo Domingo and Haiti. Not satisfied with that role, Powell yearned to find his place in history as the man who delivered the island to the United States. The Minister's repeated suggestions for accomplishing that goal met with sharp rebuffs, but the State Department did instruct him to keep a close watch over the activities of European powers there. This was an all-day, every-day task, since Santo Domingo was in a more or less permanent state of revolution. Troop landings from foreign ships had become commonplace.

Early in 1903 Powell devised a plan whereby the company's claim might be paid off by having United States agents collect import duties on various products. Dominican officials were reluctant at first to go quite that far, and suggested instead a reciprocity treaty with the United States, throwing in an offer of naval bases at Samana and Manzanilla bays as part of the bargain. Meanwhile, however, Powell had learned from certain Dominican "revolutionaries" that they were willing to go just as far—even further—if the United States would "assist them in bringing peace to the Republic, and repress these factional struggles for all time." "In other words," Powell reported to the Secretary of State, "that our Government will do for them what was done for Cuba."[11]

Roosevelt Corollary

This was something new, but it should not have been totally unexpected. It took no great intelligence, after all, to see that here was a way for the ins to stay in power permanently, or a chance for the current outs to maneuver the situation (if they acted quickly enough) to reverse the situation.

Late in 1903, American naval commanders in the area arranged matters so that Carlos Morales and his supporters won the key battle for control of the government. Minister Powell lost no time in warning Morales to settle up with the United States. He could not expect diplomatic recognition for his regime until all private claims were satisfactorily adjusted, the desired naval bases granted, and financial controls turned over to Washington. The Minister had gone out on a limb, since Roosevelt wanted stability without responsibility. "I have about the same desire to annex it," the President wrote of Santo Domingo,

---

[11] William F. Powell to Hay, November 13, 1903, in U.S. State Department, Dominican Republic Dispatches.

"as a gorged boa constrictor might have to swallow a porcupine wrong-end to." Nevertheless, the President agreed that the only way to prevent future revolutions would be for the United States to undertake a customs receivership. On December 30, 1904, Morales formally requested that the United States take over Santo Domingo's customs. Under the watchful guns of American naval vessels, apparently stationed close by to protect Morales from his opponents until the agreement had been consummated, he signed a protocol embodying the necessary provisions.

TR sent the document to the Senate in February 1905, with a preamble that soon became famous as the "Roosevelt Corollary" to the Monroe Doctrine; i.e., the United States could not justly deny Europeans the right to protect their bona fide interests without at the same time taking corrective steps. The protocol ran into strong opposition, but TR ordered the navy to collect the customs anyway. Then he requested Hay's successor, Elihu Root, to make confirmation of the Dominican protocol his first order of business.

ROOT'S GOOD NEIGHBOR POLICY

Roosevelt once explained to a good friend that the "rest of mankind will be the better because we dig the Panama Canal and keep order in its neighborhood." Root convinced Congress that the President also needed the Dominican protocol (slightly watered down), but the new Secretary was greatly concerned that neither the Roosevelt Corollary nor the Platt Amendment seemed likely to produce the systematic remedy needed to prevent violence and revolution; besides, there was growing resentment against the unilateral imposition of these policies in South America. "The South Americans now hate us," Root admitted in a private letter, "largely because they think we despise them and try to bully them. I really like them and intend to show it." His chance to do so came as the result of an invitation to visit Rio de Janeiro in 1906. The Secretary promptly expanded the visit into a goodwill tour to all major South American countries. He assured each of them that the United States had no further territorial ambitions, and that the hemisphere had common interests in closer political and economic relations.

Upon his return to the United States, Root admonished his fellow citizens that Latin America had left the "stage of militarism" and moved now into "the stage of industrialism." If U.S. businessmen did not soon adapt their policies to this change, European rivals certainly would, and thus preempt markets and investment opportunities needed to absorb the nation's surplus energy. Root called for federally subsidized steamship lines, but warned that businessmen themselves would have to find the best way to get the markets.

Yet government had an obligation to do what it could to establish the proper climate, Root thought, and he appealed to Andrew Carnegie for funds to build a Central American "Court of Justice," so that the administration could "succeed in substituting some kind of an arbitration for a miscellaneous dogfight," still going on in those five nations. In addition the State Department initiated and promoted cultural and scientific exchanges with Latin America, such as the 1908 Pan American Scientific Congress, at which, explained a department officer, the United States hoped to substitute "the instruction of the United States for that of the old world."[12]

Roosevelt's famous maxim, "Speak softly and carry a big stick," has become, in the hands of later interpreters, a toothy caricature of his foreign policy. In some cases he is given credit for an elementary understanding of balance-of-power politics, but he is seldom credited with understanding the system he sought to modernize and advance. He understood the system, and told the nation what it must do in his first annual message to Congress:

> An additional reason for caution in dealing with corporations is to be found in the international commercial conditions of today. The same business conditions which have produced the great aggregations of corporate and individual wealth have made them very potent factors in international commercial competition. Business concerns which have the largest means at their disposal and are managed by the ablest men are naturally those which take the lead in the strife for commercial supremacy among the nations of the world. America has only just begun to assume that commanding position in the international business world which we believe will more and more be hers.

TR understood power, and its purpose.

Suggestions for Further Reading

Three recent books are useful for looking into the connections between foreign and domestic policy in this period: Ray Ginger, *Age of Excess: The United States from 1877 to 1914* (New York, 1965); Gabriel Kolko, *The Triumph of Conservatism* (New York, 1963); and Robert Wiebe, *The Search for Order, 1877–1920* (New York, 1967).

Howard K. Beale's *Theodore Roosevelt and the Rise of America to World Power* (Baltimore, 1956) is the place to begin for TR, but the older studies by

---

[12] Henry Jones to Paul S. Reinsch, October 29, 1907, in Paul S. Reinsch papers, Wisconsin State Historical Society (Madison, Wis.).

Tyler Dennett, *Roosevelt and the Russo-Japanese War* (New York, 1925), and Howard C. Hill, *Roosevelt and the Caribbean* (Chicago, 1927), are still useful.

On China, see C. S. Campbell, Jr., *Special Business Interests and the Open Door Policy* (New Haven, Conn., 1951); Thomas McCormick, *China Market: America's Quest for Informal Empire, 1893–1901* (Chicago, 1967); Jerome Israel, *Progressivism and the Open Door* (Pittsburgh, 1971); Raymond A. Esthus, *Theodore Roosevelt and Japan* (Seattle, 1966); and Charles E. Neu, *An Uncertain Friendship: Theodore Roosevelt and Japan, 1906–1909* (Cambridge, Mass., 1967). The sharply conflicting interpretations in the first three and the last two will offer the reader a chance to make up his own mind.

On the Caribbean and Latin America, see David F. Healy, *The United States in Cuba, 1898–1902* (Madison, Wis., 1963); Dana G. Munro, *Intervention and Dollar Diplomacy in the Caribbean, 1900–1921* (Princeton, N.J., 1964); and Scott Nearing and Joseph Freeman, *Dollar Diplomacy: A Study in American Imperialism* (New York, 1925). Once again variety is the spice of life.

Of special interest is Charles A. Beard, *The Idea of National Interest: An Analytical Study in American Foreign Policy* (New York, 1934). This chapter attempts to follow up some of the ideas first suggested here.

See also the general bibliography at the end of this volume.

CHAPTER 15

Dollars
and
Bullets
(1909–1913)

President Taft explained on December 3, 1912:

> The diplomacy of the present administration has sought to respond to modern
> ideas of commercial intercourse. This policy has been characterized as sub-
> stituting dollars for bullets.... It is an effort frankly directed to the increase
> of American trade upon the axiomatic principle that the Government of the
> United States shall extend all proper support to every legitimate and beneficial
> American enterprise abroad. How great have been the benefits of this
> diplomacy, coupled with the maximum and minimum provisions of the
> tariff law, will be seen by some consideration of the wonderful increase in
> the export trade of the United States.

Tested by the "wonderful increase" in exports, dollar diplomacy was indeed
a success: overall, exports were up 27 percent in those four years, from $1.6 bil-
lion to $2.5 billion annually. It had taken the country a century to surpass the
$1 billion figure annually; it took only fifteen years, from 1897 to 1911, to double
the figure. Foreign investment increased from $2 billion in 1909 to $2.5 billion
in 1913.

But William Howard Taft had been a personal failure in the White House. He found the presidency as burdensome and tiring as TR had found it exhilarating and satisfying. Neither temperamentally nor physically suited to the strenuous personal diplomacy of a Roosevelt, Taft tried too hard to eliminate the subjective element. When this proved impossible, he became peevish and obstinate. And the country became disenchanted with Taft. Republican insurgents wanted Teddy back, and joined the Progressive party with that objective in mind. This third party's campaign platform did not repudiate dollar diplomacy; it complained that Taft had not gone far enough:

> It is imperative to the welfare of our people that we enlarge and extend our foreign commerce. In every way possible our federal government should cooperate in this important matter. Germany's policy of cooperation between government and business has in a comparatively few years made that nation a leading competitor for the commerce of the world....

Accepting the judgment of his contemporary critics, historians often treat Taft as an unhappy episode between TR and Wilson. But in those four years the government and corporate leaders made a significant effort to come to grips with the major tendencies in relations between twentieth-century industrial nations.

Knox Succeeds Root

THE PRINCIPAL DIFFERENCES between TR's Secretary of State, Elihu Root, and Taft's appointee, Philander C. Knox, pertained to the proper role the government should play in American expansion. Root had held to the view that government's obligation was to provide business with a fair field and no favor. Beyond that, circumstances dictated what else should or could be done. TR's Secretary of State also feared that government partnership with selected chosen instruments of private enterprise would produce state capitalism at home and increasing rivalries abroad, especially in China. Taft and Knox, on the other hand, fully embraced what Herbert Croly, the Progressives' seer, called the "New Nationalism." "Call it paternalism, if you will," Knox once declared,

> but it is rational to hold that a fatherland owes to its children the duty of assuring them opportunity for self-advancement. The Department of State can help in this by securing for our citizens equal and fair opportunity abroad commensurate with that which the National Government aims to

secure for them at home. . . . As in the Darwinian struggle for existence, the condition is inexorable, and the fittest survive.[1]

State Department "Darwinists" only nudged the evolutionary process a little so as to ensure that the strongest and fittest American enterprises could compete in the world marketplace.

"Combinations" for Foreign Competition

WHILE ROOT HESITATED at the thought of business-government partnerships, he had always encouraged "association of individual private enterprise" to accomplish "really great things" in "the true American fashion." Businessmen and bankers interested in foreign expansion, on the other hand, worried that the really great things were being done in true German or true English fashion. References to German and English industrial success and constantly improving efficiency abound in this period. "I happen to know a number of Americans doing business in the Central American Republics," one congressman wrote Knox, "and it is the almost universal opinion that our Government has not given its citizens the strong support and backing which the citizens of England and Germany have received."[2]

Most often mentioned by State Department correspondents were such things as the lack of branch banks to aid exporters and investors with credit and exchange needs in foreign countries, and the unclear status of foreign trade combinations under the Sherman Antitrust Act. Under American laws dating from the Civil War era, it was almost impossible for national banks to do foreign and domestic business under the same charter. The Sherman Act, said National Association of Manufacturers spokesmen, was just as confining:

> The policy of all other nations but our own is to foster enterprise, encourage manufacturers to produce their goods in the most economical possible way, in other words by cooperation of corporations. Germany pursues this plan, and it has very much to do with her wonderful increase in export trade.[3]

---

[1] Speech copy, dated December 11, 1911, in William Howard Taft papers, Library of Congress.

[2] Julian Kahn to Philander C. Knox, November 26, 1909, in U.S. State Department file no. 6369/328.

[3] A. B. Farquhar to Richard B. Watrous, November 18, 1911, in Taft papers.

Assistant Secretary of State Francis M. Huntington-Wilson once tried to amend the Sherman Act on his own in a speech to the Pan American Commercial Congress, contending that recent Supreme Court decisions permitted, if they did not encourage, cooperation among corporations for foreign trade purposes. And Knox tried to get a favorable ruling from the Attorney General:

> The point is simply this—are American manufacturers and businessmen free to combine for the more efficient exploitation of foreign markets by dividing the field or otherwise? As a matter of policy it would be well if all combination for efficiency in the field of foreign commerce might be encouraged so long as it promoted instead of hurt our export trade.[4]

Measures to correct these shortcomings were delayed, however, until businessmen and government spokesmen adopted the rubric "commercial preparedness" to take advantage of the momentum of World War I forces to put them over the top. Meanwhile, Taft tackled that persistent tariff question, with disastrous results.

Reciprocity or the Alternative—Again

No OTHER ISSUE stirred up Republican troubles so much as the 1909 Payne-Aldrich tariff. Taft made the situation worse by praising the act as "the best tariff" ever passed by Congress, but his ineptitude does not begin to explain the President's full predicament. In 1907 a National Association of Manufacturers committee had called for a new program of reciprocity treaties and a "scientific" tariff board. Out of 1,260 members polled by the committee, 1,040 desired reciprocity treaties. "We are the greatest manufacturing nation on earth," concluded the NAM. "The protective policy has vastly helped us to this situation. It must not now be turned against us, but must be adapted to present-day conditions."[5] But how? TR had not seen the way to do it without splitting the party. Taft had advocated downward revision of the tariff for a long time. In 1908 he had been unsuccessful in efforts to commit the party to state that revision would be the first order of business of the new administration. After the election Taft decided to take on the high-tariff forces anyway, and, against TR's advice, called a special session of Congress to con-

---

[4] Knox to the Attorney General, November 22, 1911, in U.S. State Department file no. 600.1116/3.

[5] From a copy of the NAM Report in the papers of Oscar Strauss, Library of Congress.

sider the problem. In the ensuing struggle, the President found himself caught between a minority group of serious reformers (men he distrusted) and stand-patters. Reformers claimed that he then abandoned them; but Taft insisted that the Payne-Aldrich bill created a "very scientific" tariff. In so far as the bill established a commission to investigate the international commercial situation, this claim was justified.

Free trade had brought Great Britain to the pinnacle of world economic power in the nineteenth century, but all indications pointed to changes in European economic policies. No matter how successful American industry might be in reproducing the English success story, therefore, it would still have to get around or through the maze of new European tariff regulations. One device considered and adopted by the tariff commission was a so-called bargaining tariff with minimum and maximum schedules. The principle was simple: deny nations that discriminated against American products access to the U.S. domestic market until they were ready to grant the United States full equality in their markets. Besides the European situation itself, American policy-makers were alarmed at the decline of tariff equality in European colonies. Soon, it was thought, no territory of consequence would be open to American enterprise on a fair competitive basis, unless these powers were faced with the possible loss of U.S. markets.

Taft's problem was that while the new tariff commission faithfully reported these developments and the suggested remedy, the Payne-Aldrich "minimum" rates were so high that there was little or no incentive for foreign nations to lower their barriers. The President tried out a more limited solution in the proposed Canadian Reciprocity Treaty of 1911. If successful, a reciprocity treaty with the Canadians could reduce domestic criticism of the Payne-Aldrich tariff and establish a good working model for other commercial pacts. Agrarian interest groups attacked the proposed treaty, charging it would turn the United States into a dumping ground for Canadian farm surpluses. But the House of Representatives remained favorable to the plan. "If we could sweep away all tariffs between the two countries," read the House report, "it would have the effect upon our trade of another Louisiana Purchase."

Representative Champ Clark saw it as the fulfillment of an old dream: "I am for it, because I hope to see the day when the American flag will float over every square foot of the British North American possessions clear to the North Pole." Clark's indiscretion, and others like it, produced an adverse reaction in Canada, ending all hope for the treaty, and with it any possibility that President Taft would find his way out of the tariff thicket onto high ground. Woodrow Wilson gained the presidency with a promise to lower tariffs. But he had hardly settled into the White House before he too discovered that there was much more to the question than he had once supposed. In 1916 he had to admit as much, and support a bill to create a new tariff commission.

Central American Anachronisms

Taft had given Knox and his aides broad authority to deal with Central American affairs; but he cautioned the Secretary in December 1909 that what he expected was "some final right to compel the peace between the Central American Governments," even if he had to "knock their heads together."[6] Root had sought to avoid that, taking the initiative in 1907 to call a Central American peace conference. In North American eyes, Nicaragua's determination to control Honduras was the key problem. The Root-sponsored Central American peace conference produced a general peace treaty between all five of the countries in the area, Guatemala, Honduras, El Salvador, Costa Rica, and Nicaragua. And a Central American Court of Justice was created to ensure that justice and equity replaced bloodletting and irrationality.

Philander Knox had little faith in Central American treaties, and less in Central Americans. Guatemalan dictator Manuel Estrada Cabrera understood this, and was careful not to test the new Secretary. His guiding rule, he once remarked to an American diplomat, was never to make the mistake his principal rival, Nicaraguan ruler José Santos Zelaya, had made by offending the government of the United States. "He has thus violated the first rule of behavior for a dictator of the Caribbean area," explained a delighted Cabrera, who sat back to watch the fun.[7]

Taft's Secretary of State wanted to settle the Central American situation by applying a modified Platt Amendment solution in Honduras. Zelaya had other things in mind: subversion in Honduras, military force against El Salvador, and British capital in Nicaragua to check American economic imperialism. Washington had served public notice on Zelaya not to do these things, first by sending warships to the area, then by demanding that he settle all pending issues with American companies. He was told that if the peace were broken or the private questions not resolved satisfactorily, the Department of State would wash its hands of the matters and refer them to Congress.

---

[6] Taft to Knox, December 22, 1909, in Taft papers.
[7] Hugh R. Wilson, *Education of a Diplomat* (New York, 1938), pp. 48–49.

Zelaya's opponents inside Nicaragua included the United Fruit Company and a general of his own party, Juan J. Estrada. In October 1909 Estrada led a revolt against the government, using money from various sources, including the United Fruit Company and Guatemala, which contributed $90,000. Although diplomatically "neutral," the State Department had determined to support any rival of Zelaya who could stay in power long enough to conclude something like a Platt Amendment treaty with Washington. Juan J. Estrada was as good a candidate as any, perhaps better. "Nicaragua is rich in natural resources," Estrada told American officials and naval officers, "and under proper administration would be a credit to the Americas and a field for American commerce, instead of a pest under your country's nose."[8]

Estrada finally succeeded in establishing himself in power, but he needed a lot of hand-holding and more visible support from the United States. His demands for special protection exceeded what the Taft administration could give, and he resigned in March 1911 without signing over the necessary financial controls. Later that same year, however, a treaty known as the Knox-Castrillo Convention was signed with his successor, Adolfo Díaz. It provided for a U.S. loan of $15 million, guaranteed by control of Nicaraguan customhouses. In addition, American bankers were to be permitted to establish a bank in that country, as well as to build railways with Nicaragua's money. Despite special pleading from President Taft, Congress refused to ratify the pact. The interested bankers, Brown Brothers and J. and W. Seligman and Company, then took matters into their own hands and negotiated a private contract calling for a $1.5 million loan secured by a lien on Nicaraguan customs. Under the terms of this contract, the bankers could nominate an American citizen to collect the customs; the nominee would then be approved by the Secretary of State and "appointed" by Nicaragua. The bankers also reserved the right "to solicit of the United States of America protection against violation of the present contract, and aid in enforcing its execution."

Knox did his part by ordering the American chargé d'affaires in Managua to keep the Nicaraguan legislature in session until the contract was approved. But the Nicaraguan assembly, meanwhile, had been trying to write a new constitution to protect the country against precisely such infringements on its political and economic independence. Though the assembly succeeded in promulgating such a constitution, the bankers and the State Department simply ignored it and went ahead with supplementary loans to the Díaz government

---

[8] Drew Linard to Assistant Secretary of State, July 5, 1909, in U.S. State Department file no. 6369/131.

in exchange for the concessions that had first appeared in the Knox-Castrillo Convention. Díaz' opponents called for a new election, then proclaimed a revolution. Washington's response was swift and unequivocal. "We think," explained Assistant Secretary of State F. M. Huntington-Wilson in a memorandum on intervention, "that if the United States did its duty promptly, thoroughly and impressively ... it would strengthen our hand and lighten our task, not only in Nicaragua itself in the future, but throughout Central America and the Caribbean and would even have some moral effect in Mexico."[9]

It took two thousand Marines and eight warships to accomplish America's duty "thoroughly and impressively." The leader of the revolution was sent into exile in Panama on board the U.S.S. *Cleveland,* and U.S. Marines guarded the polls on November 2, 1912, when Díaz was reelected for a four-year term.

Meanwhile the administration continued its efforts to negotiate British financial power out of Honduras. In January 1909 Root had advised the American minister there of his "confidential opinion" that Washington would be pleased to be of service to Honduras "and to contribute towards bringing about such a satisfactory result as has been recently attained in Santo Domingo." Knox soon learned that the British were pressuring Honduras to accept *their* plan for a debt settlement, basing their case on the unhappy fact that Honduras owed British investors more than $120 million. The State Department then enlisted J. P. Morgan and Company to make the loan, because of that firm's friendly relations with the British Bondholders' Council. The State Department suggested to the White House that a frank appeal be made to Congress: "The obligation cannot be escaped. Is it better to meet it with dollars or bullets?" Such conventions were the only way to "give the very large and increasing number of American citizens the protection they ought to have in these turbulent countries."[10] On another occasion Knox put it in simple cost analysis terms:

> During the course of a year it is many times necessary for the United States to send forces to the ports of some of the Central American republics in order to afford protection to foreign life and property. This is done at enormous expense, an informal estimate from some of the naval officers showing that the annual cost to this Government amounts to over $1,000,000.

Congress refused once again to accept such responsibility in Honduras or Nicaragua and the Platt Amendment system remained unfinished, until Woodrow Wilson and William Jennings Bryan added some new arguments.

---

9 F. M. Huntington-Wilson to William Howard Taft, August 26 and 30, 1912, in Taft papers.
10 Huntington-Wilson to Taft, February 26, 1911, in ibid.

"Dollar diplomacy"

Battleships for South America

DOLLAR DIPLOMACY's only unqualified success came in South America, where the techniques employed were, of course, much different. In 1908 Argentine-Brazilian rivalries had led to the beginning of a naval armaments race. Buenos Aires looked to its long-time economic connections in London for an advantageous contract for battleships with which to intimidate its opponent. But the Bethlehem Steel Company's Charles M. Schwab spied an opening in the British economic hold on Argentina, and jumped at the chance to steam through it. The State Department liked the idea, too, and instructed its legation to request an equal opportunity to bid on the ship contract.

Argentina responded that while it was willing enough to open the competition, it also needed a loan to finance the purchases. A "very strong group, headed by J. P. Morgan and Company," Secretary of State Root cabled his minister, desired to offer terms for such a loan. In January 1910, after some diplomatic pressure had been exerted, word came that the United States companies had been awarded the battleship contract. "It is the first time in our history," proclaimed Schwab, "that the United States has received a contract of this magnitude and description.... It is, to my mind, the best step ever made towards the further development of commercial relations with foreign countries." And it was only the beginning! chimed in the American minister in the Argentine capital. Already it looked as though new railroad contracts would be given to United States concerns in this former bastion of British economic influence, even though a London firm had been willing to sell below cost to meet the American bid.

American shipbuilders were anxious to repeat their success in Chile, a country where Germany had been supreme. Using the technique that had been successful in Argentina and the cooperation of the U.S. Navy, which displayed the latest American armor plate in Chilean ports, the State Department pressed Santiago to apply for an American loan. This time the effort fell short as European and British firms combined to turn back the American upstarts. But the *London Times* warned against complacency:

> This latest move, coupled with the recent complete American defeat of all competitors for Argentine awards for battleships, seems to [indicate] ... the approaching American commercial absorption of the southern continent, which will be assisted by the opening of the Panama Canal. In [our] opinion our American cousins can only be amicably combatted by the resolute combination of the enormous British financial interests already involved, with whom these countries would prefer to deal.

During contract bidding the State Department encouraged its representatives to cable complete details of the technical requirements for the ships, whatever the cost. "Think of the money we have spent on the China loan," said a Department spokesman, "and think of the important effect of our success in this matter, and you will see that the wise thing to do is to cable without any limit to length."

The China Consortium

THE REFERENCE to the China loan concerned the voluminous telegram traffic between Washington and Peking and between Washington and European capitals during the summer of 1909, when the United States sought to reclaim at least part of the position it had lost with the failure of the America China Development Company. Since that time TR and Root had grown increasingly doubtful about the China business, especially about any involvement in Manchurian politics. Taft, on the other hand, had become increasingly enthusiastic about the possibilities of that "Asian Minnesota." In 1907 he had told the American Chamber of Commerce in Shanghai that the American government would view foreign obstacles to development of the China trade with "deep concern." Though he admitted no one could predict how far Washington would go to protect this growing interest, they could be sure that in the future "there will be no reason to complain of seeming government indifference...."

Far off in Mukden, Manchuria, American Consul Willard Straight read reports of this speech with rising excitement. He was even more impressed with Taft's determination some weeks later when the two met face to face in Vladivostok. The Secretary of War began their conversation by remarking that he had been very much encouraged by his Shanghai reception, and by evidence that the Chinese seemed to be turning to America as their one disinterested friend. Straight leaped at the chance to relate his thoughts on how American capital could be invested profitably in China, and to present a specific plan he had already worked out with Tang Shao-yi, like Taft a Yale graduate and now a provincial governor directly under the viceroy of Manchuria.

Straight had first come to Mukden in 1905, the year Japan acquired the South Manchurian Railway. American railroad magnate E. H. Harriman had tried to buy out the Japanese in order to link up the SMRR to a worldwide transportation system, but he failed and Manchuria came under Tokyo's economic dominance. Tang Shao-yi had a new proposal in mind, said Straight, a plan for American investment in a Manchurian bank, an institution that could take the lead in developing the province's natural resources and building its transportation network.

Taft liked the idea, yet he wondered if there were really much of a chance to get the necessary funds. Tang had the solution to that problem, too, explained Straight: Why not use the Boxer indemnity funds? Each of the powers had exacted enormous sums from China to pay for damage done to their nationals' persons and property during the Boxer Rebellion, but the United States had put these funds aside to pay for the training of Chinese students in American universities. The Secretary thought this over, and replied that if the suggestion came from the Chinese, it might just work, at that.

When E. H. Harriman lent his weight to the scheme, Secretary Root ordered Straight back to Washington for consultations in preparation for the visit of a special ambassador from Peking, whose mission ostensibly was to thank the United States for returning the Boxer indemnity funds. The ambassador was none other than Tang Shao-yi himself. Consul Straight was instructed to act as a go-between for Tang and "certain powers that be in Wall Street," which were "beginning to think of Manchuria as a field for investment."[11] Unfortunately Tang's real mission was already known in Europe and Japan even before he arrived in the United States. Ambassador Kogoro

---

[11] William Phillips to Willard Straight, September 9, 1908, in Willard Straight papers, Cornell University.

Takahira quickly came forth with a proposed Japanese-American diplomatic exchange on China and Manchuria which Root had to weigh against the chance to make a real effort to outmaneuver the powers, including Japan. Straight waited nervously for the Secretary of State to make up his mind, but Root proved unwilling to risk an open break with Tokyo; besides, his interpretation of the Open Door policy was based on keeping political and economic affairs separate. He had been willing to move quite far toward full partnership between the government and the bankers in the Caribbean area and South America, but the risks in China were just too great.

Although the November 30, 1908, Root-Takahira Agreement did not mention Manchuria specifically, it said that Japan and the United States had exchanged views on all Chinese questions, and agreed to preserve the status quo and to defend the principle of equal opportunity. Charging the agreement was little more than a sellout, Straight protested its signing without success. As he predicted, the Root-Takahira exchange, in combination with other adverse developments, temporarily checked the plans of those on both sides of the Pacific who were interested in pushing American capital into Manchuria.

All that was forgotten, however, a few months later when President Taft delivered his inaugural address. "In the international controversies that are likely to arise in the Orient growing out of the question of the open door and other issues," Taft declared,

> the United States can maintain her interests intact and can secure respect for her just demands. She will not be able to do so, however, if it is understood that she never intends to back up her assertion of right and her defense of her interest by anything but mere verbal protest and diplomatic note.

Even as the Japanese press boasted of having subverted the Tang scheme, these passages were going out to American diplomatic representatives as the new administration's first instructions to its embassies and legations. A few weeks later, the ambassadors and ministers found out what the State Department had in mind as the administration's first "assertion of right" on behalf of American national interest: a demand for an equal share in an Anglo-German-French loan contract to build the Hankow-Canton railway—the very same concession that had been the scene of the America China Development Company's recent disgrace. Moreover, Knox was willing to tread where Root had feared to go; that is, he was willing to organize and support a consortium of the four most powerful financial institutions on "Wall Street" as the chosen instrument of American policy.

As a partner in one of these firms, Thomas Lamont of J. P. Morgan and Company, later explained, European nations had long recognized the need for just such close cooperation: "Great Britain and Germany have built up their overseas trade by methods both cautious and courageous. They have gained strong positions in new markets like South America and the Far East by first creating the demand for their wares and then by supplying and financing that demand." Knox's initial objective was to secure a full share in the Hankow-Canton contract so that American firms would have an equal chance to bid on future railway supplies and locomotives, but his ultimate goal was nothing less than Manchuria itself.

KNOX NEUTRALIZES MANCHURIA

At a White House dinner one evening during the protracted negotiations over American participation in the Hukuang Railways loan (Hankow-Canton line), Taft poked the Chinese minister in the ribs and remarked jovially, "We only want your trade...." The President and his Secretary of State both regarded the Hukuang loan as only the opening wedge in a much broader campaign for the China market, useful primarily to establish America's claims to equality and its ability to carry out financial promises in a well-coordinated plan involving leading bankers from several countries. Knox had solemnly warned the consortium bankers not to expect immediate profits from this venture, but to undertake it as a necessary obligation to their country's future economic interests.

The American group selected Willard Straight to represent it in China; but only one or two of the bankers and E. H. Harriman knew what else the former consul hoped to accomplish on their behalf. Harriman's part called for him to purchase the Chinese Eastern Railway from Russia, while Straight contacted Tang Shao-yi to resume Manchurian loan discussions. Americans would then control both key railroads. Harriman died before he could complete his part of the negotiations, but Straight succeeded in persuading the Chinese to sign a preliminary loan contract for a competing line parallel to the South Manchurian Railroad. He presumed that Russia could be dealt with later, and Japan thus forced into an isolated position in which it could threaten no one. Thus, he prophesied, would Manchuria be restored to its rightful owner, China, in fact as well as in name. "With the bank in running order we should then with China, and our associates, British or German or French as the case might be, be able to undertake the commercial and industrial development of this region."[12]

---

[12] Straight to Huntington-Wilson, September 25, 1909, in ibid.

Straight and Knox differed on how to deal with the Russians, however; Knox was determined to take control of the situation following Harriman's untimely death. Straight urged that something approximating the Root-Takahira Agreement be offered St. Petersburg, as well as a full share in the whole enterprise; but when, in fact, the Russian ambassador in Washington suggested his country was interested in the international consortium, the State Department brushed aside these hints. Then, on November 6, 1909, Knox asked the British to join the United States in a comprehensive plan whereby *all* Manchurian railroads would be put under "an economic, scientific, and impartial administration ... vesting in China the ownership of the railroads through funds furnished for that purpose by the interested powers willing to participate."

Knox listed the reasons why he thought the plan feasible: First, despite American coolness, the Russians seemed interested in cooperating in some project of this sort. Second, American financial participation could be counted on. Third, even if the suggestion was not entirely acceptable to the Japanese, Washington had a good lever to force Japan's hand in the Chinchow-Aigun contract, which had been ratified in an unpublished imperial decree. What Knox had failed to take into account, and what unraveled his supposedly foolproof logic, was that if Russia and Japan decided to put aside their differences to meet this outside threat, then London would lose all interest in the plan, since it would threaten to disrupt the Anglo-Japanese alliance. Instead of neutralizing Manchuria, Knox maladroitly neutralized pro-Americans in St. Petersburg, who might have been willing to cooperate in a different scheme. Strong warnings to the Chinese from the Russian capital and from Tokyo killed the Chinchow-Aigun contract. "The only remedy for the situation," observed Straight, "is a strong China. Japan and Russia will oppose China's regeneration and we alone can bring it on."[13] Next to the Great China Market illusion, the persistence of American determination to deal with Peking as it should be, and not as it was, has been truly remarkable.

The situation in 1909 was even less conducive to any kind of success than it had been six years earlier when Washington had tried to put China on the gold standard, but the same men who had been involved in that venture assured Secretary Knox that "the currency question lies at the root of the introduction of foreign capital and the extension of railways and other modern improvements in China."[14] So in January 1910 the American minister in Peking

---

13 Straight to Henry P. Davison, March 26, 1910, in ibid.

14 Charles Conant to Knox, September 15, 1909, in U.S. State Department file no. 2112/88.

suggested to the Chinese that they employ an American expert to develop a currency reform plan. Six months later the Foreign Office asked if the Americans were interested in a loan to put China on the gold standard.

When the American banking group was asked for an opinion and nudged into a reply by the State Department, preliminary negotiations were undertaken. Little progress was made because the American group insisted upon inviting its three European partners to participate in this and all future China business. Knox wanted to do something more; he wanted to reverse previous attitudes (and mistakes) by inviting Russia and Japan to join the feast. Peking was appalled: here the Americans were, having proposed themselves as China's saviors since 1899, now joining with China's traditional enemies to control and dominate the country's economic future. It was too much!

Taft's critics at home agreed. The China consortium business is difficult enough to straighten out today; at the time it was almost impossible to figure out what was going on. Some dissenters were just plain fed up with Knox's "chosen instruments," whether the question was Latin America or the Far East. Others opposed cooperating with European bankers anywhere. Still others read the accounts of American connivance with Japan and Russia as a retreat from John Hay's Open Door policy. But Theodore Roosevelt objected to *any* policy that would involve the United States politically in Manchuria, whether pursued in cooperation with others or by competing on a catch-as-catch-can basis. "The 'open door' policy in China was an excellent thing," he wrote privately to Taft,

> but as has been proved by the whole history of Manchuria, alike under Russia and Japan, the "open door" policy as a matter of fact completely disappears as soon as a powerful nation determines to disregard it, and is willing to run the risk of war rather than forgo its intention.[15]

Since an alliance with China was nonsense, Roosevelt concluded, an American military effort in Manchuria would require an army comparable to Germany's and a navy equal to the British fleet. Taft and Knox disagreed, as did American policy-makers for the next four decades. Whether America would ever have to fight for Manchuria or whether it would ever be willing to was a speculative question, said Knox in reply to Roosevelt's letter, but it was certainly unwise to prejudice our policy by admitting to the world "that we would not, under any circumstances, go to war. We can at least allow others to draw their own conclusions."[16]

---

[15] Theodore Roosevelt to Taft, December 22, 1910, in Philander C. Knox papers, Library of Congress.

[16] Quoted in Henry Pringle, *William Howard Taft,* 2 vols. (New York, 1938), 2:685–86.

What conclusions were the Chinese to draw? Neither Roosevelt nor Taft thought very much about that. But the answer to that question began to be apparent in September 1911, when revolutionaries overturned the Manchu dynasty. The uprising had been triggered by the international consortium's efforts to enforce the Hukuang contract. No amount of persuasion could bring the American bankers to the aid of the Manchus.

Woodrow Wilson dedicated his presidential campaign to an attack on monopolies, asserting they blocked both foreign and domestic economic growth. The consortium came under the heading of monopoly, or, as Knox preferred to call it, the chosen instrument of American policy. The Taft administration had, in fact, discouraged competition from other American bankers who wanted to wildcat in China. Those days were over. The future belonged to the fittest, but the process of natural selection had to be controlled and properly directed.

Straight had concluded that America's failure stemmed from a different cause. "We are at the present time endeavoring to bring down the Chinese goose with a number of air guns," he wrote J. P. Morgan and Company in November 1911, "while our competitors are chasing the same bird with shot which are perhaps no better than that which we, ourselves, use but which are infinitely more effective because fired from an eight bore goose gun."

It seemed clear that everyone had to give this problem of government-business cooperation a lot more thought.

Suggestions for Further Reading

There is, obviously, a good deal of overlap in works on the Roosevelt and Taft eras, but in addition to those books cited at the end of the last chapter, see Henry Pringle, *William Howard Taft,* 2 vols. (New York, 1938), and Walter and Marie Scholes, *The Foreign Policies of the Taft Administration* (Columbia, Mo., 1970), for surveys of foreign policy issues during Taft's short, unhappy presidency.

The China consortium has been the subject of several books, the most recent being Charles Vevier, *The United States and China, 1906–1913* (New Brunswick, N.J., 1955); but see also Herbert Croly, *Willard Straight* (New York, 1924).

See also the general bibliography at the end of this volume.

CHAPTER 16

New Freedoms and Old Imperatives (1913–1917)

Woodrow Wilson's 1912 campaign speeches seldom touched on specific foreign policy questions. Once or twice he mentioned the overthrow of the Manchus in China, but only to illustrate the worldwide scope of the movement against special privilege. In Canton, Ohio, William McKinley's home, the Democratic candidate praised that Republican's foresight in seeing that the nation must soon "enter into reciprocal relations of trade with the chief countries of the world....He saw that we had made for ourselves a straitjacket...."

The straitjacket analogy had long been Wilson's favorite description of Republican tariff policies. He had used it several times before, and would return to it several more times during his presidency. Wilson viewed imperialism in much the same way as John A. Hobson, the English writer, did: "Imperialism is a depraved choice of national life, imposed by self-seeking interests which appeal to the lusts of quantitative acquisitiveness and of forceful domination surviving in a nation from early centuries of animal struggle for existence."

By striking down high tariffs, one was presumably also striking at "quantitative acquisitiveness." Imperialism and special privilege went hand in hand, and could be overcome only through strength of character.

But, like other Americans, Wilson made a crucial distinction between the colonial policies of European nations and this country's conquest of the North American continent. Moreover, the Wilson-Hobson thesis offered the President no satisfactory answer to the challenge of the century's first great revolutions in Mexico, China, and Russia.

Genesis of the "New Freedom"

Product of a postbellum southern Presbyterian childhood, Wilson brought north a set of political beliefs that underwent gradual modification, but never entirely left him either at Princeton University or in the New Jersey governor's mansion. The high protective tariff, for example, always represented the unchecked power and privilege of northern capital. He criticized dollar diplomacy as an outgrowth of that power, but his own view (and later academic analysis) of American democracy was Turnerian and expansionist. Where William James sought a moral equivalent to war, Wilson was looking for a moral equivalent to the country's lost frontier.

"It is true," he said on February 1, 1912,

> that we needed a frontier so much that after the Spanish War we annexed a new frontier some seven thousand miles off in the Pacific. But that is a long way, and it takes the energy of a very young man to seek that outlet in the somewhat depressing climate of the Philippines.

If the colonial solution was ruled out on both moral and pragmatic grounds, what was to be done about America's persistent problems?

> You have got, in order to relieve the plethora, in order to use the energy of the capital of America, to break the chrysalis that we have been in. We have bound ourselves hand and foot in a smug domestic helplessness by this jacket of a tariff we have wound around us.[1]

Wilson polled more than 6 million votes in 1912, TR just over 4 million, and Taft 3.5 million. But the Socialist candidate, Eugene Debs, received nearly a million votes, too, more than twice as many as in 1908. Wilson envisioned a liberal and a liberated capitalist society, which would serve the interests of

---

[1] Woodrow Wilson, *The Public Papers of Woodrow Wilson,* ed. Ray Stannard Baker and William E. Dodd, 8 vols. (New York, 1924–1928), 2:360.

all mankind. To achieve that society, he listed four essential measures in the presidential campaign: a lower tariff, a new banking and currency law, strong antitrust laws, and, if necessary, government aid to a revitalized merchant marine.

The new Secretary of State, William Jennings Bryan, whose anti-imperialist credentials were even better than Wilson's, summed up the economic power of righteousness during an interview with a *St. Louis Post-Dispatch* reporter on April 19, 1913:

> We have, so to speak, been busy watching the spigot and neglecting the bung hole, and we have been doing it because of the short-sighted policy that allowed the man at the spigot to dictate the policy. The effort to get a few dollars by the employment of unfair and offensive methods has prevented our industries from securing that large and lucrative business which would have come with a more liberal policy—for a just policy is a liberal policy.

Bryan went on to explain that what had to be done was to restore the nation's honor and tradition of fair dealing: "When the people of all other nations understand this, they will welcome American capital and American capitalists." Lest the reporter miss his point, the Secretary added: "The preceding administration attempted to till the fields of foreign investment with a penknife; President Wilson intends to cultivate it with a spade."

The assumption, again put forth in Hobsonian terms, was that once America reformed itself, it would be able to go out into the world far more effectively. That it would also *need* to go out into the world did not bother American policy-makers, because the nation's destiny was to fulfill its old promise as the world's last, best hope.

A Beginning

PRESIDENT WILSON attacked the tariff issue first, calling Congress into special session to enact the Underwood tariff of 1913, the first general downward revision since the Civil War. It never really had much chance to operate before the outbreak of World War I, and then both the Allies and the Central Powers made it plain that whatever the outcome, prewar trade methods were obsolete. Before the war Wilson was sure, as he wrote his ambassador in Great Britain, that "the passing of commercial supremacy to the United States will be dated in the economic histories from the tariff act of 1913...."[2]

---

2 Quoted in Ray Stannard Baker, *Woodrow Wilson: Life and Letters*, 8 vols. (New York, 1927–1939), 4:128–29.

The President also succeeded quickly in obtaining the Federal Reserve Act, a thorough banking reform measure that also permitted national banks to establish overseas branches. Long desired by exporters and investors, this provision, Secretary Bryan promised the National Foreign Trade Convention in 1914, would "do more to promote trade in foreign lands than any other one thing that has been done in our history."[3]

The Democrats were proving to be, as William Randolph Hearst had once advised them to be, as ardent expansionists as they had been in Jefferson's day. There remained the question of permitting exporters to combine for more effective penetration of foreign markets. "We have learned the lesson now," Secretary of Commerce William C. Redfield told the National Foreign Trade Convention,

> that our factories are so large that their output at full time is greater than America's market can continuously and regularly absorb. And because the markets of the world are greater and steadier than the markets of any country can be, and because we are strong, we are going out, you and I, into the markets of the world to get our share.[4]

Redfield brought convention leaders to the White House, where Wilson also assured them: "There is nothing in which I am more interested than the fullest development of the trade of this country and its righteous conquest of foreign markets."[5] But the delegates wanted something more; they wanted legislative assurance that foreign trade combinations, like those of Great Britain and Germany, would be exempt from prosecution under the Sherman Antitrust Act. In succeeding years, the foreign trade conventions adopted the theme of "commercial preparedness" to take advantage of the growing concern about national weaknesses in the face of the European challenge to America's traditional policy of neutrality. President Wilson supported both preparedness campaigns in 1916, remarking to a magazine reporter that he wanted legislation to facilitate cooperation: "American firms must be given definite authorization to cooperate for foreign selling operations, in plain words to organize for foreign trade just as the 'rings' of England and cartels of Germany are organized."[6]

Indeed, the transformation of the "New Freedom" into something approximating the "New Nationalism" espoused by Theodore Roosevelt in the 1912

---

[3] *Official Report of the National Foreign Trade Convention, 1914* (New York, 1914), p. 207.

[4] Ibid., p. 211.

[5] Ibid., p. 205.

[6] George Creel, "The Next Four Years: An Interview with the President," *Everybody's Magazine*, 36 (February 1917):129–39.

campaign became evident in legislative measures affecting foreign economic policies even sooner than it did in domestic questions. Suffice it here to note that development as an ongoing phenomenon was speeded up by events discussed at greater length in the next chapter.

With Philip Dru in Darkest Mexico and Central America

WILSON'S POLICIES toward the Caribbean and Central America did not depart from his predecessors' efforts to extend Platt Amendment pacification treaties to the area's remaining unstable governments. The President's close friend and political counselor, Colonel Edward M. House, had already rationalized the situation in his anonymous 1912 novel, *Philip Dru: Administrator*. A West Point graduate who led a bloodless coup d'état against the entrenched oligopoly in the United States, Dru found himself confronted with the provocative behavior of a Mexican dictator, whose atavistic attitudes threatened hemispheric stability and progress. As House wrote the scene: "Mexico and the Central American Republics had obstinately continued their old time habit of revo-

Colonel Edward M. House

lutions without just cause, with the result that they neither had stable governments within themselves, nor any hope of peace with each other."

When moral suasion failed, Dru turned from the task of rewriting the American constitution (to accommodate it to government by the expert commissions he had established) to lead the forces of American progressivism against the Mexican tyrant. During a battlefield truce, Dru confronted the dictator with this last argument: "Our citizens and those of other countries have placed in your Republic vast sums for its development, trusting to your treaty guarantees, and they feel much concern over their properties, not only to the advantage of your people, but to those to whom they belong."

The battle won, House closed this episode in Dru's history with a benediction: "In another generation, this beautiful land will be teeming with an educated, prosperous and contented people, who will regard ... [this battle] as the birthplace of their redemption."

The actual course of events was startlingly like this script, from beginning to end. Wilson received a warning that Central American intriguers were circulating rumors that when the Democrats came to power, Washington's restraining influence would be withdrawn. The President vowed to his Cabinet that "if he could prevent it," he "was not going to let them" have more revolutions. Following the meeting, the White House issued a statement to the press that the United States desired the kind of friends in the hemisphere who acted in the interests of peace and honor, and "who protect private rights and respect the restraints of constitutional provision."[7]

Such a statement blurred distinctions between the customhouse "revolutions," which had produced a dreary succession of petty tyrants, and the social upheaval already under way in Mexico in 1913. Leaving that aside, there was also more than a little hypocrisy and arrogance about a demand that these governments practice "constitutional" restraint. In Cuba's case, for example, the American-imposed constitution protected the interests of the United States even at the expense of Cuba's freedom of action, if not its economic welfare. As one of the founders of the Progressive weekly, *The New Republic,* pointed out in 1917: "Peace, sanitation, industrial promotion and an economic or legal compulsion to work constitute the tools of imperialism, as they are applied to agricultural countries in the tropical and sub-tropical world." The test that determined whether or not a nation could remain independent in the modern era was not whether or not it had a "democratic" government and a "consti-

---

[7] Baker, *Wilson,* 4:68f.

tution," but whether it had the capacity to control and utilize its resources.

Secretary of State William Jennings Bryan, the former Populist, was frankly eager to extend the Platt Amendment's benefits all around the Caribbean and Central America. His enthusiasm surprised the President, causing him to comment to Colonel House in 1915 that "while Mr. Bryan was always using the 'soft pedal' in negotiations with Germany, he had to restrain him when he was dealing with Santo Domingo, Haiti and such small republics."[8] Bryan drew upon his own earlier experiences in the American West in formulating a proposal to lend Central American and Caribbean governments Washington's credit rating with international bankers. His argument was that if the United States, in effect, cosigned future loans, these countries would have to make far fewer concessions to foreign bankers to get the needed money, and, in turn, far fewer occasions would arise when the bankers would call upon their governments to collect debts.

The Bryan plan presumed, of course, that the United States would exercise close supervision over financial relations between these small countries and the international bankers. But, said the Secretary of State, the fact that the United States stood ready to preserve order would usually make it unnecessary to do so—and would steadily improve the countries' ability to borrow money on favorable terms. Wilson thought the plan too "novel and radical," but promptly approved a more conventional pact Bryan then negotiated with Nicaragua, the so-called Bryan-Chamorro Treaty, which embodied the full protectorate Knox had originally proposed in 1912, even adding to it a $3 million advance for a naval base at the Gulf of Fonseca and sole rights to construct a canal through the country.

Bryan also put the final touches on the Santo Domingo protectorate. Control of the customhouse had proved insufficient as a check on the outbreak of new revolutions there, despite Bryan's repeated warnings, sent through the American minister, that "revolution would never again bring a government into power here." In the summer of 1914 American diplomatic officials managed to secure a truce between rival factions long enough to present them with an ultimatum: Once hostilities ceased, representatives of the various contenders were to meet and settle upon one man for the provisional presidency. This man would then agree to step aside following national elections supervised by the United States. Having assured itself that the elections were valid, Washington would recognize the new government—and support it against both external and internal disturbances. "No opportunity for argument should be

---

8 Diary entry, June 24, 1915, in the Diary of Colonel Edward M. House, Edward M. House papers, Yale University.

given to any person or faction," the Secretary had explained in forwarding the plan to his representatives. "It is desired that you present plan and see that it is complied with."[9] Lyndon Johnson's representatives made it plain to Dominican leaders years later, in 1965, that they regarded the most recent outburst on the island as a violation of these terms, and acted accordingly.

Meanwhile, on the other side of Hispaniola, Haiti continued to resist the imposition of American financial control, responding to Bryan's overtures with counteroffers of concessions and special preferences for American capitalists. Such offers were beneath the State Department's dignity; besides, as the Secretary's new-found adviser on Haitian affairs, Samuel McRoberts, vice-president of the National City Bank, had often pointed out, no holdings would ever be safe until someone guaranteed stability. As Bryan put it to those in power in Port-au-Prince:

> While we desire to encourage in every proper way American investments in Haiti, we believe that this can be better done by contributing to stability and order than by favoring special concessions to Americans. American capital will gladly avail itself of business opportunities in Haiti when assured of peace and quiet necessary for profitable production.[10]

"Gosh! I'm gettin' tired dopin' these 'internal disturbances'"

---

[9] *Foreign Relations, 1914*, pp. 241–46.
[10] Ibid., pp. 370–71.

Frustrated by the continued instability and bloodletting in Haiti, Bryan suggested to Wilson in April 1915 "a plan similar to that which The Netherlands adopts in Java—namely, having a resident Advisor." He thought the plan was also used "in some of the provinces of India" by the British. This way the government remained in the hands of natives, but an outside representative "advised" local officials. Hence, concluded the Secretary, such a plan might be less offensive than foreign customs officials. (Bryan had learned about British rule in India while on a world tour in 1902; but at that time he felt no sympathy for British methods or manners.) Probably all that would be necessary, therefore, was to make clear what we wanted "with a good sized ship there ready to enforce the demand."[11] The situation got so bad, however, that there was no government in Port-au-Prince to receive the ultimatum. Though he had tried to prevent such a denouement, Bryan did not hesitate to recommend military intervention, initiating an occupation that lasted for nearly fifteen years.

Bryan's successor, Robert Lansing, explained the purposes of the occupation with the same aplomb once evidenced by the narrator of *Philip Dru.* "Haiti should appreciate," Lansing noted,

> that means for economic and industrial development cannot come from within and that foreign capital must be sought and secured, and this cannot be expected unless there is reasonable assurance against internal dissensions. Therefore the period during which peace in Haiti is assured will measure the extent to which foreigners may be expected to invest in the country.[12]

It was not that U.S. businessmen *had to have* Haitian or Nicaraguan markets and investment opportunities—in point of fact, American investment in Haiti never reached significant levels—but they were deemed essential to bring about a lasting resolution of the issues between the American metropolis and the surrounding underdeveloped area, in line with other political and economic foreign policies. In 1916 the administration completed the conversion of the Caribbean into an American lake with the purchase of the Danish West Indies. United States authority remained unchallenged for four decades, until Fidel Castro came to power in Cuba.

The Mexican Revolution

AT FIRST Wilson treated the Mexican situation he had inherited from Taft as something like a Caribbean revolution, if on a much larger scale. One differ-

---

[11] Bryan to Woodrow Wilson, April 2, 1915, in William Jennings Bryan papers, Library of Congress.

[12] *Foreign Relations, 1915*, pp. 440–41.

ence, of course, was that during the short reign of Francisco Madero, 1910–1913, Mexico had seemed to be moving in the direction of stable political democracy. That made it all the more necessary, thought the President, to take a firm line with the usurper Victoriano Huerta, who had overthrown the legitimate government in February 1913. As his understanding of the situation grew, so did his sympathy for the "submerged masses" of Mexico, whose rulers had contributed to the revolution by parceling out Mexico's natural resources to various bidders, American as well as European. Wilson also became convinced that British oil interests were the principal factor in Huerta's ability to remain in power; consequently, he looked suspiciously upon every suggestion that America should come to terms with Huerta.

In the days of Porfirio Díaz, 1876–1910, Mexico had become a foreign investor's paradise. American investments, as William Howard Taft once noted, had already risen to nearly $2 billion. By 1910, the year Díaz fell from power, American citizens controlled 43 percent of all property values in Mexico —10 percent more than the Mexicans themselves. Taft was worried that he would be forced to intervene if Madero failed to establish his rule quickly. But even while Díaz still controlled the Mexican government there had been rumblings of anti-Americanism, and antiforeign feelings generally. These had been expressed in proposed mining laws designed to bring all foreign companies under much stricter control.

"A SORT OF WAR."

U.S. gunner: "We have strict orders to aim only at Huerta"

Díaz had even made a late effort to counterbalance American capital with new European investments, but despite these palliatives, the old dictator lost control of his own *científicos,* who turned increasingly to other alternatives, including a young upper-class idealist, Francisco I. Madero. Peasant leaders were bent on carrying out a much more sweeping revolution. Yet even Madero's election slogans, "Mexico for the Mexicans" and "Lands for the Landless," portended dark days ahead for foreign investors. When Díaz attempted to thwart the electoral process in 1910, Madero and his supporters simply seized power.

Americans in Mexico split over what to do about Madero. Some aligned themselves with Ambassador Henry Lane Wilson, who from the beginning did everything he could to undermine the new government. In the Ambassador's group there were many who hoped that the nephew of the old dictator, Félix Díaz, might somehow get a chance to restore the *ancien régime.* Against these hard-liners stood another group that thought the best way to deal with the Madero problem (and the upsurge in the countryside as well) would be to employ financial controls. The head of the Mexican National Railways, himself an American, contacted banking friends in the United States during 1912, explaining that "financial supervision is the alternative to intervention ... and as such is preferable."[13]

With full State Department backing, efforts to achieve such supervision through controlled loans were in fact initiated that year, but Madero's inability to put down Félix Díaz' counterrevolution prevented serious negotiations. Early in 1913, General Victoriano Huerta threw in his lot with the old dictator's nephew, and the new allies made short work of the Madero government. They were applauded from the wings by Ambassador Wilson, who even offered the American Embassy as a meeting place for the conspirators. In what became known as the "Compact of the Embassy," the two agreed that Huerta should become provisional President, while Díaz named the Cabinet. Huerta also promised to support Díaz for President once order had been restored. Ambassador Wilson encouraged them to look northward for financial aid, and they assured him that they "believed it to be best for the interests of this country to deal to as great an extent as possible with American financial interests."[14]

But Knox and Taft were uncertain about what to do next. The Ambassador's deep involvement in the overthrow of a legitimate government

---

[13] Montgomery Schuyler to Philander C. Knox, December 28, 1912, in U.S. State Department file no. 812.51/52.

[14] H. L. Wilson to Knox, February 26, 1913, in U.S. State Department file no. 812.51/60.

was embarrassing, and became more so somewhat later when he was implicated in consultations prior to Madero's assassination. There were only a few weeks left until the end of their stewardship of American foreign affairs. And, finally, would not diplomatic recognition be useful as a lever to ensure compliance with the "Compact of the Embassy," as well as to encourage the new regime to undertake early financial negotiations with U.S. banking corporations? So, for a variety of reasons, Secretary Knox decided to wait, advising his ambassador in Mexico City: "It is left to you to deal with this whole matter of keeping Mexican opinion, both official and unofficial, in a salutary equilibrium between a dangerous and exaggerated apprehension and a proper degree of wholesome fear."

Henry Lane Wilson protested that it was all-important to extend diplomatic recognition to the provisional government before it became embroiled in the schemes of European governments and bankers, but to no avail. And there the situation stood when Woodrow Wilson entered the White House. A few weeks after his inauguration, a New York banker and E. N. Brown, head of the Mexican railways, came to Colonel House's apartment to discuss the absolute necessity of enforcing the "Compact of the Embassy." If this new government did not survive, they warned, intervention would become a certainty. House told the President a few days later that while he agreed that formal diplomatic recognition was out of the question, nonetheless Ambassador Wilson should not be recalled until "after the election occurred." But the more the President learned about Mexican affairs, the less he believed that Huerta could be counted on to carry out his agreements. Moreover, the method he had used to gain power was a backward step and a bad example for the entire hemisphere. Meanwhile, however, Huerta gained diplomatic recognition from Spain and Great Britain, making it unnecessary for him to abide by his "bargain" with Félix Díaz, if he chose to ignore it.

British support for Huerta was more than an annoyance to the Wilson administration. It meant that nonrecognition, for example, would not work, since other European powers would eventually follow London's lead. As the summer months came on, Cabinet discussions of the insidious power wielded by British capital became more frequent and more heated.

At last the President and Secretary Bryan hit upon a plan that they hoped would end the impasse: to modify the "Compact of the Embassy" to meet their needs. Wilson chose a special agent, John Lind, former governor of Minnesota, to offer Huerta a large loan in exchange for the General's promise to hold new elections, in which he would not be a candidate for the presidency. The plan underestimated Huerta and the force of Mexican revolutionary nationalism.

Even Huerta's opponents applauded his refusal to be bought off for "twenty pieces of silver." Increasingly, Wilson saw the contest as a test of wills with the Mexican leader. "I have made myself his insuperable stumbling block," he wrote an admirer.

This aspect of the Mexican crisis bothered many of the President's countrymen, as well as foreign diplomats, many of whom concluded that Wilson really had no solution to the crisis beyond driving Huerta from power. Was it not likely, therefore, that chaos would follow the General's ouster? Responding directly to British criticism, the President declared that "the United States Government intends not merely to force Huerta from power, but also to exert every influence it can exert to secure for Mexico a better government under which all contracts and business and concessions will be safer than they have been."[15] Wilson's frequent expressions of interest in commercial expansion were difficult to reconcile with his repeated expressions of distrust of financial interests and special concessionaires. His promise to secure a better Mexican government, under which all business transactions would be protected, confounded the British, who read hypocrisy into every other word uttered by the President and his Secretary of State.

And while Wilson had made promises about his long-range goals in Mexico, his famous "Mobile Speech" of October 27, 1913, raised further questions in the corridors of European foreign offices. Designed to cover several issues, the speech began with the President's fullest explanation for his refusal to follow a de facto recognition policy (America's traditional practice) toward Mexico. A restatement was needed because Huerta had in fact held elections on October 26, 1913, which at least approached the validity of those sponsored by the United States elsewhere in the area. Second, the speech restated a promise that America had no territorial ambitions. The remainder of the speech concerned the "one peculiarity about the history of the Latin American States ... 'concessions' to foreign capitalists...." After detailing the power that special interests had in the domestic affairs of host states, Wilson concluded:

> What these States are going to see ... is an emancipation from the subordination, which has been inevitable, to foreign enterprise.... I rejoice in nothing so much as in the prospect that they will now be emancipated from these conditions, and we ought to be the first to take part in assisting in that emancipation.

In the context of British-American disagreements over Mexico, it was not surprising that the Mobile Speech suggested to the Foreign Office that a campaign to clear out all European investments in Mexico was now in the offing.

---

[15] Baker, *Wilson*, 4:292–93.

The better government that President Wilson had talked about for Mexico, then, would be expected to protect only remaining investments—American concessions. European diplomats observed, for example, that Wilson had not departed from Taft's reliance upon selected bankers to help create a stable climate in the area. Wilson's foreign critics also noted that America's concern for constitutional government was highly selective, and that the United States had lost no time in recognizing the Peruvian military junta that overthrew President Billinghurst in February 1914. In short, it appeared to Europeans that Woodrow Wilson's Mexican policy was primarily designed to pave the way for complete American hegemony.

"The present policy of the government of the United States is to isolate General Huerta entirely," Bryan advised his chargé d'affaires in Mexico City, "to cut him off from foreign sympathy and aid from domestic credit, whether moral or material, and to force him out."[16] Still Huerta hung on. Finally, in April 1914, Washington found the excuse it had been looking for in the arrest and detention of a few American sailors by Mexican officers in Tampico. Acting on this insult to the nation's honor, the President ordered the seizure of the customhouse in Vera Cruz. He had done so, he said later, to prevent the unloading of an arms shipment, erroneously thought to be of German origin, intended for the central government.

U.S. occupation of Vera Cruz

---

[16] *Foreign Relations, 1914*, p. 443.

For all the moral rhetoric Wilson wrapped around it, this act was as blatant in design and execution as anything TR or Taft ever engineered. It was, in fact, outright aggression against a foreign government. The drums of war were already sounding in the background. The *New York Times* reported on April 20, 1914: "From early in the evening until a late hour last night thousands of persons assembled in Times Square and scanned eagerly the bulletins displayed in the Times Building on the Mexican situation."

In Washington, the President admitted to his advisers that he was "oppressed with the thought that he might be the cause of the loss of lives of many young men." He asked them to "invoke divine guidance during the interval before [their] next meeting."[17] Something like a *deus ex machina* ending did in fact appear in an offer from Argentina, Brazil, and Chile to mediate the crisis. Huerta accepted, then resigned, clearing the way for each side to step back from the edge of war.

The Mexican Revolution: Phase II

HAVING SECURED General Huerta's resignation, Wilson and Bryan had no intention of allowing the dust to settle before undertaking new initiatives. The State Department had stationed representatives near several of Huerta's likely heirs, all of whom had fought for the right to share in the leadership of the Mexican Revolution. The strongest group, the "Constitutionalists," were led by an improbable revolutionary, the conservative landholder Venustiano Carranza. Secretary Bryan promptly cautioned Carranza that the United States was the "only first-class power that can be expected to take the initiative in recognizing the new government." He and Wilson now seemed confident that British diplomacy had been bested once and for all. The Secretary of State then instructed the Mexican Constitutionalist leader on what was expected of him:

> First, the treatment of foreigners, foreign lives, foreign property, foreign rights, and particularly the delicate matter of the financial obligations, the legitimate financial obligations of the government now superseded. Unless the utmost care, fairness and liberality are shown in these matters the most dangerous complications may arise.[18]

U.S. advice cannot be turned down, Bryan felt compelled to add a few days later, "without deep and perhaps fatal consequences to the cause of the present

17 Josephus Daniels, *The Wilson Era: Years of Peace, 1910–1917* (Chapel Hill, N.C., 1944), p. 189.

18 *Foreign Relations, 1914*, pp. 568–69.

revolution...." It is hard to say which was more presumptuous here, the assumption that Carranza would emerge victorious in the contest among the contenders for power or the bald assertion that the winning faction could, and should, turn over control and management of the Mexican Revolution to the United States. Better information from American agents in Mexico might have made the situation clear to Washington: no man could hope to control the government who did not respond to the drive and direction of the revolution, which was moving directly away from Washington's growing paternalism. Even had he wanted to, Carranza could not have complied with Bryan's "advice" and remained in the running.

But Bryan's successor, Robert Lansing, took Carranza's refusals for simple defiance, and reacted accordingly. "The reasons for furnishing [Pancho] Villa with an opportunity to obtain funds is this," he explained to the President. "We do not wish the Carranza faction to be the only one to deal with in Mexico. Carranza seems so impossible that an appearance, at least, of opposition to him will give us an opportunity to invite a compromise of factions...."[19] Lansing was on the verge of committing the United States to a second intervention in August 1915—based upon this reasoning and the dubious reliability of men like Pancho Villa—when President Wilson intervened instead against State Department plans, and ordered Lansing to extend limited recognition to Carranza's government.

Over the next eighteen months, however, Mexican-American relations did not improve; they grew worse. In 1916 the United States sent General Pershing with a military expedition into Mexico to punish its erstwhile ally against Carranza, Pancho Villa, for his border raids into Texas. Some policy-makers fervently hoped that the General's orders might be expanded to include the bigger problem in Mexico City, since their complaint was that those in charge in the Mexican capital could not maintain law and order in the countryside. Carranza countered these charges by pointing out that private American interests were supporting local leaders against the central government. Pershing failed to track down Villa, however, and was recalled following a serious clash with Carranza's troops at Carrizal.

The emerging issue was the revolution itself: Wilson wanted to impose his own standards, the criteria of American liberalism, on Mexico's revolution. Tensions reached a high point with the announcement early in 1917 of a new Mexican constitution. Certain articles in that document had been foreshadowed in the latter days of Porfirio Díaz, but now they were codified as the funda-

---

[19] Robert Lansing to Wilson, August 8, 1915, in U.S. State Department file no. 812.00/15751½.

mental law of the land. Article 27, for example, stated that all subsoil natural resources belonged to the Mexican government. Aliens could own land or exploit mineral resources only if they agreed in advance not to invoke the protection of their governments in disputes about their property. With these and other explicit checks upon the operation of private enterprise, the constitution produced a mixture of shock and dismay in Washington. Nothing in the "New Freedom" or the "New Nationalism" had contemplated such a potentially revolutionary change, at home or abroad. The decision to go to war against Germany and the Central Powers postponed the time when Washington would have to come to terms with the Mexican situation, but the revolution remained a serious challenge throughout the remaining years of the Wilson administration.

Restoring the "Original" Open Door Policy in China

WHEN TAFT admitted Russia and Japan (under pressure) to the consortium in 1912, Tokyo understood that the powers were to coordinate their China policies as far as possible. Woodrow Wilson's abrupt decision to pull American financiers out of the consortium raised Japanese suspicions that they had been deceived. But the American bankers were also angered about the way the President announced his decision, and about the language he used in a public statement, which seemed to imply that they had been caught in a disreputable attempt to exploit China. Nevertheless, his announcement had discussed America's undiminished desire to participate fully in the development of China's "almost untouched" resources. To facilitate this participation, the President declared, he would seek legislation to provide the country's merchants, manufacturers, contractors, engineers, *and bankers* with facilities comparable to those of "their industrial and commercial rivals."

In Cabinet discussions, Wilson further clarified his stand on the international consortium. If he had requested the bankers to go ahead in this big power combine, he explained, "we would have got nothing but mere influence in China and lost the proud position which America secured when Secretary Hay stood for the Open Door in China after the Boxer uprising."[20] Once again the United States could challenge Russian policy in Manchuria or Japanese behavior in China proper, not as a rival, but from the "proud position" of China's protector and friend.

---

[20] *Foreign Relations, 1913,* p. 170.

Wilson's new ambassador to China, Professor Paul S. Reinsch, found the American business community there dispirited by recent events and discouraged by Washington's new policy. At once he undertook to restore their confidence and to uplift the sagging spirits of the Chinese themselves. Reinsch proposed that the United States construct a series of dams on the Huai River to control flooding, the scourge of Chinese agriculture. These dams would demonstrate what the railroad loans had so miserably failed to prove: that the United States, acting alone, could carry out major development projects in China, relying solely upon its own financial resources. The Ambassador even persuaded the Chinese government to give the American Red Cross an option on the project for a year, during which it could raise the money to begin work, but the outbreak of the European war collapsed even the most conservative foreign ventures. The simple truth was that American bankers had to marshal every available capital source in order to withstand the initial shock caused by the war.

Japan, on the other hand, was in a position to take advantage of the war to improve its position in China at once, and moved quickly to drive the Germans out of their leasehold on the Shantung peninsula. A few months later Tokyo secretly presented Peking with what became known as the "Twenty-One Demands," essentially a series of proposals by which it hoped to consolidate its Manchurian and Chinese gains during the war. Reinsch was appalled; but Secretary Bryan and his aides reacted cautiously until they learned the full extent of Japan's claims. Then Wilson decided that he must make it plain to all parties that the United States could not recognize any of the Twenty-One Demands, despite a previous telegram Bryan had sent to Tokyo accepting at least some of them.

This decision was followed by a State Department campaign to encourage American business to go after the China trade, on pain of losing future markets. But the thought of challenging Japan directly disturbed many of those who were interested in China; the experiences of the Taft administration had not exactly boosted confidence in China's ability to resist outside pressures and develop a stable government. The alternative seemed to be to work with Japan, not against it. Judge Elbert H. Gary, the steel magnate; Frank A. Vanderlip, the banker who founded the American International Corporation; and Vanderlip's chief troubleshooter, Willard Straight, led a movement to encourage Japanese-American cooperation. To Reinsch's amazement and consternation, they even wanted to convert the old Huai dam project into the base from which to launch their Japanese-American partnership!

When the Japanese formally inquired about the administration's attitude toward economic cooperation, they met an ambiguous response in the State

Department. Secretary Lansing at times seemed inclined simply to write off Manchuria, as Theodore Roosevelt had done, so he could concentrate on finding a way to get Japan out of Shantung. But Reinsch had his own ideas on all these questions, and proceeded to steal the initiative from everyone by encouraging the Chinese to follow America's lead in February 1917 by breaking off diplomatic relations with the Central Powers. He promised the Chinese that by taking this step, and then going to war with the Allies, they could assure themselves an equal place at the peace table. China's voice would be heard and Japan would have to return the Shantung peninsula to Peking's control. Reinsch's boldness sent tremors through the State Department, but when Japan followed suit by encouraging China to enlist in the war under *its* auspices, there was little Lansing could do to prevent the United States from becoming even more deeply involved in China's internal affairs.

The Mexican and Chinese policies pursued by the Wilson administration developed in the background of World War I, and the European conflict exercised a powerful influence on the development of each. In the former situation, for instance, the revelation of the "Zimmerman Note," in which Germany supposedly promised to help Mexico get back its "lost territories" from the United States if Carranza helped out in case war broke out between Germany and the United States, had a double impact, shoving America both away from its neutral position in regard to the European war and toward efforts to reach a *modus vivendi* with Mexico City. Similarly, when the General Board of the Navy proposed building a force equal to that of the world's most powerful navy in October 1915, many congressmen voted for new naval bills to counter Japan's rising threat in Asia. One's perspective on other questions is improved by keeping the war in mind, but its influence was to heighten previous concerns, not to exclude them. What the war demonstrated most of all was the inextricable character of America's growing involvements.

Suggestions for Further Reading

Arthur S. Link's monumental biography of Woodrow Wilson is the beginning point for readers interested in both foreign and domestic policy. For this chapter see *The Road to the White House* (Princeton, N.J., 1947), *The New Freedom* (Princeton, 1956), and *The Struggle for Neutrality, 1914–1915* (Princeton, 1960). See also N. Gordon Levin, *Woodrow Wilson and World Politics* (New York, 1968).

Mexican problems are treated in a long list of books, but see first Howard F. Cline, *The United States and Mexico* (New York, 1963), and then be sure to go to Peter Calvert, *The Mexican Revolution, 1910–1914: The Diplomacy of Anglo-American Conflict* (Cambridge, Mass., 1968), for a strikingly fresh perspective on the Mexican Revolution's impact on world affairs.

In addition to works on the Far East cited earlier, see Paul Reinsch's own neglected account, *An American Diplomat in China* (New York, 1922), and Tien-yi Li, *Woodrow Wilson's China Policy, 1913–1917* (New York, 1952). Focusing primarily on a later period is Burton F. Beers, *Vain Endeavor: Robert Lansing's Attempts to End the American-Japanese Rivalry* (Durham, N.C., 1962), but it should be read as background for what comes next.

See also the general bibliography at the end of this volume.

CHAPTER 17

America
Abandons
"Neutrality"
(1914–1917)

In the century following the War of 1812, the history of America's inability to remain "neutral" in its very first wartime test had gathered dust in textbooks. Unable to live with the British maritime system, President James Madison had risked taking a divided nation into a war that nearly ruined the Jeffersonians before it was over. Woodrow Wilson remembered these events, however, and remarked on the irony that Madison had been the last President from Princeton before his own election. As Wilson meant to imply, the similarity did not end there. Both had contended for "peace without victory," based not on "a balance of power, but a community of power." Each chose war rather than acquiesce to European "systems." Madison fought England, but had no sympathy for Napoleon's "continental" system. Wilson went to war against Germany, but refused to join the Allies or accept their war aims.

Neutrality Challenged: The Guns of August

AMERICANS GENERALLY condemned Germany's invasion of little Belgium without inquiring further into the origins of the war. The spike-helmeted German militarist grimaced over Europe in editorial cartoons, but few feared him as a direct threat to American security in August 1914. The war itself was another matter. It had come at a bad time for both Wilson and the nation. The death of his wife, on August 6, 1914, left him temporarily enervated just when key decisions had to be made. For the nation, the outbreak of war meant a serious disruption of its foreign trade. On August 14 the president of the New York Chamber of Commerce observed glumly, "Europe has placed an embargo on the commerce of the world." Cotton and wheat exports were the most obvious losses, but the whole economy of the nation relied upon agricultural surpluses to adjust the international balance of trade. In 1914 the United States was still a debtor to Europe by upwards of $3 billion; it counted on these exports to settle its yearly account. If they were cut off, even for one year, the glut on the home market would ruin the price structure.

President Wilson had called Democratic congressional leaders to the White House on July 31, 1914, to warn them that if war did come, the American economy would be in danger for at least six months, or until Great Britain established its naval supremacy. America's great harvests would "waste in the warehouses" or "rot in the fields." Hence Congress must provide the nation with its own merchant ships so that if and when war came, American trade could be sent to sea in neutral bottoms. Wilson had raised these points in the 1912 campaign, but neither he nor Congress had done anything about the problem. Now, even if Congress responded instantaneously, it was too late.

Without a large merchant fleet, America's defense of neutral shipping was hampered. It was harder to contend for abstract justice than demand respect for its ships on the high seas. Even so, Wilson and Bryan still had the choice of insisting that America's right to trade with Germany in noncontraband goods be recognized or of bending before the soon-to-be-announced British mercantile system. It was an old dilemma.

Britannia Rules the Seas: Neutrality Thwarted

"EXPERIENCE WARNS US," James Madison had said in 1812, "of the fatal tendencies of a commerce unrestricted with Great Britain, and restricted by her pleasure and policy elsewhere." The State Department had had another century of experience with Great Britain's sea power, and was engaged in an effort to persuade the belligerents to accept the 1909 Declaration of London (a liberal maritime code favoring neutral rights proposed by a conference of naval powers initiated, ironically, by Great Britain itself) when the first wartime order-in-council was announced to the world on August 20, 1914. Now there would have to be a clash between America's neutral interests and Britain's war needs.

Great Britain had never ratified the Declaration of London, nor had the other signatories. It therefore had no standing in international law. The State Department, including those who favored the British cause, wanted to give it that standing.

Washington was particularly anxious about cotton, securely placed on the declaration's "free list" of items that could never be declared contraband. London had been evasive about cotton. Cotton-state senators like Oklahoma's Robert Owen thought Secretary Bryan should try to pin down a specific guarantee; otherwise the cotton-growing areas stood to lose more than $250 million immediately, and larger sums in the future. Perplexed by the problems confronting America, Bryan replied that the belligerents had "inferentially" agreed that "they will not declare contraband the articles listed" in the Declaration of London.[1]

Inferences are risky things to run an export business on while waiting for some final word; they are even more unsatisfactory as a foreign policy base. When London continued to delay, Wilson told the State Department he wanted a note with "teeth in it." The night the requested paper came over from Bryan's office, Colonel House was dining with the President. Shocked by its denunciatory language, House persuaded Wilson not to send it until its phrases were at least modified. He asked for and received the President's permission to consult privately with the British ambassador before any note was dispatched. These two easily reached an agreed modification. The note—and American policy—were changed.

In regard to House's actions, it might be well to remember that Bryan had also taken every opportunity to gain a little time before committing the nation to an irrevocable course. Yet the Colonel's intervention undercut any serious effort to secure acceptance of the Declaration of London, and the administration's final note on the matter trailed off weakly in a sentence reserving the right to lodge later protests against any British policies that proved injurious. Relieved, Sir Edward Grey, the British Foreign Minister, almost immediately enlarged the contraband list to include "strategic" raw materials—though not

---

[1] Robert Owen to William Jennings Bryan, August 20, 1914; Bryan to Owen, August 25, 1914; in U.S. State Department file no. 763.72112/104.

yet cotton—and advised the Admiralty only that it should exercise a sense of proportion in interrupting American trade.

American business firms, unable to deal in inferences, thus had to come to terms with the British maritime system on their own. And these terms, of course, meant that American trade would become a vastly important aid to those who ruled the seas. "The British," wrote a student of the Allied blockade against Germany,

> secured the beginnings of a system of trade controls over neutral commerce in both Europe and America, without evoking more than polite notes of protest from the United States Government. The latter had shown itself willing to permit its citizens to make private agreements if American trade and industries would thus be benefited. It even went further and of its own accord adopted measures that made the execution of these agreements easier. Having received this degree of toleration, the British government felt quite safe in perfecting and extending its system of coercion in Europe.[2]

No one in government was happy about this situation, and Wilson did continue to press Congress for shipping bills to build an American merchant fleet, but as the war went on the State Department became extremely sensitive to criticism that it had abdicated its responsibilities. After 1915 the new Secretary of State, Robert Lansing, accused complainants of "pro-German sentiment" or "purely selfish interests." In his *War Memoirs,* Lansing even asserted that those who protested that the British prevented them from trading with neutrals secretly wanted to trade with the Germans; these dissidents, he said, were the "loudest in their protests and most persistent in sending their senators and representatives and attorneys to the Department of State to demand vigorous action by the government." Lansing's touchiness revealed the administration's basic predicament: unable to respond to the demand that the government protect the right to trade with *all* belligerents, the Secretary dismissed such complaints, and even attributed them to motives substantiated by nothing but his own subjective judgment. Little wonder Lansing urged the President to abandon the pretense after the Germans initiated submarine warfare; little wonder, too, that Wilson soon found neutrality a labyrinth from which there was no exit, save the one he had hoped to avoid.

"The Worst of Contrabands": Credits and Loans

Soon after the war began, the French government requested J. P. Morgan and Company to float a $100 million loan in the United States. Unsure of their posi-

---

[2] Marion C. Siney, *The Allied Blockade of Germany, 1914–1916* (Ann Arbor, Mich., 1957), p. 59.

tion, the bankers asked for a ruling from the Department of State. Secretary Bryan, on the other hand, was very sure of the proper attitude for a neutral government: "Loans by American bankers to any foreign nation which is at war is [*sic*] inconsistent with the true spirit of neutrality."[3] The Secretary's statement appeared in the *New York Times* on August 16, 1914. There was nothing in international law to support his position; it was argued at the time and later that such a ban was unneutral because prejudicial to the Allies, who were more deeply involved in international finance. Even so, Wilson seemed uneasy about removing the ban, remarking upon one occasion, "It was my duty to discourage the loans to belligerents."[4]

Bryan had contended that loans of any kind constituted the "worst of contrabands" because money "commands all other things." He also feared that powerful economic interests would line up behind the combatants, creating special pressure on the administration. The bankers, of course, had a different view. One recalled that at the time the first request came from Paris he had just been shown

> a front page of the *New York Times* ... and I happened to notice ... a telegram from Pittsburgh stating that there were 100,000 steel men idle in the Pittsburgh district. That gives a picture of our industrial situation at that time. There was great dullness in our industries, and there was every reason for us to stimulate those industries with an export business, if we could.[5]

Using this argument, the bankers approached the administration a second time in late October, explaining that what the Allies now sought was not really a "loan" but private short-term "credits." Wilson seized upon this distinction as a way out of what he now professed to see as an exaggerated concern for spiritual "neutrality." Yet he was careful not to stir up things with a newspaper statement approving "credits." He told Acting Secretary of State Lansing that his approval should be conveyed verbally to the interested parties, although he still felt that in the case of a public loan, the "purchasers of bonds are loaning their savings to the belligerent government, and are, in fact, financing the war."[6]

---

[3] Quoted in Arthur S. Link, *Woodrow Wilson and the Progressive Era, 1910–1917* (New York, 1954), p. 151.

[4] Cited in Ray Stannard Baker, *Woodrow Wilson: Life and Letters,* 8 vols. (New York, 1924–1928), 5:188–89.

[5] U.S. Senate, 74th Cong., 2nd sess., Special Committee to Investigate the Munitions Industry, *Hearings* (Washington, D.C., 1937), p. 7530. Hereafter cited as Munitions Industry Hearings.

[6] "Memorandum by the Acting Secretary of State of a Conversation with the President," October 23, 1914, in *Foreign Relations, The Lansing Papers,* 1:140.

Within a few months, nonetheless, it became necessary to amend Bryan's ban a second time to permit "long-term" credits, and finally to repudiate it altogether so as to permit flotation of public loans.

This last decision came in August 1915, when the Allies informed the United States that they could not continue war purchases in America without a $500 million loan. Treasury Secretary William Gibbs McAdoo put before the President two reasons for abandoning what was left of the Bryan policy: (1) the great prosperity that had come with war orders would disappear if the administration failed to make it possible for the Allies to obtain long-term credits; (2) if, as even the Central Powers conceded, the munitions trade and other war trade were legal, then the government was not being truly neutral if it prevented one party from securing needed goods by banning loans. Wilson could take his choice; either rationale would produce the desired change. McAdoo, however, was perfectly candid about his position. "It is not a question in my mind," he told a member of the Federal Reserve Board, "as to whether the protection of American interests affects favorably, or adversely, any one, or all of the belligerents. Our duty is to protect American interests. . . ."[7]

Lansing favored the loan because he was pro-British, for "balance of power" reasons. But all avenues seemed to lead American policy-makers to the same position. When America entered the war in April 1917, it had loaned the Allies approximately $2.3 billion; Germany had obtained only $27 million. Yet the loans were not the cause of the decision to go to war, as revisionists argued so vehemently in the 1930s. Foreign policy was not made at the bankers' behest. The loans represented only an agreement among policy-makers that desired ends could be achieved by this means. There was a massive economic stake in Allied victory, but not in Allied war aims.

Submarine Warfare: Differentiated Neutrality

LOAN DECISIONS in August 1915 were made in the midst of a political crisis with Germany over submarine warfare. The crisis had begun when a German U-boat commander had fired his last torpedo into the British passenger liner *Lusitania* on May 7, 1915. It sank within twenty minutes, carrying down with it 1,198 men, women, and children—including 128 Americans. The nature of submarine warfare appalled many Americans. Bryan, however, tended to view

---

[7] Munitions Industry Hearings, p. 10168.

CUNARD

EUROPE VIA LIVERPOOL
LUSITANIA
Fastest and Largest Steamer
now in Atlantic Service Sails
SATURDAY, MAY 1, 10 A. M.
Transylvania, Fri., May 7, 5 P.M.
Orduna, - - Tues. May 18, 10 A.M.
Tuscania, - - Fri., May 21, 5 P.M.
LUSITANIA, Sat., May 29, 10 A.M.
Transylvania, Fri., June 4, 5 P.M.

Gibraltar–Genoa–Naples–Piraeus
S.S. Carpathia, Thur., May 13, Noon

NOTICE!
TRAVELLERS intending to
embark on the Atlantic voyage
are reminded that a state of
war exists between Germany
and her allies and Great Britain
and her allies; that the zone of
war includes the waters adjacent to the British Isles; that,
in accordance with formal notice given by the Imperial German Government, vessels flying
the flag of Great Britain, or of
any of her allies, are liable to
destruction in those waters and
that travellers sailing in the
war zone on ships of Great
Britain or her allies do so at
their own risk.

IMPERIAL GERMAN EMBASSY
WASHINGTON, D. C., APRIL 22, 1915.

The Lusitania

it in the context of an appalling war, while Wilson differentiated between attacks on American property and those that resulted in the loss of American
lives. When the German government had announced the establishment of a war
zone around the British Isles in February 1915, it insisted that it was only
countering Britain's illegal and inhumane blockade against the Central Powers.
The State Department rejected this argument, warning Berlin that if American
ships or lives were lost, the United States would hold Germany strictly accountable.

As dangerous incidents began to pile up toward the inevitable crisis, Secretary Bryan asked Wilson to reconsider the American position. He questioned
whether individual American citizens, knowing that they were running risks
by traveling in designated war zones, should demand that their country extend
them the kind of protection that might involve the nation in an international
crisis. "Once accept a single abatement of right," Wilson replied, "and many
other humiliations would certainly follow, and the whole fine fabric of international law might crumble under our hands piece by piece."[8]

---

[8] *Foreign Relations, Lansing Papers*, 1:400–406.

Bryan hardly had time to formulate an answer to that argument when he and the rest of the nation were overtaken by the *Lusitania* crisis. Lansing put an end to talk about warning Americans off belligerent ships, as Bryan had suggested, by pointing out that if it were done in the wake of the *Lusitania*'s sinking, the announcement would suggest that the government had neglected its duty in not having made such a statement before the tragedy. President Wilson probably would have taken the same stand regardless of Lansing's new argument, but the episode illustrated yet another tangle in the increasingly confused pattern of American neutrality.

So Bryan struggled to word the *Lusitania* note to Germany in such a way as to prevent a rupture of diplomatic relations—after the fashion of House's intervention the year before, when a draft note on the Declaration of London had threatened a serious break with England. He also proposed a press release stating that the United States expected Germany to give a satisfactory response; Wilson refused, declaring the idea "Pickwickian." Then Bryan asked to include a final sentence in the note reiterating American friendship for Germany; the President asserted that the note already had quite enough of that kind of sentiment in it. When Bryan made one last effort to persuade Wilson to warn Americans not to travel on belligerent vessels, Wilson snapped that such a policy would be weak and futile.

The first *Lusitania* note of May 13, 1915, virtually demanded that the Germans cease their submarine warfare against merchantmen. Berlin's reply evaded the central issue, leading Wilson to prepare to repeat his stand in a second note. Rather than go on with a course he felt sure would end disastrously, and which it was now apparent he could not alter, Bryan resigned, and Robert Lansing succeeded the Great Commoner at the head of the State Department.

The new Secretary based his policy on an absolute conviction that sometime in the future America would join the Allies. In preparing the second *Lusitania* note, therefore, he advised the President to avoid all extraneous issues: "I believe that brevity will impress the German Government with the earnestness of our purpose, to insist on our rights, and will also cause a feeling in this country that this Government does not intend to prolong the controversy indefinitely."[9] Brevity brought issues to a climax. And Lansing explained in his *War Memoirs* why he had followed an opposite policy in regard to British violations of neutral rights:

> I did all that I could to prolong the disputes by preparing, or having prepared, long and detailed replies, and introducing technical and controversial matters in

---

[9] Robert Lansing to Woodrow Wilson, July 14, 1915, in Woodrow Wilson papers, Library of Congress.

the hope that before the extended interchange of arguments came to an end something would happen to change the current of American public opinion or to make the American people perceive that German absolutism was a menace to their liberties and to democratic institutions everywhere. Fortunately this hope and effort were not in vain.[10]

From Lansing's frank account it would appear that either Wilson knew of these policies and approved them, if only by his silence, or that if he did not understand what the Secretary was doing, he was not nearly in such complete control of American foreign policy as has been assumed. In either case, it will hardly do to speak of American policy from 1914 to 1917 as disinterested or genuinely neutral.

Negotiations were still going on when another U-boat sank the British liner *Arabic,* with the loss of two more American lives. Lansing now urged the President to consider asking Congress for a declaration of war, before the United States forfeited its remaining influence with both belligerents. If that happened, American desires for a peace settlement guaranteeing freedom of the seas were likely to be ignored. This soul-searching was interrupted by the German ambassador's public statement that no more passenger ships would be sunk without warning, provided they did not seek to escape or offer resistance. The ambassador, Count Johann von Bernstorff, had issued the declaration on his own initiative, but Berlin backed him up and the crisis eased at once. In March 1916 the Germans torpedoed the *Sussex,* a French passenger liner, causing injuries to eighty persons, including several Americans. Wilson threatened to sever diplomatic relations unless Germany abided by Bernstorff's promise. The German Foreign Office did repeat the pledge, but added a proviso that unrestricted submarine warfare could be abandoned only if Britain were forced to give up the blockade.

The House-Dru Missions to Europe

LANSING'S POINTED SUGGESTION, during the *Lusitania* crisis, that Wilson could influence the peace settlement only by entering the war against Germany had been aimed at countering Colonel House's continuing advice to the President. The new Secretary of State had only the vaguest idea of what House was up to, but he had witnessed Bryan's growing embarrassment ever since September of 1914, when the Colonel had shortstopped the Department's protest to London.

---

[10] Robert Lansing, *The War Memoirs of Robert Lansing* (Indianapolis, 1935), p. 112.

It was clear that the President relied on House to conduct his "peace" initiatives.

House, in turn, seemed to follow the ideas of his creation, Philip Dru, who, having solved America's domestic problems and pacified Latin American revolutionaries, turned to the problem of big power relations. As Dru saw it, the problem centered on the need to stabilize Anglo-German-American relations so that rivalries in colonial and underdeveloped areas would not lead to war between the nations most responsible for protecting Western civilization from outsiders. Dru had imagined that German ambitions, perhaps the most difficult problem for the other two, might be eased by encouraging that restless country to engage itself in South America. In the novel that solution helped to prevent war, but in real life Colonel House failed to bring it off.

House had gone to Europe in the summer of 1914 to urge England and the western European nations to consider some such alternative. After the war began he allowed himself to believe that his mission had nearly succeeded: if only the Kaiser's advisers had not panicked at the thought and demanded war! The Colonel had in mind reopening his prewar discussions when he intervened to prevent the dispatch of the State Department's protest that September, a plan he immediately put into operation in the following weeks. He sounded out the German, French, and British ambassadors on the chance for serious negotiations to end the war; but no matter what they told him, House was already convinced that such an opportunity existed. Count von Bernstorff invited him to come to Berlin to pursue the proposal, but, with the President's approval, House began the mission by going to London in January 1915. There he stayed—and stayed—until Wilson finally asked if he were not jeopardizing the chance for real negotiations with Germany.

House replied that Germany had not as yet agreed to begin talks on the basis of an evacuation of Belgium and an indemnity to that country, the fundamental *sine qua non* of his plan. In other words, the world had to be restored just as it was before everything went out of control; then America could help build a better international society. He bolstered his position with a questionable assertion that Sir Edward Grey was seriously interested in having the President mediate between the warring powers. House had proposed that when the belligerents actually got to the negotiation stage, President Wilson would issue a call for a "second peace convention" to take up world issues, while the nations that had been fighting would settle local issues between them in a simultaneous conference. If that happened, something worth all the destruction and death might yet emerge from the war. "He has come to look upon it," House wrote of the British Foreign Minister, "as one of the hopes of the future, and if we accomplish nothing else, you will be able to do the most important world's work within sight."[11]

When he finally got to Berlin, without having gained his first objective, House broached the possibility of greater German-American cooperation in South America after the war, a notion that surprised Foreign Office officials, who inquired if the Monroe Doctrine had recently been amended. The Colonel had returned to England before the *Lusitania* was sunk. He advised the President that British leaders were watching American behavior closely to see if the United States would take a firm stand against submarine warfare: "Our action in this crisis will determine the part we will play when peace is made, and how far we may influence a settlement for the lasting good of humanity. We are being weighed in the balance, and our position amongst nations is being adjudged by mankind."[12] What influence House's appeal had on Wilson's determination to press the issue cannot be gauged. Lansing believed it had led to the President's promise, in the *Lusitania* note, that he would also press Great Britain to guarantee genuine freedom of the seas. He also thought that an invitation to Germany to cooperate in that effort had been included in order to fulfill some secret plan House had devised. In point of fact, however, House was considerably less "neutral" than Lansing feared. He had undertaken his peace missions believing that the American position vis-à-vis the Allies was different than it could be in regard to Germany, "for we are bound up more or less in their success. . . . If we lost their good will we will not be able to figure at all in peace negotiations and we will be sacrificing too much in order to maintain all our commercial rights."[13] Once again all avenues led to one, and only one, way out.

The Confluence of Events and Ideas

ON JULY 30, 1915, the liberal journalist Oswald Garrison Villard wrote Secretary Lansing, "Why does the United States say to England that the laws of blockade can be altered during war, and insist to Germany that the laws governing attacks on ships cannot be altered?" The administration always gave the same answer to this question: Submarine warfare took American lives; the British blockade only interrupted American goods on the way to market. But

[11] Edward M. House to Wilson, February 23, 1915, in Wilson papers.

[12] House to Wilson, May 9, 1915, in Edward M. House papers, Yale University.

[13] House to Wilson, May 25, 1915, in ibid.

in the fall of 1915 public patience with British policy was wearing extremely thin, despite the war boom caused by Allied purchases. Cotton had been declared contraband, but the British immediately arranged to purchase the entire export surplus. Even so, London's blacklisting of firms that refused to go along with these special purchasing arrangements or to confine their trade to the Allies and friendly neutrals brought renewed demands that something be done about London's cavalier attitude toward American rights. These grew much stronger following Bernstorff's pledge that Germany would stop sinking unarmed ships without warning.

Convinced that a German triumph would mean victory for "militarism," if not yet a direct threat to the United States, Wilson confessed to House in September 1915 that he had never been sure that the United States had done the right thing in remaining neutral when Germany started the war. The President's worried state of mind stimulated the Colonel's fertile imagination, and a new peace plan emerged full grown: it was a "positive policy," said House, designed to extricate the United States from its paralyzing dilemma, win the peace, and forestall future militarism and naval adventurism. All in one package. Wilson would set the plan in motion by asking the Allies if they would agree to have the United States demand that all hostilities cease. Since this would be done only after the Allies and the United States had agreed on acceptable peace terms, such a call would receive a favorable reply from London and Paris. If the Central Powers agreed to a cease-fire and to the proposed peace terms, the plan would constitute a master stroke. What if Berlin did not go along? "We could then push our insistence to a point where diplomatic relations would first be broken off, and later the whole force of our Government— and perhaps the force of every neutral—might be brought against them."[14]

Wilson liked the plan, but he modified it by inserting the word "probably" before a statement to the British that the United States would go to war against Germany if Berlin refused peace terms. He made the change, he told House, because he could not quite say it was "inevitable" that "we should take part to force terms on Germany." When House delivered the memorandum in London, the "probably" stood out like a sore thumb. It provided Sir Edward Grey with an out, for, while he was more eager than ever for the United States to come into the war, he still wanted it to happen as a result of Wilson's outrage at German behavior, not in return for British acceptance of American foreign policy goals. He had more than enough "understandings" to handle already. As House talked with British and French leaders in the early months of 1916, he

---

14 Edward M. House, *The Intimate Papers of Colonel House,* ed. Charles Seymour, 4 vols. (Boston, 1926–1928), 2:84–86.

came increasingly to realize how much Allied secret treaties for dividing up the spoils of victory reduced the chances not only for the success of his mission, but of a peace settlement acceptable to the United States.

These impressions were confirmed in several ways. To begin with, there was Sir Edward's refusal to invoke the President's aid in summoning a conference to end the war. A February 1916 House-Grey memorandum had stipulated that at some opportune moment the Allies might call upon the United States to put in motion the President's plan for ending the war. Such a moment never came, even after House had prodded Grey with warnings that the time was very late for the Allied cause. In his disappointment House wrote: "A situation may arise, if the Allies defeat Germany, where they may attempt to be dictatorial in Europe and elsewhere."[15]

A second confirmation came in reports that both the Central Powers and the Allies had well-advanced plans for the "war after the war," the struggle for economic supremacy in the postwar world. By 1916 both sides had to consider seriously the possibility that the war might end inconclusively, in which case there would soon develop a bitter struggle for investments and markets. Then each side would build up its military strength for a new showdown, and the cycle would begin all over again. A gloomy outlook, not only for Europe but for America as well, because it could mean that the United States would become trapped in a permanent state of "preparedness." That would mean the final defeat of long-cherished hopes of escaping from the domination of Old World politics. Indeed, the influence of European attitudes on American institutions would grow stronger and stronger.

At their June 1916 economic conference in Paris, the Allies outlined a far-reaching postwar program of exclusive trade pacts aimed against both enemy and *neutral* countries. The conference envisioned state-sponsored inter-Allied agreements among certain key industries, cartel fashion, so as to promote their growth as export combines competing with the rest of the world. Informing Wilson of these resolutions, Lansing warned that if they were adopted, "the consequent restrictions upon profitable trade with these commercial allies will cause a serious, if not critical, situation for nations outside the Union by creating unusual and artificial conditions."[16]

It almost seemed as if the only solution was to join the Allies in the war, so that it would not be necessary to join them in the war after the war. Wilson also received a warning from the chairman of the Senate Foreign Relations

---

[15] Diary entry, May 13, 1916, in House papers.

[16] Lansing to Wilson, June 23, 1916, in *Foreign Relations, Lansing Papers*, 1:311–12.

Committee; he wrote the President, "It seems to me that the most important thing of immediate concern with which we have to deal concerns 'preparedness' to meet what under present conditions will be an over-mastering rivalry in the commercial world." The world was closing in on Woodrow Wilson and his conception of neutrality. It was becoming clear, he confided to House, that "there lies latent" in British policy "the wish to prevent our merchants getting a foothold in markets which Great Britain has hitherto controlled and all but dominated."[17]

For a long time Wilson had held out against a military preparedness campaign of the sort urged by Theodore Roosevelt. The former President was still banking on that "alternative," but Wilson was not ready to accept it. At least not alone. If the only way America could make itself respected was to build a navy, then so be it—and woe to those who would provoke a conflict after that. But the trouble with military preparedness alone was, as it had always been, that the solution was only temporary. It was not nearly enough even to assure that the United States would have its wishes respected at the end of the war.

Hence Wilson sought a third alternative. He had been thinking about it during House's peace missions; now he led the campaign for a different preparedness, diplomatically by setting forth conditions that he felt would undermine all the secret treaties and entangling alliances that had caused this dreadful war in the first place, and economically by supporting federal legislation to permit American export combines. His misgivings about Allied war aims had brought him this far, and he took the country into the war, when it became necessary, not as an "Allied" power, but as an "associated" nation determined to put forward its own peace aims at the conference table.

To Make the World Safe

THE LAST MONTHS of 1916 were agonizing ones for Robert Lansing. The Secretary of State feared that Wilson's ever growing commitment to the future and to a "league to enforce peace" had blinded him to the immediate issue of war and peace. Lansing had done all he could to prevent a break with the Allies, but Wilson's indignation now seemed evenly divided between both sides. Even worse, it appeared that the Germans were ready to talk seriously about peace,

---

[17] Wilson to House, July 23, 1916, copy in Ray Stannard Baker papers, Library of Congress.

though Lansing was unduly alarmed on that score, because Berlin's demands were no less those of a conqueror than London's, and, given the actual war situation, even less realistic. His suffering reached a high point when Wilson went before Congress on January 22, 1917, to call for a peace without victory.

Lansing had prolonged the disputes with the British Foreign Office over neutral rights in the expectation that something would happen—that Germany would do something to change the current of public opinion. Once again he was proved right. On January 31, 1917, Berlin announced the resumption of unrestricted submarine warfare. The decision had been taken after a long debate and constituted a triumph for those who argued that nothing the United States could do as an active belligerent could be worse than the situation as it existed at that moment. But even after the decision became known in Washington, Lansing found the President undecided about war. When the Secretary stated at a Cabinet meeting that the Allies had to win because democracies were never aggressive or unjust, Wilson cut him off with the remark that maybe it would be better for the world if the war ended in a draw. Lansing was unsure of the President right down to the last moment before Wilson went to Congress to ask for a declaration of war. "If you agree with me that we should act now," he pleaded with Colonel House on March 19, 1917, "will you not please put your shoulder to the wheel."[18]

Robert Lansing

---

[18] Lansing to House, March 19, 1917, in House papers.

Germany's fateful decision to resume submarine warfare triggered the final sequence of events leading to the American declaration of war. It solved Lansing's growing problems with the issue of neutral rights; it forced Wilson to put aside, momentarily at least, his serious doubts about the Allied cause; it provided a clear moral choice between the belligerents. But America went to war not because of submarine warfare, but because a neutrality policy that would serve the country's immediate interests and yet keep it economically uninvolved with the Allies could not be defined, and because neutrality could not protect America's political independence or assure the triumph of principles it deemed essential to its future well-being. It fought the war to reestablish and preserve American freedom of action on both those levels. Wilson assumed that America's goals were those of all people. The assumption and the dream built around it were confronted with a fundamental challenge even before the war ended.

Suggestions for Further Reading

In addition to the volumes of Arthur S. Link's biography of Wilson cited in the preceding chapter, one should see *Confusions and Crises, 1915–1916* (Princeton, N.J., 1964) and *Campaigns for Progressivism and Peace, 1916–1917* (Princeton, N.J., 1966). Other books on Wilson include Harley Notter, *The Origins of the Foreign Policy of Woodrow Wilson* (Baltimore, 1937), and Edward Buehrig, *Woodrow Wilson and the Balance of Power* (Bloomington, Ind., 1955).

Daniel Smith's important study *Robert Lansing and American Neutrality* (Berkeley, Calif., 1958) corrects the tendency to see World War I as Mr. Wilson's war. Also see his *The Great Departure: The United States and World War I, 1914–1920* (New York, 1965). And Lansing's *War Memoirs* (Indianapolis, 1935), written to answer critics, remain among the most revealing by an American statesman.

Charles C. Tansill, *America Goes to War* (Boston, 1938), has become the standard revisionist account, while Ernest R. May, *The World War and American Isolation, 1914–1917* (Cambridge, Mass., 1959), is now regarded as the most balanced.

Of special interest is Gaddis Smith's slim volume, *Britain's Clandestine Submarines, 1914–1915* (New Haven, Conn., 1964), a test case of the ineffectiveness of American neutrality.

See also the general bibliography at the end of this volume.

CHAPTER 18

A Race
Between
Peace and
Anarchy
(1917–1921)

Wilson cut the Gordian knot of neutrality only to find himself entangled in the complexities of Old World diplomacy. Pre-Versailles efforts to extricate American policy reached a high point with his "Fourteen Points" speech on January 8, 1918. But this statement enumerating American war aims had also been occasioned by a pressing need to counter the new "new diplomacy" emanating from Lenin's revolutionary government in Russia. The Soviet challenge perplexed all the Allies, but it created special difficulties for the American President, who had counted on support for the Fourteen Points from many of the groups now influenced by Bolshevik appeals for world peace and universal self-determination. Wilson's freedom of action all but disappeared in the revolutionary-reactionary crunch, and though he did get the "large convention" he and Colonel House had envisioned when they first began efforts to end the war in 1915, the peace treaty itself would resemble neither the letter nor the spirit of the Fourteen Points. Wilson had once imagined a League of Nations to uphold the settlement; he now declared it was the only hope of correcting whatever wrongs had been written into the Versailles Treaty.

The Russian Challenge

TWO MONTHS after America entered the war, one of Wilson's frequent correspondents wrote: "We went into a war to free Cuba and came out of it with a heavy responsibility in the Philippines. The present war is vastly greater and we may come out of it with vastly greater responsibilities for the future of Russia."[1] The March 1917 Revolution in Russia brought to an end the ancient rule of the tsars and delighted Americans who favored the Allied cause; now it could be truly said that the war was a struggle between democracy and autocracy. Renewed interest in Russia's future antedated the overthrow of Nicholas II, however. Secretary of State Lansing, for one, had been anxious for some indication of how St. Petersburg would see its place in the postwar scheme of things. He, along with other policy-makers, was concerned lest Russia be absorbed into the political or economic sphere of either alliance. Some still feared Russia would eventually become dominant on the European continent; others believed it more likely that the party that dominated Russia would soon control Europe.

These considerations, and a quite earnest desire to improve economic relations, prompted the appointment of David Francis, former governor of Missouri, as ambassador to Russia. Francis was instructed to conclude negotiations for a new commercial treaty before St. Petersburg committed itself irrevocably to the kinds of policies laid down at the 1916 Paris Economic Conference. It was important that those policies not be given a chance to solidify into a new Russian orthodoxy. The Ambassador did his work well, establishing strong Russian connections for the National City Bank, which in turn gave the Kerensky government a $50 million credit. Francis also played the key role in securing a Treasury advance of $100 million for the provisional government. The loan was made "on condition that the entire amount be disbursed in America."[2]

But Ambassador Francis was out of his depth when it came to assessing the political situation. In a long-shot gamble to fortify the provisional government

---

[1] Charles R. Crane to Woodrow Wilson, June 21, 1917, in Woodrow Wilson papers, Library of Congress.

[2] David R. Francis, *Russia from the American Embassy* (New York, 1921), p. 124.

against its foes, domestic and foreign, Washington sent the "Root Commission" to Russia. Headed by former Secretary of State Elihu Root, the commission was a hodgepodge of technical experts, financiers, labor leaders, and moderate (very moderate) socialists. Root himself expected to be "awfully bored" on the "damned expedition," and took along a "large package of novels ... and ... two cases of Haig and Haig." The commission recommended still another $100 million Treasury advance and more technical missions, but Secretary Lansing was understandably depressed at the optimism of some commission members when they returned home. In a private memorandum comparing the situation to the French Revolution, he concluded: "The demoralized state of affairs will grow worse and worse until some dominant personality arises to end it all."[3]

Lenin

The "dominant personality" turned out to be Lenin, who came to power on November 7, 1917, after proclaiming a policy of peace and land to the peasants. The "imperialist governments" on both sides of the war would resist this proposal, Lenin declared. "But we hope that revolution will soon break out in all the belligerent countries...." From now on it was to be Lenin versus Wilson, liberal capitalism against bolshevism. All other issues were debated against that background.

---

[3] August 9, 1917, in Robert Lansing, *War Memoirs* (Indianapolis, 1935), pp. 337–38.

Lansing Talks It Over with the Japanese

THE COLLAPSE of the provisional government in Russia came at just the worst time for the Secretary of State's endeavor to arrive at a new understanding with Japan concerning China and Manchuria. Talks with special Ambassador Viscount Kikujiro Ishii during September and October of 1917 had produced a draft agreement on the model of the Taft-Katsura Memorandum and the Root-Takahira Agreement. And like those earlier exchanges, the Lansing-Ishii Agreement of November 2, 1917, failed to make clear what either nation had actually promised to do or not to do. Lansing had encouraged the talks for two reasons: (1) to prevent China from playing Japan off against the United States, a possibility raised most recently by Ambassador Reinsch's unwelcome success in getting China to declare war on the Central Powers; and (2) to initiate a new diplomatic effort to persuade the European powers as well as Japan to give up their spheres of influence in China.

The Secretary had made plain his purposes in the discussions with Ambassador Ishii, pointing out that a joint reaffirmation of the Open Door policy would be useful to Japan against nations that wanted to go back to old ways after the war. Since Germany had already been eliminated from Shantung, a Tokyo-Washington alliance would leave only Russia, Great Britain, and France —all weakened by the war—to deal with and convince. Ishii said he appreciated the Secretary's logic, but his government required formal recognition of Japan's special interests in any joint statement they might issue. Lansing tried to square the circle with an ingenious distinction between special interests based on geographical proximity, which could be allowed, and those claimed simply to secure "paramount" political influence, which could not be allowed. Ishii thought something might be worked out along these lines. As both men realized, they were honing very fine distinctions indeed. How it worked out would depend upon everything falling into place on either side.

The Russian Revolution tipped the balance Japan's way, at least temporarily. The issue came to a head on January 18, 1918, when London proposed that Japan be named the Allied "mandatory" for the Trans-Siberian Railroad, ostensibly to aid anti-Bolshevik elements and to prevent a "Germanized" Russia from dominating the scene. Lansing saw at once a connection between Britain's support for Tokyo's mandate and the undoing of his own carefully worked-out plans. The history of China's partition, as far as it had gone, was filled with such temporary arrangements. Bitterly anti-Bolshevik, the Secretary was eager to seize any chance to bring about Lenin's downfall—any chance except a Japanese take-over of the Trans-Siberian Railroad and Manchuria proper. On

February 8, 1918, therefore, the State Department replied to the British suggestion in a note to the embassy stating that it hoped for "a change for the better," but if intervention finally became necessary, the United States would prefer a multilateral undertaking.

The Decision to Intervene

IN THE Fourteen Points speech, Wilson had told Congress that the "treatment accorded Russia by her sister nations in the months to come will be the acid test of their good will, of their comprehension of her needs as distinguished from their own interests, and of their intelligent and unselfish sympathy." His words were meant as a warning to those who might be tempted to take advantage of Russia's time of troubles to exploit the country according to old imperialist patterns. Lansing and Wilson agreed that British sponsorship of the Japanese mandate in Siberia was just such a bargain, and the harbinger of even worse things unless it could be headed off at the outset. Neither believed that Lenin and his "perverse idealists" could control Russia for any great length of time, but in whatever time they had, the Bolsheviks might do great damage.

There was the possibility—soon to be a reality—of a separate peace with Germany. Some (including Wilson for a time) saw the Bolshevik surrender to outrageous German demands as proof that Lenin and his coterie were German agents. Not only had Russian negotiators at Brest-Litovsk behaved in what the Allies and the United States regarded as an irresponsible fashion; by their blatant appeals to class interests the Bolsheviks threatened the social structure everywhere. Lansing wrote Wilson that Lenin's appeals to the workers of the world were directed "to the proletariat of all countries, to the ignorant and mentally deficient, who by their numbers are urged to become masters. Here seems to me to lie a very real danger in view of the present social unrest throughout the world."[4]

At least a month before the Fourteen Points speech, Lansing and Wilson had decided not to have any formal dealings with Lenin's government—ever. Indeed, the administration had instructed American representatives on the Inter-Allied Finance Council that the United States was prepared to aid financially "any movement," however slight its chances for success, that offered a

---

[4] Lansing to Wilson, January 2, 1918, in *Foreign Relations, Lansing Papers,* 2:346–48.

program "for the reestablishment of a stable government and the continuance of a military force on the German and Austrian fronts." A State Department message singled out General Alexei Kaledin as the strongest prospect; Washington urged that he be aided by the Allies, using American funds. The cable ended with a strict injunction to keep all this secret.[5]

This message was promptly conveyed to British and French officials on the Inter-Allied Finance Council, but the results' were anything but satisfactory from Washington's point of view. Instead of stimulating a unified policy toward the Bolsheviks, the State Department's message "contributed" to an Anglo-French decision to delimit "geographic areas in southern Russia in which each of the two powers would take such action as might be possible."[6] When the British then proposed, less than three weeks later, that Japan be given a mandate over Siberia, the issue of secret pacts among the Allies, and America's seeming inability to do anything about them, took on new significance.

For nearly six months Wilson agonized over the problem of intervention against the Bolsheviks. At the end of March 1918 the American ambassador in Japan was instructed to contact Thomas Masaryk, political leader of Czechoslovak forces then making their way across Siberia to Vladivostok, from which point they hoped to find a way to join Allied forces on the Western front. What Lansing wanted to know was whether Masaryk thought there was any possibility of organizing effective resistance to the Central Powers "within Russia." Further contacts and reports from diplomatic and military observers in the Far East convinced Wilson that the Czechs represented at least "the shadow of a plan that might be worked." At a White House conference on July 6, 1918, a formal decision was made to land Marines at Vladivostok to help Czech forces hold the city. From this base the United States would then send additional aid to the interior to "help the Czecho-slovaks consolidate their forces" along the Trans-Siberian Railroad and to "steady any efforts at self-government or self-defense in which the Russians themselves may be willing to accept assistance."[7]

Wilson obviously hoped to check Japanese ambitions with this plan, but things went wrong from the beginning. On the eve of the European armistice, Secretary of War Newton D. Baker wrote Wilson, "I heartily wish it were possible for us to arrange affairs in such a way as to withdraw entirely from

[5] Ibid., pp. 345–46.

[6] George F. Kennan, *Russia Leaves the War* (Princeton, N.J., 1956), p. 178.

[7] *Foreign Relations, Russia, 1918*, 2:262–63.

that expedition." The President had his own doubts about the value of military intervention, but he could not pull out of Siberia until he had had a chance to study all other alternatives at Versailles.

False Hopes

IN EARLY OCTOBER 1918 the German government sent a message addressed to Wilson through the Swiss minister in Washington. Berlin formally requested an immediate armistice, and accepted, "as the basis for negotiations, the program laid down by the President of the United States." All of a sudden here it was —the chance to end the war and begin the peace on American terms. The President informed the Allies of the German message and allowed them to state terms for a cease-fire, but he refused to share the actual negotiations with any other power. On his own, Wilson told Germany that further negotiations would be impossible if the Allies had to "deal with the military masters and monarchial autocrats" of the Kaiser's regime. Germany promptly transformed itself into a republic and the Kaiser fled into exile.

The President then sent Colonel House to the Allies with his terms for *them*. Prime Minister David Lloyd George got to the heart of the matter at once: "If we agree to this armistice," he asked, "do you think we are accepting Wilson's terms—all of them?"

"I certainly do," answered House.[8]

After several discussions, with House finally raising the possibility of a separate peace between Germany and the United States, the European leaders yielded—but not quite completely. Lloyd George insisted that there were several interpretations of Point Two of the Fourteen Points, "Freedom of the Seas." He would agree only to discuss the issue at the peace conference. House felt confident that this reservation and others stipulated by Lloyd George and by the French Premier, Georges Clemenceau, did not invalidate agreement with the substance of American terms. Besides, as Wilson put it in a cable to House, "England cannot dispense with our friendship in the future and the other Allies cannot without our assistance get their rights as against England."[9] Or so it seemed in this moment of triumph.

The November 11 armistice ended more than four years of fighting. Concerned about the countries on Germany's eastern frontiers, Allied military

---

8 Stephen Bonsal, *Unfinished Business* (New York, 1944), pp. 1–2.

9 Wilson to Edward M. House, October 29, 1918, cited in Ray Stannard Baker, *Woodrow Wilson: Life and Letters*, 8 vols. (New York, 1924–1928), 8:529.

representatives had inserted into the armistice agreement a clause forbidding the German high command to evacuate those regions until "the Allies think the moment suitable, having regard to the internal situation of these territories." In other words, not until the Bolshevik menace abated. German officers were relieved, even boasting that they had "succeeded in establishing a common ground" with their former enemies.

In Washington, meanwhile, various presidential advisers urged Wilson to restore his freedom of action by dissolving the key wartime inter-Allied councils and agencies, lest they become tools of Old World diplomacy. "At the peace conference," said Allen Dulles, "the economic power of the United States must be entirely unrestricted, as this force in our hands may be of powerful assistance in enabling us to secure the acceptance of our views."[10] Herbert Hoover, director of the Federal Food Administration and soon to be a highly valued adviser at Versailles, also insisted on this point, and wanted Congress to provide a demonstration of "calm and shrewd financial leadership ... to banish the specter of Bolshevism" and set the world on the path to economic recovery. Although the President and Congress were already at odds, the legislators responded to Hoover's appeal by authorizing $100 million for relief to liberated countries.

Like Franklin Roosevelt in 1945, Wilson went to Europe confident in his principles and sure of his bargaining power. He was so sure of his position that he told Prime Minister Lloyd George in private pre-Versailles discussions that he was primarily interested in the League of Nations, not in details of the peace settlement. Nor did he oppose Lloyd George's suggestion that the "matter" of the "Freedom of the Seas" could be "left for further consideration after the League of Nations had been established and proved its capacity in actual working." The ease with which this went over came as a "great relief" to British aides, who congratulated Lloyd George on being "as successful as had Castlereagh before the Conference of Vienna in virtually excluding this thorny question from the Conference."[11] It also came as a surprise to members of the American delegation, the first of many.

Ordeal by Peacemaking

ON THE TRIP over to Europe aboard the U.S.S. Washington, the President had told the American delegation that the "poison of Bolshevism" was readily

10 Allen Dulles to State Department, November 21, 1918, in U.S. State Department file no. 600.001/591.

11 Arno J. Mayer, *Politics and Diplomacy of Peacemaking: Containment and Counter-Revolution at Versailles, 1918–1919* (New York, 1967), p. 269.

accepted by many because it was a protest against the way the world had worked. It was to be their business at the peace conference to fight for a new order, "agreeably if we can, disagreeably if necessary." At the first meeting of the commission appointed to draft a League of Nations covenant on January 25, 1919, Wilson restated America's purposes in going to war: "The United States in entering the war never for a moment thought it was intervening in the politics of Europe, Asia, or of any part of the world." The United States would, in fact, feel that its part had been played in vain if there ensued from this conference "merely a body of European settlements."

The trouble was that specific terms in the peace treaty could not be separated from the League of Nations; that body would guarantee that whatever settlement emerged would provide "continuous superintendence of the peace of the world by the Associated Nations of the World." The terms of the Versailles Treaty, therefore, would determine whether the League of Nations became, as Wilson hoped, a parliament of man, or, as critics feared, a new version of the Holy Alliance.

This fact was well illustrated in the first problem discussed at Versailles, the question of Germany's African colonies and the future of the Ottoman Empire. Point 5 of the Fourteen Points promised "a free, open-minded, and absolutely impartial adjustment of all colonial claims," with "strict observance of the principle that in determining all such questions ... the interests of the populations concerned must have equal weight" with claims listed by those seeking title. At Versailles the British dominion governments immediately put in a claim for outright annexation of the African colonies and the German islands in the Pacific, while the French announced their intention to hold the British to wartime agreements parceling out the Ottoman Empire. Japan then brought up its claim to Germany's Pacific island outposts north of the equator. Appalled, Wilson declared that the "world would say that the Great Powers first portioned out the helpless parts of the world, and then formed a League of Nations."[12] He had put his finger on what critics would indeed say; but the President settled for a "compromise" League mandate system, with different categories of territories defined according to supposed possibilities for ultimate self-government. For all practical purposes, the awarding of mandates followed the outlines sketched out in the "secret treaties." Each power holding a League mandate was required to submit annual reports to the organization, but those sitting in judgment would pronounce their decisions with their own reports next on the docket.

To justify this compromise to himself and the nation, President Wilson had to accept a key Allied argument at Versailles (which set a precedent for later

<hr>

[12] *Foreign Relations, Paris Peace Conference,* 3:762–65.

decisions): the "Huns" had ruthlessly exploited their colonies "without thought of the interest or even the ordinary human rights of their inhabitants." The Allies' colonial policies, on the other hand, were good, and entitled them to administer the areas formerly controlled by Germany. Nor could he stop there. Wilson felt he had to participate in the mandate system—to give it his blessing, so to speak—by accepting an Allied request that he recommend to Congress that the United States accept responsibility for Armenia. "When you cease to be President," Premier Clemenceau gibed, "we will make you Grand Turk." The remark pointed up Wilson's dilemma: either he accepted these unpalatable compromises, and the remarks that went with them, or he denounced the Allies and thereby gave up any chance for a League of Nations. Wilson's greatest political problem, perhaps, was that his conscience would not permit him to admit that any decision he had participated in was in fact a compromise with principle. He alienated friends with these insistences, and gave opponents an easy target.

Secretary of State Lansing did not believe in the League of Nations and was not so burdened with the need to justify the mandate system or to participate in it. The Allies, he charged, would be amply paid or overpaid for their responsibilities, while the United States would have to pay for the privilege of being a mandatory. "We would get an unproductive jumble of mountains and a port with little or no commerce, while they would have great productive areas, profitable ports and valuable railways."[13] Other members of the American delegation were growing more and more uneasy about the course of the peace conference for quite different reasons. Fully Wilsonian in their outlook, they found the President's behavior inexplicable.

But the President also had to answer to congressional critics, who took the occasion of his mid-February trip back to the United States to demand that reservations for the Monroe Doctrine be put in the League Covenant. When Wilson placed these requests before his colleagues at Versailles, his personal bargaining position was further reduced. And there was still the Bolshevik specter.

The Imminent Crisis

"FROM THE LOOK of things the crisis will soon be here," Colonel House wrote in his diary on March 22, 1919. "Rumblings of discontent every day. The people want peace. Bolshevism is gaining ground everywhere. Hungary has

---

[13] "The Unequal Burden of Proposed Mandates," June 20, 1919, in Robert Lansing papers, Library of Congress.

The Big Four: Orlando, Lloyd George, Clemenceau, Wilson

just succumbed. We are sitting upon an open powder magazine and some day a spark may ignite it."[14] President Wilson had returned to Paris with a new sense of urgency. "At this moment," he told Lloyd George, Clemenceau, and Italian Prime Minister Vittorio Emanuele Orlando, "there is a race going on between peace and anarchy and the public is beginning to show its impatience."

Wilson proposed that they meet twice daily as the "Big Four" to settle the most difficult remaining problems, "and the rest will proceed quickly." So for the remainder of the conference the Big Four grappled with the reparations issue, a proposal for guaranteeing French security, border questions, and Japan's claim to Shantung. As they talked, each kept an ear open to news from central and eastern Europe.

On the first of these questions, American and British experts were in general agreement that Germany could pay no more than $35 billion. The French refused to set any maximum. Both Lloyd George and Wilson warned that Germany would refuse to sign any treaty that did not specify its obligations and the time period for reparations payments. "The Weimar government is without credit," Wilson insisted.

----

14 Edward M. House, *The Intimate Papers of Colonel House,* ed. Charles Seymour, 4 vols. (Boston, 1926–1928), 4:389.

If it cannot remain in power, it will be replaced by a government with whom we cannot negotiate.... We owe it to the cause of world peace to save Germany from the temptation to abandon herself to Bolshevism; we know only too well the connection between the Bolshevik leaders and Germany.[15]

The French answer, then as before, came down to a counterassertion that if bolshevism was really that great a threat, then the solution was to mount a military offensive against it, using local troops from eastern European countries, staffed with Allied officers, and supported financially by the United States. On the first day of the Versailles conference, the commander in chief of the Allied armies, Marshal Foch, had proposed sending two divisions to Poland. Wilson demurred, citing the larger context of the "social danger of Bolshevism." When Foch renewed his call in late March for the organization of a military barrier against bolshevism, "behind which we can proceed to clean up the region," the President replied that "any attempt to check a revolutionary movement by means of deployed armies is merely trying to use a broom to sweep back a high tide. Besides," he added, "armies may become impregnated with the very Bolshevism they are sent to combat."[16]

Wilson could refuse to participate in such adventurism, but he could not sway the French on reparations. Indeed, on the following day Lloyd George reversed himself and praised the French formula for the establishment of a commission to determine German indebtedness at a later date. It provided, he said, "a way to avoid subsequent discussions in our respective parliaments ... because we have not asked enough." Once Wilson agreed to this "compromise," he found himself justifying his decision in the same way he had resolved the colonial crisis: he accepted the Allied insistence on Germany's sole responsibility for the war, and its formal inclusion in the war guilt clause of the peace treaty.

The President's inability to prevent England and France from pursuing what he and the rest of the American delegation believed were not only unwise but immoral policies came as a bitter disappointment. The President made one appeal to the people of Italy over the heads of their representatives on the question of the frontier with Yugoslavia and the disposition of the port city of Fiume—with disastrous results. He was unable as well to find any way to use Allied war debts and other financial obligations to bring about a change in their policies. In short, he had nothing left but the moral authority of a compromised League of Nations.

---

[15] Paul Mantoux, *Paris Peace Conference 1919: Proceedings of the Council of Four (March 24–April 18)* (Geneva, 1964), p. 14.

[16] Ibid., p. 35.

The Final Blow: Shantung

WILSON'S FINAL COMPROMISE at Versailles caused him a special agony. And it became a favorite issue with his critics during the domestic fight over the Versailles Treaty and the League of Nations. Japan had remained discreetly silent at Paris on all issues except those directly concerning its interests. These were two: a request that a racial equality clause be included in the Covenant of the League of Nations, and a demand that Japan's succession to German rights in Shantung be recognized in the peace treaty. Since the President could not grant the Japanese delegates their request for racial equality, he was in a weak position to deny them Shantung—a claim they based on Anglo-Japanese understandings.

On April 18, 1919, the President called upon his Big Four colleagues to strengthen his hand by renouncing "our" zones of influence in China. Lloyd George said he was willing to consider the question, but later decided that "we could not do so ... because we should have to allow the Japanese in" on economic projects in the Yangtze River valley. Wilson met separately with the Chinese delegates in his Paris apartment on April 22. He told them that Great Britain and France were bound to Japan by treaties, and they "were bound to keep these Treaties because the war had largely been fought for the purpose of showing that Treaties could not be violated." Then he posed a classroom argument, asking them to consider what would have happened if Germany had won the war. The Kaiser "had wanted to get France and Great Britain out of the way and afterwards to get everything else he could. One result of the war undoubtedly had been to save the Far East in particular, since that was an unexploited part of the world."[17] Wilson's abstract theorizing was of little use to the Chinese, who had come to Versailles believing Reinsch's promise that things would be made right at the peace table.

When they learned that the Big Four had acceded to Japan's claim, a member of their delegation told an American newspaper correspondent, "There is no hope now for China save in revolution." The American delegation was almost equally shaken by the decision. Lansing spoke for both conservatives and liberals when he wrote, "It must be admitted in honesty that the League is an instrument of the mighty to check the normal growth of national power and national aspirations among those who have been rendered impotent by defeat."[18]

---

[17] *Foreign Relations, Paris Peace Conference,* 5:138–48.
[18] "The Terms of Peace to Germany," May 8, 1919, in Lansing papers.

The Crusade Comes to an End

AT HOME Wilson faced a congressional alliance united along similar lines. Led by the chairman of the Senate Foreign Relations Committee, Henry Cabot Lodge, and Progressives like Hiram Johnson and William E. Borah, the "irreconcilables" prepared to take the treaty and Covenant apart clause by clause. When Secretary Lansing appeared before the Foreign Relations Committee, Senator Johnson opened up on Article 10, under which all members pledged to protect one another against external aggression. Citing the several different interpretations of that obligation which the President had offered during the past few months, the Senator asked if the United States would be bound by the Covenant to go to the aid of France, or would "we be free to accept the advice of the league only if our own judgment justified such action... ?" Concealing his private reservations, Lansing replied that he could not be expected to interpret the President's language for the Senator.

Then it was former Secretary of State Philander C. Knox's turn: Did the United States have a moral obligation under Article 10? "I presume in honor that we would have to follow out the general purposes of that article," said Lansing.

> Senator Knox. "In other words, if the council of the League of Nations directed us to resort to arms against China in order to prevent her from regaining her rights in Shantung, we would be bound to do it?"
> Secretary Lansing. "If Congress approved."
> Senator Knox. "No, I am not talking about Congress, I am talking about the obligations we have assumed under the treaty."
> Secretary Lansing. "I do not think that is an absolute obligation."
> Senator Knox. "It is one thing or the other, Mr. Secretary. We either have liberty of action, or we are bound by our agreement...."[19]

Lansing did not get out of this no-man's-land between Johnson and Knox until he had admitted that the United States was bound to act in some way to fulfill its obligations under Article 10; but he insisted that it had the freedom to choose the means by which it would act. No one was satisfied by these answers, especially not the President. Though the Versailles conference had used up practically all of his remaining physical reserves, Wilson determined to take his message to the people on a cross-country tour. The League of Nations, he said again and again, was the only alternative to a permanently

---

[19] U.S. Senate, 66th Cong., 1st sess., Committee on Foreign Relations, *Treaty of Peace with Germany: Hearings Before the Committee on Foreign Relations* (Washington, 1919), pp. 198–201.

Wilson shortly before his death

militarized America; it was the only way that international wrongs, including those in the Versailles Treaty itself, could ever be righted; it was the only way that the nation could justify the sacrifices of those who had died to make the world safe for democracy.

After his speech at Pueblo, Colorado, on September 25, 1919, Wilson at last gave out. The rest of the tour was canceled, even though the President seemed to regain his strength after a short rest. A few days after his return to Washington, the President suffered a stroke that left him partially paralyzed for the remaining years of his life. The first votes on the treaty came on November 19, 1919, while Wilson was still gravely ill. Lodge may have wanted passage of a treaty, but not the President's version. Wilson had sent word that he would accept nothing except that version. The "irreconcilables" voted with the Democrats against Lodge on the "Lodge reservations," and with Lodge against the Democrats on the original treaty. They swung the balance of power in the Senate on that fateful day, but disillusionment with the "Great Crusade" had long since set in across the land. Revelations of the secret treaties and the compromises they had forced at Versailles were a big factor, and those opposed to the President's foreign policy, whether conservative or liberal, despaired of the League of Nations as an effective answer to the challenges presented by the disruption and social breakdown of the old order. In a second vote on March 19, 1920, enough Democrats voted for the Lodge reservations to give the amended treaty a simple majority, but not the two-thirds necessary for ratification. So the League fight ended, but America could not—and did not—withdraw from the world.

Before setting out on his cross-country speaking tour, Wilson had called the Senate Foreign Relations Committee to the White House for one final appeal. It was an unsatisfactory meeting for both sides. Near the end, the President declared that without the treaty there could be no assurance of foreign markets or business stability at home. "The nations that ratify the Treaty, such as Great Britain, Belgium, and France, will be in a position to lay their plans for controlling the markets of Central Europe without competition from us if we do not presently act."[20]

Wilson usually did not deal in such specifics when discussing the treaty and the League of Nations, but on the tour he often discussed what Brooks Adams had once called reciprocity or the alternative. In Los Angeles, Wilson, like Adams, recalled William McKinley's predictions:

> This new day was dawning upon . . . [McKinley's] heart, and his intelligence was beginning to draw the lines of the new picture which has been completed and sketched in a constructive document that we shall adopt and that, having adopted it, we shall find to reflect a new glory upon the things we did.

Wilson's private secretary had obtained McKinley's last speech for the President, "in which he discussed Americanism, and said the age of isolation was past."

"I think we ought to impress the fact upon the people," added Joseph Tumulty, "that provincialism on the part of America means playing the game alone. It means increased taxation and a nation in arms." Reciprocity or the alternative.

Some Important Loose Ends

THE WAR had put off the reckoning time for the United States and the Mexican Revolution, but Secretary of State Lansing had not forgotten about Carranza or his constitution. His aim, the Secretary told a representative of American oil interests on May 16, 1917, was to get the Mexican leader into a position where he depended absolutely upon the United States for a loan; then the Department of State could establish all the essential and proper conditions for the granting of such aid. If the success of this approach was to be ensured

---

[20] Quoted in David Houston, *Eight Years with Wilson's Cabinet*, 2 vols. (New York, 1926), 2:7–9.

before Carranza took the revolution too far, he would have to be convinced that Mexico would not be able to secure European financial help after the war, as Huerta had attempted to do in the first phase of the Mexican-American conflict.

Lansing met with Thomas W. Lamont of J. P. Morgan and Company on October 4, 1918, and asked that his firm take the lead in the creation of an international committee of bankers to deal with the Mexican problem. It was essential, said the Secretary, that there be no question about American pre-dominance on this committee. Here was one instance where America's new economic power *could* be translated into political leverage against European competitors, because, given the war-devastated state of Europe's finances and its war debts to the United States, such a committee was the only likely way they could recoup anything on past advances to Mexico.

Washington expected that Carranza would come to terms with the com-mittee sometime in the summer of 1919. When he did not, Lansing lost patience again and began planning for intervention. Once again Wilson inter-ceded—quite literally from a sickbed—but pressures were rapidly mounting for strong action. The Mexican constitution, moreover, was no longer simply a Mexican issue. Senator Albert Fall, long an advocate of intervention in Mexico, wrote the State Department that his correspondents in South America had informed him that the countries there looked to Mexico for leadership, and that so "long as Mexico is allowed to run wild we will have additional difficulties" in that area. Lansing had already recognized that there was a serious issue in Colombia, which was considering petroleum legislation similar to that adopted by Mexico. He was anxious that Colombia not only reject such policies, but set an "example" that could be followed by other nations that needed foreign capital to develop their "potential riches."[21] Carranza's over-throw in May 1920 ended talk of intervention, but the administration was still engaged in negotiations with the new regime over "general principles" when the Republicans came to power.

The State Department had also been working on a financial solution to complement the Lansing-Ishii understanding, or rather to give it some mean-ingful definition. Realizing that Japanese opposition could block American efforts to sustain the Open Door policy through development loans, Lansing had sought the President's approval for an attempt to resurrect the China consortium, and to increase U.S. financial backing for it by including large banks from the Midwest and the Pacific Coast. Economic discussions with the Japanese were actually going on at the same time the Shantung issue was

---

[21] *Foreign Relations, 1919*, 1:779–80.

being discussed at Versailles. In effect, the United States put up the stakes for Great Britain and France so that the international consortium could absorb the Japanese forward movement in China and contain it without war. The record of the first consortium did not encourage American officials to believe that the new one would speed up China's economic development, especially with that country still in revolutionary turmoil, but it might have negative usefulness in restraining the Japanese from unilateral action.

Once again it was Tom Lamont who took the message to the other concerned powers. In Tokyo, the banker was able to reach an agreement on two levels: first, it was agreed that the consortium should be considered solely a matter of economic relations between bankers of several countries, thus divorcing governments from responsibility for its private arrangements; and second, it was further agreed that Japan's special interests in south Manchuria and Mongolia would be recognized, if not by governments, at least by the consortium. Lamont warned the State Department that the Japanese still had to learn table manners, and must not be allowed a free hand in Siberia or China proper. As for south Manchuria and Mongolia, American capitalists would not want to buck Japan in that area anyway. "To tell the truth," Lamont confided to a State Department aide, "the question of the Anglo-Japanese Alliance is especially on my mind." Wilson's successors took up that issue, as we shall see, at the 1921 Washington Naval Conference.

Woodrow Wilson, meanwhile, had become thoroughly disgusted with Allied selfishness. "I am almost inclined to refuse to permit this country to be a member of the League of Nations," he confided in a moment of anger.[22] Outbursts against British and French policies became frequent in the last months of his term. He had long suspected, for example, that they had schemed for special concessions in a post-Bolshevik Russia. Despairing of Allied cooperation on a Russian policy acceptable to the United States, Wilson withdrew American forces from Siberia. But he still refused to deal directly with Lenin.

The President also ordered the State Department to keep a close watch on Anglo-French maneuvers in Germany; he believed that they were plotting to control the situation there, and through Germany to gain control of Russia. Though his new advisers in the State Department doubted if Allied plans went quite so far, they were disposed to see the reparations issue in a political light. A big reason for not easing the pressure on Allied war debts was their hope that it afforded at least some control over Anglo-French policy; but the Allies simply turned the tables on this matter, contending that nothing could

---

22 "The President's Feelings as to the Present European Situation," August 20, 1919, in Lansing papers.

be done about easing Germany's reparations obligations without American concessions on the debts. So that impasse continued.

Meanwhile, the United States sought to consolidate and enlarge upon policies first made in response to the 1916 Allied Economic Conference. Wilson had hoped to reverse the trend toward neo-mercantilist state trading organizations at Versailles, but at the same time he supported the Webb-Pomerene Act and later the Edge Act, which gave American manufacturers and bankers legal authority to organize for foreign trade without fear of prosecution under the Sherman Antitrust Act. Once the Edge Act became law, a call went out to American bankers to organize a "Hundred Million Dollar Foreign Trade Financing Corporation." They met at Chicago on December 10 and 11, 1920, and heard Herbert Hoover declare that America stood at the "changing point in our national economics," where the British Empire had stood in 1860, when it was no longer possible to take full value in commodities from other nations in exchange for surplus production. America had to build up the capacity of foreign nations to absorb its goods, and perform a service for all mankind by lifting the world's standard of living. It was an idealized, even a Wilsonian vision of the world. Though he thought the President had made a mistake in not accepting some reservations in order to get ratification, Hoover's admiration for Woodrow Wilson never failed. The two had agreed at Versailles that "there is but one way to wipe out Bolshevism: determine the frontiers and open every door to commercial intercourse."[23]

Wilson had delivered that verdict in response to the French demand for military intervention; Hoover tried to carry it out in the next decade.

Suggestions for Further Reading

Still useful for information on the Versailles Conference is Ray Stannard Baker, *Woodrow Wilson and World Settlement*, 3 vols. (New York, 1922), but for special insight into both Wilson and Herbert Hoover see the latter's *The Ordeal of Woodrow Wilson* (New York, 1958).

The following present various sides of America's dilemma at the peace conference and after: Arno Mayer, *Wilson vs. Lenin: Political Origins of the New Diplomacy* (New York, 1964) and *Politics and Diplomacy of Peacemaking* (New York, 1967); John M. Thompson, *Russia, Bolshevism, and the Versailles Peace* (Princeton, N.J., 1966).

---

[23] Mantoux, *Paris Peace Conference*, p. 35.

On the motives for the intervention against Russia, see George F. Kennan, *Russia Leaves the War* (Princeton, 1956) and *The Decision to Intervene* (Princeton, 1958); and William Appleman Williams, *American-Russian Relations, 1781–1947* (New York, 1952).

Of special interest is James Weinstein, *The Corporate Ideal in the Liberal State: 1900–1918* (Boston, 1968), and Carl Parrini, *Heir to Empire: United States Economic Diplomacy, 1916–1923* (Pittsburgh, 1969). Ideally, these two books should be read in succession. And finally, William Reynolds Braisted, *The United States Navy in the Pacific, 1909–1922* (Austin, Tex., 1971).

See also the general bibliography at the end of this volume.

CHAPTER 19

Starting
Over
Again
(1921–1925)

*It was hard to take Warren Gamaliel Harding seriously. The Re-*publicans seemed to be trying to prove that they could win the presidency in 1920 with any "available man," even an undistinguished senator from Marion, Ohio. But unlike his chosen domestic advisers, the men Harding picked to counsel him on foreign questions were exceptionally capable. Both Secretary of State Charles Evans Hughes and Commerce Secretary Herbert Clark Hoover had initially favored participation in a postwar association of nations, but each shared the doubts of fellow Republicans (and a great many others) about the Versailles Treaty system and Article 10 of the League Covenant. Neither wanted to waste any more time fighting old battles. Everything had to be done over again. Only this time the Republicans would see to it that the nation's foreign policies were built upon "practical conceptions of national interest arising from some immediate exigency or standing out vividly in historical perspective."

Harding, Hughes, and Hoover:
On the Road to Normalcy

THERE WERE PLENTY of immediate exigencies for the new administration, from disputes over tiny islands to the reconstruction of an entire continent. Harding knew what had to be done. "I am quite as convinced as the most bitter 'irreconcilable' that the country does not want the Versailles League," he wrote Senator Lodge. "I am equally convinced that the country does wish us ... to bring nations more closely together for counsel and advice."[1]

Hughes translated Harding's wishes into concrete achievements, using both public conferences and private negotiations. The new Secretary of State felt that the Wilsonians had first gone wrong when they assumed that "helpful cooperation in the future will be assured by the attempted compulsion of an inflexible rule." A community of "ideals, interests, and purposes," asserted Hughes, was more likely to "be promoted by freedom of conference."

Hoover had joined the Cabinet only after he received assurances of a veto power over foreign economic policy decisions. He and Hughes often clashed on policy questions, and neither was a man to yield without a fight. But they agreed on one fundamental: economic "normalcy" meant a situation in which the United States had access to world markets and assured outlets for American capital. Before the war the United States had owed something over $3 billion to Europeans; now it was a creditor nation, which the rest of the world owed more than $12 billion. To Hughes and Hoover it was simply absurd to think that Europe could send, or America could absorb, sufficient dollar imports to balance the debt in the reconstruction period—perhaps even over the long haul. There had to be an alternative means of keeping Europe supplied with the needed dollars. Hughes and Hoover agreed that American capital investments in Europe would serve two purposes: they would provide the stimulus to recovery and sustain high levels of economic activity on a worldwide basis. If the world market was constantly growing, America would prosper, Europe would prosper, and the United States would not have to take European surpluses. Judicious and reproductive investments would play a role outside of Europe as well, opening up new areas for future trade. Between 1922 and 1929 the United States exported capital at an average rate of $733 million—a minimum of $454 million in 1926, a maximum of $1 billion in 1929.

Efforts to channel these investments into nonspeculative ventures and to use the dollar politically—to check arms spending, for example, or to isolate

---

[1] Warren G. Harding to Henry Cabot Lodge, December 29, 1920, in Warren G. Harding papers, Ohio Historical Society (Columbus, O.).

nonrecognized governments—were largely unsuccessful. This development contributed to the economic collapse at the decade's end, though it is hard to see how a more conservative loan policy by itself would have prevented the debacle. Looking back on those years, Hoover wrote in his *Memoirs* that even if one wrote off a billion dollars in bad loans as a total loss, "it certainly was a cheap method of unemployment and agricultural relief. We were the only large nation engaged in the World War which did not have continuous unemployment and constant drains on the Treasury for relief of the unemployed some time during the decade."

This viewpoint was not confined to Hoover and Hughes; it was shared by various interest groups. "Economic isolation does not seem possible or desirable," said the president of the American Farm Bureau Federation, O. E. Bradfute. "It would require...[an] overnight adjustment in agricultural production. This seems less possible than to bring economic order to Europe." Most agricultural leaders in the 1920s felt that the government was not doing enough to expand farm exports and demanded special legislation to stimulate foreign buying. Few Americans questioned the wisdom of the nation's economic foreign policies at the time, though many came up with accusations and answers in the aftermath of the world depression. In 1928, for example, Franklin D. Roosevelt promoted the Federal International Investment Trust, a speculative loan venture he and several associates had devised to "fill an urgent need for expanded facilities in our international financial relations."[2] During the presidential campaign four years later, Roosevelt reserved his most caustic criticisms for Republican *Alice in Wonderland* economics: foreign loans and high tariffs.

In writing the 1922 Fordney-McCumber tariff, however, the Republicans had had in mind something beyond protection for special interest groups. Ever since the 1916 Paris Economic Conference of the Allies, American leaders had feared the resurgence of extreme economic nationalism after the war in both inter-European arrangements and imperial preference schemes. The Fordney-McCumber tariff was designed to protect the United States against one form of that nationalism, currency depreciation and dumping; but even more than that, it was designed to assure the United States equality of treatment both in Europe and in colonial areas. Special clauses in the law authorized the President to raise tariff rates against nations that discriminated against the United States. Secretary of State Hughes then undertook to negotiate a series of new tariff treaties with European and Latin American countries embodying the nondiscrimination principle. Assistant Secretary of State J. Reuben Clark explained:

---

[2] Roosevelt to Norman H. Davis, October 28, 1928, in Norman H. Davis papers, Library of Congress.

We believe in the open door and desire equality of treatment, and equality of commercial opportunity. We have no means of securing this equality if it is not freely granted. These clauses are expected to provide these means. They are primarily defensive and not offensive.... They are necessary to our well being and development.[3]

The Ratio of Security in Asia

SECRETARY HUGHES solved the immediate problem of peace with Germany simply by lifting from the Versailles Treaty all the sections dealing with rights accorded the United States and incorporating them into a new treaty, which the Germans and the Senate readily accepted. The Asian situation, however, could not be reduced to a single treaty, and would require the most careful diplomacy on several levels. Although the Japanese had agreed to cooperate in the second China consortium, they still held the Shantung peninsula and remained in Siberia. There was also the matter of Yap Island in the Pacific, formerly a German cable center and now claimed as a mandate by Japan, along with other islands. Wilson had demanded at Versailles that Tokyo return Shantung to the Chinese and internationalize the facilities on Yap, but neither issue had been resolved.

A long-standing problem in dealing with Japan was the Anglo-Japanese alliance; every American Secretary of State since Elihu Root had come up against that wall. So far no one had found a way to scale it. But the alliance was coming up for renewal in 1921 and the British dominions reportedly opposed a new pact. If that were true, it might be possible to dismantle the alliance—or trade it for something else. Hughes had something to trade that interested both London and Tokyo: a huge naval building program inherited from the wartime preparedness campaign. The 1916 naval bill had authorized $133 million as a first step in building a fleet to equal the combined strength of potential opponents. When the war ended, there was a pause while everyone waited to see if a new naval race would develop.

Inside the State Department, meanwhile, a memorandum on the advantages of establishing a "grand fleet" in the Pacific was being circulated. The effect of such a fleet in and on China, Hughes was advised, would counteract "the belief in American weakness and lack of serious purpose, which resulted from our acknowledgement (in the Lansing-Ishii notes of 1917) of Japan's

---

[3] For this quotation and the discussion of the Fordney-McCumber tariff in general I am indebted to Carl Parrini, *Heir to Empire: United States Economic Diplomacy, 1916–1923* (Pittsburgh, 1969), pp. 230f.

'special interests' in China."[4] But the Secretary had little faith in Chinese nationalism, even if it were backed up by an American fleet. He preferred to seek an understanding among the principal powers interested in China, but only if he could first eliminate the special relationship between Great Britain and Japan. When Undersecretary of State Henry P. Fletcher suggested to a British Foreign Office representative that the Anglo-Japanese alliance prevented full cooperation between the English-speaking powers, he was given the reply that "often when they had a bad elephant in India they put him between two good elephants to make him behave, and that that might be tried in the case of Japan."

Neither Fletcher nor Hughes was much impressed with tales from the British raj in India, or in a tripartite alliance in which the United States would always be in the middle or on the outside. To avoid this alternative, or something equally objectionable, the Secretary took up Senator William E. Borah's suggestion for a tripartite disarmament conference and expanded it into a multination conference on disarmament and Far Eastern problems generally. Great Britain accepted the invitation promptly, but Japan agreed to come only after voicing reservations. At the opening of the Washington Conference on November 12, 1921, Hughes startled the roomful of diplomats by offering

Washington Conference

---

[4] J. V. A. MacMurray, memorandum, April 21, 1921, in U.S. State Department file no. 811.30/131.

the most candid disarmament proposal ever delivered in public or, for that matter, in secret. If the other powers would agree to a ten-year shipbuilding holiday, the United States would scrap thirty capital ships already under construction! Hughes then outlined a plan for a treaty establishing a 5:5:3 ratio of capital ships for the United States, Great Britain, and Japan. The Secretary's speech won tremendous approval from American observers, and left the foreign delegations stunned.

It was an audacious stroke, and it worked. Japan held up the treaty until the United States agreed not to fortify its Pacific islands, but the Secretary saw no reason not to accept that condition. "The prospect of making Guam a first-class naval base for the purpose of exerting a more effective naval force in the Western Pacific area as against Japan was nothing but a picture of the imagination," he wrote the Secretary of War, who had expressed some concern about the concession. "Congress would never have authorized, in time of peace, the development of Guam as a challenge to Japan and even if we had made the attempt the challenge would have been taken up and the issue forced before it would have been possible to develop it into a base of any great military value."[5] The French also delayed the final signing of a naval treaty with demands that cruisers, destroyers, and submarines be excluded, a point the Secretary reluctantly conceded in order to get them to accept last place in the scale. The treaty was signed on February 6, 1922, and provided for a ratio of 5:5:3:1.7:1.7, the last two figures representing France and Italy.

Once the new security framework had been established, Hughes was free to concentrate on political problems. He prefaced his initial remarks to the Committee on Pacific and Far Eastern Questions with the comment that "no one in this gathering desired to set bounds to the progress or development of any other; that there should be equal opportunity for all; and that if the door were open, Japan was at the threshold."[6] Having made the American position clear, the Secretary turned to a discussion of Chinese questions—the return of leased territories, elimination of extraterritoriality, tariff reform, electrical communications, removal of foreign post offices, and control of the Chinese Eastern Railroad. The Chinese delegates protested this approach, but Hughes rebuffed them and warned their government through the American ambassador "that a policy of insisting obstinately upon impractical points of view may defeat the hopes of China and of China's friends that the Conference may help in ameliorating some at least of the existing unfortunate conditions."[7]

---

[5] Charles Evans Hughes to Sinclair Weeks, April 11, 1922, in U.S. State Department file no. 500A4/425.

[6] U.S. Senate, 67th Cong., 2nd sess., document no. 126: *Conference on Limitation of Armaments* (Washington, 1922), p. 443.

[7] Hughes to J. G. Schurman, December 7, 1921, in *Foreign Relations, 1922*, 1:274.

Reassured by Hughes's plain intentions to deal *with* the powers *about* China rather than the reverse, Great Britain and Japan headed the lesser powers in the direction the Secretary wanted them to go. The result was the first multilateral affirmation of the Open Door policy in the so-called Nine Power Treaty. It was a major accomplishment, but of uncertain duration without the termination of the Anglo-Japanese alliance.

With British cooperation, the Secretary solved that problem by offering the conference leaders a consultative pact guaranteeing the signators' rights in the Pacific, and pledging them to consider jointly the steps to be taken to meet any exigency. Critics charged that Hughes had simply added two new names to the Anglo-Japanese alliance, but that was not so. He had, in fact, done away with the obnoxious pact and substituted something quite different. Confident of the final outcome, Hughes later remarked that the Four Power Treaty had superseded not only the Anglo-Japanese alliance, but the Lansing-Ishii Agreement as well.

While Secretary Hughes clearly wanted to (and would in fact) base his China policy on a close understanding with Japan, he just as certainly desired to maximize his future options. This did not mean that his policy went unchallenged. Senator Borah was incensed by the Four Power Treaty, and charged it was no more than a screen behind which the powers "will do China in." China's protests were given even less attention. Still divided by a revolution that would take nearly three more decades to complete, China had never seemed more at the mercy of the powers, or more in need of whatever aid the United States was willing to give. Yet the Washington Conference decisions pushed Sun Yat-sen and the Kuomintang closer to the Soviet Union. Hughes was never willing to jeopardize "close relations" with Japan to meet Sun's appeals for aid, or inclined to take the "Communist" threat seriously enough to counteract it with a new China policy. His successors inherited both a Japanese problem and a Chinese Communist problem; but they owed to the Secretary the creation of a flexible treaty system that made policy changes at least possible. Even a Hughes critic recognized that Japan could not be gotten out of China all at once, and that the elimination of the Anglo-Japanese alliance was the key. Writing about one who took an all-or-nothing viewpoint, Stanley K. Hornbeck advised former Ambassador Paul Reinsch, "It would seem that he has never studied the parable of the bundle of faggots and that he thinks it necessary ... either to break the whole bundle all at once or to leave all the sticks both new and old untouched."[8] What Hornbeck saw was that under

---

[8] Stanley K. Hornbeck to Paul S. Reinsch, September 5, 1921, in Paul S. Reinsch papers, Wisconsin State Historical Society (Madison, Wis.).

different conditions (and perhaps under a different Secretary of State) the Washington Treaty system provided an admirable basis for a vigorous defense of American interests in China.

The Three Rs: Reparations, Recovery, and Refinancing

AMERICAN POLICY-MAKERS thought the disarmament conference set an example of proper postwar international behavior. President Harding hoped the bankers would now be more willing to take direction in refusing loans to nations that continued to spend large amounts for arms; Secretary Hughes thought there was a general lesson in the conference's reaffirmation of the Open Door policy. Europeans, however, seemed to need special tutoring. The final reparations settlement the Allies imposed on Germany obligated that country to pay $32 billion (plus billions more in interest), and, said Washington's representatives, would discriminate against the United States. How? By making Germany into an Allied appendage in Central Europe. The only way that Germany could ever free itself from the reparations burden, moreover, would be to become so efficient in producing goods for the export trade that it undersold America in European and world markets. As early as July 1921 the State Department received the details of a supposed German-British plan for cooperation in the Russian market. The Weimar official who told American officials about this arrangement added that "his hope had always been to obtain such an agreement with American financial circles."[9]

The German diplomat had closed his statement, Hughes was informed, by expressing an earnest desire that American capital should at least "come into this agreement as the doors will be wide open." The Harding administration and its successors always opposed any idea of working through Germany to reach Russia, but the threat posed by an Anglo-German alliance in that direction could not be ignored. Neither could the developing Russo-German rapprochement, which was formalized with the signing of the Rapallo agreements in April 1922.

Germany's early default on its reparations payments alerted American policy-makers that this was the time to act. But what could be done? "I think this government would be very glad to be helpful in a practical and constructive way," Harding informed the State Department. But he was waiting

---

[9] Ellis Loring Dresel to Hughes, July 8, 1921, in U.S. State Department file no. 741.62/18.

for someone to submit a concrete plan. When the right idea did come along, it emerged from several different sources all at once.

One unlikely source was Captain Eddie Rickenbacker, who went before banking groups with a speech that posed the solution in highly undiplomatic language: "...A loan must...be made on such terms and conditions as will enable America to dictate and control the use of the money, and thereby the policy of Germany. And of course it must be administered by the best business brains we have." Otherwise, continued the man who had accounted for "twenty-six Huns" as America's premier flying ace during the war, we would see the rise of a German-Bolshevik alliance:

> Such an alliance, including as it would, the hordes of men and industrial resources of Russia, the ambitions of Japan—which are as militaristic and as grasping as those of pre-war Germany—the daring of Turkey, directed by the organizing and executive genius of the Germans, would surely bring into the balance China which is in a leaderless chaotic condition, and India which is rebellious against the British rule.
>
> Germany is a tramp—out of a job, hungry, poorly clothed and desperate. It is for us to decide whether he will become a citizen or an I.W.W.

There was a final stake in German recovery which he saved for the last: "American commerce—American agriculture—American industry—cannot produce a profit until we have a market for the surplus."[10]

Wilson had failed at Versailles to persuade the Allies to rethink the reparations problem; his advisers had expected that the war debts would give him great leverage, but he never found the means or the opportunity to use America's new economic power to force their compliance. Hughes had several advantages five years later when he confronted the Europeans with the "Dawes Plan" (named for an American delegate to the Reparations Commission, Charles G. Dawes) on a take-it-or-leave-it basis. First, the French had already failed to force payments out of the Germans with a military occupation of the Ruhr. Second, British and French policies and interests on the continent had once again begun to diverge. And finally, Paris needed State Department blessing for other financial transactions with American bankers.

Under these circumstances, agreement was reached in October 1924 on a private loan of $200 million to Germany. American conditions required scaled-down reparations payments, and a U.S. reparations tsar who would oversee the German economy and determine when and how much could be paid in any given year. America's share of the initial loan was set at $110 million, a sum

---

[10] Rickenbacker Machine Company to Hughes, January 4, 1923, in U.S. State Department file no. 862.51/1601.

subscribed ten times over when J. P. Morgan and Company put the issue on the open market. In the months and years that followed, Americans supplied more than 80 percent of the funds borrowed by German public credit institutions and utilities, 75 percent of the money sent to local governments, 68 percent of that borrowed by private concerns, and 56 percent of that sent to large industrial corporations. Large industrial corporations in the United States, meanwhile, tied themselves to German organizations such as the I. G. Farbenindustrie, or opened up branch factories. The president of General Motors, Alfred P. Sloan, wrote after World War II:

> So far as we in General Motors are concerned, we were glad to have been able to operate in Germany, prewar, and it was frequently passed on to us by the German Economic Ministry that we had contributed much to the expansion of industry in Germany and to the advancement of their technological position in the areas in which we were operating.[11]

Occasional warnings from the State or Commerce Department about speculative loans or the danger of overextension had little effect on the rapid growth of American investment in Germany. Nor were investors much inclined to listen for rumblings inside Germany, such as the October 1925 speech of banker and financial expert Hjalmar Schacht. The Balkanization of Europe by the Versailles Treaty, he asserted,

> has not only erected unnatural customs barriers, but has filled the small nations, formerly Germany's customers, with an ambition for economic autonomy, the absurdity of which will, however, be shown by Europe's steady development into one large economic territory. But even then ... Germany will not be able to thrive and fulfill her obligations under the Dawes Plan as long as the possibility is not given her to obtain raw materials for her industry and necessary food stuffs from colonies and settlements of her own.[12]

Official concern about German policy toward eastern Europe and Soviet Russia, never really absent since the Treaty of Brest-Litovsk and the Rapallo Treaty, surfaced again in 1925 when American capitalists proposed to finance large-scale efforts by German middlemen to penetrate the Russian market. The administration vetoed the plan, but it was hampered in proposing an effective alternative by virtue of its continuing refusal to enter into diplomatic relations with Moscow.

---

11 Alfred P. Sloan to Bernard Baruch, November 30, 1945, in Bernard M. Baruch papers, Princeton University.

12 J. G. Schurman to Secretary of State, October 12, 1925, in U.S. State Department file no. 862.51/2081.

Waiting for a New Kerensky:
America's Russian Dilemma

ALTHOUGH PRESIDENT HARDING had expressed some interest in hearing arguments on the proposition, the Republicans forsook one possibility for checking later German and Japanese excesses by failing to "start over again" when it came to political relations with the Soviet Union. Wilson's ban endured throughout the decade, yet policy-makers eagerly seized upon whatever opportunities arose to get a peep at developments inside Russia or to establish economic foundations for good relations with the still expected post-Soviet government. The Soviets, on the other hand, made several overtures to Washington in anticipation of a restoration of full relations.

In a letter to labor leader Samuel Gompers a month after assuming his duties in the State Department, Secretary Hughes described Russia as a "gigantic economic vacuum," and said it would remain so for as long as "the present political and economic system continues."[13] To Soviet diplomat Maxim Litvinov he wrote that the Russian people's only hope was to restore a secure basis for production: "Production is conditioned upon the safety of life, the recognition of firm guarantees of private property, the sanctity of contract, and the rights of free labor."[14] When major firms came forward with proposals for indirect dealings with Moscow, however, the State Department quietly gave its blessing, except when the transactions involved long-term credits that might promote Russian industrialization under the Soviets. The distinction proved unrealistic and troublesome from the beginning. One of the earliest requests for a State Department go-ahead, for example, came from the Baldwin Locomotive Company, which had devised a way for exporting a hundred locomotives to Russia through a British intermediary. Clearly, rail transportation was crucial not only to distribution, but to any economic plan devised by Lenin and his government. The sale would mean an income of from $5 to $6 million for the company, noted a State Department officer, and it was "anxious to take the order as they are running at present on half time." The Department decided that there was nothing to be gained "by way of economic pressure on the Bolsheviks, by refusing it, which could be compared with the advantage resulting from so large a contract."[15]

---

[13] Hughes to Samuel Gompers, April 5, 1921, in *Foreign Relations, 1921,* 2:769–73.

[14] Hughes to Maxim Litvinov, March 25, 1921, in U.S. State Department file no. 661.1115/275A.

[15] D. C. Poole to F. M. Dearing, May 18, 1921, in U.S. State Department file no. 661.1115/-318.

In the end, the deal fell through, but the way in which the State Department handled the matter suggests the problems of trying to do business without formal relations. A far more successful venture was the effort of the American Relief Administration, under the direction of Herbert Hoover, to relieve famine inside the Soviet Union. Hoover had first proposed this plan in 1919, but the Bolsheviks rejected it on the grounds that the conditions for the aid were aimed at the destruction of the new regime. With the civil war all but won, the Russians initiated a request for American aid and agreed to Hoover's conditions for its distribution. The ARA raised more than $50 million for food, supplies, and seed plantings, which it delivered over a twenty-two-month period. Hughes gave the plan full support. "Full information will be obtained in this way," he observed, "without the risk of complication through government action."

Hoover was equally candid, and more optimistic: "The relief measures ... will build a situation which, combined with other factors, will enable the Americans to undertake the leadership in the reconstruction of Russia when the proper moment arrives."

By 1925 American exports to the Soviet Union had increased ninefold over 1923 totals, to nearly $70 million. And plans were being laid for really big things. W. Averell Harriman, son of the man who had proposed to "girdle the globe" by connecting up American, Chinese, and Russian railroads, had been granted a concession by the Soviets over manganese deposits in Stalin's home province of Georgia. He was then asked by the Soviets to supply a $35 million loan to German industrialists to enable them to extend export credits to Moscow. Although American bankers and German industrialists were prepared to cooperate, the plan was stopped in Washington, largely at Hoover's insistence. The Secretary of Commerce had long taken the position that

> permanent American foreign commerce can never be based upon the reshipment of goods at the hands of other nationalities. The hope of our commerce lies in the establishment of American firms abroad, distributing American goods under American direction: in the building of direct American financing abroad, and, above all, in the installation of American technology in Russian industries.[16]

Harriman was thus blocked by the administration. Left to their own devices, the Germans extended the credits from local financial resources and boasted they had stolen a march on commercial rivals.

No matter how Hughes and Hoover tried to resolve the dilemma, it was becoming obvious that Washington's response to the Bolshevik challenge had

---

16 Herbert Hoover to Hughes, December 1, 1921, in U.S. State Department file no. 661.-6215/1a.

to be rethought. Lenin's New Economic Policy and his decision to concentrate his efforts on "socialism in one country" offered American policy-makers the rationale for a full-scale reevaluation without repudiating the original non-recognition policy, but the process was to be a long one.

Correcting a Serious Error: The Lausanne Conference

BOTH SOVIET RUSSIA and the United States were unofficial participants at the 1922–1923 Lausanne Conference, which took up the Turkish Straits question specifically, and which had broad significance for a variety of other questions connected with the disposition of the Ottoman Empire. At Versailles, once again, Wilson had been checked in every attempt to forestall an Anglo-French division of the spoils. The League mandate system, as it applied to the Near East especially, was nothing more than a fig leaf to cover the systematic exploitation of the area's natural resources. Oil constituted the most important of these, and therefore supplied the immediate incentive for a positive policy in the Middle East.

While the United States Senate was refusing to ratify the Treaty of Versailles, the British and French were reaching agreement on who should have what from Turkey. Their negotiations led to the so-called San Remo Agreement of April 1920, which awarded Britain control of the Turkish Petroleum

Cartoonist's view of the Lausanne Conference

Company, a former German concern, and the right to build a pipeline through the new French sphere of influence to a port on the eastern Mediterranean. Acquiescence in this agreement was part of the price exacted from Turkey in the Treaty of Sèvres. Having settled their affairs there, the European victors sought to arrange things between them and the Soviets for a concession covering the whole oil-bearing region of southeastern Russia and the Caucasus.

Citing its role in bringing about the victory over the Central Powers, the State Department (under Democrats and Republicans alike) had refused to recognize the validity of the San Remo Agreement. More positively, it produced a rival claimant to the concession held by the Turkish Petroleum Company, the old Colby M. Chester concession, which went back to the "chosen instrument" policy of Taft's dollar diplomacy. Meanwhile, the Department vigorously pursued its new-style dollar diplomacy in southeastern Europe and Iran. In Rumania, loans were withheld until favorable oil legislation was assured; in Albania, economic pressure was successfully applied on the new government to prevent a British takeover; and in Yugoslavia, similar understandings preceded American loans. Preliminary negotiations between the government of Iran and the United States led to a hasty British decision to grant the Standard Oil Company of New Jersey a concession in the northern part of the country. But on the broader issue of recognizing the Open Door policy throughout the Middle East, London stood firm.

Then the Turkish Revolution, led by Kemal Ataturk, overturned the old regime, and with it the Treaty of Sèvres. The Lausanne Conference was assembled to produce a new arrangement for the Turkish Straits, but it also gave the United States a second chance to press for acceptance of the Open Door policy. Once again London tried to compromise the issue, offering a quarter share in the Turkish Petroleum Company. Hughes refused—for the record—and then set about trying to adjust matters so as to reconcile principle and practicality. The British had been anxious to keep from a confrontation with the United States because of the possibility that *both* America and the Soviet Union would take Turkey's part at Lausanne. Hughes, on the other hand, had to go carefully in insisting upon the Open Door policy to avoid being backed into a corner where he would have to choose between the Allies (with whom he was trying to build a community of interest) and the new Turkish government (which wanted Washington's support and was prepared to pay for it with favorable concessions). In no instance—not in China or anyplace else—had the Secretary given serious consideration to an alternative means of securing adherence to the Open Door policy by aligning the United States with revolutionary nationalist movements. The pattern was repeated at the opening of the

Lausanne Conference in November 1922, when the American delegation called upon the powers negotiating with Turkey to honor the principle of equal access for all nations in settling the Straits question and matters relating to concessions for the development of natural resources.

Almost immediately the Americans were sought out by a member of the Turkish delegation, who suggested the best way for the United States to assure itself equal opportunity would be to negotiate a separate treaty—"before the Allies had signed theirs." "When I told him that this was not our present intention," recorded the American ambassador to Turkey, "he replied that in any case we should find the 'open door' whenever we wished to enter, but he distinctly conveyed the impression that the policy of the open door means 'first come, first served.'" Washington was advised of this private conversation, but Hughes instructed the American delegation to make it clear to the Allies "that we would not sign such a treaty until the Turks had signed a treaty of peace with the Allies."[17] Hughes thus managed to avoid an awkward situation and to keep his Middle Eastern policy in harmony with the principles established at the Washington Conference governing relations among the leading powers and underdeveloped areas. He even succeeded in obtaining a favorable commercial treaty with Turkey, which ironically came under fire from religious groups and failed in the Senate by six votes. In the course of the Lausanne Conference, the British declared themselves in favor of the Open Door policy throughout the Middle East. It was not yet possible to test that promise everywhere, but Hughes was satisfied that he had made a good beginning.

A New Look at the Monroe Doctrine

HUGHES USED the centenary anniversary of the Monroe Doctrine to state a new interpretation of that pronouncement. In the recent past, he said, an effort had been made to find a basis for intervention policies in the Monroe Doctrine. But these originated elsewhere, from international law, specific treaties, self-defense, or the need to protect the interests of humanity. The problem, therefore, was not to modify or repudiate the Monroe Doctrine, but to avoid abusing the valid right of intervention, which he preferred to call "nonbelligerent interposition." In all instances, "interposition" should be limited to immediate exigencies, and not extended and expanded into long-term control.

---

[17] Joseph C. Grew, *Turbulent Era: A Diplomatic Record of Forty Years, 1904–1945*, 2 vols. (Boston, 1952), 1:522, 588.

Although he made it plain that the United States would not accede to any demand that the Monroe Doctrine be made multilateral, the Secretary undertook to eliminate Wilsonian errors in applying the doctrine. American Marines were withdrawn from the Dominican Republic in 1924 and from Nicaragua the following year. He avoided the temptation to interevene in Cuba when President Alfredo Zayas chose to ignore the advice of Ambassador Enoch Crowder. Loans to Caribbean countries were more carefully regulated than similar investments elsewhere, however, in an effort to protect borrower and lender from excesses. "Taking the decade as a whole," concluded a State Department economic adviser, "the Government was roughly successful in its pur poses."

Credit for settling the one outstanding issue with Colombia, the long-delayed treaty awarding the country $25 million for the loss of Panama, went to the Republicans, although they only put the final push behind the agreement in the Senate. Dollars flowed into Colombia, increasing total investments from $30 million in 1920 to more than $280 million by 1929. In Chile copper provided the incentive for a similar boom, pushing totals from $15 million to $800 million by the end of the decade. Little Uruguay also shared in the general expansion, as a stream of money poured into packing plants, telegraphs, telephones, cables, power plants, and even sewer systems, pushing the total dollar figure from a prewar level of $5 million to $77 million by 1927. Estimates for South America as a whole reveal an increase of $1.5 billion in the same period. Long predominant in the Caribbean and Central America, the dollar moved into the lead now in South America as well.

A Mexican "solution," however, still eluded Hughes, but he kept trying. He sought formal treaty assurances from Álvaro Obregón and Plutarco Elías Calles, Carranza's successors, that the 1917 constitution would not be used to deprive American citizens of their more than $300 million investment in mines and petroleum. Until the United States received such guarantees, the Secretary of State refused to consider diplomatic recognition of any government in Mexico City. Obregón was anxious to consolidate the gains made by the revolution, repair the destruction of a decade of civil war, and secure his own rule. Still, to agree to such a pact would have forced Obregón to relinquish the revolution's principal gains. "It would have built a legal fence around almost the only lucrative enterprise in Mexico, one marked 'Mexicans Keep Out.' "[18] At last Hughes saw that further pressure would not force a treaty out of Obregón, and might create a worse situation. Moreover, the Mexicans had demonstrated a willingness to guarantee legitimate oil concessions acquired between 1876 and 1917 by

18 Howard F. Cline, *The United States and Mexico* (New York, 1963), p. 206.

means of a gentleman's agreement known as the "Extra-Official Pact." It was not iron-clad, and the State Department still had some doubts, but recognition was accorded Obregón on August 31, 1923. If Obregón's word stood behind the agreement, it seemed wise for the United States to stand behind the Mexican ruler; so when an uprising threatened his government, he was saved from defeat by prompt aid from north of the border in the form of arms and active military cooperation, including bombing raids against revolutionaries.

The "Extra-Official Pact" came unstuck in a very short time, and Hughes's successor had to renew the search for a permanent solution. When one looks back on Republican diplomacy in the 1920s, it now seems evident that many of its successes had been put together in similar fashion, with extraofficial understandings or arrangements. Even those grounded in firmer stuff depended upon continued prosperity as a condition for their success. Nevertheless, Charles Evans Hughes brought to the Department of State a much-needed flexibility, which checked the descent into futile rigidity that had marked Woodrow Wilson's last days in the White House. Nor did his solutions do violence to Wilson's original goals, and those of traditional policy-makers.

Suggestions for Further Reading

No really satisfactory study of Hughes's period as Secretary of State exists yet, but see Merlo J. Pusey, *Charles Evans Hughes*, 2 vols. (New York, 1951). There are several worthwhile works on Hoover, the best being Joseph Brandes, *Herbert Hoover and Economic Diplomacy: Department of Commerce Policy, 1921–1928* (Pittsburgh, 1962). A very good little book that surveys loan policies is Herbert Feis, *The Diplomacy of the Dollar* (New York, 1966).

On Asia, two studies are musts: Dorothy Borg, *American Policy and the Chinese Revolution, 1925–1928* (New York, 1968), and Akira Iriye, *After Imperialism: The Search for a New Order in the Far East, 1921–1931* (Cambridge, Mass., 1965). For a surprising new look at what happened to the Far East with the breakdown of the Anglo-Japanese alliance, see Malcolm D. Kennedy, *The Estrangement of Great Britain and Japan, 1917–1935* (Berkeley, Calif., 1969).

On Latin America, see Wilfrid Hardy Callcott, *The Western Hemisphere: Its Influence on United States Policies to the End of World War II* (Austin, Tex., 1968). Robert Freeman Smith's *The United States and Cuba: Business and Diplomacy, 1917–1960* (New York, 1960) is particularly strong on the 1920s.

European questions are dealt with in Selig Adler, *The Isolationist Impulse: Its Twentieth-Century Reaction* (New York, 1957), and Roland Stromberg, *Collective Security and American Foreign Policy from the League of Nations to NATO* (New York, 1963). See also Harold G. Moulton and Leo Pasvolsky, *War Debts and World Prosperity* (Washington, D.C., 1932).

See also the general bibliography at the end of this volume.

CHAPTER 20

The Destruction
of the
Washington
Treaty System
(1925-1933)

Frank B. Kellogg's assignment was to preserve and, if possible, extend the Washington Treaty system. He gave his name to the most ambitious and famous effort in that direction, the 1928 Kellogg-Briand Pact, which obligated the signers to renounce war "as an instrument of national policy in their relations with one another." The unreality of it all was illustrated by the Soviet Union's adherence to the antiwar treaty, for in this instance the United States had seemingly undertaken binding responsibilities toward a government whose existence it professed not to recognize.

But like other incongruities in the 1920s, this anomaly did not prove serious until the onset of the Great Depression. American postwar policy, according to critics, now stood exposed as a jerry-built dollhouse, held together with paper treaties and paper dollars. When the first economic shock waves hit, Kellogg's successor, Henry L. Stimson, tried to paste over the tears and rips, but everywhere demands were heard for a new order; in many places new men responded with totalitarian blueprints.

The First Signs of Trouble: Central America and Mexico

WHEN POLITICAL TROUBLES returned to Nicaragua in 1926, so did the Marines. A former president of the American Bar Association, United States senator from Minnesota, and ambassador to Great Britain, Secretary Kellogg was perfectly suited to the framework established by President Calvin Coolidge's strong statement in 1925: "The person and property of a citizen are a part of the general domain of the nation, even when abroad.... There is a distinct and binding obligation on the part of self-respecting governments to afford protection to the persons and property of their citizens, wherever they may be." The messenger Kellogg sent to Nicaragua with this pronouncement was Henry L. Stimson, who warned rebels that they could either turn over their arms to the Marines and accept the conservative Adolfo Díaz, who *was* friendly to Americans and their property, or face "forcible disarmament."[1] Stimson stayed awhile to set

U.S. intervention in Nicaragua

---

[1] L. Ethan Ellis, "Frank B. Kellogg," in *An Uncertain Tradition: American Secretaries of State in the Twentieth Century,* ed. Norman Graebner (New York, 1961), pp. 149–67.

in motion a new plan for replacing the local police with a more efficient national guard, staffed and advised by American officers.

During the Nicaraguan trouble, Kellogg told the Senate Foreign Relations Committee that much of the problem originated elsewhere, in Mexico, where fast-growing Bolshevik influence was committed to "the destruction of what they term American imperialism." Kellogg had said on an earlier occasion that Mexico was "now on trial before the world." Now he seemed to be saying that the verdict was in. The issue—as ever—was the 1917 constitution. Faced with rising discontent in his own party, President Calles had supported legislation limiting oil concessions obtained before the promulgation of the new constitution to fifty years. Surprised at the adverse reaction in the United States, he told American officials that fifty years seemed plenty long enough to develop and exhaust the old concessions. That was not the right way to look at it, commented spokesmen for the oil companies. As one of them explained,

> It was necessary for the oil companies to remember that it involved their general policy on oil developments outside of Mexico in countries such as the Argentine, Colombia, Peru, Ecuador, and Venezuela; that the companies must remember that if they gave way in a matter of principle in Mexican disputes, they would be forced to do so likewise in those other countries.[2]

The State Department was also being urged to take strong action by Americans with large Mexican landholdings. Their properties were threatened with expropriation as part of the new economic and sociological program of the Mexican Revolutionary party. And to top it off, Calles and the American ambassador, James R. Sheffield, distrusted and disliked one another. When the Mexican President hinted that he would welcome a chance to talk with a special emissary about this new phase of the long-standing Mexican-American dispute, Kellogg sent him Dwight R. Morrow, a partner in J. P. Morgan and Company. It is difficult to say whether Morrow was really more flexible than his predecessor, because Calles summoned the new ambassador to Chapultepec Castle within days of his arrival in Mexico City and suggested they settle the matter then and there. The Mexican President reassured Morrow that his government wanted American investments, and would protect them; but the oil companies had created their own problem with boasts that they were beyond Mexican law. Morrow explained that the companies feared that if a fifty-year limit could be set today, tomorrow it might be reduced to forty years, and the next day to ten, and then... ? How could these really unimportant differences be reconciled? asked Calles. Morrow thought the best way would be for

---

[2] Dwight R. Morrow to Frank B. Kellogg, December 24, 1927, in U.S. State Department file no. 812.6363/2469.

the Mexican Supreme Court to rule that the holdings were guaranteed in perpetuity. Calles promised that he would have his ruling within two months.

Actually, it took less than two weeks. Then Calles recommended that the offending articles in the petroleum laws be rescinded and made to conform with the court decision. A new petroleum code was issued on March 27, 1928; in return, Ambassador Morrow commissioned Marxist artist Diego Rivera to paint murals extolling the virtues of the Revolution on the walls of Cuernavaca's city hall. He also sent America's newest hero, Charles Lindbergh, on a goodwill flight to Mexico City. All in all, it was a good bargain: ten years without further interference in the oil fields, in exchange for lots of goodwill.

Lindbergh and Ambassador Morrow

When Sleeping Dragons Awake:
Kellogg and Chinese Nationalism

HUGHES AND HIS AIDES had always deprecated the possibility of working with Chinese nationalism. Kellogg did not entirely agree. While he wanted to maintain the friendly connections reestablished between Tokyo and Washington, he doubted that the Four Power Treaty would provide a way to come to terms with the rising force of Chinese nationalism. In the summer of 1925 a strike of Chinese employees in Japanese-owned factories, which rapidly spread out into a violent antiforeign demonstration, led the Secretary of State to propose an international conference so that concrete recommendations could be made for restoring complete tariff autonomy to China. He also suggested that an international commission be sent to China to look into the question of relinquishing some or eventually all of the extraterritorial rights acquired by the powers at the time of the Boxer Rebellion. Once the conference was scheduled, the Secretary instructed the American minister in China that he should remain cooperative in dealing with the treaty powers, but he should be sure to preserve America's "complete independence." If the others proved unwilling to restore China's tariff autonomy, the United States could then pursue independent negotiations for a bilateral treaty, one guaranteeing most-favored-nation treatment for American commerce. "In other words," concludes a recent study, "the United States would endeavor to bring about a new order in the Far East based on Sino-American understanding and the new tariff arrangement."[3]

The conference did agree to restore China's tariff autonomy by 1929, but Japanese suspicions had been aroused by Kellogg's initiative; so much so that Japan sought assurances that Coolidge had not put his Secretary of State up to repeating Woodrow Wilson's 1913 turnabout in search of what Wilson had called the "original" Open Door policy. In 1927 Tokyo tried to float a private loan on the American market to provide funds for the South Manchurian Railroad. The political aspects of the loan were discussed in a Cabinet meeting, and Coolidge frankly raised the question whether such a loan might not imply acceptance of Japan's claim to special rights throughout Manchuria. The matter dragged on for several months until pressure built up from two directions: the American bankers wanted to go ahead with the plan, but the Chinese had got wind of the proposal and were even more anxious to prevent it—and thus convert Kellogg's modest initiative into open support against the Japanese. Japan's control of the South Manchurian Railroad, declared the Chinese Foreign Minister, was both "a symbol and instrument of alien domination over a large and rich portion of Chinese territory."[4] In this instance the Department avoided a firm commitment to either position by suggesting to the bankers that adverse publicity had probably affected the public's confidence in such a loan.

Struggling to gain control of all China, the Kuomintang (now under Chiang Kai-shek) continued to press the Manchurian issue. On December 31, 1928, Kuomintang forces seized the Russian-owned Chinese Eastern Railroad and hoisted the Nationalist flag over its administrative buildings. The Japanese, who normally rejoiced at every difficulty encountered by their Russian rivals, were troubled this time by the precedent that might be set if the Nationalists

---

[3] Akira Iriye, *After Imperialism: The Search for a New Order in the Far East, 1921–1931* (Cambridge, Mass., 1965), p. 74.

[4] Herbert Feis, *The Diplomacy of the Dollar* (New York, 1966), pp. 36–39.

succeeded in their purpose. Both Moscow and Tokyo, moreover, thought that the Americans had encouraged the Nationalists to gamble with such exploits, if not specifically, then generally, since the time of the 1925 tariff conference. When a small war broke out between China and Russia, the new Secretary of State, Henry L. Stimson, thought the situation presented a real opportunity to test the recently completed Kellogg-Briand Pact. In his concern to demonstrate that the treaty system really would work in a crisis, Stimson found himself lecturing the Chinese ambassador on the inviolability of Bolshevik property rights, and calling his government to task for ignoring its contractual obligations to the Soviets under the antiwar pact! Whatever else happened, it was marvelous irony.

Stimson suggested the interposition of a neutral "Commission of Conciliation," which recalled to the Japanese the 1909 Knox neutralization plan and the more recent inter-Allied commission that, under the leadership of an American engineer, ran the Chinese Eastern Railroad from 1918 until 1922. His plan received little support from any of the powers, but a later proposal that the Kellogg Pact signatories all join in reminding the combatants of their obligations produced notes to the two capitals from thirty-seven of the fifty-five signers. The war ended shortly thereafter, but the American initiative did not seem to have much to do with its resolution. Stimson would soon get a second chance to try out the Kellogg-Briand Pact in Manchuria. Meanwhile, American diplomats were careful to note that Japan had not been among those in support of the pact in this crisis.

The Smashup in Europe and America

BEFORE THE DAWES PLAN ran down, Washington replaced it with a new model, the "Young Plan," which further reduced Germany's reparations payments and set off another German boom on the American market. Herbert Hoover had run for President in 1928 on the promise of even greater prosperity through foreign trade. Reminding his audiences that he had "reorganized the Department of Commerce for the promotion of American trade abroad on a greater scale than had ever been achieved or ever attempted by any government anywhere in the world," the Republican candidate elaborated on the way this had been accomplished. "We mobilized our manufacturers and exporters; cooperated with them in laying out and executing strategic plans to expand our foreign trade in all directions."[5]

---

[5] Herbert Hoover, *The New Day* (New York, 1929), pp. 73–75.

Although he had expressed private doubts about the soundness of at least some of the banking operations, especially the German boom, Hoover entered the presidency brimming with confidence about the international situation. "It seems to me," he wrote his Secretary of State on September 17, 1929,

> that there is the most profound outlook for peace today that we have had at any time in the last half century.... It occurs to me that the dangers of war during the next six or ten years ... are inconceivably less than they have been at any period since the Great War.[6]

The Crash

Then came the crash. It began on the New York stock market, where on Black Thursday, October 24, 1929, 13 billion shares were dumped by investors, triggering a fall of 32 percent in industrial stocks within two months. The panic was, of course, only symptomatic of larger faults in the system, but the psychological effect of the market collapse on America's international position —which depended so much upon its ability to sustain responsibilities as the leading creditor nation in the world—was almost instantaneous. Foreign commerce suffered first. Imports, especially raw materials, fell from $4.4 billion in 1929 to $1.3 billion in 1933. Exports plummeted from $5.2 billion to $1.6 billion in the same four years. Foreign loans held up for a bit, then they too dropped to mere fractions of recent levels. New direct investments disappeared by 1932.

Hoover's first response was directed toward restoring the country's faith in its economic institutions. As the depression deepened, the President took up the

---

[6] *Foreign Relations, 1929,* 1:241.

theme that the economic trouble had come to America from Europe and Latin America. Congress, of course, seized upon Hoover's statements as an excuse to raise the tariff even higher to protect domestic producers. Caught between conflicting demands, the President found himself unable to pursue a consistent policy. On the one hand, he signed the 1930 Smoot-Hawley tariff, which raised the average duty on protected goods to 59 percent, the highest in the twentieth century. On the other hand, he continued to insist that the depression could be conquered only through international cooperation. Whether the new tariff really made all that much difference was somewhat beside the point: it was proof enough of America's state of mind, an economic nationalist state of mind.

The following spring brought a near-collapse in Germany. If Germany defaulted on its public and private obligations, not only would the complicated reparations and debt settlement be undone, with unforeseeable consequences for all Europe, but news of the failure would force bank liquidations inside the United States. American bank holdings in central Europe, Hoover learned to his dismay, totaled more than $1.7 billion; even worse, many of these were short-term notes without any collateral. To a great degree the postwar political settlement depended upon these interlocking economic arrangements. As they came apart, so did the Versailles system. In March, for example, Germany and Austria announced a customs union between the two countries. At the same time word came from Vienna of an impending financial crisis. France was willing to help the Austrians, but only if they agreed to abandon the customs union. The provisions of the Versailles Treaty proscribed such a union, but Paris' insistence on the letter of the treaty at this critical moment infuriated many American policy-makers. By May 1931 French pressure had driven the largest bank in Austria, the Creditanstalt, to the edge of insolvency.

Hoover waited out the situation as long as he could, then proposed a one-year moratorium on all intergovernment debts and a similar plan for private obligations. These proposals were acts of political courage and wisdom, but they required a full reassessment of long-range policies on debts and reparations if the moratoria were to be more than stopgap measures. Hoover managed to establish the debt moratoria, but he was not given the time or the circumstances to work out policies that might have led to long-range solution to the problem. "I felt that the situation was weakening and that the political forces in motion might result in revolution and overthrow if any financial crisis should develop," he later explained in his memoirs. Hoover had stalled the "political forces in motion" in Germany, but when they began again, they did not stop until the National Socialists were in power.

Indeed, the moratorium itself inadvertently produced forces elsewhere that endangered the remaining foundations of the postwar economic order. The standstill on German payments led to a run on the Bank of England, which forced Britain to go off the gold standard and devalue the pound in September 1931. Japan followed suit in December. Currency devaluation by one or two trading nations raised fears among all the others that they would have to devalue their own currencies beneath the new levels of the pound and the yen in order to restore their competitive position in foreign markets. And the longer a nation waited, the greater its leap would have to be. To nations embattled at home, it mattered little that such gains as could be made this way would last only until the next round of leaps, or that the momentum of forces thus let loose might soon carry the world into chaos.

The European nations did make one effort to prevent that from happening, at the 1932 Lausanne Conference, which proposed a mutual cancellation of war debts and reparations. But it came just as the American presidential campaign got under way. Since Wilson's first unsuccessful efforts at Versailles, American policy-makers had tried various means to persuade Paris and London to reduce reparations. At the beginning, Washington had hinted at substantial debt reductions, but there was some question about Congress' willingness to go along with such a plan. Nevertheless, by putting special conditions on the "private" Dawes and Young plans, it had effected reductions by other means.

Even without the depression and the presidential campaign, it would have been difficult for any President to propose a simple forgiving of the war debts. They had become, in the years of disillusionment, an emotional issue. Hoover saw that only something dramatic would have a chance, so he called for a world economic conference to stabilize national currencies and reduce trade barriers. When the major powers accepted the idea, Hoover dedicated himself to holding together the dissolving world order. But by the time the conference met in June 1933, there was nothing left to build on.

Letdown in Latin America

HOOVER HAD ENTERED office with high hopes for America's relations with Latin America. Immediately following the 1928 election he set out on a tour through the southern half of the hemisphere, declaring that "we have a desire to maintain not only the cordial relations of governments with each other but with the relations of good neighbors."

Secretary Stimson then made explicit what had once been implied in Hughes's time (though Kellogg had demurred): the United States would henceforth recognize Latin governments upon demonstration of a "*de facto* capacity to fulfill obligations" as members of the world community. Intervention under the guise of *de jure* recognition policies (that is, the effort to determine the rightful government of a foreign nation) was to come to an end. Publication in 1930 of the so-called Clark Memorandum, named for a State Department expert on Latin America, was taken (as Hoover intended it should be) as a formal renunciation of any intervention rights claimed under the so-called Roosevelt Corollary to the Monroe Doctrine.

Despite the reservations of certain State Department officials and others inside the government, Hoover also moved to eliminate the remaining military occupations in Haiti and Nicaragua. He wanted, he told a special commission appointed for the purpose, recommendations on means of carrying out a Haitianization" policy in Haiti's Department of Public Works, Sanitary Service, and Technical Service of Agriculture. Hoover also authorized the establishment of a Haitian security force patterned on the already functioning Nicaraguan *Guardia Nacional*. The 5,763 American sailors and Marines on duty in Nicaragua in 1928 were reduced by 1932 to fewer than 1,000, including 200 who were serving in the *Guardia Nacional*. Hoover complemented the declining military presence with increased emphasis on the building of good roads. "Good roads and banditry are antagonistic," explained the State Department.[7] When the first complaint arose that the administration had abandoned American propertyholders, Stimson brushed aside the objection:

> Lives and property in the interior of Nicaragua are to be protected by the Guardia, and if the company is not satisfied with that protection it has two alternatives: either to provide for its own protection—the Secretary understood that the company had two machine guns already—or to withdraw, and he hoped they would not do that.[8]

Succeeding administrations in Washington pursued the same policy, to the satisfaction of dictator Anastasio Somoza, who preserved order in the interior of Nicaragua for no fewer than twenty-three years.

In South America, however, the expectations of Hoover and Stimson fell short of realization. Of the ten republics of South America, only Colombia, Uruguay, and Venezuela escaped revolutionary upheavals between 1930 and 1932. And in the Caribbean, where "Haitianization" had been pronounced a success, the Cuban dictatorship of Gerardo Machado was in serious trouble. In both South America and the Caribbean, moreover, few of the disturbances were *caudillo*-inspired, but arose from popular unrest. This was a development of

---

[7] Wilfrid Hardy Callcott, *The Western Hemisphere: Its Influence on United States Policies to the End of World War II* (Austin, Tex., 1968), pp. 256–57.

[8] Memorandum of a conversation with officials of the Standard Fruit and Steamship Company, April 21, 1931, in Henry L. Stimson papers, Yale University.

the first importance, one not contemplated in the philosophies or policies (even with the Hughes-Kellogg-Stimson adjustments) pursued since 1898. What brought these situations to the eruption point was the onset of the Great Depression. Cuba's share of the American sugar market, for example, fell from 49.4 percent to 25.3 percent in 1933. The American ambassador in Havana reported that the issue for most Cubans was not the dictatorship, but poverty, especially in the cities. The troubles were "economic and communistic." From Chile came reports that American investors feared that the government intended to seize their properties or demand cash payments from them in order to satisfy angry insurgents.

American policies offered little substantive aid to Latin American governments struggling with internal discontent and external debts. Hoover even issued a press statement denying that he was planning to call for a Latin American moratorium on debt payments. Latin American governments responded to the depression in the same way as European governments, with high tariffs and trade controls. In addition to these problems, there were new outbreaks of fighting between countries. Peru and Colombia clashed over a territory known as Leticia, a corner of the Amazon jungle presumed to be of some worth to someone. "I am getting quite blue over the way in which all Latin America is showing up," lamented Secretary Stimson privately.

> If we try to take the lead for them, at once there is a cry against American domination and imperialism. But in Leticia the action of Peru has been so unprovoked and so without any defense, that we may have to intervene to protect the treaties which are being smashed. It is Manchuria once again on a small scale.[9]

Japan Kicks Over the Traces

BY THE END of Hoover's term, American policy-makers were judging developments in all parts of the world in relation to Japan's 1931 forward movement into Manchuria. Stimson had made a special effort to uphold the treaty structure in the Far East, invoking the Kellogg-Briand Pact when the 1929 "war" broke out along the tracks of the Chinese Eastern Railway. At the London Naval Conference the following year, the Secretary carefully guided the delegates around a series of pitfalls and came home with a new treaty providing for an extension of the shipbuilding holiday until 1936 and an expansion of the ratio principle to include heavy and light cruisers.

---

[9] Diary entry, November 11, 1932, in Stimson papers.

To get the treaty, Stimson gave Japan a somewhat more favorable ratio in this last category, so that it now stood at 10:10:7. Meanwhile he restored Hughes's policy of extending free advice to the Chinese, and upon occasion lecturing their diplomats on China's responsibilities to the powers. At least once he even warned an American business concern not to allow the Chinese to entice it into an unwise expansion in the face of Japanese opposition.

But the economic bonds of the Japanese-American rapprochement proved to be as flimsy as those holding together the political arrangements of the 1920s. In Tokyo the government that signed the London Treaty came under sharp attack from Japanese generals and admirals. The civilian government won; but it was to be the last time for more than a decade and a half. On September 18, 1931, Japanese military forces in Manchuria began a forward movement that civil officials could not (or would not) reverse. When the fighting stopped, Japan was in full control of the province, which it renamed Manchukuo and ruled through a puppet emperor.

It was hard for Japanese "liberals" to argue down the generals with economic facts. In 1929 the United States had absorbed 40 percent of Japan's exports; but by the end of that year the New York silk market had collapsed, reducing the world price of Japan's major export by 50 percent. The Smoot-Hawley tariff did not take silk off the free list, but it raised the levy on a variety of other exports from 5 to 200 percent. Throughout the decade Japanese policymakers would argue that American trade policies were no less an international issue than was Japanese policy in Manchuria and China.

Yet Stimson thought he could encourage and support Japanese liberals through a carefully measured response, which would reveal to the militarists the folly of their policies. At a Cabinet meeting early in October the Secretary admitted the difficulty facing anyone who sought to uphold the Washington Treaty system:

> This fight has come on in the worst part of the world for peace treaties. The peace treaties of modern Europe ... no more fit the three great races of Russia, Japan, and China, who are meeting in Manchuria, than ... a stovepipe hat would fit an African savage. Nevertheless they are parties to these treaties and the whole world looks on to see whether the treaties are good for anything or not....[10]

The search for a proper response led Hoover and Stimson back to the League of Nations, which, after reminding both parties of their obligations under the Kellogg Pact, proceeded to establish a Commision of Enquiry. The

---

[10] Diary entry, October 9, 1931, in ibid.

State Department feared this was a roundabout way of doing nothing. President Hoover encouraged his Secretary of State to bring into play all the moral force he had available, but warned that he would not countenance anything beyond that. Stimson pressed Tokyo and Peking to enter bilateral negotiations under an American aegis, but the Japanese became especially intransigent as their military forces moved into south Manchuria. The Secretary was furious. They had upset "the whole applecart," and "nobody would trust Japan again."[11]

It was hard to say whether Stimson was more distressed at the forward movement of the Japanese army or at the prospect of never being able to trust them again. He regarded both with equal concern—and pessimism. But Hoover still refused to reconsider his ban on an economic boycott against Japan or any other coercive measure. Besides, there was reason to question what effectiveness a boycott would have at this point, except perhaps to stimulate retaliatory acts against American raw cotton. Lacking international support and under severe limitations, Stimson devised a nonrecognition doctrine. What he had forsworn in Latin America, *de jure* recognition requirements, he now put forward in Asia. But what neither man anticipated, especially not Hoover, was the lengths to which this policy would be extended by others.

After arranging things in London and Paris, Washington sent out its note to Peking and Tokyo on January 7, 1932: This nation could not recognize as legal any de facto situation or treaty that might impair America's treaty rights in China or the territorial and administrative integrity of that country. Great Britain's "supporting" note, however, nullified much of the effect of a joint protest because it did not refer to the territorial integrity of China. So, in this first test of the effectiveness of Hughes's accomplishment at the Washington Conference, the shadow of the Anglo-Japanese alliance still fell between theory and action.

The Far Eastern situation actually got worse after the dispatch of the American note. On January 28, 1932, Japan seized Shanghai. Stimson appealed to Hoover to permit him at least to hint at plans for serious countermeasures, however vaguely. The important thing, he felt, was that Japan was afraid of "our great size and military strength," and Tokyo would respond even to the "unconscious elements" of these advantages. The most Hoover would allow along these lines was a public letter addressed to Senator William E. Borah, dated February 23, 1932. In this "letter," which the Secretary of State later referred to as "in many ways the most significant state paper" he had authored, Stimson reviewed yet again the history of the Open Door policy, emphasizing

---

[11] Robert H. Ferrell, *American Diplomacy in the Great Depression* (New York, 1970), pp. 147–48.

that the Nine Power Treaty had elevated that American initiative to the status of "international policy," though he stopped short of calling it international law. Then he tried to suggest what might happen in the future, couching his words in the most diplomatic manner possible:

> The willingness of the American government to surrender its then commanding lead in battleship construction and to leave its positions at Guam and in the Philippines without further fortification, was predicated upon, among other things, the self-denying covenants contained in the Nine Power Treaty, which assured the nations of the world not only of equal opportunity for their Eastern trade but also against the military aggrandizement of any other power at the expense of China. One cannot discuss the possibility of modifying or abrogating those provisions of the Nine Power Treaty without considering at the same time the other promises upon which they were really dependent.

Whether Tokyo was adept at reading between the lines of the Borah letter or not, Hoover was; and he waited until Stimson was out of the country to have another State Department official affirm that the United States would always employ peaceful means in international affairs. Nevertheless, the doctrine, whether in Stimson's terms or in Hoover's milder version, became the central issue in Japanese-American relations. Franklin D. Roosevelt endorsed it after his election, and every attempt to reconstruct a semblance of Japanese-American understanding in the remainder of the decade floundered on that issue.

Postscript to a Bad Ending

HOOVER FELT BESIEGED in the 1932 presidential campaign. His opponent took all sides of every argument, and from each position blasted away at Republican policies, both foreign and domestic. Hoover's predicament was largely self-made, though certainly not exclusively the handiwork of selfish "isolationist" Republicans. The outgoing President still hoped that the proposed World Economic Conference could halt the descent into chaos—and initiate a plan for world recovery, political and economic. Roosevelt's promised "New Deal" seemed to Hoover to be the only serious obstacle to American participation in an international plan "to remove the obstructions to world consumption and rising prices." To the extent that the President believed this to be the real situation, he was deceived. Nonetheless, he made one last effort to persuade Roosevelt to abandon the "New Deal" and commit himself to the administration's plan to exchange a reduction of the war debts for a promise that the world powers, in particular Great Britain, would stabilize their currencies and reduce trade barriers.

> What is required is a group of the best brains of England, to sit down with a group of the best and most expert brains of the United States to work out a plan to reverse the economic forces now working in the world. This will be a discussion which will take weeks and months. No concession should be given to the British until that project is complete and then only if it shows results to the United States.[12]

It was no use. Hoover thought Roosevelt deliberately refused to comprehend "the problem with which the world is confronted and which we have tried to get before him." Roosevelt and his advisers thought Hoover refused to comprehend that the country did not have "weeks and months" to spend in discussion, holding in abeyance domestic recovery plans on the chance that the world's nations could come up with an answer to the depression in time to save American institutions. Hoover asked too much; Roosevelt gave too little. Neither had much choice.

Suggestions for Further Reading

Two books by Robert H. Ferrell provide a political overview of these years· *Peace in Their Time. The Origins of the Kellogg-Briand Pact* (New York, 1969) and *American Diplomacy in the Great Depression* (New York, 1970). See also Selig Adler, *The Uncertain Giant, 1921–1941: American Foreign Policy Between the Wars* (New York, 1965).

Kellogg is treated in L. Ethan Ellis, *Frank B. Kellogg and American Foreign Relations, 1925–1929* (New Brunswick, N.J., 1961), while Henry L. Stimson's *On Active Service in Peace and War* (New York, 1948) is still the best source on Stimson, although it should be supplemented with Elting Morison's *Turmoil and Tradition: A Study of the Life and Times of Henry L. Stimson* (Boston, 1960).

Hoover's approach to Latin America is presented in Alexander De Conde, *Herbert Hoover's Latin American Policy* (Stanford, Calif., 1951). The best special study is Hans Schmidt, *The United States Occupation of Haiti, 1915–1934* (New Brunswick, N.J., 1971).

Of special interest is Raymond G. O'Connor, *Perilous Equilibrium: The United States and the London Naval Conference of 1930* (Lawrence, Kans., 1962), and Armin Rappaport, *Henry L. Stimson and Japan, 1931–1933* (Chicago, 1963).

See also the general bibliography at the end of this volume.

---

[12] Hoover to Stimson, January 15, 1933, in Stimson papers.

CHAPTER 21

American Foreign Policy in a Closed World (1933–1937)

As the long interregnum following Franklin Roosevelt's election dragged on through the fourth winter of the Great Depression, anxious advisers urged the President-elect to make clear his intention to deal with America's economic problems on a domestic basis. Others warned him of the dreadful consequences that "isolationism" would surely have for the country. Like almost everyone in both groups, Roosevelt had qualms about either course in a world where nations had retreated behind trade barriers and now resembled medieval walled cities, each well armed and surrounded by a variety of vassal fiefdoms. Japan had initiated a "coprosperity sphere" in Manchuria; Great Britain had barricaded its empire within the "Ottawa Preference System"; and, most recently, Germany had come under the rule of the National Socialist party. After three years of New Deal experimentation, Roosevelt was still uncertain about the course the country should take. "The rest of the world," he said in a message to Congress, "—ah, there's the rub."

FDR and the Brains Trusters' Formula

THE MEN who helped Roosevelt in the shaping of the New Deal opposed further efforts to solve the problem of the depression through international action. At best, they reasoned, foreign trade recovery was ancillary to the central problem: the anarchy of concentrated economic power. The recovery formula proposed by the Brains Trust consisted of two primary measures, the National Industrial Recovery Act and the Agricultural Adjustment Act; both were designed to coerce producers into a cooperative plan to reduce output to consumable levels. "It is not easy to think of a civilization which is not constantly pushing out its frontiers in terms of goods and services," admitted one Brains Truster, "though geography is beginning to be a restricted field."[1]

Their victory was far from complete. Roosevelt listened to other advisers on political questions like disarmament, and followed his own inclinations in endorsing Henry L. Stimson's Far Eastern policy. His long-time interest in the navy, going back even beyond the time he served as Assistant Secretary of the Navy under Wilson, no doubt had much to do with the President-elect's continuing interest in political questions in the Pacific basin and its rimlands. Throughout the 1920s Roosevelt had maintained a keen interest in foreign affairs, though he modified his big-navy views in writings on the need for cooperation with Japan and a new approach to Latin American countries. In the 1920 campaign, for example, Vice-Presidential Nominee Roosevelt boasted of having written the Haitian constitution, but a few years later he called for an end to Republican "big stick" policies. It was, he said, "an announced Democratic doctrine not to interfere in the internal affairs of our neighboring sister republics."

Roosevelt's disinclination to get involved with the League of Nations was, despite the doubts of anti-Wilson critics, apparently quite sincere. He explained this defection by pointing out that the League had not developed according to Woodrow Wilson's vision, "nor have the principal members shown a disposition to divert the huge loans spent on armaments into the channels of legitimate trade, balanced budgets and payment of obligations."[2] These disparagements were not made merely for effect; they reflected the new President's actual suspicions of continued European conniving, even in the final weeks leading up to the London Economic Conference.

---

[1] Adolf A. Berle, Jr., "Private Business and Public Opinion," *Scribner's Magazine*, 95 (February 1934):81–87.

[2] Extract from Franklin Roosevelt, *Looking Forward*, in *Franklin D. Roosevelt and Foreign Affairs, 1933–1937*, ed. Edgar Nixon, 3 vols. (Cambridge, Mass., 1969), 1:23–24.

Out with the Old: The London Economic Conference

ROOSEVELT HAD FELT for some time that Hoover's World Economic Conference was little more than an international version of the discredited national "commissions" with which Hoover had tried to get the economy moving at home, and which had failed so miserably. Roosevelt wavered a bit during the interregnum, but he came back to this conviction shortly before the conference convened in June 1933. Besides, he had taken the United States off the international gold standard and wanted a chance to see how that attempt to boost prices worked out before agreeing to tie the country's currency to any new international standard. His suspicions of British motives were borne out when, on the eve of the international meeting, London negotiated a special trade agreement with Argentina which State Department experts reported would result in discriminations against American trade. "They wanted to use the conference for such arrangements as would enable them to sell in American markets," wrote one of the architects of the New Deal, "without making it easier for American products to be exported."[3]

Despite the President's doubts, which he had not tried to hide, Secretary of State Cordell Hull, who headed the American delegation, left for London amidst a brief flurry of press releases proclaiming his intention to seek a general agreement to reduce trade barriers. All the President authorized Hull to say, however, was that the United States would negotiate bilateral treaties with any country that showed an interest in that kind of limited bargaining. Even so, the new Secretary of State could not resist the temptation to lecture the assembled delegates on their responsibilities to join in a cooperative movement toward freer trade and multilateralism.

Hull was very much on his own here, because Roosevelt had already turned down his plea to make tariff reform a priority item of the New Deal. To this curious picture was added a third element when the President's special emissary, Raymond Moley, suddenly appeared in London to announce the United States' readiness to negotiate a currency stabilization agreement. Surprisingly, when an agreement was reached, Roosevelt immediately repudiated it in his "bombshell" message of July 2, 1933. "The sound internal economic system of a nation is a greater factor in its well-being," the President said, "than the price of its currency in changing terms of the currencies of other nations." Did this mean the administration had opted for a policy of self-containment? Hull cabled Washington in great distress. Roosevelt's reassurance that he could offer

---

3 Rexford G. Tugwell, *The Democratic Roosevelt* (New York, 1957), p. 291.

to negotiate bilateral reciprocal trade agreements in Washington did little to relieve the Secretary's mind. Whether the proposed currency stabilization agreement would really have curtailed New Deal planning as much as the President feared is still a moot question, but Roosevelt never regretted this decision. A State Department official who talked with the President noted in his diary that Roosevelt had told him that the "bombshell" message would counteract the impression that America always came away from conference tables the loser. "For better or worse, he has proved to the public that Europe cannot force us to accept what he does not want and the psychological effect, at least here, should be very valuable."[4]

How Americans could take much psychological comfort from the disintegration of the London Conference seems surprising today, but at the time New Deal nationalism was no less emotional than World War I outbursts had been. Roosevelt had asked and received wartime emergency powers to deal with the depression. So had leaders in other countries. Some had seized power and destroyed representative government; others had not. But in both cases, the foreign policies of depression-struck nations were posited upon the assumption that one nation's gain was another's loss.

Political cooperation could not succeed where economic multilateralism had failed. The fate of the Geneva Disarmament Conference later that summer reinforced decisions for unilateralism. In this instance, however, FDR did try to meet the Europeans halfway by making a tentative offer to forsake neutral trading rights with a belligerent power that was designated an aggressor by the community of nations— provided, that is, the United States agreed with the judgment.

Roosevelt told the Geneva Conference that the United States would join in such a boycott only if the European powers first adopted a disarmament agreement among themselves, a condition that was never fulfilled. In the fall Germany denounced Anglo-French proposals and all the doings of the Geneva Conference and withdrew under a barrage of Hitlerian rhetoric. Strong congressional opposition had arisen to giving the President discretionary power to embargo goods even against an aggressor, but Roosevelt's decision to retract the American offer was based on his own disinclination to become involved to any degree in what might become a political alliance with America's former allies. Roosevelt fully shared in the national disillusion of the mid-1930s, though he never became an isolationist of the sort pictured in stereotypes.

---

4 Diary entry, July 6, 1933, in J. Pierrepont Moffat papers, Harvard University.

Hull versus Peek: The Trade War Within

ROOSEVELT WAS TORN, for example, between the logic and requirements of the NRA and the AAA and his Secretary of State's economic internationalism. Hull nearly suffered a fit of apoplexy upon learning that the President had been listening to George N. Peek's recommendations for a national trade policy. "His efforts," Hull later commented, "and those of his associates, aided at times by the President, came perilously near supplanting my whole set of international economic policies." At the outset of the New Deal, however, there was nothing to supplant. Hull's operating assumptions were not shared by the President—at least, not for the moment.

Agricultural surpluses were FDR's main concern, and Peek insisted that the best (indeed the only) way to get these out of the country was through bilateralism: barter, export subsidies, or any other mechanism that would show immediate results. That was the way to lift the deadweight off the whole price structure and free the economy.

The Secretary of State had to demonstrate that Peek was wrong, that multilateralism was still the only valid policy for America, and, more important, that it could bring results in a shrinking world. The Hull-Peek battle raged for almost two years, and was fought on almost every policy front: Latin America, Europe, and the Far East. A major victory for Hull was the 1934 Reciprocal Trade Agreements Act, but while it was a step back from the unmitigated protectionism of the Smoot-Hawley tariff, it left essential questions unanswered. Hull wanted to implement it with the unconditional most-favored-nation policy of the early 1920s. He and his aides argued that such clauses were the only way to protect America's share of the foreign trade of nations that bought more than they sold in the American market. Books have been written on this subject, but the rudiments can be covered simply by saying that the aim of such clauses is to prevent two nations from arranging things between them in any way that might discriminate against the trade of a third country. In theory it is advantageous for all powers to subscribe to the most-favored-nation principle; in practice, and under certain conditions, this is not always true. It may be that two nations can aid one another only by discriminating against a third.

Peek contended that this was the case in the 1930s, and moreover, that a balance sheet of past trade figures would reveal that only selected special interest groups in America had profited from multilateralism anyway. The nation as a whole had not. Peek never quite convinced Roosevelt, but late in December 1933 the President announced during a press conference that he did not think there was very much in sight, given world conditions, "except through bilateral treaties, which might be extended to take in a few other countries."

The Challenge Repulsed

IN JUNE 1934 Peek offered Roosevelt a "good Yankee horse trade" with Germany: cotton for needed commodities on a strictly barter basis. Thoroughly alarmed, the State Department reacted at once: "To give in on this essential point to Germany would be inviting similar action which tends to drive our trade to a dollar for dollar exchange basis against our ultimate interests."[5] For the next several months the intra-administration conflict stayed at a high level of intensity, to which the Germans added in a variety of ways and which was climaxed by Berlin's denunciation of its own most-favored-nation treaty with the United States.

Hull claimed the final victory when Roosevelt refused to approve the deal. Whatever the President's motives for his action, and they were no doubt complex, the State Department's triumph reestablished several key points in American economic policy, and these had a permanent effect on New Deal foreign policy. First, the nation's international economic policies had to serve the long-term interests of the country, not just relieve temporary problems. Second,

Franklin Roosevelt and Cordell Hull

---

[5] Diary entry, June 6, 1934, in ibid.

America's economic interests were worldwide; what happened in one part of the world deeply affected the situation elsewhere. Third, however advantageous this particular barter transaction might prove to be, it promoted German policies (rearmament, autocracy, extreme nationalism) detrimental to United States interests throughout Europe. "It is the policy of the State Department," Hull wrote FDR,

> to maintain the ... doctrine of equality of commercial and industrial treatment. .... This doctrine is the corner stone of our present foreign policy and of our reciprocal trade agreement program. ...
>
> This program and this policy have been constantly thrust in the face of Germany, of Japan, and other countries which seemed bent on preferences and discriminations, especially against us. This broad and consistent course is calculated to avoid giving any country any ground or pretext to discriminate, much less driving it to do so.[6]

Hull's aides supplied the White House with other memoranda on the general question of American trade policy and the specific question of the German agreement. These sealed the victory, though other factors no doubt weighed heavily with the President. Agricultural prices, for example, were up, easing the pressure on the administration from the farm bloc. Roosevelt's antipathy to the Nazi regime and all its works made a barter deal with Germany a bad choice for Peek's last stand.

Once these are all accounted for, however, Roosevelt must have been impressed with the big vote of confidence Hull received from key business leaders, including Thomas J. Watson, president of the International Business Machines Corporation. In a letter to Roosevelt stressing the activities of England and Germany in "South America and with other outside countries," Watson concluded, "When we realize that the United States with six percent of the world's population manufactures fifty percent of all the goods manufactured, it convinces me that we should increase our efforts towards restoring and increasing our foreign trade."[7] Latin America was a good place to begin, because its products were not generally competitive with U.S. manufactures, and because England, Germany, and Japan were indeed making serious efforts to move into these markets.

---

[6] Cordell Hull to Franklin D. Roosevelt, December 14, 1934, in *Roosevelt and Foreign Affairs*, 2:319–21.

[7] Thomas B. Watson to Roosevelt, July 6, 1935, in Franklin Delano Roosevelt papers, Franklin D. Roosevelt Library (Hyde Park, N.Y.), official file no. 614–A.

Dedicating the Good Neighbor Policy

ROOSEVELT HAD DEVOTED only one paragraph of his first inaugural address to actual foreign policy concerns: he said he would dedicate "this Nation to the policy of the good neighbor—the neighbor who resolutely respects himself and, because he does so, respects the rights of others." Though he did not mention Latin America specifically, New Deal officials used the phrase "Good Neighbor policy" to describe Roosevelt's determination to remove the remaining occupation forces from the Caribbean and Central America and henceforth practice nonintervention in the area.

Both Hull and Roosevelt often referred to the Good Neighbor policy in conversations with world leaders, contrasting their faith in nonintervention and military withdrawal with the forward movements of Germany and Japan. "The results were bad," Hull once told the Japanese ambassador, commenting on the use of U.S. Marines in Latin America, "and we brought them out. Since then we have found it more profitable to practice the 'Good Neighbor Policy.' "[8] From the beginning, however, Roosevelt had something much more positive in mind than nonintervention. He had expected the London Economic Conference to fail, and when it did, he urged Hull to give first priority to trade agreements with Latin American countries. Just before his inauguration FDR had talked with Secretary Stimson about the situation in the Caribbean, particularly in Haiti and Cuba. Not satisfied with Stimson's advice and assurances, the President-elect sent special representatives to Havana to investigate the growing unrest and antipathy to President Gerardo Machado.

These aides and Special Ambassador Sumner Welles agreed that the only way to forestall real trouble on the island would be to hold out a bigger share of the American sugar market as an inducement to Machado to grant political reforms. A fair agreement, Welles reported to the State Department in May, would serve the dual purpose of "distracting the attention of the public from politics" and assuring the United States of "practical control of a market it has been steadily losing for the past ten years."[9] Before Welles could complete negotiations, however, the smoldering unrest exploded into a general strike. Machado was forced out, and his successors were less amenable to Welles's

---

[8] Cited in Lloyd C. Gardner, *Economic Aspects of New Deal Diplomacy* (Madison, Wis., 1964), p. 47.

[9] Sumner Welles to Hull, May 13, 1933, in Charles Taussig papers, Franklin D. Roosevelt Library.

neighborly advice. The new regime, led by Ramón Grau San Martín, even talked about changing Cuba's fundamental relationship to the United States!

For four months (September 1933 to January 1934) Washington waited, publicly refusing diplomatic recognition to a government it thought too "radical" and privately encouraging various Cubans to form a government that could and would "protect life, property, and individual liberty."[10] Throughout this period Ambassador Welles paid special attention to the new chief of staff, Fulgencio Batista, who he thought represented the only force for stability. Grau San Martín was overthrown by the army on January 15, 1934, and Batista began a twenty-five-year career as Cuba's most powerful strongman, sometimes ruling through others, sometimes holding the presidency himself. Diplomatic recognition was granted to this new government after it gave assurances of its intentions toward the United States, a bargain sealed with the long-delayed commercial agreement Welles had promised and two large loans totaling $8 million. The 1934 reciprocal trade agreement with Cuba was the first completed under the new Hull program. In return for a subsidy to Cuban sugar, the United States received concessions all along the line.

Despite its careful avoidance of overt military intervention in Cuba, American policy revived suspicions of big-stick diplomacy. These came out at the Inter-American Conference at Montevideo in November 1933, when Mexico introduced a resolution calling for absolute nonintervention by any nation in the internal or external affairs of any other hemisphere nation. Hull signed the resolution on behalf of the United States delegation, qualifying his acceptance of the principle with verbal reservations about certain legal obligations (the Platt Amendment, for example), and then went back to work to secure other resolutions in line with his trade proposals. It was this aspect of the Montevideo Conference that most interested European observers.

American exports to Latin America had declined from $628.2 million in 1930 to a low of $194.5 million in 1932. Succeeding years saw marked improvements, especially in 1934, when U.S. exports climbed back up to $307.3 million—a one-year increase of more than 42 percent. The Cuban trade pact accounted for a significant part of this gain, much of it at Japan's expense. German competition was less easily overcome. Hitler's Finance Minister, Hjalmar Schacht, had put together what he called a "New Plan," consisting of barter transactions, blocked credits, and export subsidies. American officials declared it to be the very antithesis of the Good Neighbor policy, a point

---

[10] Robert Freeman Smith, *The United States and Cuba: Business and Diplomacy, 1917–1960* (New York, 1960), pp. 150–51.

Hull had used in persuading the President to turn down Peek's Yankee horse trade.

The New Plan began to make noticeable inroads in 1935, when German trade increased by 47 percent, followed by another big gain in 1936. In certain countries, Brazil and Chile especially, German trade threatened to outstrip American trade in absolute figures; but the most ominous trends noted in a 1936 interdepartment report on German gains in Latin America concerned comparative developments on selected items. United States cotton cloth exports had declined 27 percent in 1935, but German exports had gone up 170 percent and were now nearly 20 percent of the American totals; iron and steel mill products from the United States had decreased by 20 percent, but German exports had increased by 131 percent and were now 95 percent of the U.S. figure. In every one of the twenty categories listed, Germany had increased its trade both in absolute terms and as a percentage of the market. Germany's new plan was effective, concluded this report, because Latin American countries "finally decided they would sooner sell to Germany on Germany's terms than run the risk of not being able to dispose of their products in other markets."[11] Brazil's major export to Germany, for example, was cotton, a commodity that the Roosevelt administration was almost desperate to get out of the country.

Growing German-American economic rivalry in Latin America was in the background of a discussion held in the State Department on November 24, 1936, between the German ambassador and Assistant Secretary of State Francis B. Sayre. At issue was a possible German-American trade agreement, but when the ambassador asked if his country would have to accept the most-favored-nation principle, not only in that specific pact but in its trade policies with all nations, Sayre replied that while the United States did not wish to dictate to any nation, his government would of course be interested in "the effects of German policy upon American trade" generally.[12]

When Roosevelt went to the 1936 Buenos Aires Conference, his personal prestige was at a high point. The last troops had been withdrawn from Haiti; new treaties had been signed with Panama and Cuba; and the United States had formally renounced its right of intervention under the Platt Amendment. Roosevelt's keynote speech calling for hemispheric unity was well received; but Hull's resolutions reaffirming the principles of equality of trade treatment and the elimination of discrimination met with consistent opposition from the host country, Argentina, making the conference something less than a total

---

[11] Laurence Duggan, "German Trade with Latin America in the Past Two Years," November 16, 1936, in U.S. State Department file no. 610.6231/29B.

[12] Memorandum by Francis Sayre, November 24, 1936, in *Foreign Relations, 1936*, 2:252–54.

success. Meanwhile, events in Mexico, where President Lázaro Cárdenas had initiated a broad reform program, presaged the most serious challenge to the Good Neighbor policy yet, one that would see all the unresolved issues come together in a full-scale crisis.

Japan's Bid for a New "Understanding"

ROOSEVELT HAD TOLD Secretary Stimson at Hyde Park on January 9, 1933, that he believed Japan "would ultimately fail through the economic pressure against the job she had undertaken in Manchuria."[13] Meanwhile, of course, he would endorse the nonrecognition policy the Secretary had devised to persuade the Japanese leaders to return to the world of the Washington treaties. They also talked about how to make the best use of the navy to keep Japan's recalcitrant militarists from completely jumping the track before diplomatic pressure had had a chance to work. Then in June 1933 FDR issued an executive order allotting $238 million for a naval building program—the largest single shipbuilding project undertaken by any nation since the end of World War I. He had discovered upon entering office, he explained to a critic, that the United States had not kept up its navy to treaty levels, "with the net result that our Navy was and probably is actually inferior to the Japanese Navy." Moreover, the President added darkly, "the whole scheme of things in Tokio [sic] does not make for an assurance of non-aggression in the future."[14]

Shortly before the London Economic Conference, the United States had extended a $50 million credit to China for the purchase of wheat and cotton, despite expressions of concern from some State Department officials who feared the Japanese would contend the arrangement violated the 1920 consortium agreement. There were many rumors that summer that China was encouraging the League of Nations to supplant the moribund consortium altogether with a new plan for international financial and technical aid. It was true that the Chinese were attempting something of this sort, but it was not true that the United States was prepared to take part in such a plan.

Nevertheless, in April 1934 the Japanese formally declared their opposition to all such projects, on the grounds that they had a special responsibility for the maintenance of peace in East Asia. Less than a month later the Japanese

---

[13] Diary entry, January 15, 1933, in Henry L. Stimson papers, Yale University.

[14] Roosevelt to the Reverend Malcolm E. Peabody, August 19, 1933, in *Roosevelt and Foreign Affairs,* 1:370.

ambassador in Washington asked for a confidential meeting with Secretary Hull to discuss a "highly" important matter. The gist of the ambassador's presentation came down to a desire for a new bilateral understanding, something on the order of the Lansing-Ishii Agreement. The State Department had anticipated this move and was ready with its brief against the proposal. To begin with, said Stanley K. Hornbeck's memorandum to the President, the Japanese had tried to make it appear that the Lansing-Ishii Agreement affirmed precisely what the United States had always declined to affirm. However innocent the Japanese might try to make a new exchange seem, it would be calculated to "limit our freedom of action and to enable Japan to go further afield, with our assent, real or inferred, in pursuance of her policy of making her influence paramount in Eastern Asia." But the final argument, concluded the chief of the Far Eastern Division, was that the United States had, and could have, "no 'Far Eastern policy' as a thing separate from and different from our foreign policy in general."[15] This statement helps to explain why the United States refused to abandon Stimson's nonrecognition doctrine concerning "Manchukuo," even after it became clear that it would take no steps to force Japan out. To the Japanese, American insistence upon abstractions and general rules seemed inexplicable. It left Tokyo stranded between a desire for at least minimal cooperation with the United States and its perception of the Asian situation.

These apparent abstractions were not the products of "idealism," however, but of what Woodrow Wilson called the "higher realism": the conviction that America's survival under the kind of institutions it had evolved depended upon a friendly climate outside the country as well as inside it. Freedom and free enterprise were indivisible; the world could not survive half free and half slave, it would become all one thing or the other. Japan's behavior in Manchuria could not be condoned without setting a precedent that, if followed by others (or by Japan itself), would bring on the final crisis of world capitalism.

Hornbeck and his superiors did not want war with Japan. After Roosevelt and Hull rejected the Japanese bid, the chief of the Far Eastern Division made a sincere effort to restore cooperation by resurrecting the banking consortium. His initiatives were thwarted on all sides: the Chinese wanted absolutely nothing to do with it; the British had their own "new plans" for Asia; and the Japanese charged it was no more than the old scheme to deny them economic opportunities in China. But Hornbeck also faced strong opposition from Treasury Secretary Henry Morgenthau, Jr., who had been

---

[15] Stanley K. Hornbeck to Hull, April 5, 1934, in *Roosevelt and Foreign Policy*, 2:54–71.

Chiang Kai-shek reviewing his troops

developing his own plan to convert the administration's foreign silver purchase program into direct financial aid for Chiang Kai-shek's Chinese Nationalist government. At first Roosevelt opposed all proposals for economic aid to China, citing past failures and commenting on the need for China to stand on its own feet, even if it took "many years and possibly several revolutions."

Secretary Morgenthau refused to take this for a final answer, and produced evidence that the British and the Japanese were ready to step in if the United States refused to act. "This thing is awfully big," Morgenthau once wrote, "it's an international battle between Great Britain, Japan and ourselves and China is the bone in the middle."[16] Roosevelt relented, allowing the Treasury Department to adjust the silver purchases so as to provide China with an important new source of income. Estimates of the actual effectiveness of this aid vary considerably, but at the very least it demonstrated American determination to keep a foot in the Open Door.

Naval Geopolitics

THE TREASURY'S successful bid to pursue an independent policy in regard to China illustrated another aspect of America's Far Eastern strategy in the

---

[16] Diary entry, August 14, 1935, in diary of Henry J. Morgenthau, Jr., Franklin D. Roosevelt Library.

mid-1930s: prevention of a new Anglo-Japanese "understanding," even a negative one. London had never been enthusiastic about the Stimson Doctrine, complaining it was a posture instead of a policy. Washington, on the other hand, suspected that British hints about the need for a new beginning covered a desire to reach an accommodation with Japan that would facilitate expansion at China's expense. Faced with Hitler's rearmament program in Europe, London seemed to be increasingly willing to let bygones be bygones in Asia. This concern was much in evidence in bilateral and tripartite naval talks in 1934 and 1935. The Japanese had announced that the 1922 tonnage ratio of 5:5:3 in capital ships no longer afforded them adequate security. Although the British were as reluctant as the Americans to see a change in the ratio, they had been seeking a private agreement on the limitation of actual building of new ships.

American naval diplomacy aimed at isolating Japan in such a way as to prevent subsequent private agreements between Tokyo and London. If the United States yielded to the demand for full naval equality, or otherwise showed any disposition to weaken itself in the Orient, England and Japan "might join forces in attempting to exclude the United States from the Asiatic market."[17] With neither side prepared to concede any of the other's claims, the talks soon reached an impasse. Japan gave the required two-year notice of its decision to terminate the 1922 agreement on December 29, 1934—the same day the Navy Department announced that the 1935 naval maneuvers would be held west of Hawaii. The United States also implemented a number of long-range plans to counter the anticipated Japanese buildup, including the doubling of naval air strength. FDR rebuilt the Great White Fleet, but like his cousin Theodore, the President was increasingly aware that Japanese-American conflicts would not be resolved by a simple show of force.

The Political Economy of Japanese-American Rivalry

IN WHITE HOUSE strategy sessions at the time of the naval talks, the President had expressed his concern about Japanese "seizure of markets throughout the world by underselling, particularly in textiles."[18] For three decades the United States had waited for the Great China Market to materialize. It never

---

17 Memorandum of a conversation at the White House, October 2, 1934, in Moffat papers.
18 Diary entry, October 24, 1934, in ibid.

did. As the 1930s wore on, American concern about Japanese expansion into Manchuria and north China underwent something of a transformation. At first Washington's primary objection had been that by closing off Manchuria, Japan threatened world order. That consideration remained a factor, but as Tokyo consolidated its positions on the Asian mainland, and integrated the raw materials from these areas into its economy, policy-makers also became worried about Japan's ability to compete in third markets elsewhere in Asia or in Latin America. Japan remained America's best customer for raw cotton, but even that situation might change once the Japanese-Manchurian-Chinese bloc became a reality.

The Commerce Department presented a series of reports to the President in May of 1935 which illustrated the growing problem. In the Philippines, for example, America's share of the textile market had fallen alarmingly in 1934, from 67 percent to 40 percent, while Japan's had increased from 23 percent to 53 percent. That particular situation might be remedied in a number of ways, but overall, American finished cotton exports had decreased by 60 percent from 1925–1929 levels, a decline the Department's advisers said was almost entirely the result of Japanese price competition. The Department recommended the negotiation of gentlemen's agreements to limit Japanese exports to the Philippines and the United States, a policy the administration adopted, but this approach did not get to the heart of the problem.

Japan's invasion of China proper following the Marco Polo Bridge incident on July 7, 1937, forced Secretary of Commerce Dan C. Roper to face the Japanese problem head-on. If the Japanese succeeded, he wrote the President, they would be growing cotton within China, endangering not only third markets, but the $100 million annual sales to Japan as well. From that point on, the general decline in exports of both raw cotton and finished cotton would produce a domestic crisis. "This would call for drastic readjustments on the part of our cotton growers, in fact, a recharting of the economy of the South and definite Federal production control procedures."[19] The rising sun in Asia cast long, bleak shadows across the Pacific. American policy-makers resolved to make one last effort to persuade Japan to return to the framework established at the Washington Naval Conference in 1922, but they held out few hopes to the President that the effort would succeed.

---

[19] Dan Roper to Roosevelt, November 26, 1937, in Roosevelt papers, President's Secretary's file no. 22.

Neutrality or Neutral Rights

THE PRESIDENT's brief sally into the Geneva Disarmament Conference in 1933 was typical of the administration's European "policy" in these four years. He had been urged to recognize the Soviet Union by men who thought there might be a chance to work out some sort of joint approach between the two non-European giants to give the revisionist powers some second thoughts before going too far. These advisers were apparently misled somewhat by Roosevelt's desire to have a number of men around him who encouraged his "internationalism." His performance as President, however, revealed him to be a cautious leader in these years.

He remained aloof, for example, both from advisers who wanted closer cooperation with the European democracies against Hitler and from Russian Foreign Minister Maxim Litvinov, who repeatedly hinted that "collective security" would succeed only if the United States took a strong role on the European stage. In fact, Russian-American relations actually grew worse after formal diplomatic recognition in November 1933. A number of issues arose between the two countries concerning interpretations of pledges Litvinov was supposed to have offered in order to obtain the exchange of ambassadors. These matters probably could have been settled by presidential intervention, but Roosevelt preferred that the State Department handle them, a somewhat unusual procedure since only the President and Litvinov actually knew what private understandings lay behind the written communiqués on their discussions.

However that may be, Roosevelt had apparently decided that diplomatic recognition of the Soviet Union suggested the possibility of combined action later—that is, it opened up his political options a bit. At the time, it had also been assumed that diplomatic recognition would open up America's economic options and offer a large new market for several categories of production. This proved not to be the case, although certain trade pacts were arranged in later years.

When Mussolini moved against Ethiopa, Russian and American negotiators were bogged down in endless quibbling over how much the Soviet Union had agreed to pay on Russia's prerevolutionary war debts, and by what means. The total amount at issue was $75 million. The money was not important, insisted Ambassador William C. Bullitt, but the principle was. And the Soviets had also broken their pledge not to interfere in America's internal affairs, Bullitt complained, by allowing American Communists to take a prominent role at the Seventh Communist International meeting in Moscow during the summer of 1935.

Suspicious of Russian motives, fearful of Fascist aggression, and concerned about domestic crises, Congress passed a neutrality act. Testimony before a special committee had produced an interpretation of the role of bankers and munitions-makers in American entrance into World War I, which distorted more serious investigations of the political economy of American capitalism and the foreign policy it produced. New acts were passed in 1936 and 1937, but Congress found itself able to do little more than legislate against a dead President's mistakes. The "cash and carry" provision of the 1937 act, for example, was an attempt to "avoid the provocative incidents that had contributed to war in 1917, yet at the same time guarantee Americans the chance to benefit financially from any war that broke out."[20] To the extent that they were sold to the public as insurance against war, the neutrality laws were a sham.

Roosevelt tried to use the 1935 act to block Italian aggression in Africa; he failed, but the attempt showed the inability of such acts to sustain genuine neutrality. The outbreak of civil war in Spain during July of 1936 demonstrated their inability to contribute to world peace as well. In a remarkable speech at Chautauqua, New York, on August 14, 1936, Roosevelt denounced those who said that

> if they could produce and ship this and that and the other article to belligerent nations, the unemployed of America would all find work. They would tell you that if they could extend credit to warring nations that credit would be used in the United States to build homes and factories and pay our debts. They would tell you that America once more would capture the trade of the world.

Roosevelt's seeming acceptance of the "merchants of death" thesis, or some variant of it, was codified in the 1937 "cash and carry" provisions. In such a mood the country avoided serious thinking about its own—and the world's—real problems. The issue was not, and never had been, the manipulation of foreign policy by special interest groups for their own benefit. As the war in Spain assumed the character of a *European* civil war, American policy-makers brooded about past errors. By keeping up the pretense of noninvolvement and neutrality, they failed to keep their options open, they neglected chances to head off the impending crisis, and they set the stage for a divisive debate over a second crusade to make the world safe for democracy.

---

[20] Robert Divine, *The Illusion of Neutrality* (Chicago, 1962), pp. 194–96.

Suggestions for Further Reading

Background on the New Deal may be found in William E. Leuchtenburg, *Franklin D. Roosevelt and the New Deal, 1932–1940* (New York, 1963), and in Howard Zinn, ed., *New Deal Thought* (New York, 1966). A good introduction to its diplomacy is Herbert Feis, *1933: Characters in Crisis* (Boston, 1966).

Robert Divine's *The Illusion of Neutrality* (Chicago, 1962) covers that topic with exceptional insight and clarity, but see also John E. Wiltz, *In Search of Peace: The Senate Munitions Inquiry, 1934–1936* (Baton Rouge, La., 1963).

Far Eastern crises are explored from two angles in William L. Neumann, *America Encounters Japan: From Perry to MacArthur* (Baltimore, 1963), and Dorothy Borg, *The United States and the Far Eastern Crisis of 1933–1938* (Cambridge, Mass., 1964). Latin American relations and conditions are covered in J. Fred Rippy, *Latin America and the Industrial Age,* 2nd ed. (New York, 1947), and Bryce Wood, *The Making of the Good Neighbor Policy* (New York, 1954).

Of special interest is Charles A. Beard, *The Open Door at Home* (New York, 1934), a citizen-historian's effort to be "relevant" in the best sense of the word.

See also the general bibliography at the end of this volume.

CHAPTER 22

Rendezvous with Destiny (1937–1941)

By midsummer 1937 world politics had assumed a shape that compelled American leaders to reevaluate the nation's immediate situation and its future options. It was not a hopeful undertaking. In November 1936 Germany, Japan, and Italy had signed the Anti-Comintern Pact. Although the three had exchanged no formal military commitments, the pact stirred great concern in the United States. And events following its signing—Japan's invasion of north China and the intervention of Germany and Italy in the Spanish Civil War—bore out the worst fears of those who perceived in the alliance a worldwide fascist conspiracy. As policy-makers pondered these developments, the nation suffered an abrupt economic downturn at home which threatened to wipe out whatever progress had been made by the New Deal's national recovery program. This unhappy sequence suggested two conclusions to Roosevelt's advisers: (1) the Brains Trust's assumption that world and national problems could be dealt with separately had proved false; and (2) with fascism on the march, America's seeming inability to find the path to economic recovery weakened its foreign policies and endangered domestic institutions. Roosevelt's impatience with old remedies—Cordell Hull's reciprocity treaties, for example—mounted with each new crisis.

"Henry," the President told Treasury Secretary Morgenthau after Munich, "these trade treaties are just too goddamned slow. The world is marching too fast. They're just too slow."[1] They were thought too slow even in Latin America, where German penetration and local nationalist movements threatened the United States' hegemony.

Expropriation Day in Mexico

GERMAN ECONOMIC INFLUENCE in Mexico played a significant, though probably not decisive, part in Washington's response to the decision of President Lázaro Cárdenas in March 1938 to expropriate foreign-owned oil properties. Ambassador Josephus Daniels, Roosevelt's former chief in the Navy Department during the Wilson era, kept the President fully alerted to the danger that an unwise policy could drive Mexico toward unfriendly powers. State Department strategy in this second act of the oil crisis conceded Mexico's right to nationalize the properties, but sought to bring pressure on Cárdenas to negotiate a settlement that would allow the companies to regain a managerial role. A settlement that left the Mexican government in full control of the oil fields, reasoned State Department officers, would set a bad precedent.

After establishing its intention to insist upon prompt and adequate compensation, the State Department successfully argued for a reduction in the special price the Treasury paid for Mexican silver, a key source of revenue for Mexico. The Department also supported the companies' boycott of Mexican oil where and when it could. The companies had always assumed that if their dispute over the wages they paid Mexican workers came to a showdown, expropriation would fail, because Cárdenas had too few tankers or tank cars to move the crude oil. Since the oil would do him no good underground, Cárdenas, like Calles before him, would come to terms. Although Roosevelt thought the companies' demands exorbitant and was skeptical of the effectiveness of State Department pressure against Mexican nationalism, he went along with the Secretary of State's defense of contractual obligations and orderly processes—for a time.

---

[1] John Morton Blum, *From the Morgenthau Diaries: Years of Crisis* (Boston, 1959), p. 524.

Hull wanted the Mexican government to accept the principle of arbitration in settling the dispute; Cárdenas regarded that proposal as an unacceptable challenge to Mexican sovereignty. The impasse lasted for more than two years. Neither side thought the issue was simply the nationalization of the fields, or how much money the companies finally got back on investments they valued at half a billion dollars. "The subject is now of increasing importance," read a memorandum prepared in the Legal Division of the Department of State, "due to the fact that so many nations are coming under the control of dictators who are able to change overnight their domestic laws pertaining to private property."[2] To Mexicans, on the other hand, the subject was the Revolution—*their right* to a revolution.

The oil boycott failed, in part because a maverick American shipping entrepreneur, William Rhodes Davis, supplied Mexico with the means to sell its oil in the world market. On its own, the Mexican government negotiated a larger barter arrangement with Italy, which proved once again that rival political-economic systems afforded the Latin American countries new options and increased bargaining power vis-à-vis the industrial powers. Within a year, Mexico was earning more than a million dollars a month from petroleum sales abroad.

On January 31, 1939, President Roosevelt met with the Senate Military Affairs Committee, some of whose members thought the administration was not doing enough to punish Mexico. "All right," replied the President, "suppose we did not buy any Mexican silver. We are buying today, in small amounts, much less than we did. If we stopped buying Mexican silver, they would sell it to somebody else." As for the suggestion that the government stop American tourists from going to Mexico and spending dollars there, Roosevelt commented matter-of-factly: "The President of Mexico would, I am inclined to think, sell more oil to Italy and Germany to make up for that amount. There isn't very much more you could do."[3] Then Roosevelt lectured the senators on the realities of the world situation, drawing a parallel with the era of the Napoleonic Wars. The Axis powers, he concluded, threatened to put up a fence around the United States, and thereby gain domination of world trade. A tough policy against Mexico would only supply them with important fencing materials.

Following the outbreak of the European war that fall, State Department officials divided on the course to follow to resolve the extended crisis. On one

---

[2] Cited by Bryce Wood, *The Making of the Good Neighbor Policy* (New York, 1961), p. 233.

[3] Transcript in Franklin Delano Roosevelt papers, Franklin D. Roosevelt Library (Hyde Park, N.Y.), President's personal file no. 1–P, pp. 20–21.

side were Ambassador Daniels and his supporters, who wanted to accept Mexican proposals for a joint commission to determine the value of the properties; on the other were those who agreed with the oil companies that a settlement should be deferred until Mexico's need for foreign investment finally created an atmosphere favorable to their position. The business community also divided on the Mexican question. The board of directors of the American Chamber of Commerce in Mexico, for example, complained that the oil companies were seeking to put Mexico under a total boycott, to prevent any sales at all, at a time when German agents had invaded Mexico with offers to sell typewriters, electrical appliances of all kinds, and other goods, at prices below American prices and on favorable credit terms.[4]

Finally, in September 1941, Hull called the oil men to the State Department and explained that Mexico had agreed to a tentative solution. It was not the kind of solution they had sought, but the world situation did not permit the United States to delay further. Mexico had agreed to pay $40 million on outstanding agrarian claims going back more than a decade, Hull said, and a joint committee of experts was to determine the compensation to be paid to the oil companies. The United States would resume its silver purchase agreement with Mexico at prenationalization prices, and the Export-Import Bank was to grant Mexico a $30 million loan to complete the Mexico City–Guatemala section of the Pan American Highway. This last stipulation was the most significant new element, not only in the Mexican situation, but in the "second phase" of the Good Neighbor policy generally. Prior to the Mexican oil crisis, Washington defined its Good Neighbor policy as non-intervention in the purely domestic affairs of other hemisphere countries. In return, the United States expected cooperation with its economic policies and respect for its citizens' private investments. Clearly that definition and those expectations were not adequate or unchallenged after 1938.

The Framework of Hemisphere Defense

THE SHIFT to a "positive" Good Neighbor policy had begun almost accidentally with an Export-Import Bank public works loan to Haiti in 1938; but it was only the place where the shift occurred that was really accidental. The following year President Roosevelt granted Nicaraguan dictator Anastasio Somoza

---

[4] Diary entry, November 19, 1938, Josephus Daniels papers, Library of Congress.

a loan from Public Roads Administration funds to build an east-west highway to stabilize the political situation in his country and to promote its economic development. Then came government loans to American companies for special purposes, such as clearing out Axis-controlled airlines. With these loans the original functions of the Export-Import Bank were expanded into something approximating the national development corporations used by both friendly and unfriendly European nations.

At first Congress refused the President's June 1939 request for an additional $500 million appropriation for the Export-Import Bank so that it could continue and enlarge these new functions, but it changed its mind after the German *Blitzkrieg* in Poland and the swift fall of France. "Should England go down," wrote two journalists who enjoyed special access to administration policy-makers and their thoughts, "a Hitler-organized Europe would be in a position to apply enormous pressure on the raw materials producing economies of all South America.... Much of South America might then be absorbed bloodlessly into the Nazi scheme from a central purchasing bureau in Berlin."[5]

The threat may have seemed greater than it actually was, but there was no denying the very real concern American leaders felt, not about a military conquest but about the fatal link-up of a "Hitler-organized Europe" with Latin American nations already bound to the Axis through crisscrossing barter arrangements. Following Germany's victory over France, there was some talk, to be sure, of the short leap from Dakar in French North Africa over to Brazil, but these speculations were built upon other long-standing fears. Brazil had been a problem area for some time. Even after the State Department succeeded in negotiating a reciprocity treaty with that country, its operation had been checked by prior arrangements between Brazil and Germany. Moreover, dictator Getulio Vargas was suspected of holding pro-Axis sympathies. Roosevelt himself thought of Brazil as he calculated fascist gains late in 1937. "Brazil was veering that way," he told Henry Morgenthau.

Vargas was very much interested in the development of his country's steelmaking capability. American private investors had looked into the situation in 1938, but concluded that a steel complex there was not especially feasible. So had British companies with large iron ore holdings. Japanese and German concerns, on the other hand, announced they were interested in the project. Roosevelt's efforts to persuade United States Steel to reconsider its position failed, but he could and did take up Vargas' suggestion that the Export-Import Bank loan Brazil $20 million to initiate the Volta Redonda complex.

---

[5] Forrest K. Davis and Ernest L. Lindley, *How War Came* (New York, 1942), pp. 126–27.

Roosevelt used the Brazilian situation to illustrate the need for American businessmen to "learn more about South America" in a conference with business paper editors on January 12, 1940. Vargas had told him in 1936, said the President, that he wanted national ownership of Brazilian utilities. "He looked at me and said, 'What would the people of New York City do if the subways were all owned in Canada?' 'Oh,' I said, 'why there would be a revolution.' He said, 'Well, perhaps you can understand our feelings a little bit.'" The President ended his comments by noting that the British were going to have to sell back many of the "tramways" and other utilities they owned, not only in Latin America but throughout the world, in order to finance the war. The United States should finance these transfers whenever and wherever possible: "I think it is rather an interesting thought on our foreign trade."[6]

In the months before Pearl Harbor, newly created inter-American financial and economic commissions laid plans not only for the combined war effort, but, through the office of Nelson Rockefeller, Roosevelt's newly appointed Coordinator of Inter-American Affairs, to realize the President's ideas and thereby "make permanent the cultural and commercial ties between the American Republics" resulting from the revised Good Neighbor policy and the war's new opportunities. The expectation that war's end would see a vast expansion of American government-financed projects in Latin America proved unwarranted, however, as Rockefeller stressed the primary postwar development role of "individual and private groups throughout the Americas."[7]

At Sea in Asia

JAPANESE SPOKESMEN always insisted that their actions in China were modeled on the United States' Monroe Doctrine. Taking this claim at face value, Cordell Hull argued that Japanese leaders misunderstood that policy, especially since the advent of the Good Neighbor policy. Less than a week after the July 7, 1937, invasion of north China, Hull told the Japanese ambassador that advanced nations must accept "great responsibility for world leadership with a constructive program like the basic program proclaimed at Buenos Aires for the purpose of restoring and preserving stable conditions of business and of

---

6 Roosevelt papers, January 12, 1940, President's personal file no. 1–P.

7 See Lloyd Gardner, *Economic Aspects of New Deal Diplomacy* (Madison, Wis., 1964), p. 199f.

peace."[8] The Japanese replied that Asian conditions, as well as conditions throughout most of the world, were in no way comparable to those in the Western Hemisphere. There was a serious "Bolshevik" threat, for example, in the Far East. That was so, countered the Americans, but Japanese policy only encouraged the spread of lawlessness and disorder—preconditions for revolution and bolshevism. This dialogue, in various forms, continued right down to the eve of the Japanese attack on Pearl Harbor.

Early in October 1937, without consulting his advisers, Roosevelt publicly suggested quarantining certain areas to prevent an "epidemic of world lawlessness." Reporters covering his speech presumed that the President meant economic or military sanctions against Japan, but in his news conference immediately afterward Roosevelt refused to be drawn into a discussion of specifics. He would only say, "There are a lot of methods in the world that have never been tried yet."[9] On October 6 the League of Nations Assembly called for a meeting of the signatories of the Nine Power Treaty, along with other interested states (a euphemism for Russia), "to seek a method of putting an end to the Sino-Japanese conflict by agreement." In the "Quarantine Speech," as it was now already called, Roosevelt had concluded with the admonition "There must be positive endeavors to preserve peace." He saw the call for a Nine Power meeting as an opportunity to do something positive to restore healthy conditions to Asia.

As he worked out American policy for the Brussels Nine Power Conference with Chief Delegate Norman Davis, however, he discovered that the language of the Quarantine Speech itself had conveyed the impression of sanctions to both Americans and Europeans. Any plan advanced by the American delegation, therefore, had to overcome this ambiguity. The State Department worked out what it felt was a "constructive" proposal calling for new commitments from Japan, China, and the other powers. When it was reduced to its essentials, all it promised Japan was fair treatment in China on economic matters in return for military disengagement and a return to the framework of the Washington treaties. "All the economic provisions are in accord with our trade policy," noted its authors. "If accepted by Japan and the other Powers, it would give valuable impetus to the universal acceptance of this policy."[10]

---

[8] Department of State, *Peace and War: United States Foreign Policy, 1931–1941* (Washington, D.C., 1943), pp. 368–70.

[9] See Dorothy Borg's excellent account of the whole "Quarantine Speech" episode in *The United States and the Far Eastern Crisis of 1933–1938* (Cambridge, Mass., 1964), chap. 13.

[10] Memorandum of a conversation with Roosevelt, October 19, 1937, Norman Davis papers, Library of Congress.

When the conference opened, the other delegations still wanted to know what Roosevelt had meant in the Quarantine Speech. Japan's refusal to come to Brussels only added to speculation about possible sanctions and made the task of the American delegation, which had brought no such proposal, even more difficult. Russia's Maxim Litvinov did his best to channel discussions toward cooperative coercion against Japan. There were strong overtones in his presentation of Russia's desire for united action against Germany, which further confused the situation. Pushed by members of his own delegation, and himself unsure of Roosevelt's instructions, Davis submitted a plan for sanctions to the State Department. Washington's answer came back within forty-eight hours: None of the measures he had suggested were acceptable, nor was the United States in any position to participate in any joint effort to carry them out if proposed by another nation.

The Brussels Conference, concluded the American ambassador in Japan, had been a disaster. It had only convinced Japanese militarists that concerted action against their policies was not to be considered a serious threat.

The sinking of the U.S.S. *Panay*, a gunboat assigned to protect the Standard Oil Company's vessels on the Yangtze River, by Japanese planes touched off a brief war scare late in December 1937, and momentarily led Roosevelt to consider a unilateral quarantine of Japan, either by naval blockade in the mid-Pacific or by cutting off foreign exchange. Tokyo's prompt response

Sinking of U.S.S. Panay *on the Yangtze River*

to American demands for proper amends ended the scare, but Roosevelt had begun to encourage the Chinese government in its refusal to negotiate terms with Japan. "So far as an independent Chinese Republic goes," the President explained to Secretary Hull, "Japanese terms which we have seen are utterly impossible."[11]

Over the next several months, certain of the President's advisers, led by Secretary of the Treasury Morgenthau, urged him to accept responsibility for the survival of an "independent Chinese Republic" with more than words. Hull too thought the United States had arrived at "the Oriental crossroads of decision," but the Secretary refused to be pushed into provoking Japanese retaliation by approving a large loan to China. This left Morgenthau in a state of angry frustration. Roosevelt was not to be pushed, either, but he did approve of special new credits to China, extended under the guise of normal commercial transactions. The largest of these was a $25 million arrangement for the shipment of tung oil to the United States. Even these transactions were seen by some as gestures of defiance, not sound policy. They could worsen relations with Japan, yet could not affect the outcome in China.

In 1939 the internal conflict over the course to follow in Asia intensified. Those who desired stronger action against Japan asserted that the administration's "moral embargoes" on airplane parts and financial credits amounted to little more than polite wrist-slapping; those who argued for "moderation" protested each new pressure on Japan as misconceived and provocative. Congressional support for a firm line with Japan surfaced in a surprising place when "isolationist" Senator Arthur Vandenberg demanded abrogation of the 1911 Japanese-American commercial treaty. Hull had contemplated this step as a compromise between administration factions, believing it represented perhaps the last chance to convey America's determination to support the Open Door policy short of direct measures against Japan. Although he did not like the idea of seeming to respond to congressional rhetoric, since it made the decision not quite so much of a compromise, Hull announced that on July 26, 1939, the United States had given the Japanese government the required six months' notice that the treaty would be terminated.

Hull's middle-of-the-road tactics were pushed in the direction of the hard-liners by an event completely beyond his control: the outbreak of the European war on September 1, 1939. It encouraged them to press for a complete embargo against Japan. Though Roosevelt rejected that advice, the war obviously sharpened his interest in checking Japan's expansion. He instructed

---

[11] Elliott Roosevelt, ed., *F.D.R.: His Personal Letters, 1928–1945*, 2 vols. (New York, 1950), 2:741–42.

Morgenthau to "do everything we can that we can get away with" to help China economically.[12] Henceforth America's Far Eastern policy was closely tied to the progress of the war in Europe.

Munich and After

Press comments on the Quarantine Speech had given a somewhat misleading impression that the President was talking about immediate sanctions against Japan. One reason that Roosevelt tried to dispel that notion was that he had been groping for a way to expand America's "neutral" position to meet the European situation as well. Indeed, in the days following that speech the President gave much of his attention to a memorandum submitted by Under Secretary of State Sumner Welles proposing that he "inquire of the other governments of the world whether they will be willing to take part in a world conference" for the purpose of reexamining all the basic issues of the 1930s. After further discussions with Welles and other State Department officials, the President decided to specify the need for political adjustments to "remove those inequities which exist by reason of the nature of certain of the settlements reached at the termination of the Great War."[13]

Hull vehemently opposed the idea, which appeared to encourage British appeasement, and won the day. The Secretary's policy seemed to be aimed at bolstering others in the defense of international order while reserving American commitments to the last possible moment. As he once explained to former Secretary of State Henry L. Stimson, he had hoped to get twenty or thirty nations in line behind his trade agreement policies so as to force Germany back into international respectability. But he now had to admit that the domestic economic situation was so threatening that it was unlikely such an approach would have a chance to succeed.

The Munich crisis in September 1938 confirmed these impressions. Great Britain and France went into this conference unprepared physically or spiritually to resist Germany's demands for the dismemberment of Czechoslovakia. The result was foreordained, though Prime Minister Neville Chamberlain tried to make it seem that he and his French colleagues had recognized on their own the need to complete the destruction of the Versailles system to

---

12 William L. Neumann, *America Encounters Japan: From Perry to MacArthur* (Baltimore, 1963), p. 255.

13 Cited in William L. Langer and S. Everett Gleason, *The Challenge to Isolation* (New York, 1952), p. 23.

Neville Chamberlain and Axis leaders

assure Europe of "peace in our time." Ironically, the Munich crisis gave Hull his biggest prewar reciprocal trade treaty. Since 1933 he had been waiting for the right moment to press for an agreement with Great Britain, the kind of agreement that would lay the basis for a full-scale attack on the Ottawa Preference System. "When war was threatening and Germany was pounding at our gates," one of his aides told a British negotiator, "it seemed ... tragic that we had not been able to reach and sign an agreement."[14] As late as October 1938 the Foreign Office was still insisting that American terms would worsen the already "miserable" trade situation of the Empire, but political exigencies could no longer be ignored and the pact was signed.

Following Hitler's move to absorb the rest of Czechoslovakia in March 1939, the process of Anglo-American entente picked up speed. Roosevelt successfully urged Congress to repeal the arms embargo section of the most recent neutrality law and restore "cash and carry" provisions. From the Munich crisis through 1940 England and France spent more than $1.4 billion on American war materials. Believing themselves safeguarded by the neutrality acts, Americans rejoiced at the upturn in trade without much concern that they were being drawn into war once again.

---

[14] Memorandum by the Assistant Secretary of State, September 9, 1938, in *Foreign Relations, 1938*, 2:53–55.

More and more the public debate on foreign policy centered narrowly on Roosevelt's conduct of the nation's affairs and less and less on calculations of real national interest, a development made inevitable by the 1940 presidential campaign. Nevertheless, the statements of the America First Committee and the Committee to Defend America by Aiding the Allies suggested that the underlying issues most troubling to Americans, isolationists and interventionists alike, were (1) the effect of an Axis victory on America's ability to determine its future options, and (2) the dangers to social and political institutions inherent in full-scale mobilization. In other words, could America adjust to a Europe organized by Hitler and Stalin, a possibility raised by the Nazi-Soviet pact of August 1939, and still preserve a liberal capitalist democracy? Or would the effort to prevent a totalitarian victory only produce a fascist or communist government at home? No one had a foolproof answer to these questions; most tried to escape confronting them head-on, a choice aided and abetted by the rhetoric of political campaigning.

Hands Across the Sea: The Destroyer-Base Deal and Lend-Lease

FRANCE FELL in six weeks. Predictions of the time it would take for Germany to defeat Britain ranged from six weeks more to an indefinite number of years. Some said the war would end not with the occupation of Great Britain but with the establishment of a government of British Fascists who would cooperate fully with Hitler. Either prospect deeply disturbed Roosevelt and his advisers. Congress voted $18 billion for military preparedness, but it hedged on other questions of equal importance for national defense. This situation left Roosevelt with the responsibility (others said opportunity) of making foreign policy by executive agreement. No previous President, moreover, had centralized power in the executive so strongly as Roosevelt, who had declared in his 1933 inaugural address that he would ask Congress for "broad executive power to wage a war against the emergency as great as the power that would be given me if we were in fact invaded by a foreign foe."

By adding Henry L. Stimson and Frank Knox, leading Republican interventionists, to the Cabinet in June 1940, thus creating a national unity government like those established in Great Britain during both wars, the President had sought to increase the power and public support of the executive still further. Without doubt the most important step taken by Roosevelt that summer was the September 3 executive agreement transferring some fifty World War I destroyers from the United States Navy to the British fleet in exchange for ninety-nine-year leases on bases in the British West Indies. When Roosevelt told Congress of the agreement, he asserted: "This is not inconsistent in any sense with our status of peace. Still less is it a threat against any nation. It is an epochal and far-reaching act of preparation for continental defense in the face of grave danger." Prime Minister Winston S. Churchill, who had initiated the destroyer-bases deal upon taking office the previous May, was more candid in his memoirs, pointing out that it

> was a decidedly unneutral act by the United States. It would, according to all the standards of history, have justified the German Government in declaring war.... And it was the first of a long succession of increasingly unneutral acts in the Atlantic which were of utmost service to us.[15]

Neither Roosevelt nor Churchill thought that Hitler would take up the gauntlet; and the President did have increasing support in Congress for a policy of all-out aid short of actual war. On the other hand, his repeated insistence that such acts were "defensive" or "not inconsistent with our status of peace" troubled even interventionists. Roosevelt and Republican candidate Wendell Willkie promised the same thing: aid to the Allies but no declaration of war. "I have said this before," Roosevelt declared at the height of the campaign, "but I shall say it again and again and again: Your boys are not going to be sent into any foreign wars."

The election over, Roosevelt moved swiftly to formulate a plan for making American arms available on credit to the Allies. On November 9, 1940, the President announced a rule of thumb for the division of the nation's arms output, fifty-fifty between United States forces and British and Canadian forces. But the question of how the British would pay for their share had yet to be solved. Seeking to "eliminate the dollar sign," as well as another war-debt tangle, the President came up with the notion of lend-lease. This proposal obviously required congressional approval beforehand, so there was to be something like a national debate on foreign policy after all. Antiadministration forces fully recognized that here was their last chance to check the President's supporters. The vote on H.R. 1776, introduced as "An Act Further to Promote the Defense of the United States," was passed 317 to 71 in the House and 60 to 31 in the Senate.

Although many Americans still liked to think that the bill passed by Congress on March 11, 1941, protected them from "foreign wars," a belief

---

[15] Winston S. Churchill, *Their Finest Hour* (Boston, 1949), pp. 404–405.

the administration had not tried to discourage, some presidential advisers hoped Roosevelt would drop the pretenses he had found necessary in the past and candidly inform the nation it must now prepare for war. Congress, said Secretary of War Stimson, "has declared war to this extent at least." Stimson had even told senators in an off-the-record conference that lend-lease would allow the United States to coordinate and *control* Allied war policy. It would supply a bond between the Allies as they neared the war's end.

Secretary Hull was also thinking about the postwar world, and the use to which lend-lease could be put as a means of establishing the multilateral trade liberalism he had failed to establish in the 1930s. It would all be different then, but these were matters to be mulled over in the future. Right now the first challenge was the organizing of an Allied victory.

Roosevelt may even have clung to the illusion that America's contribution would consist of maintaining the "arsenal of democracy" and supplying naval and air power if the United States did declare war. The President had called for the production of 50,000 war planes, and Churchill encouraged him to think in these terms. "He looks forward with our help to mastery in the air," observed the President's closest adviser after talking with the Prime Minister, "and then Germany with all her armies will be finished. He believes that this war will never see great forces massed against one another." Emboldened by Congress' action, Roosevelt extended American patrols far outside territorial waters, on the dubious grounds that by passing the Lend-Lease Act, the legislators had intended to ensure the safe delivery of munitions to England. Then he defended the occupation of Greenland in April 1941 as within "the area of the Monroe Doctrine." He sent American soldiers to relieve British forces in Iceland, justifying the action by the supposed need to make sure that "such outposts in our defense-frontier remain in friendly hands."

Stimson, for one, was increasingly worried by the President's "rather disingenuous attitude" and rationalizations. But each step of the way, Roosevelt convinced himself he was acting under the broad mandate of congressional intention—even if he did not always tell Congress what he was doing. He did not tell it or the American people, for instance, that he was using the navy patrols to report the presence of German submarines to the British fleet. And when the inevitable "incident" took place—a submarine attack on the U.S. destroyer *Greer* on September 4, 1941—he insisted publicly that it had been "proceeding on a legitimate mission," and used the affair as an excuse to expand the patrols. Henceforth, he declared, American ships would shoot on sight any German or Italian vessels that entered waters "the protection of which is necessary for American defense." How was such an area to be defined? It was "the vast expanse of the Atlantic Ocean" wherever American patrols were operating.[16] Precedents were being set; and when they came home to roost years later, the shock would shake the nation's institutions to their foundations.

Roosevelt gambled that the end would justify the means: should the Germans avoid American patrols, lend-lease supplies would get through to England; should they decide to accept the challenge, the attacks would bring America into the war on the administration's terms. Roosevelt cemented his "common law" alliance with Great Britain at the August 1941 Atlantic Conference, at which he and Prime Minister Churchill drew up a preliminary statement of war aims.

Atlantic Conference: Roosevelt and Churchill

The Atlantic Charter

THE IDEA of an Anglo-American policy statement had originated as the best way to counter rumors (and whatever substance there was) of a secret understanding between Churchill and Stalin to divide up postwar Europe. Turning

---

16 Off-the-record conference in Hull's office, March 7, 1941, in Henry L. Stimson papers, Yale University.

on his sometime ally, Hitler had attacked Russia on June 22, 1941. As soon as he heard the news, Prime Minister Churchill sent forth envoys to the Russian dictator to coordinate military plans, and, American observers feared, to pave the way for an early political understanding, lest the Soviet Union attempt to bargain with Germany as Lenin had done in 1918.

The prospect of trying to undo whatever Churchill might agree to in a moment of fear, or of facing another revelation of secret treaties at war's end, appalled Roosevelt's advisers. They suggested that the United States extend lend-lease to the Soviets and take immediate steps to forestall an Anglo-Russian political agreement. Consequently, the President urged the Prime Minister to issue a public statement making it clear "that no postwar commitments as to territories, populations or economies have been given." This correspondence led to the Atlantic Conference, where once again the President asked Churchill to draw up a statement of broad principles "which should guide our policies along the same road."

The Prime Minister produced a document for Roosevelt's approval on the following day, August 10, 1941. The President's advisers thought that it did not go nearly far enough in at least one particular, so they changed it to conform to their vision of the postwar economic world. When Churchill demurred, Roosevelt intervened to prevent an impasse, but not until he had lectured the Prime Minister on the economic issue, making it plain that the question would have to be faced sooner or later.

Though Secretary Hull, who had been left in Washington, was not entirely satisfied with the wording of the Atlantic Charter, Roosevelt had accomplished most of what he had set out to do. Point 3—"They respect the right of all peoples to choose the form of government under which they will live; and they wish to see sovereign rights and self-government restored to those who have been forcibly deprived of them"—certainly seemed to bar any arrangement between Britain and Russia that would substitute their own domination of Europe for Hitler's. The Atlantic Charter marked the beginning of wartime diplomacy and of the emergence of the United States as a political factor in the postwar settlement. Wilson had lost the peace in the neutrality period, thought Roosevelt and his advisers; this time they must not fail to convert their second chance into something worth the cost of the coming war.

Churchill had come to the conference seeking answers to more immediate problems: the American decision to freeze Japanese assets had brought the British up short. If Japan went to war, the Empire's lifelines would be cut, further jeopardizing the situation in the European theater. Churchill proposed a joint warning as the best means of restraining Tokyo, or, failing that, of assuring that the United States would go to war should the Japanese attack

Singapore or any other Empire strong point. Unable to give such a promise, Roosevelt said that he would formally warn the Japanese against any further encroachments. This "assurance" that the United States would look out for its own interests hardly sufficed as a substitute, at least so far as the British were concerned, but Roosevelt explained that the Japanese had presented their own proposals for a comprehensive settlement. Their terms were completely unacceptable, noted the Prime Minister in a message to his colleagues, but the President's idea was "to negotiate about these unacceptable conditions and thus procure a moratorium of, say, thirty days in which we may improve our position in the Singapore area and the Japanese will have to stand still."[17]

Japan Closes the Door

THE LAST ROUND of Japanese-American negotiations had begun on April 14, 1941, when Special Ambassador Kichisaburo Nomura came to Hull's apartment in the Wardman Park Hotel for the first of a prolonged series of discussions that continued until the very eve of the attack on Pearl Harbor. Proponents of an embargo on war materials still had not persuaded the President to drop the other shoe and cut off all supplies of aviation fuel and oil to the Japanese, but he had taken several steps to increase economic pressure on Japan during 1940.

Nomura and Kurusu arriving at Hull's residence

---

[17] Churchill to Anthony Eden, August 11, 1941, in Churchill, *The Grand Alliance* (Boston, 1950), p. 439.

As the moderates had predicted, Japanese policy-makers responded in two ways: first by taking advantage of the war in Europe to force French Indochina and the Netherlands East Indies to guarantee supplies of raw materials and oil, second by moving closer to Germany and Italy diplomatically. In September 1940 Roosevelt responded to a Japanese ultimatum on Indochina by cutting off American scrap iron and steel exports. It was Japan's turn to raise the stakes, which it did by joining the Axis Tripartite Pact on September 27, 1940. The pact committed Tokyo to come to its partners' aid if they should be "attacked" by a power not then in the European war. Suspecting as much, American policy-makers insisted that future negotiations with the Japanese depended on their renunciation of any such pledge.

Of equal importance, the Tripartite Pact had created a new framework for old disputes in Japanese-American relations. Previously it had been possible to go on thinking that at some time Japan's bluff would have to be called, but that since it was only a bluff, the Japanese would throw in their hand. Now that was all changed. When Nomura arrived in Washington, he was assured by Roosevelt that "there is plenty of room in the Pacific for everybody." Hull's statement of the American negotiating position, however, simply presented earlier principles as prerequisites to serious negotiations. In other words, there could be serious discussions only after the Japanese accepted American terms. Nomura restated his government's arguments. With negotiations at an impasse, Japanese leaders declared at a secret meeting on July 2, 1941, "We will not be deterred by the possibility of being involved in a war with England and America."

Three weeks later Ambassador Nomura informed Sumner Welles that Japan had concluded an agreement with Vichy France for the occupation of southern Indochina. Welles said this act rendered further conversations pointless, but Roosevelt overruled him and offered Nomura a "neutralized" Indochina with access to its raw materials as an alternative to Japan's military occupation of the colony. Continuation of Tokyo's move southward, he warned, threatened a general war in the Far East. No reply had been received from Nomura's superiors when the United States froze Japanese assets on July 26, 1941.

Upon Roosevelt's return from the Atlantic Conference with Churchill, Nomura presented Prime Minister Fuminaro Konoye's answer: a counter-proposal for a Pacific conference between the two of them. To Secretary Hull's chagrin, the President seemed taken with the idea. Hull's concern, of course, was that the President's Indochina plan and Konoye's suggestion that they sit down and talk it over might well remove the negotiations from the framework he had constructed at the outset of the talks, and, he insisted to Roosevelt, from principles established in the Open Door policy. As he told Secretary of War Stimson, he was afraid that the "President would commit himself to something." Consequently, he had insisted that there be no conference unless Japan agreed beforehand to evacuate China and refrain from attacking Siberia. Moreover, no promise made by the United States should become effective "until the evacuation had taken place." Roosevelt, reported Hull, "agreed to all of this."[18]

Once Roosevelt had "agreed to all of this," further negotiations with the Japanese were indeed pointless. Stimson wanted the State Department to stall the negotiations, however, "so as to be sure that Japan was put in the wrong and made the first bad move—overt move," and in order to "get that big stick in readiness." It was still hard for Roosevelt to believe that the Japanese would take the fatal plunge into war, although he wavered a bit (along with some State Department policy-makers) in November, when he considered offering Tokyo a six-month "truce" and the resumption of trade in certain items. "I reminded him," noted Stimson, "that it has always been our historic policy since the Washington Conference not to leave the Chinese and Japanese alone together, because the Japanese were always able to overslaugh the Chinese and the Chinese know it."[19]

As Stimson had predicted, the Chinese opposed the plan, as did the British (for somewhat different reasons), and the offer was never made. On November 25, 1941, the President met with the "War Cabinet." Hull reported the negotiations had come to an end and an attack was likely within the next few days. Then they discussed "the difficult proposition" that if it did come, "the question was how we should maneuver them into the position of firing the first shot without allowing too much danger to ourselves."[20] Certain historians later seized upon this statement in Henry L. Stimson's diary as proof that Roosevelt and his colleagues plotted to allow the attack on Pearl Harbor. A more plausible explanation was offered by Professor Richard N. Current, who pointed out that the discussion was concerned with a new thrust in the Japanese move southward. The problem was how to maneuver the situation so that an attack on British or Dutch possessions would unite the country behind a war policy.[21] In the event, the December 7, 1941, attack on the Pacific Fleet at Pearl Harbor

---

[18] Diary entry, October 6, 1941, in Stimson papers.

[19] Diary entry, November 6, 1941, in ibid.

[20] Diary entry, November 25, 1941, in ibid.

[21] Richard N. Current, *Secretary Stimson: A Study in Statecraft* (New Brunswick, N.J., 1954). Professor Current's interpretation may have some bearing on Stimson's instructions to the Western Defense Command on November 27, 1941: "Negotiations with Japan have been termi-

resolved the problem. "When the news first came that Japan had attacked us," Stimson wrote in his diary that night, "my first feeling was of relief that the indecision was over and that a crisis had come in a way which would unite all our people." On December 11, Germany and Italy solved another potential problem for American policy-makers by declaring war upon the United States.

Pearl Harbor on December 7, 1941

Suggestions for Further Reading

Cordell Hull's *Memoirs,* 2 vols. (New York, 1948), are filled with self-justifications, but they contain a wealth of material for the student and the historian. The standard scholarly interpretation of American policy before World War II is William L. Langer and S. Everett Gleason, *The Challenge to Isolation, 1937–1940* (New York, 1952), and *The Undeclared War, 1940–1941* (New York, 1953). A great many revisionist positions are put forth in Harry Elmer Barnes, ed.,

---

nated without agreement on disputed points. Japanese future action unpredictable but action possible any moment. If hostilities cannot, repeat cannot, be avoided, the United States desires that Japan commit the first overt act. This policy should not, repeat not, be construed as restricting you to a course of action that might jeopardize the successful defense of the Philippines. Prior to hostile Japanese action you are directed to take such reconnaissance and other measures as you deem necessary. Should hostilities occur you will carry out the tasks assigned in revised Rainbow Five which were delivered to you by General Brereton." Stimson may have hoped that Japanese attacking southward would encounter American reconnaissance and would then fire the first shot without endangering the bases in the Philippines.

Perpetual War for Perpetual Peace: A Critical Examination of the Foreign Policy of Franklin Delano Roosevelt and Its Aftermath (Caldwell, Idaho, 1953), but other books should be consulted on both sides of the question.

In a different category are studies by Paul Schroeder, *The Axis Alliance and Japanese-American Relations, 1941* (Ithaca, N.Y., 1958), and Richard N. Current, *Secretary Stimson: A Study in Statecraft* (New Brunswick, N.J., 1954). Neither establishment histories nor revisionist studies, these monographs are critical of American policy in insightful ways.

Herbert Feis, *The Road to Pearl Harbor: The Coming of the War Between the United States and Japan* (Princeton, N.J., 1950), and Arnold Offner, *America's Appeasement of Germany* (Cambridge, Mass., 1968), should be read carefully. There will never be agreement on Hitler's intentions toward the New World, but see James V. Compton, *The Swastika and the Eagle: Hitler, the United States, and the Origins of World War II* (Boston, 1967).

On Latin America see D. M. Dozer, *Are We Good Neighbors?* (Gainesville, Fla., 1961).

See also the general bibliography at the end of this volume.

CHAPTER 23

Big Three
Diplomacy
(1942–1945)

President Roosevelt relied on personal diplomacy during the war.
He was his own Secretary of State at Big Three summit conferences, which
irked Cordell Hull and emphasized differences between the White House
and the State Department on certain questions. But the President's aim was
not to outflank his postwar planners. Roosevelt was determined not to lose
the peace by repeating Wilson's fatal error; he would not allow himself to
be trapped in a situation where his options were limited and his initiatives
checked by preexisting secret treaties or understandings.

The Atlantic Charter was preventive diplomacy, and had to be followed
up with positive steps as soon as possible. Yet the President, often reflecting
national indecision, was himself ambiguous on key issues, a fact that helps to
explain why the wartime summit meetings never did resolve major political
problems.

Postwar economic planning, on the other hand, followed on a straight
line from the assumption that the United States would have primary responsibility for world recovery. Policy-makers interpreted that mandate to mean
the restoration and expansion of "an integrated and—as far as possible—

automatic world economy, largely free of interference by national governments...."[1] In other words, the United States would make use of its national power to reduce the power of state intervention in other national economies and its own. For this reason, Secretary Hull and his aides often carried the day in White House discussions on the postwar world by pointing out that arrangements that contradicted economic premises or jeopardized their operation endangered the reconstruction of a stable world order. How long had it taken the Great Depression to ruin the Versailles and Washington Treaty systems? Hull asked. The same fate was in store for any postwar political organization unless it was based on sound economic thinking.

The Continuing Challenge of Old World Diplomacy

DESPITE CHURCHILL's commitment to the Atlantic Charter, American policymakers feared that at some critical moment the British would backslide into a spheres-of-influence agreement with Russia. Indeed, the moment seemed to have arrived in the days just after Pearl Harbor, when Foreign Minister Anthony Eden traveled to Moscow in quest of a still uncompleted Anglo-Russian alliance against Nazi Germany. Stalin had made it plain that he expected Sir Anthony's concurrence on two points: the need for an understanding on postwar aims and plans for the organization of the peace (by which he meant recognition of Russia's frontiers as defined in the Nazi-Soviet pact), and the need for mutual military aid against Germany (by which he meant the opening of a second front in western Europe).

As Hull explained to Roosevelt, the State Department was fully aware of these demands, and had dispatched a protest to London on December 5, 1941—two days before the Japanese attack formally brought the United States into the war. The United States was firmly against submitting to any "arrangements which would make the Soviet Union the dominating power of Eastern Europe if not of the whole continent."[2] Sir Anthony's steadfast refusal to repudiate British pledges to the United States and to the principles of the Atlantic Charter was cheered in Washington, but in London Churchill's advisers still faced the horrifying possibility that Russia might yet seek a

---

[1] William Y. Elliott et al., *The Political Economy of American Foreign Policy* (New York, 1955), p. 206.

[2] Cordell Hull to Franklin D. Roosevelt, February 4, 1942, in *Foreign Relations, 1942*, 3:504–12.

separate peace with Germany once it had blunted the initial thrust of Hitler's armies. Roosevelt again urged the Prime Minister not to accede to Stalin's demands when they met in Washington at year's end for the first of their many wartime strategy conferences, warning him that to yield would only lead to new Russian demands for the eastern half of Poland.

In January and February of 1942 the British government was subjected to new military and political pressures, prompting the Prime Minister to cable Roosevelt to appeal this decision: "The Atlantic Charter ought not to be construed so as to deny to Russia the frontiers which she occupied when Germany attacked."[3] To a man, the President's close advisers insisted there must be no compromise, that America's response to Russian demands ought to be in the form of military and economic aid against Germany—a course of action that would have the added advantage of quickly bringing into play America's only effective levers against Old World diplomacy, its industrial power and technological advantages. The President therefore asked Stalin to send Foreign Minister V. M. Molotov to Washington to hear American proposals, proposals the British could not offer for a variety of reasons.

The Russian Foreign Minister met with Roosevelt and his military advisers on May 29 and 30 and June 1, 1942. The President had several far-reaching proposals to make in these conversations, but he emphasized at the outset that he was "glad that the frontier problem had not been mentioned" in the recently signed Anglo-Russian mutual assistance treaty. Molotov remarked dourly that his countrymen had very different views on that point, and came to the heart of the matter: Could the United States mount an early offensive operation that would force Hitler to pull approximately forty divisions from the eastern front? If so, he continued, Germany could be beaten within the year, or at least its ultimate defeat could be assured. Turning to Chief of Staff George C. Marshall, Roosevelt restated Molotov's question: Could a western front be opened in 1942? Marshall replied affirmatively. "The President," recorded the official minutes of the meeting, "then authorized Mr. Molotov to inform Mr. Stalin that we expect the formation of a second front this year."[4]

The Molotov-Roosevelt conversations produced evidence of Roosevelt's troubling ambiguity about the political structure of the postwar world. He spoke to the Foreign Minister about his plan for a wide-ranging Big Four

---

[3] Winston Churchill to Roosevelt, March 7, 1942, cited in Churchill, *The Hinge of Fate* (Boston, 1950), pp. 327–28.

[4] Robert Sherwood, *Roosevelt and Hopkins: An Intimate History* (New York, 1948), pp. 562–63.

trusteeship to manage the transition from war to peace, and to share a permanent "role as guarantors of eventual peace." Hull was always worried by such talk, which he believed promoted the very regionalism and spheres-of-influence policy that the President had ostensibly rejected in opting for second-front diplomacy. The Secretary tried to make Roosevelt see the possible contradiction in Big Four agreements and the principles of the Atlantic Charter. This was very touchy stuff, he insisted, and must be handled with care by American policy-makers. Roosevelt never completely resolved the problem, but his immediate concern was with British refusal to support a second front.

Churchill's seeming obstinacy infuriated Americans, who accused the British of wanting to duck the main fight so as to keep the Empire intact for the postwar world. The British counterproposal for an Anglo-American invasion of North Africa further angered some military planners, who wanted to chuck the Germany-first strategy and go after Japan. The so-called Torch operation did not appeal very much to Marshall and Roosevelt, either, but it seemed the only way to get American troops into a significant offensive operation before the end of the year.

Stalin reacted bitterly to the news, which Churchill had brought personally to Moscow, though he seemed somewhat mollified by the Prime Minister's explanations and his new promise that the British and Americans "were preparing for a very great operation in 1943."[5] Roosevelt had written, "We are coming as quickly and as strongly to your assistance as we possibly can and I hope that you will believe me when I tell you this."[6] At the conclusion of the initial phase of the Torch operation, the President invited Stalin to join him and Churchill at Casablanca to plan the next move in the European theater. The Soviet leader replied that he was too busy with the crucial Battle of Stalingrad to take time out even for such an important conference.

Had Stalin come to Casablanca, he and Roosevelt might have carried the day against the British, who had come prepared to argue down all American proposals to concentrate Allied efforts on a cross-channel attack in favor of a Mediterranean campaign. On the last day of the conference, January 24, 1943, Roosevelt gave out his famous "unconditional surrender" statement to a startled group of newsmen who had not even known the two leaders were in Morocco.

---

[5] Churchill, *Hinge of Fate*, p. 430.

[6] Roosevelt to Joseph Stalin, August 19, 1942, in USSR Ministry of Foreign Affairs, *Correspondence Between the Chairman of the Council of Ministers of the USSR and the Presidents of the USA and the Prime Ministers of Great Britain During the Great Patriotic War of 1941–1945*, 2 vols. (Moscow, 1957), 2:33.

F.D.R. and Churchill with De Gaulle at Casablanca

The President apparently wanted to convey a public promise that there would be no negotiated peace in the west. It was another attempt to seize the initiative in Big Three diplomacy. But, grumbled American strategists, while Roosevelt had proposed, Churchill had disposed. The British plan for invading Sicily would tie up American armed forces in a traditional British sphere of influence for at least another year. No wonder, then, that Churchill also insisted that the summary of conference decisions sent to Stalin "should contain no promises."[7]

On the day Roosevelt arrived back in Washington from the conference, January 31, 1943, German Field Marshal von Paulus and sixteen of his generals, along with the remnants of a 300,000-man force, surrendered at Stalingrad. The turning point of the entire war had been reached, a fact at once recognized in London and Washington, as well as in Moscow. Henceforth the second front, whenever it materialized, would determine not which side would "win," but how long it would take—and where the Allies would meet in central Europe. This did not mean that Stalin ceased pressing for an early invasion, or that Churchill suddenly lost his doubts about a cross-channel attack. Diplomatically, however, the second front was of utmost importance to the United States, which had risked considerable prestige and staked its entrance into Anglo-Russian political negotiations on being able to bring off a

---

[7] Churchill, *Hinge of Fate*, p. 685.

successful invasion when it was still a life-and-death matter to the Soviets. In the post-Casablanca, post-Stalingrad world, "unconditional surrender" had become almost irrelevant and possibly even a barrier to the attainment of American war aims—the first of a series of unanticipated consequences of war-time diplomacy. With political and military strategy askew and badly in need of recalculation, the State Department continued to move ahead with plans to restore a "liberal" world economically.

"Article 7" Diplomacy

JUST BEFORE Foreign Minister Molotov arrived in Washington in May 1942, the State Department sent to the White House a memorandum on economic matters to be taken up with the Russians. It called Roosevelt's attention to the draft lend-lease agreement that had already been communicated to the Soviet ambassador. This draft, said Hull, was practically identical to the agreement signed with the British on February 23, 1942. The key to both agreements, from an American point of view, was that they laid down broad principles governing the ultimate settlement of lend-lease balances and that they contemplated that "compensation will, to a large extent, consist of cooperation in the attainment of the basic objectives in the economic field envisaged in the Atlantic Charter."[8]

Article 7 of the agreements stated that the signatory governments agreed to early consultations "with respect to basic commercial and economic policies to be pursued after the war." Harry Hopkins noted that Hull's memorandum had nothing to do with the war on the Russian front, although this was of considerable importance to the United States. It would mean "very little to the Russians unless we really mean business." Hopkins was right: Soviet coopera-tion in the restoration of a capitalist world order was hardly to be expected, except perhaps, and only perhaps, as part of a broad agreement on political goals that would permit the newly formed Grand Alliance to continue to grow in the postwar world. Hull's aides, on the other hand, hoped that Russia could be persuaded to cooperate with American plans by promises of economic aid for reconstruction purposes. Moreover, they thought it best to explore Russian thinking from the outset to see just how far Moscow would go along, or whether it would put up obstacles. And finally, the State Department needed

---

8 Hull to Roosevelt, April 29, 1942, in Franklin Delano Roosevelt papers, Franklin D. Roo-sevelt Library (Hyde Park, N.Y.), president's secretary's files.

a Russian signature on the master lend-lease agreement to forestall likely British objections that Article 7 was simply directed at destroying the Ottawa Preference System.

Ever since Churchill had entered a caveat at the Atlantic Charter meeting against American insistence on including a statement assuring equal access to the trade and raw materials of the world, the State Department had sought a way to commit the British to wartime negotiations to end economic preferences and discriminations. After several tries at meeting new British objections to the original draft of Article 7, Hull presented it to Churchill in December 1941, when he arrived in Washington for a conference on military strategy. The Prime Minister insisted that he could not consider it until he had had an opportunity to consult with the War Cabinet after returning to London.

State Department advisers thought their British counterparts did not believe Roosevelt was much interested in the matter, and asked the President to intervene, which he did in a letter disclaiming any intention to use lend-lease as a trading weapon against imperial preference. He only wanted to ensure, he said, that there would be "bold, forthright and comprehensive discussions."[9]

No one in Washington supposed that direct economic questions relating to the Russians were half as important as those relating to Great Britain, which had controlled 40 percent of the world's prewar trade through its domination of Empire outlets. Indirectly, however, negotiations and settlements with the Soviets were crucially important, as were those with China and other powers, in order to construct a true world order to replace the now defunct gold standard system, which had broken down in the Great Depression.

As soon as the British signed the lend-lease agreement, on February 23, 1942, the administration set its planning apparatus in motion. Formal negotiations with the British began in the summer of 1943 and continued through the spring of 1944. Responsibility for developing American proposals was shared by the State Department and the Treasury Department, which worked out detailed plans for an International Monetary Fund (IMF) and the International Bank for Reconstruction and Development (IBRD). The first was designed to restore currency convertability by means of a central clearing agency from which member nations could borrow needed currencies to pay for imports. The second was aimed at providing funds for reconstruction projects that required large capital sums, such as the rebuilding of roads and dams and the development of needed utilities and technical facilities. The IBRD, later known as the World Bank, was to be capitalized at $10 billion,

---

9 Cited in Sherwood, *Roosevelt and Hopkins,* p. 507.

and its loans were to be made strictly according to business principles. As the largest contributor to each institution, the United States pretty much had its way, first in negotiations with the British planners (who wanted to reserve greater freedom of national action for member countries) and then at the 1944 Bretton Woods Conference, where the proposals were formally presented to the signatories of the United Nations Declaration.

According to the American plans, prospective member countries were to adopt nondiscriminatory economic policies and conduct their international trade on the basis of capitalist principles. Provisions for state trading countries like the Soviet Union were written into the proposal, but it was clear that by virtue of the requirements for membership in the IMF and IBRD, these institutions would play a significant role in each member's national policies. A Treasury memorandum prepared for Roosevelt's information explained the objective American planners had in mind: "We in the United States believe that the greatest freedom should be given to our own businessmen engaged in international trade. But we know that this freedom will be meaningless unless other countries accord an equal measure of freedom to their businessmen."[10]

Delegates to Bretton Woods Conference

---

10 "The Bretton Woods Proposals," undated memorandum (1944) in Roosevelt papers, official file no. 5544.

The Bretton Woods proposals would supposedly ensure that other countries did allow their businessmen an equal measure of freedom. When the plans came before Congress, it was clear that not all American businessmen were grateful for more "freedoms" proposed by New Dealers; they had seen enough in the prewar days, going back to the NRA and the AAA. The new Secretary of State, former United States Steel executive Edward R. Stettinius, answered that objection in straighforward language: "Once in a while one of my business friends speaks to me of Government planning as if it were either ridiculous or dangerous. I reply that when I was in business planning was fundamental to successful management and I don't suppose things have changed since."[11]

Congressional approval in early 1945 set the economic foundations for the peace American leaders envisioned. Progress in this area had run far ahead of political planning, which depended upon so many variables not only in Europe but in Asia as well.

The Chinese Puzzle

JUST AFTER Molotov departed Washington in June 1942, Harry Hopkins wrote the American ambassador in Great Britain that the English-speaking powers could not organize the postwar world without bringing in the Russians as equal partners. "For that matter," he added, "if things go well with Chiang Kai-shek, I would surely include the Chinese too."[12] Whether or not things went well with Chiang Kai-shek, however, American postwar planning had to include the Chinese somewhere. At the beginning it was hoped that China would somehow replace Japan as the principal stabilizing power in Asia. Roosevelt had had these hopes in mind when he originated the Big Four concept in his discussions with the Russian Foreign Minister.

To that end the United States undertook a number of special steps to improve China's internal stability and world position, beginning with a $500 million currency stabilization loan and a treaty formally abrogating all remaining extraterritorial rights, claimed by the United States since the settlement of the Boxer Rebellion in 1901. China was also invited to sign major declarations on the postwar world as an equal with the other Big Three. Even

---

11 *Congressional Record*, 91, pt. 11:1656–58.
12 Sherwood, *Roosevelt and Hopkins*, p. 578.

if things did not work out well, noted the President and his advisers in conversations with British and Russian officials, it was better to have this nation of 400 million inside such agreements than as a potential disrupter of the new order.

Economic planners also regarded China as central to their schemes, whether or not the elusive Great China Market ever materialized for American exporters. If China adopted anything like the economic policies Japan had attempted to impose on Asia, the outlook for everyone else in the area, and ultimately the world, would be increased regimentation. If China's industrialization were carried out on a free enterprise basis, on the other hand, freedom would be expanded everywhere. "It would open up new outlets for the energies of man," said *Fortune* magazine, "and these would give to freedom an economic meaning that it has lacked for more than a decade."[13]

Roosevelt sent General Joseph Stilwell to the China theater to organize Chiang's military effort against the Japanese, but the dour Stilwell soon found himself at odds with the Generalissimo's officers, who were bent on conserving the strength of their armies for the war after the war against Mao Tse-tung's Communist People's Army. Stilwell even wanted to use Mao's troops in a combined effort against the Japanese invaders in Burma, a policy that made the British very nervous as well. Generally, the British (and the Russians) regarded Roosevelt's China policy and all that talk about the Big Four as the Great American Illusion; but they feared it was an illusion that could do them serious harm before the President was disabused. The effort to make China into a strong international power could have immediate effects on European colonies in Asia, already awakened to new nationalistic feelings by the humiliation of white nations by the Japanese in the first days of the war. The President's "suggestion" that Great Britain give Hong Kong back to the Chinese as part of his campaign to build up Chiang Kai-shek's government was an indication of what could happen if this madness went too far.

Moreover, Roosevelt was prepared to suggest to Chiang the possibility of Chinese participation in trusteeships over former French Indochina and Korea. When the President revealed these plans to Anthony Eden, the Foreign Minister remarked with traditional British understatement that he "did not much like the idea of the Chinese running up and down the Pacific."[14] Nor did the Russians especially relish Roosevelt's seeming insistence that the

---

[13] "The Time Is Now," *Fortune*, 24 (September 1941):42–43.

[14] Hopkins memorandum, cited in Sherwood, *Roosevelt and Hopkins*, p. 716.

Chinese be given a prominent place at the peace table. Both allies were more than half convinced that the American proposals for China in reality amounted to a scheme to secure another sure vote for its policies in the highest councils.

Chiang Kai-shek, meanwhile, anticipated that the United States would solve his internal problems with the Communists in the course of driving the Japanese out of Southeast Asia and China. He came to the November 1943 Cairo Conference with Roosevelt and Churchill hoping to secure their agreement to joint operations in Burma, then in north China and Manchuria. He also wanted a new billion-dollar loan and assurances of adequate supplies for the duration of the war. Though Churchill opposed a Burma campaign, especially one involving American-led Chinese troops, Roosevelt was determined to make the conference a success for the Generalissimo (and for his China policy), and forced the issue. The final communiqué of the Cairo Conference elevated Chiang's role to seeming equality with those of the Big Three, but Roosevelt himself reversed the decision for a Burma campaign less than two weeks later when Prime Minister Churchill refused to agree to "Overlord," the proposed invasion of northern France, unless the Burma operation were called off. The decision naturally embittered Chiang Kai-shek, who was not consulted on matters of grand strategy by the Big Three. Indeed, after the Cairo Conference the United States followed a more traditional China policy, a combination of friendly advice and stern instruction. First priority went to European issues.

The First Summit Conference

SPECULATIONS ABOUT future relations with the Soviet Union reached new highs in the weeks following the Battle of Stalingrad. As William Hardy McNeill, the author of one of the first, and still one of the best, studies of World War II diplomacy explained: "The earlier expectation of a settlement in which the Soviet Union would be no more than a passive partner to Britain and America, restored to pre-war boundaries by the victory of its Western Allies, became ludicrously inapplicable."[15] The President openly discussed the matter of Russian expansion not only with his close advisers and British officials, but with several guests in the White House. In all these discussions, Roosevelt made the point that certain areas in eastern Europe would inevitably come under Russian

---

[15] William Hardy McNeill, *America, Britain, and Russia: Their Cooperation and Conflict, 1941–1946* (New York, 1953), p. 221.

influence. The problem, as he saw it in 1943, was to devise a policy that would encourage the Soviet Union to participate in a postwar security system that would minimize both the geographical and the political extent of Russian hegemony in eastern Europe. The proper way to go about this, the President concluded, was to make no commitments on spheres of influence in the expectation that at war's end Russia could be made to see the advantages it would derive from cooperation with the West: a leading role in the general security system and large-scale economic aid for reconstruction purposes.

Of course, as Roosevelt told British Foreign Minister Eden, if the Soviet Union was out to communize Europe, there was little hope for any policy. Eden's reply summed up the situation perfectly. "Even if these fears were to prove correct," he said, "we should make the position no worse by trying to work with Russia and by assuming that Stalin meant what he said in the Anglo-Soviet Treaty."[16] Senator Arthur Vandenberg, who was later to play a leading role in the development of cold war policy, agreed, and added that an open break with Russia could very well cost Great Britain and the United States a million more casualties. Therefore, he said in his diary, he opposed the language of a congressional resolution barring governments that indulged in "territorial aggrandizement" from all postwar associations of nations:

> Suppose Mr. Stalin were to ask us if we considered his proposed retention of Latvia, Lithuania, Estonia, East Poland, Bessarabia, etc., to be "territorial aggrandizement." We would have to fish or cut bait. We should have to say "Yes"—which would certainly infuriate Moscow.... If we said "No"—we should deny the Atlantic Charter and infuriate tens of thousands of our own people.... *We must win the war first.*[17]

The likelihood of future conflicts with the Russians increasingly dominated policy-makers' thoughts. Roosevelt had to find out, as far as possible, just what Stalin did want. His dissolution of the Comintern encouraged those who hoped the Soviet Union would henceforth behave as a "traditional" nation-state, though Russia's foreign policy under the tsars was hardly the model that American planners had in mind. But what if Stalin *had* eliminated the Comintern? doubters argued. He hardly needed a formal organization, after all, to subvert capitalist governments.

"I want to explore his thinking as fully as possible concerning Russia's post-war hopes and ambitions," Roosevelt wrote Churchill in urging a Big

---

[16] Anthony Eden, *The Reckoning* (Boston, 1965), pp. 430–32.

[17] Arthur Vandenberg, *The Private Papers of Senator Vandenberg,* ed. Arthur Vandenberg, Jr. (Boston, 1952), p. 48.

Three meeting.[18] To get a face-to-face meeting, the President had to travel all the way to Teheran, Iran, the farthest the Soviet dictator would come to see his allies. At a private discussion with Stalin just before the opening session of the formal conference, Roosevelt affirmed that his main purpose was to make final plans for the long-delayed second front. Then he moved to a different subject altogether: the possible allocation of merchant ships from the American and British fleets for Soviet use after the war. Stalin took him up on this point, expressed a desire for expanded Russian-American relations, and suggested that if equipment were made available to his country, he could provide the United States in return with a plentiful supply of raw materials.

Throughout the conference Roosevelt avoided similar tête-à-têtes with Churchill in an obvious effort to convince Stalin that he wanted no part of an Anglo-American front against Russia. Once it had been decided that Overlord would be launched the following May or June, the Big Three explored in a preliminary way a wide range of other topics. The President, for example, talked about the possible dismemberment of Germany and the role of the United States, Britain, Russia, and France in the postwar world organization. He also raised the matter of Russia's interest in a warm-water port on the Pacific, possibly Dairen in Manchuria. The State Department, meanwhile, had been urging Roosevelt to modify his regionalistic emphasis in political planning. At Teheran the President did try to outline a future world organization more in line with Hull's thinking, yet retaining a special role for the Big Four.

Roosevelt came away from Teheran convinced that Stalin could be brought around, though nothing concrete beyond a commitment to Overlord had emerged from the four days of Big Three talks. He had had another private meeting with Stalin on the final day of the conference, December 1, 1943, and assured him that when the Red Army reoccupied the three Baltic countries, "he did not intend to go to war with the Soviet Union" over the point of their future independence. While domestic politics prevented his participation in any arrangement that Stalin and Churchill might work out on Poland's future, he would "like to see the Eastern border moved further to the west and the Western border moved even to the River Oder."[19] Early in the conference Stalin had stated his intention to join in the Pacific war against Japan once Hitler had been defeated. But even as the Big Three completed their first round of summitry, events only partly within their control were creating a different reality and a different set of options.

---

[18] Roosevelt to Churchill, June 28, 1943, in *Foreign Relations, The Conferences at Cairo and Teheran*, p. 11.

[19] Minutes of Roosevelt-Stalin meeting, in ibid., p. 594.

Year of Decision: 1944

FOR SOME TIME prior to the Teheran Conference, Stalin had complained that he had not been properly consulted during armistice negotiations with Italy or in the establishment of a provisional government under General Badoglio. He had even proposed a three-power commission to consider all questions concerning negotiations with governments dissociating themselves from Germany, like Italy, but also, presumably, those in eastern Europe such as Rumania, Hungary, and Bulgaria. In March 1944 the Soviet Union formally exchanged representatives with the Badoglio government, somewhat to the annoyance of British and American officials, who felt they had not been properly consulted by the Russians on this step.

Soviet representatives in Washington and London explained that their government had been in an unequal position in Italy, a situation now corrected by this step. But their explanation did not end there; it went on to describe the deterioration of the Badoglio regime and the existence of an anti-Fascist junta. Such a situation aided the enemy, and could be ended only if the two competitors joined forces. The Russian action, therefore, was intended to bring them together for the common good. The wording of the explanation concerned British and American officials, although they were far from certain as to its meaning. One interpretation, which gained widespread acceptance as the Red Army pursued the Germans into eastern Europe, posited that Moscow had recognized the Badoglio government and abandoned the Italian left in full expectation that the western allies would reciprocate when it came time to establish new regimes in Rumania and Hungary.

By the summer of 1944 British policy-makers were prepared, indeed anxious, to bargain for the best terms they could get, specifically a free hand to restore a pro-British monarchy in Greece and sustain a measure of influence in Yugoslavia. Churchill solicited Roosevelt's views but did so in the context of a warning that there was no margin for further delay. At Secretary Hull's urging, the President advised both Stalin and Churchill that any arrangement they might make could only be temporary, and would be subject to review at the next Big Three meeting. Roosevelt had pointed out to the Soviet Premier at Teheran that domestic politics would not permit him to participate in such diplomatic maneuvering, even if he wanted to do so. But the State Department's objections were on different grounds. Any concession to Old World spheres of influence would undermine the postwar political and economic systems then being developed even before they had had a chance to operate.

Similarly, Hull opposed the so-called Morgenthau Plan for the deindustrialization of postwar Germany. He was supported by Secretary of War Stimson, who warned Roosevelt that it was based upon a false assumption —that Great Britain's recovery depended upon its ability to recapture foreign markets lost to Germany. "This is an argument," said Stimson, "addressed to a shortsighted cupidity of the victors and the negation of all that Secretary Hull has been trying to accomplish since 1933."[20] Faced with conflicting opinions within his own circle of advisers, the President retreated from his provisional acceptance of something like the Morgenthau Plan, and held the German question in abeyance.

The number of issues demanding Big Three consideration was growing rapidly. Besides southeastern Europe and Germany, there was Poland. A Polish government in exile had existed in London since the early days of World War II. Its very vocal demands frayed the nerves of each of the Big Three; but Stalin made clear at every wartime conference and in private negotiations that he could not compromise with the so-called Curzon Line as the new boundary for *any* Polish government. Russia had been attacked twice through Poland; it must not happen again. Roosevelt and Churchill agreed—in principle—that both the boundary and the government of Poland must provide the Soviet Union with the sense of security that could come only from having a friendly nation as its neighbor. Not satisfied with these assurances or with the willingness of his allies to force these views on the London Poles, Stalin created his own Polish government in exile and granted it formal diplomatic recognition on January 1, 1945. Thus the stage was set for a showdown between rival security systems that might well open a fatal fissure in the Grand Alliance.

There were also Far Eastern matters pending. The President's military advisers still wanted Russian participation in the war against Japan, but the terms were yet to be agreed upon. Washington's frail hopes that Chiang Kai-shek would somehow resolve China's internal crisis dwindled away. If advancing Russian troops were to link up with Mao's forces somewhere in Manchuria or north China, the result might well be disastrous unless a prior political agreement had been reached between the Soviet Union and the Chinese Nationalists. Even then it would be a precarious situation at best. Hence Roosevelt sent Vice-President Henry Wallace to China in midsummer 1944 to try to persuade the Generalissimo to liberalize his government by taking in dissident factions, including Communists, and to settle all outstanding issues with the Soviet

---

[20] Henry L. Stimson to Roosevelt, September 15, 1944, in Henry L. Stimson papers, Yale University.

Union. The President even offered to "introduce" the contending parties to one another, since, explained Wallace, the Communists and the Nationalists "were all Chinese, they were basically friends."[21] The working premise of this policy was that Russian-style communism could come to China only through contacts with the Soviet Union. The Chinese Communists were widely assumed to be agrarian reformers, though they would certainly be susceptible to whatever influence predominated in postwar China.

Roosevelt's reelection in November presumably freed his hand for the arduous work of peacemaking; but the web of wartime diplomacy had become tangled in so many places that some advisers urged him to make a new start. Early in January 1945, Secretary of the Treasury Morgenthau proposed that the United States offer the Soviet Union a $10 billion credit. "If we were to come forward now and present to the Russians a concrete plan to aid them in the reconstruction period," said Morgenthau, "it would contribute a great deal towards ironing out many of the difficulties we have been having with respect to their problems and policies."[22] Meanwhile, in Moscow, Ambassador Averell Harriman had been presented with a request for a $6 billion credit by Foreign Minister Molotov. Harriman and other State Department officers argued that since economic aid for reconstruction was really the only lever available to American diplomats, it should be used as effectively as possible to obtain formal commitments from the Russians. Roosevelt told his advisers that nothing should be done until he had had a chance to talk with Stalin at the forthcoming Yalta Conference. The time for final decisions had arrived —or had it?

Postponement Triumphant: The Yalta Conference

ONCE AGAIN Roosevelt was obliged to travel great distances to see Joseph Stalin. Roosevelt's health was failing, many of his closest advisers were sick or absent, and the burdens of decision-making were approaching the unbearable. Stung by increasing criticism that the administration had yielded to British and Russian "imperialism" all along the line, the State Department had prepared a series of proposals designed to reinvigorate the Atlantic Char-

---

21 Notes by John Carter Vincent, June 21, 1944, in U.S. Department of State, *United States Relations with China: With Special Reference to the Period 1942–1949* (Washington, D.C., 1949), pp. 549–51.

22 Henry Morgenthau to Roosevelt, January 1, 1945, in *Foreign Relations, The Conferences at Malta and Yalta*, pp. 309–10.

Churchill, Roosevelt, and Stalin at Yalta Conference

ter, make it applicable to eastern Europe, and put its principles into almost immediate operation. These measures, the proposed Declaration of Liberated Europe and European High Commission, were to be put forward as stop-gaps until the new United Nations Organization could begin functioning.

Roosevelt presented the Declaration of Liberated Europe and urged its adoption by the Big Three, but he refused to push for the European High Commission, the machinery needed to make it more than yet another pious restatement of Allied war aims. On almost every issue at Yalta (February 4–11, 1945), the President backed away from final decisions. Nor did he offer new proposals, as he had done in 1942 when Molotov came to Washington for the first serious diplomatic exchange between the two countries. Although speculation that the United States would now set forth serious proposals concerning possible economic aid for Russian reconstruction had spread far beyond the confines of the State Department into usually well-informed journals, the records of the conference do not indicate that Roosevelt talked seriously with Stalin on the subject.

The outstanding exception to postponement was the Stalin-Roosevelt Far Eastern agreement. According to its terms, Russia was to come into the Pacific war not later than three months after Germany's defeat. In addition, the Soviet dictator agreed to negotiate a formal pact of friendship and alliance with Chiang Kai-shek, thus cutting off the Chinese Communists from Russian support—or so it was hoped. In return, it was agreed at Yalta that the status of Outer Mongolia, a Russian satellite, would remain unchanged; that the southern half of Sakalin Island and the Kurile Islands, north of Japan, would be returned to Russia; that the Manchurian port of Dairen would be internationalized and Port Arthur leased to the Soviets for a naval base; and that the Chinese Eastern Railroad and South Manchurian Railroad were to be operated jointly by Russia and China. The terms of this agreement were to be kept secret from Chiang Kai-shek for the time being, but they could not become operative until his approval had been obtained by Roosevelt. Postwar controversy about Big Three diplomacy at Yalta began with the revelation of the Far Eastern agreement in 1946—an ironic ending for Roosevelt's quite sincere efforts to uplift China.

The Polish problem—there were now two governments claiming to represent that country—occupied several plenary sessions, but the final Declaration on Poland, calling for the reorganization of Stalin's Polish provisional government "on a broader democratic basis," was so ambiguous that one American adviser declared, "This is so elastic that the Russians can stretch it all the way from Yalta to Washington without ever technically breaking it."[23] At the completion of the reorganization process the new government was to plan for free and democratic elections—a perfect solution in theory, but one unlikely ever to be realized.

When Stalin pressed for a decision on the dismemberment of Germany, the President noted that "the permanent treatment of Germany might grow out of the question of the zones of occupation," and referred the matter to the foreign ministers for further study. Stalin pressed even harder for a commitment on reparations; Roosevelt, much to Prime Minister Churchill's dismay, agreed that the figure of $20 billion, with half going to the Soviet Union, should be taken as a "basis for discussion" by the Allied Reparations Commission.

On board ship during the return trip from the Crimean Conference, the President related some of his difficulties in dealing with Churchill and Stalin to American newsmen. He discussed the colonial question and the Prime Minister's "Victorian" attitude toward anything that might conceivably touch on the preservation of the Empire. What he did not tell them was that Churchill's insistence on limiting every wartime declaration, from the Atlantic Charter to the Declaration on Liberated Europe, to a statement on European continental boundaries had seriously complicated the process of bargaining with the Soviet Union. And it worked both ways. Roosevelt could not award

---

23 William D. Leahy, *I Was There* (New York, 1950), p. 314.

Port Arthur to the Russian navy and then insist that Great Britain hand over Hong Kong to China. At the conclusion of his talk with the newsmen, Roosevelt commented, "The Atlantic Charter is a beautiful idea." But he did not finish the point: It could not be implemented without dividing the victorious allies.

In the weeks following the Yalta Conference, the Polish problem worsened, arguments developed over charges and and countercharges that each side was attempting to deal separately with the remnants of the Third Reich, and American policy-makers grew increasingly fearful that these issues would plague the San Francisco Conference on the organization of the United Nations, scheduled to begin on April 25, 1945. On April 5 the President held a news conference at Warm Springs, Georgia, where he had gone for a few days' rest before returning to the world's work. He was questioned about the Russian demand for three votes in the proposed United Nations General Assembly. "It is not really of great importance," he began. "It is an investigatory body only. I told [Secretary] Stettinius to forget it.... It is the little fellow who needs the vote in the Assembly. This business about the number of votes in the Assembly does not make a great deal of difference."

Roosevelt died a week later of a massive cerebral hemorrhage, unable to complete the business that he did think made a great deal of difference. The policy of postponement died with him.

Suggestions for Further Reading

Books on various aspects of wartime diplomacy have grown so numerous that any selection fails to do justice to areas and viewpoints. But it is best to begin with a book that describes what Roosevelt at least thought he was doing, Robert Sherwood's *Roosevelt and Hopkins: An Intimate History* (New York, 1948). This book is filled with primary material, some of it still unavailable elsewhere. An excellent survey, and a continuing source of others' opinions, is William Hardy McNeill, *America, Britain, and Russia: Their Cooperation and Conflict, 1941–1946* (New York, 1953).

Richard N. Gardner, *Sterling-Dollar Diplomacy* (Oxford, 1956), is indispensable for Anglo-American economic diplomacy. Winston Churchill's own story, his six-volume *Second World War* (Boston, 1948–1953), is similarly indispensable for Anglo-American political relations.

Of special interest on Germany is John M. Blum, *From the Morgenthau Diaries: Years of War, 1941–1945* (Boston, 1967). See Arthur Bliss Lane, *I Saw*

Poland Betrayed (Indianapolis, 1948), for one side of the story on Poland, and William L. Neumann, *After Victory: Churchill, Roosevelt, Stalin, and the Making of the Peace* (New York, 1967), for an account of the difficulties posed by Poland and all other issues. Diane Shaver Clemens, *Yalta* (New York, 1970), explores in depth the background and issues before the Big Three as the European war came to an end. For an unusually candid memoir on political aspects of strategic surrender, see Allen Dulles, *The Secret Surrender* (New York, 1966).

On the Far East see Tang Tsou, *America's Failure in China* (Chicago, 1963), and Herbert Feis, *China Tangle* (Princeton, N.J., 1953).

Of special interest is Gabriel Kolko, *The Politics of War* (New York, 1968), and Barbara Tuchman, *Stilwell and the American Experience in China* (New York, 1971).

See also the general bibliography at the end of this volume.

CHAPTER **24**

The Cold War Begins (1945–1952)

The San Francisco Conference on the organization of the United Nations (then called the United Nations Organization) revealed to the world that the victors were divided on several key issues concerning the peace. Up to that time Allied communiqués and Office of War Information press releases had satisfied all but the most skeptical that the Grand Alliance would surmount the problems of peace-making as it had the problems of coalition warfare. Among those most surprised that things were not as they had seemed was the new President, Harry S. Truman. His determination—bolstered by many of Roosevelt's wartime advisers—to prevent any deterioration of America's position vis-à vis the two allies during the critical weeks ahead, when he himself would still be learning the essentials of that position, accounted for the American delegation's willingness to debate the Polish issue publicly with the Russians. But Truman's "decisiveness" only speeded up the time of reckoning for each of the Big Three; it did not, just as Stalin's supposed paranoia did not, cause the cold war.

The 1945 Conferences

TRUMAN SENT Ambassador Averell Harriman to San Francisco to repeat to the American delegation what he had said in the White House concerning Russian ambitions:

> All men who have dealt with Russia know of the Russian attempt to chisel, by bluff, pressure, and other unscrupulous methods to get what they wish.... While we cannot go to war with Russia, we must do everything we can to maintain our position as strongly as possible in Eastern Europe. Russia is building a tier of friendly states there and our task is to make it difficult for her to do so, since to build one tier of states implies the possibility of further tiers, layer on layer.[1]

The issue was not just Poland, or even all of eastern Europe: that area was merely the present locus of the conflict.

Acting upon Harriman's advice, and with the concurrence of a majority of the War Cabinet, President Truman had made the Polish issue the subject of his first face-to-face meeting with Russian Foreign Minister Molotov two days before, on April 23, 1945. In blunt language he told Molotov that the Soviet government had not carried out the Yalta agreements on Poland, and that he expected Russian cooperation with American and British efforts to remedy the situation at San Francisco. Truman concluded his lecture with a reminder that President Roosevelt had made it plain in his last message to Stalin on April 1 that no policy, foreign or domestic, could succeed within the United States unless it had public support. "The President added that legislative appropriation was required for any economic measures in the foreign field and that he could not hope to get these measures through Congress unless there was public support for them."[2]

This oblique reference to all pending (and future) proposals concerning American economic aid for Russian reconstruction had been decided upon as the best strategy, at least for the moment, for employing that leverage to its best advantage. Since 1941 the United States had sent the Soviet Union more than $11 billion in lend-lease aid, with fewer strings attached than to the aid extended to any other ally. With a quarter of Russia's prewar capital equipment destroyed or otherwise not in use, American aid had played a significant part in Soviet victories on the eastern front. It was presumed that with the

---

[1] Minutes of the sixteenth meeting of the United States delegation, San Francisco, April 25, 1945, in *Foreign Relations, 1945*, 1:386–402.

[2] Memorandum of a conversation between Harry S. Truman and Vyacheslav Molotov by Charles E. Bohlen, April 23, 1945, in *Foreign Relations, 1945*, 5:256–58.

even more immense economic problems of reconstruction looming before him, Stalin would weigh Truman's warning carefully—unless, of course, the Russian dictator had something else in mind.

No agreement was reached at San Francisco on the composition of a Polish provisional government that could be admitted to the United Nations. In the weeks that followed, the President indicated a willingness to settle for less than he had demanded in his first interview with Molotov. He made it plain in a variety of ways, however, that the United States expected to have a voice in eastern European affairs, because those affairs could not be separated from larger issues at the peace table. America's public disapproval of Russian policy in Hungary, Rumania, and Bulgaria had been expressed in a non-recognition policy, which Truman reaffirmed at the Potsdam Conference at the end of July. Stalin countered with references to Western policy in Italy and Greece. "The Russians had no rights in Italy," he said. His representative "had never been on the Control Commission." Moreover, Stalin asserted, "there was a far less democratic government in Argentina which in spite of this had been admitted to the United Nations. If a government is not Fascist a government is democratic."[3]

Churchill, Truman, and Stalin at Potsdam Conference

---

[3] Llewellyn Thompson minutes of the Eighth Plenary Meeting, Potsdam Conference, July 24, 1945, in *Foreign Relations, Potsdam*, 2:357–68.

That definition failed to satisfy President Truman, who soon became impatient not only with Stalin's tactics, but with Britain's willingness to bargain at his level in order to protect its interests in the Mediterranean. Truman and the rest of the American delegation were convinced that a division of Europe into spheres of influence would produce economic and political conflicts in the Balkans, and sooner or later these would spread throughout Europe, ending in yet another world war involving the United States. The President introduced several proposals for the internationalization of European waterways, but these collided head-on with Russian demands for a share of control in the Dardanelles. Like Wilson and Roosevelt before him, Truman felt himself being dragged against his will into the tangled nets of Old World diplomacy.

American policy on German reparations at Postdam, on the other hand, actually promoted a division of central Europe into spheres of influence. Unable to arrive at a Big Three agreement on a dollar figure in post-Yalta reparations negotiations in Moscow, and increasingly disturbed at Russia's removal of capital equipment from East Germany, Secretary of State James F. Byrnes proposed that the Big Three take the bulk of their reparations from their respective occupation zones. When Molotov complained that the Soviet Union had a right to an equal share of the industrial properties in the Ruhr, located in the British zone, Byrnes offered not a dollar figure but 25 percent of all industrial plants finally declared available for reparations. In exchange, the Soviets were to supply certain raw materials from their zone to the three western zones. The outlook for an all-German agreement depended upon fulfillment of those conditions, a not very hopeful situation.

Enter the Bomb

THE BIG THREE adjourned the Berlin conference with an understanding that their foreign ministers would meet again at the end of three months to begin the actual work of drafting peace treaties. News of the first successful test of an atomic "device" had reached President Truman shortly after the Potsdam Conference began. Secretary of War Stimson noted that the President was "very greatly reinforced" by this report, which came as he was about to undertake his first (and last) venture in personal diplomacy. But aside from the boost it gave him personally, and the hope that American possession of this powerful new weapon might make Russia more manageable in Europe, there was no thought-out "atomic diplomacy" at Potsdam.

The "Bomb"

Not that American leaders recoiled from "peaceful" uses of the bomb, but it was as yet untested in wartime. After talking it over with Prime Minister Churchill, Truman decided to tell Stalin enough about the new weapon to protect himself against later charges by the Russians that military information had been kept from them. The real significance of Truman's attitude at Potsdam, therefore, was not that it was a break with past policies, but rather that it was a *continuation* of policies previously determined upon when development of the bomb began. The Grand Alliance had never been solid enough to permit open disclosure about work on the bomb to the Russians. And speculations by both American and British leaders about the postwar political effects of the bomb, if indeed it worked, had begun not in the weeks before Potsdam, but as early as 1942 and 1943.

It was Secretary of War Stimson who urged a break with past policies following the bombing of Hiroshima and Nagasaki and the Japanese surrender. Stimson feared that Byrnes and his aides in the State Department viewed the weapon "as a substantial offset to the growth of Russian influence on the continent." They "wished to have the implied threat of the bomb," he confided to his diary, to back them up at the forthcoming Foreign Ministers' Conference in London. It would be the worst kind of folly to go into the conference with that attitude, Stimson told the President. No progress would be made on any peace treaty, and the Russians could be expected to respond by going all-out to develop their own bomb.[4]

---

[4] See Henry L. Stimson and McGeorge Bundy, *On Active Duty in Peace and War* (New York, 1948), pp. 641–48.

Truman's Cabinet discussed Stimson's fears and his proposal to enter into direct negotiations with the Russians on sharing information on atomic energy and control of the bomb. But no decision was reached before the London Conference convened in mid-September. In some ways the London meeting was simply a rehash of the Potsdam arguments, with the Russians countering criticisms of the Rumanian and Bulgarian regimes with charges against British policy in Greece. Molotov also introduced complaints against American occupation policy in Japan. Byrnes met these charges indirectly by pressing for a broadening of the peacemaking process. "Our fight...for the right of the smaller states to participate in the peace," Byrnes wrote later, "won for us the good opinion of those states. And it forced the Soviets to begin to re-orient their policy."[5]

But it did not get the Soviets out of eastern Europe. The longer those countries remained under Russia's domination, thought Byrnes, the less likely it was that they would ever be able to participate in all aspects of the peace. Already the Russians had signed bilateral trade pacts with many of them, pacts that would discriminate against western trade and also, and more importantly, would form the nucleus of a future ruble bloc. Compared to the possibility that such a political-economic bloc might stimulate similar policies in western Europe and the British Empire, the loss of direct trade with eastern Europe was a minor matter. But the only way to combat the development of a bloc, said the State Department in a policy memorandum, was to make sure that the peace treaties with eastern European countries contained provisions securing "unconditional most-favored-nation treatment to the nationals, corporations and associations of each signatory Allied State," and that these provisions would "supersede any other treaties, agreements, or arrangements which are inconsistent" with such a clause.[6] That was a direct challenge to Russian hegemony.

At London, and later at the Moscow Foreign Ministers' Conference in December, Byrnes had hoped to persuade the Soviets to agree to a general peace conference where treaties following this guideline could be drafted. At Moscow he traded diplomatic recognition of less than satisfactory governments in Rumania and Bulgaria for a promise that such a conference could be held in 1946. The United States had already taken a similar gamble in recognizing the Hungarian government, and had been pleased with Soviet willingness to allow a noncommunist government to come to power. But the ability of that

---

[5] James F. Byrnes, *Speaking Frankly* (New York, 1947), pp. 102–105.
[6] Dean Acheson to Byrnes, September 18, 1945, in *Foreign Relations, 1945*, 2:236–38.

government, as indeed of all coalition governments in the area, to survive any serious East-West rupture was simply out of the question.

The Long Peace Conference, April–December 1946

As SPECIAL INDUCEMENTS to the Russians, Secretary Byrnes had proposed the possibility of a Big Four "security" treaty to prevent Germany from rearming and offered to discuss United Nations control of atomic energy. But the atmosphere surrounding the opening of peace negotiations in April 1946 was anything but conducive to Russian-American cooperation on any issue. In January, at the first session of the UN General Assembly, the United States and Great Britain had supported an Iranian complaint that the Soviets were seeking to establish a satellite regime in the northwestern region of Iran known as Azerbaijan. Britain and the United States had rival interests in present and future oil concessions in Iran and in other Middle Eastern matters. No doubt as eager to please the Shah as to thwart Russian aspirations, Washington took a very strong position on Azerbaijan. Then in March Winston Churchill delivered his famous "Iron Curtain" address at Fulton, Missouri, which celebrated America's atomic monopoly as a God-given agency to prevent the imposition of "Communist or neo-Fascist ... totalitarian systems upon the free democratic world" and drew a line from "Stettin in the Baltic to Trieste in the Adriatic" between the free and the unfree. To all this Stalin retorted with charges that the former Prime Minister had enunciated an Anglo-American "racial theory" reminiscent of Hitler's and that Churchill would like Hungary and Austria to be ruled again "by some king from the House of Habsburg."[7] Finally, and more serious than such rhetorical pyro-technics, Allied control councils in Berlin and Vienna had so far failed to agree upon unified economic policies in the zones controlled by the Allies. The situation in Germany was so bad that the American military commander, General Lucius Clay, wanted to halt reparations shipments until the Russians agreed upon all-zone economic centralization.

When Clay actually carried out this threat in May, a new phase in the struggle for control of Europe began. Writing later about the atmosphere as the Paris Peace Conference began, Byrnes admitted, "It is not surprising that Mr. Molotov regarded the American proposals to guarantee equality of oppor-

---

[7] Reprinted in Thomas G. Paterson, ed., *The Beginnings of the Cold War* (Boston, 1970), pp. 6–7.

tunity in economic affairs and free navigation on the Danube simply as additional efforts at imperial expansion and capitalist domination."[8] Nonetheless, Byrnes pushed ahead, confident that a decent respect for the opinions of the nations assembled at Paris would bring the Russians into line. Senator Tom Connally, one of the godfathers of the UN in Congress and a member of the American delegation at Paris, was somewhat troubled by the way things were working out. The UN's "original job," said Connally, "was not to *make* peace, but to preserve and extend peace after it has been re-established."[9] Others on the American delegation did not share Connally's doubts. Senator Arthur Vandenberg, for example, took a leading role in demanding that the "Conference . . . endorse the economic provisions of the Atlantic Charter, to which we have all subscribed, and . . . seek the adherence of Rumania [and other former enemy satellites] to the principles through the treaty provisions."[10]

Byrnes's efforts at Paris were interrupted by a surprising development in the United States. Former Vice-President Henry A. Wallace, now Secretary of Commerce, speaking at a political rally sponsored by liberal groups in Madison Square Garden on September 12, 1946, denounced the proponents of a get-tough-with-Russia policy. "The real peace treaty we now need," Wallace asserted, "is between the United States and Russia." Such a peace treaty, he continued, would have to be based on mutual respect for American political dominance in the Western Hemisphere and Russian hegemony in "their sphere of influence," eastern Europe. Wallace's speech was doubly distasteful to Byrnes and his aides: not only did it cast doubt on United States policies at Paris, but it was never to be admitted, even by implication, that the Monroe Doctrine area constituted anything like a "sphere of influence" in the European sense.

Truman quickly purged the heretical Wallace from his Cabinet, and the former Vice-President's supporters (who believed that he was FDR's rightful heir) banded together to form the Progressive party, which nominated Wallace on an anti–cold war platform in 1948. Russia's rejection of the "Baruch Plan" for the international control of atomic energy, on the other hand, seemed to prove the Progressives wrong in their estimate of Soviet intentions. Had the situation been reversed, with Russia holding the monopoly and proposing to share its control only after the completion of steps ensuring that the United States could not develop an independent atomic capacity, the reaction would no doubt have been different. The truth was, of course, that no plan had much

---

8 Byrnes, *Speaking Frankly,* p. 129.

9 *State Department Bulletin,* 15 (August 4, 1946):206–207.

10 Ibid. (October 20, 1946), p. 713.

chance of success until there was relative parity between the two superpowers, unless (as Stimson had insisted) there were prior Big Three accord on both political and military questions. But Byrnes's "public diplomacy" had gone much too far in the other direction for anyone to try to return to Roosevelt-style Big Three diplomacy. Even if the Secretary of State had wished to do so, political opposition in the United States would have blocked the attempt.

Yet despite these interruptions and reversals, the 1946 Paris Peace Conference was remarkably successful from the administration's point of view. Each of the proposed peace treaties contained nondiscrimination clauses, though qualified by an initial eighteen-month time limit. American policy-makers thought that was an adequate period to test Russian intentions and their own ability to restore the European and world economy. As it turned out, of course, they had overestimated western Europe's recovery ability and underestimated the impact of events in other areas of the world. "We cannot permit the door to be closed against our trade in eastern Europe," Henry Wallace had declared in Madison Square Garden, "any more than we can in China." But after the failure of General George C. Marshall's mission to China in 1947 and the inability of the British to contain the Communist threat in the Mediterranean, it was necessary to sacrifice whatever influence remained in eastern Europe in order to draw ideological boundaries around what remained of the "free world."

Five Decades of Frustration: General Marshall in China

THE YALTA Far Eastern agreement had been reconsidered several times in the weeks before Potsdam. But no matter how anxious American policy-makers were to keep the Russians from entering Manchuria in force, there was one political factor that precluded an attempt to abrogate the Yalta agreement. The situation inside China had so far deteriorated in 1944 and 1945 that it was essential to have as much outside support for Chiang Kai-shek as possible, and by the terms of the Yalta agreement, Stalin was pledged to negotiate a treaty of friendship and alliance with the Chinese government. If Russian occupation of Manchuria was to be forestalled, it must be done by ending the Pacific war quickly.

The atomic bombs dropped on Hiroshima and Nagasaki did bring a

Area hit by atomic bomb

speedy end to the war with Japan, but not before the Red Army had swept into Manchuria. Hence a Sino-Russian treaty became all the more important. When the treaty was signed, there was general relief that at least the United States had gained a breathing spell in which to prevent the outbreak of full-scale civil war in China. This mission was assigned to General George C. Marshall, the architect of the Normandy invasion and victory on the western front. His experience with coalition warfare, however, in no way prepared him for what awaited him in China.

As American policy-makers viewed the situation in the fall of 1945, there was no viable alternative to such a mission. "You are quite right that we are surrounded by a sea of international troubles," wrote one of Byrnes's top aides to a friend. "If we start cleaning up China by force we might just as well make up our minds to police the world."[11] Marshall was instructed to speak to Chiang with the "utmost frankness," particularly in regard to economic and military assistance. He was to say that "a China disunited and torn by civil strife could not be considered realistically as a proper place for American assistance."[12] Chiang would simply have to understand that he must broaden

[11] Joseph Grew to Barrett Wendell, November 16, 1945, in Joseph Grew papers, Harvard University.

[12] Truman to George C. Marshall, December 15, 1945, in U.S. Department of State, *United States Relations with China* (Washington, D.C., 1949), pp. 605–606.

Chiang Kai-shek

his government, even to include the Communists, provided that Mao agreed to abide by the rules laid down by General Marshall. After several weeks in China, Marshall reported that he was still not certain that Chiang understood what was expected of him.

He understood well enough, but the Generalissimo was somehow convinced that despite such warnings, in the end the Americans would put aside such minor complaints and reservations in order to achieve common goals. When, in other words, the inevitable military showdown came, the United States would support Chiang against Mao. Even so, Marshall managed to obtain a temporary truce between the contending forces which stipulated that the Chinese Nationalists would be allowed to move soldiers into Manchuria as the Russians withdrew. This uneasy peace was broken in April 1946 by the Communist attack on Changchun, thus bringing to an end the brief experiment in coalition government.

Mao Tse-tung

Despite further warnings that Chiang should seek to consolidate his position in China proper, the Generalissimo moved in force against Communist positions in Manchuria. A few early victories led him to boast that the Communist issue would be settled within six months to a year. He invited General Marshall to become his chief of staff and preside over the final strategy sessions leading to victory. Unpersuaded by Chiang's optimism, American policy-makers issued their final warnings that the United States would not become involved in a civil war and settled into a posture of watchful waiting. Marshall returned home in January 1947, blaming a "dominant group of reactionaries" in the Kuomintang and rigid doctrinaires among the Communists for the failure of his mission.

Developments in China soon prompted a reappraisal of General Douglas MacArthur's occupation policies in Japan. Since Japan's surrender the Pacific commander had enjoyed almost a free hand in initiating and administering whatever economic reforms he found necessary to supplement his efforts to democratize Japan. Japan's economy had not responded by mid-1947, however, and with China in the throes of an increasingly hopeless struggle, Washington became concerned about the situation. A parade of economic experts visited MacArthur that summer, but none of their recommendations could have any effect until the administration settled upon a new policy for Japan. At a Cabinet meeting on November 7, 1947, Marshall, now Secretary of State, reviewed the "critical instability" in China and "stated that the objective of our policy from this point on would be the restoration of balance of power in both Europe and Asia and that all actions would be viewed in the light of this objective."[13]

Even the slightest indication that the United States was once more looking toward Japan to stabilize Asia alarmed Chinese leaders of all political viewpoints. Others were also worried. The British and Australians, noted Secretary of the Navy James V. Forrestal, were reportedly "becoming increasingly suspicious that the United States was interested in restoring Japan to economic soundness in order to have her as a bulwark against Russia."[14] Chiang's most vocal supporters in Congress, the so-called China lobby, approved of building bigger and better bulwarks against the Communists, but they resented the way the administration had written off China as a lost cause. They responded with a series of attacks on the Yalta Far Eastern agreement and Roosevelt's Russian policy in general. "How is it to be explained," wrote the Reverend William R. Johnson, a former missionary and a pro-Chiang publicist,

---

[13] James V. Forrestal, *The Forrestal Diaries*, ed. Walter Millis (New York, 1951), pp. 340–41.
[14] Ibid., p. 284.

that in the brief period of 15 months between the issuance of the Cairo Declaration on December 1, 1943 and the Yalta agreement of February 11, 1945, America's China Policy was completely reversed from that of the restoration and defense of China's territorial integrity to the surrender to Russia, in effect, of more than Japan had taken from China together with a pledge accepting for the United States the responsibility of forcing China to deliver all that was promised?[15]

It was a sticky question, made all the more difficult by the developing cold war in Europe. Instead of facing it head-on, the administration sought to mollify critics by requesting Congress to provide Chiang with $570 million in economic aid. But the 1948 China Aid Act only sharpened the debate as the Nationalist armies continued to crumble before the Communist onslaught. The Generalissimo managed to escape from the mainland with several thousands of his soldiers to Taiwan, where he established a rump government in Taipei and another Chinese dilemma for American policy-makers. Even as Mao's armies began their final offensive, in April 1949, Congress was considering Senator Pat McCarran's new bill to provide $1.5 billion in economic, financial, and military aid to the Nationalist regime by means of a loan secured by Chinese customs. Oblivious of actual events in China, the Americans thus finished the Open Door policy as they had begun it—with yet another unrealized scheme to stabilize Chinese nationalism.

The "loss" of China had an immediate impact on both domestic and foreign policy. A young Massachusetts congressman attacked his own party's Far Eastern record since 1945 with the charge:

> The continued insistence that aid would not be forthcoming unless a coalition government with the Communists was formed, was a crippling blow to the National Government. . . . This is the tragic story of China whose freedom we once fought to preserve. What our young men had saved our diplomats and our President have frittered away.[16]

Representative John F. Kennedy's complaint, like that of the more committed regular China lobby spokesmen, included the charge that the China Aid Act of 1948 was "only a fraction of what we were sending to Europe" through the Truman Doctrine and the Marshall Plan. Unlike many of the China lobbyists, however, Kennedy supported programs that the administration said were necessary to save Europe from communism.

---

[15] Reprinted in Ross Y. Koen, *The China Lobby in American Politics* (New York, 1960), p. 67.

[16] January 30, 1949.

"Containment" as a World View

THE THEORETICAL BASIS for those policies was formulated in an article, "The Sources of Soviet Conduct," which appeared in the July 1947 issue of *Foreign Affairs Quarterly*. Its author had not permitted his name to be used, so the article was signed only by an "X." This strange procedure was assumed to be designed to protect some career diplomat, but later another explanation emerged:

> Since this article represented the newly formulated position of the United States Government, it would have been self-defeating to put it forward simply as the thought of one man, even if the discipline of the career service had not limited the public expression of personal views by its members.[17]

Nor was the author's identity a very well-guarded secret; he was soon revealed by Washington newsmen to be George Frost Kennan, the recently appointed head of Secretary of State Marshall's policy planning staff.

Kennan, who had been trained as a Russian expert in the 1920s and had served in the Moscow embassy in the 1930s and again as Ambassador Harriman's chargé d'affaires, had first put together a comprehensive explanation of Russia's postwar behavior in a famous "long telegram" he had sent to Washington in January 1946. That message was widely discussed inside the administration; it so impressed Navy Secretary Forrestal, for example, that he had the career diplomat recalled from Moscow and installed as the leading foreign policy expert at the new National War College. The "Mr. X" article, a revised version of that earlier analysis, made both the author and his recommendations for countering the Russian threat, the so-called containment policy, known throughout the country.

Briefly, Kennan suggested that the origins of current Russian foreign policy could be found in an ideology inherited from the old Bolsheviks, combined with the circumstances of the dictatorial power exercised by the Soviet leaders for the past three decades. During all those years Russian foreign policy was apparently little affected by external circumstances. This was a crucial point in the author's thesis. Since the war's end, Soviet policy had been moving like "a fluid stream" toward a general goal:

> Its main concern is to make sure that it has filled every nook and cranny available to it in the basin of world power. But if it finds unassailable barriers in its path, it accepts these philosophically and accommodates itself to them. The main thing is that there should always be pressure, increasing constant pressure, toward the desired goal.

---

[17] Louis Halle, *The Cold War as History* (New York, 1967), p. 106.

This was "basic to the internal nature of Soviet power," and would be so "until the internal nature of Soviet power is changed." But if the United States responded by a "long-term, patient but firm and vigilant containment of Russian expansive tendencies," managed without "threats or blustering," it could not only turn back the threat, but in so doing "promote tendencies which must eventually find their outlet in either the breakup or the gradual mellowing of Soviet power."

Truman addressing Congress

Although first published in July 1947, Kennan's article had been written before President Truman asked Congress on March 12 to appropriate $400 million for Greece and Turkey in order to "support free peoples who are resisting attempted subjugation by armed minorities or by outside pressures." Indeed, Kennan later revealed that he thought the Truman Doctrine, with its ringing declaration that at "the present moment in world history nearly every nation must choose between alternative ways of life," an inappropriate application of "containment," both in theory and in practice. In Greece, civil war had raged since the British had sought to restore the monarchy in 1945; so far as Turkey was concerned, Kennan believed that the government could stand up to Russian demands for territorial revisions and joint control of the Black Sea Straits without American military aid. Congressional conservatives like Senator Robert A. Taft and Virginia's Harry Byrd objected on somewhat similar grounds. "I cannot escape the conclusion," Byrd declared, "that the effort to dramatize this as an imminent crisis has been over-emphasized and exaggerated." No doubt Russian policy was every bit as unscrupulous as the administration said it was, but "if we act independently and arm nations to oppose communism, can we assume that Russia will not follow our lead and establish a counterpolicy?"[18]

Truman had been advised by other congressional leaders that he would have to "scare hell" out of Congress and the American people if he expected to get the money to help the Greek and Turkish governments. A week before, in a speech at Baylor University, Truman had pointed out that political and economic questions were "indivisible." A resurgence of protectionism in the United States, the President warned his audience, would have a disastrous effect on the economic policies of some other nations, pushing them away from free enterprise and toward state control. Much of the world was headed toward regimentation, economic and political. If that trend were not reversed, the government of the United States would be under pressure to use "these same devices to fight for markets and for raw materials."

"When the process of reconversion at home is completed," Under Secretary of State Dean Acheson added a few weeks later, "we are going to find ourselves far more dependent upon exports than before the war to maintain levels of business activity to which our economy has become accustomed." We would therefore have to "concentrate our emergency assistance in areas where it will be most effective in building world political and economic stability, in promoting human freedom and democratic institutions, in fostering liberal trading policies, and in strengthening the authority of the United Nations." And the President's Committee on Foreign Aid, headed by Averell Harriman, tied up the remaining loose ends:

> The deterioration of the European economy ... would force European countries to resort to trade by government monopoly—not only for economic but for political ends. The United States would almost inevitably have to follow suit. The resulting system of state controls, at first relating to foreign trade, would soon have to be extended into the domestic economy to an extent that would endanger the survival of the American system of free enterprise....

Doubts remained, nonetheless, about the administration's unilateral response to the Greek-Turkish crisis, with only an afterthought to the propriety of going ahead without United Nations sanction and support. The reason was obvious, of course: fear that Russia would block American policy. But the blocking of U.S. policy was not the sole consideration. If the Soviets had vetoed the American plan, the United States would have found itself in the position of

18 *Congressional Record*, April 22, 1947, p. 3889.

having to defy the Russians directly, and perhaps making the crisis greater than it was.

Ironically, the "X" article helped to resolve doubts about the administration's unilateral action, as well as to silence liberal criticisms that the Greek and Turkish governments were undemocratic and did not represent the will of the people. By portraying the Russian-American conflict as an ideological struggle without geographical or political boundaries, Kennan appeared to be justifying the very rhetoric he privately deplored. The final sentences of the "X" article, for example, fitted perfectly with the message of the Truman Doctrine:

> The thoughtful observer of Russian-American relations will find no cause for complaint in the Kremlin's challenge to American society. He will rather experience a certain gratitude to Providence which, by providing the American people with this implacable challenge, has made their entire security as a nation dependent on their pulling themselves together and accepting the responsibilities of moral and political leadership that history plainly intended them to bear.

The Marshall Plan was much more to Kennan's liking. Developed in high-level State Department planning sessions, the plan was unveiled in Secretary Marshall's commencement speech at Harvard University on June 5, 1947. The Secretary of State proposed that the nations of Europe—including the Soviet Union if it agreed to the ground rules—get together and work out a reasonable plan for recovery and reconstruction. Once the Europeans agreed among themselves on what needed to be done and what each could do, the United States would provide large-scale economic assistance to ensure the success of their efforts. The Marshall Plan eventually supplied western European nations with something over $17 billion, and with doubt marked the turning point in the recovery of postwar Europe. But it had other consequences for Europe's political development. Even without the gloss of Truman Doctrine rhetoric, the plan's anticommunist emphasis was plain enough, and it significantly aided some conservative governments against leftist opposition and modified socialist experimentation in other countries. The Russians, as expected, refused to open their economic records to public scrutiny or to stipulate certain quotas of raw materials for the West as their membership and initiation fee. When the Soviets stalked out of the preliminary planning conference, Czechoslovakia, which had been seeking a neutral role for itself, also left, further completing the division of Europe. Russian objections to the Marshall Plan had another, more elementary source: Washington's determination to include the western zones of Germany in the program. "We must," Under Secretary of State Dean Acheson had recently declared, "push ahead with the reconstruction of those two great workshops of Europe and Asia—Germany and Japan—upon which the ultimate recovery of the continents so largely depends."[19]

Berlin Blockade

THE FIRST ANNOUNCEMENT of the Marshall Plan had come only a few weeks after the Big Four foreign ministers had failed once again to agree on a method of reuniting Germany. In September 1946 the United States and Great Britain had merged their zones into a single economic unit, "Bizonia," and urged the French to make it "Trizonia." At the March–April 1947 Moscow Foreign Ministers' Conference, the Russians proposed immediate steps toward the formation of a strong central government for Germany, but they insisted on making that government responsible for renewed reparations shipments out of current production. The American delegation, to which this demand was unacceptable in any form, suspected that Stalin felt the time had come for such a move because under current circumstances it would have delivered both parts of Germany to Communist control.

The Marshall Plan signaled to the Russians that the United States was not going to negotiate about any issue, let alone one as important as Germany's future, until European recovery was assured. And since the integration of German resources was regarded as essential to European recovery, it was obvious that the West intended to develop and exploit the status quo. For the record, the United States agreed to meet with the Russians in one final Big Four attempt to negotiate reunification at London in late fall 1947. That conference fell apart without even the usual promise to try again. But the United States delegation made good use of the breakdown to lay the foundations for its next move by releasing to the press Secretary Marshall's statements on Germany's future: "The United States Delegation considers that the establishment of a German Government is an urgent necessity.... More than two years ago Mr. Byrnes at Stuttgart declared that the United States favored the establishment of a Provisional Government for Germany." The absence of any reference to the Soviet Union in this and other statements on the establishment of a German government did not go unnoticed by the Russians, who promptly accused the Western powers of negotiating in bad faith. Congressional hearings in the United States, meanwhile, had already established the administration's intention to go ahead with a West German currency reform.

---

[19] In *America in the Cold War,* ed. Walter LaFeber (New York, 1969), pp. 56–60.

East-West tension in central Europe reached a high point early in 1948, when, following an argument over western plans for Germany, the Soviet representative on the Allied Control Council walked out of a regularly scheduled meeting, thereby bringing to an end any remaining pretense of Big Four cooperation. Eleven days later, on March 31, 1948, the Russians began obstructing surface traffic from the western zones into Berlin. In the first week of June, the United States, Britain, and France informed German leaders in their zones that they might begin working to establish a German federal republic. This announcement was followed by the actual implementation of a West German currency reform, at first limited to areas outside Berlin, but then extended to the western zones of the former capital, deep within the Soviet zone. The next day, June 24, the Russians imposed a full blockade against any traffic between the western zones and Berlin, itself divided into four occupation zones.

It lasted almost exactly one year. In that period the United States demonstrated its determination and ability to maintain its key position far behind the Iron Curtain by making the fullest use of its technological capability in the Berlin airlift, which kept the city supplied with every necessity of life. This success in turn assured German confidence in Western support not only in Berlin, but for the Federal Republic, which came into being just a few weeks before the blockade was lifted in June 1949.

Airlift over blockaded Berlin

Against the background of the blockade, which had stirred great resentment and fear throughout Europe, the United States also pushed forward plans for the North Atlantic Treaty Organization, designed "to meet any attack from the East." On April 12, 1949, the United States and Great Britain jointly announced that they had agreed on the facilities to be made available in England for American atomic bombers. Plans for a radar warning net stretching for some nine hundred miles across Europe from north to south were also announced as evidence of the rapid progress that had already been made in preparing for the eventuality of an attack. Looking back on those critical months from a distance of twenty years, an American policy-maker wrote:

> The Alliance was not exclusively or even primarily [designed] to deter an impending or threatened Soviet military attack.... There was a deeper and more underlying motive than the fear of a direct invasion of the West.... [It was the] contrast between Soviet strength and purpose on the one hand and Western European weakness and lack of concentrated direction on the other which prompted the formation of a Western security system. The system was intended at a minimum, to offset, morally and physically, the overriding, and to put it mildly, unbenign influence from the east.[20]

Behind such a shield as NATO promised to provide, the "real threat of internal subversion" would disappear, to be replaced by a renewed sense of strength and purpose.

This testimony does not supersede earlier evidence concerning NATO's origins, but it does supplement it in ways that help to demonstrate the breadth of the containment world view, as understood and acted upon by American leaders. The lifting of the Berlin blockade, after the formation of the German Federal Republic and the signing of the NATO pact, was taken by some as evidence that Russia was ready to concede defeat in its efforts to take over West Germany and the continent. Whatever satisfaction Americans took from these developments was cut short by President Truman's statement on September 23: "We have evidence that within recent weeks an atomic explosion occurred in the U.S.S.R."

NSC-68 and Korea

THE PRESIDENT'S ANNOUNCEMENT was doubly shocking to the American public. Cold war military strategy had been formulated on the assumption that Amer-

---

[20] John J. McCloy, *The Atlantic Alliance: Its Origins and Future* (New York, 1969), pp. 22–26.

ica's atomic monopoly permitted it (1) to take certain risks, otherwise unacceptable, to preserve the peace and restore the world capitalist order, and (2) to devote the rest of the nation's energies to nonmilitary purposes. Congress was especially dedicated to these propositions. It refused the President's request for universal military training legislation in 1948 but appropriated large amounts for the Air Force. Even those who doubted congressional wisdom in these matters were no more prepared to call for full-scale mobilization early in the cold war. Thus Defense Secretary Forrestal testified on the 1949 defense budget, "It is not possible for us—at present, if ever—to maintain in peacetime anything approaching what might be called an adequate military establishment."[21]

Russia's development of an atomic bomb, years before the West had expected it could produce one, called for a new look at America's cold war strategy. "It seems to me," one of Truman's advisers wrote on October 5, 1949, "that the time has come for a quantum jump in our planning (to borrow a metaphor from our scientist friends)—that is to say, that we should now make an intensive effort to get ahead with the super."[22] There was no doubt in the President's mind that he should try to get ahead with the "super"— that is, the hydrogen bomb—but more than that was needed. A committee of top Defense and State Department officials reported to Truman that the most critical time would come around 1954, when it could be expected that the Russians would have attained something approximating atomic parity. But this estimate, contained in a document that was to become known as NSC-68 (National Security Council paper no. 68), was paired with a warning that the then existing balance of power would demand "virtual abandonment by the United States of trying to distinguish between national and global security." And the costs of a "global" security policy would run high, probably as much as $50 billion a year.

Marshall's successor, Dean Acheson, had meanwhile been preparing the nation for an era of protracted conflict in a series of speeches early in 1950. To the suggestion that Russia's acquisition of atomic weapons offered an opportunity to reexamine cold war issues, Acheson answered: "No good would come from our taking the initiative in calling for conversations at this point. ... The only way to deal with the Soviet Union, we have found from hard experience, is to create situations of strength." But eliminating weaknesses in

---

[21] Quoted in Warner Schilling, Thomas Y. Hammond, and Glen Snyder, *Strategy, Politics, and Defense Budgets* (New York, 1962), pp. 61–62.

[22] Lewis Strauss, *Men and Decisions* (New York, 1962), pp. 216–17.

the "free world" position was only the beginning: "The times call for a total diplomacy equal to the task of defense against Soviet expansion and to the task of building the kind of world in which our way of life can flourish."[23]

The phrase "total diplomacy" implied the primacy of foreign policy; but although Truman had directed his Secretary of State to make these speeches, his own actions still followed priorities set by a Congress oriented to domestic politics. Indeed, the President had just ordered Secretary of Defense Louis Johnson to halve the $30 billion defense budget recommended by the Joint Chiefs of Staff. Little wonder that Acheson said he sometimes felt like a man standing on a dock with an oar, trying to row the dock away. Then came the North Korean attack of June 24, 1950—and everything began to move.

The administration's critics later charged that Acheson had invited the attack in one of his speeches earlier that year when he had not included South Korea within a defense perimeter running from the Aleutians to Japan and south around the Philippines. It was also pointed out that he had excluded Taiwan and Chiang Kai-shek from American protection. Whether or not Acheson's speech precipitated the North Korean decision to strike at Syngman Rhee's government, the American decision to intervene on South Korea's behalf has raised other historical problems. Not all of the answers are clear yet.

Since 1945, when American and Russian occupation forces met at the thirty-eighth parallel, Korea had remained divided. Although the Big Three were pledged to a restoration of that unhappy country's independence, no agreement had been reached on how it could be accomplished. As a result, the occupiers had established semipermanent regimes after the pattern of other divisions caused by the cold war. But American policy-makers did not feel they had as large a stake in Syngman Rhee's continued survival as they had in those other situations. The Joint Chiefs, for example, had repeatedly warned against becoming "so irrevocably involved in the Korean situation that an action taken by any faction in Korea *or by any other power in Korea* could be considered a casus belli for the United States."[24] Similarly, when Defense Secretary Louis Johnson asked the Joint Chiefs about Taiwan's strategic importance in the fall of 1949, "they were of the opinion that they shouldn't even do the limited thing of sending a mission over to check into the... situation."[25]

23 Reprinted in *State Department Bulletin,* 22 (March 20, 1950):427–29, and Department of State, *Strengthening the Forces of Freedom* (Washington, D.C., 1950), pp. 21–28.

24 Cited in Matthew Ridgway, *The Korean War* (New York, 1967), p. 7.

25 U.S. Senate, 82nd Cong., 1st sess., Joint Committee on Armed Services and Foreign Relations, *Hearings: The Military Situation in the Far East* (Washington, D.C., 1951), p. 2577. Hereafter cited as *Hearings: Military Situation.*

The attack, which came after a series of military probes by both sides, occurred while Truman was at home in Independence, Missouri. By the time he had returned to Washington by airplane, and without seeing any intelligence reports on Russian intentions, he had decided that it demonstrated "beyond all doubt that communism has passed beyond the use of subversion to conquer independent nations and will now use armed invasion and war." In addition, he announced that he had interposed the Seventh Fleet between Taiwan and the Chinese mainland. Further light was shed on the President's decision when portions of a letter he had sent to former Secretary of State Henry L. Stimson on July 7, 1950, were published: "I remember very well your suggestions in the early thirties when Japan went into Manchuria. Had your suggestions been followed I rather think the second world war would not have come about. I was thinking of those things when the decision was made."[26]

To others in the administration, especially Secretary of State Acheson, the Korean situation provided a clear lesson for those who still held back from facing a new set of realities; for instance, the necessity of rearming Germany. American intervention was ratified after the fact by a United Nations resolution, passed in the temporary absence of the Russian delegate to the Security Council.

American and South Korean forces were pushed back to a small area around Pusan by the momentum of the initial North Korean thrust. The situation had yet to be stabilized even in that area when the American delegate to the Security Council, Warren R. Austin, called upon the United Nations to "see that the people of Korea attain complete individual and political freedom." "Shall only a part of the country be assured this freedom?" Austin asked. "I think not. . . . Korea's prospects would be dark if any action of the United Nations were to condemn it to exist indefinitely as 'half slave and half free,' or even one-third slave and two-thirds free."[27]

General Douglas MacArthur's brilliant amphibious landing at Inchon on September 15 gave some substance to this aspiration, especially when his forces in the south joined the counterattack and moved swiftly to the thirty-eighth parallel. MacArthur wanted to make a public announcement that he was crossing that symbolic barrier, but the administration informed him that it desired "to avoid having to make an issue of the thirty-eighth parallel until we have accomplished our mission."[28] In mid-October Truman and MacArthur met

---

[26] Truman to Stimson, July 7, 1950, in William Hillman, *Mr. President* (New York, 1952), p. 55.

[27] U.S. Mission to the United Nations, press release no. 930, August 17, 1950.

[28] Cited in John W. Spanier, *The Truman-MacArthur Controversy and the Korean War* (New York, 1965), p. 100.

on Midway Island to discuss the final phases of the Korean war; they even planned for postwar elections in North Korea as the best way to avoid anything that might "undermine the present Korean Government."[29] And MacArthur assured the President that the Chinese Communists would not intervene: There would be military victory in Korea, and for the first time a Communist capital would be liberated!

When they were questioned later about the massive Chinese attack that occurred only weeks after the Midway conference, administration witnesses admitted they had been "fooled" by the Chinese, but made it clear that they thought MacArthur's assurances were largely to blame. Following the Chinese sweep across the Yalu, the General called for air attacks on their Manchurian bases and the use of Chinese Nationalist troops in Korea. When these and other requests were refused, MacArthur contrived in a number of ways to get his case before the American public. Finally, on April 10, 1951, President Truman relieved the General of all his commands and recalled him to the United States. The final straw had been MacArthur's distortion of a diplomatic initiative to begin talks on a settlement approximating the *status quo ante* into a military threat to bomb China proper unless Communist commanders in Korea surrendered. With MacArthur out of the way—but not without a full congressional investigation of the military situation in the Far East, ranging all the way back to Yalta and even to John Hay's Open Door notes— such talks actually began in July 1951. But before a truce was signed, the talks went on for a period twice as long as the first phase of the war.

General Douglas MacArthur

---

[29] Cited in Richard Rovere and Arthur M. Schlesinger, Jr., *The General and the President* (New York, 1951), pp. 257–62.

Korea: Aftermath and Consequences

A STALEMATE had become inevitable in Korea unless the United States was prepared either to commit armed forces on a large scale to do battle against the full force of Chinese infantry, poor in equipment but endless in numbers, or to risk the use of atomic weapons. Neither course was at all feasible. America's allies were a bit nervous about some of Truman's efforts to plant atomic fears in Peking's mind, but he was determined to keep a close watch on the situation to prevent what General Omar N. Bradley, chairman of the Joint Chiefs, testified "would involve us in the wrong war, at the wrong place, at the wrong time, and with the wrong enemy."[30]

Bradley also asserted that "our global strategy is paying off and I see no reason to let impatience alter it in the Far East." These words recalled NSC-68 and Acheson's "situations of strength" speech. The answer to Mac Arthur and other critics, therefore, was that the intervention in Korea had been *part of* a strategy; it could not be allowed to dominate policy-planning. The Korean war had been a testing time and a learning time. The profits from this experience were not to be squandered away to correct a miscalculation. In the atomic era, for example, it was likely that there would be other "tests," other "limited" wars. This meant high military budgets; annual defense spending rose from $12 billion in 1950 to nearly $44 billion by 1953, when the truce was signed. Thereafter military spending would average around 10 percent of the nation's gross national product.

The Korean war had other consequences in Asia. It ended any possibility that Japan would play a neutral role in the cold war. Negotiations for a Japanese peace treaty had begun in the months before the outbreak of full-scale fighting in Korea, and the United States made it plain that it planned to go ahead with such a treaty regardless of Russian or Chinese Communist objections. Indeed, a few American policy-makers later admitted that the $58 million appropriated for a bomber base on Okinawa in 1949 and the decision to negotiate a separate peace treaty involving "the indefinite retention of an American military presence in Japan" might have been factors in the timing of the North Korean attack.[31] The Japanese peace treaty was signed in September 1951, along with a Japanese-American security pact under which the United States "consented" to maintain its forces there for ten years to deter a foreign attack. And to assure other allies that Japan would not backslide into its former be-

[30] *Hearings: Military Situation*, pp. 729–34, 742–43.
[31] George F. Kennan, *Memoirs: 1925–1950* (Boston, 1967), p. 395.

havior pattern, Washington signed security pacts with Australia and New Zealand.

The Korean war provided a boost to NATO and, more important, to the rearmament of Germany as part of the defense system. In the United States, however, the war and the prolonged truce negotiations had become a nightmare in which the specter of "McCarthyism" was set loose in a nation already haunted by "security" risks and tales of treason in high places. So great was the repugnance against the war that it almost shattered the "containment" world view altogether. The Democratic party had lost the 1952 election before the campaign began, unless the Republicans could somehow manage to snatch defeat from the jaws of victory. But this time they took no chances. They nominated Dwight Eisenhower, a man for all points of view, who promised peace in Korea and "liberation" from "containment."

Suggestions for Further Reading

More books have been published on the origins of the cold war in recent years than on any other subject. For an overall view, see Martin F. Herz, *Beginnings of the Cold War* (Bloomington, Ind., 1966); Marshall D. Shulman, *Stalin's Foreign Policy Reappraised* (Cambridge, Mass., 1963); Coral Bell, *Negotiation from Strength* (New York, 1963); Louis Halle, *The Cold War as History* (New York, 1967); Herbert Feis, *From Trust to Terror* (New York, 1970); and Joyce and Gabriel Kolko, *The Limits of Power* (New York, 1972).

On the atomic bomb, see Herbert Feis, *The Atomic Bomb and the End of World War II* (Princeton, N.J., 1966), and Gar Alperovitz, *Atomic Diplomacy* (New York, 1964); on the Marshall Plan, Joseph M. Jones, *The Fifteen Weeks* (New York, 1955), and Harry B. Price, *The Marshall Plan and Its Meaning* (Ithaca, N.Y., 1955). Asian policy still needs general treatment, but for a critical view see Edward Friedman and Mark Selden, *America's Asia: Dissenting Essays on Asian-American Relations* (New York, 1971). The best volume on Korea remains David Rees, *Korea: The Limited War* (New York, 1964), but Allen Whiting, *China Crosses the Yalu* (New York, 1960), is required reading for fuller understanding of the conflict. Latin America is covered in detail by David Green, *The Containment of Latin America* (Chicago, 1971). Memoirs by leading figures such as Truman, and Dean Acheson's *Present at the Creation* (New York, 1970), round out the story.

See also the general bibliography at the end of this volume.

CHAPTER 25

From Kansas
to Camelot
(1952–1962)

The 1952 presidential campaign was bitterly waged amidst daily headlines of a Korean stalemate, mounting war costs, and a rampant hunt for disloyal Americans. Republicans exploited these events by nominating General Dwight D. Eisenhower, Supreme Commander of the NATO military forces. Although Eisenhower was a sophisticated officer and complex personality, his birth and childhood in Abilene, Kansas, at the turn of the century enabled many people to view him as a personification of the traditional middle-American values they desperately sought to recapture. His military background offered hope to an electorate sick of Korea, a feeling he played upon in October when he promised to "go to Korea" to help end the conflict.

Eisenhower handily defeated the Democratic nominee, Adlai Stevenson of Illinois, in the November elections. The President-elect and his Secretary of State, John Foster Dulles, vowed to turn their backs on Republican "isolationists" and follow instead the Acheson-Truman policies in dealing with Stalin. Within a year, however, Stalin was dead. Within two years the bipolar world of the two superpowers splintered in Europe and Indochina. A "third world" emerged, with the Suez crisis of 1956 symbolizing this transformation. American policy assumptions, however, changed little. After eight years of Republican diplomacy, John F. Kennedy led the Democrats back to the White House in 1961. Kennedy accepted the strategies of the Eisenhower administration, differing only in his intensity in fighting the cold war to a victorious conclusion in the new third world, even if this meant the commitment of a great American military force. Neither Eisenhower nor even Dulles had been willing to make that kind of commitment.

Eisenhower and Dulles

DULLES: ASSUMPTIONS OF POLICY

In 1952 Dulles was the public spokesman for Republican foreign policy. Few Americans had his experience and knowledge of diplomatic affairs. "Foster has been studying to be Secretary of State since he was five years old," Eisenhower once remarked privately. A grandson of one Secretary of State and a nephew of another, Dulles served on several American foreign missions between 1907 and 1921. During the 1920s, as senior partner in the powerful law firm of Sullivan and Cromwell in New York City, he helped Washington officials and private corporations rebuild central Europe. Between 1945 and 1951 he had been intimately involved in Truman's foreign policies as an adviser.

Eisenhower conferring with Dulles

During and after the 1952 campaign, Dulles' foreign policy statements rested on a rigid assumption: communism was "not only the gravest threat that ever faced the United States," he told a Senate committee early in 1953, "but the gravest threat that has ever faced what we call western civilization, or, indeed, any civilization which was dominated by a spiritual faith."[1] He argued that the Truman-Acheson policy of "containment" was too weak. An offensive "liberation" of eastern Europe was required, but Dulles, and particularly Eisenhower, emphasized that "liberation" must be accomplished by peaceful means.

More important, the Secretary of State frequently reminded listeners that Lenin and Stalin had prophesied "the shortest way to Paris is via Peiping." Dulles consequently turned his attention from Europe, which had been the focus of Acheson's concern, to the newly emerging nations in Asia, Latin America, and Africa, with the aim of saving them from communism by integrating them into the West's political-economic system. On this he tolerated no compromise. By 1956 he could say that neutrality, as practiced in such third-world nations as India, had "increasingly become an obsolete conception and, except under very exceptional circumstances, it is an immoral and short-sighted conception."

In this race for the third world, however, the United States could not hope to match the Soviets "man for man, gun for gun," for that meant "bankruptcy." The Republicans, after all, had come to power in 1952 promising to "liberate" Communist areas, but also to balance the budget and reduce taxes at home. Eisenhower would not tolerate the building of a great conventional American army. He deemed it too expensive and also useless against the Communists. The President and Secretary of State proposed that their allies abroad assume this burden in order to protect themselves, while the United States would meanwhile establish greater strategic bombing forces to carry its new nuclear weapons. Such a policy not only was cheaper for Americans, but enabled them to maintain their nuclear supremacy over both foes and friends. If Red armies marched "anywhere, we could and would strike back where it hurts, by means of our own choosing," Dulles warned in 1952.[2] By 1954 this had been labeled the doctrine of "massive retaliation." How well nuclear bombs could control revolutionary movements in the huts and jungles of Southeast Asia, Africa, and Latin America remained to be seen.

---

[1] U.S. Senate, 83rd Cong., 1st sess., Committee on Foreign Relations, *Nomination of John Foster Dulles, Secretary of State Designate,* January 15, 1953 (Washington, D.C., 1953), pp. 10–11.

[2] John Foster Dulles, "A Policy of Boldness," *Life,* May 19, 1952, p. 151.

1953–1954: A NEW COLD WAR

The world in which Eisenhower and Dulles planned to work out their policies changed drastically and dramatically in March 1953, when Moscow announced Stalin's death. Some American experts predicted a leadership crisis that would paralyze Soviet power. Instead, a collective leadership led by Georgi Malenkov and Nikita Khrushchev firmly assumed the reins, and on March 15 seized the diplomatic initiative when Malenkov publicly asked for more conciliatory East-West relations. Eisenhower later admitted that the Soviet "peace offensive" confused Washington officials[3]—as well it might, given the assumptions with which men such as Dulles had come to power. The President could only respond that the United States would settle for nothing less than a negotiation of all major global problems. This all-or-nothing reply was a successful stall for time, but American policy assumptions changed little during the next three years. A settlement ended the fighting in Korea in July 1953. Dulles nevertheless remained cool toward negotiation on other selected issues. On August 8 the administration became even more tense, for Malenkov announced that the Soviets had successfully tested a hydrogen bomb. After a nine-year American monopoly of nuclear power, a strategic balance was appearing. Dulles began to fear that beneath this umbrella of nuclear equality communism would become more aggressive in western Europe and particularly in the newly emerging nations.

He believed this threat was becoming real in the Middle East. The area possessed two-thirds of the world's crude oil reserves and nearly 90 percent of the noncommunist reserves, but was torn by the existence of the new state of Israel and antiforeign nationalist movements in the Arab nations. One such nationalist group, headed by Mohammed Mossadegh, had seized power in Iran in 1951, then nationalized the Anglo-Iranian Oil Company. A year later an army coup drove out a corrupt monarchy in Egypt and instituted a regime soon to be headed by General Gamal Abdel Nasser. Nationalism seemed to be contagious.

Acheson had been patient with Mossadegh, but in June 1953 Dulles cut off all assistance to the Iranian government. During the summer Mossadegh moved closer to the Soviets. Dulles responded through the Central Intelligence Agency, which joined with the Shah of Iran and disaffected Iranian army units to destroy the Mossadegh regime with a counterrevolution. In October negotiations commenced on the vital oil question. American oil companies had been

---

[3] Dwight D. Eisenhower, *The White House Years: Mandate for Change, 1953–1956* (Garden City, N.Y., 1963), pp. 148–49.

unsuccessfully attempting to break the British control of Iranian oil fields since the turn of the century, but now, through the mediation of State Department officials, five major United States companies obtained a 40 percent interest in a new oil consortium.

Dulles gave the same response to a similar revolutionary problem in Latin America. Incredibly poor and peopled largely by diverse Indian tribes living in isolated mountain communities, Guatemala had long been controlled by strong-handed dictators while European and particularly American coffee and fruit growers, along with a handful of the Guatemalan elite, exploited the nation's wealth. In 1944 a revolution deposed the current dictator and introduced attempts at democratic reform, which were doomed to failure by the country's inexperience in democratic processes and the determined opposition of both the conservatives and the Communists. In 1951 Jacobo Arbenz Guzmán, a left-leaning militarist, came to power. In 1952 and 1953 the Arbenz government seized extensive landholdings of the United Fruit Company, among others, as part of its land reform program, and, because of the impoverished state of the Guatemalan treasury, was unable to pay the promised compensation immediately.

Faced with constant attempts by the conservatives to overthrow him, Arbenz tried to buy arms from the United States, but was refused. He then turned to the Communist bloc and succeeded in obtaining arms. On May 17, 1954, the U.S. State Department, without mentioning that Arbenz had turned first and fruitlessly to the United States for aid, announced that Communist arms were entering Guatemala. American aid, military and economic, now quickly flowed to Colonel Carlos Castillo Armas, a former Guatemalan army officer who led dissident forces stationed in Nicaragua and Honduras. On June 18 Castillo Armas invaded Guatemala and quickly seized power. Dulles applauded the invasion, recognized Castillo Armas, and pledged economic aid. The United States meanwhile blocked Soviet moves within the United Nations to condemn the American involvement in the affairs of another sovereign country.

Castillo Armas received $70 million in American aid, executed several hundred followers of Arbenz, was elected President by a yes-no plebescite with about 10 percent of the population voting, restored a quarter-million acres to United Fruit, and signed an investment guarantee agreement to protect foreign investors. That string of successes stabilized neither the economy nor the political situation of Guatemala, and did not prevent Castillo Armas' assassination by one of his own palace guards in July 1957. By 1958 the little nation, always bipolarized politically, was more widely split than ever, with both the conservatives and the leftists making strong showings. A gravely weak economy based on banana and coffee exports slid further, with nearly half of Guatemala's $75 million in dollar reserves flowing out of the country in 1959. When a combination of natural and political disasters caused the United Fruit Company to close down most of its operations in the country, Guatemala was reduced to a one-crop economy. The nation entered a period of chaos, economic stagnation, and finally guerrilla terrorism.

"Massive retaliation" was irrelevant to these revolutions in Latin America and the Middle East. But apparently so were some counterrevolutionary devices engineered in Washington.

INDOCHINA: ENDING ONE EMPIRE, BEGINNING ANOTHER

While Guatemala's attempt at internal reform came to a halt, Indochina endured both an ongoing revolution and an anticolonial war against French control. The conflict had begun in 1946 when the Indochinese nationalist leader, Ho Chi Minh, and the French were unable to agree upon terms for the nation's autonomy. Until 1950 the United States remained on the sidelines, but after a Communist government moved into control in China, the American attitude hardened. On May 8, 1950, a month before the major involvement in Korea, the State Department announced support for the French and their puppet Vietnamese government, headed by Bao Dai. Between 1950 and 1954 the United States spent $1.2 billion aiding the French, thereby paying for nearly 80 percent of France's effort to defeat Ho. The Truman administration largely rationalized this huge expenditure by emphasizing the need to keep Paris officials committed to the western European alliance as well as to Indochina.

By mid-1953, however, both Congress and the State Department began to see they were on the losing side. Dulles privately confided to British Foreign Secretary Anthony Eden that perhaps France was, "by a process of historical evolution, inevitably ceasing to be a great power."[4] The ineptitude of the French in Southeast Asia and their reluctance to agree with the United States on the need to rearm Germany were beginning to wear American patience thin.

During April 1954 Ho's forces surrounded the main French army at Dien Bien Phu. Dulles answered French pleas for help by requesting congressional and Allied support for intervention. Leading Senate figures, however, led by Democrat Lyndon Johnson of Texas, refused to support the proposed intervention unless the Allies promised extensive help, and this the British refused to

---

[4] Anthony Eden, *Full Circle: The Memoirs of Anthony Eden* (Boston, 1960), p. 108.

do. Vice-President Richard Nixon threatened that the President might "take the risk now by putting our boys in" in order to stop future Communist expansion, but fortunately the decision was Eisenhower's, not Nixon's. There was no American intervention, the French garrison fell, and France prepared to negotiate its evacuation from Indochina at an international conference called at Geneva, Switzerland.

On July 20, 1954, that conference worked out an agreement between Ho's government and the French. Vietnam would be temporarily divided at the seventeenth parallel, with·withdrawal of French troops from the north and the far greater withdrawal of Ho's troops from the south; a national election would be held within two years to unify the country; and neither North nor South Vietnam would join a military alliance or allow foreign bases on its soil. The United States, preferring to maintain its freedom of action, refused to sign any agreement with a Communist-supported government such as Ho's, which had just obtained half of Vietnam. Instead the United States issued a unilateral declaration of its own, warning against "any renewal of the aggression," and pledged to work for "free elections supervised by the United Nations."[5]

The elections were never held. As French forces left Indochina, American military advisers moved in to attempt to rebuild the South Vietnamese military, now under the control of President Ngo Dinh Diem. Faced with the failure of "massive retaliation" to bail out the French at Dien Bien Phu, Dulles created the Southeast Asia Treaty Organization (SEATO), a NATO-like structure composed of Pakistan, the Philippines, Thailand, Australia, France, New Zealand, Great Britain, and the United States, for the purpose of preventing future Communist aggression. The Asian signatories, however, were considerably less committed to Dulles' view of the world than the NATO partners. They joined SEATO primarily to obtain more American military and economic aid for their own economies, and, as in the case of Pakistan, to gather support for fighting such noncommunist enemies as India.

By the summer of 1955 Dulles was so confident of the American position that he and Diem refused even to discuss the promised elections. Vietnam, like Korea, remained divided, but unlike Syngman Rhee in South Korea, Diem could not establish a solid governmental base. His failure to carry out important land and political reforms sharpened internal dissent. In 1960 he was nearly overthrown by a military coup engineered by his own generals. North Vietnam, then China began aiding the South Vietnamese rebellion headed by the newly established National Liberation Front (NLF).

---

[5] U.S. Department of State, *American Foreign Policy, 1950–1955, Basic Documents*, 2 vols. (Washington, D.C., 1957), 1:785–88.

THE THIRD WORLD THREAT

Iran, Guatemala, and Southeast Asia demonstrated the extent to which the cold war had shifted from confrontation in Europe to American involvement in far-flung areas undergoing nationalist revolutions. This again became apparent during April 1955 when China appeared at the Bandung Conference of Asian nations, where nearly 60 percent of the world's population was represented. The Chinese made a highly effective plea for peaceful coexistence and neutrality, but nevertheless reiterated their determination to "liberate" Taiwan from the control of Chiang Kai-shek. The Eisenhower administration responded to this challenge by warning China that any invasion of Taiwan would meet American resistance. On January 23, 1955, Congress voted overwhelmingly (409–3 in the House and 85–3 in the Senate) to give Eisenhower power to meet any military crisis in the Formosa Straits area. The threat abated by late 1955, although it revived in 1958 and the Chinese periodically shelled the offshore islands, held by Chiang, during the next decade.

The immediate military threat had been stifled, but Dulles devoted considerable time to worrying over China's new policy of peaceful coexistence. He believed that Mao's government, encouraged by the new Russian regime headed by Nikita Khrushchev, intended to lower the West's guard with soft words. The Chinese and Soviets made direct appeals to noncommunist nationalist groups, convinced that nationalism in the third world was basically anti-capitalist and anti-West. Early in 1955 Khrushchev responded to the American rearming of West Germany, and also solidified Russian control of eastern Europe, by creating the Warsaw Pact, which tied together the Soviet bloc's military plans and strategies under Russian control. Dulles became deeply concerned that "the wolf has put on a new set of sheep's clothing," but Russian "policy remains the same."[6]

THE SUMMIT AND AFTER (1955)

Dulles' concern deepened when Khrushchev agreed to evacuate Soviet troops from Austria, thereby reuniting that country after ten years of East-West division. The Soviet leader then pushed for a summit conference. Dulles was convinced the Soviets hoped to use such a conference to appeal to the newly emerging nations. Eisenhower, Prime Minister Anthony Eden of Great Britain, and Premier Nikolai Bulganin, who played front man for Khrushchev, met at Geneva in July 1955. They soon mired down on the issue of German reunification.

---

6 "Press and Radio News Conference ... May 15, 1955," in conference dossiers, John Foster Dulles papers, Princeton University.

The West played from a position of strength, for late in 1954 Eden and Dulles had overcome France's strong opposition to Acheson's plan for rearming West Germany. In May 1955, on the eve of the summit, German troops entered the NATO structure and the West restored full sovereignty to Konrad Adenauer's government. Dulles was confident that he had trapped Khrushchev: if the Russian wanted to negotiate German reunification, the Western powers had extremely powerful cards to play because of the now-independent Adenauer government and West German remilitarization. But if the Russians refused to negotiate this issue, as indeed they did, Dulles believed he had blunted the new Sino-Soviet offensive toward the third world. Since the Russians refused to negotiate on Germany, Dulles believed he had shown the world that Khrushchev was emphasizing peace merely for Soviet propaganda purposes.

Dulles continued to work hurriedly to integrate other newly emerging areas into the American system. In 1955 he negotiated the Baghdad Pact, joining together Turkey, Iraq, Iran, Pakistan, and Great Britain in a treaty that, with NATO and SEATO, was to form a wall of military alliances around communism. But in this instance, the United States merely closely cooperated with the pact nations, remaining out of the formal alliance in order to avoid the looming traps of Middle Eastern nationalism and the threatening Arab-Israeli confrontation.

The Eisenhower administration also streamlined its foreign aid program in order, in Dulles' words, to win the "bitterly competitive" contest over which system was to lead in the development of the newly emerging nations. An Asian Economic Development Fund was created, and in 1957, when Congress raised military assistance programs by 40 percent, the bulk of the increase went to Burma and especially to Indonesia and South Vietnam. Finally, in late 1955 the United States and Great Britain pledged the Egyptian government of General Nasser nearly $70 million to build the huge Aswan Dam in order to control the floodwaters of the Nile and power a vast industrial complex that Nasser hoped to construct.

COLD WAR WATERSHED: SUEZ AND HUNGARY

In May 1956 Dulles spelled out the rising importance of the newly emerging peoples for his NATO allies. The Western nations must work together to protect the "so-called underdeveloped countries which are exposed to the Soviet economic tactics," the Secretary of State solemnly warned.

If those tactics should prevail, the world ratio as between Communist dominated peoples and free peoples would change from a ratio [in terms of world population] of two-to-one in favor of freedom to a ratio of one-to-three against freedom. That would be an almost intolerable ratio given the industrialized nature of the Atlantic Community and its dependence upon broad markets and access to raw materials.[7]

Dulles' fears had increased during late winter of 1955–1956 when the United States learned of Nikita Khrushchev's denunciation of Joseph Stalin at the Twentieth Congress of the Communist party in Moscow. American officials, although surprised by such explicit condemnation of Stalin, generally agreed with Dulles that this was only another layer of sheep's clothing over the Russian wolf. Leaders in the Communist bloc nations, however, having learned the hard way that Stalin was to be honored and revered, were confused. By condemning Stalin, Khrushchev had also condemned a quarter century of Soviet history and opened Pandora's box.

Noting the growing discontent within the Soviet bloc, Dulles began re-evaluating his offer to Nasser to help build the Aswan Dam. Congressional pressure also built, particularly from southern congressmen who bitterly complained that American money would help grow competitive Egyptian cotton. Spokesmen for American Jews disliked aiding Egypt, which had vowed to destroy Israel ever since it had been established as a nation. Dulles decided to withdraw the Aswan offer, convinced that the Soviets would not be able to help Nasser build the dam.

This proved to be one of the grossest miscalculations of the cold war era. Nasser retaliated by seizing the Suez Canal, thereby eliminating the last vestige of British power around the canal area, controlling the vital passageway for the flow of oil to the western European economy, and taking the millions of dollars in annual profits from the canal for Egypt. After negotiations failed, Israeli forces suddenly attacked, driving the Egyptian army back across the Sinai Desert toward Suez. With careful coordination, Great Britain and France demanded that Nasser stay away from the canal, and when he refused, they began bombing Egyptian targets. Dulles was trapped between his fear that the Soviets would enter the war on the side of the Arabs and his determination to support his NATO friends. He decided to sacrifice his allies. The United States demanded an end to the fighting and pressured the British, French, and Israelis to withdraw their forces by threatening to shut off the flow of oil to western Europe.

---

7 "NATO Meeting, Etc." file, May 1–7, 1956, in ibid.

During the turmoil, Khrushchev seized the opportunity to restore Soviet control over the Communist bloc. On October 31 he made an example of the Hungarians, who had gone further than other Communist powers by threatening both to allow noncommunist parties to exist and to withdraw from the Warsaw military pact. Soviet tanks crushed Hungarian resistance during the first week of November. Despite his talk of encouraging "liberation," Dulles realized the West could only watch helplessly.

Crushing the Hungarian revolt

AFTER SUEZ: SPLINTERING THE SUPERPOWERS

The aftereffects of October–November 1956 have been profound. The NATO alliance, upon which Dulles had built many hopes and patterned alliances elsewhere, suffered perhaps a fatal blow. France, for example, accelerated its development of nuclear weapons so that in the future it could be militarily and politically more independent of the United States.

In the Middle East, a power vacuum existed, but Nasser had escaped with the prestige to move into that vacuum over a period of time. During the crisis, moreover, Khrushchev had loudly backed Nasser, threatening French and British cities with extinction if the fighting were not halted. The Soviet presence suddenly became a very tangible factor in Middle Eastern politics. Dulles could only retort that it had been his pressure, not Khrushchev's, that forced the British, French, and Israeli troops to withdraw and leave the canal in Nasser's hands.

But Dulles was also fearful that Nasser might push his luck by attempting to extend his, and perhaps Russia's, power over other Mediterranean areas. The United States responded in early 1957 with the Eisenhower Doctrine, pledging to aid any Middle Eastern government that might be threatened by Communist-supported aggression. Embodied in a congressional resolution, the Doctrine was loosely worded. In July 1958 it was stretched to its fullest when Eisenhower ordered 14,000 American troops to land in Lebanon. The pro-Western Lebanese government had been weakened by internal dissent, which gained support when a nationalist, anti-Western regime seized power in neighboring Iraq. The American landing was a warning to Arab nations to stay out of Lebanese politics and, more specifically, a display of power to an Iraqi government that was considering nationalization of American oil holdings.

The Suez crisis demonstrated that the newly emerging nations, such as Egypt, now had the power to divide the powerful NATO alliance. Nor had the Russian bloc proved immune to splintering. Hungary displayed Communist ideology to be considerably less powerful than Hungarian nationalism, an insight that later Russian leaders would not forget. Khrushchev's condemnation of Stalin and his mishandling of the eastern European situation, moreover, had created immense strain in Soviet-Chinese relations, as had his increasing moderation toward capitalism. But overall it was clear that the two superpowers that had controlled world affairs with an iron hand for eleven years had suddenly lost their grip. The Soviets' development of nuclear weapons had created a strategic balance between the two great powers, and newly emerging nations appeared to take advantage of that balance by playing one power off against the other. The cold war could no longer be considered merely a struggle between two monolithic blocs. The key question would be which of the two superpowers could best adjust to the rapid changes occurring in the third world.

SPUTNIK

The growing instability increased on October 4, 1957, when the Soviets successfully launched the world's first manmade satellite. The satellite (*sputnik* in Russian) demonstrated Soviet missile capacity for everyone to observe, including, as Dulles most feared, the newly emerging nations. Worried that they were on the short end of a missile gap, Americans turned feverishly inward to begin crash programs in science, the teaching of mathematics, and outer-space projects.

Sputnik

Such fear was misplaced, for Soviet and American strategic capability remained equal during the next three years. One American official later characterized the missile gap argument of 1957–1961 as "a couple of millionaires arguing about who has got the most change in his pocket."[8] In 1958, however, American leaders were not certain whether they were in fact as rich in missile power as the Soviets. Some Washington sources gravely predicted that by 1960 Russian intercontinental ballistic missiles (ICBMS) would outnumber American ICBMS by 3 to 1, and that by 1964 the ratio could be as much as 15 to 1. The Chinese meanwhile urged Khrushchev to utilize his illusory missile superiority to intensify pressure on the West. The Soviet leader's refusal further split the Sino-Soviet camp, but in the pivotal area of Germany, Khrushchev did attempt to break Western control by threatening force.

A NEW EUROPE, 1957–1958

Since 1945 West Berlin, lying 110 miles within the Soviet zone of Germany, had been a Western outpost and rallying point. Khrushchev graphically described it as a "bone in my throat." Germany had begun rearming in 1955 and three years later joined with Italy, France, and the Benelux nations in forming the European Economic Community (EEC) or European Common Market.

---

[8] Oral History interview with Herbert York, June 16, 1964, John F. Kennedy Oral History Project, John F. Kennedy Library (Waltham, Mass.). Quoted with permission of Mr. York.

Common Market at formation

A new, awesome force suddenly materialized, for the EEC nations pledged to create a virtual United States of Western Europe by eliminating within a period of ten to fifteen years all tariffs and quotas that had been imposed against one another.

Khrushchev hardly cared for West Germany's military and economic integration with western Europe, but the EEC also threatened some American interests. The French viewed the EEC as a purely European power that could protect itself against American unilateral decision-making (as had occurred at Suez) in the future. But any hope of Europeans that the EEC would counterbalance American economic power quickly disappeared. United States corporations swarmed behind the Common Market tariff walls to build subsidiary plants that could exploit the vast new market.

The American corporations also fled overseas to escape a recession that had afflicted the United States economy throughout the post–Korean war years. Dulles had hoped that surplus American capital would flow into the third world and bind that area to the West. United States corporate managers, however, turned to industrialized, secure western Europe rather than to the chaotic newly emerging nations. During the decade after 1958, American investment in western Europe tripled to more than $21 billion, with over 80 percent of this in direct investment in plants under American control. Using immense capital resources and organizational and managerial skills unknown or unutilized by Europeans, United States businesses could not be excluded by the EEC. Indeed, they rapidly Americanized it.

This American success was only dimly apparent in November 1958, when Khrushchev attempted to split the Western powers and remove the bone in his throat by demanding negotiations within six months to make West Berlin a "neutral" city. If the West would not negotiate, he threatened, he would turn control of access to the city over to the East German government—a government the West refused to recognize. Dulles would not negotiate under the time limit. Khrushchev retreated, agreeing to drop the ultimatum and visit the United States in the autumn of 1959 to discuss common problems at President Eisenhower's mountain retreat at Camp David, Maryland. The Soviet leader clearly did not want to force the issue prematurely. He doubtless believed that it lay in both superpowers' interest to negotiate and settle the explosive German question so each could then devote its attention to problems within its own sphere and in the third world. The "spirit of Camp David," however, brought no concrete results. The two leaders only agreed to a summit meeting at Paris in the spring of 1960.

Hopes for a successful summit began to disappear with the snow when Khrushchev and State Department spokesmen traded blunt speeches indicating that neither side would yield on Berlin. The Chinese meanwhile attacked Khrushchev for not utilizing his supposed missile superiority against the West. Faced with an adamant West and an aroused China, Khrushchev was rescued on the eve of the summit conference when the Soviets shot down a high-flying U-2 American reconnaissance plane. Loudly condemning the United States for violating Soviet territory, Khrushchev broke up the Paris sessions.

More important, he apparently realized the U-2 had revealed that Russia's presumed missile superiority was an illusion; Eisenhower could now reveal this fact to the world if he wished. The President's restraint had been great indeed, for he could have embarrassed Khrushchev at any time since 1956, when the U-2s had begun flying, by announcing how weak the Russian missile system really was. Eisenhower instead had kept his silence while restraining trigger-happy Americans who wanted to build larger missiles faster. But now Khrushchev could no longer wage a cold war in Berlin and the newly emerging areas under the cover of a supposed missile superiority. Suddenly the familiar emphasis upon "peaceful coexistence" was missing from his speeches. Soviet and American policies hardened until the catharsis of the Cuban missile crisis two years later.

CASTRO

Between the depression of the 1930s and the seizure of power in Cuba by Fidel Castro on New Year's Day, 1959, Latin America had few years of per capita economic growth. After small booms during World War II and the Korean conflict, gross national product rose about 3 percent in the area during 1957. Since Latin America was enduring the world's greatest population growth rate of about 2.5 percent, the actual net economic growth was considerably less than 1 percent. Many Latin American one-crop economies (Venezuela with its oil, Brazil with its coffee, Cuba with its sugar) were dependent upon American investments, markets, and controls, so the United States incurred much of the blame for this lack of development.

In 1958 Vice-President Richard Nixon visited Latin America and met a hail of rocks, eggs, and epithets at some of his stops. Washington officials quickly reviewed Latin American policies, until then largely taken for granted. In 1959 the Inter-American Development Bank was established to channel funds for the development of infrastructure and for aid to investment. This marked the beginning of what the Kennedy administration would package and attempt to sell as the Alliance for Progress.

The new policies arrived a half century too late to keep Cuba within the United States' orbit. Since 1898 the Cubans had been economically integrated within the American economy, while, with few exceptions, a series of dictators

Fidel Castro

kept internal order. The last of these was Fulgencio Batista, who had ruled Cuba in the 1930s and then seized power in 1952. His ruthless methods, the frequent appearance of American military advisers in Cuban army and air force units, and a worsening of the economic balance and distribution accelerated a revolutionary movement headed by a young lawyer named Fidel Castro, who led an attack on an army post on July 26, 1953. The attack was unsuccessful, but by 1958 Castro had substantial support in the countryside, although the urban areas, where Cuban Communists and labor politicians were concentrated, were less enthusiastic. On January 1, 1959, he marched into Havana and assumed control.

The United States reluctantly recognized Castro's government. As one reporter accurately characterized Washington sentiment, however, "On one thing there was general agreement—that there was no dominant Communist influence."[9] But Castro was determined to make drastic reforms in the Cuban economy and in Cuban society. To accomplish this goal he needed money and organizational support. He found the money by seizing American and private Cuban property. Organizational support appeared as Communists and other radical groups, who had been unsure of Castro's politics, threw their weight behind his reforms, particularly after more conservative advisers left the movement. Cuban-American relations soured quickly after Castro announced his agrarian reform program in May 1959. In February 1960 the Soviets offered an agreement that would increase Soviet-bloc trade from less than 2 percent to 80 percent of total Cuban trade within two years.

The United States concluded a series of countermoves by cutting the Cuban sugar quota in the American market in July 1960. Robert Hurwitch, head of the State Department's Cuban desk from October 1960 until February 1962, best explained the early policy:

> By November of 1960 the belief was widespread, and I think it was firm United States policy, that he [Castro] was . . . beyond redemption, that he did represent the hostile element. . . .
>
> [No one thought economic sanctions would force Castro to surrender.] But it was perfectly clear that the Cuban economy was, in a sense, a Western-based economy. . . . Clearly if they were going to change from their Western orientation and enter the Sino-Soviet bloc or the Socialist camp, then they would have to shift over from a Western, or could be forced to shift over from a Western-based economy, to a Soviet one. It seemed desirable to move in this direction for a variety of reasons: one, to make the transition from the type of economic system that was prevalent before Castro came to power to a Communist, state-owned one as difficult as possible; secondly, to make

---

[9] E. W. Kenworthy in *New York Times,* January 3, 1959, p. 2.

it as burdensome as possible upon the Soviet Union.... [There was always] the thought in the back of our minds that through the economic denial program an atmosphere or a situation might be created in Cuba, that is, a situation which resulted in disgruntlement over probable rationing...a number of these effects of an economic denial program which might translate itself into open active opposition to the regime.[10]

One after the other, these assumptions proved false. Castro, his Cuban supporters, and the Soviet Union proved willing to pay a high price indeed to cut Cuba from the American economic orbit. Internal "open active opposition to the regime" never occurred in any significant fashion. In January 1961, as John F. Kennedy prepared to enter office, the Eisenhower administration finally cut diplomatic relations after Castro demanded a drastic reduction in the number of personnel staffing the American Embassy in Havana.

Kennedy and McNamara

AMERICAN EFFICIENCY IN A REVOLUTIONARY WORLD

Until his death in May 1959, Dulles had successfully pursued a single policy: maintaining the Soviet-American status quo, especially in western Europe, while protecting and attempting to integrate the newly emerging nations into the Western economic and military system. John F. Kennedy continued the central Dulles policy, but with vastly different tactics.

He and his running mate, Lyndon B. Johnson of Texas, defeated Richard Nixon by one of the smallest popular vote margins in American history. On foreign policy issues, Kennedy assumed a tough stance in regard to Castro and a more moderate position on the Chinese offshore island problem, and promised a new approach to Latin America. Above all, however, he won with a curious combination: a cool, pragmatic approach to problem-solving and an exhilarating call for dedicated national self-sacrifice so the United States would win

 what Kennedy assumed to be a contest with the Soviets over who would control world politics (and later the moon).

His inaugural address set the tone for the aggressive and wholly committed foreign policies of the 1960s. A "new generation of Americans" must prove itself worthy of carrying on the "long twilight struggle." "Let every nation know," Kennedy proclaimed, "whether it wishes us well or ill, that we shall

---

[10] Oral History interview with Robert A. Hurwitch, April 24, 1964, John F. Kennedy Oral History Project. Quoted with permission of Mr. Hurwitch.

John F. Kennedy

pay any price, bear any burden, meet any hardship, support any friend, oppose any foe to assure the survival and the success of liberty." He added, "I do not shrink from this responsibility—I welcome it." But Kennedy wanted also a national consecration to protect "liberty" anywhere: "And so, my fellow Americans: ask not what your country can do for you—ask what you can do for your country."

Having defined the world in ideological terms, Kennedy followed Dulles in focusing upon the third world. That area of Asia, Latin America, Africa, and the Middle East, the President gravely warned on May 25, 1961, was to be "the great battleground" in the struggle between "freedom and tyranny."[11] Kennedy believed this struggle required new military weapons, and he chose Robert McNamara, president of the Ford Motor Company, to head this intensified militarization as Secretary of Defense. The new weapons included increasing numbers of conventional forces, rapid development of the Special Forces ("Green Berets"), and a streamlining of Defense Department decision-making so that its highly computerized operation could play the fullest possible role in the President's councils. But McNamara also ordered a buildup of ICBMs to match the Soviets' theoretical missile capacity. The United States ran

---

[11] *Public Papers of the Presidents . . . 1961* (Washington, D.C., 1962), pp. 396–403.

this race against itself, for the Soviets did not decide to build to capacity, As McNamara admitted later, "If we had had more accurate information about planned Soviet strategic forces, we simply would not have needed to build as large a nuclear arsenal as we have today."[12]

The error was hardly accidental; Kennedy had berated the Republicans during the campaign for allowing a "missile gap" to develop, and he continued to emphasize this issue despite Eisenhower's announcements that no such gap existed. But then, Eisenhower had also emphasized the uselessness of creating large numbers of American conventional forces to fight any "twilight struggles" in the newly emerging world, and Kennedy paid no attention to that sound advice either.

THE BAY OF PIGS

Besides Dulles' strategy (although not his tactics), Eisenhower bequeathed Kennedy a several-thousand-man force of Cuban exiles training in Guatemala under American intelligence and military officers for an invasion of Cuba. The success of the plan depended upon an uprising within Cuba, superior air cover, and the destruction of Castro's air force. Kennedy ordered the invasion to begin on April 17, but cloud cover cut the effectiveness of the inadequate exile air force, Castro's planes decimated the landing beaches at the Bay of Pigs, and the invasion force was captured or destroyed. There was no internal uprising.

Kennedy assumed full responsibility for the fiasco. Given the massive newspaper publicity of the supposedly secret operation, he had no other course. His personal prestige suffered, and so did his Alliance for Progress, announced only the month before, which aimed at combining Latin American domestic reform with private and governmental development capital. Over a ten-year period this combination was supposed to increase Latin America's prosperity and political stability, and make the area immune to future Castros. Most important, in his speech accepting responsibility for the invasion, Kennedy emphasized that despite this setback, the United States would fight a "relentless struggle in every corner of the globe" against an offensive of "power and discipline and deceit." These evils would be combatted whether they appeared "in Cuba or South Vietnam."[13]

---

12 Robert McNamara, *The Essence of Security* (New York, 1968), pp. 57–58.
13 *Public Papers of the Presidents . . . 1961*, pp. 304–306.

THE CRISIS SUMMER OF 1961

Diem's weakening regime in South Vietnam was much on Kennedy's mind after the Bay of Pigs. He could hardly afford to suffer another disaster so early in his term. In this context of the Cuban and South Vietnam problems, Kennedy traveled to Europe to meet General Charles de Gaulle of France and Nikita Khrushchev.

American relations with France and Germany were deteriorating. De Gaulle did not trust the United States to defend western European interests in a nuclear conflict. He was determined to preserve the Common Market from those whom he scornfully called the "Anglo-Saxons" and so vetoed British entry into the EEC in 1963 and again in 1967. He weakened NATO, which he considered an American-controlled alliance, by withdrawing French forces and pressuring the organization to move its headquarters from Paris to Brussels. The French meanwhile went ahead full speed with the development of their own nuclear weapons. Kennedy was unable to reverse any of De Gaulle's policies during the 1961 conversations.

Nor did the President enjoy much better luck with Khrushchev. The two men did work out an approach for a temporary settlement of the deepening crisis in Laos. But Kennedy had scant success in attempting to pry from Khrushchev the assurance that the Soviets would not help revolutionary movements in the third world. The Russian leader simply refused to assume responsibility for the existence of nationalist movements over which he had no control. Khrushchev essentially argued that Russia would help nationalists in the third world to develop as rapidly as those nationalists desired; Kennedy, on the other hand, was determined to try to control the rate of change of these movements. Because of this fundamental difference, no agreement was possible.

Worse, Khrushchev reimposed the six-month limit for a Berlin settlement. Kennedy returned home to sound the alarm to the American people, using the crisis as an opportunity to accelerate the building of American military forces. In a militant speech on July 25, the President announced an increase of 25 percent in the conventional army. He mobilized units of the army reserves, meanwhile warning the Soviets not to attempt to cut off West Berlin. Civil defense preparations were stepped up and Americans were told how to build more comfortable, if not necessarily safer, air-raid shelters. But on August 13, the Soviets defused the issue by building a high concrete-and-brick wall between East and West Berlin. A forlorn, barren no-man's-land bracketed the wall on each side. Khrushchev had further insulated the Communist bloc

Section of Berlin Wall

from western Europe. He next announced resumption of Soviet nuclear testing, doubtless in an attempt to reduce the growing American lead in ICBMS. Kennedy responded by increasing underground tests, but waited until the spring of 1962 before recommencing aboveground. The cold war was picking up momentum.

VIETNAM: ANOTHER COMMITMENT

If Americans had indeed been asking themselves what they could do for their country, they were now being told what it was. And they were being asked to do it in faraway places. In the autumn of 1961 Kennedy appointed a special mission to examine the Vietnam situation. The team was headed by General Maxwell Taylor, long an advocate of building conventional army capacity to fight insurgencies, and economist Walt Whitman Rostow, who had emphasized the necessity of saving the newly emerging nations by developing antiguerrilla tactics and aid programs. Not surprisingly, therefore, the Taylor-Rostow team recommended increased numbers of military advisers to help Diem's army and government, also suggesting a 10,000-man American army to seal the infiltration routes from North Vietnam into the south. Kennedy accepted the first proposal but rejected the second. American military personnel in Vietnam grew from 1,300 in late 1961 to 10,000 a year later. Given the approach, policy-making for Vietnam gravitated out of the hands of the State Department and into the Pentagon office of McNamara, although the transference had at least the implicit assent of Secretary of State Dean Rusk.

Late in 1962 McNamara observed, "Every quantitative measurement we have shows we're winning this war." He could particularly point to the success of the strategic hamlet program, which cut off aid to the NLF by placing entire villages into fortified areas surrounded by barbed-wire fences. Failing to understand how this and other policies rapidly diminished Diem's already small support in the countryside, the American Embassy in Saigon assured Kennedy and Rusk throughout 1962 and early 1963 that the war was indeed being won. Diem meanwhile used the growing American commitment to secure his family's authoritarian regime, despite contrary advice from American officials. Thus far had American foreign policies traveled a decade after a new administration had paradoxically promised to take the offensive against communism but to end a war in Asia.

Suggestions for Further Reading

An excellent detailed survey is Seyom Brown, *The Faces of Power: Constancy and Change in U.S. Foreign Policy from Truman to Johnson* (New York, 1968). The Republican policies are explained in Dwight D. Eisenhower's two-volume *The White House Years,* subtitled *Mandate for Change, 1953–1956* and *Waging Peace, 1956–1961* (Garden City, N.Y., 1963, 1965); Richard Goold-Adams' interesting account, *John Foster Dulles: A Reappraisal* (New York, 1962); and Louis L. Gerson's more detailed and sympathetic *John Foster Dulles* (New York, 1967).

Two volumes are useful for an understanding of the 1952 transition, or lack of transition, in American policy: Coral Bell, *Negotiation from Strength* (London, 1962), and Norman A. Graebner, *The New Isolationism* (New York, 1956). The Suez crisis is examined in Herman Finer, *Dulles over Suez* (Chicago, 1964), very harsh on the Secretary of State; Hugh Thomas, *The Suez Affair* (London, 1966), emphasizing the European side; and Benjamin Shwadran, *The Middle East, Oil, and the Great Powers, 1959,* 2nd ed. (New York, 1959), which traces out some implications of the Suez crisis.

The situation in Guatemala and its aftereffects are delineated in Ronald M. Schneider's excellent *Communism in Guatemala, 1944–1954* (New York, 1958) and Milton S. Eisenhower, *The Wine Is Bitter* (New York, 1963), a general examination of policies toward Latin America.

The standard biographies are Arthur M. Schlesinger, Jr., *A Thousand Days: John F. Kennedy in the White House* (Boston, 1965), and Henry L. Trewhitt, *McNamara* (New York, 1971); but Rockefeller Brothers Fund, *Prospects for Peace: The Rockefeller Panel Reports* (Garden City, N.Y., 1961), is necessary for any understanding of the Kennedy administration, for some of its top officials wrote these reports. See David Halberstam's splendid *The Best and the Brightest* (New York, 1972).

Useful accounts of the changing American military strategy are Henry A. Kissinger, *The Necessity for Choice* (New York, 1961), and Urs Schwarz, *American Strategy* (New York, 1966). The Cuban tragedy is told in Robert F. Smith, *The United States and Cuba: Business and Diplomacy, 1917–1960* (New York, 1961); W. A. Williams, *The U.S., Cuba, and Castro* (New York, 1962); and Theodore Draper, *Castro's Revolution: Myths and Realities* (New York, 1962).

See also the general bibliography at the end of this volume.

CHAPTER **26**

Vietnamization:
Abroad and
at Home
(1962–1972)

The unsolvable problems of another Asian war dominated Amer-
ican foreign and domestic policies during the 1960s. Russian-American relations
improved somewhat despite the war, and the appearance of a postindustrial
age portended a new epoch in world history. The Vietnam struggle nevertheless dominated the decade, crippling the American ability to adapt to this
new world, for the war depressed the economy, increased sociopolitical instability, destroyed the political career of an American President, and provided
fertile ground for the growth of radical movements on both the left and the
right. The war created the gravest domestic crisis since the 1850s, another
decade when overexpansion exacerbated internal problems and brought the
nation to the edge of civil war. The "long twilight struggle" of President
Kennedy's New Frontier was exacting a heavy toll. Ironically, the morass
deepened partially as the result of Kennedy's greatest diplomatic victory, the
resolution of the Cuban missile crisis.

Crises of the New Frontier

THE BRINK OF NUCLEAR WAR

Cuba apparently rose in Soviet estimation after Secretary of Defense McNamara and other administration spokesmen informed the world in late 1961 and early 1962 that not only was the supposed Russian missile superiority a myth, but the United States enjoyed sufficient strategic power to destroy Soviet military installations with a second-strike, or retaliatory, attack. Khrushchev understood that the American claims severely reduced Soviet diplomatic leverage in central Europe and opened his leadership to charges of weakness and diplomatic bungling.

During the early summer of 1962, Soviet ships hauled sections of long-range bombers and missiles to Cuban ports. In September, Kennedy defined the missiles as defensive—that is, of the ground-to-air variety—but he warned Russia against installing ground-to-ground missiles. As late as October 14 the administration denied the emplacement of offensive weapons, but that evening a U-2 plane returned from a flight over Cuba with pictures of sites being readied for ground-to-ground long-range missiles. The President believed that such weapons ninety miles from American shores gravely threatened the nation's security, and he rejected any arguments that the placing of missiles on the border of the Soviet Union (particularly in Turkey) by the Americans justified Khrushchev's doing the same thing to the United States. The threat, moreover, was double-edged, for several leading Republicans had warned of such weapons during the previous months, and the 1962 congressional elections were only three weeks distant.

The President convened a special committee that met in utmost secrecy for a week to decide the response. Special adviser Dean Acheson and several military officers suggested a direct strike on the sites. Indeed, some members of the group were so anxious to use American power directly that Attorney General Robert Kennedy later recalled that although the special committee was comprised of "the brightest kind of group that you could get together under those circumstances," if "six of them had been President...I think that the world might have been blown up."[1] Another group within the committee, led by Robert Kennedy and McNamara, finally swayed the committee by arguing that a blockade to exclude missile parts from Cuban ports should first be tried; if the Soviets refused to honor the blockade, a military strike could then be sent. On October 22 the President dramatically told the world

---

[1] Quoted by Ronald Steel in *New York Review of Books,* March 13, 1969, p. 22.

that the blockade had been established. He warned that if any missile from Cuba hit the United States, he would order retaliation upon the Soviet Union as well as Cuba.

A week of hectic exchanges with the Russians followed. On October 26 Khrushchev sent a long letter denying that the missiles were offensive, emphasizing to Kennedy that the Soviets well understood how close the world was to nuclear war, and particularly stressing that Russia had to respond to Castro's pleas for help because of the constant threat of American invasion— the kind of invasion, Khrushchev pointedly observed, that Russia had endured at the hands of the British and Americans between 1918 and 1920. The special committee, again led by McNamara and Robert Kennedy, advised moving toward an agreement whereby the Soviets would dismantle their ground-to-ground missiles on the island in return for the United States' promise to make no further attempt to overthrow Castro by invasion.[2] By November the crisis had passed. The aftereffects, however, proved crucial.

Aftermath of Cuban missile crisis

Khrushchev's power within the Kremlin suffered, especially as the Chinese made political capital within the Communist bloc by bitterly condemning the Soviet leader's bungling in Cuba. Khrushchev nevertheless attempted to make the best of the situation, and during the summer of 1963 worked out

---

[2] The Kennedy speech and the Kennedy-Khrushchev correspondence can be found in *Department of State Bulletin*, 47 (November 12, 1962):741–46. A copy of Khrushchev's crucial letter to Kennedy of October 26 is in possession of the authors.

with Kennedy a nuclear test-ban treaty prohibiting aboveground tests of atomic or nuclear weapons. The President had enhanced the chances for such a break-through with a speech at American University in Washington, D.C., during June of 1963, in which he eloquently asked for a lessening of tensions between the United States and Russia.

THE LESSONS

Important American policy-makers believed the missile crisis had one major diplomatic result: it produced a strategic standoff between the two great powers, thereby allowing further fragmentation of both blocs and in-creasing the freedom of the newly emerging nations to maneuver in inter-national politics. Leading administration theoreticians such as Walt Rostow of the State Department's Policy Planning Staff, and later President Johnson's key foreign policy adviser, warned that an increase in nationalism could make the world even more chaotic than it already was. Rostow advised the encourage-ment of regional alliances and a commitment to stop such aggressive revolu-tionary movements as that in Vietnam.[3]

President Kennedy had another reason to follow Rostow's advice for ordering the world. By early 1963 he was probably more concerned with the outflow of gold from the United States than with any other foreign policy matter.[4] The drain resulted from increased importation of foreign goods by the United States while Americans were sending increased amounts of capital overseas for investment and for military and economic aid. More funds were leaving the country than were being received from exports, foreign investment in American companies, and profits from American overseas ventures. The deficit had to be made up from the American gold supply. At the end of World War II the United States had a virtual monopoly upon world gold reserves, with $24 billion worth in its vaults, but the deficits, beginning in the late 1950s, had reduced those holdings by 40 percent by the mid-1960s. As gold left the United States, the dollar became less stable, for its worth was based on gold. It had been accepted as the leading circulating medium in world trade because other nations knew that, at least before the 1960s, it was sup-ported by the vast gold reserve as well as an immense industrial and agri-

---

3 Walt Whitman Rostow, "Domestic Determinants of U.S. Foreign Policy: The Tocqueville Oscillation," *Armed Forces Journal*, June 27, 1970, pp. 16D–16E.

4 Oral History interview with Maurice Couve de Murville, May 20, 1964, John F. Kennedy Oral History Project, John F. Kennedy Library (Waltham, Mass.).

cultural complex. As gold fled the United States, American power dwindled in international trade. Kennedy proposed a major international conference in which leading world trading nations would agree to reduce their tariffs and hence increase trade. Such a conference was brought to a successful conclusion in 1967. The United States nevertheless continued to suffer a gold outflow, in large part because of inflation at home and huge expenditures in Vietnam.

VIETNAM, 1962–1963

In the third world, Rostow's theories of regionalism were particularly directed toward Southeast Asia. Rostow later recalled that Kennedy had accepted the domino thesis, for

> he believed the United States, in the end, would not acquiesce in the region from Saigon and Vientiane to Singapore and Djakarta falling under the hegemony of a potential enemy. He was conscious too that Burma was the military gateway to the Indian subcontinent; and that the American performance in Southeast Asia would affect profoundly the stability of other nations of the world.[5]

Given such an analysis, the only viable policy was to strengthen the Diem regime in South Vietnam. Diem, however, was not cooperating. He paid little attention to American advice, insisting upon ruthlessly suppressing internal dissent. In May 1963 the South Vietnamese army fired into a group of Buddhists who attempted to display their religious flags on Buddha's birthday, an act that contravened Diem's order that only the national flag should be shown. The Buddhists fought back, and when several monks publicly protested by burning themselves to death, Americans were suddenly faced with a new and increasingly dangerous situation.

In early September, Kennedy reaffirmed the commitment, but added that the South Vietnamese must restore order and win the war primarily through their own efforts. In retrospect, the President's words appear ominous. In late October, a small group of South Vietnamese generals decided to overthrow Diem. In a quick coup on November 1, Diem and his brother were captured and shot. The American Embassy had known of the plans and encouraged the ringleaders, although it apparently had not known of the intention to kill Diem.[6] Three weeks later the American President was murdered in

---

[5] Rostow, "Domestic Determinants," pp. 16B–16C.

[6] *The Pentagon Papers,* as published by the *New York Times* (Chicago, 1971), especially pp. 215–33.

Dallas, Texas. Lyndon Johnson became President, inheriting the terrible legacy of the Eisenhower-Kennedy commitment to a South Vietnam now on the edge of internal chaos.

Johnson

EMERGING FROM the last frontier in Texas during the 1930s, Johnson had become one of the greatest Senate leaders in the nation's history. To general surprise, the ambitious, egocentric Texan accepted second place on the 1960 Democratic ticket, and for the next three years virtually disappeared behind the Kennedy image. After entering the White House, Johnson was constantly haunted by the memory of the assassinated President and the political ambitions of Robert Kennedy. These shadows heightened Johnson's determination to be a successful President in his own right, regardless of the cost.

The new President's foreign policy differed from his predecessor's more in style than in goals. Kennedy had warned in general terms of the dangers posed by a China that had nuclear weapons and by radical movements in the newly emerging nations, but Johnson stated it bluntly: "There are 3 billion people in the world and we have only 200 million of them. We are outnumbered 15 to 1. If might did make right they would sweep over the United States and take what we have. We have what they want."[7] Both men also agreed upon the mission for the City Upon a Hill. "Woodrow Wilson once said," Johnson observed approvingly in the autumn of 1964, " 'I hope we shall never forget that we created this nation, not to serve ourselves, but to serve mankind.' " The contradiction of this statement to his earlier pronouncement was easily lost in the fervor with which the new President uttered it.

VIETNAM AND THE CAMPAIGN OF 1964

When Johnson became President, South Vietnamese politics seemed uncontrollable. The Viet Cong (NLF) strength had dramatically increased to nearly forty thousand men, and this force virtually dominated the vital Mekong Delta area. The new President immediately decided that the only acceptable solution was for "the authorities in Hanoi [to] cease and desist from their terrorist aggression." During the summer and autumn of 1964, North Vietnam

---

[7] *Public Papers of the Presidents . . . 1966* (Washington, D.C., 1967), p. 1287.

sent peace feelers to Washington, particularly through United Nations Secretary General U Thant. Johnson refused to discuss any terms, fearing that the weakness of South Vietnam would be fatal for the American bargaining position. Johnson's sensitivity to this trap intensified as the 1964 election approached.

The Republicans repudiated the liberal wing of their party and nominated Senator Barry Goldwater of Arizona. The Republican right wing, however, was no longer isolationist, as it had been during the 1930s; now it had swung close to the other extreme. Goldwater heartily endorsed NATO as "the greatest force for freedom in the world today," viewed the Communist world as monolithic, and intimated that since Communists understood only force, NATO commanders should be able to use tactical nuclear weapons without presidential approval. Johnson seized upon this last assertion to picture Goldwater as an irresponsible militarist whose reaction to a problem was too likely to be "mashing the button" that released nuclear weapons. The President solemnly berated "those that say you ought to go north [in Vietnam] and drop bombs." On the contrary, he asserted, "We don't want our American boys to do the fighting for Asian boys."[8]

The President nevertheless employed a two-edged policy. On August 2, North Vietnamese torpedo boats attacked two American destroyers in the Gulf of Tonkin, off the North Vietnamese coast. Two days later another attack occurred. Late that night Johnson announced over national television that at that moment American planes were attacking North Vietnamese bases in retaliation. North Vietnam charged that the U.S. destroyers were cooperating with South Vietnamese attacks on the North Vietnamese coast, and thus had provoked the response. Although this charge was denied at the time, four years later Secretary of Defense McNamara confirmed the truth of it.[9]

Johnson immediately asked Congress for presidential authority "to take all necessary measures to repel any armed attack against the forces of the United States and to prevent further aggression." This Tonkin Gulf Resolution passed the House 416–0, and then the chairman of the Senate Foreign Relations Committee, J. William Fulbright, Democrat of Arkansas, shepherded it through the Senate, 88–2. Congress had effectively transferred its constitutional powers to declare war to the President for use as he saw fit in Southeast Asia.

Johnson's performance as both soldier and statesman drove the Republicans down to one of the worst defeats in twentieth-century American politics. The

---

[8] Ibid., *1964*, p. 1126.

[9] U.S. Senate, 90th Cong., 2nd sess., Committee on Foreign Relations, *The Gulf of Tonkin: The 1964 Incidents* (Washington, D.C., 1968); *Pentagon Papers*, pp. 253–70.

President claimed an impressive consensus for his policies. The world, however, had altered slightly during the autumn. Nikita Khrushchev had been driven from power by a younger group of Russians led by Alexei Kosygin and Leonid Brezhnev. The colorless Kremlin leaders focused their attention on stabilizing the Communist bloc through new heavy industry programs, another attempt to resurrect Soviet agricultural production, and suppression of dissident intellectuals.

VIETNAM ESCALATION, 1964–1965

Shortly after the election, Johnson again concluded that South Vietnam's weakness precluded peace negotiations. He ordered plans drawn for the American expansion of the war to defeat the NLF. The opportunity to put this plan into effect arose on February 7, 1965, when the Viet Cong attacked the American camp at Pleiku, killing 7 Americans and wounding 109. The next day the President announced the beginning of a massive American counterattack, including systematic bombing of North Vietnam. Johnson had accepted the argument of General Curtis L. Le May, chief of staff of the Air Force, that "we are swatting flies when we should be going after the manure pile."

The bombing, however, immensely complicated the war. Until that point, North Vietnam had restrained infiltration into the south in return for an implicit understanding that the United States would not hit exposed industries and harbors. Johnson's advisers had taken the risk of provoking increased infiltration from North Vietnam on the assumption that the bombing would hinder the North Vietnamese supply effort. Instead, infiltration from the north increased from 12,400 men in 1961 to 19,000 in 1965 and over 60,000 in 1966.[10] The bombing led Russia to become more deeply involved by supplying replacement goods to the North Vietnamese, brought American military might closer to China's borders, indiscriminately killed civilians and military personnel, and violated the Geneva Accords of 1954, thereby making more difficult a negotiated peace on the basis of that agreement. In June 1966 Secretary McNamara announced another stepping up of the bombings, because under the original bombing schedule "the daily tonnage of [North Vietnamese] supplies moved overland has increased 150 percent and personnel infiltration has increased 120 percent during 1966, compared with 1965 averages."[11]

---

[10] Roger Hilsman, *To Move a Nation* (New York, 1967), p. 531.

[11] Text of statement in *New York Times,* June 30, 1966.

With the bombing policy, Johnson also rapidly increased the number of American combat troops. In 1965 the United States forces increased nine times, to 190,000. With the 635,000 South Vietnamese troops, the American command enjoyed superiority in manpower and especially firepower, but the NLF continued to gain ground. By the end of 1966 American personnel doubled to 400,000. In April 1966, for the first time, more Americans were killed in action than South Vietnamese troops.

In April 1965 Johnson had justified this effort by asserting that the United States would accept only an independent South Vietnam, although he was prepared to enter "unconditional discussions." On April 13 Hanoi issued its own four-point position: withdrawal of American troops and bases from South Vietnam, a return to the 1954 Geneva agreements pending peaceful reunification of Vietnam, settlement of South Vietnamese affairs "by the South Vietnamese people themselves in accordance with the program of the [NLF] without any foreign interference," and the peaceful reunification of the "Vietnamese people in both zones, without any foreign interference." In November 1965 the Hanoi government relayed offers for discussions through intermediaries to the State Department, but they were again rejected because of the deteriorating military and political situation in South Vietnam. Nor was the situation improving within the United States.

THE CASE OF THE DISAPPEARING CONSENSUS

Johnson's support of November 1964 was rapidly dissolving. Republicans attacked him for not winning the war, Democratic congressional leaders questioned his manipulation of the Senate on war issues, and his domestic programs aimed at creating a "Great Society" were whittled down to pay for the war.

Many Americans were not prepared to sacrifice betterment at home for war overseas. War dissenters organized teach-ins and other demonstrations to educate the public on the lack of justification, either legal or moral, for the war. Senator Fulbright repudiated his earlier cooperation with the President, asking searching questions about the effects the war was having on the society and on the constitutional restraints upon presidential powers.

The administration responded, in the President's words, that "if peace fails [in Asia], nowhere else will our achievements really be secure." The domino theory had become global. He was convinced these achievements were gravely jeopardized by "the deepening shadow of Communist China," and argued that the United States must contain China by fighting the NLF and North Vietnamese soldiers in South Vietnam. The urgency increased when

McNamara dramatically told Congress that within two or three years China would be able to launch a nuclear attack on surrounding Asian nations, and within a decade could threaten the United States itself.[12] The fear of China did not abate when clashes between Russian and Chinese troops over disputed territory in Mongolia indicated that Peking's primary foreign policy concern lay north, not south. Nor did it lessen as China immersed itself in a bloody "Cultural Revolution." Initiated by Mao Tse-tung to cleanse the Communist party of revisionists, the Cultural Revolution threw parts of the country into chaos and severely disrupted its foreign affairs. The Washington rationale for Vietnam, however, never wavered.

ANOTHER INTERVENTION: SANTO DOMINGO

Along with Great Society programs, other foreign concerns slipped down the priority list of the Johnson administration. The President unenthusiastically promised to continue the Alliance for Progress with Latin America, but by the mid-1960s that program had essentially failed. Castro continued in power, and opportunities for other Castros grew throughout the area, where population continued to outstrip economic growth, 40 percent of the people were fifteen years old or younger, illiteracy averaged 50 percent, ten million children lacked classrooms, and per capita income ranged from less than $100 annually in Bolivia to $1,120 in Venezuela, with an overall average of about $300.

"Oh, I'm Just Here As The Referee"

U.S. intervention in the Dominican Republic

---

[12] *New York Times,* March 8, 1966, p. 1.

Perhaps the most unstable area was the Caribbean, that collection of islands which the United States had controlled, along with neighboring Central America, throughout the twentieth century. One of the least stable nations was the Dominican Republic, where the brutal and corrupt dictator Rafael Leonidas Trujillo had been gunned down in 1961 after thirty years in power. A liberal reform government gained power through national elections in 1962 and lasted until September 1963, when a coup d'état engineered by the army, the church, and large landholders elevated a civilian group serving as a front for the army. When the President, Donald Reid Cabral, insisted upon running for another term in the spring of 1965, he was overthrown by middle-rank army officers. The army, however, failed to keep this affair under control. Fighting broke out late in April, and rebels soon claimed control of the capital and placed arms in the hands of thousands of civilians. On April 27 counterrevolutionary forces led by army officers attempted to retake the capital, then urged President Johnson to intervene with American troops before the island fell into the hands of Castro-style revolutionaries.

The island was moving toward political chaos, as it had done during the eras of Theodore Roosevelt and Woodrow Wilson, but this time there was also Castro. The Cuban leader was not intervening in the situation, but he frightened Washington simply by acting as an example—as his own City Upon a Hill, as it were. On April 28 Johnson moved in United States Marines "to protect American lives," but within four days these forces had increased to 32,000, to ensure, in the President's words, that "people trained outside the Dominican Republic" would not gain control.

On May 2 he announced the Johnson Doctrine: "The American nations cannot, must not, and will not permit the establishment of another Communist government in the Western Hemisphere."[13] Taken literally, this announcement justified intervention in Latin American—even in Brazil, Chile, or Peru—if Washington considered that those countries were coming under the control of Communists.

The State Department tried to justify the intervention by producing a list of fifty-eight Communists, later reduced to forty, who supposedly were gaining control of the Dominican revolution. American journalists on the scene disproved both the validity of this list and the claim that the situation was falling under Communist control. But not only was this rationale for the intervention called into question; the United States had blatantly violated its promise to abide by the Charter of the Organization of American States, whose Article

---

[13] *Public Papers of the Presidents . . . 1965* (Washington, D.C., 1966), pp. 469–74.

15 reads: "No state or group of states has the right to intervene, directly or indirectly, for any reason whatever, in the internal or external affairs of any other state." Such a violation became especially difficult to justify when Americans claimed to be fighting in Asia in order to uphold the sanctity of another treaty structure, SEATO.

AFRICA

In addition to sending troops to Vietnam and the Dominican Republic, the United States intervened directly in African affairs during the 1960s. And again, as in Southeast Asia and the Caribbean, the pivotal question was whether American power could somehow impede the attempts of nationalist African movements to transform their countries. Opportunities for rapid change were hardly lacking. In all of Africa at the end of World War II, only Ethiopia, Nigeria, South Africa, and Egypt could lay claim to independence. The rest of the vast continent was under British, French, Spanish, and Portuguese control. The Suez crisis, followed in 1957 by the termination of British control of Ghana (the first black colony to achieve independence in the postwar era), set off a chain reaction of independence movements. In 1960 alone sixteen new African states joined the United Nations. With new, untested governmental structures, racked by tribal strife, and lacking the capital and managerial experience to develop their resources independently, some of these nations encountered immense difficulties maintaining even political viability. By the mid-1960s, moreover, Chinese Communists appeared in East Africa in increasing numbers with significant offers of aid. At home, Washington officials involved with African policies were caught in the swirl of domestic civil rights conflicts, especially the emerging movement of black Americans intent upon rediscovering their historic ties with Africa.

The United States' position was also precarious because of its refusal to use sanctions to penalize South Africa for that nation's policy of *apartheid,* under which 3.6 million whites isolated and ruthlessly suppressed 15.5 million non-whites. In November 1965 the problem was compounded when Southern Rhodesia, with a white population of 200,000 and a black population of nearly 4 million, declared its independence of the British Empire and, under white control, patterned itself on the South African model.

The reluctance of the United States to commit itself fully against the policies of South Africa and Southern Rhodesia resulted largely from American economic dependence upon the two nations, especially its need for South African gold and diamonds. In West Africa, military considerations helped explain

Washington policy. In November 1970 Guinea claimed that neighboring Portuguese Guinea, under the colonial control of Lisbon, was attempting to invade Guinea. A United Nations fact-finding mission unanimously agreed with Guinea's charges. When the Security Council voted on a motion to condemn Portugal, however, the United States abstained. Since 1945 American aircraft and warships on patrol in the eastern Atlantic had refueled at bases in the Portuguese Azores. The Portuguese required in return military assistance and, apparently, noninterference in attempted anticolonial wars in Africa.

The United States played a more positive role in the Congo, the most beleaguered of all African nations. When Belgium suddenly gave the Congo its independence on June 30, 1960, the colonial power left behind an unprepared, divided country with little common political experience, much illiteracy, and, according to one observer, a cadre of less than two dozen native-born college graduates to operate the country. Nationalist Patrice Lumumba attempted to centralize control of the nation, but encountered resistance from Katanga province, under the control of Moise Tshombe. Katanga was the richest of all the Congo provinces because of its Belgian mining interests. When Belgium encouraged Tshombe's separatist policies, Lumumba asked the United Nations for help in driving Belgian soldiers out of Katanga. The troops finally left, but when Tshombe remained recalcitrant, Lumumba asked the Soviets for help. This move caused the Congolese army to desert Lumumba, arrest him, and turn him over to Tshombe—who promptly murdered him. Fearful of possible Soviet intervention, the United States worked through the United Nations and successfully pressured Tshombe to merge Katanga with the remainder of the Congo.

In 1961 and 1962 the United States checked the Soviets by supporting UN action in the Congo and threatening to intervene unilaterally if the presence of UN troops were not upheld. In 1964 Lyndon Johnson found a new situation. Former followers of Lumumba had established rebel headquarters in Stanleyville and were successful in obtaining aid from the Communist bloc. As rebellion spread, the United States acquiesced to Tshombe's assumption of the premiership of the entire country. He recruited white mercenaries from southern Africa, Europe, and the United States, while Washington provided aircraft and supplies. In November 1964 the rebels herded hundreds of white hostages into Stanleyville for a last-ditch stand. A Belgian-American rescue operation dropped paratroopers into Stanleyville to rescue the hostages (although not before the rebels shot thirty-five victims) and destroyed the Stanleyville regime. The intervention by non-African nations, however, provoked strong condemnation from other African states. The Congo quieted, and the United States replaced Belgium as the major foreign influence. During the 1964 rebellion the Central Intelligence Agency had provided Tshombe with mercenary soldiers, airplanes, and pilots, most of them exiled Cubans. This assistance was followed with some $50 million in financial aid and, after Tshombe's fall in late 1965, with a successful American effort to stabilize the regime of Joseph Mobutu.

The American intervention in the Congo and the more blatant United States military campaigns in Vietnam and the Dominican Republic formed a pattern. The strain between Russia and the United States during the Congo crisis, however, was not so great as it would have been a decade before, for in many parts of the world the two superpowers were trying to cooperate to reduce cold war tensions. In a sporadic and very indirect fashion, for example, they were trying to calm the explosive Middle Eastern situation.

THE MIDDLE EAST

The Middle East was by all odds the world's most dangerous and volatile area in the late 1960s. Here, however, the two superpowers could not act as independent agents, for the Soviets were bound up with the fortunes of the Egyptians while the United States became increasingly tied to Israel. After the Suez crisis of 1956, Russia invested heavily to build the Aswan Dam complex, and also shipped more than $1 billion in arms to Egypt and Syria, thereby providing the weapons that Nasser hoped would either shrink or eliminate Israel. For centuries Russian rulers had attempted to break through to the Mediterranean. Now the Arab-Israeli struggle provided the opportunity. Soviet warships extensively used Egyptian and other Mediterranean ports, while a Russian fleet appeared for the first time on a regular basis in the Indian Ocean.

In May 1967 skirmishes erupted along the Israeli-Syrian border. Nasser then ejected the United Nations peacekeeping force along the Egyptian-Israeli boundary of the Gaza Strip and proceeded to close off the Gulf of Aqaba, which controlled the entrance to Israel's only southern port, Elat. On June 5 Israel suddenly retaliated. In six days the troops of Israel, a nation of 3 million, drove the army of Egypt, with a population of 30 million, across the Sinai peninsula to Suez. The Israelis also defeated Jordanian and Syrian armies, and annexed such treasured ancient sites as the Old City of Jerusalem. The United States watched approvingly, but the Soviets were horrified. Both powers resorted to the hot line (a private communication system between Moscow and Washington installed after the Cuban missile crisis) to assure each other that neither would interfere in the war.

Egypt demanded that Israel withdraw from Sinai and relinquish its new claims to the north and east, but the Israelis agreed to do so only on condition that Cairo first recognize Israel's existence as a sovereign state and its right to use the Gulf of Aqaba and Suez. Hostilities again threatened in 1969 and 1970 as the Soviets rebuilt Egyptian armies, a program matched by American aid to Israel. In the autumn of 1970 the superpowers pressed Egypt and Israel to accept a cease-fire and begin discussions through a neutral UN mediator. These talks continued despite skirmishes along the border and the sudden death of Nasser in the fall of 1970. The two great powers were aiding their respective allies in the Middle East, but through 1972 both attempted to prevent an outbreak of fighting that might lead to a confrontation of the superpowers themselves.

THE BOTTOMLESS PIT: VIETNAM, 1967–1968

To the displeasure of some Americans, the United States was unable to commit sufficient power or attention to the Middle East powder keg because so much of its energy was devoted to Vietnam. By early 1967 the President had declared several bombing halts in North Vietnam in an effort to open discussions, but Ho's government refused to talk until Johnson would promise to halt the bombing unconditionally and remove American troops so that the Vietnamese could settle their own affairs.

U.S. Army troops in Vietnam

The two sides became more intransigent, particularly as Secretary of State Dean Rusk emphasized that success in Vietnam was necessary in order to contain during "the next decade or two...a billion Chinese on the mainland, armed with nuclear weapons, with no certainty about what their attitude toward the rest of Asia will be."[14] The commitment was to hold, but by early 1968 that commitment was costly. More than twenty thousand Americans had lost their lives. Secretary of Defense McNamara admitted, to the President's great displeasure, that the bombing of the North had not been as effective as the administration had hoped in stopping the southward flow of men and supplies. Meanwhile American war expenditures had doubled to more than $20 billion between 1967 and 1968. Owing to McNamara's inability to predict this rise and to Johnson's reluctance, for political reasons, to propose sufficient taxation to pay these rising costs, a dangerous inflation infected the American economy. Riots in the black ghettos of Newark, Detroit, Atlanta, Cincinnati, New York, Los Angeles, and elsewhere had left more than a hundred dead, tragic evidence of the administration's inability to better conditions at home while supervising daily bombing raids halfway around the globe.

U.S. Army troops in Detroit

---

14 Text of press conference in *New York Times,* October 13, 1967, p. 15.

The climactic blow fell between January 29 and February 11, 1968, during the *Tet* lunar new year. In a quick, surprisingly effective offensive, the North Vietnamese and NLF attacked a number of supposedly invulnerable cities, including Saigon; shelled the American Embassy; destroyed United States military installations and communications; and, in all, inflicted a humiliating defeat despite Washington's claim that 32,000 of the enemy had been killed. Johnson's advisers now reassessed the situation. At the same time, a presidential primary election in New Hampshire revealed the public's disaffection from Johnson's policies. Senator Eugene McCarthy of Minnesota condemned American policies in Vietnam and won a surprising 42 percent of the Democratic vote.

On March 31 the President told a national television audience that bombing would be halted in North Vietnam in an effort to open discussions. He then announced he would not be a presidential contender in 1968. Discussions with the North Vietnamese opened in Paris two months later. As fighting continued, however, disaffection spread in the United States. Demands on both sides hardened. No progress would be made in these talks until four years had passed.

Nixon

JOHNSON'S WITHDRAWAL opened the Democratic race to Vice-President Hubert Humphrey of Minnesota, Senator Robert Kennedy of New York, and Senator McCarthy. In June, after winning his greatest victory in the California primary, Kennedy was assassinated by a young Jordanian enraged by the Senator's position in support of Israel, which actually differed little from the positions of the other contenders. Supported by the President, Humphrey gained the nomination, but in November lost by a narrow margin to Richard Nixon. Since his defeat in 1960 and in the California gubernatorial race in 1962, Nixon had patiently bided his time, rebuilding his support among state organizations.

Nixon muted his foreign policy statements during the campaign, preferring to stand instead on a domestic "law and order" platform. He shrewdly retreated to his old device of attacking administration policies rather than advancing positive programs that could become targets for Humphrey. Nixon promised to deescalate the Vietnam conflict, but refused to say explicitly how he planned to do it.

Once in office, the new President cut military budgets during his first two years and adopted a low-profile foreign policy. The army was to be reduced from its peak 1968 strength of nineteen divisions to the pre-Vietnam sixteen divisions, perhaps even to twelve or fourteen. New stress was laid upon repairing the badly eroded American relations with France, Great Britain, and West Germany. In mid-1969 the President announced a "Nixon Doctrine" that promised the withdrawal of American combat troops from Asia while at the same time providing nuclear cover and military and economic assistance for Asian allies.

When Peru and Chile came under control of left-wing regimes and nationalized some American property, Nixon merely reiterated the Johnson Doctrine of 1965. The softness of his response was determined in part by the decision of some American corporations simply to switch their operations from Latin America to the politically more secure and prosperous nations of the European Common Market. Such a reaction partially dismantled the Johnson Doctrine of 1965. The new administration simply had no positive policy toward Latin America other than weak attempts to reduce trade barriers. The Alliance for Progress disappeared.

The success of Nixon's foreign policy program depended almost entirely on an acceleration of "Vietnamization"—that is, the gradual replacement of American ground combat troops by South Vietnamese troops, so the United States could reduce its troop strength and expenditures in Southeast Asia. In 1969 there had been 550,000 Americans in Vietnam; four years later that number had been reduced to 27,000—although Nixon simply shifted thousands of U.S. Air Force personnel from Vietnam to supposedly more secure bases in neighboring Thailand. This reduction was not accomplished, however, without a terrible shock in the spring of 1970.

CAMBODIA AND KENT STATE

Americans had high hopes for Vietnamization, despite the failure of similar programs by the French in 1950 and the United States in 1955, 1961, 1963, and 1967. No administration official, moreover, predicted the complete withdrawal of United States forces from Southeast Asia. A residual group of perhaps 50,000 Americans, particularly Air Force personnel, would be maintained there to protect the wobbly South Vietnam government. Whether that government could be maintained successfully remained to be seen; it had been propped up for nearly a decade by American firepower, and with that power largely withdrawn, the government appeared to be highly vulnerable to the military and political pressures of North Vietnam.

Vietnamization was undergoing intense strain when, in March 1970, a military regime overthrew the long-time neutral stabilizing force of Prince Norodom Sihanouk in neighboring Cambodia. The Prince fled into exile in Peking while North Vietnamese forces won a succession of victories in Cambodia, thereby consolidating their bases on the Cambodian–South Vietnamese border, from which they had long funneled supplies into South Vietnam. Vietnamization suddenly faced a severe challenge.

On April 30 President Nixon dramatically announced that at that moment American troops were invading those Cambodian bases with the intent of destroying Communist supplies and perhaps capturing the main enemy headquarters. He promised a complete withdrawal of troops from Cambodia by June 30. Large caches of supplies were destroyed, but no important numbers of enemy troops or the headquarters could be located, in part, it seems, because the plans of the secret invasion had been learned by the North Vietnamese at least four days before the incursion began. American ground combat troops were removed from Cambodia by July 1, but the necessity of the invasion demonstrated the fundamental problems of the Vietnamization policy.

Graver problems appeared at home. Cities and college campuses erupted in large demonstrations against President Nixon's invasion of Cambodia and his failure to consult Congress beforehand. Nixon responded by publicly calling the student protesters "bums." At Kent State University in northeastern Ohio, National Guard troops moved onto the campus to restore order. Kent State had been the scene of protests and violence, including the bombing of the Reserve Officers' Training Corps (ROTC) building. In a tense confrontation with jeering, stone-throwing students, the National Guard troops opened fire. A few moments later four students lay dead. The Cambodian invasion had suddenly acquired an even more tragic dimension, and so, consequently, had Vietnamization.

The tragedy at Kent State, the failure to obtain stated objectives in Cambodia, the massive national protests, Republican failures to make predicted gains in the 1970 congressional elections—none of these proved sufficiently instructive to Washington officials. In January and February of 1971, United States helicopters carried South Vietnamese troops into both Cambodia and Laos. The operation was a disaster. The South Vietnamese troops were chopped up by Communist forces and survivors rushed back to South Vietnam in headlong retreat, leaving their American equipment behind. If, as the administration claimed, the Cambodian-Laotian invasion was the acid test for Vietnamization, then Nixon's policy had failed, for the South Vietnamese were proved incapable of defending themselves even with overwhelming American air support.

THE CITY UPON A HILL TWO CENTURIES AFTER

The Cambodian-Laotian fiasco marked a turning point in American policy. Since it demonstrated that South Vietnamese forces were incapable of offensive operations outside of their country's borders, and since President Nixon could not send in large numbers of American troops once again if he hoped to be reelected in 1972, he was forced to search for new policies. But Vietnam was only one of several such failures during the 1960s. Americans began to realize that despite their employment of massive military force—whether that force was directed by Kennedy, Johnson, or Nixon—they were incapable of controlling the revolutionary anti-American forces unleashed in Africa, Asia, and Latin America in the mid-1950s and early 1960s. This realization became even clearer to Americans when their economy began to suffer from simultaneous depression and inflation. Rapidly rising prices and unemployment were among the many costs of the tremendously expensive American military commitment around the globe.

In a belated but hectic search for more workable policies, President Nixon made two major decisions in 1971. The first was in the economic realm. At home he imposed wage and price controls in the hope of cutting the inflationary spiral. In doing so he repudiated his own and his party's proclaimed faith that a "free market" system with minimal governmental interference could solve America's economic problems. Abroad he threatened some of America's best friends with trade discriminations (such as higher tariffs against Japanese and western European products) unless they quickly passed measures that would allow Americans to sell products more easily in those countries. The Nixon administration emphasized that a key to ending the nation's economic crisis was the exportation of American goods abroad. This decision helped the economy turn slightly upward early in 1972, but it did little to help the 30 million Americans who lived below the poverty level and who badly needed goods themselves. Nor did it do anything to improve the government's critical relations with Japan, America's pivotal ally in the Pacific, or with western Europe. But Americans were learning that the essense of tragedy is choice. Regardless of what Kennedy and Johnson believed, the United States could not produce both a great military establishment to control revolutionaries overseas and adequate material goods to raise living standards at home and abroad. When the United States chose to create the military complex during the 1960s, the result was failure in the third world, riots and depression at home.

Nixon's second major decision of 1971 was to visit China early the following year. The visit, which took place in February 1972, laid the groundwork for

Nixon with Mao Tse-tung

resumption of Sino-American relations after Washington had refused for twenty-three years to recognize that China existed. Since Nixon had risen in American politics between 1948 and 1968 because of his vigorous attacks upon Communists at home and abroad, the switch was particularly notable. But he had few alternatives. China was a major power containing one-quarter of the world's population and possessing nuclear weapons. Mao's government replaced Chiang Kai-shek's aged Taiwan regime in the United Nations during the autumn of 1971. Most important, the President could hold no hope for a settlement in Southeast Asia or in global arms-control negotiations unless the Chinese cooperated. And then there was always the phantom of the China Market, that specter which American exporters had chased during other periods of economic depression in the 1780s, 1840s, 1890s, and 1930s.

Three months after the China visit, in May 1972, President Nixon became the first American chief executive to visit the Soviet Union. The two governments had signed a nonproliferation treaty in January 1968, promising to stop the spread of nuclear weapons to states that did not already possess them. Late in 1969 the two powers entered into the Strategic Arms Limitation Talks (SALT) in an effort to reach agreement on controlled levels of nuclear weapons and defensive antiballistic missile systems. Both professed to want to stop the upward spiral of arms costs as well as to reach a mutually agreeable balance of power, but each nation was also determined to preserve its ability to handle any future threat from China. Neither the Russians nor the Americans believed China properly understood the diplomatic dangers of nuclear weapons. Now Nixon emphasized the mutuality of interests by going to Moscow.

The journey was primarily motivated by Nixon's hope that the publicity would make him appear to be a statesman as well as a politician to the American voter in the upcoming November presidential election, and also by his belief that the Soviets could exercise restraint upon the North Vietnamese and Egyptians. But the major result of the Moscow summit talks was an arms agreement signed by Nixon and Soviet Communist Party Secretary Leonid Brezhnev. This pact limited defensive antiballistic-missile systems to two (one of which could be constructed around each nation's capital and one around an offensive missile site), and confined American and Russian offensive missiles to those then ready or under construction. As a result of the treaty, the Russians would have more missiles, but the United States would have nearly twice as many deliverable warheads as the Soviets because of the successful American development of the MIRV (Multiple Independently Targeted Reentry Vehicle), which contained several nuclear warheads on a single missile. The offensive missile treaty was for a five-year term, and the Nixon administration used this provision in part to ask Congress for the highest peacetime military budget in the country's history; the money was needed, the administration argued, so that it could develop new and even more fantastic and destructive weapons systems to serve as a "bargaining chip" at the next round of arms limitation talks.

Henry Kissinger with North Vietnamese negotiators

Of equal importance, however, American military leaders in the Pentagon had told the President they would not support the arms limitation agreements made in Moscow unless they had new weapons to replace the old limited ones. Nixon had surrendered to this argument. If this was to be the pattern, the United States would not be able to afford many more arms limitation agreements, regardless of how such pacts at least temporarily eased Soviet-American tensions.

Thus far had the City Upon a Hill come in the two hundred years since Madison had advised solving internal problems by "extending the sphere"; in the three-quarters of a century since McKinley and Hay had defined Asia as one of those spheres; in the fifty years since Wilson had urged Americans to join a crusade to make the world safe for democracy and other American interests; and in the ten years since John Fitzgerald Kennedy had implored Americans to realize the Wilsonian dream by asking what they could do for their country. In responding once again to the old answer supplied to them, 45,000 of them had left the City Upon a Hill to fall in the bottomless pit of Vietnam.

In January 1973 this killing of Americans promised to stop. The Paris Accords, signed by the U.S., North Vietnam, South Vietnam, and the NLF, provided for a supervised cease-fire, American troop withdrawal, dismantling of U.S. bases, and release of prisoners. Key to the agreement was its acknowledgment of "the unity and territorial integrity of Vietnam" while also recognizing the South Vietnamese "right to self-determination" through an early election. Vietnamese jockeyed for position and fighting between them continued, but at last Americans had reason to hope that they were finished with their longest war and might turn to rebuilding their own tormented City Upon a Hill.

Suggestions for Further Reading

The Kennedy years are sympathetically treated in Arthur M. Schlesinger, Jr., *A Thousand Days* (Boston, 1965), but Garry Wills, *Nixon Agonistes* (Boston, 1970), is brilliant in setting Kennedy and Nixon within the context of the period from 1945 (indeed 1913) to 1970.

The missile crisis is unraveled in Elie Abel, *The Missile Crisis* (Philadelphia, 1966); Graham T. Allison, *Essence of Decision* (Boston, 1971); and Robert F. Kennedy's memoir, *Thirteen Days* (New York, 1969).

The Johnson policies, and at times their shaping by the Kennedy legacies, can be found in Philip L. Geyelin, *Lyndon B. Johnson and the World* (New York, 1966); David Halberstam, *The Best and the Brightest* (New York, 1972), on

Kennedy but interesting on Johnson also; and Johnson's own *Vantage Point* (New York, 1971), which must be approached carefully.

An excellent survey on Vietnam is Chester L. Cooper, *The Lost Crusade: America in Vietnam* (New York, 1970); indispensable is Neil Sheehan et al., *The Pentagon Papers* (Chicago, 1971), with key documents from the 1950s but particularly the 1960s. The late Bernard Fall wrote several minor classics, with *The Two Viet Nams,* 2nd rev. ed. (New York, 1967), an appropriate starting point. The Gulf of Tonkin episode is well examined in Anthony Austin, *The President's War* (Philadelphia, 1971); the *Tet* offensive in Don Oberdorfer, *Tet!* (New York, 1971); and the expanding war in Cambodia and Laos, as well as Vietnam, in an excellent collection of documents edited by Marvin and Susan Gettleman and Lawrence and Carol Kaplan, *Conflict in Indochina* (New York, 1970). Not to be overlooked is V. Brodine and Mark Selden, *Open Secret: The Kissinger-Nixon Doctrine in Asia* (New York, 1972).

An overview of American interventions around the world is provided in Richard J. Barnet, *Intervention and Revolution: The U.S. and the Third World* (New York, 1968), while specific episodes are examined in Dan Kurzman, *Santo Domingo: Revolt of the Damned* (New York, 1965); Ernest W. Lefever, *Uncertain Mandate: Politics of the U.N. Congo Operation* (Baltimore, 1967); and Rupert Emerson, *Africa and U.S. Policy* (Englewood Cliffs, N.J., 1967). The collapse of Washington's Latin American policy is well delineated in Jerome Levinson and Juan de Onís, *The Alliance That Lost Its Way* (Chicago, 1970).

The Middle East crises are examined in several books by J. C. Hurewitz, including *Soviet-American Rivalry in the Middle East* (New York, 1969), which he edited. The troubles of the Atlantic Alliance are explained by two men deeply committed to a Europe-first policy: Stanley Hoffmann, *Gulliver's Troubles, Or the Setting of American Foreign Policy* (New York, 1968), and Henry Kissinger, *The Troubled Partnership* (New York, 1965); and an especially valuable study is Richard J. Barnet and Marcus G. Raskin, *After Twenty Years: Alternatives to the Cold War in Europe* (New York, 1965).

The Nixon policies cannot be understood without Garry Wills's *Nixon Agonistes,* mentioned above; Rowland Evans and Richard Novak, *Nixon in the White House* (New York, 1971); Richard M. Scammon and Ben J. Wattenberg's fascinating analysis of the 1968 election, *The Real Majority* (New York, 1970); and D. Landau, *Kissinger: Uses of Power* (Boston, 1972).

The State Department bureaucracy is dissected by a Foreign Service officer, John Franklin Campbell, in *The Foreign Affairs Fudge Factory* (New York, 1971).

The critical international economic context is explained in an easy-to-read book by Gordon L. Weil and Ian Davidson, *The Gold War: The Story of the World's Monetary Crisis* (New York, 1970), and in Sidney E. Rolfe and Walter Damm, eds., *The Multinational Corporation in the World Economy* (New York, 1970).

See also the general bibliography on the following pages.

Bibliography

GENERAL BIBLIOGRAPHICAL AIDS, ATLASES, REFERENCES

The most comprehensive source for the student who wishes to uncover additional documents and secondary works is Oscar Handlin et al., *Harvard Guide to American History* (Cambridge, Mass., 1954), well organized and indexed, but unfortunately out of date. Even more out of date but still useful is Samuel Flagg Bemis and Grace G. Griffin, eds., *Guide to the Diplomatic History of the United States, 1775-1921* (Washington, D.C., 1935). A most useful pamphlet describing general works is Alexander De Conde, *New Interpretations in American Foreign Policy,* published in Washington, D.C. (1961), by the American Historical Association. David F. Trask et al., *A Bibliography of United States-Latin American Relations Since 1810* (Lincoln, Neb., 1968), is also most useful.

A helpful paperback atlas is Andrew Boyd, *An Atlas of World Affairs,* 6th rev. ed. (New York, 1970); some particulars of C. O. Paullin's *Atlas of the Historical Geography of the United States* (Washington, D.C., 1932) have been found incorrect by recent scholars, but it continues to be a basic source on American expansion between the seventeenth and twentieth centuries.

For specific information on population, forms of government in various nations, and an incredible array of other material, see John Paxton, *The Statesman's Year-Book: Statistical and Historical Annual of the States of the World* (New York), published annually. On the United States specifically, see Allen Johnson and Dumas Malone, eds., *Dictionary of American Biography* (New York, 1928–   ); Thomas C. Cochran and Wayne Andrews, eds., *Concise Dictionary of American History* (New York, 1962); and Thomas H. Johnson, *The Oxford Companion to American History* (New York, 1966).

DOCUMENTS

Key foreign policy documents of American history are easily accessible for the student in Ruhl Bartlett, *The Record of American Diplomacy,* 4th ed. (New York, 1964), and William A. Williams, *The Shaping of American Diplomacy* (Chicago, 1969, 1970), available in two paperback volumes and containing valuable interpretive articles. The primary source is the Department of State's *Papers Relating to the Foreign Relations of the United States,* published annually since 1862 and at present covering events into 1948. For pre-1862 documents, see U.S. Congress, *American State Papers: Documents Legislative and Executive of the Congress of the United States,* 38 vols. (Washington, D.C., 1832–1861). An extremely valuable collection for the post-1945 years is *Public Papers of the Presidents,* published annually by the U.S. Government Printing Office and containing every public utterance made by the President during that year. The Department of State's *American Foreign Policy: Current Documents* series began in 1956 and is indispensable, but the series ended, at least temporarily, in 1966 because of budgetary problems. The Council on Foreign Relations has annually published the critical public documents in its *The United States in World Affairs* series, which has a volume of documents and another of narrative. Treaties are available in D. H. Miller, ed., *Treaties and Other International Acts of the United States of America,* 8 vols. (Washington, D.C., 1931–1948), and *United States Treaties and Other International Agreements* (Washington, D.C., 1950–   ). Most valuable is G. H. Hackworth, *Digest of International Law,* 8 vols. (Washington, D.C., 1940–1944).

GENERAL AND INTERPRETIVE WORKS

The Secretaries of State are treated individually in Samuel Flagg Bemis and Robert H. Ferrell, eds., *The American Secretaries of State and Their Diplomacy* (New York, 1927–1972), now covering the Secretaries through Christian Herter, whose tenure ended in 1960. Interesting analyses of twentieth-century Secretaries of State are found in Norman A. Graebner, ed., *An Uncertain Tradition* (New York, 1961).

General surveys on important topics include Dexter Perkins, *A History of the Monroe Doctrine,* rev. ed. (Boston, 1963); John A. Logan, Jr., *No Transfer* (New Haven, Conn., 1961), which studies a fourth dimension of the Monroe Doctrine; Dexter Perkins, *The American Approach to Foreign Policy* (Cambridge, Mass., 1962); B. H. Williams, *Economic Foreign Policy of the United States* (New York, 1929); Mira Wilkins, *The Emergence of Multinational Enterprise: American Business Abroad from the Colonial Era to 1914* (Cambridge, Mass., 1970); Selig Adler, *The Isolationist Impulse* (New York, 1957); D. A. Graber, *Crisis Diplomacy: A History of U.S. Intervention Policies and Practices* (New York, 1959). The subject of U.S. intervention has now been brought into the 1960s from a different perspective by Richard J. Barnet, *Intervention and Revolution* (New York, 1968). Intellectual factors are considered in Arthur A. Ekirch, Jr., *Ideas, Ideals, and American Diplomacy: A History of Their Growth and Interaction* (New York, 1966), and Loren Baritz, *City Upon a Hill* (New York, 1964); and for the eighteenth and early nineteenth centuries, Richard W. Van Alstyne, *Genesis of American Nationalism* (Waltham, Mass., 1970), as well as Albert Weinberg's classic *Manifest Destiny* (Baltimore, 1935).

The so-called realist school has dominated American policy-making and scholarship in the post–World War II era. This school is represented by Robert E. Osgood, *Ideals and Self-Interest in America's Foreign Relations* (Chicago, 1953), an interpretation of twentieth-century American diplomacy; Kenneth W. Thompson, *Political Realism and the Crisis of World Politics* (Princeton, N.J., 1960); Louis J. Halle, *The Cold War as History* (New York, 1967); Hans J. Morgenthau, *In Defense of the National Interest* (New York, 1951); Stanley Hoffmann, *Gulliver's Troubles, Or the Setting of American Foreign Policy* (New York, 1968); and in particular several books by George F. Kennan, especially his highly popular *American Diplomacy, 1900–1950* (Chicago, 1951) and *Realities of American Foreign Policy* (Princeton, N.J., 1954); Kennan's second thoughts, both explicit and implicit, are given in his *Memoirs* (Boston, 1967). Good studies of the cold war which owe much to this school are John A. Lukacs, *A History of the Cold War* (Garden City, N.Y., 1966), and John W. Spanier, *American Foreign Policy Since World War II*, rev. ed. (New York, 1972).

During the 1960s and early 1970s the realists have been increasingly challenged by a growing revisionist school, which traces its roots back to Charles A. Beard's *The Idea of National Interest* (New York, 1933). Important general revisionist studies include D. F. Fleming, *The Cold War and Its Origins, 1917–1960*, 2 vols. (Garden City, N.Y., 1961); William Appleman Williams, *The Tragedy of American Diplomacy* (New York, 1962) and *Contours of American History* (Chicago, 1966); Richard W. Van Alstyne, *The Rising American Empire* (New York, 1960); and Garry Wills, *Nixon Agonistes* (Boston, 1970). Interesting treatments of the cold war era which are related to the revisionist school include Stephen E. Ambrose's excellent *Rise to Globalism* (Baltimore, 1971); Frederick L. Schuman, *The Cold War: Retrospect and Prospect* (Baton Rouge, 1962); and Edmund Stillman and William Pfaff, *The New Politics: America and the End of the Postwar World* (New World, 1961), as well as Richard Barnet, *Roots of War* (New York, 1972).

SELECTED TOPICS IN AMERICAN DIPLOMACY

Administration and Department of State

Alexander De Conde, *The American Secretary of State: An Interpretation* (New York, 1962); Don K. Price, ed., *The Secretary of State* (Englewood Cliffs, N.J., 1960); John Franklin Campbell, *The Foreign Affairs Fudge Factory* (New York, 1971); William Barnes and J. H. Morgan, *The Foreign Service of the United States* (Washington, D.C., 1961); H. Field Haviland, Jr., et al., *The Formulation and Administration of United States Foreign Policy* (Washington, D.C., 1960); W. F. Ilchman, *Professional Diplomacy in the United States, 1779–1939* (Chicago, 1961); H. B. Westerfield, *The Instruments of America's Foreign Policy* (New York, 1963).

Congress

H. B. Carroll, *The House of Representatives and Foreign Affairs* (Pittsburgh, 1958); A. C. F. Westphal, *The House Committee on Foreign Affairs* (New York, 1942); D. N. Farnsworth, *The Senate Committee on Foreign Relations* (Urbana, Ill., 1961); L. N. Rieselbach, *The Roots of Isolationism: Congressional Voting and Presidential Leadership in Foreign Policy* (Indianapolis, 1966); W. Stull Holt, *Treaties Defeated by the Senate* (Baltimore, 1933); C. V. Crabb, Jr., *Bipartisan Foreign Policy: Myth or Reality?* (Evanston, Ill., 1957); G. L. Grassmuck, *Sectional Biases in Congress on Foreign Policy* (Baltimore, 1951).

Indians

Angie Debo, *A History of the Indians of the United States* (Norman, Okla., 1971); Francis Paul Prucha, *American Indian Policy in the Formative Years* (Cambridge, Mass., 1962).

International Organizations,
Including United Nations

Richard N. Gardner, *In Pursuit of World Order: U.S. Foreign Policy and International Organizations,* rev. ed. (New York, 1966); Lincoln Bloomfield, *United Nations and U.S. Foreign Policy,* rev. ed. (Boston, 1967); Ruth B. Russell, *A History of the United Nations Charter: The Role of the United States, 1940–1945* (Washington, D.C., 1961).

Labor Movement

Ronald Radosh, *American Labor and United States Foreign Policy* (New York, 1969).

Law

P. E. Corbett, *Law in Diplomacy* (Princeton, N.J., 1959); and two books by Richard A. Falk, *Legal Order in a Violent World* (Princeton, N.J., 1968) and *The Status of Law in International Society* (Princeton, N.J., 1970).

Military and National Defense

Raymond G. O'Connor, ed., *American Defense Policy in Perspective* (New York, 1965); Harold Stein, ed., *American Civil-Military Decisions: A Book of Case Studies* (Birmingham, Ala., 1963); Paul Y. Hammond, *Organizing for Defense: The American Military Establishment in the Twentieth Century* (Princeton, N.J., 1961); Harold and Margaret Sprout, *The Rise of American Naval Power, 1776-1918* (Princeton, N.J., 1939); E. B. Potter, ed., *Sea Power: A Naval History* (Englewood Cliffs, N.J., 1960); Armin Rappaport, *The Navy League of the United States* (Detroit, 1962); two important studies by Walter Millis, *Arms and Men* (New York, 1956) and *Arms and the State* (New York, 1958); two volumes by Samuel P. Huntington, *The Soldier and the State* (Cambridge, Mass., 1957), to be used carefully, and *The Common Defense: Strategic Programs in National Politics* (New York, 1961); William B. Bader, *The U.S. and the Spread of Nuclear Weapons* (New York, 1968); Seymour Melman, *Pentagon Capitalism* (New York, 1970).

Missionaries

Paul A. Varg, *Missionaries, Chinese, and Diplomats: The American Protestant Missionary Movement in China, 1890–1952* (Princeton, N.J., 1958).

Presidents

Sidney Warren, *The President as World Leader* (Philadelphia, 1964); Ernest R. May, ed., *The Ultimate Decision: The President as Commander in Chief* (New York, 1960); H. M. Wriston, *Executive Agents in American Foreign Relations* (Baltimore, 1929).

Press

James Reston, *The Artillery of the Press* (New York, 1967); Bernard C. Cohen, *The Press and Foreign Policy* (Princeton, N.J., 1963); James Aronson, *The Press and the Cold War* (Indianapolis, 1970).

Public Opinion and Politics

A number of studies by Angus Campbell, including *The Voter Decides* (Evanston, Ill., 1954); V. O. Key, Jr., *Public Opinion and American Democracy* (New York, 1961); Gabriel Almond, *The American People and Foreign Policy* (New York, 1960); Louis L. Gerson, *The Hyphenate in Recent American Politics and Diplomacy* (Lawrence, Kans., 1964); Alfred O. Hero, Jr., *The Southerner and World Affairs* (Baton Rouge, 1965); Charles O. Lerche, Jr., *The Uncertain South: Its Changing Patterns of Politics in Foreign Policy* (Chicago, 1964); James N. Rosenau, ed., *Domestic Sources of Foreign Policy* (New York, 1967); Richard Scammon and Ben J. Wattenberg, *The Real Majority* (New York, 1970); Thomas A. Bailey, *The Man in the Street* (New York, 1948).

Revolution

Peter Calvert, *Revolution* (New York, 1970); Hannah Arendt, *On Revolution* (New York, 1963); Richard W. Van Alstyne, *Genesis of American Nationalism* (New York, 1968); William Appleman Willliams, *The Tragedy of American Diplomacy* (New York, 1962).

AMERICAN RELATIONS WITH SELECTED AREAS

Africa

Rupert Emerson, *Africa and U.S. Policy* (Englewood Cliffs, N.J., 1967); William A. Hance, ed., *Southern Africa and the United States* (New York, 1968); George E. Brooks, Jr., *Yankee Traders, Old Coasters, and African Middlemen* (in the nineteenth century) (Brookline, Mass., 1970), with nothing on slavery or Liberia; Charles F. Gallagher, *The United States and North Africa* (Cambridge Mass., 1963); R. W. Irwin, *The Diplomatic Relations of the United States with the Barbary Powers, 1776–1816* (Chapel Hill, N.C., 1931); Raymond W. Bixler, *The Foreign Policy of the United States in Liberia* (New York, 1957).

Arab World

John S. Badeau, *The American Approach to the Arab World* (New York, 1968); William R. Polk, *The United States and the Arab World* (Cambridge, Mass., 1965); John A. De Novo, *American Interests and Policies in the Middle East, 1900–1939* (Minneapolis, 1963).

Argentina

Harold F. Peterson, *Argentina and the United States, 1810–1960* (New York, 1964); Arthur P. Whitaker, *The United States and Argentina* (Cambridge, Mass., 1954). See also "Latin America."

Australia

C. H. Grattan, *The United States in the Southwest Pacific* (Cambridge, Mass., 1961); Werner Levi, *American-Australian Relations* (Minneapolis, 1947).

Brazil

L. F. Hill, *Diplomatic Relations Between the United States and Brazil* (Durham, N. C., 1932). See also "Latin America."

Canada

Gerald M. Craig, *The United States and Canada* (Cambridge, Mass., 1968); S. F. Wise and R. C. Brown, *Canada Views the United States* (Seattle, 1967); John S. Dickey, ed., *The United States and Canada* (Englewood Cliffs, N.J., 1964); Robert T. Wilson et al., *Canada–United States Treaty Relations* (Durham, N.C., 1963); Edgar W. McInnis, *The Atlantic Triangle and the Cold War* (Toronto, 1959).

Chile

F. B. Pike, *Chile and the United States, 1880–1962* (Notre Dame, Ind., 1963). See also "Latin America."

China

Warren I. Cohen, *America's Response to China* (New York, 1971); John K. Fairbank, *United States and China*, rev. ed. (Cambridge, Mass., 1971); Paul A. Varg, *Missionaries, Chinese, and Diplomats: The American Protestant Missionary Movement in China, 1890–1952* (Princeton, N.J., 1958); Kwang-ching Liu, *Americans and Chinese: A Historical Essay and Bibliography* (Cambridge, Mass., 1963).

Cuba

Lester D. Langley, *The Cuban Policy of the United States* (New York, 1968); Robert F. Smith, *The United States and Cuba: Business and Diplomacy, 1917–1960* (New York, 1961); P. S. Foner, *A History of Cuba in Its Relations with the United States, 1492–1845* (New York, 1962). See also "Latin America."

Eastern Europe

Robert F. Byrnes, ed., *The United States and Eastern Europe* (Englewood Cliffs, N.J., 1967). See also "Russia."

France

Henry Blumenthal, *France and the United States: Their Diplomatic Relations, 1789–1914* (Chapel Hill, N.C., 1970); Crane Brinton, *The Americans and the French* (Cambridge, Mass., 1968).

Germany

H. M. Adams, *Prussian-American Relations, 1775–1871* (Cleveland, 1960); Edgar McInnis et al., *The Shaping of Postwar Germany* (New York, 1960).

Great Britain

H. C. Allen, *Conflict and Concord: Anglo-American Relationship Since 1783* (New York, 1960); Crane Brinton, *The United States and Britain* (Cambridge, Mass., 1945).

Greece

S. A. Larrabee, *Hellas Observed: The American Experience of Greece, 1775–1865* (New York, 1957); William H. McNeill, *Greece: American Aid in Action, 1947–1956* (New York, 1957); Stephen G. Xydis, *Greece and the Great Powers, 1944–1947* (Salonika, 1963).

Haiti

Hans Schmidt, *The U.S. Occupation of Haiti, 1915–1934* (New Brunswick, N.J., 1971); R. W. Logan, *The Diplomatic Relations of the United States with Haiti, 1776–1891* (Chapel Hill, N.C., 1941); L. L. Montague, *Haiti and the United States, 1714–1938* (Durham, N.C., 1940). See also "Latin America."

India

Norman D. Palmer, *South Asia and United States Policy* (Boston, 1966); W. Norman Brown, *The United States and India and Pakistan*, rev. ed. (Cambridge, Mass., 1963); Selig Harrison, ed., *India and the United States* (New York, 1961); Harold R. Isaacs, *Scratches on Our Minds: The American Image of China and India* (New York, 1958).

Iran

L. V. Thomas and R. N. Frye, *The United States and Turkey and Iran* (Cambridge, Mass., 1951); Robert Engler, *The Politics of Oil* (New York, 1961).

Israel

Nadev Safran, *The United States and Israel* (Cambridge, Mass., 1963); John A. De Novo, *American Interests and Policies in the Middle East, 1900–1939* (Minneapolis, 1963).

Italy

H. Stuart Hughes, *The United States and Italy*, rev. ed. (Cambridge, Mass., 1965).

Japan

William L. Neumann, *America Encounters Japan: From Perry to MacArthur* (Baltimore, 1963); Edwin O. Reischauer, *The United States and Japan,* rev. ed. (Cambridge, Mass., 1965).

Korea

Fred Harvey Harrington, *God, Mammon, and the Japanese: Dr. Horace Allen and Korean-American Relations, 1884–1905* (Madison, Wis., 1944).

Latin America

Gordon Connell-Smith, *The Inter-American System* (New York, 1966); J. Lloyd Mecham, *A Survey of United States–Latin American Relations* (Boston, 1965); Dexter Perkins, *The United States and the Caribbean,* rev. ed. (Cambridge, Mass., 1966); J. Fred Rippy, *Globe and Hemisphere: Latin America's Place in the Postwar Foreign Relations of the United States* (Chicago, 1958); Arthur P. Whitaker, *The Western Hemisphere Idea* (Ithaca, N.Y., 1954).

Mexico

Howard F. Cline, *The United States and Mexico,* rev. ed. (Cambridge, Mass., 1963). See also "Latin America."

Pakistan

W. Norman Brown, *The United States and India and Pakistan,* rev. ed. (Cambridge, Mass., 1963); Norman D. Palmer, *South Asia and United States Policy* (Boston, 1966).

Panama

Sheldon B. Liss, *The Canal: Aspects of United States–Panamanian Relations* (Notre Dame, Ind., 1967). See also "Latin America."

Peru

James C. Carey, *Peru and the United States, 1900–1962* (Notre Dame, Ind., 1964). See also "Latin America."

Philippines

George E. Taylor, *The Philippines and the United States: Problems of Partnership* (New York, 1964); Milton W. Meyer, *A Diplomatic History of the Philippine Republic* (Honolulu, 1965).

Russia

William Appleman Williams, *American-Russian Relations, 1781–1947* (New York, 1952); T. A. Bailey, *America Faces Russia* (Ithaca, N.Y., 1950); C. A. Manning, *Russian Influence on Early America* (New York, 1953); Adam B. Ulam, *The Rivals: America and Russia Since World War II* (New York, 1971); Anatol Rapoport, *The Big Two: Soviet-American Perceptions of Foreign Policy* (Indianapolis, 1970).

Santo Domingo

Charles C. Tansill, *The United States and Santo Domingo, 1798–1873* (Baltimore, 1938); M. M. Knight, *The Americans in Santo Domingo* (New York, 1928). See also "Latin America."

Scandinavia

F. D. Scott, *The United States and Scandinavia* (Cambridge, Mass., 1950).

Spain

Arthur P. Whitaker, *Spain and Defense of the West* (New York, 1961).

Switzerland

Heinz K. Meier, *The United States and Switzerland in the Nineteenth Century* (The Hague, 1963).

Vietnam

Frances Fitzgerald, *Fire in the Lake: The Vietnamese and the Americans in Vietnam* (Boston, 1972).

Additional bibliography can be found in most of the above-listed volumes and also in the footnotes and suggestions for further reading at the end of each chapter of this book.

Index